CONTENTS · INHALT · SOMMARIO · CON~~TENTS~~ · CONTEÚDO ·
INDHOLD · INHOUD · OBSAH · O~~...~~

Europe · Europa · Europa · E~~...~~
Europa · Europa · Evropa · ~~...~~
1:2 000 000

MAP OF EUROPE · Übersicht Europa · Panoramica d'Europa · Vista general de Europa ·
Europa – Visão geral · Oversigtskort Europa · Overzicht Europa ·
Přehled – Evropa · Prehľad – Evropa · Przeglądowa Europy . . . . **2 - 3**

GENERAL MAP · Verkehrsübersicht · Carta sinottica · Vista general · Mapa geral de tráfego ·
Primære rejseruter · Overzichtskaart · Přehledná mapa · Prehľadná mapa · Przeglądowa . . . . . **4 - 5**

KEY PLAN · Blattübersicht · Tavola riassuntiva delle pagine · Vista de la página ·
Visão geral dos mapas · Inddeling i kortsider · Bladoverzicht · Klad listů ·
Prehľad kladu listov · Skorowidz arkuszy . . . . **6 - 7**

LEGEND · Legende · Legenda · Leyenda · Legenda ·
Signaturforklaring · Legende · Vysvětlivky · Vysvetlivky · Legenda . . . . **8 - 9**

ROAD + LEISURE TIME MAP EUROPE 1:2 000 000 · Auto + Freizeitkarte Europa ·
Carta stradale + turistica Europa · Mapa de rutas + del ocio Europa ·
Mapa de Estradas + de lazer Europa · Bil- og fritidskort Europa ·
Auto + Vrije tijd kaart Europa · Automapa + mapa pro volný čas Evropa ·
Automapa + mapa pre voľný čas Európa · Mapa samochodowa i rekreacyjna Europa

ROAD MAP · Kartenblätter · Carta stradale · Mapa de carreteras · Mapa de estradas ·
Bilkort · Autokaart · Automapa · Automapa · Mapa samochodowa . . . . **1 - 110**

INDEX WITH POSTCODES · Ortsregister mit Postleitzahlen · Indice con codici postali ·
Índice con códigos postales · Índice de lugares com códigos postais ·
Stedregister med postnumre · Plaatsnamenregister met postcode ·
Rejstřík míst s PSČ · Zoznam obcí s PSČ · Indeks miejscowości z kod pocztowy . . . . **111 - 216**

freytag & berndt
www.freytagberndt.de
© FREYTAG-BERNDT u. ARTARIA KG, 1230 VIENNA, AUSTRIA, EUROPE

AA Media Limited 2011

ISBN: 978-0-7495-6337-0

The contents of this book are believed to be correct at the time of printing. Nevertheless the Publisher can accept
no responsibility for errors or emissions, or for changes in the details given. This does not affect your statutory rights.

A04160

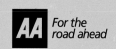

1:2 000 000

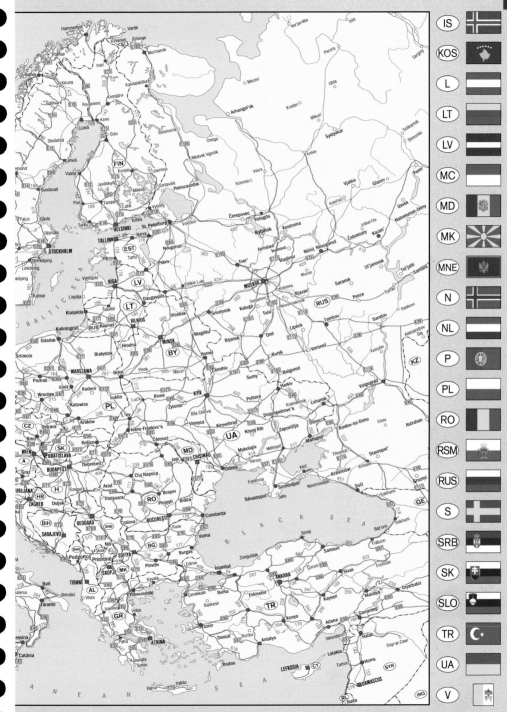

IS
KOS
L
LT
LV
MC
MD
MK
MNE
N
NL
P
PL
RO
RSM
RUS
S
SRB
SK
SLO
TR
UA
V

EUROPE

EUROPA · EUROPA · EUROPA · EUROPA ·
EUROPA · EUROPA · EVROPA · EURÓPA · EUROPA

1 : 2 000 000

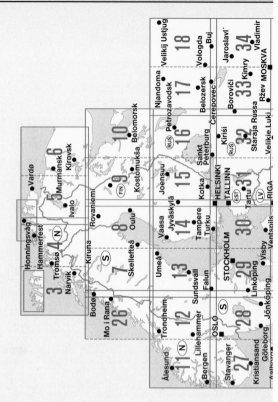

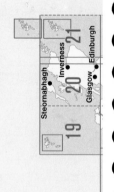

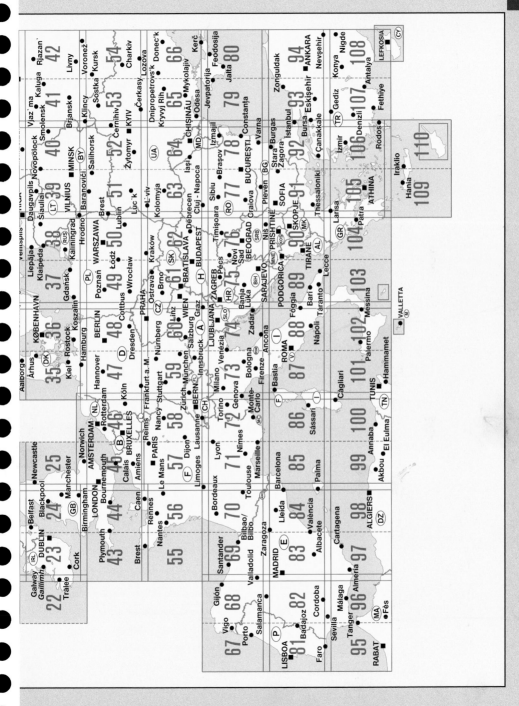

Motorway Autobahn Autostrada Autovía y autopista libre Auto-estrada	Motorvej Autosnelweg Dálnice Diaľnica Autostrady
Dual carriageway Fernverkehrsstraße, 4-spurig Strada di grande comunicazione a quattro corsie Autovía doble carril Itinerário principal com 4 faixas	Motortrafikvej, 4-sporet Autoweg, 4 rijstroken Dálková silnice, čtyřproudová Diaľková cesta štvorpruhová 4-sávos gyorsforgalmi út 4-jezdniowa
Primary route, main road Fernverkehrsstraße, Hauptstraße Strada di grande comunicazione, strada principale Carretera nacional, calle principale con número Itinerário principal, estrada principal	Vigtig hovedvej, hovedvej Autoweg, belangrijke verkeersader Dálková silnice, hlavní silnice Diaľková cesta, hlavná cesta Droga komunikacji dalekobieżnej, droga drugorzędna
Secondary Road Nebenstraße Strada secondaria Carretera secundaria Estrada secundária	Bivej Secundaire weg Vedlejší komunikace Vedľajšia cesta Droga lokalna
Motorway, dual carriageway under construction Autobahn, Fernverkehrsstraße, 4-spurig in Bau Autostrada, strada di grande comunicazione a quattro corsie in costruzione Autovía y autopista libre, autovía en construcción Auto-estrada, itinerário principal com 4 faixas em construção	Motorvej, motortrafikvej, 4-sporet, under bygning Autosnelweg, autoweg, 4 rijstroken in aanleg Dálnice, dálková silnice, čtyřproudová ve stavbě Diaľnica, rozostavaná diaľková cesta štvorpruhová Autostrada, droga komunikacji dalekobieżnej, 4-jezdniowa w budowie
Distances in kilometres (km) Entfernungen in km Distanze in km Distancias en km Distância em quilómetros	Afstande i km Afstanden in km Vzdálenosti v km Vzdialenosti v km Odległości w km
Main railway line, branch line Hauptbahn, Nebenbahn Linea ferrovia principale, linea ferrovia secondaria Ferrocarril principal, ferrcarril secundario Linha principal de caminho-de-ferro, ramal	Hovedbane, sidebane Hoofdspoorweg, secundaire spoorweg Hlavní trať, vedlejší trať Hlavná železnica, vedľajšia železnica Kolej, dworzec kolejowy, kolej lokalna
National boundary, international border crossing Staatsgrenze, Internationaler Grenzübergang Confine di Stato, posto di frontiera internazionale Territorio nacional, internacional passo de frontera Fronteira nacional, posto fronteiriço international	Rigsgrænse, international grænseovergang Staatsgrens, internationale grensovergang Státní hranice, mezinárodní hraniční přechod Štátna hranica, medzinárodný hraničný priechod Granica państwa, Międzynarodowe przejście graniczne

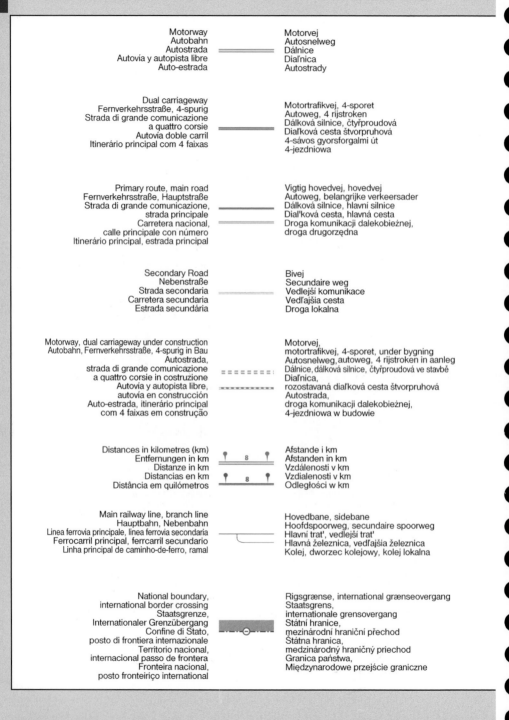

International airport, airport
Internationaler Flughafen, Flughafen
Aeroporto internazionale, aeroporto
Aeropuerto internacional, aeropuerto
Aeroporto internacional, aeroporto

International lufthavn, lufthavn
Internationale vliegveld, vliegveld
Mezinárodní letiště, letiště
Medzinárodné letisko, letisko
Miedzynarodowy port lotniczy,
port lotniczy

Car ferry
Autofähre
Traghetto per il trasporto
Ferry
Ferry-boat

Bilfærge
Veerdienst
Trajekt pro automobily
Autokompa
Prom samochodowy

Road numbers
Straßennummer
Numerazione delle strade
Numeración de las carreteras
Número de estrada

56
E85

Vejnummer
Straatnummer
Čisla silnič
Číslo cesty
Numer drogi

Manor house, castle - ruin, monastery
Schloss, Burg - Ruine, Kloster
Castello, fortezza - rovine, convento
Castillo, fortaleza - ruinas, monasterio
Palácio, castelo - ruina, convento

Slot, borg - ruin, kloster
Paleis, burcht - ruïne, klooster
Zámek, hrad - zřícenina, klášter
Zámok, ruiny hradu, kláštor
Zamek, Ruina zamku warownego, klasztor

National park
Naturschutzgebiet
Parco naturale
Parque nacional
Reserva natural

Balatonfelvidéki
N.P.

Fredet område
Natuurbeschermingsgebied
Přírodní rezervace
Chránená krajinná oblasť
Rezerwat przyrody

Lake, river, canal, wadi, seasonal lake,
swamp
See, Fluss, Kanal,Wadi,See (per.), Sumpf
Lago, fiume, canale, wadi,
lago temperaneo, palude
Lago, rio, canal, uad,
lago intermitente, pantano
Lago, rio, canal, uádi, lago
(intermitente), pântano

Sø, flod, kanal,wadi, sø (periodisk), sump
Meer, rivier, kanaal, wadi, meer met
veranderlijke oeverlijn, moerasgebied
Jezero, řeka, kanál, vádi,
jezero s nestálým břehen, bažina
Jazero, rieka, kanál, vádi,
jazero s nestálým brehom, močiar
Jezioro, rzeka, kanał, wadi,
jezioro okresowe, bagno

Salt lake, seasonal salt lake, salt flat
Salzsee, Salzsee (periodisch), Salzsumpf
Lago salato, lago salato temporanec,
sebka
Lago salado, lago salado intermitente,
saladar
Lago salgado, lago salgado (intermitente),
pântano salgado

Saltsø, saltsø (periodisk), saltsump
Zoutmeer, zoutmeer met veranderlijke
oeverlijn, zoutmoeras
Slané jezero, slané jezero s nestálým
břehem, slaniska
Slané jazero, slané jazero s nestálým
brehom, slanisko
Jeziora stone, jeziora stone okresowe,
solniska

Sand desert, rock desert, depression
Sandwüste, Steinwüste, Depression
Deserto di sabbioso, deserto roccioso,
depressione
Desierto de arena, desierto pétreo,
depresión

Deserto de areia,deserto pedregoso,
depressão
Sandørken, stenørken, sænkning
Zandwoestijn, kiezelwoestijn, depressie
Pisecné poušte, kámen poušt, deprese
Piesocné púšte, kamen púšt, deprese
Pustynie, kamien pustynia, depresja

1 : 2 000 000

0   20   40   80   120   160   200km

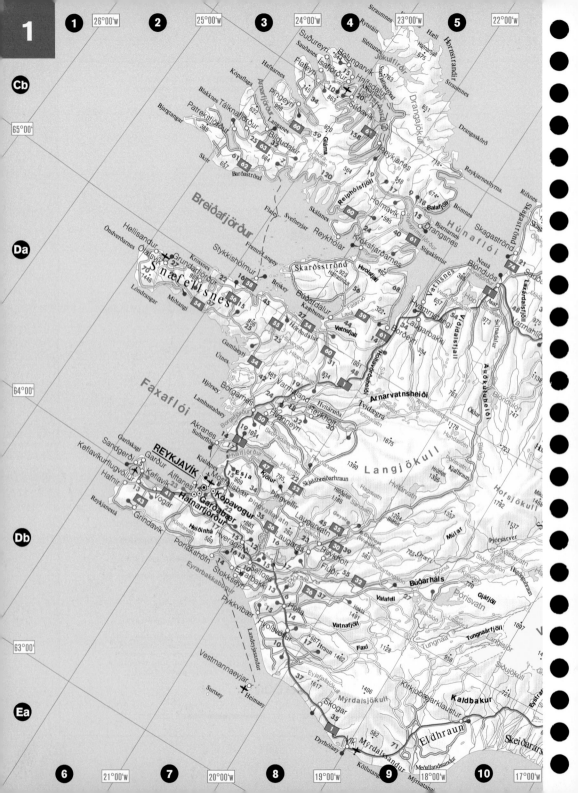

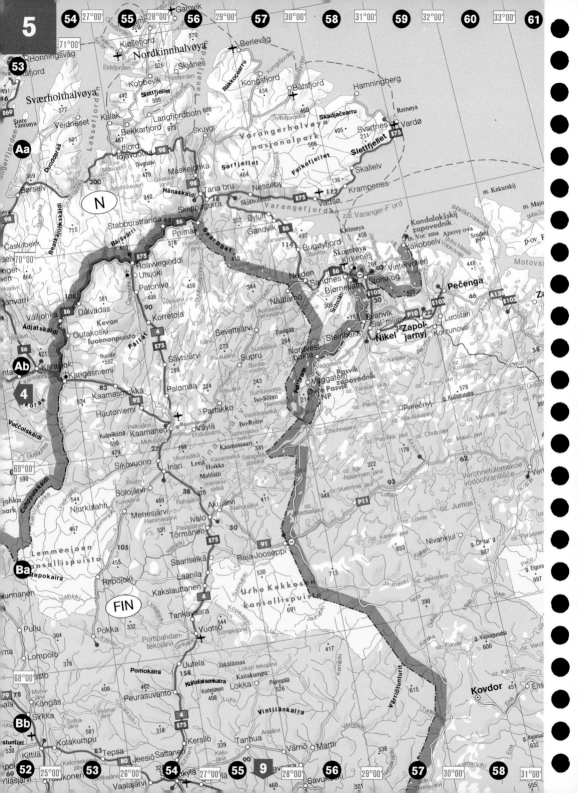

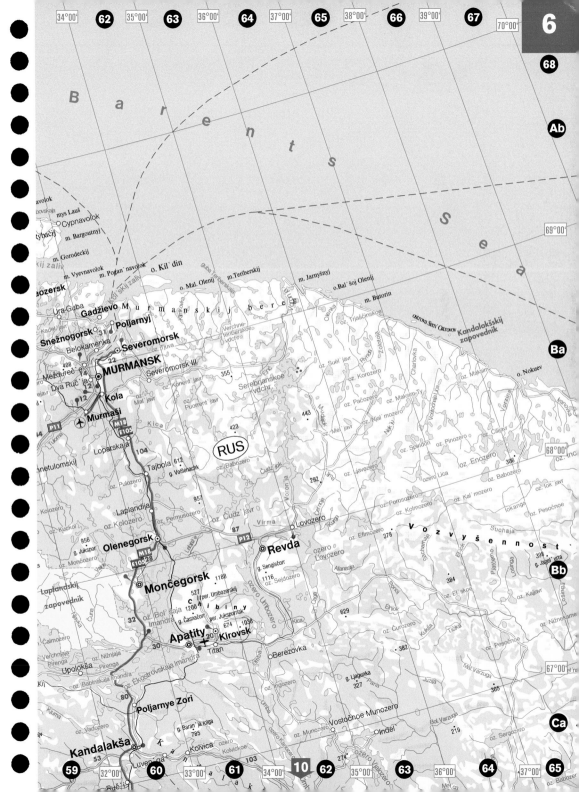

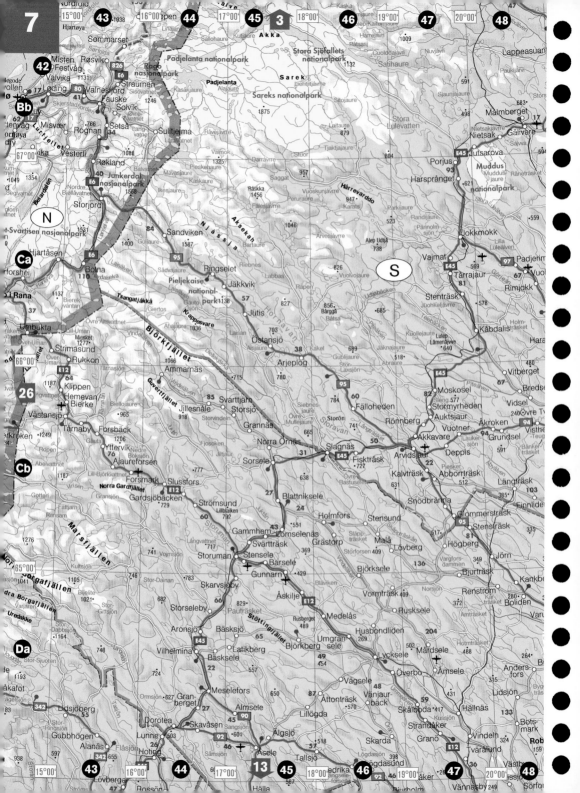

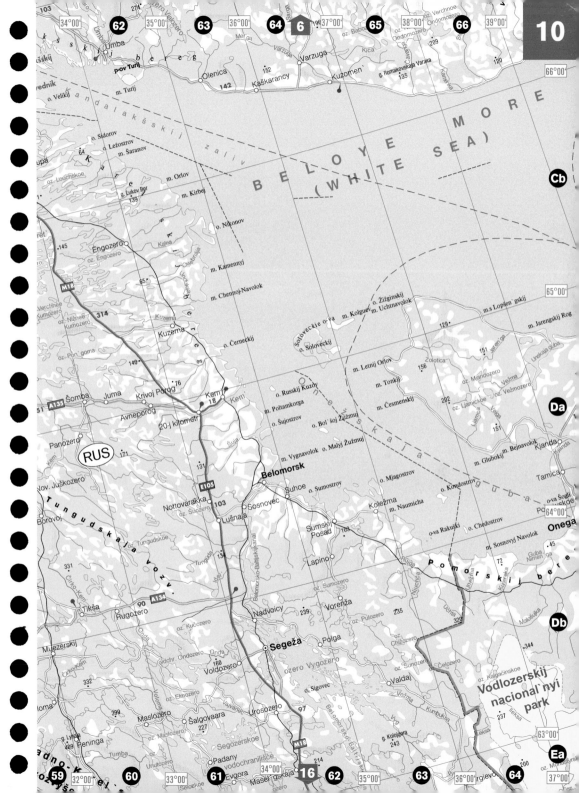

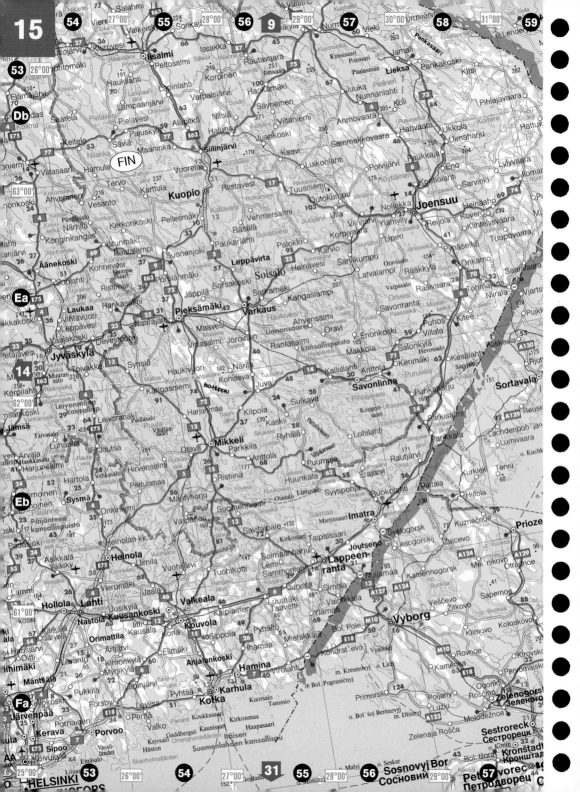

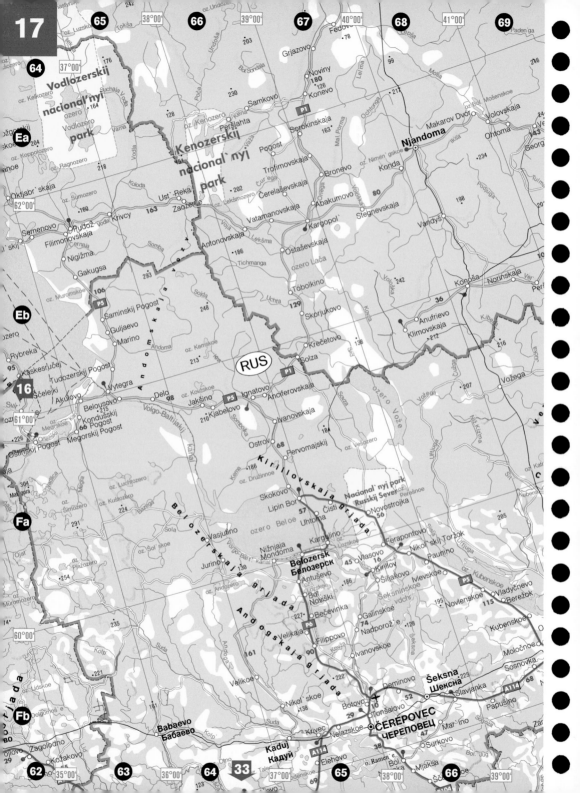

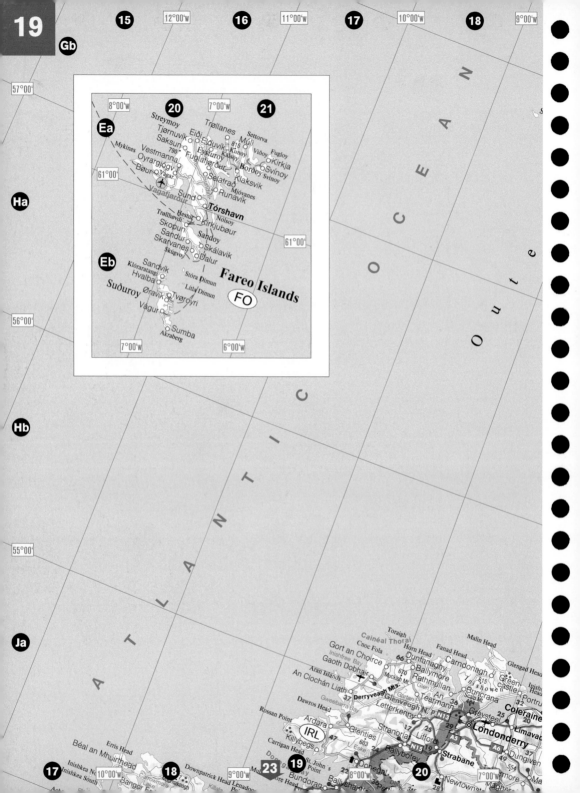

Gb

57°00'

Ha

Hb

56°00'

55°00'

Ja

15   12°00'W   16   11°00'W   17   10°00'W   18   9°00'W

Fareo Islands

20   8°00'W   7°00'W   21

Ea

Streymoy
Tjørnuvík   Trøllanes   Settorva
Saksun   Eiði Elduvík   Múli
Vestmanna   Kunoy   Viðoy   Fugloy
Oyrargjógv   790   Eysturoy   Kalsoy   Kirkja
Bøur   Vágar   Fuglafjørður   Borðoy   Svínoy
Mykines   Klaksvík
Selatrað   Mjóvanes
Vagafjørður   Sund   Runavík
Tórshavn
Hestur   Nólsoy
Trøllhøvdi   Kirkjubøur
Skopun   Sandoy
Sandur   Skálavík
Skarvanes   Dalur
Skúgvoy

Eb
Sandvík
Klóraratangi   Stóra Dímun
Hvalba   Litla Dímun
Suðuroy   Øravík   Tvøroyri
Vágur
Sumba
Akraberg

7°00'W   6°00'W

Fareo Islands
FO

61°00'

61°00'

56°00'

O   C   E   A   N

O u t e r

A   T   L   A   N   T   I   C

Toraigh
Caineál Thorai   Horn Head   Malin Head
Gort an Choirce   Cnoc Fola   Fanad Head
Inishfree Bay   Dunfanaghy   Carndonagh   Glengad Head
Gaoth Dobhair   66   Ballymore   Green-   Inishe
An Clochán Liath   670   Rathmullan   castle   Hea
Muckish Mt.   Inishowen   Buncrana   Portru
Dawros Head   37   Derryveagh Mts.   815   Scalp Mt.   464   Greysteel   Coleraine
Rossan Point   Gweebarra Bay   Glenveagh N.P.   Gártan   An   25
Ardara   Letterkenny   Clady   17   N13   19   Londonderry
Killybegs   Glenties   603   Stranorlar   25   N13   Limava
IRL   47   Carrigan Head   Eske   Lifford   29   A5   Dungiven
St. John's   22   Ballybofey   Strabane   A6   49
23   Point   Eske   N15   19   554   Ma
17   Inishkea N.   9°00'W   18   Downpatrick Head Lenadoon   Mulroy Bay   Donegal   36   20   Newtowns
Inishkea South   Bangor   Bundoran   8°00'W   Magher
Béal an Mhuirthead   10°00'W   Killala P.   Ballysha

23   19   20

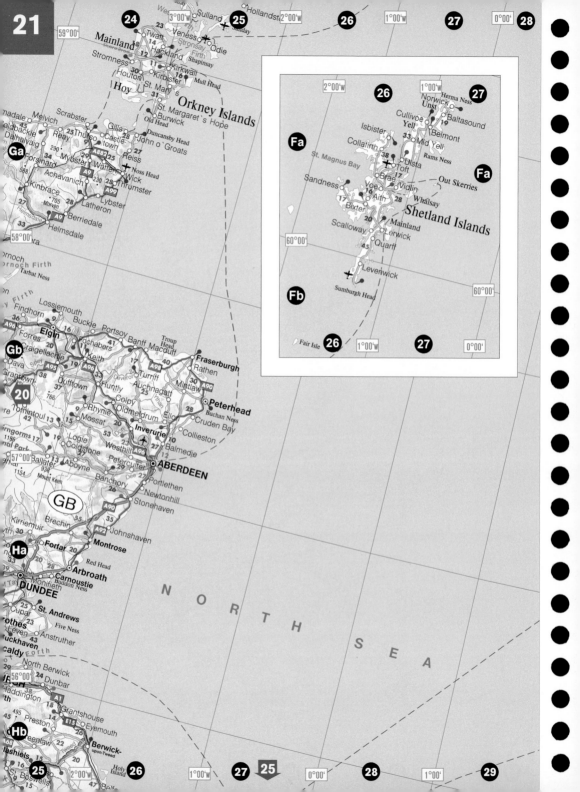

Orkney Islands

Mainland
Twatt
Sulland
Veness
Stronsay
Odie
Hackland
Sanday
Hollandsto
Stromness
Houton
Hoy
St. Mary's
Kirkister
Kirkwall
Shapinsay
Mull Head
St. Margaret's Hope
Burwick
Old Head
Duncansby Head
John o`Groats

Shetland Islands

Herma Ness
Norwick
Unst
Baltasound
Cullivoe
Yell
Belmont
Isbister
Mid Yell
Collafirth
Rams Ness
Ulsta
St. Magnus Bay
Toft
Sandness
Brae
Vidlin
Out Skerries
Voe
Bixter
Aith
Whalsay
Mainland
Scalloway
Lerwick
Quarff
Levenwick
Sumburgh Head
Fair Isle

Scrabster
Melvich
Reay
Thurso
Gills
Castletown
Reiss
Noss Head
Myster
Watten
Wick
Achavanich
Thrumster
Kinbrace
Latheron
Lybster
Morven
Berriedale
Helmsdale

Lossiemouth
Findhorn
Buckie
Portsoy
Banff
Macduff
Elgin
Forres
Fochabers
Keith
Troup Head
Rathen
Fraserburgh
Craigellachie
Turriff
Mintlaw
Dava
Dufftown
Huntly
Auchnagatt
Grantown
Rhynie
Colpy
Oldmeldrum
Peterhead
Tomintoul
Mossat
Ellon
Buchan Ness
Logie
Inverurie
Cruden Bay
Colliston
Coldstone
Westhill
Balmedie
Ballater
Aboyne
Petercultter
ABERDEEN
Banchory
Portlethen
Mount Keen
Newtonhill
Stonehaven
Kirriemuir
Brechin
Johnshaven
Forfar
Montrose
Red Head
Arbroath
Carnoustie
DUNDEE
Monifieth
Buddon Ness
St. Andrews
Five Ness
Anstruther
Leven
North Berwick
Dunbar
Grantshouse
Preston
Eyemouth
Berwick-upon-Tweed
Holy Island

NORTH SEA

GB

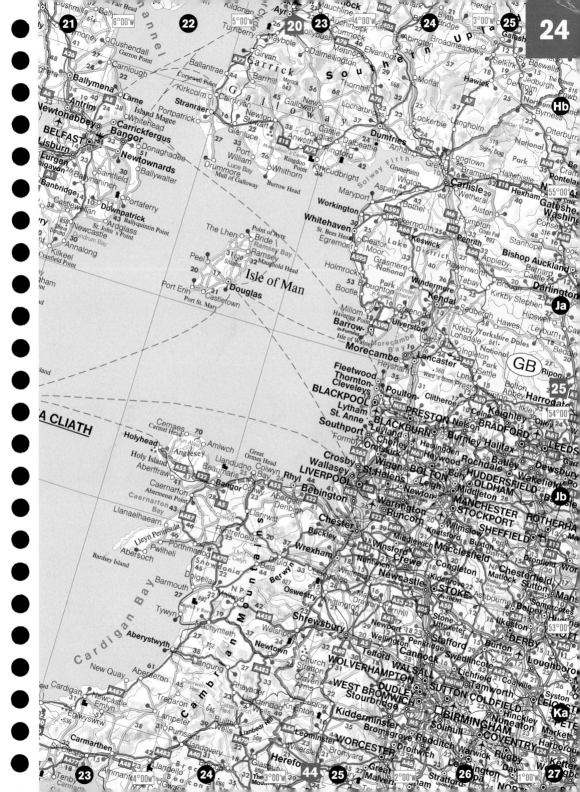

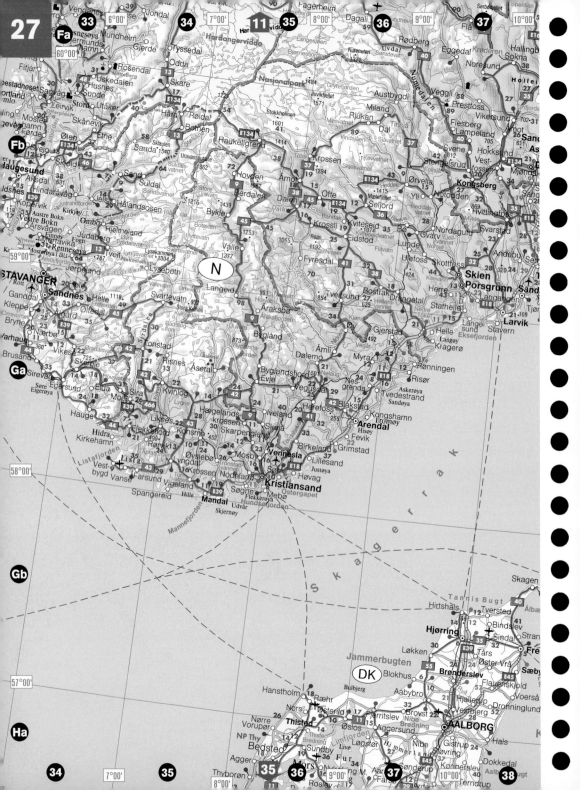

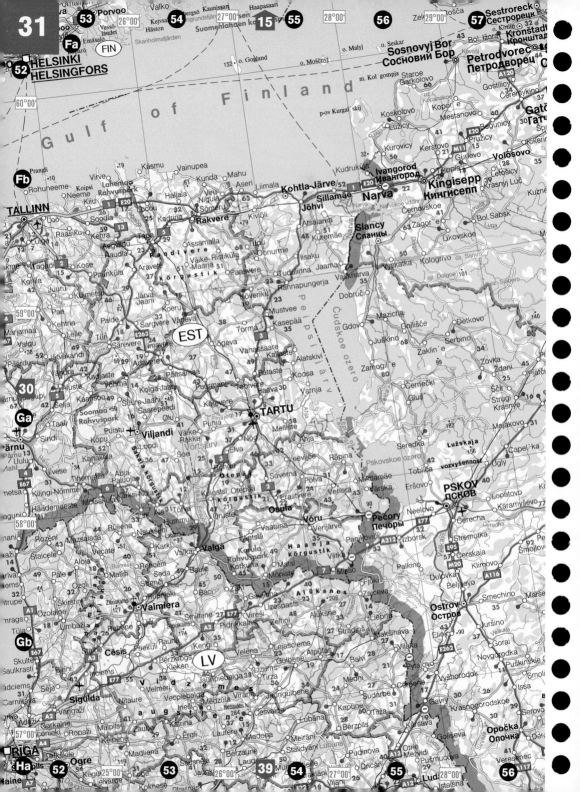

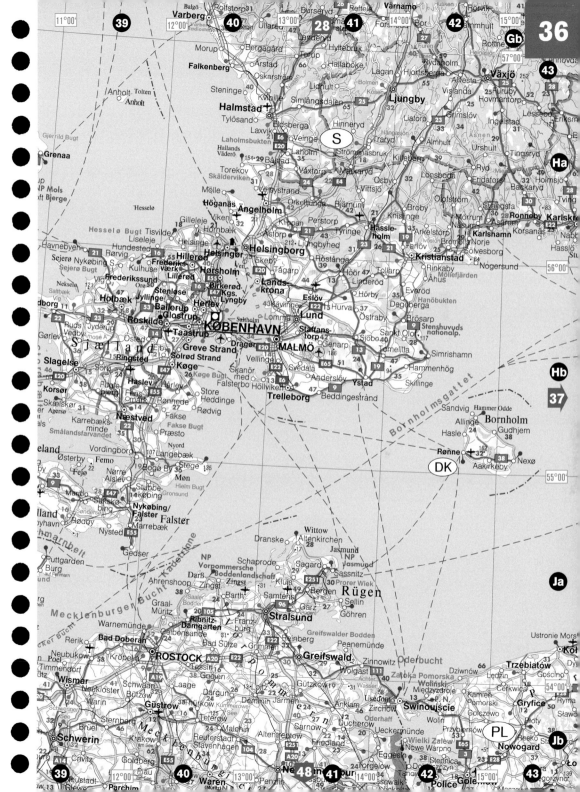

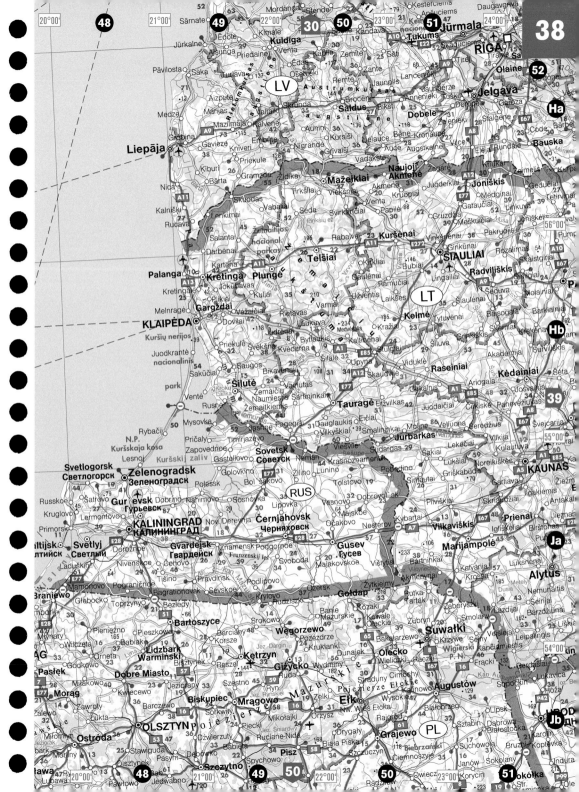

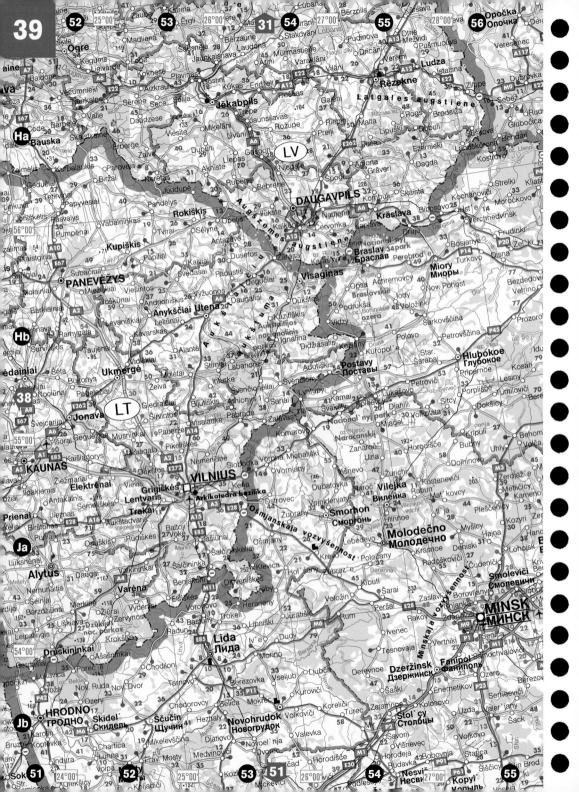

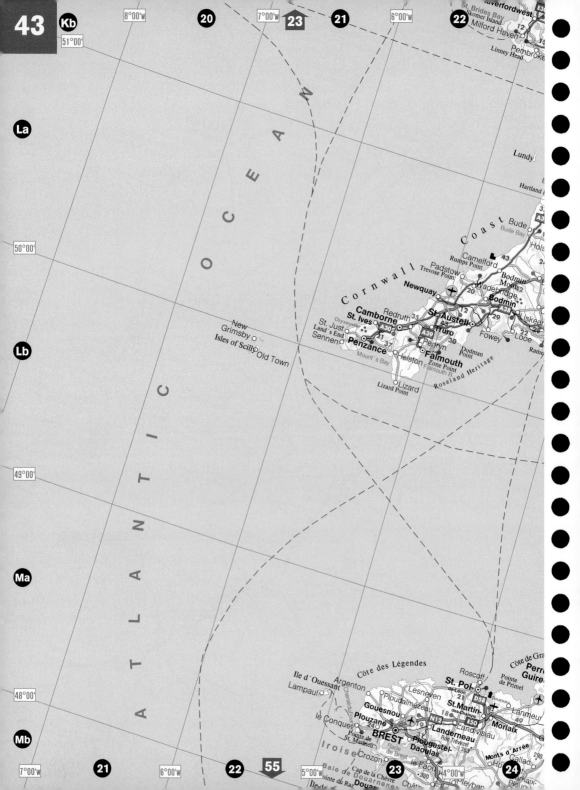

8°00'W   20   7°00'W   23   21   6°00'W   22   St. Brides Bay
Skomer Island
Haverfordwest
Milford Haven
Pembroke
Linney Head

La

O
C
E
A
N

Lundy

Hartland Point

50°00'

Coast   Bude
Bude Bay

Camelford
Rumps Point
Padstow   43
Trevose Point   Bodmin
Wadebridge   Moor
Newquay   20   Bodmin
Cornwall   Liskeard
Redruth   St. Austell   Fowey
Camborne   A30   Truro   30   Looe
St. Ives   Dodman   22   Ramo
St. Just   Penryn   Point
Land's End   A30   Falmouth
Sennen   Penzance   Zone Point
New   Mount's Bay   Helston   Falmouth B
Grimsby   Roseland Heritage
Isles of Scilly Old Town   Lizard
Lizard Point

Lb

A
T
L
A
N
T
I
C

49°00'

Ma

A
T
L
A
N
T
I
C

48°00'

Côte des Légendes   Côte de Gra
Roscoff   Perr
Ile d'Ouessant   St. Pol-   Guire
Argenton   de-Léon   Pointe
Lampaul   Lesneven   St.Martin-   de Primel
Pioudalmézeau   des-Champs   Lanmeur
Gouesnou   N12   Landivisiau   Morlaix
Plouzané   Landerneau
le Conquet   BREST   Plougastel-
Pointe de   Daoulas   Monts d'Arrée
St.Mathieu   Crozon   le Faou   Callac
Mb   Iroise   Rade   Baie de Douarnenez
Cap de la Chèvre   de Brest   Char   Pleyber
Pointe du Raz   Douar   Plouni
Île de

7°00'W   21   6°00'W   22   55   5°00'W   23   4°00'W   24

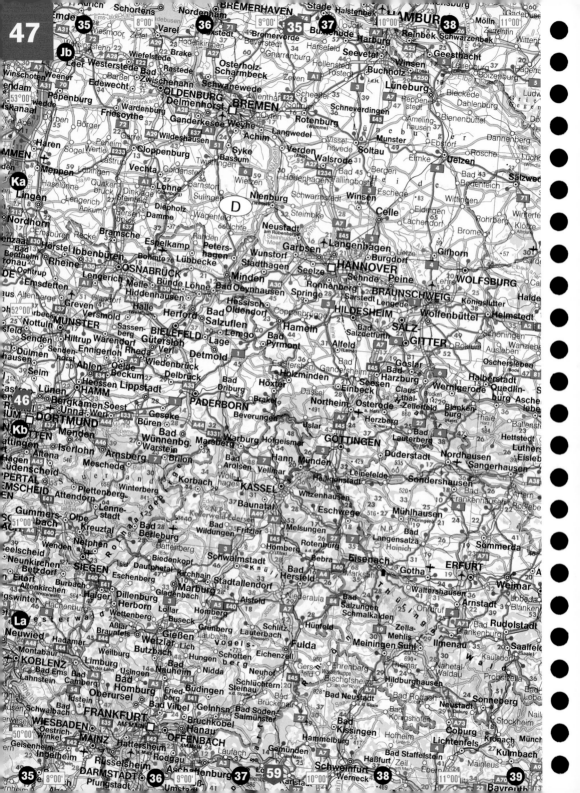

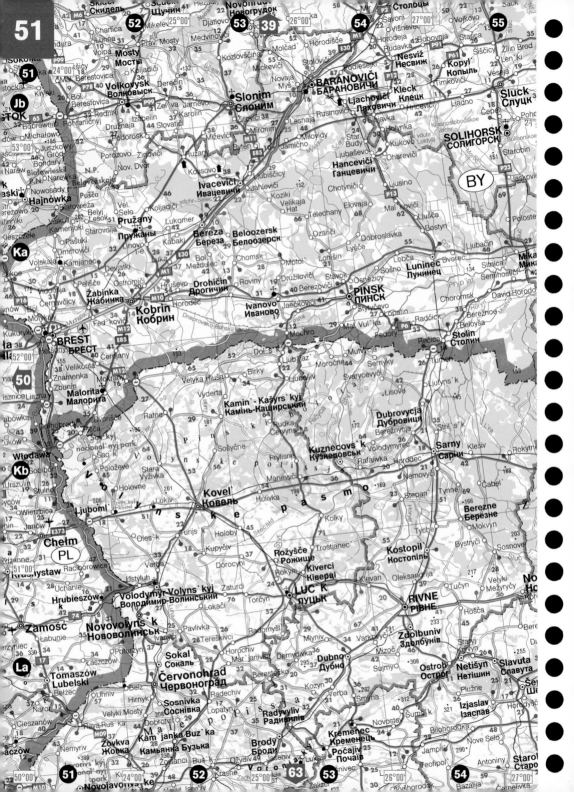

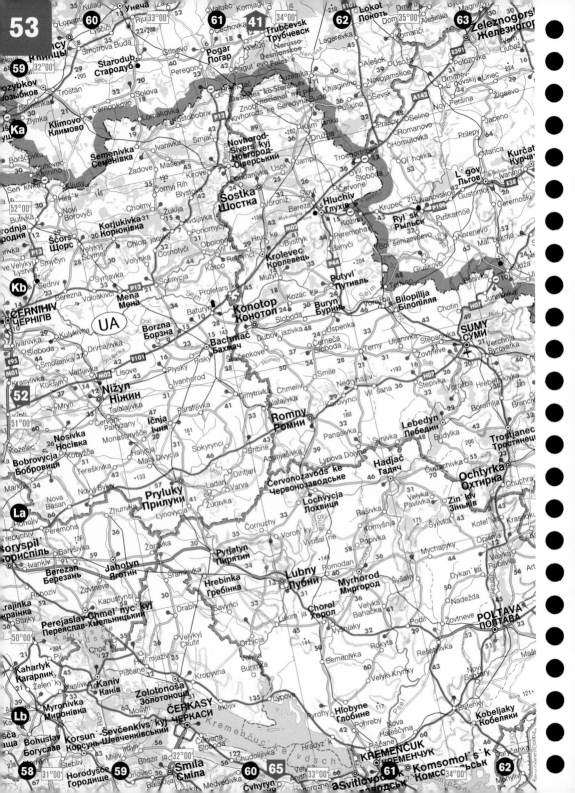

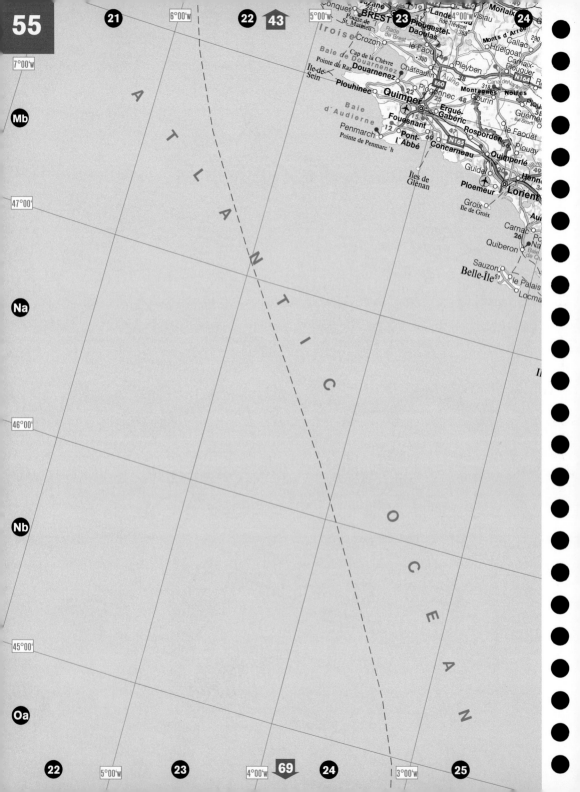

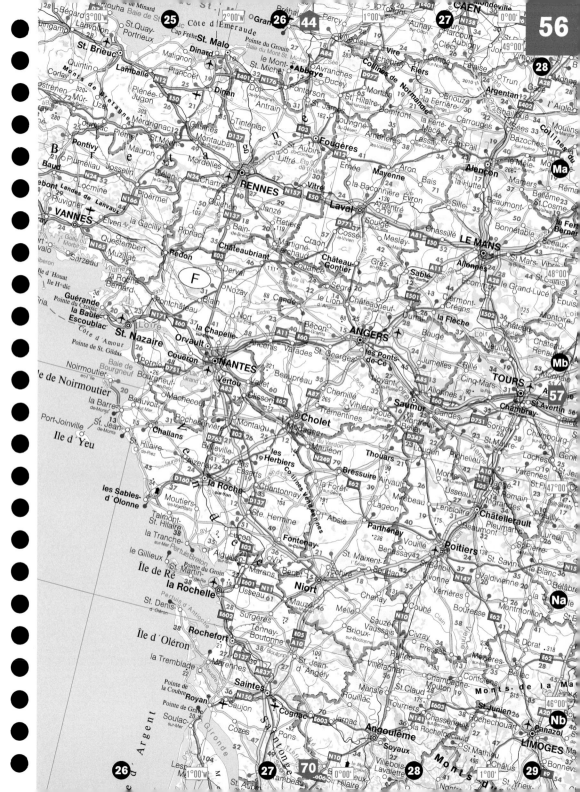

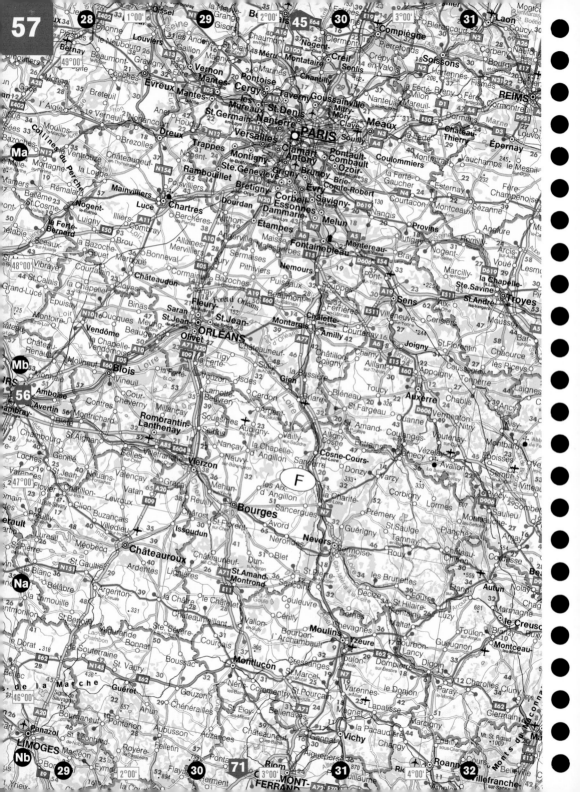

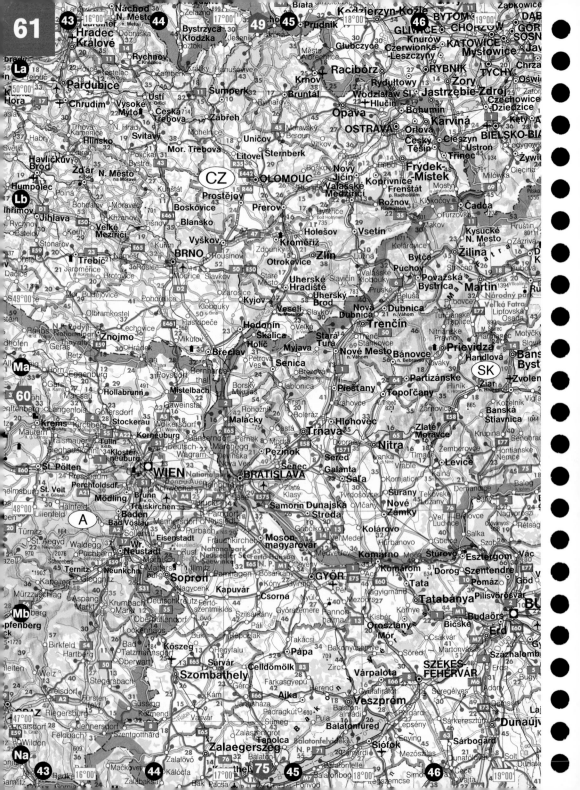

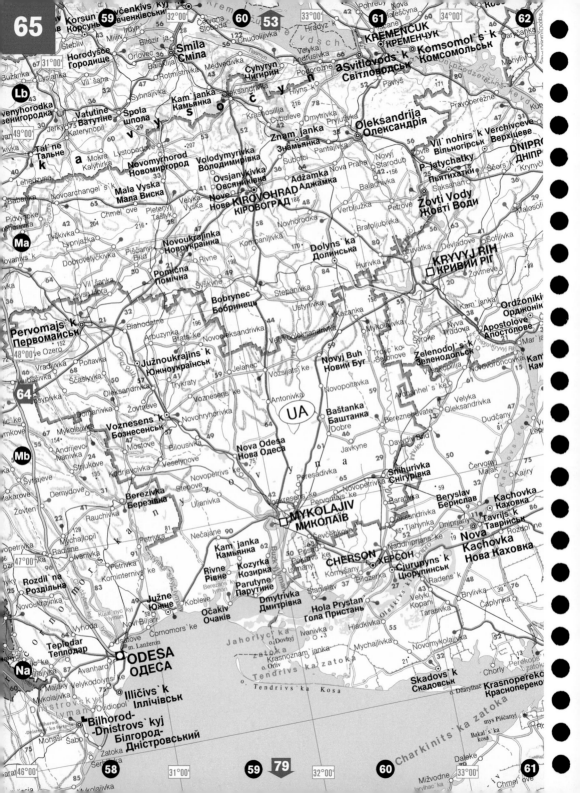

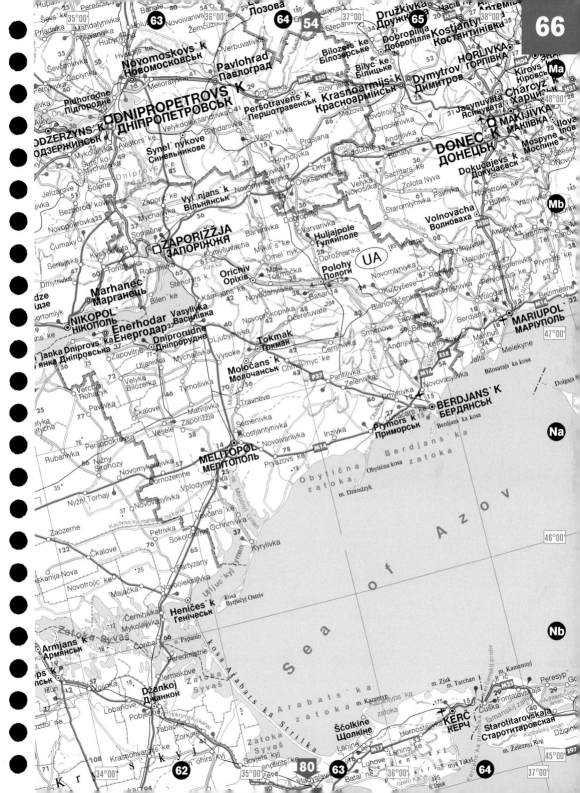

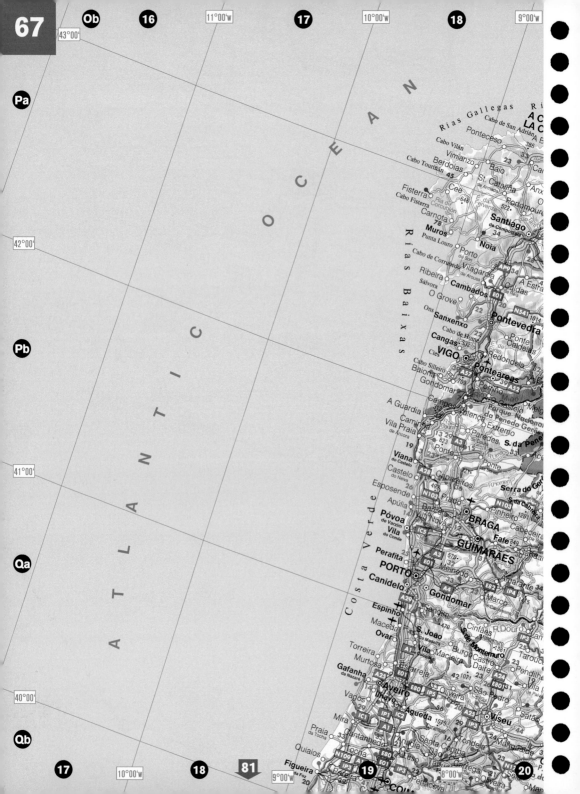

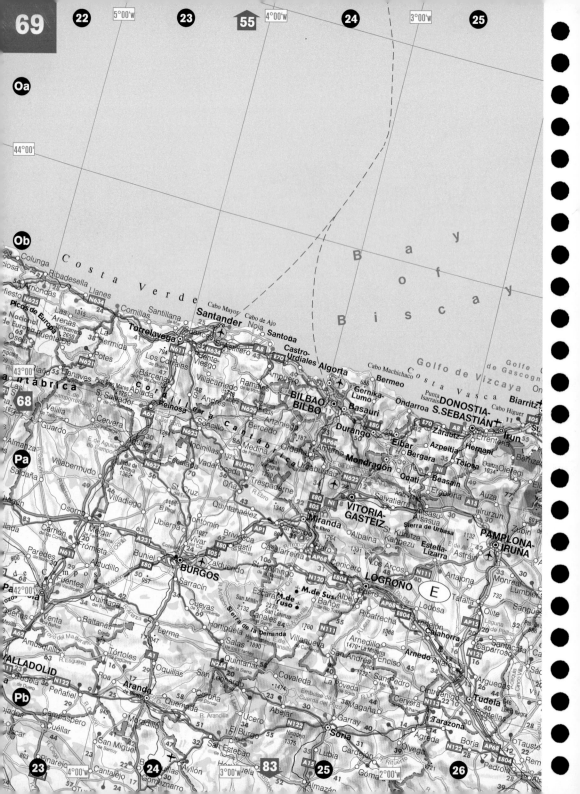

75

88

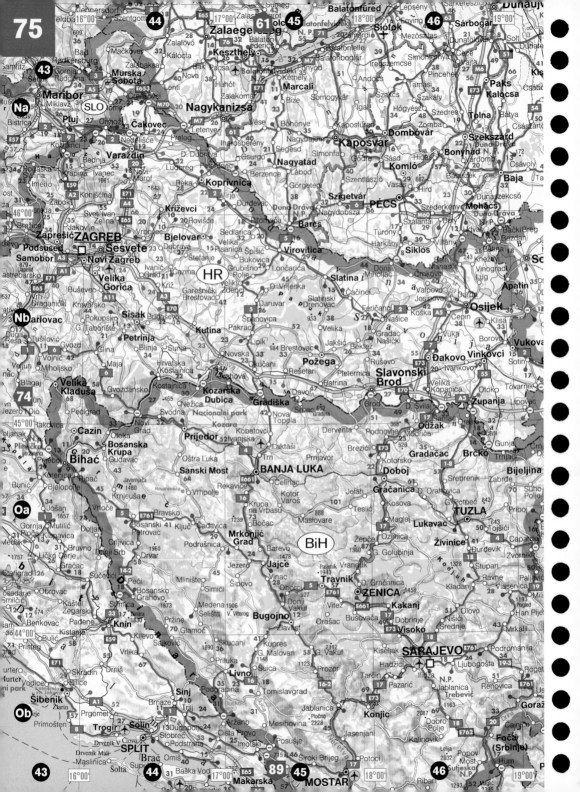

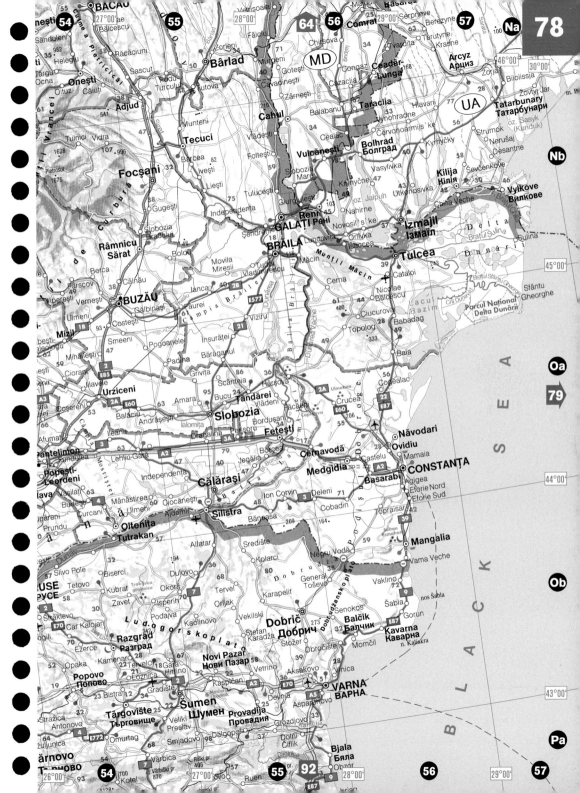

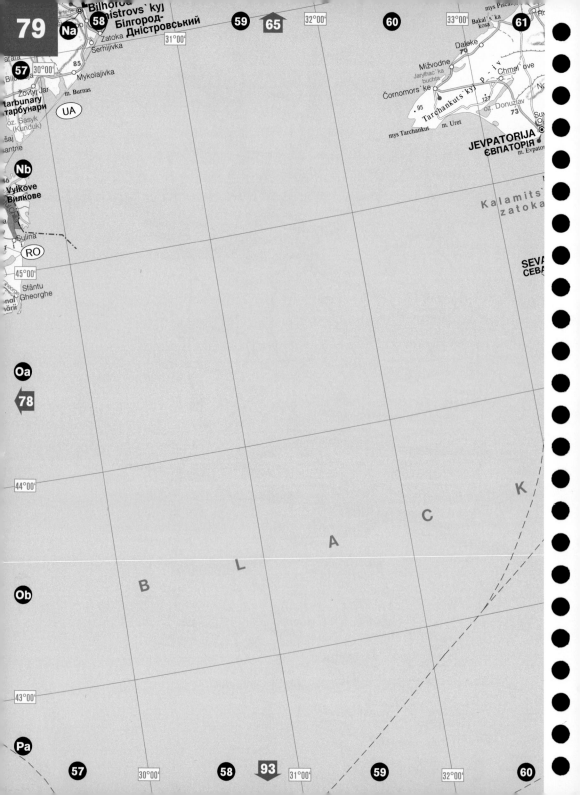

Bilhorod
58 nistrovs`kyj
Білгород-
Zatoka Дністровський
Serhijivka

59 **65** 32°00' **60** 33°00' mys Piscan

57 30°00' 85
Bilho na Mykolajivka
Žovtyj Jar m. Burnas
tarbunary
тарбунари **UA**
öz. Sasyk
(Kunduk)
šaj
santne

Nb
Vylkove
Вилкове

Sulina
RO
45°00'
Sfântu
Gheorghe
nal
ării

Oa
◀**78**

44°00'

Bakal`s`ka
kosa **61** R
Daleke
79
Mižvodne p - i - v
Jarylhac`ka  Chmel`ove
Čornomors`ke buchta
.95 oz. Donuzlav
Tarchankuts`kyj 73
mys Tarchankut m. Uret

JEVPATORIJA
ЄВПАТОРІЯ
m. Evpator

K a l a m i t s`
z a t o k a

SEVA
СЕВА

B   L   A   C   K

Ob

43°00'

Pa

57 30°00' **58** **93** 31°00' **59** 32°00' **60**

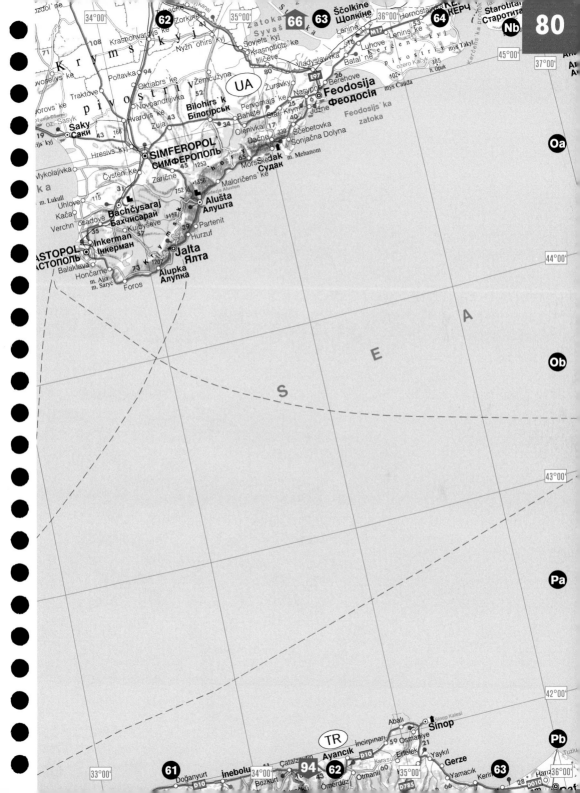

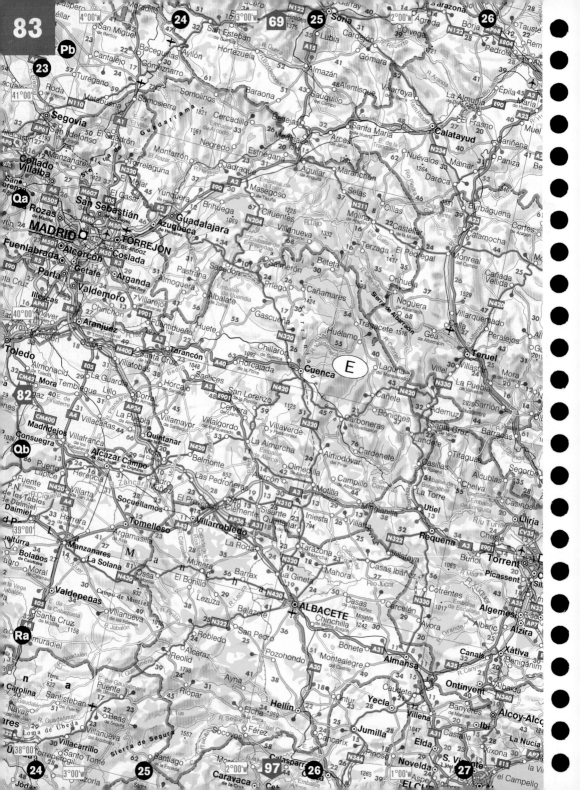

Corse

Í. Asinara
Parco Nazionale
dell' Asinara

Í s o l a   d i
S a r d e g n a

A N   S E A

G o l f o

Ajaccio

SASSARI
Porto Tórres
Alghero

Macomèr

Oristano
Golfo di
Oristano

Ghilarza

Terralba

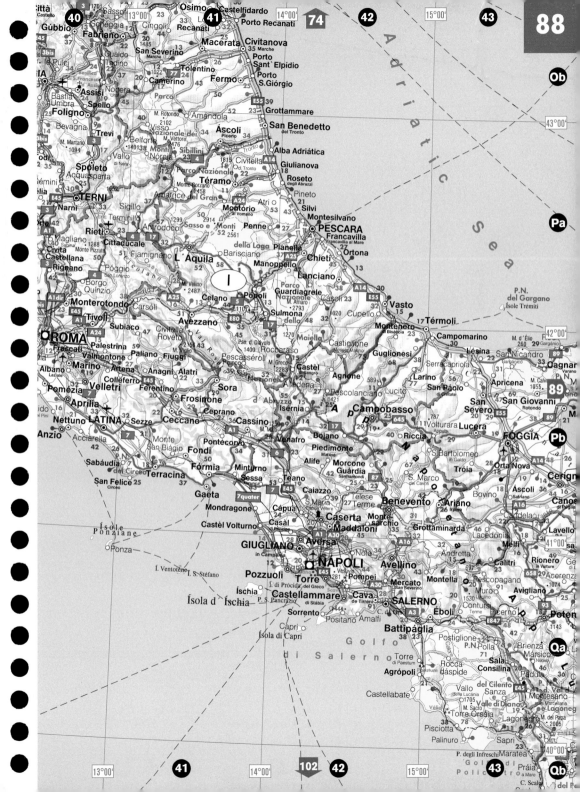

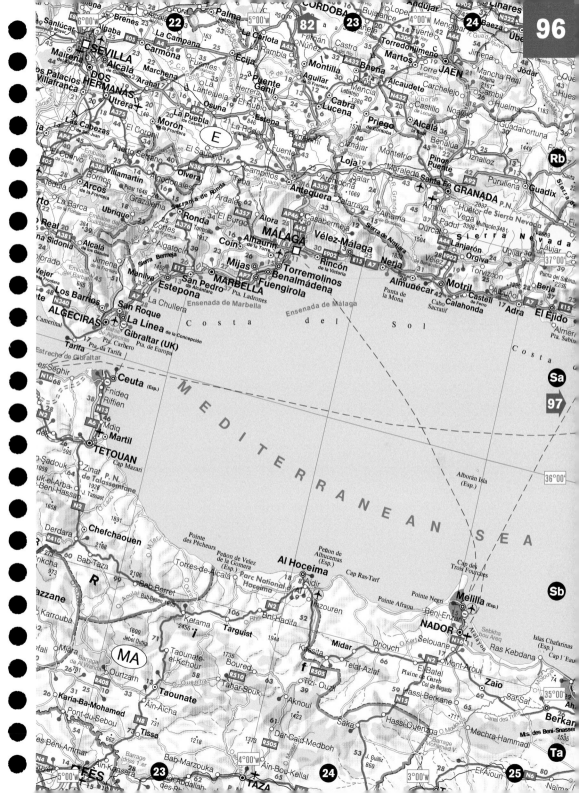

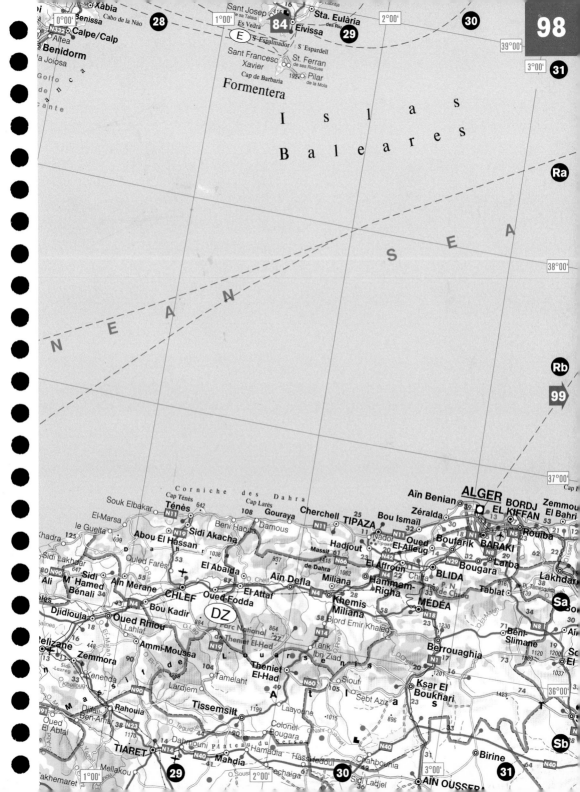

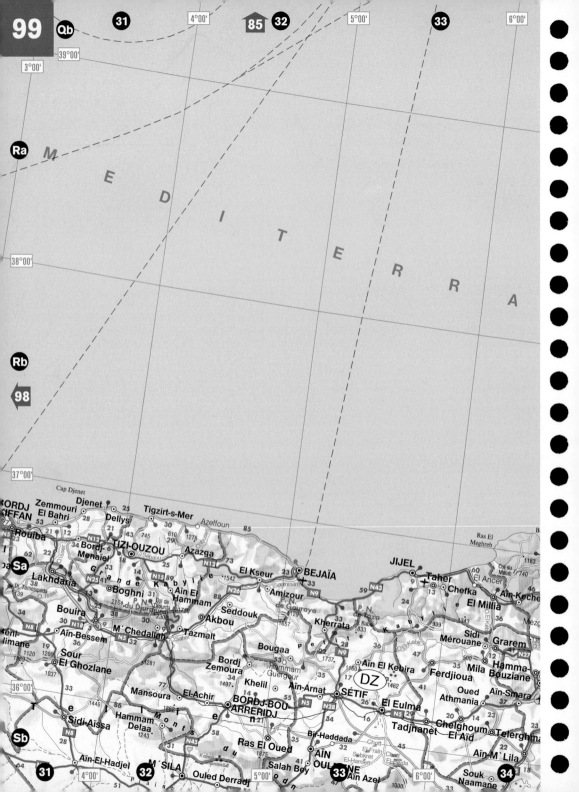

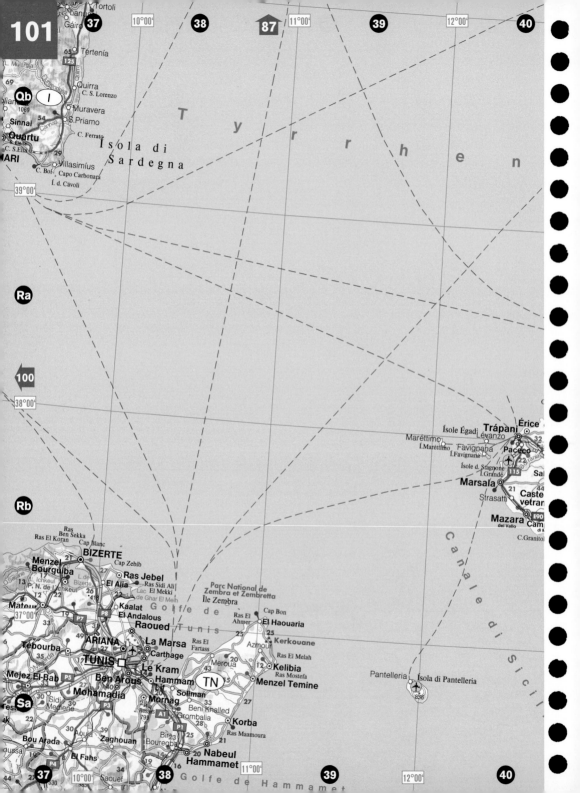

Tórtoli
37
Cántra
10°00'
38
Gáiro
87
11°00'
39
12°00'
40
L. Mularga
65
Tertenía
125
69
Quirra
C. S. Lorenzo
Qb
I
1069
Muravera
S.Priamo
Sinnai
54
Quartu
C. Ferrato
ARI
29
Villasimius
C. Boi Capo Carbonara
Í. d. Cávoli

I s o l a d i
S a r d e g n a

T
y
r
r
h
e
n

39°00'

Ra

100

38°00'

Ísole Égadi Trápani Érice
Maréttimo Lévanzo
Í.Maréttimo Favignana 32
Í.Favignana Paceco
Ísole d. Stagnone 22
Í.Grande 115 Sal
Marsala 21
Strasatti Caste
vetran

Rb

Mazara E90
del Vallo Cam
di V
C.Granitol

Ras
Ben Sekka
Ras El Koran Cap Blanc
BIZERTE
Menzel 21
Bourguiba Cap Zebib
13 Ras Jebel
I.ckeul 27
P.N. de El Alia
Mateur Íchkeul 26 Ras Sidi Ali
Lac El Mekki
19 de Ghar El Melh
33 Kaalat G o l f e d e
P7 P8 El Andalous
Tébourba 49 Raoued Ras El Cap Bon
ARIANA T u n i s Ahmer El Haouaria
35 La Marsa 25 Kerkouane
TUNIS Carthage Ras El 25
Mejez El Bab P5 Le Kram Fartass Azmour Ras El Melah
Ben Arous Hammam Meroua 20 Kelibia
Mohamadia Lif 43 12 Ras Mostefa
Sa P5 Soliman TN 25 Menzel Temine
Sidi Mornag 27
Mediene Beni Khalled Pantelleria Ísola di Pantelleria
Bou Arada J.Resas Grombalia 28 836
795 Bir Korba
Zaghouan 25 Ras Maamoura
14 21
Bouregba 20 Nabeul
El Fahs P4 Hammamet
37 10°00' 38 39 12°00' 40
Saouef 11°00' Golfe de Hammamet

Canale di Sicil

Ranal

C a n a l e   d i   S i c i l

Parc National de
Zembra et Zembretta
Île Zembra

C. Ferrato

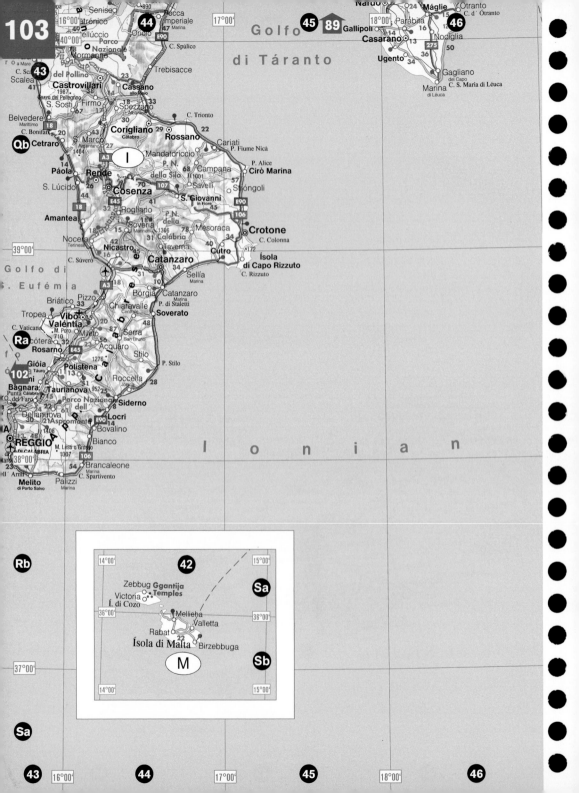

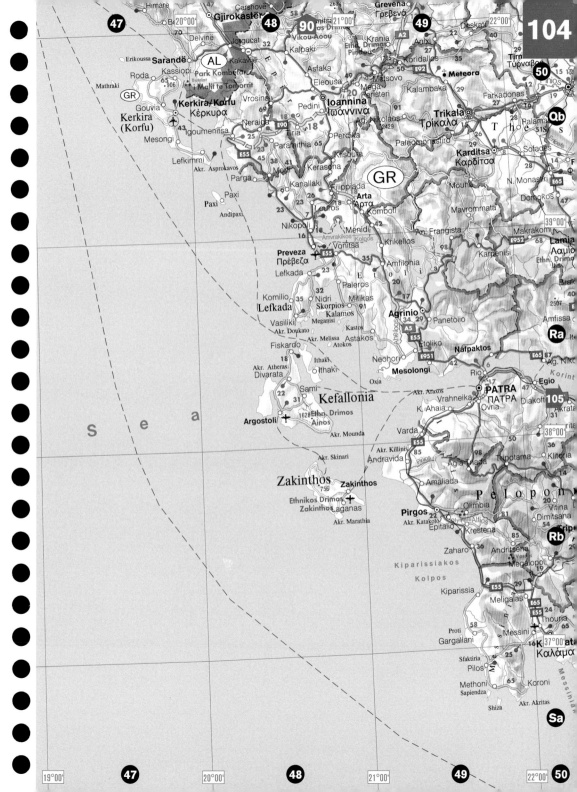

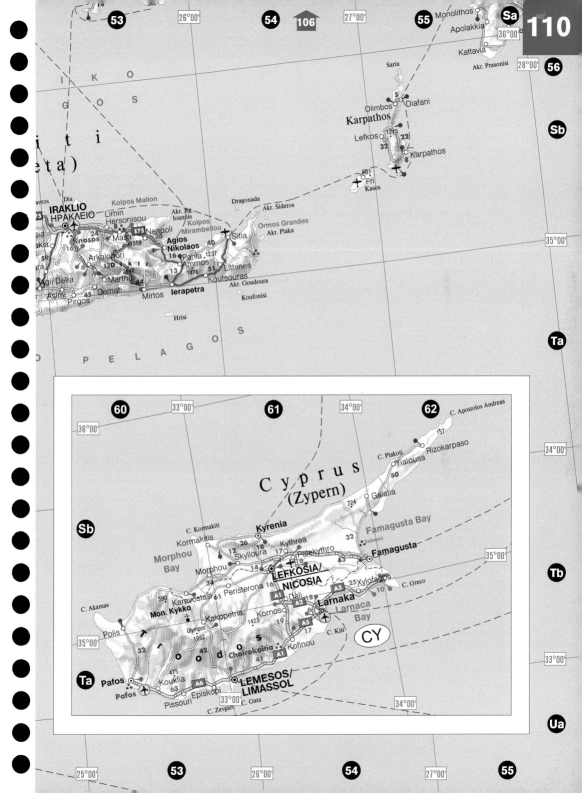

36°00'
56
Kattavia
Akr. Prasonisi 28°00'

Sb

Saria

5
Olimbos Diafani

Karpathos

Lefkos 1215
32 22

8 Karpathos

Koufonisi

601
Fri
Kasos

Ta

*I Kini
(eta)*

I K O S O
G O S

Dia
Akr. Ag.
Ioannis
IRAKLIO
HPAKΛEIO
Limin
Hersonisou
Kolpos Malion
Dragonada

Akr. Sideros
Kolpos
Mirambellou
Sitia
Ormos Grandes
Akr. Plaka

24
8
Mallia
175 Neapoli
20
Agios
Nikolaos
16
Pahia 1237
40
35°00'

Arkalohori
1559
Ammos
51
Lithines
Koutsouras
Akr. Goudoura

17 D i k t i
2148
13
1476

Agii Deka
Martha
44
Demati
45
Mirtos
Ierapetra

Asimi
Pirgos

Hrisi

P E L A G O S

---

60 33°00' 61 34°00' 62 C. Apostolos Andreas

36°00'

157
34°00'
C. Plakoti
Yialousa Rizokarpaso
50

C y p r u s
(Zypern)

Galatia
724

Sb
C. Kormakiti
Kyrenia
32 Solomis
Famagusta Bay

Kormakitis
12
26
18
Kythrea
35°00'
Morphou
Skylloura
17
Patekythro
Bay
14
Patekythro
3
Famagusta
Morphou
LEFKOSIA/
34
16
NICOSIA
25 Xylofagou
C. Akamas
590
Karavostasi 61 Peristerona
A1
Dali
A3
10 C. Greco
Tb
Mon. Kykko
Kakopetria
Kornoso
A2
Larnaca
Larnaca
Polis
Olympos
1423
19
A3
Bay
T 1952
32
r o o d o s
41
Kofinou
C. Kiti
CY
475
Choirokoitia
A1
33°00'
Ta
Pafos
Kouklia
A6
LEMESOS/
63
Episkopi
LIMASSOL
Pafos
Pissouri 33°00'
C. Zevgari C. Gata 34°00'

Ua

111

INDEX WITH POST CODES · ORTSREGISTER MIT POSTLEITZAHLEN · INDICE CON CODICI
STEDREGISTER MED POSTNUMRE · PLAATSNAMENREGISTER MET POSTCODE · REJSTŘÍK

A

5441 Abtenau 60 Mb 41
8943 Aigen im Ennstal 60 Mb 42
3804 Allentsteig 60 Ma 43
4121 Altenfelden 60 Ma 41
4813 Altmünster 60 Mb 41
3300 Amstetten 60 Ma 42
9601 Arnoldstein 74 Na 41
2870 Aspang Markt 61 Mb 44
4481 Asten 60 Ma 42
4800 Attnang-Puchheim 60 Ma 41
6094 Axams 59 Mb 39
8990 Bad Aussee 60 Mb 41
9135 Bad Eisenkappel 74 Na 42
5640 Bad Gastein 60 Mb 41
4822 Bad Goisern 60 Mb 41
5630 Bad Hofgastein 60 Mb 41
4820 Bad Ischl 60 Mb 41
4190 Bad Leonfelden 60 Ma 42
8983 Bad Mitterndorf 60 Mb 41
8490 Bad Radkersburg 75 Na 43
9462 Bad Sankt Leonhard im
         Lavanttal 60 Na 42
7431 Bad Tatzmannsdorf 61 Mb 44
2540 Bad Vöslau 61 Mb 44
4283 Bad Zell 60 Ma 42
2500 Baden 61 Mb 44
2560 Berndorf 61 Mb 44
2275 Bernhardsthal 61 Ma 44
8190 Birkfeld 61 Mb 43
5500 Bischofshofen 60 Mb 41
9150 Bleiburg 74 Na 42
6700 Bludenz 59 Mb 37
5733 Bramberg am Wildkogel
         60 Mb 40
5280 Braunau am Inn 60 Ma 41
6900 Bregenz 59 Mb 37
6252 Breitenbach am Inn 60 Mb 39
6230 Brixlegg 59 Mb 39
2460 Bruck an der Leitha 61 Ma 44
8600 Bruck an der Mur 60 Mb 43
2345 Brunn 61 Ma 44
2232 Deutsch-Wagram 61 Ma 44
7301 Deutschkreutz 61 Mb 44
8530 Deutschlandsberg 74 Na 43
9843 Döllach 60 Na 40
6950 Dornbirn 59 Mb 37
4802 Ebensee 60 Mb 41
4070 Eferding 60 Ma 42
3730 Eggenburg 61 Ma 43
6632 Ehrwald 59 Mb 38
8790 Eisenerz 60 Mb 42
7000 Eisenstadt 61 Mb 44
6352 Ellmau 60 Mb 40
4470 Enns 60 Ma 42
9181 Feistritz im Rosental 74 Na 42
8330 Feldbach 74 Na 43
6800 Feldkirch 59 Mb 37
9560 Feldkirchen in Kärnten
         74 Na 42
9170 Ferlach 74 Na 42
4890 Frankenmarkt 60 Mb 41
7132 Frauenkirchen 61 Mb 44
4240 Freistadt 60 Ma 42

8114 Friesach 60 Na 42
8403 Frohnleiten 60 Mb 43
6166 Fulpmes 59 Mb 39
8280 Fürstenfeld 61 Mb 44
8462 Gamlitz 74 Na 43
2230 Gänserndorf 61 Ma 44
3571 Gars am Kamp 61 Ma 43
2191 Gaweinstal 61 Ma 44
2093 Geras 61 Ma 43
3542 Göfl 60 Ma 43
8200 Gleisdorf 61 Mb 43
2640 Gloggnitz 61 Mb 43
3950 Gmünd 60 Ma 42
9853 Gmünd in Kärnten 60 Na 41
4810 Gmunden 60 Mb 41
2013 Göllersdorf 61 Ma 44
3345 Göstling an der Ybbs
         60 Mb 42
8010 Graz 60 Mb 43
4360 Grein 60 Ma 42
8962 Gröbming 60 Mb 41
3920 Groß Gerungs 60 Ma 42
4464 Großraming 60 Mb 42
9342 Gurk 60 Na 42
7540 Güssing 61 Mb 4
3350 Haag 60 Ma 42
2410 Hainburg an der Donau
         61 Ma 44
3170 Hainfeld 61 Mb 43
6060 Hall 59 Mb 39
5400 Hallein 60 Mb 41
6971 Hard 59 Mb 37
8244 Hartberg 61 Mb 43
8967 Haus 60 Mb 41
3860 Heidenreichstein 60 Ma 43
9844 Heiligenblut 60 Mb 40
9620 Hermagor 74 Na 41
8920 Hieflau 60 Mb 42
6294 Hintertux 59 Mb 39
6395 Hochfilzen 60 Mb 40
8785 Hohentauern 60 Mb 42
2020 Hollabrunn 61 Ma 44
6361 Hopfgarten im Brixental
         60 Mb 40
3580 Horn 61 Ma 43
9375 Hüttenberg 60 Na 42
7142 Illmitz 61 Mb 44
6460 Imst 59 Mb 38
6020 Innsbruck 59 Mb 39
6561 Ischgl 59 Mb 38
6200 Jenbach 59 Mb 39
8380 Jennersdorf 61 Na 44
8750 Judenburg 60 Mb 42
8401 Kalsdorf bei Graz 60 Na 43
8691 Kapellen 61 Mb 43
8605 Kapfenberg 60 Mb 43
5710 Kaprun 60 Mb 40
8650 Kindberg 60 Mb 43
3470 Kirchberg am Wagram
         61 Ma 43
2421 Kittsee 61 Ma 45
6370 Kitzbühel 60 Mb 40
9020 Klagenfurt am Wörthersee
         74 Na 42
3400 Klosterneuburg 61 Ma 44
8720 Knittelfeld 60 Mb 42

8580 Köflach 60 Mb 43
2100 Korneuburg 61 Ma 44
6345 Kössen 60 Mb 40
9640 Kötschach 74 Na 41
3500 Krems an der Donau 61 Ma 43
4550 Kremsmünster 60 Ma 42
5743 Krimml 60 Mb 40
2851 Krumbach Markt 61 Mb 44
5431 Kuchl 60 Mb 41
6330 Kufstein 60 Mb 40
6182 Kühtai 59 Mb 39
2136 Laa an der Thaya
         61 Ma 44
4650 Lambach 60 Ma 41
6500 Landeck 59 Mb 38
6444 Längenfeld 59 Mb 38
3550 Langenlois 61 Ma 43
9473 Lavamünd 74 Na 42
6764 Lech 59 Mb 38
8430 Leibnitz 74 Na 43
8700 Leoben/Bruck an der Mur
         60 Mb 43
4060 Leonding 60 Ma 42
9900 Lienz 60 Na 40
8940 Liezen 60 Mb 42
3180 Lilienfeld 60 Ma 43
4020 Linz 60 Ma 42
7442 Lockenhaus 61 Mb 44
5090 Lofer 60 Mb 40
3293 Lunz am See 60 Mb 43
6890 Lustenau 59 Mb 3
3712 Maissau 61 Ma 43
2452 Mannersdorf am Leithagebirge
         61 Mb 44
2293 Marchegg 61 Ma 44
4614 Marchtrenk 60 Ma 42
5571 Mariapfarr 60 Mb 41
8630 Mariazell 60 Mb 43
4490 Markt Sankt Florian 60 Ma 42
9971 Matrei in Osttirol 60 Na 40
7210 Mattersburg 61 Mb 44
5230 Mattighofen 60 Ma 41
3512 Mautern an der Donau
         60 Ma 42
6290 Mayrhofen 59 Mb 39
3390 Melk 60 Ma 43
2130 Mistelbach 61 Ma 44
6481 Mittelberg 59 Mb 38
5730 Mittersill 60 Mb 40
2340 Mödling 61 Ma 44
5310 Mondsee 60 Mb 41
7072 Mörbisch am See 61 Mb 44
6082 Mühltal 59 Mb 39
8850 Murau 60 Mb 42
8680 Mürzzuschlag 61 Mb 4
6543 Nauders 59 Na 38
4212 Neumarkt im Mühlkreis
         60 Ma 42
8820 Neumarkt im Steiermark
         60 Mb 42
2620 Neunkirchen 61 Mb 44
7100 Neusiedl am See 61 Mb 44
7350 Oberpullendorf 61 Mb 44
5562 Obertauern 60 Mb 41
9821 Obervellach 60 Na 41

7400 Oberwart 61 Mb 44
7152 Pamhagen 61 Mb 44
7111 Parndorf 61 Mb 44
9711 Paternion 74 Na 41
2380 Perchtoldsdorf 61 Ma 44
4320 Perg 60 Ma 42
3650 Pöggstall 60 Ma 43
8761 Pöls 60 Mb 42
2170 Poysdorf 61 Ma 44
4230 Pregarten 60 Ma 42
3021 Pressbaum 61 Ma 44
2734 Puchberg am Schneeberg
         61 Mb 43
3214 Puchenstuben 60 Mb 43
7083 Purbach am Neusiedlersee
         61 Mb 44
3251 Purgstall an der Erlauf
         60 Ma 43
3820 Raabs an der Thaya 60 Ma 43
9545 Radenthein 60 Na 41
5550 Radstadt 60 Mb 41
6167 Ranalt 59 Mb 39
6830 Rankweil 59 Mb 37
9863 Rennweg am Katschberg
         60 Mb 41
2070 Retz 61 Ma 43
6600 Reutte 59 Mb 38
4910 Ried im Innkreis 60 Ma 41
8333 Riegersburg 61 Mb 43
4150 Rohrbach in Oberösterreich
         60 Ma 41
8786 Rottenmann 60 Mb 42
7071 Rust 61 Mb 44
5760 Saalfelden am Steinernen Meer
         60 Mb 40
5020 Salzburg 60 Mb 41
3193 Sankt Aegyd am Neuwalde
         60 Mb 43
9433 Sankt Andrä im Lavanttal
         74 Na 42
6580 Sankt Anton am Arlberg
         59 Mb 38
8933 Sankt Gallen 60 Mb 42
9313 Sankt Georgen am Längsee
         74 Na 42
9963 Sankt Jakob im Defreggental
         60 Na 40
5600 Sankt Johann im Pongau
         60 Mb 41
9951 Sankt Johann im Walde
         60 Na 40
6380 Sankt Johann in Tirol
         60 Mb 40
4113 Sankt Martin im Mühlkreis
         60 Ma 42
5582 Sankt Michael im Lungau
         60 Mb 41
3100 Sankt Pölten 61 Ma 43
3162 Sankt Veit 61 Ma 43
9300 Sankt Veit an der Glan
         74 Na 42
5360 Sankt Wolfgang im
         Salzkammergut 60 Mb 41
4780 Schärding 60 Ma 41
3270 Scheibbs 60 Ma 43
8970 Schladming 60 Mb 41

POSTALI · ÍNDICE CON CÓDIGOS POSTALES · INDICE DE LUGARES COM CÓDIGOS POSTAIS ·
MÍST S PSČ · ZOZNAM OBCÍ S PSČ · INDEKS MIEJSCOWOŚCI Z KOD POCZTOWY

112

Schrems A . AL . AND . B **Tongeren**

 A
 AL
 AND
 B

3943 Schrems 60 Ma 43
6780 Schruns-Tschagguns 59 Mb 37
5620 Schwarzach im Pongau
    60 Mb 41
6130 Schwaz 59 Mb 39
2320 Schwechat 61 Ma 44
9871 Seeboden 60 Na 41
6100 Seefeld in Tirol 59 Mb 39
5201 Seekirchen am Wallersee
    60 Mb 41
3353 Seitenstetten 60 Ma 42
3541 Senftenberg 60 Ma 43
3443 Sieghartskirchen 61 Ma 44
9920 Sillian 74 Na 40
6450 Sölden 59 Na 39
2601 Sollenau 61 Mb 44
9800 Spittal an der Drau 60 Na 41
3620 Spitz 60 Ma 43
8770 Sankt Michael in der
    Obersteiermark 60 Mb 43
8510 Stainz 60 Na 43
6422 Stams 59 Mb 38
6642 Stanzach 59 Mb 38
7551 Stegersbach 61 Mb 44
6150 Steinach am Brenner
    59 Mb 39
9754 Steinfeld 74 Na 41
4400 Steyr 60 Ma 42
2000 Stockerau 61 Ma 44
5204 Straßwalchen 60 Mb 41
5350 Strobl 60 Mb 41
5580 Tamsweg 60 Mb 41
6410 Telfs 59 Mb 39
2630 Ternitz 61 Mb 44
8621 Thörl 60 Mb 43
2514 Traiskirchen 61 Ma 44
3133 Traismauer 61 Ma 43
4050 Traun 60 Ma 42
8784 Trieben 60 Mb 42
8793 Trofaiach 60 Mb 43
3430 Tulln 61 Ma 44
3184 Türnitz 60 Mb 43
8864 Turrach 60 Na 41
9220 Velden am Wörthersee
    74 Na 42
9500 Villach 74 Na 41
4840 Vöcklabruck 60 Ma 41
8570 Voitsberg 60 Mb 43
9100 Völkermarkt 74 Na 42
3830 Waidhofen an der Thaya
    60 Ma 43
3340 Waidhofen an der Ybbs
    60 Mb 42
2754 Waldegg 61 Mb 44
6112 Wattens 59 Mb 39
9344 Weitensfeld im Gurktal
    60 Na 42
3970 Weitra 60 Ma 42
8160 Weiz 60 Mb 43
4600 Wels 60 Ma 42
3335 Weyer 60 Mb 42
1010 Wien 61 Ma 44
2700 Wiener Neustadt 61 Mb 44
8924 Wildalpen 60 Mb 42
8410 Wildon 60 Na 43
3150 Wilhelmsburg 60 Ma 43

4580 Windischgarsten 60 Mb 42
9851 Winklern 60 Na 40
9400 Wolfsberg 60 Na 42
2120 Wolkersdorf im Weinviertel
    61 Ma 44
6300 Wörgl 60 Mb 40
3370 Ybbs an der Donau 60 Ma 43
5700 Zell am See 60 Mb 40
6280 Zell am Ziller 59 Mb 39
4755 Zell an der Pram 60 Ma 41
8740 Zeltweg 60 Mb 42

AL

6406 Ballaban 90 Qa 48
9308 Ballsh 90 Qa 47
    Bejar 90 Qa 47
5000 Berat 90 Qa 47
8504 Bicaj 90 Pb 48
7006 Bilisht 90 Qa 48
9714 Borsh 90 Qa 47
8400 Bulqizë 90 Pb 48
8000 Burrel 90 Pb 48
3007 Cërrik 90 Pb 47
6403 Çarshovë 90 Qa 48
5400 Çorovodë 90 Qa 48
9704 Delvinë 104 Qb 48
    Dobërçan 90 Qa 48
    Dukat 90 Qa 47
2000 Durrës 90 Pb 47
3000 Elbasan 90 Pb 48
7400 Erseke 90 Qa 48
9300 Fier 90 Qa 47
4030 Fierzë 90 Pa 48
4402 Fushë Arrëzi 90 Pa 48
1502 Fushë-Krujë 90 Pb 47
3300 Gramsh 90 Qa 48
6000 Gjirokastër 90 Qa 48
    Helmës 90 Qa 48
9425 Himarë 90 Qa 48
    Ibë 90 Pb 47
6011 Jorgucat 104 Qb 4
    Kakavijë 104 Qb 48
9002 Karbunara e Poshtme
    90 Qa 47
    Kassiopi 104 Qb 47
2500 Kavajë 90 Pb 47
6402 Këlcyrë 90 Qa 48
8002 Klos 90 Pb 48
4300 Koplik 90 Pa 47
7000 Korcë 90 Qa 48
1501 Krujë 90 Pb 47
5007 Kuçovë 90 Qa 47
8500 Kukës 90 Pa 48
4700 Laç 90 Pb 47
7402 Leskovik 90 Qa 48
4500 Lezhë 90 Pb 47
3400 Librazhd 90 Pb 48
9000 Lushnjë 90 Qa 47
7005 Maliq 90 Qa 48
4704 Mamuras 90 Pb 47
6302 Memaliaj 90 Qa 47
4705 Milot 90 Pb 47
    Muriqan 90 Pa 47

9307 Patos 90 Qa 47
8300 Peshkopi 90 Pb 48
3500 Pëqin 90 Pb 47
6400 Përmet 90 Qa 48
3403 Përrenjas 90 Pb 48
7016 Pirg 90 Qa 48
    Piskupat 90 Pb 48
7300 Pogradec 90 Qa 48
4400 Pukë 90 Pa 47
    Qyrsaç 90 Pa 47
    Roda 104 Qb 4
4600 Rrëshen 90 Pb 47
2503 Rrogozhinë 90 Pb 47
9306 Rroskovec 90 Qa 47
9700 Sarandë 104 Qb 48
9410 Sevaster 90 Qa 47
4503 Shëngjin 90 Pb 47
2018 Shijak 90 Pb 47
4000 Shkodër 90 Pa 47
8404 Shupenzë 90 Pb 48
6300 Tepelenë 90 Qa 48
5015 Terpan 90 Qa 48
1000 Tiranë 90 Pb 47
8003 Ulëz 90 Pb 47
9400 Vlorë 90 Qa 47
1032 Vorë 90 Pb 47

AND

AD 500 Andorra 70 Pa29
AD 400 El Serrat 70 Pa 29

B

9300 Aalst 46 La 32
3200 Aarschot 46 La 32
5300 Andenne 46 La 33
2000 Antwerpen 46 Kb 32
6700 Arlon 58 Lb 33
1730 Asse 46 La 32
7800 Ath 46 La 31
6790 Aubange 58 Lb 33
6600 Bastogne 46 Lb 33
6500 Beaumont 46 La 32
5570 Beauraing 46 La 32
6880 Bertrix 46 Lb 33
9120 Beveren 46 Kb 32
8370 Blankenberge 45 Kb 31
1420 Braine-l'Alleud 46 La 32
7090 Braine-le-Comte 46 La 32
2930 Brasschaat 46 Kb 32
8000 Brugge 45 Kb 31
1000 Brussel/Bruxelles 46 La 32
6000 Charleroi 46 La 32
6200 Châtelet 46 La 32
6460 Chimay 46 La 32
6180 Courcelles 46 La 32
5660 Couvin 46 La 32
9800 Deinze 45 La 31
9200 Dendermonde 46 Kb 32
3290 Diest 46 La 33
5500 Dinant 46 La 32

6740 Étalle 58 Lb 33
4700 Eupen 46 La 34
4400 Flémalle 46 La 33
6220 Fleurus 46 La 32
6820 Florenville 46 Lb 33
2440 Geel 46 Kb 33
5030 Gembloux 46 La 32
3600 Genk 46 La 33
9000 Gent 46 Kb 31
7041 Givry 46 La 32
6720 Habay-la-Neuve 46 Lb 33
1500 Halle 46 La 32
3500 Hasselt 46 La 33
5370 Havelange 46 La 33
2200 Herentals 46 Kb 32
4040 Herstal 46 La 33
3530 Houthalen 46 Kb 33
8650 Houthulst 45 La 30
4500 Huy 46 La 33
8900 Ieper 45 La 30
1880 Knokke-Heist 45 Kb 31
8500 Kortrijk 45 La 31
7100 La Louvière 46 La 32
6980 La Roche-en-Ardenne
    46 La 33
3000 Leuven 46 La 32
6800 Libramont-Chevigny 46 Lb 33
4000 Liège 46 La 33
2500 Lier 46 Kb 32
9160 Lokeren 46 Kb 31
3920 Lommel 46 Kb 33
6852 Maissin 46 La 33
4960 Malmédy 46 La 34
7170 Manage 46 La 32
6900 Marche-en-Famenne 46 La 33
6630 Martelange 46 Lb 33
2800 Mechelen 46 Kb 32
8930 Menen 45 La 31
8430 Middelkerke 45 Kb 30
2400 Mol 46 Kb 33
7000 Mons 46 La 31
7700 Mouscron 45 La 31
5000 Namur 46 La 32
6840 Neufchâteau 46 Lb 33
8620 Nieuwpoort 45 Kb 30
9400 Ninove 46 La 32
1400 Nivelles 46 La 32
8400 Oostende 45 Kb 30
1340 Ottignies-Louvain-la-Neuve
    46 La 32
9700 Oudenaarde 45 La 31
5600 Philippeville 46 La 32
8970 Poperinge 45 La 30
5580 Rochefort 46 La 33
8800 Roeselare 45 La 31
9600 Ronse 45 La 31
6870 Saint Hubert 46 Lb 33
4780 Saint Vith 46 La 34
4100 Seraing 46 La 33
9100 Sint Niklaas 46 Kb 32
3800 Sint-Truiden 46 La 33
7060 Soignies 46 La 32
4900 Spa 46 La 33
8700 Tielt 45 La 31
3300 Tienen 46 La 32
3700 Tongeren 46 La 33

113

INDEX WITH POST CODES · ORTSREGISTER MIT POSTLEITZAHLEN · INDICE CON CODICI
STEDREGISTER MED POSTNUMRE · PLAATSNAMENREGISTER MET POSTCODE · REJSTŘÍK

B

BG

Tournai

B · BG

Simeonovgrad

7500 Tournai 45 La 31
2300 Turnhout 46 Kb 32
4800 Verviers 46 La 33
8630 Veurne 45 Kb 30
6690 Vielsalm 46 La 33
1800 Vilvoorde 46 La 32
1410 Waterloo 46 La 32
1300 Wavre 46 La 32
4190 Werbomont 46 La 33
9230 Wetteren 46 Kb 31
8380 Zeebrugge 45 Kb 31

BG

8280 Ahtopol 92 Pa 55
7538 Ajdemir 78 Oa 55
8500 Ajtos / Айтос 92 Pa 55
9154 Aksakovo 78 Ob 55
5560 Aleksandrovo 77 Ob 52
7570 Alfatar 78 Ob 55
7970 Antonovo 78 Ob 54
3770 Arčar 77 Ob 50
6750 Ardino 91 Pb 53
4230 Asenovgrad / Асеновград 91 Pa 52
9000 Asparuhovo 78 Ob 55
9600 Balčik / Балчик 78 Ob 56
5583 Bălgarene 91 Ob 52
4360 Banja 91 Pa 52
2770 Bansko 91 Pb 51
4580 Batak 91 Pb 52
3900 Belogradčik 77 Ob 50
4470 Belovo 91 Pa 52
4130 Belozem 91 Pa 53
6865 Benkovski 91 Pb 53
3500 Berkovica / Берковица 91 Ob 51
7334 Biserci 78 Ob 54
7777 Bistra 78 Ob 54
9101 Bjala/Obzor / Бяла 92 Pa 55
7100 Bjala/Pavliken 77 Ob 53
3200 Bjala Slatina / Бяла Слатина 77 Ob 51
2700 Blagoevgrad / Благоевград 91 Pa 51
2660 Boboševo 91 Pa 50
4114 Boljarci 91 Pa 52
8720 Boljarovo 92 Pa 54
4824 Borino 91 Pb 52
3240 Borovan 77 Ob 51
2140 Botevgrad / Ботевград 91 Pa 51
5971 Brest 77 Ob 52
2360 Breznik 91 Pa 50
4160 Brezovo 91 Pa 53
8000 Burgas / Бургас 92 Pa 55
2780 Car Kalojan 78 Ob 54
8260 Carevo 92 Pa 55
2087 Čelopeč 91 Pa 52
7139 Cenovo 77 Ob 53
4850 Čepelare 91 Pb 52
6462 Čerepovo 92 Pa 54
2287 Cerovo 91 Ob 51

5980 Červen Brjag / Червен Бряг 77 Ob 52
6200 Čirpan / Чирпан 91 Pa 53
2940 Dăbnica 91 Pb 51
6554 Dăbovec 92 Pb 53
9250 Dălgopol 78 Ob 55
9160 Devnja 78 Ob 55
6400 Dimitrovgrad / Димитровград 91 Pa 53
3750 Dimovo 77 Ob 50
9300 Dobrič / Добрич 78 Ob 55
2777 Dobrinište 91 Pb 51
7000 Dolapite 77 Ob 53
2040 Dolna Banja 91 Pa 51
5855 Dolna Mitropolija 77 Ob 52
9120 Dolni Čiflik 78 Pa 55
3958 Dolni Lom 77 Ob 50
2560 Dolno Ujno 91 Pa 50
4831 Dospat 91 Pb 52
5137 Draganovo 77 Ob 53
2210 Dragoman 91 Pa 50
5370 Drjanovo 91 Pa 53
7650 Dulovo 78 Ob 55
2600 Dupnica / Дупница 91 Pa 51
7150 Dve Mogili 77 Ob 53
5146 Džuljunica 77 Ob 53
5070 Elena 91 Pa 53
6064 Elhovo / Елхово 92 Pa 54
2100 Elin Pelin 91 Pa 51
2180 Etropole / Етрополе 91 Pa 51
7274 Ezerce 78 Ob 54
5300 Gabrovo / Габрово 91 Pa 53
6280 Gălăbovo 92 Pa 53
3785 Gămzovo 77 Oa 50
9780 Gara Hitrino 78 Ob 54
9500 General Toševo 78 Ob 56
5970 Gigen 77 Ob 52
2570 Gjueševo 91 Pa 50
2900 Goce Delčev / Гоце Делчев 91 Pb 51
6395 Goljam Izvor 91 Pb 53
3458 Gorna Luka 77 Ob 50
5100 Gorna Orjahovica / Горна Оряховица 77 Ob 53
9689 Gorun 78 Ob 56
8990 Gradec 92 Pa 54
5910 Gradište/Levski 77 Ob 53
9803 Gradište/Šumen 78 Ob 54
4198 Graf Ignatievo 91 Pa 52
9106 Grozdjovo 78 Ob 55
6199 Gurkovo 91 Pa 53
3329 Hărlec 77 Ob 51
6540 Harmanli / Харманли 92 Pb 53
6300 Haskovo / Хасково 91 Pb 53
4180 Hisarja 91 Pa 52
4890 Hvojna 91 Pb 52
2050 Ihtiman / Ихтиман 91 Pa 51
7400 Isperih 78 Ob 54
6570 Ivajlovgrad 92 Pb 54
5750 Jablanica 91 Ob 52
6167 Jagoda 91 Pa 53
2790 Jakoruda 91 Pa 51
8600 Jambol / Ямбол 92 Pa 54
8210 Kableškovo 92 Pa 55

4370 Kalofer 91 Pa 52
4173 Kalojanovo 91 Pa 52
2889 Kamenar 78 Ob 54
9980 Kaolinovo 78 Ob 55
9390 Karapelit 78 Ob 55
6600 Kărdžali / Кърджали 91 Pb 53
4300 Karlovo / Карлово 91 Pa 52
8400 Karnobat / Карнобат 92 Pa 54
9930 Kaspičan 78 Ob 55
9650 Kavarna Каварна 78 Ob 56
6100 Kazanlăk / Казанлък 91 Pa 52
1532 Kazičene 91 Pa 51
5050 Kilifarevo 91 Pa 53
2500 Kjustendil / Кюстендил 91 Pa 50
3230 Kneža 77 Ob 52
9481 Kolarci 78 Ob 55
2077 Koprivštica 91 Pa 52
2030 Kostenec 91 Pa 51
2230 Kostinbrod / Костинброд 91 Pa 51
8970 Kotel 92 Pa 54
3643 Kovačica 77 Ob 51
3320 Kozloduj 77 Ob 51
2840 Kresna 91 Pb 51
3060 Krivodol 77 Ob 51
6900 Krumovgrad 91 Pb 53
8877 Krušare 92 Pa 54
8148 Kruševec 92 Pa 55
5860 Kruševene 77 Ob 52
5881 Kruševica 77 Ob 51
7300 Kubrat 78 Ob 54
3800 Kula 76 Ob 50
5570 Letnica 77 Ob 53
6540 Levka 92 Pb 54
5900 Levski / Левски 77 Ob 53
6550 Ljubimec 92 Pb 53
3600 Lom 77 Ob 51
5500 Loveč / Ловеч 91 Ob 52
7290 Loznica 78 Ob 54
5770 Lukovit 77 Ob 52
4900 Madan 91 Pb 52
6180 Măgliž 91 Pa 53
8350 Malko Tărnovo 92 Pb 55
8000 Meden Rudnik 92 Pa 55
3100 Mezdra / Мездра 91 Ob 51
2826 Mikrevo 91 Pb 51
3330 Mizija 77 Ob 51
9221 Momčil 78 Ob 56
6800 Momčilgrad 91 Pb 53
3400 Montana / Монтана 77 Ob 51
8230 Nesebăr 92 Pa 55
2595 Nevestino 91 Pa 50
5940 Nikopol 77 Ob 52
7645 Nova Černa 78 Ob 54
8900 Nova Zagora / Нова Загора 92 Pa 54
1280 Novi Iskăr / Нови Искър 91 Pa 51
9900 Novi Pazar / Нови Пазар 78 Ob 55
8958 Novoselec 92 Pa 54
5922 Obnova 77 Ob 52

4522 Oborište 91 Pa 52
9630 Obročište 78 Ob 56
8250 Obzor 92 Pa 55
7680 Okorš 78 Ob 55
7900 Omurtag 78 Ob 54
7840 Opaka 78 Ob 54
3300 Orjahovo 77 Ob 51
9490 Orljak 78 Ob 55
3665 Orsoja 77 Ob 51
6960 Padalo 92 Pb 53
4500 Panagjurište / Панагюрище 91 Pa 52
1137 Pančarevo 91 Pa 51
8317 Pănčevo 92 Pa 54
4270 Părvomaj / Първомай 91 Pa 53
5200 Pavlikeni / Павликени 77 Ob 53
4400 Pazardžik / Пазарджик 91 Pa 52
6664 Pčelarovo 91 Pb 53
2825 Pelovo 77 Ob 52
2300 Pernik / Перник 91 Pa 51
4550 Peštera / Пещера 91 Pa 52
2850 Petrič / Петрич 91 Pb 51
2070 Pirdop 91 Pa 52
5800 Pleven / Плевен 77 Ob 52
4000 Plovdiv / Пловдив 91 Pa 52
7431 Podajva 78 Ob 54
5138 Polikraište 77 Ob 53
6276 Polski gradec 92 Pa 54
5180 Polski Trămbeš 77 Ob 53
7131 Polsko Kosovo 77 Ob 53
8200 Pomorie / Поморие 92 Pa 55
4528 Popinci 91 Pa 52
7800 Popovo / Попово 78 Ob 54
8290 Primorsko 92 Pa 55
9200 Provadija / Провадия 78 Ob 55
6260 Radnevo / Раднево 92 Pa 53
2400 Radomir 91 Pa 50
4640 Rakitovo 91 Pb 52
4150 Rakovski / Раковски 91 Pa 52
3660 Rasovo 77 Ob 51
7200 Razgrad / Разград 78 Ob 54
2760 Razlog / Разлог 91 Pb 51
8567 Rečica 92 Pa 54
8281 Rezovo 92 Pb 56
2630 Rila 91 Pa 51
8630 Roza 92 Pa 54
4340 Rozino 91 Pa 52
4960 Rudozem 91 Pb 52
8540 Ruen 92 Pa 55
7000 Ruse / Русе 77 Ob 53
3930 Ružinci 77 Ob 50
9680 Šabla 78 Ob 56
2000 Samokov / Самоков 91 Pa 51
2800 Sandanski / Сандански 91 Pb 51
2950 Satovča 91 Pb 51
9634 Senokos 78 Ob 56
4490 Septemvri 91 Pa 52
5400 Sevlievo 91 Ob 53
7500 Silistra 78 Oa 55
6490 Simeonovgrad 92 Pa 53

Simitli — (BG) · (BiH) — **Živinice** — (BG) (BiH)

2730 Simitli 91 Pb 51	3700 Vidin / Видин 77 Ob 50	76250 Gradačac 75 Oa 46	71243 Pazarić 75 Ob 46
6150 Šipka 91 Pa 53	9000 Vinica 78 Ob 55	78400 Gradiška 75 Nb 45	71243 Peći 75 Oa 44
8895 Šivačevo 92 Pa 54	3734 Vojnica 77 Ob 50	88340 Grude 89 Ob 45	77227 Pećigrad 75 Nb 43
8559 Šivarovo 92 Pa 55	3000 Vraca / Враца 91 Ob 51	Gudavac 75 Oa 44	Podgradina 75 Ob 44
2143 Skravena 91 Pa 51	8321 Zagorci 92 Pa 55	32260 Gunja 75 Oa 46	74217 Podnovlje 75 Oa 46
8240 Slănčev brjag 92 Pa 55	7330 Zavet 78 Ob 54	71240 Hadžici 75 Ob 46	70266 Podrašnica 75 Oa 44
8800 Sliven / Сливен 92 Pa 54	3738 Žeglica 77 Ob 50	71360 Han Pijesak 75 Oa 46	Podromanija 75 Ob 46
7070 Slivo Pole 78 Ob 54	8690 Zimnica 92 Pa 54	Hum 89 Ob 46	Popov Most 89 Ob 46
9820 Smjadovo 78 Ob 55	4980 Zlatograd 91 Pb 53	71210 Ilidža 75 Ob 46	88240 Posušje 75 Ob 45
4700 Smoljan / Смолян 91 Pb 52	3170 Zverino 91 Ob 51	78216 Ivanjska 75 Oa 45	88208 Potoci 89 Ob 45
3450 Smoljanovci 77 Ob 50		88420 Jablanica/Konjic 75 Ob 45	75249 Priboj 75 Oa 46
1000 Sofia / София 91 Pa 51		Jablanica/Sarajevo 75 Ob 46	79101 Prijedor 75 Oa 44
4751 Sokolovci 91 Pb 52	(BiH)	70101 Jajce 75 Oa 45	80202 Priluka 75 Ob 44
4330 Sopot 91 Pa 52		Jasenjani 75 Ob 45	Prnjavor 75 Oa 45
8130 Sozopol 92 Pa 55	78000 Banja Luka 75 Oa 45	74264 Jelah 75 Oa 45	88440 Prozor 75 Ob 45
8300 Sredec/Burgas 92 Pa 55	Barevo 75 Oa 45	70206 Jezero 75 Oa 45	79285 Pržine 75 Oa 44
6066 Sredec/Radnevo 91 Pa 53	77000 Bihać 75 Oa 43	72240 Kakanj 75 Oa 46	Ravne 75 Oa 46
7560 Središte 78 Ob 55	76300 Bijeljina 76 Oa 47	71230 Kalinovik 75 Ob 46	Ravno 89 Pa 45
4210 Stambolijski / Стамболийски 91 Pa 52	89230 Bileća 89 Pa 46	71250 Kiseljak 75 Ob 46	Rekavice 75 Oa 45
2737 Stanke Lisičkovo 91 Pb 50	Bočac 75 Oa 45	75280 Kladanj 75 Oa 46	73290 Renovica 75 Ob 46
6000 Stara Zagora / Стара Загора 91 Pa 53	79224 Bosanska Kostajnica 75 Nb 44	79280 Ključ 75 Oa 44	Ribari 89 Ob 46
4175 Starosel 91 Pa 52	77240 Bosanska Krupa 75 Oa 44	Kobatovci 75 Oa 45	77215 Ripač 75 Oa 43
9371 Stefan Karadža 78 Ob 55	Bosanski Petrovac 75 Oa 44	88400 Konjic 75 Ob 45	73220 Rogatica 75 Ob 47
9350 Stožer 78 Ob 55	77270 Bosanski Grahovo 75 Oa 44	74253 Kosova 75 Oa 46	73260 Rudo 76 Ob 47
7076 Štrăklevo 78 Ob 54	77256 Bravsko 75 Oa 44	78220 Kotor Varoš 75 Oa 45	Sajković 75 Ob 44
5150 Stražica 77 Ob 53	76101 Brčko 75 Oa 46	74215 Kotorsko 75 Oa 46	79260 Sanski Most 75 Oa 44
2344 Studena 91 Pa 51	Brezići 75 Oa 46	79240 Kozarska Dubica 75 Nb 44	71000 Sarajevo 75 Ob 46
9700 Šumen / Шумен 78 Ob 54	80260 Brod 75 Nb 45	77253 Krnjeuša 75 Oa 44	Simići 75 Oa 44
8470 Sungurlare 92 Pa 54	70230 Bugojno 75 Oa 45	78206 Krupa na Vrbasu 75 Oa 45	80227 Skucani 75 Ob 44
6500 Svilengrad / Свиленград 92 Pb 54	77260 Busovača 75 Oa 45	80320 Kupres 75 Ob 45	78420 Srbac 75 Nb 45
5250 Svištov 77 Ob 53	75406 Caparde 75 Oa 46	78250 Laktaši 75 Oa 45	Srebrenik 75 Oa 46
2260 Svoge 91 Pa 51	77220 Cazin 75 Oa 43	80101 Livno 75 Ob 45	71385 Srednje 75 Oa 46
8658 Tamarino 92 Pa 54	Crljivica 75 Oa 44	76278 Lončari 75 Oa 46	88360 Stolac 89 Ob 45
7700 Tărgovište / Търговище 78 Ob 54	76328 Crnjelovo Donje 75 Oa 47	Lug 89 Pa 46	75283 Stupari 75 Oa 46
5990 Teliš 7 Ob 52	79287 Čađavica 75 Oa 44	75300 Lukavac 75 Oa 46	76321 Suho Polje 75 Oa 47
9450 Tervel/Dobrič 78 Ob 55	73280 Čajniče 75 Ob 47	88380 Ljubinje 89 Pa 46	79229 Svodna 75 Nb 44
9769 Tervel/Loznica 78 Ob 54	88300 Čapljina 89 Ob 45	Ljubogošta 75 Ob 46	76230 Šamac 75 Nb 46
5700 Teteven / Тетевен 91 Pa 52	78240 Čelinac 75 Oa 45	88320 Ljubuški 89 Ob 45	70270 Šipovo 75 Oa 45
7340 Tetovo 78 Ob 54	89243 Čemerno 89 Ob 46	74250 Maglaj 75 Oa 46	88220 Široki Brijeg 89 Ob 45
8880 Topolčane 92 Pa 54	74400 Derventa 75 Oa 45	78223 Maslovare 75 Oa 45	80249 Šuica 75 Ob 45
6560 Topolovgrad 92 Pa 54	74101 Doboj 75 Oa 46	Medena Selišta 75 Oa 44	71244 Tarčin 75 Ob 46
4260 Topolovo 91 Pb 53	Dobrinje 75 Oa 46	80243 Mesihovina 75 Ob 45	74270 Teslić 75 Oa 45
2460 Trăn 91 Pa 50	Dobro Polje 75 Ob 46	75446 Milići 75 Oa 47	75265 Tojšići 75 Oa 46
7092 Trăstenik 77 Ob 53	73247 Dobrun 76 Ob 47	Mliniše 75 Oa 44	80240 Tomislavgrad 75 Ob 45
5350 Trjavna / Трявна 91 Pa 53	Donja Gračanica 75 Oa 45	74480 Modriča 75 Oa 46	72270 Travnik 75 Oa 46
5600 Trojan / Троян 91 Pa 52	75323 Donja Orahovica 75 Oa 46	88101 Mostar 89 Ob 45	89103 Trebinje 89 Pa 46
2160 Trudovec 91 Pa 51	76297 Donji Svilaj 75 Nb 46	Mrkalji 75 Oa 46	78252 Trn 75 Oa 45
7622 Tutrakan 78 Oa 54	70220 Donji Vakuf 75 Oa 45	70260 Mrkonjić Grad 75 Oa 45	76310 Trnjaci 75 Oa 46
8890 Tvărdica 92 Pa 53	80260 Drvar 75 Oa 44	88390 Neum 89 Pa 45	75000 Tuzla 75 Oa 46
2060 Vakarel 91 Pa 51	76311 Dvorovi 76 Oa 47	88820 Nevesinje 89 Ob 46	73208 Ustiprača 75 Ob 47
9672 Vaklino 78 Ob 56	75272 Đurđevik 75 Oa 46	79246 Nežica 75 Nb 44	77230 Velika Kladuša 75 Nb 43
5128 Vărbica 78 Pa 54	73300 Foča 75 Ob 46	71383 Nišići 75 Oa 46	70202 Vinac 75 Oa 45
9000 Varna / Варна 78 Ob 55	89240 Gacko 89 Ob 46	78418 Nova Topola 75 Nb 45	71300 Visoko 75 Ob 46
9941 Vekilski 78 Ob 55	80230 Glamoč 75 Oa 44	74475 Novi Grad 75 Nb 44	73240 Višegrad 76 Ob 47
9850 Veliki Preslav 78 Ob 54	76318 Glavčice 75 Oa 47	70225 Oborci 75 Oa 45	72250 Vitez 75 Oa 45
5000 Veliko Tărnovo / Велико Търново 91 Ob 53	73110 Goražde 75 Ob 46	74470 Odžak 75 Nb 46	75440 Vlasenica 75 Oa 46
4600 Velingrad / Велинград 91 Pa 52	Gornja Golubinja 75 Oa 45	71340 Olovo 75 Oa 46	Vranduk 75 Oa 46
8127 Vetren 92 Pa 55	Gornja Meka Gruda 89 Ob 46	Orahova 75 Nb 45	77256 Vrhpolje 75 Oa 44
9220 Vetrino 78 Ob 55	Gornji Malovan 75 Ob 45	Orašac 75 Oa 45	77254 Vrtoče 75 Oa 44
	Gornji Potpeć 75 Oa 46	Orašje 75 Nb 46	76333 Zabrđe 75 Oa 46
	70240 Gornji Vakuf 75 Ob 45	79263 Oštra Luka 75 Oa 44	72000 Zenica 75 Oa 45
	75320 Gračanica 75 Oa 46	77244 Otoka 75 Oa 44	Zlavast 75 Oa 45
		72238 Ozimica 75 Oa 46	75400 Zvornik 75 Oa 47
		Paljevići 75 Oa 47	72230 Žepče 75 Oa 46
			88268 Žitomislići 89 Ob 45
			75270 Živinice 75 Oa 46

115

INDEX WITH POST CODES · ORTSREGISTER MIT POSTLEITZAHLEN · INDICE CON CODICI
STEDREGISTER MED POSTNUMRE · PLAATSNAMENREGISTER MET POSTCODE · REJSTŘÍK

BY

Achremovcy BY Kletnoe

BY

211972 Achremovcy 39 Hb 55
213912 Aleksandrovka 40 Jab 57
211424 Azino 40 Hb 56
211035 Babiniči/Orša 40 Ja 58
211322 Babiniči/Vitebsk 40 Hb 58
211206 Babinoviči 40 Ja 58
213901 Baceviči 40 Jab 57
211011 Baran`/ Барань 40 Ja 58
225401 Baranoviči / Барановичи
  51 Jab 54
247180 Barsuki 40 Jab 58
231371 Bastuny 39 Ja 53
211730 Behoml` 39 Ja 56
213514 Bel` 1-ja 40 Jab 59
211126 Belaja Lipa 40 Ja 57
231314 Belica 39 Jab 53
213680 Belinkoviči 41 Jab 60
225215 Beloozersk / Белоозерск
  51 Ka 53
225531 Beloyša 51 Kb 54
225162 Belyj Lesok 51 Ka 52
213051 Belyniči 40 Jab 57
231381 Benjakoni 39 Ja 53
225895 Bereza / Береза 51 Ka 52
211732 Berezino/Lepel` 39 Ja 56
223311 Berezino/Minsk / Березино/
  Минск 40 Jab 57
225532 Berežnoe 51 Kb 55
225763 Berezoviči 51 Ka 53
231306 Berezovka/Lida 39 Jab 53
222822 Berezovka/Mar`ina Horka
  39 Jab 55
211350 Bešenkoviči 40 Hb 57
211438 Bezdedoviči 39 Hb 56
211640 Bihosovo 39 Hb 55
223942 Bobovnja 51 Jab 54
222040 Bobr 40 Ja 57
213801 Bobrujsk / Бобруйск
  40 Jab 57
211371 Bočejkovo 40 Hb 57
213661 Bochany 41 Jab 60
211510 Bohuševsk 40 Ja 58
231770 Bol`šaja Berestovica
  51 Jab 52
213857 Bol`šie Bortniki 40 Jab 57
225033 Bol`šie Motykaly 51 Ka 51
225221 Bol`šoe Meždulec`e
  51 Ka 53
211123 Bol`šoj Ozereck 40 Ja 57
222511 Borisov / Борисов 40 Ja 56
247611 Borisovščina 52 Ka 56
247401 Boroviki 52 Ka 57
223053 Borovljany 39 Ja 55
247846 Borovoe 52 Kb 56
247511 Borščevka 52 Ka 58
247087 Borščovka 52 Ka 59
211957 Bosjanye 39 Hb 55
225654 Bostyn 51 Ka 54
211550 Botali 40 Hb 58
223338 Božino 40 Jab 56
247631 Brahin 52 Kb 58
211961 Braslav / Браслав 39 Hb 55
225000 Brest / Брест 51 Ka 51

231722 Bruzhi 38 Jab 51
222460 Bubny 39 Ja 55
211044 Buda 40 Ja 58
247350 Buda-Košelevo 52 Ka 58
211356 Budilovo 40 Hb 57
247538 Budka 52 Ka 58
247862 Bujnoviči 52 Kb 56
213353 Bychov / Быхов 40 Jab 58
213111 Bystrik 40 Jab 58
222131 Bytča 40 Ja 56
225281 Byten` 51 Ka 53
211150 Čašniki / Чашники 40 Ja 57
213204 Čausy / Чаусы 40 Jab 59
247152 Čečersk 52 Ka 58
213315 Čečeviči 40 Jab 57
247922 Čeljuščeviči 52 Ka 56
225730 Čepeli 51 Ka 55
211164 Čereja 40 Ja 57
213530 Čerikov 40 Jab 59
225030 Černavčicy 51 Ka 51
222118 Černeviči 4 Ja 56
213974 Černevka 40 Ja 58
225914 Černjany 51 Kb 52
213022 Černoruč`e 40 Ja 58
223210 Červen` / Червень
  40 Jab 56
247321 Červonnaja Sloboda
  52 Ka 56
231605 Chartica 39 Jab 55
211127 Chodcy 40 Ja 57
231543 Chodiloni 39 Jab 52
213513 Chodorovcy 39 Jab 53
213460 Chodosy 40 Jab 59
247600 Chojniki / Хойники
  52 Kb 57
247505 Cholmeč 52 Ka 58
213570 Cholmy 40 Jab 59
225620 Chomsk 51 Ka 53
225544 Choromsk 51 Ka 55
213250 Choronevo 40 Jab 58
213660 Chotimsk 41 Jab 60
225441 Chotyniči 51 Ka 54
222011 Chudovcy 40 Ja 57
223227 Chutor 40 Jab 56
247410 Čirkoviči 52 Ka 57
220013 Cnjanka 39 Jab 55
223115 Čudeniči 39 Ja 55
213860 Dačnoe 52 Jab 56
225540 David-Horodok 51 Ka 55
247034 Davydovka 52 Ka 58
223141 Deniski 39 Ja 55
247303 Derbin 52 Ka 57
231952 Derečin 51 Jab 52
222680 Derevnoe 39 Jab 54
  (Dernoviči) 52 Kb 57
225895 Devjatki 51 Ka 52
211950 Disna 39 Hb 56
222391 Djahili 39 Ja 55
231471 Djatlovo 39 Jab 53
223313 Dmitroviči/Berezino
  40 Jab 57
225062 Dmitroviči/Žabinka
  51 Ka 51
213004 Dobrejka 40 Ja 58
247821 Dobrin` 52 Kb 57
211223 Dobromysli 40 Ja 58

225742 Dobroslavka 51 Ka 54
247050 Dobruš / Добруш 52 Ka 59
211720 Dokšicy 39 Ja 55
222031 Dokudovo 40 Ja 56
222424 Dolhinovo 39 Ja 55
  (Dovljady) 52 Kb 57
247261 Dovsk 40 Jab 58
213970 Dribin 40 Ja 59
225830 Drohičin / Дрогичин
  51 Ka 53
225821 Družiloviči 51 Ka 53
231971 Družnaja 51 Jab 52
231013 Dubatovka 39 Ja 54
213266 Dubno 40 Jab 59
247415 Dubrova/Svetlohorsk
  52 Ka 57
247953 Dubrova/Žitkoviči
  52 Ka 57
247623 Dubrovica 52 Ka 58
211495 Dubrovka 40 Hb 57
213318 Dubrovo 40 Jab 57
247710 Dudiči 52 Ka 57
231331 Dudy 39 Jab 55
222840 Dukora 39 Jab 55
225652 Dvorec/Luninec 51 Ka 54
231474 Dvorec/Slonim 39 Jab 53
225921 Dvorišče 51 Kb 51
222720 Dzeržinsk / Дзержинск
  39 Jab 55
247820 El`sk / Ельск 52 Kb 57
225441 Elovaja 51 Ka 54
213543 Elovka 40 Jab 59
222710 Ênerhetikov 39 Jab 55
211033 Esipovo-Krasnoe 40 Ja 58
213033 Evdokimoviči 40 Ja 59
211580 Ezerišče 40 Hb 58
222750 Fanipol` / Фаниполь
  39 Jab 55
247938 Fastoviči 52 Ka 56
225115 Fed`koviči 51 Ka 52
247140 Fedorovka 52 Ka 59
225254 Federy 51 Kb 54
247260 Hadiloviči 40 Jab 58
223121 Hajna 39 Ja 55
222136 Hanceviči/Borisov
  39 Ja 56
225440 Hanceviči/Solihorsk /
  Ганцевичи/Солигорск
  51 Ka 54
231345 Heraneny 39 Ja 53
225011 Heršony 51 Ka 51
231463 Hezhaly 39 Jab 53
247607 Hlinišče 52 Kb 57
247553 Hlinnaja Sloboda 52 Ka 57
222417 Hlinnoe 39 Ja 54
211800 Hlubokoe / Глубокое
  39 Ja 55
213844 Hluša 52 Jab 56
213860 Hlusk 52 Jab 56
247849 Hluškeviči 52 Kb 55
231120 Hol`šany 39 Ja 54
213536 Holoviči 40 Ja 57
225363 Holynka 51 Ka 54

246000 Homel`/Dobruš / Гомель/
  Добруш 52 Ka 59
211657 Homel`/Polock 40 Hb 56
222516 Hora 40 Ja 56
211478 Horbačevo 40 Hb 57
213410 Horki / Горки 40 Ja 59
225883 Horodec 51 Ka 52
222610 Horodeja 51 Jab 54
225328 Horodišče/Baranoviči
  51 Jab 54
222378 Horodišče/Vilejka 39 Ja 55
211540 Horodok / Городок
  40 Hb 58
247524 Horval` 52 Ka 58
231741 Hoža 39 Jab 51
222643 Hriceviči 51 Ka 54
230000 Hrodno / Гродно 39 Jab 51
225885 Hruševo 51 Ka 53
211582 Hurki 40 Hb 58
211521 Iduta 40 Ja 56
222135 Ikany 39 Ja 56
222431 Il`ja 39 Ja 55
231712 Indura 51 Jab 51
211913 Iody 39 Hb 55
231330 Iv`e 51 Jab 53
225250 Ivaceviči / Ивацевичи
  51 Ka 53
225800 Ivanovo / Иваново
  51 Ka 53
222370 Ivenec 39 Jab 54
231922 Izabelin 51 Jab 52
223144 Izbišče 40 Jab 56
225802 Jaečkoviči 51 Ka 53
225270 Jahleviči 51 Ka 53
223337 Jakšicy 40 Jab 56
225355 Jamično 51 Ka 54
247261 Jamnoe 40 Jab 58
213472 Janovka 40 Ja 59
231945 Jarnevo 51 Jab 52
213742 Jasen` 40 Jab 56
223733 Jaskoviči 51 Ka 55
211250 Jazvino 40 Hb 57
211467 Juchoviči 39 Ha 56
231350 Juratiški 39 Ja 53
211018 Jurcevo 40 Ja 58
247722 Juroviči 52 Kb 57
225246 Kabaki 51 Ka 52
211070 Kaceviči 51 Ka 53
213902 Kaličenka 40 Jab 57
247380 Kalinino 52 Ka 58
247710 Kalinkoviči / Калинковичи
  52 Ka 57
223817 Kalinovka 52 Ka 56
211862 Kamai 39 Hb 54
225063 Kamenjuki 51 Ka 51
223132 Kameno 39 Ja 56
225050 Kamjanec 51 Ka 51
247732 Kaplіči 52 Ka 57
211983 Karasino 39 Hb 54
231720 Karolin/Hrodno 38 Jab 51
231931 Karolin/Slonim 51 Jab 52
222350 Kibuti 39 Ja 54
211873 Kirov 52 Kb 57
213940 Kirovsk 40 Jab 57
222640 Kleck / Клецк 51 Jab 54
222861 Kletnoe 40 Jab 56

POSTALI · ÍNDICE CON CÓDIGOS POSTALES · INDICE DE LUGARES COM CÓDIGOS POSTAIS ·
MÍST S PSČ · ZOZNAM OBCÍ S PSČ · INDEKS MIEJSCOWOŚCI Z KOD POCZTOWY

116

Klevica — BY — **Pribytki** — BY

231113 Klevica 39 Ja 53
213900 Kličev 40 Jab 57
213600 Klimoviči / Климовичи
        40 Jab 59
211463 Kljasticy 39 Hb 56
211029 Kljukovka 40 Ja 58
213011 Knjažicy 40 Ja 58
213125 Knjažnicy 40 Jab 58
225860 Kobrin / Кобрин 51 Ka 52
211625 Kochanoviči 39 Hb 56
211060 Kochanovo 40 Ja 58
247835 Kočišče 52 Kb 56
211321 Kojtovo 40 Hb 58
213908 Kolbča 40 Jab 57
211876 Koleevcy 39 Hb 54
225169 Koljadiči/Pružany 51 Ka 52
231904 Koljadiči/Volkovysk
        51 Jab 52
222661 Kolosovo 39 Jab 54
247650 Komarin 52 Kb 58
222394 Komarovo 39 Ja 54
247920 Kopatkeviči 52 Ka 56
231710 Koptevka 39 Jab 51
211346 Kopti 40 Hb 58
223910 Kopyl` / Копыль 51 Jab 55
211038 Kopys` 43 Ja 57
231430 Koreliči 39 Jab 54
247542 Korovatiči 52 Ka 58
211486 Kosari 39 Hb 56
225262 Kossovo 51 Ka 53
222420 Kosteneviči 39 Ja 55
213640 Kostjukoviči / Костюковичи
        40 Jab 60
247045 Kostjukovka / Костюковка
        52 Ka 58
211453 Kostrovo 39 Ha 56
247605 Kozelyž`e 52 Kb 57
213577 Kožemjakino 40 Jab 59
225271 Koziki 43 Ja 53
211994 Kozjany 39 Hb 54
247738 Kozloviči 52 Ka 57
231482 Kozlovščina 51 Jab 53
223141 Kozyri 39 Ja 55
213510 Krasnaja Buda 40 Jab 59
222320 Krasnoe 39 Ja 54
213560 Krasnopol`e 40 Jab 59
247813 Krasnovka 52 Ka 57
231022 Krevo 39 Ja 54
213500 Kričev / Кричев 40 Jab 59
211725 Kripuli 39 Ja 55
222211 Krivaja Bereza 39 Ja 56
222914 Krivonosy 52 Ka 56
247392 Krivsk 52 Ka 58
213205 Krotki 40 Jab 59
213180 Kruhloe 40 Ja 57
247085 Kruhovec-Kalinino 52 Ka 59
247111 Krupejki 52 Kb 58
222010 Krupki 40 Ja 57
213317 Kučin 40 Jab 58
225457 Kukovo 51 Ka 54
211841 Kuropol`e 39 Hb 54
231407 Kuroviči 39 Jab 53
247211 Lebedevka 52 Ka 58
222315 Lebedevo 39 Ja 54
247840 Lel`čicy 52 Kb 56
223648 Len`ki 51 Jab 55

213421 Lenino 40 Ja 59
211180 Lepel` / Лепель 40 Ja 56
211486 Lesiny 39 Ja 56
225356 Lesnaja 51 Ka 53
231300 Lida / Лида 39 Jab 53
225149 Linovo 1-e 51 Ka 52
211200 Liozno 40 Hb 58
231335 Lipniški 39 Ja 53
225370 Ljachoviči / Ляховичи
        51 Jab 54
225662 Ljubačin 51 Ka 55
223810 Ljuban` / Любань 52 Ka 56
225458 Ljubaševo 51 Ka 54
231425 Ljubča 39 Jab 54
225256 Ljubiščicy 51 Ka 53
213416 Ljubiž 40 Ja 58
213930 Ljuboniči 40 Jab 57
225683 Ljušča 51 Ka 54
225430 Ljusino 51 Ka 54
213543 Lobanovka 40 Jab 59
225673 Lobča 51 Ka 54
247100 Loev 52 Kb 58
225740 Lohišin 51 Ka 53
223110 Lohojsk 39 Ja 55
225747 Lopatin 51 Ka 54
222122 Lošnica 40 Ja 56
213629 Lozovica 40 Jab 60
225892 Luka 51 Ka 52
211876 Lukašovo 39 Hb 55
231744 Lukavica 38 Jab 51
225204 Lukomer 51 Ka 52
211161 Lukoml` 40 Ja 57
225650 Luninec / Лунинец
        51 Jab 54
231606 Lunna 51 Jab 52
211870 Lyntupy 39 Hb 54
225741 Lyšče 51 Ka 54
247759 Machnoviči 52 Kb 56
225439 Mal`koviči 51 Ka 54
231780 Malaja Berestovica
        51 Jab 51
225745 Malaja Vul`ka 51 Kb 54
247230 Maleviči 52 Ka 57
247563 Maloduša 52 Ka 58
225910 Malorita / Малорита
        51 Kb 52
222810 Mar`ina-Horka / Марьина
        Горка 40 Jab 56
222442 Mat`kovcy 39 Ja 55
223326 Mateviči 40 Jab 57
213122 Medvedevka 40 Jab 58
231481 Medvinoviči 51 Jab 53
247754 Meleševiči 52 Kb 57
247158 Merkuloviči 40 Ka 58
223119 Metličicy 39 Ja 55
213136 Mežisjatki 40 Jab 58
213759 Mezoviči 40 Jab 56
231230 Michališki 39 Ja 54
225340 Mickeviči 51 Jab 53
225687 Mikaševiči / Микашевичи
        51 Ka 54
231611 Mikelevščina 39 Jab 52
247846 Milaševiči 52 Kb 55
225354 Milovidy 51 Ka 53
220000 Minsk / Минск 39 Jab 55

211930 Miory / Миоры 39 Hb 55
231444 Mir 39 Jab 54
225283 Mironim 51 Ka 53
213804 Miževiči 51 Ka 53
222380 Mjadel` 39 Ja 54
225812 Mochro 51 Kb 53
213110 Mohilev / Могилев
        40 Jab 58
225917 Mokrany 51 Kb 52
213412 Mokrec 39 Jab 53
225340 Molčad` 51 Jab 53
222310 Molodečno / Молодечно
        39 Ja 54
231331 Morino 39 Jab 53
247963 Morochorovo 52 Ka 56
211469 Moročkovo 39 Hb 56
222223 Mostišče 39 Jab 54
231600 Mosty / Мосты 51 Jab 52
225822 Motol` 51 Ka 53
247760 Mozyr` / Мозырь 52 Ka 57
213470 Mstislavl` / Мстиславль
        40 Ja 59
222137 Mstiž 39 Ja 56
247930 Muljarovka 52 Ka 56
213642 Murin Bo 40 Jab 60
223125 Myšicy 39 Ja 55
222418 Naroč` 39 Ja 54
247800 Narovlja / Наровля
        52 Ka 57
211062 Nekljudovo 40 Ja 57
211121 Nemojta 40 Ja 57
211371 Neseno 40 Ja 57
222620 Nesviž / Несвиж 51 Jab 54
211280 Nikiticha 40 Hb 57
211340 Nikonoviči 40 Jab 58
213354 Nižnjaja Toščica 40 Jab 58`
247019 Novaja Huta 52 Ka 59
225331 Novaja Myš` 51 Jab 53
231757 Novaja Ruda 39 Jab 52
247622 Novaja Rudnja 52 Kb 57
213021 Novobraščino 40 Ja 58
247868 Novoe Poles`e 52 Kb 56
231470 Novoel`nja 39 Jab 53
231400 Novohrudok / Новогрудок
        39 Jab 53
211162 Novolukoml` / Новолукомль
        40 Ja 57
211440 Novopolock / НовополоцкН
        40 Hb 56
222121 Novoselki/Borisov 40 Ja 56
247942 Novoselki/Petrikov
        52 Ka 56
211170 Novozaslonovo 40 Ja 56
222044 Novye Denisoviči 40 Ja 57
222911 Novye Dorohi 52 Ka 56
247266 Novye Žuraviči 40 Jab 58
231540 Novyj Dvor/Ščučin
        39 Jab 52
231983 Novyj Dvor/Volkovysk
        51 Ka 52
247273 Novyj Krivsk 40 Jab 58
211934 Novyj Pohost 39 Hb 55
213343 Obidoviči 40 Jab 58
211132 Obol` 40 Ja 58
225450 Ohareviči 51 Ka 54
247221 Oktjabr` 52 Ka 58

211147 Oktjabr`skij/Čašniki /
        Октябрьский/Чашники
        40 Ja 57
247300 Oktjabr`skij/Svetlohorsk
        52 Ka 56
231784 Olekšicy 51 Jab 51
211998 Opsa 39 Hb 54
211030 Orša / Орша 40 Ja 58
211420 Osetno 40 Hb 57
211448 Osinovka 40 Hb 58
213760 Osipoviči 40 Jab 56
211227 Osipovo 40 Ja 58
213176 Osman-Kasaevo 40 Jab 57
231100 Ošmjany 39 Ja 53
225751 Osnežicy 51 Ka 54
213106 Osovec 40 Jab 57
225889 Ostromiči 51 Ka 52
247292 Ostrov 52 Ka 57
231210 Ostrovec 39 Ja 53
231364 Ostrovno 40 Hb 57
225757 Ozariči/Pinsk 51 Ka 53
247742 Ozariči/Svetlohorsk 52 Ka 57
247991 Ozerany 52 Ka 55
223417 Ozero 39 Jab 55
247520 Ozerščina 52 Ka 58
231753 Ozery 3 Jab 52
247413 Pariči 52 Ka 57
213426 Paršino 40 Ja 59
225056 Pašuki 51 Ka 51
222226 Pekalin 40 Ja 56
225054 Pelišče 51 Ka 51
211932 Perebrod`e 39 Hb 55
222361 Peršai 39 Ja 54
247940 Petrikov / Петриков
        52 Ka 56
211853 Petroviči 39 Hb 55
211805 Petrovščina 39 Hb 55
225710 Pinsk / Пинск 51 Ka 54
        (Pirki) 51 Kb 58
211111 Plamja 40 Ja 57
223130 Pleščenicy 39 Ja 55
213570 Pobeda 40 Jab 59
211160 Počaeviči 40 Ja 57
225361 Podlesejki 51 Jab 54
231923 Podorosk 51 Ka 52
211965 Podrukša 39 Hb 54
223320 Pohost 40 Jab 57
223715 Pohost 2-j 51 Ka 55
231773 Pohraničnyj 51 Jab 51
247416 Poles`e/Svetlohorsk
        52 Ka 57
        Poles`e/Volosoviči
        40 Jab 59
222312 Poločany 39 Ja 54
211400 Polock / Полоцк 40 Hb 56
247979 Polosteviči 51 Ka 55
211847 Polovo 39 Hb 55
223334 Poplavy 40 Jab 56
231742 Poreč`e 39 Jab 52
231982 Porozovo 51 Ka 52
211721 Porplišče 39 Ja 54
211840 Postavy / Поставы
        39 Hb 54
223220 Pravda 40 Jab 56
231619 Pravye Mosty 51 Jab 52
247042 Pribytki 52 Ka 59

117

INDEX WITH POST CODES · ORTSREGISTER MIT POSTLEITZAHLEN · INDICE CON CODICI
STEDREGISTER MED POSTNUMRE · PLAATSNAMENREGISTER MET POSTCODE · REJSTŘÍK

BY

Pripernoe BY **Zvonec**

211820 Pripernoe 39 Hb 55
211817 Prozoroki 39 Hb 56
211602 Prudinki 39 Hb 56
247768 Prudok 52 Ka 57
222917 Prussy 52 Ka 56
225140 Pružany / Пружаны
    51 Ka 52
222832 Puchoviči 40 Jab 56
211280 Pušča 40 Hb 57
211177 Pyšno 40 Ja 56
213250 Raboviči 40 Jab 58
222440 Rabun 39 Ja 55
225525 Radčick 51 Kb 54
222322 Radoškoviči 39 Ja 55
231390 Radun` 39 Ja 53
247233 Raduša 52 Ka 57
222365 Rakov 39 Jab 55
213208 Rebjatki 40 Jab 59
247500 Rečica/Homel / Речица/
    Гомель 52 Ka 58
225502 Rečica/Stolin 51 Kb 54
211045 Red`ki 40 Ja 58
247832 Remezy 52 Kb 57
213980 Rjasna 40 Jab 59
211100 Rjasno 40 Ja 57
231909 Rodniki 51 Jab 52
213621 Rodnja 40 Jab 60
247902 Roh 52 Ka 56
247250 Rohačev 40 Jab 58
211026 Romal`dovo 40 Ja 58
247311 Romanišči 52 Ka 57
211460 Rossony 40 Hb 54
225849 Roviny 51 Ka 53
211351 Rubež 40 Ja 57
247114 Ručaevka 52 Kb 58
222621 Rudavka 51 Jab 54
223322 Rudenki 40 Jab 57
223221 Rudnja/Minsk 40 Jab 56
211435 Rudnja/Novopolock
    40 Hb 56
247136 Rudnja-Stolbunskaja
    52 Ka 59
222357 Rum 39 Ja 54
225396 Rusinoviči 51 Ka 54
225154 Ružany 51 Ka 52
222824 Šack 39 Jab 55
223013 Samochvaloviči 39 Jab 55
213480 Šamovičina 40 Ja 59
247186 Sapožki 40 Jab 58
222362 Šarai 39 Ja 54
211910 Šarkovščina 39 Hb 55
222675 Šaški 39 Jab 54
213412 Sava 40 Ja 58
213850 Saviči/Bobrujsk 40 Jab 57
247734 Saviči/Chojniki 52 Kb 58
222695 Savoni 39 Jab 54
247235 Ščedrin 52 Ka 57
247673 Ščibrin 40 Jab 58
222923 Ščitkoviči 40 Jab 56
231510 Ščučin / Щучин 39 Jab 52
213342 Selec/Bychov 40 Jab 58
213135 Selec/Mohilev 40 Jab 58
213475 Selec/Mstislavl` 40 Jab 59
211461 Seljavščina 40 Hb 56
225556 Semihostiči 51 Ka 55
223056 Senica 39 Jab 55

211120 Senno / Сенно 40 Ja 57
222825 Serheeviči 39 Jab 55
213119 Sidoroviči 40 Jab 58
247731 Šiiči 52 Ka 57
211349 Šilki 40 Hb 58
247853 Simoniči 52 Kb 56
213874 Simonoviči 52 Jab 56
222652 Sinjavka 51 Ka 54
223820 Šipiloviči 52 Ka 56
213484 Širki 40 Ja 59
211271 Sirotino 40 Hb 57
223643 Šiščicy 51 Jab 55
211712 Sitcy 39 Ja 55
225685 Sitnica 51 Ka 55
213950 Skaček 40 Jab 57
231761 Skidel` / Скидель
    39 Jab 52
213010 Šklov / Шклов 40 Ja 58
247824 Skorodnoe 52 Kb 56
247761 Skryhalov 52 Ka 56
213240 Slavhorod 40 Jab 59
213331 Sledjuki 40 Jab 58
222215 Sloboda 39 Ja 55
213841 Slobodka/Bobrujsk
    40 Jab 57
213910 Slobodka/Kličev 40 Jab 57
231220 Slobodka/Smorhon
    39 Ja 53
231800 Slonim / Слоним 51 Jab 53
231933 Slovatiči 51 Ka 52
223610 Sluck / Слуцк 51 Jab 55
211574 Smal`ki 40 Hb 57
223216 Smiloviči 39 Jab 56
211014 Smol`jany 40 Ja 58
213691 Smol`ki 41 Jab 60
222210 Smoleviči / Смолевичи
    39 Ja 56
231000 Smorhon` / Сморгонь
    39 Ja 54
211464 Sokolišče 39 Hb 56
211373 Sokorovo 40 Hb 57
223710 Solihorsk / Солигорск
    51 Jab 54
222927 Solon 52 Jab 56
247530 Soltanovo 52 Ka 58
231733 Sopockin 38 Jab 51
211491 Soročino 40 Hb 56
225739 Sošno 51 Ka 54
213728 Sosnovyj 40 Jab 58
247405 Sosnovyj Bor 52 Ka 57
223813 Sosny 52 Ka 57
247631 Speriž`e 52 Kb 58
211339 Stajki 40 Hb 58
213815 Starica 51 Jab 55
223730 Starobin 51 Ka 55
211240 Staroe Selo 40 Hb 57
211080 Staroe Sokolino 40 Ja 57
225177 Starovolja 51 Ka 52
225393 Starye Budy 51 Ka 54
222901 Starye Dorohi / Старые
    Дороги 52 Jab 56
211829 Staryj Šarabai 39 Hb 55
211210 Stasevo 40 Hb 55
225752 Stavok 51 Ka 54
222660 Stolbcy / Столбцы
    39 Jab 54

225510 Stolin / Столин 51 Kb 54
225312 Stoloviči 51 Jab 54
211607 Strelki 39 Hb 56
213138 Studenka/Senno 40 Ja 57
222228 Studenka/Smoleviči
    40 Jab 56
225745 Stytyčevo 51 Ka 54
211260 Šumilino 40 Hb 57
211330 Suraž 40 Hb 58
213982 Susloviki 40 Jab 58
222396 Švakšty 39 Ja 54
213261 Svensk 40 Jab 58
247140 Svetiloviči 52 Ka 59
247400 Svetlohorsk / Светлогорск
    52 Ka 57
213714 Svisloč` 40 Jab 56
213847 Syčkovo 40 Jab 57
213347 Tajmonovo 40 Jab 58
223830 Tal` 52 Ka 55
213328 Tarnovo 39 Jab 54
213177 Techtin 40 Jab 57
225275 Telechany 51 Ka 53
247070 Terechovka 52 Ka 59
247003 Terjucha 52 Ka 59
222686 Tesnovaja 39 Jab 54
213186 Teterino 40 Ja 57
223920 Timkoviči 51 Jab 54
213130 Tišovka 40 Jab 58
225081 Tokari 40 Ja 57
211070 Toločin / Толочин 40 Ja 57
231352 Traby 39 Ja 53
213372 Trokeli 39 Ja 53
211727 Tumiloviči 39 Ja 55
231146 Turkovo 39 Hb 56
247980 Turov 52 Ka 55
222044 Uchvala 40 Ja 57
211736 Uhly 39 Ja 55
211375 Ulla 40 Hb 57
223831 Ureč`e 52 Ka 55
247023 Urickoe 52 Ka 58
211480 Ušači 40 Hb 56
211628 Ust`e 39 Hb 55
247374 Uvaroviči 52 Ka 58
223400 Uzda 39 Jab 55
222283 Uzla 39 Ja 54
247536 Uznož 52 Ka 58
247826 Valavsk 52 Kb 56
223413 Valer`jany 39 Jab 55
231403 Valevka 39 Jab 53
211569 Varchi 40 Hb 57
213260 Vas`koviči 40 Jab 58
247550 Vasileviči 52 Ka 57
225274 Velikaja Hat` 51 Ka 53
225165 Velikoe Selo 51 Ka 52
225912 Velikorita 51 Kb 52
211620 Verchnedvinsk 39 Hb 55
247984 Veresnica 52 Ka 55
222742 Vertniki 39 Jab 55
222631 Veseja 51 Jab 55
247965 Vetčin 52 Ka 56
247120 Vetka 52 Ka 59
211430 Vetrino 39 Hb 56
225067 Vidomlja 51 Ka 51
211990 Vidzy 39 Hb 54
222410 Vilejka / Вилейка 39 Ja 54

225176 Viskuli 51 Ka 51
222696 Višnevec 39 Jab 54
231005 Višnevo 39 Ja 54
213166 Višov 40 Jab 57
210000 Vitebsk / Витебск 40 Hb 58
223408 Vojkovo 39 Jab 55
231012 Vojnidenjaty 39 Ja 54
225066 Vojskaja 51 Ka 51
211730 Volča 39 Ja 56
211713 Volkolata 39 Ja 55
213232 Volkoviči/Čausy 40 Jab 58
231405 Volkoviči/Novohrudok
    39 Jab 53
231900 Volkovysk / Волковыск
    51 Jab 52
247164 Volosoviči 40 Ka 59
222340 Voložin 39 Ja 54
211914 Voložinki 39 Hb 55
231908 Volpa 51 Jab 52
231220 Vornjany 39 Ja 54
231221 Vorona 39 Ja 53
213330 Voronino 40 Jab 58
231370 Voronovo 39 Ja 53
247116 Voschod 52 Ka 58
231414 Vseljub 39 Jab 53
225066 Vysokoe/Brest 50 Ka 51
211024 Vysokoe/Orša 40 Ja 58
213672 Zabelyšin 41 Jab 60
225110 Žabinka / Жабинка
    51 Ka 52
247365 Zabolot`e 52 Ka 58
222353 Zabrez`e 39 Ja 54
213642 Zabyčan`e 40 Jab 59
211331 Zadubrov`e 40 Hb 58
222671 Zajamnoe 39 Jab 54
222926 Zaluž`e 52 Ka 55
211168 Zamoš`e 40 Ja 56
222382 Zanaroč` 39 Ja 54
211417 Zaozer`e 40 Hb 56
213903 Zapol`e 40 Jab 57
247552 Zaščeb`e 52 Ka 57
223036 Zaslavl` 39 Ja 55
247501 Zaspa 52 Ka 57
211047 Zastenki 40 Ja 56
211498 Zavečel` 40 Hb 54
225013 Zbunin 51 Kb 51
223031 Ždanoviči 39 Jab 55
211609 Zel`ki 39 Hb 56
231930 Zel`va 51 Jab 52
211423 Zelenka 40 Hb 56
222133 Zembin 40 Ja 56
223141 Žerdjaž`e 39 Ja 55
223649 Žilin Brod 51 Jab 55
225156 Zinoviči 51 Ka 52
231822 Ziroviči 51 Jab 53
247960 Žitkoviči / Житковичи
    52 Ka 55
247210 Žlobin / Жлобин 52 Ka 58
225013 Znamenka 51 Kb 51
222160 Žodino / Жодино 40 Ja 56
231102 Župrany 39 Ja 54
222452 Žurichi 39 Ja 54
223312 Žurovka 40 Jab 57
213613 Zvenčatka 40 Jab 60
247627 Zvenjatskoe 52 Kb 58
247262 Zvonec 40 Jab 58

POSTALI · ÍNDICE CON CÓDIGOS POSTALES · INDICE DE LUGARES COM CÓDIGOS POSTAIS ·
MÍST S PSČ · ZOZNAM OBCÍ S PSČ · INDEKS MIEJSCOWOŚCI Z KOD POCZTOWY

118

Aarau Jeseník

 CH

5000 Aarau 58 Mb 36
3715 Adelboden 58 Na 35
6780 Airolo 73 Na 36
6463 Altdorf 59 Na 36
9450 Altstätten 59 Mb 37
7473 Alvaneu 59 Na 37
8580 Amriswil 59 Mb 37
9050 Appenzell 59 Mb 37
9320 Arbon 59 Mb 37
7055 Arosa 59 Na 37
7310 Bad Ragaz 59 Na 37
5400 Baden 59 Mb 36
4710 Balsthal 58 Mb 35
4000 Basel 58 Mb 35
6500 Bellinzona 73 Na 37
3000 Bern 58 Na 35
6710 Biasca 73 Na 36
2500 Biel 58 Mb 35
7402 Bonaduz 59 Na 37
8180 Bülach 59 Mb 36
1630 Bulle 58 Na 35
3400 Burgdorf 58 Mb 35
1874 Champéry 72 Na 34
7000 Chur 59 Na 37
7260 Davos 59 Na 37
2800 Delémont 58 Mb 35
8953 Dietikon 59 Mb 36
7180 Disentis/Mustér 59 Na 36
9642 Ebnat-Kappel 59 Mb 37
8767 Elm 59 Na 37
6032 Emmen 58 Mb 36
6390 Engelberg 59 Na 36
6162 Entlebuch 58 Na 36
3984 Fiesch 72 Na 36
8500 Frauenfeld 59 Mb 36
1700 Fribourg (Freiburg) 58 Na 35
3714 Frutigen 58 Na 35
1200 Genève (Genf) 72 Na 34
6074 Giswil 58 Na 36
8750 Glarus 59 Mb 37
3999 Gletsch 58 Na 36
2540 Grenchen 58 Mb 35
3918 Grindelwald 58 Na 36
3780 Gstaad 58 Na 35
9100 Herisau 59 Mb 37
8810 Horgen 59 Mb 36
7130 Ilanz 59 Na 37
8308 Illnau 59 Mb 36
3232 Ins 58 Mb 35
3800 Interlaken 58 Na 35
3210 Kerzers 58 Na 35
7250 Klosters 59 Na 37
3098 Köniz 58 Na 35
8280 Kreuzlingen 59 Mb 37
6010 Kriens 58 Mb 36
7522 La Punt 73 Na 37
2300 La-Chaux-de-Fonds 58 Mb 34
4900 Langenthal 58 Mb 35
3550 Langnau im Emmental 58 Na 35
1000 Lausanne 58 Na 34
4410 Liestal 58 Mb 35
6600 Locarno 73 Na 36

6900 Lugano 73 Na 36
6000 Luzern 58 Mb 36
7516 Maloja 73 Na 37
1920 Martigny 72 Na 35
3860 Meiringen 58 Na 36
6850 Mendrisio 73 Nb 37
1870 Monthey 72 Na 34
1820 Montreux 58 Na 34
1110 Morges 58 Na 34
2740 Moutier 58 Mb 35
3985 Münster 72 Na 36
2000 Neuchâtel (Neuenburg) 58 Na 34
8212 Neuhausen am Rheinfall 59 Mb 36
8867 Niederurnen 59 Mb 37
1260 Nyon 58 Na 34
4104 Oberwil 58 Mb 35
6718 Olivone 73 Na 36
4600 Olten 58 Mb 35
1937 Orsières 72 Na 35
1530 Payerne 58 Na 34
6695 Peccia 73 Na 36
2900 Porrentruy 58 Mb 35
7742 Poschiavo 73 Na 38
1987 Pralong 72 Na 35
1009 Pully 58 Na 34
8640 Rapperswil 59 Mb 36
4153 Reinach 58 Mb 36
1680 Romont 58 Na 34
8630 Rüti 59 Mb 36
3906 Saas-Fee 72 Na 35
1450 Sainte Croix 58 Na 34
6565 San Bernardino 73 Na 37
6690 San Carlo 73 Na 36
9000 Sankt Gallen 59 Mb 37
7500 Sankt Moritz 73 Na 37
6060 Sarnen 58 Na 36
8200 Schaffhausen 59 Mb 36
6430 Schwyz 59 Mb 36
3960 Sierre 72 Na 35
1950 Sion 72 Na 35
4500 Solothurn 58 Mb 35
3700 Spiez 58 Na 35
8712 Stäfa 59 Mb 36
3922 Stalden 72 Na 35
6370 Stans 59 Na 36
7542 Susch 59 Na 38
3600 Thun 58 Na 35
7430 Thusis 59 Na 37
8610 Uster 59 Mb 36
9240 Uzwil 59 Mb 37
7132 Vals 59 Na 37
1896 Vouvry 72 Na 34
8880 Walenstadt 59 Mb 37
8304 Wallisellen 59 Mb 36
6484 Wassen 59 Na 36
8620 Wetzikon 59 Mb 36
4800 Winterthur 59 Mb 36
5610 Wohlen 58 Mb 36
6110 Wolhusen 58 Mb 36
1400 Yverdon-les-Bains 58 Na 34
3920 Zermatt 72 Na 35
7530 Zernez 59 Na 38
8702 Zollikon 59 Mb 36

6300 Zug 59 Mb 36
8000 Zürich 59 Mb 36

 CY

Dali 108 Sb 61
Episkopi 110 Ta 60
Famagusta 108 Sb 61
Galatia 108 Sb 61
Kakopetria 110 Ta 60
Karavostasi 108 Sb 60
Kofinou 110 Ta 61
Kormakitis 108 Sb 61
Kornos 110 Ta 61
Kouklia 110 Ta 60
Kyrenia 108 Sb 61
Kythrea 108 Sb 61
Larnaka 110 Ta 61
Lefkosia/Nicosia 108 Sb 61
Lemesos/Limassol 110 Ta 61
Morphou 108 Sb 60
Pafos 110 Ta 60
Palekythro 108 Sb 61
Peristerona 108 Sb 61
Pissouri 110 Ta 60
Polis 110 Sb 60
Rizokarpaso 108 Sb 62
Skylloura 108 Sb 61
Xylofagou 108 Ta 61
Yialousa 108 Sb 62

 CZ

588 51 Batelov 60 Lb 43
345 26 Bělá nad Radbuzou 60 Lb 40
294 21 Bělá pod Bezdězem 48 La 42
256 01 Benešov 60 Lb 42
382 82 Benešov nad Černou 60 Ma 42
266 01 Beroun 60 Lb 42
340 01 Bešiny 60 Lb 41
418 01 Bilina 48 La 41
678 01 Blansko 61 Lb 44
388 01 Blatná 60 Lb 41
336 01 Blovice 60 Lb 41
592 13 Bohdalov 61 Lb 43
735 51 Bohumín 61 Lb 46
364 71 Bochov 60 La 41
348 02 Bor 60 Lb 40
373 12 Borovany 60 Ma 42
680 01 Boskovice 61 Lb 44
753 62 Boškov 61 Lb 45
250 01 Brandýs nad Labem 60 La 42
382 06 Brloh 60 Ma 42
602 00 Brno 61 Lb 44
550 01 Broumov 49 La 44
792 01 Bruntál 61 Lb 45
690 02 Břeclav 61 Ma 44
262 72 Březnice 60 Lb 41

411 84 Bříza 48 La 42
569 92 Bystřice 61 Lb 44
257 51 Bystřice 60 Lb 42
768061 Bystřice pod Hostýnem 61 Lb 45
286 01 Čáslav 60 Lb 43
407 21 Česká Kamenice 48 La 42
363 01 Česká Lípa 48 La 42
560 02 Česká Třebová 61 Lb 44
370 01 České Budějovice 60 Ma 42
282 01 Český Brod 60 La 42
463 43 Český Dub 48 La 43
381 01 Český Krumlov 60 Ma 42
737 01 Český Těšín 61 Lb 46
398 04 Čimelice 60 Lb 42
380 01 Dačice 60 Lb 43
405 02 Děčín 48 La 42
518 01 Dobruška 49 La 44
263 01 Dobříš 60 Lb 42
472 01 Doksy 48 La 42
543 74 Dolní Kalná 49 La 43
344 01 Domažlice 60 Lb 40
345 20 Draženov 60 Lb 40
544 01 Dvůr Králové nad Labem 49 La 43
351 01 Františkovy Lázně 60 La 40
744 01 Frenštát pod Radhoštěm 61 Lb 46
738 01 Frýdek-Mistek 61 Lb 46
464 01 Frýdlant 48 La 43
382 79 Frymburk 60 Ma 42
742 45 Fulnek 61 Lb 45
582 81 Habry 60 Lb 43
788 33 Hanušovice 61 La 44
580 01 Havlíčkův Brod 61 Lb 43
539 01 Hlinsko 61 Lb 43
748 01 Hlučín 61 Lb 46
695 01 Hodonín 61 Ma 45
769 01 Holešov 61 Lb 45
534 01 Holice 61 La 43
341 01 Horažďovice 60 Lb 41
382 26 Horní Planá 60 Ma 42
346 01 Horšovský Týn 60 Lb 40
508 01 Hořice 49 La 43
268 01 Hořovice 60 Lb 41
267 24 Hostomice 60 Lb 42
500 02 Hradec Králové 61 La 43
671 27 Hrádek 60 Ma 44
753 01 Hranice 61 Lb 45
675 55 Hrotovice 61 Lb 44
396 01 Humpolec 60 Lb 43
693 01 Hustopeče 61 Ma 44
350 02 Cheb 60 La 40
357 35 Chodov 48 La 40
430 01 Chomutov 48 La 41
463 31 Chrastava 48 La 42
537 01 Chrudim 61 Lb 43
382 08 Chvalšiny 60 Ma 42
466 01 Jablonec nad Nisou 48 La 43
551 01 Jaroměř 49 La 43
675 51 Jaroměřice nad Rokytnou 61 Lb 43
790 70 Javorník 49 La 45
270 33 Jesenice 60 La 41
790 01 Jeseník 61 La 45

119

INDEX WITH POST CODES · ORTSREGISTER MIT POSTLEITZAHLEN · INDICE CON CODICI
STEDREGISTER MED POSTNUMRE · PLAATSNAMENREGISTER MET POSTCODE · REJSTŘÍK

CZ

D

Jičín   CZ · D   **Altenkirchen**

506 01 Jičín 48 La 43
586 01 Jihlava 61 Lb 43
377 01 Jindřichův Hradec 60 Lb 43
431 11 Jirkov 48 La 41
432 01 Kadaň 48 La 41
394 70 Kamenice nad Lipou
     60 Lb 43
382 41 Kaplice 60 Ma 42
360 01 Karlovy Vary 48 La 40
733 01 Karviná 61 Lb 46
387 11 Katovice 60 Lb 41
331 51 Kaznějov 60 Lb 41
345 06 Kdyně 60 Lb 41
272 01 Kladno 60 La 42
431 51 Klášterec nad Ohří 48 La 41
339 01 Klatovy 60 Lb 42
691 72 Klobouky u. Brna 61 Lb 44
349 52 Kokašice 60 Lb 40
280 02 Kolín 60 Lb 43
798 52 Konice 61 Lb 44
507 32 Kopidlno 48 La 43
742 21 Kopřivnice 61 Lb 46
517 41 Kostelec nad Orlicí 61 La 44
675 55 Kouty 61 Lb 43
561 69 Králíky 61 La 44
331 41 Kralovice 60 Lb 41
278 01 Kralupy nad Vltavou
     48 La 42
358 01 Kraslice 48 La 40
357 31 Krásno 48 La 40
794 01 Krnov 61 La 45
767 01 Kroměříž 61 Lb 45
417 41 Krupka 48 La 41
594 51 Křižanov 61 Lb 44
679 72 Kunštát 61 Lb 44
664 34 Kuřim 61 Lb 44
284 01 Kutná Hora 60 Lb 43
697 01 Kyjov 61 Lb 45
544 01 Lanžov 49 La 43
671 63 Lechovice 61 Ma 44
460 01 Liberec 48 La 43
411 17 Libochovice 48 La 42
363 01 Litoměřice 48 La 42
784 01 Litovel 61 Lb 45
436 03 Litvínov 48 La 41
512 51 Lomnice nad Popelkou
     48 La 43
363 01 Louny 48 La 41
410 02 Lovosice 48 La 42
394 26 Lukavec 60 Lb 42
756 11 Lužná 61 Lb 46
353 01 Mariánské Lázně 60 Lb 40
340 37 Měčín 60 Lb 41
276 01 Mělník 48 La 42
793 95 Město Albrechtice 61 La 45
692 01 Mikulov 61 Ma 44
262 34 Milevsko 60 Lb 42
257 86 Miličín 60 Lb 42
262 31 Milín 60 Lb 42
471 24 Mimoň 48 La 42
338 43 Mirošov 60 Lb 41
382 32 Mirovice 60 Lb 42
363 01 Mladá Boleslav 48 La 42
391 43 Mladá Vožice 60 Lb 42
664 42 Modřice 61 Lb 44
789 85 Mohelnice 61 Lb 44

592 54 Moravec 61 Lb 44
571 01 Moravská Třebová
     61 Lb 44
676 02 Moravské Budějovice
     61 Lb 43
793 05 Moravský Beroun 61 Lb 45
434 01 Most 48 La 41
739 98 Mosty u Jablunkova
     61 Lb 46
270 64 Mšec 48 La 41
277 35 Mšeno 48 La 42
547 01 Náchod 49 La 44
675 71 Náměšť nad Oslavou
     61 Lb 44
335 01 Nepomuk 60 Lb 41
277 11 Neratovice 48 La 42
384 11 Netolice 60 Lb 42
257 56 Neveklov 60 Lb 42
373 33 Nové Hrady 61 Lb 44
592 31 Nové Město na Moravě
     61 Lb 44
549 01 Nové Město nad Metují
     49 La 44
473 01 Nový Bor 48 La 42
504 01 Nový Bydžov 48 La 43
742 41 Nový Jičín 61 Lb 46
394 04 Nový Rychnov 60 Lb 43
288 02 Nymburk 60 La 43
340 22 Nýrsko 60 Lb 41
671 51 Olbramkostel 61 Ma 43
772 00 Olomouc 61 Lb 45
391 61 Opařany 60 Lb 42
746 01 Opava 61 Lb 45
289 04 Opočnice 60 La 43
735 33 Orlová 61 Lb 46
700 00 Ostrava 61 Lb 46
363 01 Ostrov 48 La 40
765 02 Otrokovice 61 Lb 45
395 01 Pacov 60 Lb 43
530 12 Pardubice 61 La 43
393 01 Pelhřimov 60 Lb 43
790 82 Písečná 49 La 45
363 01 Písek 60 Lb 42
348 15 Planá 60 Lb 40
391 11 Planá nad Lužnicí
     60 Lb 42
300 00 Plzeň 60 Lb 41
345 22 Poběžovice 60 Lb 40
441 01 Podbořany 48 La 41
290 01 Poděbrady 60 La 43
691 23 Pohořelice 61 Ma 44
572 01 Polička 61 Lb 44
588 13 Polná 61 Lb 43
100 00 Praha 60 La 42
383 01 Prachatice 60 Lb 41
796 01 Prostějov 61 Lb 45
535 01 Přelouč 61 La 43
750 01 Přerov 61 Lb 45
334 01 Přeštice 60 Lb 41
742 58 Příbor 61 Lb 46
261 01 Příbram 60 Lb 42
341 61 Rabí 60 Lb 41
338 28 Radnice 60 Lb 41
269 01 Rakovník 60 La 41
337 01 Rokycany 60 Lb 41
665 01 Rosice 61 Lb 44

413 01 Roudnice nad Labem
     48 La 42
683 01 Rousínov 61 Lb 44
382 18 Rožmberk nad Vltavou
     60 Ma 42
262 42 Rožmitál pod Třemšínem
     60 Lb 41
756 61 Rožnov pod Radhoštěm
     61 Lb 46
408 01 Rumburk 48 La 42
516 01 Rychnov nad Kněžnou
     61 La 44
795 01 Rýmařov 61 Lb 45
252 30 Řevnice 60 Lb 42
251 01 Říčany 60 Lb 42
538 07 Seč 61 Lb 43
264 01 Sedlčany 60 Lb 42
387 32 Sedlice 60 Lb 41
391 01 Sezimovo Ústí 60 Lb 42
274 01 Slaný 48 La 42
763 21 Slavičín 61 Lb 45
687 64 Slavkov 61 Ma 45
684 01 Slavkov u Brna 61 Lb 44
378 81 Slavonice 60 Ma 43
392 01 Soběslav 60 Lb 42
507 43 Sobotka 48 La 43
356 01 Sokolov 48 La 40
345 61 Staňkov 60 Lb 41
250 01 Stará Boleslav 60 La 42
686 02 Staré Město 61 Lb 45
333 01 Stod 60 Lb 41
588 33 Stonařov 60 Lb 43
386 01 Strakonice 60 Lb 41
349 01 Stříbro 60 Lb 40
342 01 Sušice 60 Lb 41
582 92 Světlá nad Sázavou
     60 Lb 43
568 02 Svitavy 61 Lb 44
785 01 Šternberk 61 Lb 45
787 01 Šumperk 61 Lb 44
363 01 Tábor 60 Lb 42
347 01 Tachov 60 Lb 40
588 56 Telč 60 Lb 43
373 01 Temelín 60 Lb 42
415 01 Teplice 48 La 41
666 01 Tišnov 61 Lb 44
36401 Toužim 60 La 40
539 52 Trhová Kamenice 61 Lb 43
374 01 Trhové Sviny 60 Ma 42
541 01 Trutnov 49 La 43
674 01 Třebíč 61 Lb 43
273 75 Třebíz 48 La 41
379 01 Třeboň 60 Lb 42
330 11 Třemošná 60 Lb 41
739 61 Třinec 61 Lb 46
511 01 Turnov 48 La 43
375 01 Týn nad Vltavou 60 Lb 42
257 41 Týnec nad Sázavou
     60 Lb 42
686 06 Uherské Hradiště 61 Lb 45
688 01 Uherský Brod 61 Lb 45
512 63 Újezd 48 La 43
273 51 Unhošt 60 La 42
783 91 Uničov 61 Lb 45
400 01 Ústí nad Labem 48 La 42
562 01 Ústí nad Orlicí 61 Lb 44

411 45 Úštěk 48 La 42
384 32 Vacov 60 Lb 41
76601 Valašské Klobouky 61 Lb 46
757 01 Valašské Meziříčí 61 Lb 45
407 47 Varnsdorf 48 La 42
696 74 Velká nad Veličkou
     61 Ma 45
594 01 Velké Meziříčí 61 Lb 44
391 81 Veselí nad Lužnicí 60 Lb 42
698 01 Veselí nad Moravou
     61 Ma 45
385 01 Vimperk 60 Lb 41
749 01 Vítkov 61 Lb 45
258 01 Vlašim 60 Lb 42
389 01 Vodňany 60 Lb 42
384 51 Volary 60 Ma 41
259 01 Votice 60 Lb 42
543 01 Vrchlabí 49 La 43
755 01 Vsetín 61 Lb 45
345 07 Všeruby 60 Lb 40
566 01 Vysoké Mýto 61 Lb 44
682 01 Vyškov 61 Lb 44
382 73 Vyšší Brod 60 Ma 42
789 01 Zábřeh 61 Lb 44
281 44 Zásmuky 60 Lb 43
768 02 Zdounky 61 Lb 45
349 62 Zhoř 60 Lb 40
760 01 Zlín 61 Lb 45
671 81 Znojmo 61 Ma 44
330 08 Zruč nad Sázavou 60 Lb 43
564 01 Žamberk 61 La 44
696 34 Žarošice 61 Lb 44
438 01 Žatec 48 La 41
591 01 Žďár nad Sázavou 61 Lb 43
582 63 Ždírec nad Doubravou
     61 Lb 43
364 52 Žlutice 60 La 41

D

52062 Aachen 46 La 34
73430 Aalen 59 Ma 38
93326 Abensberg 60 Ma 39
77855 Achern 58 Ma 36
28832 Achim 47 Jab 37
09221 Adorf/Vogtland 48 La 40
86444 Affing 59 Ma 38
48683 Ahaus 46 Ka 34
59227 Ahlen 47 Kb 35
22926 Ahrensburg 35 Jab 38
18347 Ahrenshoop 36 Ja 40
86551 Aichach 59 Ma 39
25767 Albersdorf 35 Ja 37
72458 Albstadt 59 Ma 37
31061 Alfeld (Leine) 47 Kb 37
85391 Allershausen 59 Ma 39
52477 Alsdorf 46 La 34
36304 Alsfeld 47 La 37
84032 Altdorf 60 Ma 40
58762 Altena 47 Kb 35
48341 Altenberge 47 Ka 35
04600 Altenburg 48 La 40
24161 Altenholz 35 Ja 38
18556 Altenkirchen 36 Ja 41

POSTALI · ÍNDICE CON CÓDIGOS POSTALES · INDICE DE LUGARES COM CÓDIGOS POSTAIS ·
MÍST S PSČ · ZOZNAM OBCÍ S PSČ · INDEKS MIEJSCOWOŚCI Z KOD POCZTOWY

120

Altenkirchen (Westerwald) Cuxhaven

57610 Altenkirchen (Westerwald) 46 La 35	94086 Bad Griesbach im Rottal 60 Ma 41	27211 Bassum 47 Ka 36	26919 Brake 47 Jab 36
17087 Altentreptow 36 Jab 41	38667 Bad Harzburg 47 Kb 38	35088 Battenberg (Eder) 47 Kb 36	33034 Brakel 47 Kb 37
25845 Alterkoog 35 Ja 36	36251 Bad Hersfeld 47 La 37	34225 Baunatal 47 Kb 37	49565 Bramsche 47 Ka 35
84503 Altötting 60 Ma 40	87541 Bad Hindelang 59 Mb 38	02625 Bautzen 48 Kb 42	09618 Brand-Erbisdorf 48 La 41
55232 Alzey 59 Lb 36	61348 Bad Homburg 47 La 36	95444 Bayreuth 59 Lb 39	14770 Brandenburg an der Havel 48 Ka 40
92224 Amberg 60 Lb 39	53604 Bad Honnef 46 La 35	36179 Bebra 47 La 37	35619 Braunfels 47 La 36
21385 Amelinghausen 47 Jab 38	97688 Bad Kissingen 47 La 38	59269 Beckum 47 Kb 36	06242 Braunsbedra 48 Kb 39
56626 Andernach 46 La 35	97631 Bad Königshofen im Grabfeld 47 La 38	14547 Beelitz 48 Ka 40	38100 Braunschweig 47 Ka 38
16278 Angermünde 48 Jab 42		15848 Beeskow 48 Ka 42	25821 Bredstedt 35 Ja 36
17389 Anklam 36 Jab 41	06628 Bad Kösen 48 Kb 39	92339 Beilngries 59 Lb 39	79206 Breisach am Rhein 58 Ma 35
49577 Ankum 47 Ka 35	93444 Bad Kötzting 60 Lb 40	14806 Belzig 48 Ka 40	28195 Bremen 47 Jab 36
09456 Annaberg-Buchholz 48 La 41	55545 Bad Kreuznach 59 Lb 36	64625 Bensheim 59 Lb 36	27568 Bremerhaven 35 Jab 36
06925 Annaburg 48 Kb 41	79189 Bad Krozingen 58 Mb 35	92334 Berching 59 Lb 39	27432 Bremervörde 35 Jab 37
91522 Ansbach 59 Lb 38	99947 Bad Langensalza 47 Kb 38	29303 Bergen 47 Ka 37	64395 Brensbach 59 Lb 36
99510 Apolda 47 Kb 39	04651 Bad Lausick 48 Kb 40	18528 Bergen (Rügen) 36 Ja 41	75015 Bretten 59 Lb 36
39619 Arendsee (Altmark) 48 Ka 39	37431 Bad Lauterberg im Harz 47 Kb 38	50126 Bergheim 46 La 34	59929 Brilon 47 Kb 37
59755 Arnsberg 47 Kb 36	04924 Bad Liebenwerda 48 Kb 41	51465 Bergisch-Gladbach 46 La 35	38465 Brome 47 Ka 38
99310 Arnstadt 47 La 38	07356 Moorbad Lobenstein 47 La 39	59192 Bergkamen 47 Kb 35	63486 Bruchköbel 47 La 36
06556 Artern 47 Kb 39		10115 Berlin 48 Ka 41	76646 Bruchsal 59 Lb 36
95659 Arzberg 60 La 40	97980 Bad Mergentheim 59 Lb 37	16321 Bernau 48 Ka 41	19421 Brüel 36 Jab 39
63739 Aschaffenburg 59 Lb 37	61231 Bad Nauheim 47 La 36	06406 Bernburg/Saale 48 Kb 39	25541 Brunsbüttel 35 Jab 37
06449 Aschersleben 47 Kb 39	53474 Bad Neuenahr-Ahrweiler 46 La 35	02994 Bernsdorf 48 Kb 42	74722 Buchen (Odenwald) 59 Lb 37
35614 Aßlar 47 La 36		49593 Bersenbrück 47 Ka 35	21244 Buchholz in der Nordheide 47 Jab 37
57439 Attendorn 47 Kb 35	97616 Bad Neustadt an der Saale 47 La 38	57518 Betzdorf 47 La 35	
84072 Au in der Hallertau 59 Ma 39		91282 Betzenstein 59 Lb 39	66663 Büdingen 47 La 37
08280 Aue 48 La 40	32545 Bad Oeynhausen 47 Ka 36	27616 Beverstedt 35 Jab 36	77815 Bühl 59 Ma 36
08209 Auerbach/Vogtland 48 La 40	23843 Bad Oldesloe 35 Jab 38	37688 Beverungen 47 Kb 37	32257 Bünde 47 Ka 36
91275 Auerbach in der Oberpfalz 59 Lb 39	31812 Bad Pyrmont 47 Kb 37	88400 Biberach an der Riß 59 Ma 37	57299 Burbach 47 La 36
86150 Augsburg 59 Ma 38	83435 Bad Reichenhall 60 Mb 40	35216 Biedenkopf 47 La 36	33142 Büren 47 Kb 36
26603 Aurich 35 Jab 35	96479 Bad Rodach bei Coburg 47 La 38	33602 Bielefeld 47 Ka 36	39288 Burg 48 Ka 39
39393 Ausleben 47 Ka 39		26553 Bienenbüttel 47 Jab 38	23769 Burg auf Fehmarn 36 Ja 39
87727 Babenhausen 59 Ma 38	79713 Bad Säckingen 58 Mb 36	16359 Biesenthal 48 Ka 41	89331 Burgau 59 Ma 38
71522 Backnang 59 Ma 37	31162 Bad Salzdetfurth 47 Ka 38	74321 Bietigheim-Bissingen 59 Ma 37	31303 Burgdorf 47 Ka 38
93077 Bad Abbach 60 Ma 40	32105 Bad Salzuflen 47 Ka 36		84489 Burghausen 60 Ma 40
83043 Bad Aibling 60 Mb 40	36433 Bad Salzungen 47 La 38	48727 Billerbeck 46 Kb 35	84508 Burgkirchen 60 Ma 40
34454 Bad Arolsen 47 Kb 37	88348 Bad Saulgau 59 Ma 37	97653 Bischofsheim an der Rhön 47 La 38	91330 Burglengenfeld 60 Lb 40
27624 Bad Bederkesa 35 Jab 36	06905 Bad Schmiedeberg 48 Kb 40		90559 Burgthann 59 Lb 39
48455 Bad Bentheim 46 Ka 35	65307 Bad Schwalbach 47 La 36	01877 Bischofswerda 48 Kb 42	72393 Burladingen 59 Ma 37
57319 Bad Berleburg 47 Kb 36	23611 Bad Schwartau 35 Jab 38	39629 Bismark (Altmark) 48 Ka 39	35418 Buseck 47 La 36
95460 Bad Berneck am Fichtelgebirge 59 La 39	23795 Bad Segeberg 35 Jab 38	54634 Bitburg 46 Lb 34	25761 Büsum 35 Ja 36
	55566 Bad Sobernheim 58 Lb 35	06749 Bitterfeld 48 Kb 40	96155 Buttenheim 59 Lb 39
07422 Bad Blankenburg 47 La 39	37242 Bad Soden-Salmünster 47 La 37	38889 Blankenburg (Harz) 47 Kb 38	35510 Butzbach 47 La 36
29389 Bad Bodenteich 47 Ka 38		99444 Blankenhain 47 La 39	18246 Bützow 36 Jab 39
24576 Bad Bramstedt 35 Jab 37	96231 Staffelstein 47 La 38	89143 Blaubeuren 59 Ma 37	21614 Buxtehude 47 Jab 37
97769 Bad Brückenau 47 La 37	18334 Bad Sülze 36 Ja 40	74572 Blaufelden 59 Lb 37	03205 Calau 48 Kb 41
65520 Bad Camberg 47 La 36	83646 Bad Tölz 59 Mb 39	21354 Bleckede 47 Jab 38	39240 Calbe/Saale 48 Kb 39
18209 Bad Doberan 36 Ja 39	72574 Bad Urach 59 Ma 37	66440 Blieskastel 58 Lb 35	39359 Calvörde 47 Ka 39
33014 Bad Driburg 47 Kb 37	61118 Bad Vilbel 47 La 36	71032 Böblingen 59 Ma 37	75365 Calw 59 Ma 36
04849 Bad Düben 48 Kb 40	88339 Bad Waldsee 59 Mb 37	46395 Bocholt 46 Kb 34	26409 Carolinensiel 35 Jab 35
67098 Bad Dürkheim 59 Lb 36	34537 Bad Wildungen 47 Kb 37	44787 Bochum 46 Kb 35	44575 Castrop-Rauxel 46 Kb 35
06231 Bad Dürrenberg 48 Kb 40	19336 Bad Wilsnack 48 Ka 39	94327 Bogen 60 Ma 40	29221 Celle 47 Ka 38
56130 Bad Ems 46 La 35	91438 Bad Windsheim 59 Lb 38	04668 Böhlen 48 Kb 40	93413 Cham 60 Lb 40
83093 Bad Endorf 60 Mb 40	33181 Bad Wünnenberg 47 Kb 36	49163 Bohmte 47 Ka 36	09111 Chemnitz 48 La 40
29883 Bad Fallingbostel 47 Ka 37	88410 Bad Wurzach 59 Mb 37	17268 Boizenburg (Elbe) 47 Jab 38	38678 Clausthal-Zellerfeld 47 Kb 38
06567 Bad Frankenhausen 47 Kb 39	26160 Bad Zwischenahn 47 Jab 36	23946 Boltenhagen 35 Jab 39	49661 Cloppenburg 47 Ka 36
	76530 Baden-Baden 59 Ma 36	53103 Bonn 46 La 35	96450 Coburg 47 La 38
16259 Bad Freienwalde (Oder) 48 Ka 42	72270 Baiersbronn 59 Ma 36	73441 Bopfingen 59 Ma 38	48653 Coesfeld 46 Kb 35
	72336 Balingen 59 Ma 36	56154 Boppard 47 La 35	31863 Coppenbrügge 47 Ka 37
74177 Bad Friedrichshall 59 Lb 37	06493 Ballenstedt 47 Kb 39	24582 Bordesholm 35 Ja 38	01640 Coswig 48 Kb 41
94072 Bad Füssing 60 Ma 41	96047 Bamberg 59 Lb 39	26904 Börger 47 Ka 35	03042 Cottbus 48 Kb 42
37581 Bad Gandersheim 47 Kb 38	22941 Bargteheide 35 Jab 38	46325 Borken (Westfalen) 46 Kb 34	74564 Crailsheim 59 Lb 38
53177 Bad Godesberg 46 La 35	49406 Barnstorf 47 Ka 36	26757 Borkum 35 Jab 34	95473 Creußen 59 Lb 39
01816 Bad Gottleuba 48 La 41	26676 Barßel 47 Jab 35	04758 Borna 48 Kb 40	08451 Crimmitschau 48 La 40
	18356 Barth 36 Ja 40	16321 Börnicke 48 Ka 40	19089 Crivitz 36 Jab 39
		46236 Bottrop 46 Kb 34	27472 Cuxhaven 35 Jab 36

121

INDEX WITH POST CODES · ORTSREGISTER MIT POSTLEITZAHLEN · INDICE CON CODICI
STEDREGISTER MED POSTNUMRE · PLAATSNAMENREGISTER MET POSTCODE · REJSTŘÍK

D

Dachau   D   Halle an der Saale

85221 Dachau 59 Ma 39	37574 Einbeck 47 Kb 37	09599 Freiberg 48 La 41
25899 Dagebüll 35 Ja 36	99817 Eisenach 47 La 38	79098 Freiburg im Breisgau
04774 Dahlen 48 Kb 40	07607 Eisenberg 48 La 39	58 Mb 35
21368 Dahlenburg 47 Jab 38	15890 Eisenhüttenstadt 48 Ka 42	21729 Freiburg (Elbe) 35 Jab 37
15936 Dahme 48 Kb 41	53783 Eitorf 46 La 35	83395 Freilassing 60 Mb 40
17291 Damme 47 Ka 36	29351 Eldingen 47 Ka 38	85354 Freising 59 Ma 39
16259 Dannenberg 47 Jab 39	88430 Ellwangen 59 Ma 38	01705 Freital 48 La 41
17159 Dargun 36 Jab 40	25335 Elmshorn 35 Jab 37	72250 Freudenstadt 59 Ma 36
64283 Darmstadt 59 Lb 36	06918 Elster/Elbe 48 Kb 40	94078 Freyung 60 Ma 41
37586 Dassel 47 Kb 37	04910 Elsterwerda 48 Kb 41	61169 Friedberg 47 La 36
54550 Daun 46 La 34	97483 Eltmann 59 Lb 38	17098 Friedland/Neubrandenburg
35232 Dautphetal 47 La 36	26721 Emden 35 Jab 35	36 Jab 41
94469 Deggendorf 60 Ma 40	56281 Emmelshausen 46 La 35	88045 Friedrichshafen 59 Mb 37
33129 Delbrück 47 Kb 36	79312 Emmendingen 58 Ma 35	25718 Friedrichskoog 35 Ja 36
04509 Delitzsch 48 Kb 40	46446 Emmerich 46 Kb 34	25840 Friedrichstadt 35 Ja 37
27749 Delmenhorst 47 Jab 36	44888 Emsbüren 46 Ka 35	14662 Friesack 48 Ka 40
17109 Demmin 36 Jab 41	48282 Emsdetten 46 Ka 35	77948 Friesenheim 58 Ma 35
79211 Denzlingen 58 Ma 35	79346 Endingen am Kaiserstuhl	26169 Friesoythe 47 Jab 35
06844 Dessau 48 Kb 40	58 Ma 35	34560 Fritzlar 47 Kb 37
32756 Detmold 47 Kb 36	04439 Engelsdorf 48 Kb 40	36037 Fulda 47 La 37
49356 Diepholz 47 Ka 36	78234 Engen 59 Mb 36	16798 Fürstenberg/Havel 48 Jab 41
35683 Dillenburg 47 La 36	59320 Ennigerloh 47 Kb 36	82256 Fürstenfeldbruck 59 Ma 39
89407 Dillingen an der Donau	89155 Erbach 59 Ma 37	15517 Fürstenwalde (Spree)
59 Ma 38	92681 Erbendorf 60 Lb 40	48 Ka 42
84130 Dingolfing 60 Ma 40	85435 Erding 60 Ma 39	17291 Fürstenwerder 48 Jab 41
91550 Dinkelsbühl 59 Lb 38	50374 Erftstadt 46 La 34	90762 Fürth 59 Lb 38
49713 Dinklage 47 Ka 36	99084 Erfurt 47 La 39	93437 Furth im Wald 60 Lb 40
01744 Dippoldiswalde 48 La 41	84030 Ergolding 60 Ma 40	87629 Füssen 59 Mb 38
71254 Ditzingen 59 Ma 37	84061 Ergoldsbach 60 Ma 40	19205 Gadebusch 35 Jab 39
04720 Döbeln 48 Kb 41	41812 Erkelenz 46 Kb 34	76571 Gaggenau 59 Ma 36
03253 Doberlug-Kirchhain 48 Kb 41	15537 Erkner 48 Ka 41	74405 Gaildorf 59 Ma 37
03159 Döbern 48 Kb 42	91052 Erlangen 59 Lb 39	27777 Ganderkesee 47 Jab 36
19303 Dömitz 47 Jab 39	29348 Eschede 47 Ka 38	84140 Gangkofen 60 Ma 40
78166 Donaueschingen 59 Mb 36	92676 Eschenbach in der Oberpfalz	30823 Garbsen 47 Ka 37
86609 Donauwörth 59 Ma 38	60 Lb 39	85748 Garching bei München
84405 Dorfen 60 Ma 40	35713 Eschenberg 47 La 36	59 Ma 39
41539 Dormagen 46 Kb 34	37632 Eschershausen 47 Kb 37	39638 Gardelegen 47 Ka 39
26892 Dörpen 47 Ka 35	37269 Eschwege 47 Kb 38	82467 Garmisch-Partenkirchen
44135 Dortmund 46 Kb 35	52249 Eschweiler 46 La 34	59 Mb 39
27632 Dorum 35 Jab 36	32339 Espelkamp 47 Ka 36	49681 Garrel 47 Ka 36
18556 Dranske 36 Ja 41	45127 Essen 46 Kb 35	29471 Gartow 48 Jab 39
03116 Drebkau 48 Kb 42	84051 Essenbach 60 Ma 40	16307 Gartz/Oder 48 Jab 42
01067 Dresden 48 Kb 41	73728 Esslingen 59 Ma 37	18574 Garz (Rügen) 36 Ja 41
21706 Drochtersen 35 Jab 37	77955 Ettenheim 58 Ma 35	21502 Geesthacht 47 Jab 38
17398 Ducherow 36 Jab 41	76275 Ettlingen 59 Ma 36	52511 Geilenkirchen 46 La 34
37115 Duderstadt 47 Kb 38	53879 Euskirchen 46 La 34	94333 Geiselhöring 60 Ma 40
47051 Duisburg 46 Kb 34	23701 Eutin 35 Ja 38	65366 Geisenheim 47 La 35
48249 Dülmen 46 Kb 35	04895 Falkenberg/Elster 48 Kb 41	73312 Geislingen an der Steige
52349 Düren 46 La 34	14612 Falkensee 48 Ka 41	59 Ma 37
40213 Düsseldorf 46 Kb 34	16833 Fehrbellin 48 Ka 40	04643 Geithain 48 Kb 40
96106 Ebern 59 La 38	17258 Feldberg 48 Jab 41	18182 Gelbensande 36 Ja 40
16227 Eberswalde 48 Ka 41	83620 Feldkirchen-Westerham	63571 Gelnhausen 47 La 37
29574 Ebstorf 47 Jab 38	59 Mb 39	45899 Gelsenkirchen 46 Kb 35
90542 Eckental 59 Lb 39	91555 Feuchtwangen 59 Lb 38	97737 Gemünden am Main
24340 Eckernförde 35 Ja 37	70794 Filderstadt 59 Ma 37	47 La 37
26188 Edewecht 47 Jab 35	03238 Finsterwalde 48 Kb 41	77723 Gengenbach 58 Ma 36
84307 Eggenfelden 60 Ma 40	24937 Flensburg 35 Ja 37	39307 Genthin 48 Ka 40
76344 Eggenstein 59 Lb 36	09557 Flöha 48 La 41	07545 Gera 48 La 40
17367 Eggesin 36 Jab 42	24787 Fockbek 35 Ja 37	82538 Geretsried 59 Mb 39
89584 Ehingen 59 Ma 37	91301 Forchheim 59 Lb 39	82110 Germering 59 Ma 39
98660 Ehrenberg 47 La 38	03149 Forst/Lausitz 48 Kb 42	76726 Germersheim 59 Lb 36
94428 Eichendorf 60 Ma 40	00669 Frankenberg 48 La 41	76593 Gernsbach 59 Ma 36
36124 Eichenzell 47 La 37	67227 Frankenthal 59 Lb 36	54568 Gerolstein 46 La 34
85072 Eichstätt 59 Ma 39	15230 Frankfurt/Oder 48 Ka 42	97447 Gerolzhofen 59 Lb 38
04838 Eilenburg 48 Kb 40	60311 Frankfurt am Main 47 La 36	36129 Gersfeld(Rhön) 47 La 37
29578 Eimke 47 Ka 38	18461 Franzburg 36 Ja 40	66453 Gersheim 58 Lb 35

59590 Geseke 47 Kb 36	
31180 Giessen 47 La 36	
38518 Gifhorn 47 Ka 38	
45964 Gladbeck 46 Kb 35	
35075 Gladenbach 47 La 36	
49219 Glandorf 47 Ka 36	
08371 Glauchau 48 La 40	
25348 Glückstadt 35 Jab 37	
83703 Gmund am Tegernsee	
59 Mb 39	
27442 Gnarrenburg 47 Jab 37	
17179 Gnoien 36 Jab 40	
47574 Goch 46 Kb 34	
02633 Göda 48 Kb 42	
18586 Göhren 36 Ja 41	
19399 Goldberg 36 Jab 40	
25862 Goldelund 35 Ja 37	
49424 Goldenstedt 47 Ka 36	
14778 Golzow 48 Ka 40	
73033 Göppingen 59 Ma 37	
02826 Görlitz 48 Kb 42	
14828 Görzke 48 Ka 40	
38640 Goslar 47 Kb 38	
99867 Gotha 47 La 38	
37073 Göttingen 47 Kb 37	
18181 Graal-Müritz 36 Ja 40	
19300 Grabow 48 Jab 39	
85567 Grafing bei München	
60 Ma 39	
17291 Gramzow 48 Jab 42	
16775 Gransee 48 Jab 41	
26736 Greetsiel 35 Jab 35	
17489 Greifswald 36 Ja 41	
07973 Greiz 48 La 40	
48268 Greven 47 Ka 35	
41515 Grevenbroich 46 Kb 34	
04668 Grimma 48 Kb 40	
18507 Grimmen 36 Ja 41	
23743 Grömitz 35 Ja 38	
48599 Gronau 46 Ka 35	
16348 Groß Schönebeck 48 Ka 41	
64823 Groß-Umstadt 59 Lb 36	
01558 Großenhain 48 Kb 41	
01983 Großräschen 48 Kb 42	
35305 Grünberg 47 La 36	
82031 Grünwald 59 Ma 39	
03172 Guben 48 Kb 42	
51643 Gummersbach 46 Kb 35	
74831 Gundelsheim 59 Lb 37	
89312 Günzburg 59 Ma 38	
91710 Gunzenhausen 59 Lb 38	
39317 Güsen 48 Ka 39	
18273 Güstrow 36 Jab 40	
33330 Gütersloh 47 Kb 36	
17506 Gützkow 36 Jab 41	
57627 Hachenburg 47 La 35	
65589 Hadamar 47 La 36	
23683 Haffkrug 35 Ja 38	
59846 Hagen 46 Kb 35	
19230 Hagenow 47 Jab 39	
35708 Haiger 47 La 36	
72401 Haigerloch 59 Ma 36	
57250 Hainichen 48 La 41	
38820 Halberstadt 47 Kb 39	
39340 Haldensleben 47 Ka 39	
06108 Halle an der Saale 48 Kb 39	

POSTALI · ÍNDICE CON CÓDIGOS POSTALES · INDICE DE LUGARES COM CÓDIGOS POSTAIS ·
MÍST S PSČ · ZOZNAM OBCÍ S PSČ · INDEKS MIEJSCOWOŚCI Z KOD POCZTOWY

122

Halle (Westfalen)　　　　(D)　　　　Ludwigsburg　　(D)

33790	Halle (Westfalen) 47 Ka 36
25469	Halstenbek 35 Jab 37
45721	Haltern 46 Kb 35
20095	Hamburg 35 Jab 37
24805	Hamdorf 35 Ja 37
31785	Hameln 47 Ka 37
59065	Hamm 47 Kb 35
97762	Hammelburg 47 La 37
46499	Hamminkeln 46 Kb 34
63450	Hanau 47 La 36
30159	Hannover 47 Ka 37
34346	Hannoversch Münden 47 Kb 37
21073	Harburg 47 Jab 37
86655	Harburg(Schwaben) 59 Ma 38
49733	Haren 46 Ka 35
21698	Harsefeld 47 Jab 37
49740	Haselünne 47 Ka 35
97437	Haßfurt 59 La 38
67454	Haßloch 59 Lb 36
65795	Hattersheim am Main 47 La 36
45525	Hattingen 46 Kb 35
39539	Havelberg 48 Ka 40
59073	Heessen 47 Kb 35
25746	Heide 35 Ja 37
69117	Heidelberg 59 Lb 36
01809	Heidenau 48 La 41
89518	Heidenheim an der Brenz 59 Ma 38
37308	Heilbad Heiligenstadt 47 Kb 38
74072	Heilbronn 59 Lb 37
23774	Heiligenhafen 35 Ja 38
52525	Heinsberg 46 Kb 34
38350	Helmstedt 47 Ka 39
93155	Hemau 59 Lb 39
21745	Hemmoor 35 Jab 37
64646	Heppenheim 59 Lb 36
35745	Herborn 47 La 36
89542	Herbrechtingen 59 Ma 38
32049	Herford 47 Ka 36
54411	Hermeskeil 58 Lb 34
71083	Herrenberg 59 Ma 36
91217	Hersbruck 59 Lb 39
16835	Herzberg 48 Ka 40
04916	Herzberg/Elster 48 Kb 41
37412	Herzberg am Harz 47 Kb 38
31840	Hessisch Oldendorf 47 Ka 37
06333	Hettstedt 48 Kb 39
66265	Heusweiler 58 Lb 34
32120	Hiddenhausen 47 Ka 36
98646	Hildburghausen 47 La 38
31134	Hildesheim 47 Ka 37
48163	Hiltrup 47 Kb 35
26759	Hinte 35 Jab 35
92242	Hirschau 60 Lb 39
29693	Hodenhagen 47 Ka 37
95032	Hof 48 La 39
34369	Hofgeismar 47 Kb 37
97461	Hofheim in Unterfranken 47 La 38
16540	Hohen Neuendorf 48 Ka 41

06188	Hohenthurm 48 Kb 40
21279	Hollenstedt 47 Jab 37
96142	Hollfeld 59 Lb 39
83607	Holzkirchen 59 Mb 39
37603	Holzminden 47 Kb 37
34576	Homberg (Efze) 47 Kb 37
35315	Homberg (Ohm) 47 La 37
66424	Homburg 58 Lb 35
72160	Horb am Neckar 59 Ma 36
25997	Hörnum 35 Ja 36
48477	Hörstel 47 Ka 35
37671	Höxter 47 Kb 37
02977	Hoyerswerda 48 Kb 42
36088	Hünfeld 47 La 37
35410	Hungen 47 La 36
50354	Hürth 46 La 34
25813	Husum 35 Ja 37
94116	Hutthurm 60 Ma 41
49477	Ibbenbüren 47 Ka 35
55743	Idar-Oberstein 58 Lb 35
65510	Idstein 47 La 36
89257	Illertissen 59 Ma 38
66557	Illingen 58 Lb 35
98693	Ilmenau 47 La 38
87509	Immenstadt im Allgäu 59 Mb 38
55218	Ingelheim am Rhein 47 Lb 36
85051	Ingolstadt 59 Ma 39
54666	Irrel 46 Lb 34
58636	Iserlohn 47 Kb 35
85737	Ismaning 59 Ma 39
25524	Itzehoe 35 Jab 37
17126	Jarmen 36 Jab 41
07743	Jena 47 La 39
39319	Jerichow 48 Ka 40
06917	Jessen/Elster 48 Kb 40
16247	Joachimsthal 48 Ka 41
21635	Jork 35 Jab 37
52428	Jülich 46 La 34
14913	Jüterbog 48 Kb 41
67657	Kaiserslautern 58 Lb 35
01917	Kamenz 48 Kb 42
24376	Kappeln 35 Ja 37
76133	Karlsruhe 59 Lb 36
97753	Karlstadt 59 Lb 37
19294	Karstädt 48 Jab 39
34117	Kassel 47 Kb 37
87600	Kaufbeuren 59 Mb 38
07338	Kaulsdorf 47 La 39
77694	Kehl 58 Ma 35
93309	Kelheim 60 Ma 39
25548	Kellinghusen 35 Jab 37
92253	Kemnath 60 Lb 39
47906	Kempen 46 Kb 34
87435	Kempten (Allgäu) 59 Mb 38
54344	Kenn 58 Lb 34
47623	Kevelaer 46 Kb 34
83088	Kiefersfelden 60 Mb 40
24103	Kiel 35 Ja 38
85110	Kipfenberg 59 Ma 39
94261	Kirchdorf im Wald 60 Ma 41
35274	Kirchhain 47 La 36
85551	Kirchheim bei München 59 Ma 39

73230	Kirchheim unter Teck 59 Ma 37
67292	Kirchheimbolanden 59 Lb 35
55606	Kirn 58 Lb 35
97318	Kitzingen 59 Lb 38
14532	Kleinmachnow 48 Ka 41
47533	Kleve 46 Kb 34
08248	Klingenthal 48 La 40
38486	Klötze (Altmark) 47 Ka 39
18569	Kluis 36 Ja 41
23948	Klütz 35 Jab 39
56068	Koblenz 46 La 35
03099	Kolkwitz 48 Kb 42
50667	Köln 46 La 34
15711	Königs Wusterhausen 48 Ka 41
01936	Königsbrück 48 Kb 41
86343	Königsbrunn 59 Ma 38
97922	Königshofen 59 Lb 37
38154	Königslutter 47 Ka 38
53639	Königswinter 46 La 35
78462	Konstanz 59 Mb 37
54329	Konz 58 Lb 34
34497	Korbach 47 Kb 36
06366	Köthen / Anhalt 48 Kb 39
18292	Krakow am See 36 Jab 40
02957	Krauschwitz 48 Kb 42
47796	Krefeld 46 Kb 34
16766	Kremmen 48 Ka 41
57223	Kreuztal 47 La 35
96317	Kronach 47 La 39
18236	Kröpelin 36 Ja 39
24848	Kropp 35 Ja 37
86381	Krumbach (Schwaben) 59 Ma 38
95326	Kulmbach 59 La 39
97900	Külsheim 59 Lb 37
92245	Kümmersbruck 60 Lb 39
74653	Künzelsau 59 Lb 37
94550	Künzing 60 Ma 41
15910	Kuschkow 48 Ka 41
16866	Kyritz 48 Ka 40
18299	Laage 36 Jab 40
29331	Lachendorf 47 Ka 38
32791	Lage 47 Kb 36
56112	Lahnstein 46 La 35
77933	Lahr 59 Ma 35
68623	Lampertheim 59 Lb 36
94405	Landau an der Isar 60 Ma 40
76829	Landau in der Pfalz 59 Lb 36
86899	Landsberg am Lech 59 Ma 38
84028	Landshut 60 Ma 40
27607	Langen 35 Jab 36
89129	Langenau 59 Ma 38
30851	Langenhagen 47 Ka 37
27299	Langwedel 47 Ka 37
93138	Lappersdorf 60 Lb 40
49688	Lastrup 47 Ka 35
35321	Laubach 47 La 37
01979	Lauchhammer 48 Kb 41
97922	Lauda 59 Lb 37
21481	Lauenburg (Elbe) 47 Jab 38
63846	Laufach 47 La 37
88471	Laupheim 59 Ma 37

36341	Lauterbach (Hessen) 47 La 37
66822	Lebach 58 Lb 34
15326	Lebus 48 Ka 42
25917	Leck 35 Ja 36
26789	Leer 47 Jab 35
38165	Lehre 47 Ka 38
69181	Leimen 59 Lb 36
37327	Leinefelde 47 Kb 38
04109	Leipzig 48 Kb 40
04703	Leisnig 48 Kb 40
32657	Lemgo 47 Ka 36
38268	Lengede 47 Ka 38
49838	Lengerich/Lingen 47 Ka 35
49838	Lengerich/Osnabrück 47 Ka 35
57368	Lennestadt 47 Kb 36
19309	Lenzen 48 Jab 39
88299	Leutkirch im Allgäu 59 Mb 38
51373	Leverkusen 46 Kb 34
35423	Lich 47 La 36
54619	Lichtenborn 46 La 34
96215	Lichtenfels 47 La 39
09350	Lichtenstein 48 La 40
16559	Liebenwalde 48 Ka 41
15868	Lieberose 48 Kb 42
28865	Lilienthal 47 Jab 36
09121	Limbach-Oberfrohna 48 La 40
65594	Limburg an der Lahn 47 La 36
88131	Lindau 59 Mb 37
15864	Lindenberg 48 Ka 42
88161	Lindenberg im Allgäu 59 Mb 37
49808	Lingen 47 Ka 35
59555	Lippstadt 47 Kb 36
25992	List 35 Hb 36
02708	Löbau 48 Kb 42
07747	Lobeda 47 La 39
39279	Loburg 48 Ka 40
17321	Löcknitz 48 Jab 42
32584	Löhne 47 Ka 36
49393	Lohne (Oldenburg) 47 Ka 36
97816	Lohr am Main 59 Lb 37
17094	Loitz 36 Jab 41
35457	Lollar 47 La 36
01623	Lommatzsch 48 Kb 41
49624	Löningen 47 Ka 35
79539	Lörrach 58 Mb 35
66679	Losheim am See 58 Lb 34
08294	Lößnitz 48 La 40
27612	Loxstedt 35 Jab 36
32312	Lübbecke 47 Ka 36
15907	Lübben/Spreewald 48 Kb 41
03222	Lübbenau/Spreewald 48 Kb 41
23552	Lübeck 35 Jab 38
19386	Lübz 48 Jab 40
29439	Lüchow (Wendland) 47 Ka 39
15926	Luckau 48 Kb 41
14943	Luckenwalde 48 Ka 41
58507	Lüdenscheid 47 Kb 35
59348	Lüdinghausen 46 Kb 35
71634	Ludwigsburg 59 Ma 37

123

INDEX WITH POST CODES · ORTSREGISTER MIT POSTLEITZAHLEN · INDICE CON CODICI
STEDREGISTER MED POSTNUMRE · PLAATSNAMENREGISTER MET POSTCODE · REJSTŘÍK

D

Ludwigsfelde	**D**	**Quakenbrück**

14974 Ludwigsfelde 48 Ka 41
67059 Ludwigshafen am Rhein
　　　59 Lb 36
19288 Ludwigslust 48 Jab 39
21335 Lüneburg 47 Jab 38
44532 Lünen 47 Kb 35
06295 Lutherstadt Eisleben
　　　48 Kb 39
06886 Lutherstadt Wittenberg
　　　48 Kb 40
24321 Lütjenburg 35 Ja 38
17279 Lychen 48 Jab 41
39104 Magdeburg 48 Ka 39
84048 Mainburg 59 Ma 39
95336 Mainleus 47 La 39
55116 Mainz 47 Lb 36
17139 Malchin 36 Jab 40
17213 Malchow 48 Jab 40
23714 Malente 35 Ja 38
02694 Malschwitz 48 Kb 42
85077 Manching 59 Ma 39
68159 Mannheim 59 Lb 36
35037 Marburg 47 La 36
09496 Marienberg 48 La 41
88677 Markdorf 59 Mb 37
04416 Markkleeberg 48 Kb 40
99819 Marksuhl 47 La 38
97828 Marktheidenfeld 59 Lb 37
87616 Marktoberdorf 59 Mb 38
95615 Marktredwitz 60 La 40
45768 Marl 46 Kb 35
34431 Marsberg 47 Kb 36
14913 Marzahna 48 Ka 40
93142 Maxhütte-Haidhof 60 Lb 40
56727 Mayen 46 La 35
53894 Mechernich 46 La 34
88074 Meckenbeuren 59 Mb 37
53340 Meckenheim 46 La 35
08393 Meerane 48 La 40
98617 Meiningen 47 La 38
04838 Meißen 48 Kb 41
86405 Meitingen 59 Ma 38
25704 Meldorf 35 Ja 37
49324 Melle 47 Ka 36
34212 Melsungen 47 Kb 37
96117 Memmelsdorf 59 Lb 38
87700 Memmingen 59 Mb 38
58706 Menden 47 Kb 36
49716 Meppen 47 Ka 35
06217 Merseburg 48 Kb 39
66663 Merzig 58 Lb 34
59872 Meschede 47 Kb 36
39624 Meßdorf 48 Ka 39
66693 Mettlach 58 Lb 34
72555 Metzingen/Reutlingen
　　　59 Ma 37
28790 Meyenburg 48 Jab 40
64720 Michelstadt 59 Lb 37
83714 Miesbach 59 Mb 39
17268 Milmersdorf 48 Jab 41
87719 Mindelheim 59 Ma 38
32423 Minden 47 Ka 36
17252 Mirow 48 Jab 40
09648 Mittweida 48 La 40
39291 Möckern 48 Ka 39
47441 Moers 46 Kb 34

17237 Möllenbeck 48 Jab 41
23879 Mölln 35 Jab 38
41061 Mönchen-Gladbach 46 Kb 34
52156 Monschau 46 La 34
67590 Monsheim 59 Lb 36
56410 Montabaur 47 La 35
85368 Moosburg an der Isar
　　　60 Ma 39
54497 Morbach 58 Lb 35
74821 Mosbach 59 Lb 37
72116 Mössingen 59 Ma 37
69427 Mudau 59 Lb 37
84453 Mühldorf am Inn 60 Ma 40
99974 Mühlhausen (Thüringen)
　　　47 Kb 38
45438 Mülheim an der Ruhr
　　　46 Kb 34
56218 Mülheim-Kärlich 46 La 35
79379 Mülheim 58 Mb 35
15299 Müllrose 48 Ka 42
95213 Münchberg 48 La 39
80331 München 59 Ma 39
29633 Munster 47 Ka 38
48143 Münster 47 Kb 35
82418 Murnau am Staffelsee
　　　59 Mb 39
71540 Murrhardt 59 Ma 37
04688 Mutzschen 48 Kb 40
72202 Nagold 59 Ma 36
98553 Nahetal-Waldau 47 La 38
95119 Naila 48 La 39
16515 Nassenheide 48 Ka 41
14641 Nauen 48 Ka 40
06618 Naumburg/Saale 48 Kb 39
74172 Neckarsulm 59 Lb 37
73450 Neresheim 59 Ma 38
57250 Netphen 47 La 36
89231 Neu-Ulm 59 Ma 38
17033 Neubrandenburg
　　　48 Jab 41
18233 Neubukow 36 Ja 39
86633 Neuburg an der Donau
　　　59 Ma 39
15366 Neuenhagen bei Berlin
　　　48 Ka 41
41517 Neuenhaus 46 Ka 34
85375 Neufahrn bei Freising
　　　59 Ma 39
87600 Neugablonz 59 Mb 38
15320 Neuhardenberg 48 Ka 42
36119 Neuhof 47 La 37
23992 Neukloster 36 Jab 39
92318 Neumarkt in der Oberpfalz
　　　59 Lb 39
84494 Neumarkt-Sankt Veit
　　　60 Ma 40
24534 Neumünster 35 Ja 37
53819 Neunkirchen 46 La 35
66538 Neunkirchen 58 Lb 35
16816 Neuruppin 48 Ka 40
86356 Neusäß 59 Ma 38
41460 Neuss 48 Kb 34
31535 Neustadt am Rübenberge
　　　47 Ka 37
91413 Neustadt an der Aisch
　　　59 Lb 38

93333 Neustadt an der Donau
　　　59 Ma 39
07806 Neustadt an der Orla
　　　48 La 39
67433 Neustadt an der Weinstraße
　　　59 Lb 36
96465 Neustadt bei Coburg
　　　47 La 39
23730 Neustadt in Holstein
　　　35 Ja 38
01844 Neustadt in Sachsen
　　　48 Kb 42
19306 Neustadt-Glewe 48 Jab 39
17235 Neustrelitz 48 Jab 41
93073 Neutraubling 60 Ma 40
56564 Neuwied 46 La 35
63667 Nidda 47 La 37
25899 Niebüll 35 Ja 36
36272 Niederaula 47 La 37
14823 Niemegk 48 Ka 40
06429 Nienburg 48 Kb 39
31582 Nienburg (Weser) 47 Ka 37
02906 Niesky 48 Kb 42
66625 Nohfelden 58 Lb 35
26506 Norddeich 35 Jab 35
25946 Norddorf 35 Ja 36
26506 Norden 35 Jab 35
26954 Nordenham 35 Jab 36
26548 Norderney 35 Jab 35
22844 Norderstedt 35 Ja 37
99734 Nordhausen 47 Kb 38
26871 Nordhorn 46 Ka 35
86720 Nördlingen 59 Ma 38
37154 Northeim 47 Kb 37
24589 Nortorf 35 Ja 37
48301 Nottuln 46 Kb 35
90317 Nürnberg 59 Lb 39
72622 Nürtingen 59 Ma 37
83131 Nußdorf am Inn 60 Mb 40
82487 Oberammergau 59 Mb 39
46045 Oberhausen 46 Kb 34
77704 Oberkirch 58 Ma 36
78727 Oberndorf am Neckar
　　　59 Ma 36
87561 Oberstdorf 59 Mb 38
61440 Oberursel 47 La 36
92526 Oberviechtach 60 Lb 40
55430 Oberwesel 46 La 35
83119 Obing 60 Ma 40
97199 Ochsenfurt 59 Lb 38
48607 Ochtrup 46 Ka 35
59302 Oelde 47 Kb 36
08606 Oelsnitz 48 La 40
65375 Oestrich-Winkel 47 La 36
86732 Oettingen in Bayern
　　　59 Ma 38
63065 Offenbach am Main 47 La 36
77652 Offenburg 58 Ma 35
99885 Ohrdruf 47 La 38
74613 Öhringen 59 Lb 37
09526 Olbernhau 48 La 41
26121 Oldenburg 47 Jab 36
23758 Oldenburg in Holstein
　　　35 Ja 38
57462 Olpe 47 Kb 35
16515 Oranienburg 48 Ka 41

04758 Oschatz 48 Kb 41
39387 Oschersleben/Bode
　　　47 Ka 39
49074 Osnabrück 47 Ka 36
39606 Osterburg (Altmark)
　　　48 Ka 39
25836 Osterhever 35 Ja 36
94486 Osterhofen 60 Ma 41
27711 Osterholz-Scharmbeck
　　　47 Jab 36
37520 Osterode am Harz 47 Kb 38
02899 Ostritz 48 Kb 42
01458 Ottendorf-Okrilla 48 Kb 41
21762 Otterndorf 35 Jab 36
87724 Ottobeuren 59 Mb 38
28876 Oyten 47 Jab 37
33098 Paderborn 47 Kb 36
26871 Papenburg 47 Jab 35
19370 Parchim 48 Jab 39
17309 Pasewalk 48 Jab 42
94032 Passau 60 Ma 41
16306 Passow 48 Ka 42
17449 Peenemünde 36 Ja 41
91257 Pegnitz 59 Lb 39
49696 Peheim 47 Ka 35
31224 Peine 47 Ka 38
82380 Peißenberg 59 Mb 39
86971 Peiting 59 Mb 38
03185 Peitz 48 Kb 42
17217 Penzlin 48 Jab 41
19348 Perleberg 48 Jab 39
14641 Pessin 48 Ka 40
32469 Petershagen 47 Ka 36
85276 Pfaffenhofen an der Ilm
　　　59 Ma 39
84347 Pfarrkirchen 60 Ma 40
84076 Pfeffenhausen 60 Ma 39
75158 Pforzheim 59 Ma 36
87459 Pfronten 59 Mb 38
88630 Pfullendorf 59 Mb 37
64319 Pfungstadt 59 Lb 36
94431 Pilsting 60 Ma 40
25421 Pinneberg 35 Jab 37
66953 Pirmasens 58 Lb 35
01796 Pirna 48 La 41
82152 Planegg 59 Ma 39
94447 Plattling 60 Ma 40
19395 Plau am See 48 Jab 40
08523 Plauen 48 La 40
58840 Plettenberg 47 Kb 35
24306 Plön 35 Ja 38
94060 Pocking 60 Ma 41
07381 Pößneck 47 La 39
14467 Potsdam 48 Ka 41
91278 Pottenstein 59 Lb 39
86554 Pöttmes 59 Ma 39
24211 Preetz 35 Ja 38
14727 Premnitz 48 Ka 40
17291 Prenzlau 48 Jab 41
16928 Pritzwalk 48 Jab 40
07330 Probstzella 47 La 39
54595 Prüm 46 La 34
50259 Pulheim 46 Kb 34
16949 Putlitz 48 Jab 40
23769 Puttgarden 36 Ja 39
49610 Quakenbrück 47 Ka 35

POSTALI · ÍNDICE CON CÓDIGOS POSTALES · INDICE DE LUGARES COM CÓDIGOS POSTAIS ·
MÍST S PSČ · ZOZNAM OBCÍ S PSČ · INDEKS MIEJSCOWOŚCI Z KOD POCZTOWY

124

06484 Quedlinburg 47 Kb 39	02929 Rothenburg (Oberlausitz)	29690 Schwarmstedt 47 Ka 37	15913 Straupitz 48 Kb 42
01454 Radeberg 48 Kb 41	48 Kb 42	21493 Schwarzenbek 47 Jab 38	15344 Strausberg 48 Ka 41
01445 Radebeul 48 Kb 41	83700 Rottach-Egern 59 Mb 39	08340 Schwarzenberg 48 La 40	14943 Stülpe 48 Ka 41
78315 Radolfzell am Bodensee	91187 Röttenbach 59 Lb 39	16303 Schwedt/Oder 48 Jab 42	70173 Stuttgart 59 Ma 37
59 Mb 36	78628 Rottweil 59 Ma 36	54338 Schweich 46 Lb 34	25923 Süderlügum 35 Ja 36
32369 Rahden 47 Ka 36	92444 Rötz 60 Lb 40	97421 Schweinfurt 59 La 38	98527 Suhl 47 La 38
76437 Rastatt 59 Ma 36	15562 Rüdersdorf bei Berlin	19053 Schwerin 36 Jab 39	27232 Sulingen 47 Ka 36
26180 Rastede 47 Jab 36	48 Ka 41	01855 Sebnitz 48 La 42	72172 Sulz am Neckar 59 Ma 36
23626 Ratekau 35 Jab 38	07407 Rudolstadt 47 La 39	82229 Seefeld 59 Ma 39	92237 Sulzbach-Rosenberg
14712 Rathenow 48 Ka 40	83324 Ruhpolding 60 Mb 40	39615 Seehausen (Altmark)	59 Lb 39
40878 Ratingen 46 Kb 34	65428 Rüsselsheim 47 Lb 36	48 Ka 39	28857 Syke 47 Ka 36
23909 Ratzeburg 35 Jab 38	07318 Saalfeld (Saale) 47 La 39	15306 Seelow 48 Ka 42	25980 Sylt-Ost 35 Ja 36
83064 Raubling 60 Mb 40	66111 Saarbrücken 58 Lb 34	53819 Seelscheid 46 La 35	83342 Tacherting 60 Ma 40
88212 Ravensburg 59 Mb 37	66740 Saarlouis 58 Lb 34	30926 Seelze 47 Ka 37	39590 Tangermünde 48 Ka 39
49509 Recke 47 Ka 35	18551 Sagard 36 Ja 41	38723 Seesen 47 Kb 38	24963 Tarp 35 Ja 37
94209 Regen 60 Ma 41	38228 Salzgitter 47 Ka 38	21217 Seevetal 47 Jab 37	97941 Tauberbischofsheim
93047 Regensburg 60 Lb 40	38226 Salzgitter 47 Ka 38	31319 Sehnde 47 Ka 37	59 Lb 37
93128 Regenstauf 60 Lb 40	29410 Salzwedel 47 Ka 39	95100 Selb 48 La 40	04425 Taucha 48 Kb 40
95111 Rehau 48 La 40	18573 Samtens 36 Ja 41	18586 Sellin 36 Ja 41	03185 Tauer 48 Kb 42
66780 Rehlingen-Siersburg	06526 Sangerhausen 47 Kb 39	59379 Selm 46 Kb 35	14513 Teltow 48 Ka 41
58 Lb 34	53757 Sankt Augustin 46 La 35	48308 Senden/Dülmen 47 Kb 35	17268 Templin 48 Jab 41
19217 Rehna 35 Jab 39	66386 Sankt Ingbert 58 Lb 35	89250 Senden/Neu-Ulm 59 Ma 38	18195 Tessin 36 Ja 40
21465 Reinbek 47 Jab 38	25826 Sankt Peter-Ording 35 Ja 36	48324 Sendenhorst 47 Kb 35	17166 Teterow 36 Jab 40
18519 Reinberg 36 Ja 41	66606 Sankt Wendel 58 Lb 35	01968 Senftenberg 48 Kb 41	06502 Thale/Harz 47 Kb 39
42853 Remscheid 46 Kb 35	17392 Sarnow 36 Jab 41	57072 Siegen 47 La 36	54424 Thalfang 58 Lb 35
24768 Rendsburg 35 Ja 37	31157 Sarstedt 47 Ka 37	72488 Sigmaringen 59 Ma 37	98660 Themar 47 La 38
21391 Reppenstedt 47 Jab 38	48336 Sassenberg 47 Kb 36	84359 Simbach am Inn 60 Ma 41	66636 Tholey 58 Lb 35
18230 Rerik 36 Ja 39	18546 Sassnitz 36 Ja 41	55469 Simmern 46 Lb 35	17168 Thürkow 36 Jab 40
39264 Reuden 48 Ka 40	24986 Satrup 35 Ja 37	71063 Sindelfingen 59 Ma 36	90993 Tiengen 59 Mb 36
17153 Reuterstadt Stavenhagen	18569 Schaprode 36 Ja 41	78224 Singen 59 Mb 36	23999 Timmendorf 36 Jab 39
36 Jab 40	23683 Scharbeutz 35 Ja 38	74889 Sinsheim 59 Lb 36	95643 Tirschenreuth 60 Lb 40
72760 Reutlingen 59 Ma 37	27383 Scheeßel 47 Jab 37	59494 Soest 47 Kb 36	79822 Titisee-Neustadt 59 Mb 36
33378 Rheda-Wiedenbrück	25560 Schenefeld 35 Ja 37	49751 Sögel 47 Ka 35	79674 Todtnau 58 Mb 35
47 Kb 36	96110 Scheßlitz 59 Lb 39	42659 Solingen 46 Kb 35	25832 Tönning 35 Ja 36
77866 Rheinau 58 Ma 35	16552 Schildow 48 Ka 41	29614 Soltau 47 Ka 37	04860 Torgau 48 Kb 40
48431 Rheine 47 Ka 35	04435 Schkeuditz 48 Kb 40	99610 Sömmerda 47 Kb 39	17358 Torgelow 48 Jab 42
79618 Rheinfelden 58 Mb 35	53937 Schleiden 46 La 34	99706 Sondershausen 47 Kb 38	21255 Tostedt 47 Jab 37
16831 Rheinsberg 48 Jab 40	07907 Schleiz 48 La 39	96515 Sonneberg 47 La 39	24610 Trappenkamp 35 Ja 38
76287 Rheinstetten 59 Ma 36	24837 Schleswig 35 Ja 37	87527 Sonthofen 59 Mb 38	83301 Traunreut 60 Mb 40
14728 Rhinow 48 Ka 40	04936 Schlieben 48 Kb 41	24966 Sörup 35 Ja 37	83278 Traunstein 60 Mb 40
18311 Ribnitz-Damgarten 36 Ja 40	36110 Schlitz 47 La 37	27367 Sottrum 47 Jab 37	14959 Trebbin 48 Ka 41
01589 Riesa 48 Kb 41	36381 Schlüchtern 47 La 37	78549 Spaichingen 59 Ma 36	91757 Treuchtlingen 59 Ma 38
02956 Rietschen 48 Kb 42	98574 Schmalkalden 47 La 38	67346 Speyer 59 Lb 36	54290 Trier 58 Lb 34
17207 Röbel (Müritz) 48 Jab 40	04626 Schmölln 48 La 40	03130 Spremberg 48 Kb 42	07819 Triptis 48 La 39
06317 Röblingen am See 48 Kb 39	29640 Schneverdingen 47 Jab 37	31832 Springe 47 Ka 37	53844 Troisdorf 46 La 35
09306 Rochlitz 48 Kb 40	24217 Schönberg (Holstein)	21680 Stade 35 Jab 37	83308 Trostberg 60 Ma 40
67806 Rockenhausen 58 Lb 35	35 Ja 38	35260 Stadtallendorf 47 La 37	72070 Tübingen 59 Ma 37
26935 Rodenkirchen 35 Jab 36	39218 Schönebeck/Elbe 48 Ka 39	31655 Stadthagen 47 Ka 37	78532 Tuttlingen 59 Mb 36
63110 Rodgau 47 La 36	01474 Schönfeld-Weißig 48 Kb 41	48703 Stadtlohn 46 Kb 34	27239 Twistringen 47 Ka 36
93426 Roding 60 Lb 40	86956 Schongau 59 Mb 38	82319 Starnberg 59 Ma 39	88662 Überlingen 59 Mb 37
38489 Rohrberg 47 Ka 39	38364 Schöningen 47 Ka 38	39418 Staßfurt 48 Kb 39	31600 Uchte 47 Ka 36
38325 Roklum 47 Ka 38	72270 Schönmünzach 59 Ma 36	31634 Steimbke 47 Ka 37	17373 Ueckermünde 36 Jab 42
30952 Ronnenberg 47 Ka 37	76650 Schopfheim 58 Mb 35	90547 Stein 59 Lb 39	29525 Uelzen 47 Ka 38
29571 Rosche 47 Ka 38	26419 Schortens 35 Jab 35	36396 Steinau an der Straße	31311 Uetze 47 Ka 38
83022 Rosenheim 60 Mb 40	63679 Schotten 47 La 37	47 La 37	89073 Ulm 59 Ma 37
06862 Roßlau/Elbe 48 Kb 40	78713 Schramberg 59 Ma 36	49439 Steinfeld (Oldenburg)	56766 Ulmen 46 La 35
06571 Roßleben 47 Kb 39	86529 Schrobenhausen 59 Ma 39	47 Ka 36	59423 Unna 47 Kb 35
18055 Rostock 36 Ja 40	18258 Schwaan 36 Jab 40	39576 Stendal 48 Ka 39	61250 Usingen 47 La 36
36199 Rotenburg 47 Kb 37	91126 Schwabach 59 Lb 39	19406 Sternberg 36 Jab 39	31770 Uslar 47 Kb 37
27356 Rotenburg (Wümme)	73525 Schwäbisch Gmünd	78333 Stockach 59 Mb 37	71665 Vaihingen an der Enz
47 Jab 37	59 Ma 37	23617 Stockelsdorf 35 Jab 38	59 Ma 36
91154 Roth 47 Lb 39	74523 Schwäbisch Hall 59 Lb 37	96342 Stockheim 47 La 39	26316 Varel 35 Jab 36
90552 Röthenbach an der Pegnitz	86830 Schwabmünchen 59 Ma 38	52222 Stolberg 46 La 34	85591 Vaterstetten 59 Ma 39
59 Lb 39	34613 Schwalmstadt 47 La 37	18435 Stralsund 36 Ja 41	49377 Vechta 47 Ka 36
91541 Rothenburg ob der Tauber	92421 Schwandorf 60 Lb 40	17335 Strasburg 48 Jab 41	42549 Velbert 46 Kb 35
59 Lb 38	28790 Schwanewede 47 Jab 36	94315 Straubing 60 Ma 40	34246 Vellmar 47 Kb 37

D

DK

Verden (Aller)   D . DK   Jyllinge

27283 Verden (Aller) 47 Ka 37	
33415 Verl 47 Kb 36	
33775 Versmold 47 Ka 36	
94234 Viechtach 60 Lb 40	
68519 Viernheim 59 Lb 36	
41747 Viersen 46 Kb 34	
78048 Villingen-Schwenningen 59 Ma 36	
84137 Vilsbiburg 60 Ma 40	
94474 Vilshofen 60 Ma 41	
27374 Visselhövede 47 Ka 37	
79235 Vogtsburg 58 Ma 35	
85088 Vohburg an der Donau 59 Ma 39	
89269 Vöhringen 59 Ma 38	
83661 Vorderriß 59 Mb 39	
48691 Vreden 46 Ka 34	
66687 Wadern 58 Lb 34	
49419 Wagenfeld 47 Ka 36	
79183 Waldkirch 58 Ma 35	
84478 Waldkraiburg 60 Ma 40	
93449 Waldmünchen 60 Lb 40	
90993 Waldshut-Tiengen 58 Mb 36	
74731 Walldürn 59 Lb 37	
29664 Walsrode 47 Ka 37	
99880 Waltershausen 47 La 38	
88239 Wangen 59 Mb 37	
39614 Wanzleben 47 Ka 39	
34414 Warburg 47 Kb 37	
26203 Wardenburg 47 Jab 36	
17192 Waren (Müritz) 48 Jab 40	
48231 Warendorf 47 Kb 35	
19417 Warin 36 Jab 39	
18119 Warnemünde 36 Ja 40	
26802 Warsingsfehn 35 Jab 35	
59581 Warstein 47 Kb 36	
83512 Wasserburg am Inn 60 Ma 40	
26826 Weener 47 Jab 35	
92637 Weiden in der Oberpfalz 60 Lb 40	
95466 Weidenberg 60 Lb 39	
79576 Weil am Rhein 58 Mb 35	
35781 Weilburg 47 La 36	
99423 Weimar 47 La 39	
88250 Weingarten 59 Mb 37	
69469 Weinheim 59 Lb 36	
71384 Weinstadt 59 Ma 37	
91781 Weißenburg in Bayern 59 Lb 38	
06667 Weißenfels 48 Kb 39	
89264 Weißenhorn 59 Ma 38	
02943 Weißwasser (Oberlausitz) 48 Kb 42	
86650 Wemding 59 Ma 38	
57482 Wenden 47 La 35	
08412 Werdau 48 La 40	
14542 Werder (Havel) 48 Ka 40	
59457 Werl 47 Kb 35	
97440 Werneck 59 Lb 38	
38855 Wernigerode 47 Kb 38	
97877 Wertheim 59 Lb 37	
49757 Wertle 47 Ka 35	
46483 Wesel 46 Kb 34	
17255 Wesenberg 48 Jab 40	
25764 Wesselburen 35 Ja 36	

26556 Westerholt 35 Jab 35	
25980 Westerland 35 Ja 36	
26655 Westerstede 47 Jab 35	
25849 Westertilli 35 Ja 36	
35435 Wettenberg 47 La 36	
35578 Wetzlar 47 La 36	
28844 Weyhe 47 Ka 36	
26215 Wiefelstede 47 Jab 36	
65183 Wiesbaden 47 La 36	
69168 Wiesloch 59 Lb 36	
26639 Wiesmoor 35 Jab 35	
31613 Wietzen 47 Ka 37	
72218 Wildberg 59 Ma 36	
27793 Wildeshausen 47 Ka 36	
26382 Wilhelmshaven 35 Jab 36	
08112 Wilkau-Haßlau 48 La 40	
29308 Winsen (Aller) 47 Ka 37	
21423 Winsen (Luhe) 47 Jab 38	
59955 Winterberg 47 Kb 36	
29416 Winterfeld 47 Ka 39	
23966 Wismar 36 Jab 39	
25946 Wittdün 35 Ja 36	
06452 Witten 46 Kb 35	
19322 Wittenberge 48 Jab 39	
19243 Wittenburg 47 Jab 39	
29378 Wittingen 47 Ka 38	
54516 Wittlich 46 Lb 34	
26409 Wittmund 35 Jab 35	
16909 Wittstock/Dosse 48 Jab 40	
37213 Witzenhausen 47 Kb 37	
17348 Woldegk 48 Jab 41	
06766 Wolfen 48 Kb 40	
38300 Wolfenbüttel 47 Ka 38	
34466 Wolfhagen 47 Kb 37	
82515 Wolfratshausen 59 Mb 39	
38440 Wolfsburg 47 Ka 38	
17438 Wolgast 36 Ja 41	
39326 Wolmirstedt 48 Ka 39	
67547 Worms 59 Lb 36	
85457 Wörth 60 Ma 39	
76744 Wörth am Rhein 59 Lb 36	
16269 Wriezen 48 Ka 42	
46286 Wulfen 46 Kb 35	
15838 Wünsdorf 48 Ka 41	
95632 Wunsiedel im Fichtelgebirge 60 La 40	
31515 Wunstorf 47 Ka 37	
42275 Wuppertal 46 Kb 35	
97070 Würzburg 59 Lb 37	
04808 Wurzen 48 Kb 40	
25938 Wyk 35 Ja 36	
46509 Xanten 46 Kb 34	
06895 Zahna 48 Kb 40	
19246 Zarrentin 35 Jab 38	
16792 Zehdenick 48 Ka 41	
97475 Zeil am Main 59 La 38	
01619 Zeithain 48 Kb 41	
06712 Zeitz 48 Kb 40	
56856 Zell (Mosel) 46 La 35	
98544 Zella-Mehlis 47 La 38	
54492 Zeltingen-Rachtig 46 Lb 34	
39261 Zerbst 48 Kb 40	
54314 Zerf 58 Lb 34	
15758 Zernsdorf 48 Ka 41	
26340 Zetel 35 Jab 35	
07937 Zeulenroda 48 La 39	

27404 Zeven 47 Jab 37	
14793 Ziesar 48 Ka 40	
18374 Zingst 36 Ja 40	
17544 Zinnowitz 36 Ja 41	
17419 Zirchow 36 Jab 42	
90513 Zirndorf 59 Lb 38	
02763 Zittau 48 La 42	
15806 Zossen 48 Ka 41	
09405 Zschopau 48 La 41	
53909 Zülpich 46 La 34	
86441 Zusmarshausen 59 Ma 38	
66482 Zweibrücken 58 Lb 35	
08056 Zwickau 48 La 40	
94227 Zwiesel 60 Lb 41	

DK

6200 Aabenraa 35 Hb 37	
9440 Aabybro 27 Gb 37	
3720 Aakirkeby 36 Hb 42	
9000 Aalborg 27 Gb 37	
9620 Aalestrup 35 Ha 37	
9600 Aars 35 Ha 37	
5560 Aarup 35 Hb 38	
6534 Agerskov 35 Hb 37	
7770 Agger 35 Ha 36	
9670 Aggersund 27 Gb 37	
3770 Allinge 36 Hb 42	
8592 Anholt 36 Ha 39	
9510 Arden 35 Ha 37	
5610 Assens 35 Hb 37	
7490 Aulum 35 Ha 36	
8963 Auning 35 Ha 38	
5935 Bagenkop 35 Ja 38	
2750 Ballerup 36 Hb 40	
7190 Billund 35 Hb 37	
9881 Bindslev 27 Gb 38	
3460 Birkerød 36 Hb 40	
8850 Bjerringbro 35 Ha 37	
9492 Blokhus 27 Gb 37	
5400 Bogense 35 Hb 38	
4793 Bogø By 36 Ja 40	
6000 Bramdrupdam 35 Hb 37	
6740 Bramming 35 Hb 36	
7330 Brande 35 Hb 37	
5464 Brenderup 35 Hb 37	
9460 Brovst 27 Gb 37	
8654 Bryrup 35 Ha 37	
9700 Brønderslev 27 Gb 37	
5600 Bøjden 35 Hb 38	
6070 Christiansfeld 35 Hb 37	
8970 Dalbyover 35 Ha 38	
9280 Dokkedal 35 Ha 38	
2791 Dragør 36 Hb 40	
9330 Dronninglund 27 Gb 38	
8400 Ebeltoft 35 Ha 38	
6040 Egtved 35 Hb 37	
4623 Ejby 36 Hb 40	
6700 Esbjerg 35 Hb 36	
5600 Faaborg 35 Hb 38	
4640 Fakse 36 Hb 40	
9640 Farsø 35 Ha 37	
8420 Fejrup 35 Ha 38	
6200 Felsted 35 Ja 37	

4700 Fensmark 36 Hb 39	
7200 Filskov 35 Hb 37	
8585 Fjellerup 35 Ha 38	
9690 Fjerritslev 27 Gb 37	
9330 Flauenskjold 27 Gb 38	
7000 Fredericia 35 Hb 37	
7470 Frederiks 35 Ha 37	
9900 Frederikshavn 27 Gb 38	
3600 Frederikssund 36 Hb 40	
3300 Frederiksværk 36 Hb 40	
4250 Fuglebjerg 36 Hb 39	
4874 Gedser 36 Ja 39	
3250 Gilleleje 36 Ha 40	
9260 Gistrup 27 Ha 37	
7323 Give 35 Hb 37	
2600 Glostrup 36 Hb 40	
6510 Gram 35 Hb 37	
8500 Grenaa 36 Ha 38	
2670 Greve Strand 36 Hb 40	
7200 Grindsted 35 Hb 36	
6300 Gråsten 35 Ja 37	
3760 Gudhjem 36 Hb 42	
4281 Gørlev 36 Hb 39	
5683 Haarby 35 Hb 38	
6100 Haderslev 35 Hb 37	
8370 Hadsten 35 Ha 38	
9560 Hadsund 35 Ha 38	
9370 Hals 27 Gb 38	
8450 Hammel 35 Ha 38	
7730 Hanstholm 27 Gb 36	
3790 Hasle 36 Hb 42	
4690 Haslev 36 Hb 39	
4583 Havnebyen 36 Hb 39	
3200 Helsinge 36 Ha 40	
3000 Helsingør 36 Ha 40	
6854 Henne Strand 35 Hb 36	
2730 Herlev 36 Hb 40	
7400 Herning 35 Ha 36	
5874 Hesselager 35 Hb 38	
3400 Hillerød 36 Hb 40	
9850 Hirtshals 27 Gb 37	
9320 Hjallerup 27 Gb 38	
9800 Hjørring 27 Gb 37	
9500 Hobro 35 Ha 37	
4300 Holbæk 36 Hb 39	
7500 Holstebro 35 Ha 36	
6670 Holsted 35 Hb 36	
6100 Hoptrup 35 Hb 37	
3100 Hornbæk 36 Ha 40	
8543 Hornslet 35 Ha 38	
8783 Hornsyld 35 Hb 37	
8700 Horsens 35 Hb 38	
8300 Hov 35 Hb 38	
3390 Hundested 36 Hb 39	
7760 Hurup 35 Ha 36	
7790 Hvidbjerg 35 Ha 36	
6960 Hvide Sande 35 Ha 36	
6280 Højer 35 Ja 36	
7752 Hørdum 35 Ha 36	
8362 Hørning 35 Ha 38	
2970 Hørsholm 36 Hb 40	
4652 Hårlev 36 Hb 40	
7430 Ikast 35 Ha 37	
7130 Juelsminde 35 Hb 38	
4450 Jyderup 36 Hb 39	
4040 Jyllinge 36 Hb 40	

POSTALI · ÍNDICE CON CÓDIGOS POSTALES · INDICE DE LUGARES COM CÓDIGOS POSTAIS ·
MÍST S PSČ · ZOZNAM OBCÍ S PSČ · INDEKS MIEJSCOWOŚCI Z KOD POCZTOWY

126

Kalundborg — DK · DZ — **Chaabat-El-Leham**

DK

DZ

4400 Kalundborg 36 Hb 39	8550 Ryomgård 35 Ha 38	7100 Vejle 35 Hb 37	44260 Aïn Benian 98 Sa 30
4736 Karrebæksminde 36 Hb 39	7730 Ræhr 27 Gb 36	7570 Vemb 35 Ha 36	44000 Aïn Defla 98 Sa 29
7470 Karup 35 Ha 37	4970 Rødby 36 Ja 39	9380 Vestbjerg 27 Gb 37	Aïn El Berd 97 Sb 27
5300 Kerteminde 35 Hb 38	4970 Rødbyhavn 36 Ja 39	9940 Vesterø Havn 28 Gb 38	Aïn El Hadid 98 Sb 28
6933 Kibæk 35 Ha 36	7860 Røddinge 35 Ha 36	8800 Viborg 35 Ha 37	15200 Aïn El Hammam 99 Sa 32
8420 Knebel 35 Ha 38	6630 Rødding 35 Hb 37	6920 Videbæk 35 Ha 36	19400 Aïn El Kebira 99 Sa 33
8305 Kolby Kås 35 Hb 38	8840 Rødkærsbro 35 Ha 37	4560 Vig 36 Hb 39	Aïn Merane 98 Sa 28
6000 Kolding 35 Hb 37	4673 Rødvig 36 Hb 40	5700 Vindeby 35 Hb 38	Aïn Oulmene 99 Sb 33
8560 Kolind 35 Ha 38	3700 Rønne 36 Hb 42	7830 Vinderup 35 Ha 36	Aïn Oussera 98 Sb 30
2800 Kongens Lyngby 36 Hb 40	4683 Rønnede 36 Hb 40	8600 Virklund 35 Ha 37	25130 Aïn-Abid 100 Sa 34
9293 Kongerslev 35 Ha 38	4581 Rørvig 36 Hb 39	7840 Virksund 35 Ha 37	19100 Aïn-Arnat 99 Sa 33
4220 Korsør 36 Hb 39	8471 Sabro 35 Ha 38	9300 Voerså 27 Gb 38	10400 Aïn-Bessem 99 Sa 31
6340 Kruså 35 Ja 37	4990 Sakskøbing 36 Ja 39	6500 Vojens 35 Hb 37	Aïn-El-Hadjel 99 Sb 31
3630 Kulhuse 36 Hb 39	4912 Sandby 36 Ja 39	6623 Vorbasse 35 Hb 37	Aïn-El-Türck 97 Sb 27
5772 Kværndrup 35 Hb 38	3770 Sandvig 36 Hb 42	4760 Vordingborg 36 Hb 39	Aïn-Fakroun 100 Sb 34
1000 København 36 Hb 40	8600 Silkeborg 35 Ha 37	5970 Ærøskøbing 35 Ja 38	21250 Aïn-Kechera 99 Sa 34
4600 Køge 36 Hb 40	9870 Sindal 27 Gb 38	6870 Ølgod 35 Hb 36	Aïn-Kihal 97 Sb 26
4772 Langebæk 36 Ja 40	9990 Skagen 27 Gb 38	5853 Ørbæk 35 Hb 38	04300 Aïn-M'Lila 99 Sa 34
5550 Langeskov 35 Hb 38	8660 Skanderborg 35 Ha 37	8830 Ørum 35 Ha 37	25140 Aïn-Smara 99 Sa 34
8870 Langå 35 Ha 37	7800 Skive 35 Ha 36	7742 Øslos 27 Gb 37	Aïn-Tédélès 97 Sb 28
7620 Lemvig 35 Ha 36	6900 Skjern 35 Hb 36	9750 Øster Vrå 27 Gb 38	Aïn-Tellout 97 Ta 27
3450 Lillerød 36 Hb 40	4230 Skælskør 36 Hb 39	4944 Østerby 36 Ja 39	Aïn-Témouchent 97 Sb 26
3360 Liseleje 36 Ha 39	6780 Skærbæk 35 Hb 36	9940 Østerby Havn 28 Gb 39	Aït El Khadra 97 Sb 28
5953 Lohals 35 Hb 38	4200 Slagelse 36 Hb 39	7700 Østerild 27 Gb 36	06751 Akbou 99 Sa 32
9670 Løgstør 27 Ha 37	2680 Solrød Strand 36 Hb 40	8000 Århus 35 Ha 38	16000 Alger 98 Sa 31
6240 Løgumkloster 35 Hb 36	4180 Sorø 36 Hb 39	5792 Årslev 35 Hb 38	06300 Amizour 99 Sa 32
9480 Løkken 27 Gb 37	6971 Spjald 35 Ha 36		Ammi-Moussa 98 Sb 29
8723 Løsning 35 Hb 37	4780 Stege 36 Ja 40	**Føroyar**	23000 Annaba 100 Sa 35
7930 Maribo 36 Ja 39	3660 Stenløse 36 Hb 40	386 Bøur 19 Ea 20	Arzew 97 Sb 27
4873 Marrebæk 36 Ja 39	4660 Store Heddinge 36 Hb 40	235 Dalur 19 Eb 21	15300 Azazga 99 Sa 32
6470 Mommark 35 Ja 38	9970 Strandby 27 Gb 38	470 Eiði 19 Ea 20	Azeffoun 99 Sa 32
5330 Munkebo 35 Hb 38	5500 Strib 35 Hb 37	478 Elduvík 19 Ea 21	21300 Azzaba 100 Sa 35
9632 Møldrup 35 Ha 37	7600 Struer 35 Ha 36	530 Fuglafjørður 19 Ea 21	16210 Baraki 98 Sa 31
4900 Nakskov 36 Ja 39	4850 Stubbekøbing 36 Ja 40	850 Hvalba 19 Eb 21	06000 Bejaïa 99 Sa 33
3730 Nexø 36 Hb 43	9530 Støvring 35 Ha 37	765 Kirkja 19 Ea 21	Belarbi 97 Sb 27
9240 Nibe 27 Ha 37	7950 Sundby 27 Ha 36	175 Kirkjubøur 19 Eb 21	Ben Badis 97 Ta 27
6430 Nordborg 35 Hb 37	7451 Sunds 35 Ha 37	700 Klaksvík 19 Ea 21	36220 Ben Mehidi 100 Sa 35
6720 Nordby 35 Hb 36	5700 Svendborg 35 Hb 38	737 Múli 19 Ea 21	02240 Beni Haoua 98 Sa 29
5390 Nordskov 35 Hb 38	9300 Sæby 27 Gb 38	400 Oyrargjógv 19 Ea 20	Beni-Saf 97 Sb 26
7700 Nors 27 Gb 36	5985 Søby 35 Ja 38	620 Runavík 19 Ea 21	26400 Béni-Slimane 98 Sa 31
5800 Nyborg 35 Hb 38	7260 Sønder Omme 35 Hb 36	436 Saksun 19 Ea 20	Bensekrane 97 Sb 26
4800 Nykøbing/Falster 36 Ja 39	6400 Sønderborg 35 Ja 37	210 Sandur 19 Eb 21	23100 Berrahal 100 Sa 35
7900 Nykøbing Midtjylland	9541 Sønderup 35 Ha 37	680 Sandvík 19 Eb 21	Berriche 100 Sb 35
35 Ha 36	6950 Søndervig 35 Ha 36	497 Selatrað 19 Ea 21	Berrouaghia 98 Sa 30
4500 Nykøbing Sjæland 36 Hb 39	2630 Taastrup 36 Hb 40	220 Skálavík 19 Eb 21	36240 Besbes 100 Sa 35
6830 Nymindegab 35 Hb 36	6880 Tarm 35 Hb 36	236 Skarvanes 19 Eb 21	Bir-Haddada 99 Sb 33
4880 Nysted 36 Ja 39	7000 Taulov 35 Hb 37	240 Skopun 19 Eb 21	Birine 98 Sb 31
4700 Næstved 36 Hb 39	9575 Terndrup 35 Ha 38	970 Sumba 19 Eb 21	Bjord Emir Khaled 98 Sa 30
4840 Nørre Alslev 36 Ja 39	8653 Them 35 Ha 37	186 Sund 19 Ea 21	09000 Blida 98 Sa 30
6830 Nørre Nebel 35 Hb 36	7700 Thisted 27 Gb 36	465 Svínoy 19 Ea 21	15425 Boghni 99 Sa 31
7700 Nørre Vorupør 27 Ha 36	6990 Thorsminde 35 Ha 36	445 Tjørnuvík 19 Ea 20	16120 Bordj El Kiffan 98 Sa 31
8300 Odder 35 Hb 38	7680 Thyborøn 35 Ha 36	100 Tórshavn 19 Ea 21	34145 Bordj Zemoura 99 Sa 32
5000 Odense 35 Hb 38	6360 Tinglev 35 Ja 37	798 Trøllanes 19 Ea 21	Bordj-Bou-Arreridj 99 Sa 32
6857 Oksby 35 Hb 36	8400 Tirstrup 35 Ha 38	800 Tvøroyri 19 Eb 21	35200 Bordj-Menaïel 99 Sa 31
4000 Osted 36 Hb 39	6862 Tistrup 35 Hb 36	900 Vágur 19 Eb 21	42415 Bou Ismaïl 98 Sa 30
4720 Præstø 36 Hb 40	3220 Tisvilde 36 Ha 40	350 Vestmanna 19 Ea 20	Bou Kadir 98 Sa 29
7442 Pårup 35 Ha 37	6520 Toftlund 35 Hb 36	827 Øravik 19 Eb 21	Bou-Hanifia-El-Hamamat
8900 Randers 35 Ha 38	8305 Tranebjerg 35 Hb 38		97 Sb 27
8600 Resenbro 35 Ha 37	9881 Tversted 27 Gb 38		Bou-Tlélis 97 Sb 27
6760 Ribe 35 Hb 36	6270 Tønder 35 Ja 36		09400 Boufarik 98 Sa 30
6950 Ringkøbing 35 Ha 36	7160 Tørring 35 Hb 37	**DZ**	19300 Bougaa 99 Sa 33
4100 Ringsted 36 Hb 39	9830 Tårs 27 Gb 38		09350 Bougara 98 Sa 31
4000 Roskilde 36 Hb 40	6990 Ulfborg 35 Ha 36	Abdelmalek Ramdan	Bouguirat 97 Sb 28
7870 Roslev 35 Ha 36	6800 Varde 35 Hb 36	97 Sa 28	10000 Bouira 99 Sa 31
5900 Rudkøbing 35 Ja 38	6600 Vejen 35 Hb 37	02215 Abou El Hassan 98 Sa 29	Boumahra Ahmed 100 Sa 35
4291 Ruds Vedby 36 Hb 39	6853 Vejers Strand 35 Hb 36	Aïn Azel 99 Sb 33	Chaabat-El-Leham 97 Sb 26

DZ
E

Chahbounia — DZ . E — Almanza

Chahbounia 98 Sb 30
18250 Chefka 99 Sa 33
43200 Chelghoum El Aïd 99 Sa 34
42300 Cherchell 98 Sa 30
Chetaibi 100 Rb 35
Chiffa 98 Sa 30
Chlef 98 Sa 29
21200 Collo 100 Sa 34
Colonel-Bougara 98 Sb 29
25000 Constantine 100 Sa 34
Dahmouni 98 Sb 29
42145 Damous 98 Sa 29
35100 Dellys 99 Sa 31
35210 Djenet 98 Sa 31
Djidiouia 98 Sb 28
Djilali-Ben-Amar 98 Sb 28
36200 Dréan 100 Sa 35
44340 El Abadia 98 Sa 29
09200 El Affroun 98 Sa 30
El Amria 97 Sb 26
El Ancer 99 Sa 34
44340 El Attaf 98 Sa 29
19600 El Eulma 99 Sa 33
El Ghomri 97 Sb 28
23200 El Hadjar 100 Sa 35
36100 El Kala 100 Sa 36
25100 El Khroub 100 Sa 34
06310 El Kseur 99 Sa 32
El Malah 97 Sb 26
16300 El Millia 99 Sa 34
36200 El Tarf 100 Sa 36
El-Achir 99 Sa 34
21400 El-Arrouch 100 Sa 34
El-Bordj 97 Sb 28
02255 El-Marsa 98 Sa 28
43301 Ferdjioua 99 Sa 33
Froha 97 Sb 28
Gdyel 97 Sb 27
Ghazaouet 97 Sb 26
42135 Gouraya 98 Sa 29
43100 Grarem 99 Sa 34
24000 Guelma 100 Sa 35
42200 Hadjout 98 Sa 30
Hamadia 98 Sb 29
25230 Hamma-Bouziane 99 Sa 34
Hammam Delaa 99 Sb 32
Hammam Guergour 99 Sa 33
Hammam Rabbi 97 Ta 28
Hammam-Bou-Hadjar 97 Sb 27
Hammam-Righa 98 Sa 30
Hassi-El-Ghella 97 Sb 26
Hassi-fedoul 98 Sb 30
24180 Héliopolis 100 Sa 35
Hennaya 97 Ta 26
18000 Jijel 99 Sa 33
Kenenda 98 Sb 28
21210 Kerkera 100 Sa 34
27370 Khadra 98 Sa 28
34235 Khelil 99 Sa 33
44225 Khemis Miliana 98 Sa 30
06600 Kherrata 99 Sa 34
Ksar El Boukhari 98 Sb 30
Laayoune 98 Sb 30
Lahlaf 98 Sb 29

10200 Lakhdaria 99 Sa 31
Lamtar 97 Sb 27
09300 Larba 98 Sa 31
Lardjem 98 Sb 29
02256 le Guelta 98 Sa 28
10100 M`Chedallah 99 Sa 32
41220 M`Daourouch 100 Sa 35
Maghnia 97 Ta 26
Mahdia 98 Sb 29
Mansoura 99 Sa 32
Maoussa 97 Sb 28
Mascara 97 Sb 28
26000 Médéa 98 Sa 30
Mellakou 98 Sa 29
Mers-El-Kébir 97 Sb 27
43000 Mila 99 Sa 34
44200 Miliana 98 Sa 30
Mohammadia 97 Sb 28
Mostaganem 97 Sb 28
M'sila 99 Sb 32
42240 Nador 98 Sa 30
Nechmeya 100 Sa 35
Nédroma 97 Sb 26
Oran 97 Sb 27
43240 Oued Athmania 99 Sa 34
Oued El Abtal 98 Sb 28
09230 Oued El-Alleug 98 Sa 30
Oued Rhiou 98 Sb 28
Oued Tiélat 97 Sb 27
Oued-Fodda 98 Sa 29
24300 Oued-Zénati 100 Sa 35
Ouled Derradj 99 Sb 32
02180 Ouled Farès 98 Sa 29
Oum El Bouaghi 100 Sb 35
Rahouia 98 Sb 29
Ras El Oued 99 Sb 33
Rechaiga 98 Sb 29
Relizane 98 Sb 28
Remchi 97 Sb 26
16012 Rouiba 98 Sa 31
Sabra 97 Ta 26
Salah Bey 99 Sb 33
21435 Salah Bouchaour 100 Sa 34
Sebt Aziz 98 Sb 30
06500 Seddouk 99 Sa 32
41500 Sedrata 100 Sa 35
Sénia 97 Sb 27
19000 Sétif 99 Sa 33
Sfizef 97 Sb 28
02210 Sidi Akacha 98 Sa 29
Sidi Ali 97 Sa 28
Sidi Amar 97 Sb 28
Sidi Bou-Djenane 97 Ta 26
Sidi Ladjel 98 Sb 30
Sidi Lakhdar 97 Sa 28
Sidi M`Hamed Bénali 98 Sa 28
43150 Sidi Mérouane 99 Sa 34
Sidi Mezghiche 100 Sa 34
Sidi-Aïssa 99 Sb 31
Sidi-Aissa 97 Sb 28
Sidi-Bel-Abbès 97 Sb 27
Sig 97 Sb 27
Siouf 98 Sb 30
Sirat 97 Sb 28

21000 Skikda 100 Sa 34
Sougueur 98 Sb 29
02225 Souk Elbakar 98 Sa 29
Souk Naamane 98 Sa 30
41000 Souk-Ahras 100 Sa 35
Sour El Ghozlane 99 Sa 31
Stidia 97 Sb 27
26600 Tablat 98 Sa 31
43220 Tadjnanet 99 Sa 33
16200 Taher 99 Sa 33
Takhemaret 97 Sb 28
21265 Tamalous 100 Sa 34
Tamelaht 98 Sb 28
Tarik Ibn Ziad 98 Sb 30
06270 Tazmalt 99 Sa 32
Teghalimet 97 Ta 27
43250 Telerghma 99 Sa 34
02200 Ténès 98 Sa 29
Terga 97 Sb 26
Terni 97 Ta 26
Theniet El-Had 98 Sb 30
Tiaret 98 Sb 29
Tighennif 97 Sb 28
15600 Tigzirt-s-Mer 99 Sa 32
42000 Tipaza 98 Sa 30
Tissemsilt 98 Sb 29
15000 Tizi-Ouzou 99 Sa 32
Tlemcen 97 Ta 26
Youb 97 Ta 27
Zemmora 98 Sb 28
35260 Zemmouri El Bahri 99 Sa 31
42320 Zéralda 98 Sa 30
25200 Zighout Youcef 100 Sa 34

E

15142 A Baiuca 68 Ob 19
27520 A Barrela 68 Pa 20
36880 A Cañiza 67 Pa 19
15070 A Coruña/La Coruña 68 Ob 19
36680 A Estrada 67 Pa 19
27100 A Fonsagrada 68 Ob 20
36780 A Guardia 67 Pb 19
32540 A Gudiña 68 Pa 20
27720 A Pontenova 68 Ob 20
32350 A Rúa de Valdeorras 68 Pa 20
27730 Abadín 68 Ob 20
30640 Abanilla 97 Ra 26
42146 Abejar 69 Pb 25
39211 Abiada 69 Ob 24
22392 Abizanda 70 Pa 28
04510 Abla 89 Rb 25
32870 Aceredo 67 Pb 19
14430 Adamuz 82 Ra 23
05296 Adanero 82 Qa 23
46140 Ademuz 83 Qa 26
04770 Adra 96 Sa 24
25797 Adrall 70 Pa 29
25691 Àger 84 Pa 28
42100 Àgreda 69 Pb 26
13410 Agudo 82 Ra 23
19283 Aguilar de Anguita 83 Pb 25

34800 Aguilar de Campoo 69 Pa 23
14920 Aguilar de la Frontera 96 Rb 23
30880 Águilas 97 Rb 26
06940 Ahillones 82 Ra 22
22330 Ainsa 70 Pa 28
03200 Alacant/Alicante 97 Ra 27
50630 Alagón 83 Pb 26
06840 Alange 82 Ra 21
16214 Alarcón 83 Qb 25
37800 Alba de Tormes 82 Qa 22
02070 Albacete 83 Ra 26
46860 Albaida 83 Ra 27
09216 Albaina 69 Pa 25
19117 Albalate de Zorita 83 Qa 25
26120 Albelda de Iregua 69 Pa 25
46260 Alberic 83 Qb 27
12140 Albocàsser 84 Qa 28
04800 Albox 97 Rb 25
18700 Albuñol 96 Sa 24
06510 Alburquerque 81 Qb 21
41500 Alcalá de Guadaíra 96 Rb 22
11180 Alcalá de los Gazules 96 Sa 22
23680 Alcalá la Real 96 Rb 24
43530 Alcanar 84 Qa 28
30820 Alcantarilla 97 Rb 26
49500 Alcañices 68 Pb 21
44600 Alcañiz 84 Pb 27
14480 Alcaracejos 82 Ra 23
02300 Alcaraz 83 Ra 25
23660 Alcaudete 96 Rb 23
45662 Alcaudete de la Jara 82 Qb 23
13600 Alcázar de San Juan 83 Qb 24
14610 Alcolea 82 Rb 23
41449 Alcolea del Río 82 Rb 22
06131 Alconchel 81 Ra 20
12006 Alcora 84 Qa 27
28920 Alcorcón 83 Qa 24
43460 Alcover 84 Pb 29
03203 Alcoy-Alcoi 83 Ra 27
22251 Alcubierre 84 Pb 27
46172 Alcublas 83 Qb 27
07400 Alcúdia 85 Qb 31
10160 Alcuéscar 82 Qb 21
13380 Aldea del Rey 82 Ra 24
42225 Alentisque 83 Pb 25
26540 Alfaro 69 Pa 26
29491 Algatocín 96 Sa 22
11270 Algeciras 96 Sa 22
46680 Algemesí 83 Qb 27
11680 Algodonales 96 Sa 22
48990 Algorta 69 Ob 25
18120 Alhama de Granada 96 Rb 24
30840 Alhama de Murcia 97 Rb 26
29130 Alhaurín de la Torre 96 Sa 23
06894 Aljucén 82 Qb 21
25100 Almacelles 84 Pb 28
13400 Almadén 82 Ra 23
13270 Almagro 82 Ra 24
02640 Almansa 83 Ra 26
24170 Almanza 68 Pa 22

POSTALI · ÍNDICE CON CÓDIGOS POSTALES · INDICE DE LUGARES COM CÓDIGOS POSTAIS ·
MÍST S PSČ · ZOZNAM OBCÍ S PSČ · INDEKS MIEJSCOWOŚCI Z KOD POCZTOWY

128

Almazán (E) **Cañada Vellida**

42200 Almazán 83 Pb 25	26580 Arnedo 69 Pa 25	27640 Becerreá 68 Pa 20	27880 Burela 68 Ob 20
25126 Almenar 84 Pb 28	31417 Arrako 70 Pa 27	47670 Becilla de Valderaduey	09070 Burgos 69 Pa 24
12590 Almenara 84 Qb 27	33540 Arriondas 68 Ob 22	68 Pa 22	31412 Burgui 70 Pa 26
37115 Almenara de Tormes	10900 Arroyo de la Luz 82 Qb 21	37700 Béjar 82 Qa 22	12530 Burriana 84 Qb 27
68 Pb 22	21280 Arroyomolinos de León	14280 Belalcázar 82 Ra 22	07458 Ca`n Picafort 85 Qb 31
06200 Almendralejo 82 Ra 21	82 Ra 21	50130 Belchite 84 Pb 27	12180 Cabanes 84 Qa 28
04070 Almería 97 Sa 25	07570 Artà 85 Qb 31	37789 Beleña 82 Qa 22	33686 Cabañaquinta 68 Ob 22
04711 Almerimar 97 Sa 25	31140 Artajona 69 Pa 26	16640 Belmonte/Mota del Cuervo	06600 Cabeza del Buey 82 Ra 22
13580 Almodóvar del Campo	08271 Artés 84 Pb 29	83 Qb 25	13192 Cabezarados 82 Ra 23
82 Ra 23	25730 Artesa de Segre 84 Pb 29	33830 Belmonte/Oviedo 68 Ob 21	21580 Cabezas Rubias 81 Rb 20
16215 Almodóvar del Pinar	31480 Artieda 70 Pa 27	42248 Beltejar 83 Pb 25	30370 Cabo de Palos 97 Rb 27
83 Qb 26	01474 Artziniega 69 Ob 24	24300 Bembibre 68 Pa 21	14940 Cabra 96 Rb 23
14720 Almodóvar del Río 82 Rb 22	15810 Arzúa 68 Pa 19	14913 Benajemí 96 Rb 23	10070 Cáceres 82 Qb 21
19115 Almoguera 83 Qa 25	15320 As Pontes de García	29639 Benalmádena 96 Sa 23	11070 Cádiz 95 Sa 21
45420 Almonacid de Toledo	Rodríguez 68 Ob 20	18564 Benalúa de las Villas	18730 Calahonda 96 Sa 24
82 Qb 24	03680 Aspe 97 Ra 27	96 Rb 24	26500 Calahorra 69 Pa 26
21730 Almonte 95 Rb 21	24700 Astorga 68 Pa 21	22440 Benasc/Benasque 70 Pa 28	44200 Calamocha 83 Qa 26
03160 Almoradí 97 Ra 27	31190 Astráin 69 Pa 26	49600 Benavente 68 Pa 22	44570 Calanda 84 Qa 27
45900 Almorox 82 Qa 23	34450 Astudillo 69 Pa 23	12580 Benicarló 84 Qa 28	21300 Cañañas 81 Rb 21
22270 Almudévar 70 Pa 27	31797 Auza 69 Pa 26	12560 Benicàssim 84 Qa 28	30420 Calasparra 97 Ra 26
18690 Almuñécar 96 Sa 24	05070 Ávila 82 Qa 23	03500 Benidorm 98 Ra 27	50300 Calatayud 83 Pb 26
13760 Almuradiel 82 Ra 24	33400 Avilés 68 Ob 22	46830 Benigánim 83 Ra 27	36650 Caldas de Reis 67 Pa 19
46440 Almussafes 83 Qb 27	21400 Ayamonte 81 Rb 20	03720 Benissa 84 Ra 28	06292 Calera de León 82 Ra 21
29500 Álora 96 Sa 23	22800 Ayerbe 70 Pa 27	09569 Bercedo 69 Ob 24	12589 Càlig 84 Qa 28
03590 Altea 84 Ra 27	40520 Ayllón 82 Pb 24	15128 Berdoias 67 Ob 18	03710 Calpe/Calp 84 Ra 28
31800 Altsasu-Alsasua 69 Pa 25	02125 Ayna 83 Ra 25	33887 Berducedo 68 Ob 21	13370 Calzada de Calatrava
46600 Alzira 83 Qb 27	46620 Ayora 83 Qb 26	08600 Berga 84 Pa 29	82 Ra 24
32668 Allariz 68 Pa 20	44590 Azaila 84 Pb 27	20570 Bergara 69 Ob 25	49332 Camarzana de Tera
44145 Allepuz 83 Qa 27	41870 Aznalcóllar 82 Rb 21	04760 Berja 96 Sa 25	68 Pa 21
24150 Ambasaguas 68 Pa 22	20730 Azpeitia 69 Ob 25	06930 Berlanga 82 Ra 22	36630 Cambados 67 Pa 19
24524 Ambasmestas 68 Pa 21	06920 Azuaga 82 Ra 22	48870 Bermeo 69 Ob 25	32375 Cambela 68 Pa 20
43870 Amposta 84 Qa 28	19200 Azuqueca de Henares	49200 Bermillo de Sayago 68 Pb 21	32100 Cambeo 68 Pa 20
39840 Ampuero 69 Ob 24	83 Qa 24	31790 Berrizaun 69 Ob 26	23120 Cambil 96 Rb 24
01470 Amurrio 69 Ob 25	06070 Badajoz 81 Ra 21	15300 Betanzos 68 Ob 19	43850 Cambrils 84 Pb 29
47177 Amusquillo 69 Pb 23	08910 Badalona 84 Pb 30	16870 Beteta 83 Qa 26	10620 Caminomorisco 82 Qa 21
44500 Andorra 84 Qa 27	14850 Baena 96 Rb 23	48070 Bilbao/Bilbo 69 Ob 25	06460 Campanario 82 Ra 22
07150 Andratx 84 Qb 30	23440 Baeza 82 Ra 24	22500 Binéfar 84 Pb 28	47310 Campaspero 69 Pb 23
23740 Andújar 82 Ra 23	23710 Bailén 82 Ra 24	25752 Biosca 84 Pa 29	16210 Campillo de Altobuey
17160 Anglès 85 Pb 30	15150 Baio 67 Ob 19	17300 Blanes 85 Pb 30	83 Qb 26
22123 Angüés 70 Pa 27	36300 Baiona 67 Pa 19	33720 Boal 68 Ob 21	37550 Campillo de Azaba 82 Qa 21
29200 Antequera 96 Rb 23	25600 Balaguer 84 Pb 28	40560 Boceguillas 83 Pb 24	06443 Campillo de Llerena
15684 Anxeriz 67 Ob 19	02320 Balazote 83 Ra 25	10320 Bohonal de Ibor 82 Qb 22	82 Ra 22
45250 Añover de Tajo 83 Qb 24	22650 Balneario de Panticosa	25652 Boixols 84 Pa 29	29320 Campillos 96 Rb 23
31430 Aoiz-Agoitz 69 Pa 26	70 Pa 27	13260 Bolaños de Calatrava	13610 Campo de Criptana
21200 Aracena 81 Rb 21	34240 Baltanás 69 Pb 23	82 Ra 24	83 Qb 24
41600 Arahal 96 Rb 22	22234 Ballobar 84 Pb 28	22340 Boltaña 70 Pa 28	15359 Campo do Hospital
09400 Aranda de Duero 69 Pb 24	33158 Ballota 68 Ob 21	21710 Bollullos Par del Condado	68 Ob 20
28300 Aranjuez 83 Qa 24	03450 Banyeres de Mariola	81 Rb 21	07630 Campos 85 Qb 30
42250 Arcos de Jalón 83 Pb 25	83 Ra 27	02691 Bonete 83 Ra 26	27440 Canabal 68 Pa 20
11630 Arcos de la Frontera	17820 Banyoles 85 Pa 30	16311 Boniches 83 Qb 26	26326 Canales de la Sierra
96 Sa 22	26320 Baños de Río Tobía	24850 Boñar 68 Pa 22	69 Pa 24
30600 Archena 97 Ra 26	69 Pa 25	17462 Bordils 85 Pa 30	46650 Canals 83 Ra 27
29300 Archidona 96 Rb 23	42213 Baraona 83 Pb 25	50540 Borja 69 Pb 26	02490 Cancarix 83 Ra 26
29550 Ardales 96 Sa 23	22300 Barbastro 84 Pa 28	11640 Bornos 96 Sa 22	22889 Candanchú 70 Pa 27
22583 Arén 70 Pa 28	11160 Barbate 95 Sa 22	25550 Bòssost 70 Pa 28	22591 Candasnos 84 Pb 28
05400 Arenas de San Pedro	06160 Barcarrota 81 Ra 21	27340 Bóveda 68 Pa 20	05480 Candeleda 82 Qa 22
82 Qa 22	08070 Barcelona 84 Pb 30	41320 Brenes 82 Rb 22	33787 Canero 68 Ob 21
05200 Arévalo 82 Pb 23	39420 Bárcena de Pié de Concha	19400 Brihuega 83 Qa 25	36940 Cangas 67 Pa 19
13710 Argamasilla de Alba	69 Ob 23	09240 Briviesca 69 Pa 24	33800 Cangas del Narcea 68 Ob 21
83 Qb 24	45593 Bargas 82 Qb 23	10950 Brozas 82 Qb 21	18810 Caniles 97 Rb 25
13440 Argamasilla de Calatrava	12420 Barracas 83 Qa 27	14650 Bujalance 82 Rb 23	04450 Canjáyar 97 Rb 25
82 Ra 23	02639 Barrax 83 Qb 25	50177 Bujaraloz 84 Pb 27	37400 Cantalapiedra 68 Pb 22
28500 Arganda del Rey 83 Qa 24	48970 Basauri 69 Ob 25	30180 Bullas 97 Ra 26	40320 Cantalejo 83 Pb 24
31513 Arguedas 69 Pa 26	18800 Baza 97 Rb 25	09230 Buniel 69 Pa 24	44140 Cantavieja 84 Qa 27
18100 Armilla 96 Rb 24	23280 Beas de Segura 83 Ra 25	46360 Buñol 83 Qb 27	41320 Cantillana 82 Rb 22
26589 Arnedillo 69 Pa 25	20200 Beasain 69 Ob 25	44330 Burbáguena 83 Pb 26	44168 Cañada Vellida 83 Qa 27

129

INDEX WITH POST CODES · ORTSREGISTER MIT POSTLEITZAHLEN · INDICE CON CODICI
STEDREGISTER MED POSTNUMRE · PLAATSNAMENREGISTER MET POSTCODE · REJSTŘÍK

E

| Cañamares | E | Garray |

16890 Cañamares 83 Qa 25
10820 Cañaveral 82 Qb 21
16300 Cañete 83 Qa 26
14660 Cañete de las Torres 82 Rb 23
49440 Cañizal 68 Pb 22
31380 Caparroso 69 Pa 26
07580 Cala Ratjada 85 Qb 31
08786 Capellades 84 Pb 29
30400 Caravaca de la Cruz 97 Ra 26
15100 Carballo 67 Ob 19
04140 Carboneras 97 Rb 26
16350 Carboneras de Guadazaón 83 Qb 26
02153 Carcelén 83 Qb 26
23192 Carchelejo 96 Rb 24
42138 Cardejón 83 Pb 25
16373 Cardenete 83 Qb 26
14445 Cardeña 82 Ra 23
08261 Cardona 84 Pb 29
50400 Cariñena 83 Pb 26
41410 Carmona 96 Rb 22
15293 Carnota 67 Pa 18
15175 Carral 68 Ob 19
34120 Carrión de los Condes 69 Pa 23
30200 Cartagena 97 Rb 27
21450 Cartaya 81 Rb 20
29160 Casabermeja 96 Sa 23
26230 Casalarreina 69 Pa 25
10190 Casar de Cáceres 82 Qb 21
10162 Casas de Don Antonio 82 Qb 21
02151 Casas de Juan Núñez 83 Qb 26
10360 Casas de Miravete 82 Qb 22
02200 Casas Ibáñez 83 Qb 26
43787 Caseres 84 Pb 28
16321 Casillas de Ranera 83 Qb 26
46171 Casinos 83 Qb 27
50700 Caspe 84 Pb 27
03420 Castalla 83 Ra 27
10340 Castañar de Ibor 82 Qb 22
22466 Castejón de Sos 70 Pa 28
18740 Castell de Ferro 96 Sa 24
19328 Castellar de la Muela 83 Qa 26
08860 Castelldefels 84 Pb 29
12070 Castelló de la Plana/Castellón de la Plana 84 Qb 27
09258 Castil de Peones 69 Pa 24
06680 Castilblanco 82 Qb 22
50696 Castiliscar 69 Pa 25
23670 Castillo de Locubín 96 Rb 24
18816 Castril 97 Rb 25
14840 Castro del Río 96 Rb 23
39700 Castro-Urdiales 69 Ob 24
49127 Castronuevo 68 Pb 22
06420 Castuera 82 Ra 22
46470 Catarroja 83 Qb 27
02660 Caudete 83 Ra 26
41370 Cazalla de la Sierra 82 Rb 22
23470 Cazorla 97 Rb 25
45680 Cebolla 82 Qb 23

05260 Cebreros 82 Qa 23
15350 Cedeira 68 Ob 19
15270 Cee 67 Pa 18
30430 Cehegín 97 Ra 26
32800 Celanova 68 Pa 20
44370 Cella 83 Qa 26
26350 Cenicero 69 Pa 25
19269 Cercadillo 83 Pb 25
10663 Cerezo 82 Qa 21
25200 Cervera 84 Pb 29
34840 Cervera de Pisuerga 69 Pa 23
16444 Cervera del Llano 83 Qb 25
26520 Cervera del Río Alhama 69 Pa 26
51010 Ceuta 96 Sb 22
30530 Cieza 97 Ra 26
19420 Cifuentes 83 Qa 25
19339 Cillas 83 Qa 26
31592 Cintruénigo 69 Pa 26
24800 Cistierna 68 Pa 22
13070 Ciudad Real 82 Ra 24
37500 Ciudad Rodrigo 82 Qa 21
07760 Ciutadella de Menorca 85 Qb 31
46625 Cofrentes 83 Qb 26
29100 Coín 96 Sa 23
33320 Colunga 68 Ob 22
07070 Coll d'en Rabassa 84 Qb 30
28400 Collado Villalba 83 Qa 24
39520 Comillas 69 Ob 23
22808 Concilio 70 Pa 27
11140 Conil de la Frontera 95 Sa 21
43120 Constantí 84 Pb 29
41450 Constantina 82 Rb 22
45700 Consuegra 83 Qb 24
14070 Córdoba 82 Rb 23
49530 Coreses 68 Pb 22
10800 Coria 82 Qb 21
45880 Corral de Almaguer 83 Qb 24
21230 Cortegana 81 Rb 21
44791 Cortes de Aragón 83 Qa 27
29380 Cortes de la Frontera 96 Sa 22
09410 Coruña del Conde 69 Pb 24
28820 Coslada 83 Qa 24
42157 Covaleda 69 Pb 25
49710 Cubo de la Tierra del Vino 68 Pb 22
40200 Cuéllar 69 Pb 23
16070 Cuenca 83 Qa 25
09346 Cuevas de San Clemente 69 Pa 24
04610 Cuevas del Almanzora 97 Rb 26
18813 Cuevas del Campo 97 Rb 25
18850 Cúllar 97 Rb 25
46400 Cullera 84 Qb 27
27500 Chantada 68 Pa 20
04176 Chelva 83 Qb 26
46380 Cheste 83 Qb 27
11130 Chiclana de la Frontera 95 Sa 21

16190 Chillarón de Cuenca 83 Qa 25
13412 Chillón 82 Ra 23
02520 Chinchilla de Monte Aragón 83 Ra 26
28370 Chinchón 83 Qa 24
11550 Chipiona 95 Sa 21
04825 Chirivel 97 Rb 25
13250 Daimiel 82 Qb 24
50360 Daroca 83 Pb 26
33812 Degaña 68 Pa 21
43580 Deltebre 84 Qa 28
03700 Dénia 84 Ra 28
24730 Destriana 68 Pa 21
06400 Don Benito 82 Ra 22
20070 Donostia-San Sebastián 69 Ob 26
14860 Doña Mencía 96 Rb 23
41700 Dos Hermanas 96 Rb 22
34210 Dueñas 68 Pb 23
48200 Durango 69 Ob 25
18650 Dúrcal 96 Rb 24
41400 Écija 96 Rb 22
20600 Eibar 69 Ob 25
07800 Eivissa 84 Ra 29
50600 Ejea de los Caballeros 69 Pa 26
39610 El Astillero 69 Ob 24
05600 El Barco de Ávila 82 Qa 22
05110 El Barraco 82 Qa 23
02610 El Bonillo 83 Ra 25
13129 El Bullaque 82 Qb 23
29420 El Burgo 96 Sa 23
50730 El Burgo de Ebro 84 Pb 27
42300 El Burgo de Osma 69 Pb 24
37621 El Cabaco 82 Qa 21
03560 el Campello 97 Ra 27
45533 El Carpio de Tajo 82 Qb 23
19170 El Casar 83 Qa 24
11149 El Colorado 95 Sa 21
41760 El Coronil 96 Rb 22
28749 El Cuadrón 83 Qa 24
41749 El Cuervo de Sevilla 96 Sa 21
04700 El Ejido 97 Sa 25
50320 El Frasno 83 Pb 26
41888 El Garrobo 82 Rb 21
28710 El Molar 83 Qa 24
13194 El Molinillo 82 Qb 23
30413 El Moral 97 Ra 25
37524 El Payo 82 Qa 21
19327 El Pedregal 83 Qa 26
41360 El Pedroso 82 Rb 22
49715 El Piñero 68 Pb 22
25723 El Pont de Bar 70 Pa 29
25520 el Pont de Suert 70 Pa 28
08820 El Prat de Llobregat 84 Pb 30
16670 El Provencio 83 Qb 25
45570 El Puente del Arzobispo 82 Qb 22
33840 El Puerto 68 Ob 21
11500 El Puerto de Santa María 95 Sa 21
21750 El Rocío 95 Rb 21
41880 El Ronquillo 82 Rb 21

41568 El Rubio 96 Rb 23
41650 El Saucejo 96 Rb 22
05270 El Tiemblo 82 Qa 23
43700 El Vendrell 84 Pb 29
03200 Elche/Elx 97 Ra 27
02430 Elche de la Sierra 83 Ra 25
03600 Elda 83 Ra 27
31700 Elizondo (Baztan) 69 Ob 26
12182 Els Rosildos 84 Qa 27
26586 Enciso 69 Pa 25
50290 Épila 83 Pb 26
20211 Ergoiena 69 Pa 25
20100 Errenteria 69 Ob 26
07740 Es Mercadal 85 Qb 32
09145 Escalada 69 Pa 24
25596 Escaló 70 Pa 29
22760 Escarrilla 70 Pa 27
30350 Escombreras 97 Rb 27
06860 Esparragalejo 82 Ra 21
14220 Espiel 82 Ra 22
31200 Estella-Lizarra 69 Pa 25
41560 Estepa 96 Rb 23
29680 Estepona 96 Sa 22
19262 Estriégana 83 Pb 25
26280 Ezcaray 69 Pa 24
43730 Falset 84 Pb 28
02436 Férez 83 Ra 25
49220 Fermoselle 68 Pb 21
14520 Fernán Núñez 96 Rb 23
07750 Ferreries 85 Qb 31
15315 Ferrol 68 Ob 19
17600 Figueres 85 Pa 30
04500 Fiñana 97 Rb 25
15155 Fisterra 67 Pa 18
43750 Flix 84 Pb 28
31512 Fontellas 69 Pa 26
07748 Fornells 85 Qa 32
27780 Foz 68 Ob 20
22520 Fraga 84 Pb 28
06340 Fregenal de la Sierra 81 Ra 21
18812 Freila 97 Rb 25
34440 Frómista 69 Pa 23
29640 Fuengirola 96 Sa 23
28940 Fuenlabrada 83 Qa 24
30320 Fuente Álamo 97 Rb 26
39588 Fuente Dé 69 Ob 23
06240 Fuente de Cantos 82 Ra 21
29520 Fuente de Piedra 96 Rb 23
13680 Fuente el Fresno 82 Qb 24
14290 Fuente Obejuna 82 Ra 22
41420 Fuentes de Andalucía 96 Rb 22
50740 Fuentes de Ebro 84 Pb 27
34419 Fuentes de Valdepero 69 Pa 23
49400 Fuentesaúco 68 Pb 22
44587 Fuentespalda 84 Qa 28
28597 Fuentidueña de Tajo 83 Qa 24
23180 Fuerte del Rey 82 Rb 24
04560 Gádor 97 Sa 25
18840 Galera 97 Rb 25
43780 Gandesa 84 Pb 28
46700 Gandia 84 Ra 27
42162 Garray 69 Pb 25

POSTALI · ÍNDICE CON CÓDIGOS POSTALES · INDICE DE LUGARES COM CÓDIGOS POSTAIS ·
MÍST S PSČ · ZOZNAM OBCÍ S PSČ · INDEKS MIEJSCOWOŚCI Z KOD POCZTOWY

130

Garrucha — E — **Marmolejo** — E

04630 Garrucha 97 Rb 26	22210 Huerto 84 Pb 27	03530 La Nucia 84 Ra 27	41440 Lora del Río 82 Rb 22
16532 Gascueña 83 Qa 25	23487 Huesa 97 Rb 24	37428 La Orbada 68 Pb 22	30800 Lorca 97 Rb 26
44110 Gea de Albarracín 83 Qa 26	22070 Huesca 70 Pa 27	43892 La Platja de Miami	31210 Los Arcos 69 Pa 25
04550 Gérgal 97 Rb 25	18830 Huéscar 97 Rb 25	84 Pb 28	11370 Los Barrios 96 Sa 22
48300 Gernika-Lumo 69 Ob 25	16500 Huete 83 Qa 25	44562 La Pobla d` Alcolea	39400 Los Corrales de Buelna
28900 Getafe 83 Qa 24	18198 Huétor Vega 96 Rb 24	84 Qa 27	69 Ob 23
21500 Gibraleón 81 Rb 21	03440 Ibi 83 Ra 27	25500 La Pobla de Segur 70 Pa 28	04280 Los Gallardos 97 Rb 26
33200 Gijón/Xixón 68 Ob 22	08700 Igualada 84 Pb 29	24600 La Pola de Gordón 68 Pa 22	45140 Los Navalmorales 82 Qb 23
17070 Girona/Gerona 85 Pb 30	45200 Illescas 83 Qa 24	42169 La Póveda de Soria	41720 Los Palacios y Villafranca
37170 Golpejas 68 Pb 22	07300 Inca 85 Qb 30	69 Pa 25	96 Rb 22
42120 Gómara 83 Pb 25	09558 Incinillas 69 Pa 24	45840 La Puebla de Almoradiel	06230 Los Santos de Maimona
40518 Gómeznarro 83 Pb 24	33530 Infiesto 68 Ob 22	83 Qb 24	82 Ra 21
36380 Gondomar 67 Pa 19	16235 Iniesta 83 Qb 26	41540 La Puebla de Cazalla	45470 Los Yébenes 82 Qb 24
24160 Gradafes 68 Pa 22	20300 Irun 69 Ob 26	96 Rb 22	33440 Luanco 68 Ob 22
33820 Grado 68 Ob 21	31860 Irurzun 69 Pa 26	45516 La Puebla de Montalbán	33700 Luarca 68 Ob 21
24340 Grajal de Campos 68 Pa 22	31417 Isaba 70 Pa 27	82 Qb 23	42290 Lubia 69 Pb 25
18070 Granada 96 Rb 24	47420 Íscar 68 Pb 23	44450 La Puebla de Valverde	14900 Lucena 84 Rb 23
33730 Grandas 68 Ob 21	21410 Isla Cristina 81 Rb 20	83 Qa 27	27070 Lugo 68 Ob 20
49740 Granja de Moreruela	31689 Izalzu 70 Pa 26	14540 La Rambla 96 Rb 23	31440 Lumbier 69 Pa 26
68 Pb 22	14970 Iznájar 96 Rb 23	24640 La Robla 68 Pa 22	37240 Lumbrales 68 Qa 21
06910 Granja de Torrehermosa	18550 Iznalloz 96 Rb 24	02630 La Roda 83 Qb 25	24912 Llanaves de la Reina
82 Ra 22	22700 Jaca 70 Pa 27	41590 La Roda de Andalucia	69 Ob 23
08400 Granollers 84 Pb 30	19240 Jadraque 83 Qa 25	96 Rb 23	33500 Llanes 69 Ob 23
22430 Graus 70 Pa 28	23070 Jaén 96 Rb 24	25700 la Seu d`Urgell 70 Pa 29	25070 Lleida/Lérida 84 Pb 28
11610 Grazalema 96 Sa 22	10400 Jaraíz de la Vera 82 Qa 22	13240 La Solana 83 Ra 24	06900 Llerena 82 Ra 21
18560 Guadahortuna 96 Rb 24	10450 Jarandilla de la Vera	46313 La Torre 83 Qb 26	46160 Llíria 83 Qb 27
19070 Guadalajara 83 Qa 24	82 Qa 22	12600 La Vall d`Uixó 84 Qb 27	17310 Lloret de Mar 85 Pb 30
41390 Guadalcanal 82 Ra 22	11620 Jédula 96 Sa 22	03570 la Vila Joiosa 84 Ra 27	07620 Llucmajor 84 Qb 30
10140 Guadalupe 82 Qb 22	11470 Jerez de la Frontera	47140 Laguna de Duero 68 Pb 23	37310 Macotera 82 Qa 22
10137 Guadisa 82 Qb 22	95 Sa 21	16316 Laguna del Marquesado	28070 Madrid 83 Qa 24
18500 Guadix 96 Rb 24	06380 Jerez de los Caballeros	83 Qa 26	45710 Madridejos 83 Qb 24
03140 Guardamar del Segura	81 Ra 21	36500 Lalín 68 Pa 19	05220 Madrigal de las Altas Torres
97 Ra 27	23530 Jimena 96 Rb 24	22621 Lanave 70 Pa 27	82 Pb 22
08694 Guardiola de Berguedà	11339 Jimena de la Frontera	16330 Landete 83 Qb 26	10110 Madrigalejo 82 Qb 22
84 Pa 29	96 Sa 22	33900 Langreo 68 Ob 22	50710 Maella 84 Pb 28
34880 Guardo 69 Pa 23	23500 Jódar 96 Rb 24	18420 Lanjarón 96 Sa 24	42181 Magaña 69 Pb 25
06470 Guareña 82 Ra 21	30520 Jumilla 83 Ra 26	15685 Lanzá 68 Ob 19	49522 Mahide 68 Pb 21
23210 Guarromán 82 Ra 24	43860 l`Ametlla de Mar 84 Qa 28	26140 Lardero 69 Pa 25	02240 Mahora 83 Qb 26
44433 Gúdar 83 Qa 27	17130 l`Escala 85 Pa 31	33813 Larón 68 Pa 21	25179 Maials 84 Pb 28
37770 Guijuelo 82 Qa 22	43440 l`Espluga de Francolí	33554 Las Arenas 69 Ob 23	50368 Mainar 83 Pb 26
41210 Guillena 82 Rb 21	84 Pb 29	41730 Las Cabezas de San Juan	41927 Mairena del Aljarafe
25210 Guissona 84 Pb 29	37624 La Alberca 82 Qa 21	96 Sa 22	96 Rb 21
27300 Guitiriz 68 Ob 20	06170 La Albuera 81 Ra 21	05230 Las Navas del Marqués	29070 Málaga 96 Sa 23
27211 Guntín de Pallarés 68 Pa 20	41980 La Algaba 82 Rb 21	82 Qa 23	13420 Malagón 82 Qb 24
26200 Haro 69 Pa 25	16740 La Almarcha 83 Qb 25	16660 Las Pedroñeras 83 Qb 25	08380 Malgrat de Mar 85 Pb 30
02400 Hellín 83 Ra 26	50100 La Almunia de Doña Godina	28230 Las Rozas de Madrid	10680 Malpartida de Plasencia
13640 Herencia 83 Qb 24	83 Pb 26	83 Qa 24	82 Qb 21
20120 Hernani 69 Ob 26	24750 La Bañeza 68 Pa 22	24990 Las Salas 68 Pa 22	07500 Manacor 85 Qb 31
41567 Herrera 96 Rb 23	11570 La Barca de la Florida	04470 Láujar de Andarax	23100 Mancha Real 96 Rb 24
13200 Herrera de la Mancha	96 Sa 22	97 Rb 25	32698 Mandín 68 Pb 20
83 Qb 24	17100 la Bisbal d`Empordà	41740 Lebrija 96 Sa 21	29691 Manilva 96 Sa 22
06670 Herrera del Duque 82 Qb 22	85 Pb 31	50131 Lécera 84 Pb 27	08560 Manlleu 84 Pb 30
10700 Hervás 82 Qa 22	49155 La Bóveda de Toro 68 Pb 22	37100 Ledesma 68 Pb 22	08240 Manresa 84 Pb 29
44530 Híjar 84 Pb 27	41429 La Campana 82 Rb 22	24070 León 68 Pa 22	24210 Mansilla de las Mulas
14270 Hinojosa del Duque	14100 La Carlota 82 Rb 23	21440 Lepe 81 Rb 20	68 Pa 22
82 Ra 22	23200 La Carolina 82 Ra 24	09340 Lerma 69 Pa 24	13200 Manzanares 83 Qb 24
09141 Hontomín 69 Pa 24	29692 La Chullera 96 Sa 22	25400 les Borges Blanques	28410 Manzanares el Real
16162 Horcajada de la Torre	02110 La Gineta 83 Qb 25	84 Pb 28	83 Qa 24
83 Qa 25	10711 La Granja 82 Qa 21	02160 Lezuza 83 Ra 25	07700 Maó/Mahón 85 Qb 32
16410 Horcajo de Santiago	45760 La Guardia 83 Qb 24	45870 Lillo 83 Qb 24	45515 Maqueda 82 Qa 23
83 Qb 25	39580 La Hermida 69 Ob 23	23700 Linares 82 Ra 24	19280 Maranchón 83 Pb 25
42366 Hortezuela 83 Pb 25	17700 La Jonquera 85 Pa 30	31580 Lodosa 84 Pa 25	29600 Marbella 96 Sa 23
09640 Hortigüela 69 Pa 24	41630 La Lantejuela 96 Rb 22	26070 Logroño 69 Pa 25	41620 Marchena 96 Rb 22
16152 Huélamo 83 Qa 26	11300 La Línea de la Concepción	10120 Logrosán 82 Qb 22	04838 María 97 Rb 25
23560 Huelma 96 Rb 24	96 Sa 22	18300 Loja 96 Rb 23	50430 María de Huerva 83 Pb 27
21070 Huelva 81 Rb 21	17537 La Molina 84 Pa 29	23780 Lopera 82 Rb 23	23770 Marmolejo 82 Ra 23

E

Martos

E

Puebla de Sanabria

23600 Martos 96 Rb 24
44564 Mas de las Matas 84 Qa 27
19490 Masegoso de Tajuña
83 Qa 25
46130 Massamagrell 84 Qb 27
40163 Matabuena 83 Pb 24
08300 Mataró 85 Pb 30
47680 Mayorga 68 Pa 22
45114 Mazarambroz 82 Qb 23
30870 Mazarrón 97 Rb 26
09500 Medina de Pomar 69 Pa 24
47800 Medina de Rioseco 68 Pb 22
47400 Medina del Campo 68 Pb 23
11170 Medina Sidonia 96 Sa 22
42240 Medinaceli 83 Pb 25
27240 Meira 68 Ob 20
09100 Melgar de Fernamental
69 Pa 23
15800 Melide 68 Pa 19
52000 Melilla 96 Sb 25
10580 Membrío 82 Qb 20
45128 Menasalbas 82 Qb 23
05131 Mengamuñoz 82 Qa 24
23620 Mengíbar 82 Rb 24
50170 Mequinenza 84 Pb 28
06800 Mérida 82 Ra 21
15689 Mesón do Vento 68 Ob 19
10100 Miajadas 82 Qb 22
33600 Mieres 68 Ob 22
13170 Miguelturra 82 Ra 24
29650 Mijas 96 Sa 23
21660 Minas de Riotinto 81 Rb 21
16260 Minglanilla 83 Qb 26
09200 Miranda de Ebro 69 Pa 25
45270 Mocejón 82 Qb 24
21800 Moguer 81 Rb 21
47250 Mojados 68 Pb 23
19300 Molina de Aragón 83 Qa 26
30500 Molina de Segura 97 Ra 26
25230 Mollerussa 84 Pb 28
27826 Mondoñedo 68 Ob 20
12003 Moncofa 84 Qb 27
27748 Mondoñedo 68 Ob 20
20500 Mondragón 69 Ob 25
06260 Monesterio 82 Ra 21
27400 Monforte de Lemos 68 Pa 20
31471 Monreal 69 Pa 26
44300 Monreal del Campo
83 Qa 26
44700 Montalbán 83 Qa 27
49149 Montamarta 68 Pb 22
10170 Montánchez 82 Qb 21
25738 Montargull 84 Pb 29
19229 Montarrón 83 Qa 24
43400 Montblanc 84 Pb 29
02650 Montealegre del Castillo
83 Ra 26
18270 Montefrío 96 Rb 24
10810 Montehermoso 82 Qa 21
27560 Monterroso 68 Pa 20
06427 Monterrubio de la Serena
82 Ra 22
08585 Montesquiu 84 Pa 30
06480 Montijo 82 Ra 21
14550 Montilla 96 Rb 23
14600 Montoro 82 Ra 23

22400 Monzón 84 Pb 28
45400 Mora 82 Qb 24
43740 Móra d `Ebre 84 Pb 28
44400 Mora de Rubielos 83 Qa 27
09462 Moradillo de Roa 69 Pb 24
13350 Moral de Calatrava 82 Ra 24
18730 Moraleda de Zafayona
96 Rb 24
10840 Moraleja 82 Qa 21
49177 Moraleja de Sayago
68 Pb 21
30440 Moratalla 97 Ra 26
12300 Morella 84 Qa 27
41530 Morón de la Frontera
96 Rb 22
44410 Mosqueruela 84 Qa 27
16630 Mota del Cuervo 83 Qb 25
16200 Motilla del Palancar
83 Qb 26
18600 Motril 96 Sa 24
50450 Muel 83 Pb 26
30170 Mula 97 Ra 26
02612 Munera 83 Qb 25
44780 Muniesa 83 Pb 27
05145 Muñico 82 Qa 22
30070 Murcia 97 Rb 26
15250 Muros 67 Pa 18
15570 Narón 68 Ob 19
33520 Nava 68 Ob 22
47500 Nava del Rey 68 Pb 22
10300 Navalmoral de la Mata
82 Qb 22
05631 Navalperal de Tormes
82 Qa 22
06760 Navalvillar de Pela 82 Qb 22
08670 Navàs 84 Pb 29
23240 Navas de San Juan
82 Ra 24
10930 Navas del Madroño
82 Qb 21
31450 Navascués 70 Pa 26
33710 Navia 68 Ob 21
19245 Negredo 83 Pb 25
29780 Nerja 96 Sa 24
21670 Nerva 81 Rb 21
04100 Níjar 97 Sa 25
23140 Noalejo 96 Rb 24
24734 Nogarejas 68 Pa 21
32526 Nogueira 68 Pa 19
44113 Noguera 83 Qa 26
44414 Nogueruelas 83 Qa 27
15200 Noia 67 Pa 19
39180 Noja 69 Ob 24
22113 Novales 70 Pa 27
03660 Novelda 97 Ra 27
33416 Noblejo 68 Ob 22
50210 Nuévalos 83 Pb 26
12520 Nules 84 Qb 27
32300 O Barco 68 Pa 21
36156 O Castelo 67 Pa 19
36546 O Castro 68 Pa 19
36980 O Grove 67 Pa 19
45300 Ocaña 83 Qb 24
31720 Oieregi 69 Ob 26
44479 Olba 83 Qa 27
25790 Oliana 84 Pa 29

31390 Olite 69 Pa 26
46780 Oliva 84 Ra 27
06120 Oliva de la Frontera
81 Ra 21
06100 Olivenza 81 Ra 20
16118 Olmedilla de Alarcón
83 Qb 25
47410 Olmedo 68 Pb 23
17800 Olot 85 Pa 30
04860 Olula del Río 97 Rb 25
42110 Ólvega 69 Pb 26
11690 Olvera 96 Sa 22
12200 Onda 84 Qb 27
48700 Ondarroa 69 Ob 25
46870 Ontinyent 83 Ra 27
02652 Ontur 83 Ra 26
09530 Oña 69 Pa 24
20560 Oñati 69 Ob 25
09350 Oquillas 69 Pb 24
15680 Ordes 68 Ob 19
48460 Orduña 69 Ob 24
06740 Orellana la Vieja 82 Qb 22
45450 Orgaz 82 Qb 24
18400 Órgiva 96 Sa 24
03300 Orihuela 97 Ra 27
44366 Orihuela del Tremedal
83 Qa 26
12594 Oropesa/Benicàssim
84 Qa 28
45560 Oropesa/Talavera de la Reina
82 Qb 22
31650 Orreaga-Roncesvalles
70 Ob 26
15365 Ortigueira 68 Ob 20
24916 Oseja de Sajambre 68 Ob 22
34460 Osorno 69 Pa 23
02611 Ossa de Montiel 83 Ra 25
41640 Osuna 96 Rb 22
27392 Oural 68 Pa 20
32070 Ourense/Orense 68 Pa 20
27865 Ourol 68 Ob 20
33070 Oviedo 68 Ob 22
15380 Oza 68 Ob 19
27256 Pacios 68 Ob 20
49574 Padornelo 68 Pa 21
18640 Padul 96 Rb 24
24495 Palacios del Sil 68 Pa 21
17200 Palafrugell 85 Pb 31
34070 Palencia 69 Pa 23
07070 Palma de Mallorca
84 Qb 30
14700 Palma del Río 82 Rb 22
06476 Palomas 82 Ra 21
22221 Pallaruelo de Monegros
84 Pb 27
31070 Pamplona-Iruña 69 Pa 26
09280 Pancorbo 69 Pa 24
50480 Paniza 83 Pb 26
27135 Paradavella 68 Ob 20
34300 Paredes de Nava 68 Pa 23
28980 Parla 83 Qa 24
40122 Pascuales 82 Pb 23
19100 Pastrana 83 Qb 24
23460 Peal de Becerro 97 Rb 24
27670 Pedrafita do Cebreiro
68 Pa 20

13620 Pedro Muñoz 83 Qb 25
50690 Pedrola 83 Pb 26
03780 Pego 84 Ra 27
47011 Peñafiel 69 Pb 23
41470 Peñaflor 82 Rb 22
37300 Peñaranda de Bracamonte
82 Qa 22
14200 Peñarroya-Pueblonuevo
82 Ra 22
12598 Peñíscola 84 Qa 28
44162 Peralejos 83 Qa 26
46220 Picassent 83 Qb 27
13100 Piedrabuena 82 Qb 23
05500 Piedrahíta 82 Qa 22
05440 Piedralaves 82 Qa 23
33450 Piedras Blancas 68 Ob 22
03190 Pilar de la Horadada
97 Rb 27
07872 Pilar de la Mola 98 Ra 29
40296 Pinarejos 83 Pb 23
18240 Pinos Puente 96 Rb 24
03650 Pinoso 97 Ra 26
10600 Plasencia 82 Qa 21
88210 Plasencia del Monte
70 Pa 27
33880 Pola de Allande 68 Ob 21
33980 Pola de Laviana 68 Ob 22
33630 Pola de Lena 68 Ob 22
07460 Pollença 85 Qb 31
24400 Ponferrada 68 Pa 21
36829 Ponte Caldelas 67 Pa 19
36860 Ponteareas 67 Pa 19
15110 Pontecesco 67 Ob 19
15600 Pontedeume 68 Ob 19
36070 Pontevedra 67 Pa 19
36400 Porriño 67 Pa 19
07470 Port de Pollença 85 Qb 31
07108 Port de Sóller 84 Qb 30
17497 Portbou 85 Pa 31
66760 Porté-Puymorens 70 Pa 29
07820 Portinatx 84 Qb 29
07670 Porto Colom 85 Qb 31
07680 Porto Cristo 85 Qb 31
15970 Porto do Son 67 Pa 19
15871 Portomouro 67 Pa 19
13120 Porzuna 82 Qb 23
33424 Posada 68 Ob 22
14730 Posadas 82 Rb 22
39570 Potes 69 Ob 23
23485 Pozo Alcón 97 Rb 25
14400 Pozoblanco 82 Ra 23
02141 Pozohondo 83 Ra 26
26510 Pradejón 69 Pa 25
33120 Pravia 68 Ob 21
16800 Priego 83 Qa 25
14800 Priego de Córdoba 96 Rb 23
46530 Puçol 84 Qb 27
06630 Puebla de Alcocer 82 Ra 22
18820 Puebla de Don Fadrique
97 Rb 25
13109 Puebla de Don Rodrigo
82 Qb 23
24855 Puebla de Lillo 68 Ob 22
06191 Puebla de Obando 82 Qb 21
49300 Puebla de Sanabria
68 Pa 21

POSTALI · ÍNDICE CON CÓDIGOS POSTALES · INDICE DE LUGARES COM CÓDIGOS POSTAIS ·
MÍST S PSČ · ZOZNAM OBCÍ S PSČ · INDEKS MIEJSCOWOŚCI Z KOD POCZTOWY

132

Puente de Domingo Flórez   E   Tamames

24380 Puente de Domingo Flórez 68 Pa 21	37130 Robliza de Cojos 82 Qa 22	05350 San Pedro del Arroyo 82 Qa 23
23350 Puente de Génave 83 Ra 25	40290 Roda de Eresma 83 Pb 23	30740 San Pedro del Pinatar 97 Rb 27
14500 Puente Genil 96 Rb 23	29400 Ronda 96 Sa 22	42174 San Pedro Manrique 69 Pa 25
22753 Puente la Reina de Jaca 70 Pa 27	04740 Roquetas de Mar 97 Sa 25	11360 San Roque 96 Sa 22
39670 Puente-Viesgo 69 Ob 24	17480 Roses 85 Pa 31	34847 San Salvador de Cantamuda 69 Pa 23
05621 Puerto Castilla 82 Qa 22	11520 Rota 95 Sa 21	28700 San Sebastián de los Reyes 83 Qa 24
30860 Puerto de Mazarrón 97 Rb 26	47490 Rueda 68 Pb 23	
45577 Puerto de San Vicente 82 Qb 22	07600 S´Arenal 84 Qb 30	06500 San Vicente de Alcántara 81 Qb 20
13650 Puerto Lápice 83 Qb 24	07409 Sa Marina 84 Qb 30	03690 San Vicente del Raspeig 97 Ra 27
30890 Puerto Lumbreras 97 Rb 26	07420 Sa Pobla 85 Qb 31	37470 Sancti-Spíritus 82 Qa 21
11510 Puerto Real 95 Sa 21	08200 Sabadell 84 Pb 30	31400 Sangüesa 69 Pa 26
45672 Puerto Rey 82 Qb 22	19120 Sacedón 83 Qa 25	11540 Sanlúcar de Barrameda 95 Sa 21
11659 Puerto Serrano 96 Sa 22	13414 Saceruela 82 Ra 23	41800 Sanlúcar la Mayor 82 Rb 21
13500 Puertollano 82 Ra 23	50670 Sádaba 69 Pa 26	07820 Sant Antoni de Portmany 84 Ra 29
17520 Puigcerdà 70 Pa 29	16430 Saelices 83 Qb 25	
04640 Pulpí 97 Rb 26	46500 Sagunt/Sagunto 84 Qb 27	43540 Sant Carles de la Ràpita 84 Qa 28
21100 Punta Umbria 95 Rb 21	24320 Sahagún 68 Pa 22	17220 Sant Feliu de Guíxols 85 Pb 31
22589 Purroy de la Solana 84 Pa 28	37070 Salamanca 82 Qa 22	07871 Sant Ferran de ses Roques 98 Ra 29
18519 Purullena 96 Rb 24	18310 Salar 96 Rb 23	07860 Sant Francesc Xavier 98 Ra 29
09454 Quemada 69 Pb 24	33860 Salas 68 Ob 21	07810 Sant Joan de Labritja 84 Qb 29
23480 Quesada 97 Rb 24	09600 Salas de los Infantes 69 Pa 24	07469 Sant Josep de sa Talaia 84 Ra 29
06450 Quintana de la Serena 82 Ra 22	34100 Saldaña 69 Pa 23	25282 Sant Llorenç de Morunys 84 Pa 29
24397 Quintana del Castillo 68 Pa 21	27568 Salgueiros 68 Pa 20	07530 Sant Llorenç des Cardassar 85 Qb 31
34250 Quintana del Puente 69 Pa 23	19126 Salmerón 83 Qa 25	43570 Santa Barbara 84 Qa 28
09244 Quintanaélez 69 Pa 24	10570 Salorino 82 Qb 20	21570 Santa Bárbara de Casa 81 Rb 20
45800 Quintanar de la Orden 83 Qb 24	43840 Salou 84 Pb 29	15841 Santa Cataliña de Armada 67 Ob 19
09670 Quintanar de la Sierra 69 Pb 24	01200 Salvatierra 69 Pa 25	45370 Santa Cruz de la Zarza 83 Qb 24
16220 Quintanar del Rey 83 Qb 26	08650 Sallent 84 Pb 29	16336 Santa Cruz de Moya 83 Qb 26
50770 Quinto 84 Pb 27	39687 San Andrés/Reinosa 69 Ob 24	13730 Santa Cruz de Mudela 82 Ra 24
27320 Quiroga 68 Pa 20	26126 San Andrés/Soria 69 Pa 25	45513 Santa Cruz del Retamar 82 Qa 23
39800 Ramales de la Victoria 69 Ob 24	21510 San Bartolomé de la Torre 81 Rb 20	09125 Santa Cruz del Tozo 69 Pa 24
43513 Rasquera 84 Pb 28	27888 San Ciprián 68 Ob 20	23213 Santa Elena 82 Ra 24
36800 Redondela 67 Pa 19	16600 San Clemente 83 Qb 25	14491 Santa Eufemia 82 Ra 23
39200 Reinosa 69 Ob 23	49690 San Cristóbal de Entreviñas 68 Pa 22	07840 Santa Eulària des Ríu 84 Ra 29
50637 Remolinos 83 Pb 26	42330 San Esteban de Gormaz 69 Pb 24	18320 Santa Fe 96 Rb 24
02316 Reolid 83 Ra 25	11100 San Fernando 95 Sa 21	01110 Santa Kurutze Kanpezu 69 Pa 25
46340 Requena 83 Qb 26	40100 San Ildefonso o La Granja 83 Qa 23	42260 Santa María de Huerta 83 Pb 25
43200 Reus 84 Pb 29	30730 San Javier 97 Rb 27	24240 Santa María del Páramo 68 Pa 22
25594 Rialp 70 Pa 29	22283 San Jorge 70 Pb 27	06150 Santa Marta 82 Ra 21
24900 Riaño 68 Pa 23	04648 San Juan de los Terreros 97 Rb 26	03130 Santa Pola 97 Ra 27
27700 Ribadeo 68 Ob 20	42140 San Leonardo de Yagüe 69 Pa 24	31314 Santacara 69 Pa 26
33560 Ribadesella 69 Ob 22	28200 San Lorenzo de El Escorial 82 Qa 23	22461 Santaliestra y San Quílez 70 Pa 28
26130 Ribafrecha 69 Pa 25	16770 San Lorenzo de la Parrilla 83 Qb 25	39070 Santander 69 Ob 24
27206 Ribeira 67 Pa 19	49361 San Martin de Castañeda 68 Pa 21	07650 Santanyi 85 Qb 31
49165 Ricobayo 68 Pb 22	28680 San Martín de Valdeiglesias 82 Qa 23	15770 Santiago de Compostela 67 Pa 19
29730 Rincón de la Victoria 96 Sa 23	40332 San Miguel de Bernuy 69 Pb 24	23290 Santiago de la Espada 97 Ra 25
49348 Rioconejos 68 Pa 21	41388 San Nicolás del Puerto 82 Rb 22	24732 Santiago Millas 68 Pa 21
49326 Ríonegro del Puente 68 Pa 21	02326 San Pedro 83 Ra 25	39330 Santillana de Mar 69 Ob 23
02450 Riópar 83 Ra 25	29670 San Pedro de Alcántara 96 Sa 22	23250 Santisteban del Puerto 83 Ra 24
17500 Ripoll 84 Pa 30		26250 Santo Domingo de la Calzada 69 Pa 25
09300 Roa 69 Pb 24		05292 Santo Domingo de las Posadas 82 Qa 23
37521 Robleda 82 Qa 21		23311 Santo Tomé 97 Ra 24
02340 Robledo 83 Ra 25		39740 Santoña 69 Ob 24
		36960 Sanxenxo 67 Pa 19
		22200 Sariñena 84 Pb 27
		09620 Sarracín 69 Pa 24
		27600 Sarria 68 Pa 20
		44460 Sarrión 83 Qa 27
		42216 Sauquillo del Campo 83 Pb 25
		12400 Segorbe 83 Qb 27
		40070 Segovia 83 Qa 23
		49515 Sejas de Aliste 68 Pb 21
		19346 Selas 83 Qa 25
		24145 Sena de Luna 68 Pa 22
		04890 Serón 97 Rb 25
		41070 Sevilla 96 Rb 22
		45671 Sevilleja de la Jara 82 Qb 23
		50612 Sierra de Luna 70 Pa 27
		15884 Sigüeiro 68 Pa 19
		46460 Silla 83 Qb 27
		47130 Simancas 68 Pb 23
		16700 Sisante 83 Qb 25
		27150 Sobrado de Picato 68 Pa 20
		02435 Socovos 83 Ra 26
		13630 Socuéllamos 83 Qb 25
		06209 Solana de los Barros 82 Ra 21
		25280 Solsona 84 Pb 29
		07100 Sóller 84 Qb 30
		19275 Somolinos 83 Pb 24
		28756 Somosierra 83 Pb 24
		09572 Soncillo 69 Pa 24
		45100 Sonseca 82 Qb 24
		04270 Sorbas 97 Rb 25
		42070 Soria 69 Pb 25
		25560 Sort 70 Pa 29
		05420 Sotillo de la Adrada 82 Qa 23
		37657 Sotoserrano 82 Qa 21
		39340 Suances 69 Ob 23
		46410 Sueca 83 Qb 27
		49140 Tábara 68 Pb 22
		04200 Tabernas 97 Rb 25
		31300 Tafalla 69 Pa 26
		45600 Talavera de la Reina 82 Qb 23
		06140 Talavera la Real 82 Ra 21
		10310 Talayuela 82 Qb 22
		37600 Tamames 82 Qa 21

133

INDEX WITH POST CODES · ORTSREGISTER MIT POSTLEITZAHLEN · INDICE CON CODICI
STEDREGISTER MED POSTNUMRE · PLAATSNAMENREGISTER MET POSTCODE · REJSTŘÍK

E

EST

Tamarite de Litera · E · EST · Heltermaa

22550 Tamarite de Litera 84 Pb 28
33740 Tapia de Casariego
         68 Ob 21
16400 Tarancón 83 Qa 24
50500 Tarazona 69 Pb 26
02100 Tarazona de la Mancha
         83 Qb 26
11380 Tarifa 96 Sa 22
43070 Tarragona 84 Pb 29
25300 Tàrrega 84 Pb 29
25212 Tarroja de Segarra 84 Pb 29
50660 Tauste 69 Pb 26
46760 Tavernes de la Valldigna
         83 Qb 27
29327 Teba 96 Sa 23
27191 Teixeiro 68 Ob 20
45780 Tembleque 83 Qb 24
08220 Terrassa 84 Pb 30
44070 Teruel 83 Qa 26
19312 Terzaga 83 Qa 26
47870 Tiedra 68 Pb 22
33870 Tineo 68 Ob 20
46178 Titaguas 83 Qb 26
45070 Toledo 82 Qb 23
20400 Tolosa 69 Ob 25
13700 Tomelloso 83 Qb 24
08551 Tona 84 Pb 30
24237 Toral de los Guzmanes
         68 Pa 22
47100 Tordesillas 68 Pb 23
08570 Torelló 84 Pa 30
24450 Toreno 68 Pa 21
49800 Toro 68 Pb 22
21750 Torre de la Higuera 95 Rb 21
23640 Torre del Campo 96 Rb 24
30700 Torre-Pacheco 97 Rb 27
12596 Torreblanca 84 Qa 28
23650 Torredonjimeno 96 Rb 24
28850 Torrejón de Ardoz 83 Qa 24
10694 Torrejón el Rubio 82 Qb 21
10830 Torrejoncillo 82 Qb 21
28180 Torrelaguna 83 Qa 24
39300 Torrelavega 69 Ob 23
03320 Torrellano 97 Ra 27
06210 Torremejía 82 Ra 21
29620 Torremolinos 96 Sa 23
46900 Torrent 83 Qb 27
23320 Torreperogil 82 Ra 24
03180 Torrevieja 97 Rb 27
45500 Torrijos 82 Qb 23
09312 Tórtoles de Esgueva
         69 Pb 23
43500 Tortosa 84 Qa 28
18430 Torvizcón 96 Sa 24
30850 Totana 97 Rb 26
16150 Tragacete 83 Qa 26
32695 Trasmiras 68 Pa 20
11560 Trebujena 95 Sa 21
25620 Tremp 84 Pa 28
09540 Trespaderne 69 Pa 24
21620 Trigueros 81 Rb 21
10200 Trujillo 82 Qb 22
31500 Tudela 69 Pa 26
47320 Tudela de Duero 68 Pb 23
36700 Tui 67 Pa 19
40370 Turégano 83 Pb 23

27286 Úbeda 82 Ra 24
09141 Ubierna 69 Pa 24
11600 Ubrique 96 Sa 22
42317 Ucero 69 Pb 24
18480 Ugíjar 96 Sa 24
43550 Ulldecona 84 Qa 28
01440 Urcabustaiz 69 Pa 25
05195 Urraca-Miguel 82 Qa 23
50180 Utebo 84 Pb 27
46300 Utiel 83 Qb 26
41710 Utrera 96 Rb 22
09559 Vadenoceda 69 Pa 24
36585 Valboa 68 Pa 19
28340 Valdemoro 83 Qa 24
13300 Valdepeñas 83 Ra 24
44580 Valderrobres 84 Qa 28
10050 Valencia de Alcántara
         81 Qb 20
24200 Valencia de Don Juan
         68 Pa 22
46070 València 83 Qb 27
50615 Valpalmas 70 Pa 27
13195 Valverde 82 Ra 23
06130 Valverde de Leganés
         81 Ra 21
21600 Valverde del Camino
         81 Rb 21
10890 Valverde del Fresno
         82 Qa 21
47070 Valladolid 68 Pb 23
43800 Valls 84 Pb 29
37450 Vecinos 82 Qa 22
33770 Vegadeo 68 Ob 20
10623 Vegas de Coria 82 Qa 21
11150 Vejer de la Frontera
         95 Sa 22
45612 Velada 82 Qb 23
04830 Vélez Blanco 97 Rb 25
18670 Vélez de Benaudalla
         96 Sa 24
29700 Vélez-Málaga 96 Sa 23
34869 Velilla de Tarilonte 69 Pa 23
34200 Venta de Baños 69 Pb 23
37329 Ventosa del Río Almer
         82 Qa 22
04620 Vera 97 Rb 26
32600 Verín 68 Pb 20
32550 Viana do Bolo 68 Pa 20
08500 Vic 84 Pb 30
25530 Vielha 70 Pa 28
36200 Vigo 67 Pa 19
12540 Vila-real de los Infantes
         84 Qb 27
17137 Viladamat 85 Pa 31
27259 Viladonga 68 Ob 20
08720 Vilafranca del Penedès
         84 Pb 29
36600 Vilagarcía de Arousa
         67 Pa 19
27800 Vilalba 68 Ob 20
08800 Vilanova i la Geltrú 84 Pb 29
14640 Vila del Río 82 Rb 23
34406 Villabermudo 69 Pa 23
24100 Villablino 68 Pa 21
47820 Villabrágima 68 Pb 22
45860 Villacañas 83 Qb 24

39640 Villacarriedo 69 Ob 24
23300 Villacarrillo 83 Ra 24
40150 Villacastín 82 Qa 23
33430 Villada 68 Pa 22
09120 Villadiego 69 Pa 23
06220 Villafranca de los Barros
         82 Ra 21
45730 Villafranca de los Caballeros
         83 Qb 24
24500 Villafranca del Bierzo
         68 Pa 21
06950 Villagarcía de la Torre
         82 Ra 21
14210 Villaharta 82 Ra 23
16646 Villalgordo del Marquesado
         83 Qb 25
47600 Villalón de Campos 68 Pa 22
49630 Villalpando 68 Pb 22
11650 Villamartín 96 Sa 22
16415 Villamayor de Santiago
         83 Qb 25
47620 Villanubla 68 Pb 23
19460 Villanueva de Alcorón
         83 Qa 25
26123 Villanueva de Cameros
         69 Pa 25
14440 Villanueva de Córdoba
         82 Ra 23
50830 Villanueva de Gállego
         84 Pb 27
06700 Villanueva de la Serena
         82 Ra 22
10812 Villanueva de la Sierra
         82 Qa 21
10470 Villanueva de la Vera
         82 Qa 22
21540 Villanueva de los Castillejos
         81 Rb 20
13320 Villanueva de los Infantes
         83 Ra 24
23330 Villanueva del Arzobispo
         83 Ra 24
49708 Villanueva del Campo
         68 Pb 22
06110 Villanueva del Fresno
         81 Ra 20
14230 Villanueva del Rey
         82 Ra 22
41350 Villanueva del Río y Minas
         82 Rb 22
24235 Villaquejida 68 Pa 22
28590 Villarejo de Salvanés
         83 Qa 24
44380 Villarquemado 83 Qa 26
10695 Villarreal de San Carlos
         82 Qb 21
02600 Villarrobledo 83 Qb 25
50310 Villarroya de la Sierra
         83 Pb 26
16280 Villarta 83 Qb 26
13210 Villarta de San Juan
         83 Qb 24
44130 Villastar 83 Qa 26
45310 Villatobas 83 Qb 24
05560 Villatoro 82 Qa 22
02215 Villatoya 83 Qb 26

16111 Villaverde y Pasaconsol
         83 Qb 25
33300 Villaviciosa 68 Ob 22
14300 Villaviciosa de Córdoba
         82 Ra 22
44131 Villel 83 Qa 26
03400 Villena 83 Ra 27
15129 Vimianzo 67 Ob 18
12500 Vinaròs 84 Qa 28
49177 Viñuela de Sayago 68 Pb 22
13770 Viso del Marqués 82 Ra 24
37210 Vitigudino 68 Pb 21
01070 Vitoria-Gasteiz 69 Pa 25
09140 Vivar del Cid 69 Pa 24
27850 Viveiro 68 Ob 20
03730 Xàbia 84 Ra 28
46800 Xàtiva 83 Ra 27
32630 Xinzo de Limia 68 Pa 20
03100 Xixona 83 Ra 27
30510 Yecla 83 Ra 26
19210 Yunquera de Henares
         83 Qa 24
18128 Zafarraya 96 Sa 23
06300 Zafra 82 Ra 21
06430 Zalamea de la Serena
         82 Ra 22
09199 Zalduendo 69 Pa 24
49070 Zamora 68 Pb 22
50070 Zaragoza 84 Pb 27
20800 Zarautz 69 Ob 25
10130 Zorita 82 Qb 22
31630 Zubiri 69 Pa 26
50800 Zuera 84 Pb 27
18811 Zújar 97 Rb 25

EST

69404 Abja-Paluoja 31 Ga 53
48001 Adavere 31 Ga 53
74501 Aegviidu 31 Fb 53
63701 Ahja 31 Ga 55
68501 Ala 31 Ga 53
60201 Alatskivi 31 Ga 55
87601 Aluste 31 Ga 52
93823 Angla 30 Ga 50
66403 Antsla 31 Gb 54
93501 Arandi 30 Ga 50
73501 Aravete 31 Fb 53
87301 Are 30 Ga 52
43401 Aseri 31 Fb 54
46001 Assamalla 31 Fb 54
93824 Asuka 30 Ga 50
41303 Atsalama 31 Fb 55
88301 Audru 30 Ga 52
91001 Aulepa Dirslätt 30 Fb 51
61503 Elva 31 Ga 54
92001 Emmaste 30 Ga 50
63101 Erastvere 31 Gb 54
90502 Haapsalu 30 Ga 51
60501 Haava 31 Ga 54
93823 Haeska 30 Ga 50
45301 Haljala 31 Fb 54
94701 Hellamaa 30 Ga 51
92312 Heltermaa 30 Ga 51

POSTALI · ÍNDICE CON CÓDIGOS POSTALES · INDICE DE LUGARES COM CÓDIGOS POSTAIS · MÍST S PSČ · ZOZNAM OBCÍ S PSČ · INDEKS MIEJSCOWOŚCI Z KOD POCZTOWY

134

Hummuli   (EST) · (F)   **Anvin**

68401 Hummuli 31 Gb 54	74201 Loo 31 Fb 52	63401 Saverna 31 Ga 54	34300 Agde 71 Ob 31
86001 Häädemeeste 30 Ga 52	69603 Loodi 31 Ga 53	91301 Saxby 30 Fb 51	47000 Agen 70 Oa 28
41101 Iisaku 31 Fb 55	92202 Luidja 30 Ga 50	86817 Selja 31 Ga 52	23150 Ahun 57 Na 30
86402 Ilvese 31 Ga 52	75401 Luige 30 Fb 52	90701 Silla 30 Ga 52	73220 Aiguebelle 72 Nb 34
72401 Imavere 31 Ga 53	93601 Luulupe 30 Ga 50	40102 Sillamäe 31 Fb 55	63260 Aigueperse 57 Na 31
86007 Jaagupi 30 Ga 52	88402 Lõpe 31 Ga 53	85011 Sindi 30 Ga 52	11800 Aigues-Vives 71 Ob 30
41001 Jaama 31 Fb 55	93301 Lümanda 30 Ga 50	78102 Sipa 30 Ga 52	47190 Aiguillon 70 Oa 28
79401 Juuru 31 Fb 52	44001 Mahu 31 Fb 54	69701 Soe 31 Ga 53	36140 Aigurande 57 Na 29
73301 Järva-Jaani 31 Fb 53	66101 Matsi 31 Gb 54	74402 Soodla 31 Fb 53	05340 Ailefroide 72 Oa 34
79101 Järvakandi 31 Ga 52	62301 Melliste 31 Ga 54	71504 Suure-Jaani 31 Ga 53	89110 Aillant-sur-Tholon 57 Mb 31
48303 Jõgeva 31 Ga 54	64301 Mikitamäe 31 Gb 55	72101 Särevere 31 Ga 53	73210 Aime 72 Nb 34
41541 Jõhvi 31 Fb 55	65001 Misso 31 Gb 55	93201 Sääre 30 Gb 50	40800 Aire-sur-l`Adour 70 Ob 27
87605 Kaansoo 31 Ga 53	76302 Munalaskme 30 Fb 52	44310 Sõmeru 31 Fb 54	79600 Airvault 56 Na 27
87606 Kadjaste 31 Ga 53	76901 Muraste 30 Fb 52	86818 Taali 31 Ga 52	89390 Aisy-sur-Armançon 57 Mb 32
45201 Kadrina 31 Fb 54	93601 Mustjala 30 Ga 50	76901 Tabasalu 30 Fb 52	10160 Aix-en-Othe 57 Ma 31
92212 Kalana 30 Ga 50	49501 Mustvee 31 Ga 54	49101 Tabivere 31 Ga 54	13100 Aix-en-Provence 72 Ob 33
60201 Kallaste 31 Ga 55	93201 Mäebe 30 Gb 50	75503 Tagadi 31 Fb 52	73100 Aix-les-Bains 72 Nb 33
86204 Kanaküla 31 Ga 53	78301 Märjamaa 30 Ga 52	93822 Tagamõisa 30 Ga 50	85190 Aizenay 56 Na 26
93825 Kangrusselja 30 Ga 50	87224 Mõisaküla 31 Ga 53	93601 Tagaranna 30 Ga 50	20000 Ajaccio 86 Pb 36
93822 Karala 30 Ga 49	66002 Mõniste 31 Gb 54	10505 Tallinn 30 Fb 52	81250 Alban 71 Ob 30
69104 Karksi-Nuia 31 Ga 53	20308 Narva 31 Fb 56	45100 Tapa 31 Fb 53	73410 Albens 72 Nb 33
90112 Karuse 30 Ga 51	74203 Neeme 31 Fb 53	51004 Tartu 31 Ga 54	80300 Albert 45 La 30
40501 Kasepää 31 Ga 54	92311 Nõmba 30 Ga 50	86201 Tihemetsa 31 Ga 53	73200 Albertville 72 Nb 34
74303 Kehra 31 Fb 53	61601 Nõo 31 Ga 54	48502 Torma 31 Ga 54	81000 Albi 71 Ob 30
79001 Kehtna 31 Ga 52	91101 Nõva 30 Fb 51	86003 Treimani 30 Gb 52	61000 Alençon 56 Ma 28
76003 Keibu 30 Fb 51	70323 Oiu 31 Ga 53	46606 Tudu 31 Fb 54	20270 Aléria 87 Pa 37
76505 Keila 30 Fb 52	42202 Oonurme 31 Fb 54	42202 Tudulinna 31 Fb 55	30100 Alès 71 Oa 32
76902 Kiia 30 Fb 52	94601 Orissaare 30 Ga 51	76201 Turba 30 Fb 52	54170 Allain 58 Ma 33
74604 Kiiu 31 Fb 53	66601 Osula 31 Gb 54	94501 Tõrnimäe 30 Ga 51	28310 Allaines-Mervilliers 57 Ma 29
86303 Kilingi-Nõmme 31 Ga 52	67406 Otepää 31 Ga 54	68605 Tõrva 31 Gb 53	13190 Allauch 72 Ob 33
90201 Kirbla 30 Ga 51	46501 Paasvere 31 Fb 54	88101 Tõstamaa 30 Ga 51	71350 Allerey-sur-Saône 58 Na 32
43121 Kiviõli 31 Fb 54	79004 Pae 31 Fb 52	72230 Türi 31 Ga 53	58200 Alligny-Cosne 57 Mb 31
73301 Koeru 31 Ga 54	72712 Paide 31 Ga 53	86502 Uulu 30 Ga 52	72700 Allonnes/Le Mans 56 Mb 28
79801 Kohila 30 Fb 52	76606 Paldiski 30 Fb 52	66502 Vaabina 31 Gb 54	49650 Allonnes/Saumur 56 Mb 28
32100 Kohtla-Järve 31 Fb 55	90802 Palivere 30 Ga 51	92101 Vaemla 30 Ga 50	04260 Allos 72 Oa 34
70301 Kolga-Jaani 31 Ga 53	49102 Pataste 31 Ga 54	45401 Vainupea 31 Fb 54	38750 Alpe-d`Huez 72 Nb 34
90702 Koluvere 30 Ga 52	75001 Paunküla 31 Fb 53	68205 Valga 31 Gb 54	68130 Altkirch 58 Mb 35
60402 Koosa 31 Ga 55	93824 Pidula 30 Ga 50	78204 Valgu 30 Ga 52	01500 Ambérieu-en-Bugey 72 Nb 33
68013 Korkuna 31 Gb 54	92201 Pihla 30 Ga 50	78003 Vana-Vigala 30 Ga 52	63600 Ambert 71 Nb 31
75101 Kose 31 Fb 53	88115 Pootsi 30 Ga 52	49301 Vanassaare 31 Ga 54	37400 Amboise 57 Mb 28
29024 Kudruküla 31 Fb 56	61301 Puhja 31 Ga 54	91101 Variku 30 Fb 51	53300 Ambrières-les-Vallées 56 Ma 27
68226 Kuigatsi 31 Ga 54	71104 Puiatu 31 Ga 53	60302 Varnja 31 Ga 55	
90902 Kuijõe 30 Fb 51	49001 Puurmani 31 Ga 54	41001 Vasknarva 31 Ga 55	66110 Amélie- 85 Pa 30
79302 Kuimetsa 31 Fb 53	80010 Pärnu 30 Ga 52	65502 Verijärve 31 Gb 55	80000 Amiens 45 Lb 30
94702 Kuivastu 30 Ga 51	87201 Pärnu-Jaagupi 30 Ga 52	64201 Veriora 31 Gb 55	45200 Amilly 57 Mb 30
44105 Kunda 31 Fb 54	78028 Päärdu 30 Ga 52	65201 Viitka 31 Gb 55	69550 Amplepuis 71 Nb 32
41201 Kuremäe 31 Fb 55	48103 Põltsamaa 31 Ga 53	71011 Viljandi 31 Ga 53	44150 Ancenis 56 Mb 26
93813 Kuressaare 30 Ga 50	63303 Põlva 31 Ga 55	90101 Virtsu 30 Ga 51	55170 Ancerville 58 Ma 33
92101 Käina 30 Ga 50	75203 Raasiku 31 Fb 53	44001 Viru-Nigula 31 Fb 54	89160 Ancy-le-Franc 57 Mb 32
92413 Kärdla 30 Ga 50	44310 Rakvere 31 Fb 54	74803 Virve 31 Fb 53	52700 Andelot-Blancheville 58 Ma 33
60503 Kärevere 31 Ga 54	94601 Randküla 30 Ga 50	48401 Vägeva 31 Ga 54	
93501 Kärla 30 Ga 50	86016 Rannametsa 30 Ga 52	46202 Väike-Maarja 31 Fb 54	30140 Anduze 71 Oa 31
45001 Käsmu 31 Fb 53	42202 Rannapungerja 31 Ga 55	61103 Väike-Rakke 31 Ga 54	28260 Anet 57 Ma 29
76002 Kõmmaste 30 Fb 52	79601 Rapla 31 Ga 52	87701 Vändra 31 Ga 53	49000 Angers 56 Mb 27
71202 Kõpu 31 Ga 53	73602 Raudla 31 Fb 53	64001 Värska 31 Gb 55	91670 Angerville 57 Ma 29
92212 Kõpu 30 Ga 52	91202 Riguldi 30 Fb 51	72602 Võhma 31 Ga 53	51260 Anglure 56 Ma 31
94501 Kõrkvere 30 Ga 51	76202 Riisipere 30 Fb 52	65608 Võru 31 Gb 54	16000 Angoulême 56 Nb 28
42101 Kõveriku 31 Ga 54	90901 Risti 30 Ga 52	91201 Österby 30 Ga 51	74000 Annecy 72 Nb 34
93101 Laadla 30 Gb 50	46602 Ristiküla 31 Fb 54	67111 Õruste 31 Gb 54	07100 Annonay 71 Nb 32
90612 Laiküla 30 Ga 51	90531 Rohoküla 30 Ga 51		88650 Anould 58 Ma 34
63601 Leevijõe 31 Ga 54	74001 Rohuneeme 30 Fb 52		69480 Anse 71 Nb 32
79002 Lelle 31 Ga 53	64503 Räpina 31 Ga 55		06600 Antibes 72 Ob 35
90303 Lihula 30 Ga 51	61001 Rõngu 31 Ga 54	(F)	92160 Antony 57 Ma 30
43302 Liimala 31 Fb 54	70201 Saarepeedi 31 Ga 53		35560 Antrain 56 Ma 26
69002 Lilli 31 Gb 53	93201 Salme 30 Ga 50	80100 Abbeville 45 La 29	62134 Anvin 45 La 30
45201 Locou 31 Fb 53	72602 Sargvere 31 Ga 53	05460 Abriès 72 Oa 34	

F

Appoigny

F

Cambo-les-Bains

89380 Appoigny 57 Mb 31	54120 Baccarat 58 Ma 34	60000 Beauvais 45 Lb 30
84400 Apt 72 Ob 33	54540 Badonviller 58 Ma 34	85230 Beauvoir-sur-Mer 56 Na 25
39600 Arbois 58 Na 33	11100 Bages 71 Ob 30	49370 Bécon-les-Granits 56 Mb 27
21560 Arc-sur-Tille 58 Mb 33	65200 Bagnères-de-Bigorre	34600 Bédarieux 71 Ob 31
33120 Arcachon 70 Oa 26	70 Ob 28	22140 Bégard 44 Ma 24
46090 Arcambal 70 Oa 29	31110 Bagnères-de-Luchon	36370 Bélâbre 57 Na 29
10700 Arcis-sur-Aube 57 Ma 32	70 Pa 28	11340 Belcaire 70 Pa 29
36120 Ardentes 57 Na 29	30200 Bagnols-sur-Cèze 71 Oa 32	90000 Belfort 58 Mb 34
62610 Ardres 45 La 29	21450 Baigneux-les-Juifs 58 Mb 32	33830 Belin-Béliet 70 Oa 27
33740 Arès 70 Oa 26	35600 Bain-de-Bretagne 56 Ma 26	87300 Bellac 56 Na 29
65400 Argelès-Gazost 70 Ob 27	88240 Bains-les-Bains 58 Mb 34	01200 Bellegarde-sur-Valserine
18410 Argent-sur-Sauldre 57 Mb 30	53160 Bais 56 Ma 27	72 Na 33
61200 Argentan 56 Ma 27	42510 Balbigny 71 Nb 32	61130 Bellême 57 Ma 28
19400 Argentat 71 Nb 29	31580 Balesta 70 Ob 28	03330 Bellenaves 57 Na 31
29840 Argenton 43 Ma 23	83150 Bandol 72 Ob 33	69220 Belleville 71 Na 32
36200 Argenton-sur-Creuse	55110 Bantheville 58 Lb 33	85170 Belleville-sur-Vie 56 Na 26
57 Na 29	62450 Bapaume 45 La 30	01300 Belley 72 Nb 33
53210 Argentré 56 Ma 27	55000 Bar-de-Duc 58 Ma 33	24170 Belvès 70 Oa 28
63220 Arlanc 71 Nb 31	10200 Bar-sur-Aube 58 Ma 32	86470 Benassay 56 Na 28
13200 Arles 71 Ob 32	10110 Bar-sur-Seine 57 Ma 32	85490 Benet 56 Na 27
59280 Armentiéres 45 La 30	12160 Baraqueville 71 Oa 30	28630 Berchères-les-Pierres
19230 Arnac-Pompadour 70 Nb 29	16300 Barbezieux-Saint Hilaire	57 Ma 29
21230 Arnay-le-Duc 57 Mb 32	70 Nb 27	62600 Berck 45 La 29
53440 Aron 56 Ma 27	04400 Barcelonnette 72 Oa 34	24100 Bergerac 70 Oa 28
62000 Arras 45 La 30	50760 Barfleur 44 Lb 26	59380 Bergues 45 La 30
65240 Arreau 70 Pa 28	30430 Barjac 71 Oa 32	27300 Bernay 57 Lb 28
14117 Arromanches-les-Bains	50270 Barneville-Carteret 44 Lb 26	24320 Bertric-Burée 70 Nb 28
44 Lb 27	04330 Barrême 72 Ob 34	25000 Besançon 58 Mb 34
45410 Artenay 57 Ma 29	20119 Bastelica 86 Pa 37	34550 Bessan 71 Ob 31
81160 Arthès 71 Ob 30	20200 Bastia 87 Pa 37	51490 Bétheniville 58 Lb 32
47480 Artigues 70 Oa 28	56150 Baud 56 Mb 24	51450 Bétheny 57 Lb 32
64170 Artix 70 Ob 27	49150 Baugé 56 Mb 27	62400 Béthune 45 La 30
05140 Aspres-sur-Buëch 72 Oa 33	25110 Baume-les-Dames 58 Mb 34	54620 Beuveille 58 Lb 33
13400 Aubagne 72 Ob 33	59570 Bavay 45 La 31	34500 Béziers 71 Ob 31
07200 Aubenas 71 Oa 32	14400 Bayeux 44 Lb 27	64200 Biarritz 69 Ob 26
14700 Aubigny 56 Ma 27	54290 Bayon 58 Ma 34	41240 Binas 58 Mb 29
18700 Aubigny-sur-Nère 57 Mb 30	64000 Bayonne 70 Ob 26	40600 Biscarrosse 70 Oa 26
12470 Aubrac 71 Oa 30	33430 Bazas 70 Oa 27	67240 Bischwiller 58 Ma 35
23200 Aubusson 57 Nb 30	45480 Bazoches-les-Gallérandes	57230 Bitche 58 Lb 35
32000 Auch 70 Ob 28	57 Ma 30	44130 Blain 56 Mb 26
45300 Audeville 44 Lb 26	61530 Bazoches-sur-Hoëne	54450 Blâmont 58 Ma 34
25400 Audincourt 58 Mb 34	57 Ma 28	76340 Blangy-sur-Bresle 45 Lb 29
09800 Audressein 70 Pa 29	30300 Beaucaire 71 Ob 32	71450 Blanzy 57 Na 32
14260 Aunay-sur-Odon 44 Lb 27	39190 Beaucourt 58 Na 33	33390 Blaye 70 Nb 27
83630 Aups 72 Ob 34	45190 Beaugency 57 Mb 29	89220 Bléneau 57 Mb 30
56400 Auray 56 Mb 25	33430 Beaulac 70 Oa 27	02300 Blérancourt 45 Lb 31
31420 Aurignac 70 Ob 28	86490 Beaumont/Châtellerault	37150 Bléré 57 Mb 28
15000 Aurillac 71 Oa 30	56 Na 28	43450 Blesle 71 Nb 31
31190 Auterive 70 Ob 29	63110 Beaumont/Clermont-Ferrand	18350 Blet 57 Na 30
91410 Authon-la-Plaine 57 Ma 29	71 Nb 31	39140 Bletterans 58 Na 33
71400 Autun 57 Na 32	54470 Beaumont/Pont-à-Mousson	21360 Bligny-sur-Ouche 58 Mb 32
82340 Auvillar 70 Oa 28	58 Ma 33	41000 Blois 57 Mb 29
89000 Auxerre 57 Mb 31	82500 Beaumont-de-Lomagne	20136 Bocognano 87 Pa 37
21130 Auxonne 58 Mb 33	70 Ob 28	42130 Boën 71 Nb 32
23700 Auzances 57 Na 30	24440 Beaumont-du Périgord	76210 Bolbec 45 Lb 28
89200 Avallon 57 Mb 31	70 Oa 28	84500 Bollène 71 Oa 32
59440 Avesnes-sur-Helpe	77890 Beaumont-du-Gâtinais	52310 Bologne 58 Ma 33
46 La 31	57 Ma 30	20169 Bonifacio 87 Pb 37
84000 Avignon 71 Ob 32	27170 Beaumont-le-Roger 57 Lb 28	23200 Bonnat 57 Na 29
18520 Avord 57 Mb 30	72170 Beaumont-sur-Sarthe	72110 Bonnétable 56 Ma 28
25690 Avoudrey 58 Mb 34	56 Ma 28	28800 Bonneval 57 Ma 29
50300 Avranches 56 Ma 26	51360 Beaumont-sur-Vesle	74130 Bonneville 72 Na 34
09110 Ax-les-Thermes 70 Pa 29	58 Lb 32	33000 Bordeaux 70 Oa 27
11140 Axat 71 Pa 30	21200 Beaune 58 Mb 33	20290 Borgo 87 Pa 37
55150 Azannes-et-Soumazannes	49600 Beaupréau 56 Mb 27	19110 Bort-les-Orgues 71 Nb 30
58 Lb 33	26310 Beaurières 72 Oa 33	21520 Boudreville 58 Mb 32

57570 Boulay-Moselle 58 Lb 34
66130 Bouleternère 71 Pa 30
31350 Boulogne-sur-Gesse
70 Ob 28
62200 Boulogne-sur-Mer 45 La 29
03160 Bourbon-l`Archambault
57 Na 31
71140 Bourbon-Lancy 57 Na 31
86410 Bouresse 56 Na 28
26300 Bourg-de-Péage 71 Nb 33
01000 Bourg-en-Bresse 72 Na 33
02160 Bourg-et-Comin 57 Lb 31
07700 Bourg-Saint Andéol
71 Oa 32
23400 Bourganeuf 57 Nb 29
18000 Bourges 57 Na 30
44580 Bourgneuf-en-Retz 56 Mb 26
38300 Bourgoin-Jallieu 72 Nb 33
27500 Bourneville 45 Lb 28
23600 Boussac 57 Na 30
67330 Bouxwiller 58 Ma 35
51400 Bouy 58 Lb 32
12340 Bozouls 71 Oa 30
24310 Brantôme 70 Nb 28
81260 Brassac 71 Ob 30
63570 Brassac-les-Mines 71 Nb 31
77480 Bray-sur-Seine 57 Ma 31
50290 Bréhal 44 Ma 26
02210 Breny 57 Lb 31
79300 Bressuire 56 Na 27
29200 Brest 43 Ma 23
46130 Bretenoux 71 Oa 29
60120 Breteuil 45 Lb 30
27160 Breteuil 57 Ma 28
91220 Brétigny-sur-Orge 57 Ma 30
28270 Brezolles 57 Ma 29
05100 Briançon 72 Oa 34
45250 Briare 57 Mb 30
77170 Brie-Comte-Robert 57 Ma 30
10500 Brienne-le-Château
58 Ma 32
54150 Briey 58 Lb 33
83170 Brignoles 72 Ob 34
27800 Brionne 45 Lb 28
43100 Brioude 71 Nb 31
79170 Brioux-sur-Boutonne
56 Na 27
61220 Briouze 56 Ma 27
19100 Brive-la-Gaillarde 71 Nb 29
27270 Broglie 57 Lb 28
28160 Brou 58 Ma 29
62700 Bruay-la-Buissière 45 La 30
91800 Brunoy 57 Ma 30
88600 Bruyères 58 Ma 34
71390 Buxy 57 Na 32
36500 Buzançais 57 Na 29
08240 Buzancy 58 Lb 32
14390 Cabourg 44 Lb 27
84160 Cadenet 71 Ob 33
14000 Caen 44 Lb 27
06800 Cagnes-sur-Mer 72 Ob 35
46000 Cahors 70 Oa 29
62100 Calais 45 La 29
22160 Callac 55 Ma 24
20260 Calvi 86 Pa 36
64250 Cambo-les-Bains 70 Ob 26

POSTALI · ÍNDICE CON CÓDIGOS POSTALES · INDICE DE LUGARES COM CÓDIGOS POSTAIS ·
MÍST S PSČ · ZOZNAM OBCÍ S PSČ · INDEKS MIEJSCOWOŚCI Z KOD POCZTOWY

136

Cambrai   (F)   Domrémy-la-Pucelle   F

59400 Cambrai 45 La 31
24140 Campsegret 70 Oa 28
80670 Canaples 45 La 30
47290 Cancon 70 Oa 28
49440 Candé 56 Mb 26
37300 Candes-Saint Martin
    56 Mb 28
06400 Cannes 72 Ob 35
76450 Cany-Barville 45 Lb 28
33970 Cap Ferret 70 Oa 26
40130 Capbreton 70 Ob 26
33840 Captieux 70 Oa 27
31390 Carbonne 70 Ob 29
11000 Carcassonne 71 Ob 30
50500 Carentan 44 Lb 26
20130 Cargèse 86 Pa 36
29270 Carhaix-Plouguer 55 Ma 24
08110 Carignan 58 Lb 33
81400 Carmaux 71 Oa 30
56340 Carnac 55 Mb 24
84200 Carpentras 71 Oa 33
61320 Carrouges 56 Ma 27
59670 Cassel 45 La 30
31320 Castanet-Tolosan 70 Ob 29
47700 Casteljaloux 70 Oa 28
04120 Castellane 72 Ob 34
33480 Castelnau-de-Médoc
    70 Nb 27
11400 Castelnaudary 70 Ob 29
82100 Castelsarrasin 70 Oa 29
40260 Castets 70 Ob 26
33350 Castillon-la-Bataille
    70 Oa 27
47330 Castillonnes 70 Oa 28
81100 Castres 71 Ob 30
34160 Castries 71 Ob 31
59540 Caudry 45 La 31
22350 Caulnes 56 Ma 25
82300 Caussade 70 Oa 29
84300 Cavaillon 71 Ob 33
32150 Cazaubon 70 Oa 27
45620 Cerdon 57 Mb 30
95000 Cergy 57 Lb 30
03350 Cérilly 57 Na 30
89320 Cerisiers 57 Ma 31
68700 Cernay 58 Mb 35
33610 Cestas 70 Oa 27
89800 Chablis 57 Mb 31
25300 Chaffois 58 Na 34
71150 Chagny 58 Na 32
61500 Chailloué 56 Ma 28
11230 Chalabre 70 Pa 30
16210 Chalais 70 Nb 28
01320 Chalamont 72 Nb 33
45120 Châlette-sur-Loing 57 Ma 30
85300 Challans 56 Na 26
73190 Challes-les-Eaux 72 Nb 33
71100 Chalon-sur-Saône 58 Na 32
51000 Châlons-en-Champagne
    58 Ma 32
87230 Châlus 70 Nb 28
15200 Chalvignac 71 Nb 30
19370 Chamberet 71 Nb 29
73000 Chambéry 72 Nb 33
37310 Chambourg-sur-Indre
    57 Mb 28

37170 Chambray-lès-Tours
    56 Mb 28
74400 Chamonix-Mont-Blanc
    72 Nb 34
16350 Champagne-Mouton
    56 Nb 28
39300 Champagnole 58 Na 33
63320 Champeix 71 Nb 31
54240 Champigneulles 58 Ma 34
71600 Champlitte 58 Mb 33
48230 Chanac 71 Oa 31
38150 Chanas 71 Nb 32
24650 Chancelade 70 Nb 28
42310 Changy 57 Na 31
60500 Chantilly 57 Lb 30
85110 Chantonnay 56 Na 26
10210 Chaource 57 Ma 32
08130 Charbogne 58 Lb 32
08000 Charleville-Mézières
    46 La 32
89120 Charny 57 Mb 31
55100 Charny-sur-Meuse 58 Lb 33
71120 Charolles 57 Na 32
18290 Chârost 57 Na 30
28000 Chartres 57 Ma 29
35131 Chartres-de-Bretagne
    56 Ma 26
16260 Chasseneuil-sur-Bonnieure
    56 Nb 28
72540 Chassillé 56 Ma 27
04160 Château-Arnoux 72 Oa 34
58120 Château-Chinon 57 Na 31
72500 Château-du-Loir 56 Mb 28
53200 Château-Gontier 56 Mb 27
37110 Château-Renault 56 Mb 28
57170 Château-Salins 58 Ma 34
02400 Château-Thierry 57 Lb 31
44110 Châteaubriant 56 Mb 26
28200 Châteaudun 57 Ma 29
29150 Châteaulin 55 Ma 23
18370 Châteaumeillant 57 Na 30
28170 Châteauneuf-en-Thymerais
    57 Ma 29
63390 Châteauneuf-les-Bains
    57 Na 30
18190 Châteauneuf-sur-Cher
    57 Na 30
45110 Châteauneuf-sur-Loire
    57 Mb 30
49330 Châteauneuf-sur-Sarthe
    56 Mb 27
04270 Châteauredon 72 Oa 34
36000 Châteauroux 57 Na 29
52120 Châteauvillain 58 Ma 32
86100 Châtellerault 56 Na 28
88170 Châtenois 58 Ma 33
45230 Châtillon-Coligny 57 Mb 30
01400 Châtillon-sur-Chalaronne
    72 Na 32
36700 Châtillon-sur-Indre 57 Na 29
21400 Châtillon-sur-Seine
    58 Mb 32
15110 Chaudes-Aigues 71 Oa 30
39230 Chaumergy 58 Na 33
52000 Chaumont 58 Ma 33
60240 Chaumont-en-Vexin 57 Lb 29

49120 Chemillé 56 Mb 27
79120 Chenay 56 Na 27
23270 Chénérailles 57 Na 30
50100 Cherbourg-Octeville
    44 Lb 26
03230 Chevagnes 57 Na 31
49300 Cholet 56 Mb 27
05230 Chorges 72 Oa 34
37130 Cinq-Mars-la-Pile 56 Mb 28
86400 Civray 56 Na 28
92140 Clamart 57 Ma 30
58500 Clamecy 57 Mb 31
77410 Claye-Souilly 57 Ma 30
14570 Clécy 56 Ma 27
55240 Clefmont 58 Ma 33
71520 Clermain 57 Na 32
60600 Clermont 45 Lb 30
72200 Clermont-Créans 56 Mb 27
55120 Clermont-en-Argonne
    58 Lb 33
63000 Clermont-Ferrand 71 Nb 31
34800 Clermont-l'Hérault 71 Ob 31
25340 Clerval 58 Mb 34
36700 Clion 57 Na 29
44190 Clisson 56 Mb 26
28220 Cloyes-sur-le-Loir 57 Mb 29
71250 Cluny 57 Na 32
74300 Cluses 72 Na 34
16100 Cognac 56 Nb 27
68000 Colmar 58 Ma 35
04370 Colmars 72 Oa 34
54170 Colombey-les-Belles
    58 Ma 33
52330 Colombey-les-Deux-Églises
    58 Ma 32
31770 Colomiers 70 Ob 29
70120 Combeaufontaine 58 Mb 33
19250 Combressol 71 Nb 30
03600 Commentry 57 Na 30
55200 Commercy 58 Ma 33
60200 Compiègne 45 Lb 30
83840 Comps-sur-Artuby 72 Ob 34
29900 Concarneau 55 Mb 24
27190 Conches-en-Ouche
    57 Ma 28
15190 Condat 71 Nb 30
14110 Condé-sur-Noireau
    56 Ma 27
32100 Condom 70 Ob 28
16500 Confolens 56 Na 28
    Contres 57 Mb 29
88140 Contrexéville 58 Ma 33
51320 Coole 58 Ma 32
91100 Corbeil-Essonnes 57 Ma 30
02820 Corbeny 57 Lb 31
58800 Corbigny 57 Mb 31
81170 Cordes-sur-Ciel 71 Oa 29
71540 Cordesse 57 Mb 32
22320 Corlay 56 Ma 24
28140 Cormainville 57 Ma 29
51350 Cormontreuil 57 Lb 32
01560 Cormoz 58 Na 33
12580 Cornus 71 Ob 31
38970 Corps 72 Oa 33
70500 Corre 58 Mb 33
20250 Corte 87 Pa 37

58200 Cosne-Cours-sur-Loire
    57 Mb 30
53230 Cossé-le-Vivien 56 Mb 27
02840 Coucy-lès-Eppes 45 Lb 31
44220 Couëron 56 Mb 26
86700 Couhé 56 Na 28
11190 Couiza 71 Pa 30
89480 Coulanges-sur-Yonne
    57 Mb 31
03320 Couleuvre 57 Na 30
21400 Coulmier-le-Sec 57 Mb 32
77120 Coulommiers 57 Ma 31
41700 Cour-Cheverny 57 Mb 29
21520 Courban 58 Mb 32
03370 Courçais 57 Na 30
73120 Courchevel 72 Nb 34
63800 Cournon-d'Auvergne
    71 Nb 31
69470 Cours-la-Ville 71 Na 32
77560 Courtacon 57 Ma 31
28290 Courtalain 57 Ma 29
45320 Courtenay 57 Ma 31
10210 Coussegrey 57 Mb 32
50200 Coutances 44 Lb 26
33230 Coutras 70 Nb 27
17120 Cozes 56 Nb 27
53400 Craon 56 Mb 27
60100 Creil 57 Lb 30
60800 Crépy-en-Valois 57 Lb 30
30260 Crespian 71 Ob 32
03240 Cressanges 57 Na 31
39270 Cressia 58 Na 33
26400 Crest 71 Oa 33
29160 Crozon 55 Ma 23
83390 Cuers 72 Ob 34
31270 Cugnaux 70 Ob 29
60400 Cuts 45 Lb 31
77190 Dammarie-les-Lys 57 Ma 30
55150 Damvillers 58 Lb 33
86220 Dangé-Saint Romain
    56 Na 28
88260 Darney 58 Ma 34
40100 Dax 70 Ob 26
12300 Decazeville 71 Oa 30
58300 Decize 57 Na 31
57590 Delme 58 Ma 34
80110 Démuin 45 La 30
59220 Denain 45 La 31
44590 Derval 56 Mb 26
26150 Die 72 Oa 33
76200 Dieppe 45 Lb 29
54380 Dieulouard 58 Ma 34
57260 Dieuze 58 Ma 34
04000 Digne-les-Bains 72 Oa 34
71160 Digoin 57 Na 31
21000 Dijon 58 Mb 33
22100 Dinan 56 Ma 25
35800 Dinard 56 Ma 25
88460 Docelles 58 Ma 34
35120 Dol-de-Bretagne 56 Ma 26
39100 Dole 58 Mb 33
61700 Domfront 56 Ma 27
03290 Dompierre-sur-Besbre
    57 Na 31
88630 Domrémy-la-Pucelle
    58 Ma 33

F

Donzenac　　　　　　　　　**F**　　　　　　　　　**la Ferté-Macé**

19270 Donzenac 71 Nb 29	51230 Fère-Champenoise 57 Ma 31	46300 Gourdon 70 Oa 29
58220 Donzy 57 Mb 31	02130 Fère-en-Tardenois 57 Lb 31	56110 Gourin 55 Ma 24
51700 Dormans 57 Lb 31	68480 Ferrette 58 Mb 35	76220 Gournay-en-Bray 45 Lb 29
58390 Dornes 57 Na 31	45210 Ferrières 57 Ma 30	95190 Goussainville 57 Lb 30
59500 Douai 45 La 31	42110 Feurs 71 Nb 32	23230 Gouzon 57 Na 30
29100 Douarnenez 55 Ma 23	20114 Figari 86 Pb 37	18310 Graçay 57 Mb 29
76560 Doudeville 45 Lb 28	46110 Figeac 71 Oa 30	46500 Gramat 71 Oa 30
49700 Doué-la-Fontaine 56 Mb 27	51170 Fismes 57 Lb 31	59760 Grande-Synthe 45 Kb 30
80600 Doullens 45 La 30	23260 Flayat 71 Nb 30	60210 Grandvilliers 45 Lb 29
91410 Dourdan 57 Ma 30	61100 Flers 56 Ma 27	50400 Granville 44 Ma 26
74140 Douvaine 72 Na 34	32500 Fleurance 70 Ob 28	06130 Grasse 72 Ob 34
83300 Draguignan 72 Ob 34	45400 Fleury-les-Aubrais 57 Mb 29	81300 Graulhet 71 Ob 29
28100 Dreux 57 Ma 29	55250 Fleury-sur-Aire 58 Lb 33	27930 Gravigny 57 Lb 29
50220 Ducey 56 Ma 26	48400 Florac 71 Oa 31	70100 Gray 58 Mb 33
18130 Dun-sur-Auron 57 Na 30	09000 Foix 70 Pa 29	31330 Grenade 70 Ob 29
56110 Dun-sur-Meuse 58 Lb 33	20213 Folelli 87 Pa 37	40270 Grenade-sur-l'Adour
59140 Dunkerque 45 Kb 30	77300 Fontainebleau 57 Ma 30	70 Ob 27
11360 Durban-Corbières 71 Pa 30	85200 Fontenay-le-Comte 56 Na 27	38000 Grenoble 72 Nb 33
49430 Durtal 56 Mb 27	57600 Forbach 58 Lb 34	04800 Gréoux-les-Bains 72 Ob 33
32800 Eauze 70 Ob 28	04300 Forcalquier 72 Ob 33	53290 Grez-en-Bouère 56 Mb 27
79410 Echiré 56 Na 27	76440 Forges-les-Eaux 45 Lb 29	91350 Grigny 57 Ma 30
72220 Écommoy 56 Mb 28	13270 Fos-sur-Mer 71 Ob 32	88170 Groix 55 Mb 24
19300 Égletons 71 Nb 30	29170 Fouesnant 55 Mb 23	68500 Guebwiller 58 Mb 35
76500 Elbeuf 45 Lb 29	35300 Fougères 56 Ma 26	56160 Guémené-sur-Scorff
56250 Elven 56 Mb 25	70220 Fougerolles 58 Mb 34	55 Ma 24
68190 Ensisheim 58 Mb 35	58250 Fours 57 Na 31	57310 Guénange 58 Lb 34
68190 Ensisheim 58 Mb 35	69340 Francheville 71 Nb 32	44350 Guérande 56 Mb 25
58410 Entrains-sur-Nohain	25560 Frasne 58 Na 34	23000 Guéret 57 Na 29
57 Mb 31	52360 Frécourt 58 Mb 33	58130 Guéripy 57 Mb 31
04320 Entrevaux 72 Ob 34	83600 Fréjus 72 Ob 34	71130 Gueugnon 57 Na 32
51200 Épernay 57 Lb 31	62270 Frévent 45 La 30	35580 Guichen 56 Mb 26
67680 Epfig 58 Ma 35	60480 Froissy 45 Lb 30	56520 Guidel 55 Mb 24
88000 Épinal 58 Ma 34	31440 Fronsac 70 Pa 28	06470 Guillaumes 72 Oa 34
21460 Époisses 57 Mb 32	34110 Frontignan 71 Ob 31	05600 Guillestre 72 Oa 34
51490 Epoye 58 Lb 32	62310 Fruges 45 La 30	22200 Guingamp 44 Ma 24
41360 Epuisay 57 Mb 28	08170 Fumay 46 Lb 32	60640 Guiscard 45 Lb 31
29500 Ergué-Gabéric 55 Ma 24	47500 Fumel 70 Oa 28	02120 Guise 45 Lb 31
53500 Ernée 56 Ma 27	64440 Gabas 70 Pa 27	70700 Gy 58 Mb 33
43170 Esplantas 71 Oa 31	61230 Gacé 56 Ma 28	10250 Gyé-sur-Seine 57 Ma 32
10360 Essoyes 58 Ma 32	81600 Gaillac 71 Ob 29	40700 Hagetmau 70 Ob 27
66310 Estagel 71 Pa 30	27600 Gaillon 57 Lb 29	67500 Haguenau 58 Ma 35
12190 Estaing 71 Oa 30	20245 Galéria 86 Pa 36	80400 Ham 45 Lb 31
51310 Esternay 57 Ma 31	64290 Gan 70 Ob 27	57580 Han-sur-Nied 58 Ma 34
60190 Estrées-Saint Denis	34190 Ganges 71 Ob 31	76700 Harfleur 45 Lb 28
45 Lb 30	03800 Gannat 57 Na 31	02210 Hartennes-et-Taux 57 Lb 31
55400 Étain 58 Lb 33	05000 Gap 72 Oa 34	24390 Hautefort 70 Nb 29
91150 Étampes 57 Ma 30	13120 Gardanne 72 Ob 33	59330 Hautmont 45 La 31
71190 Étang-sur-Arroux 57 Na 32	40420 Garein 70 Oa 27	57700 Hayange 58 Lb 34
62630 Étaples 45 La 29	65120 Gavarnie 70 Pa 27	59190 Hazebrouck 45 La 30
14420 Étretat 57 Lb 28	88400 Gérardmer 58 Ma 34	57830 Héming 58 Ma 34
52410 Eurville-Bienville 58 Ma 33	54830 Gerbéviller 58 Ma 34	62110 Hénin-Beaumont 45 La 30
74500 Évian-les-Bains 58 Na 34	01170 Gex 58 Na 34	56700 Hennebont 55 Mb 24
27000 Évreux 57 Lb 29	20240 Ghisonaccia 87 Pa 37	63470 Herment 71 Nb 30
53600 Évron 56 Ma 27	45500 Gien 57 Mb 30	14200 Hérouville-Saint Clair
91000 Évry 57 Ma 30	32200 Gimont 70 Ob 28	44 Lb 27
13430 Eyguières 71 Ob 33	55200 Gironville-sous-les-Côtes	62140 Hesdin 45 La 30
24500 Eymet 70 Oa 28	58 Ma 33	02500 Hirson 46 Lb 32
87120 Eymoutiers 71 Nb 29	27140 Gisors 45 Lb 29	78550 Houdan 57 Ma 29
11200 Fabrezan 71 Ob 30	08600 Givet 46 La 32	55130 Houdelaincourt 58 Ma 33
14700 Falaise 56 Ma 27	69700 Givors 71 Nb 32	47420 Houeillès 70 Oa 28
57290 Fameck 58 Lb 34	51330 Givry-en-Argonne 58 Ma 32	29690 Huelgoat 55 Ma 24
57380 Faulquemont 58 Lb 34	76110 Goderville 45 Lb 28	83400 Hyères 72 Ob 34
83440 Fayence 72 Ob 34	08190 Gomont 58 Lb 32	84800 l'Isle-sur-la-Sorgue
76400 Fécamp 45 Lb 28	83590 Gonfaron 72 Ob 34	71 Ob 33
23500 Felletin 57 Nb 30	29850 Gouesnou 43 Ma 23	33720 Illats 70 Oa 27
57930 Fénétrange 58 Ma 35		28120 Illiers-Combray 57 Ma 29

86220 Ingrandes 56 Na 28
45620 Isdes 57 Mb 30
14230 Isigny-sur-Mer 44 Lb 26
63500 Issoire 71 Nb 31
36100 Issoudun 57 Na 29
13800 Istres 71 Ob 32
35150 Janzé 56 Mb 26
16200 Jarnac 56 Nb 27
54800 Jarny 58 Lb 33
89300 Joigny 57 Mb 31
52300 Joinville 58 Ma 33
14170 Jort 56 Ma 27
56120 Josselin 56 Mb 25
39100 Jouhe 58 Mb 33
07260 Joyeuse 71 Oa 32
49160 Jumelles 56 Mb 27
08310 Juniville 58 Lb 32
70500 Jussey 58 Mb 33
74350 Jussy 72 Na 34
77650 Jutigny 57 Ma 31
52330 Juzennecourt 58 Ma 32
68240 Kaysersberg 58 Ma 35
79240 l'Absie 56 Na 27
79240 l'Aigle 57 Ma 28
85460 l'Aiguillon-sur-Mer 56 Na 26
06440 l'Escarène 72 Ob 35
20220 l'Île-Rousse 86 Pa 36
25250 l'Isle-sur-le-Doubs
58 Mb 34
31240 l'Union 70 Ob 29
53240 la Baconnière 56 Ma 27
85550 la Barre-de-Monts 56 Na 25
44500 la Baule-Escoublac
56 Mb 25
28330 la Bazoche-Gouet 57 Ma 28
38520 la Bérarde 72 Oa 34
63150 la Bourboule 71 Nb 30
45230 la Bussière 58 Mb 31
48500 la Canourgue 71 Oa 31
02260 la Capelle 45 Lb 31
12330 la Cavalerie 71 Oa 31
43160 la Chaise-Dieu 71 Nb 31
18380 la Chapelle-d'Angillon
57 Mb 30
10600 la Chapelle-Saint Luc
57 Ma 32
44240 la Chapelle-sur-Erdre
56 Mb 26
41330 la Chapelle-Vendômoise
57 Mb 29
41270 la Chapelle-Vicomtesse
57 Mb 29
58400 la Charité-sur-Loire
57 Mb 31
36400 la Châtre 57 Na 29
13600 la Ciotat 72 Ob 33
74220 la Clusaz 72 Nb 34
38260 la Côte-Saint André
72 Nb 33
23100 la Courtine 71 Nb 30
24330 la Douze 70 Nb 28
61450 la Ferrière-aux-Etangs
56 Ma 27
72400 la Ferté-Bernard 57 Ma 28
77320 la Ferté-Gaucher 57 Ma 31
61600 la Ferté-Macé 56 Ma 27

POSTALI · ÍNDICE CON CÓDIGOS POSTALES · INDICE DE LUGARES COM CÓDIGOS POSTAIS ·
MÍST S PSČ · ZOZNAM OBCÍ S PSČ · INDEKS MIEJSCOWOŚCI Z KOD POCZTOWY

138

F

02460 la Ferté-Milon 57 Lb 31
45240 la Ferté-Saint Aubin
          57 Mb 29
41220 la Ferté-Saint Cyr 57 Mb 29
77260 la Ferté-sous-Jouarre
          57 Ma 31
76220 la Feuillie 45 Lb 29
72220 la Flèche 56 Mb 27
79380 la Forêt-sur-Sèvre 56 Na 27
12270 la Fouillade 71 Oa 30
56200 la Gacilly 56 Mb 25
30110 la Grand-Combe 71 Oa 32
34280 la Grande-Motte 71 Ob 32
50250 la Haye-du-Puits 44 Lb 26
72130 la Hutte 56 Ma 28
28240 la Loupe 57 Ma 29
38350 la Mure 72 Oa 33
27150 la Neuve-Grange 45 Lb 29
42310 la Pacaudière 57 Na 31
33190 la Réole 70 Oa 27
56130 la Roche-Bernard 56 Mb 25
24490 la Roche-Chalais 70 Nb 28
74800 la Roche-sur-Foron 72 Na 34
85000 la Roche-sur-Yon 56 Na 26
16110 la Rochefoucauld 56 Nb 28
17000 la Rochelle 56 Na 26
34330 la Salvetat-sur-Agout
          71 Ob 30
05110 la Saulce 72 Oa 33
83500 la Seyne-sur-Mer 72 Ob 33
23300 la Souterraine 57 Na 29
33260 la Teste-de-Buch 70 Oa 26
38110 la Tour-du-Pin 72 Nb 33
85360 la Tranche-sur-Mer 56 Na 26
17390 la Tremblade 56 Nb 26
86290 la Trimouille 56 Na 29
61190 la Ventrouze 57 Ma 28
51520 la Veuve 58 Lb 32
40210 Labouheyre 70 Oa 27
40420 Labrit 70 Oa 27
62140 Labroye 45 La 29
33680 Lacanau-Océan 70 Oa 26
81230 Lacaune 71 Ob 30
79200 Lageon 56 Na 27
11220 Lagrasse 71 Ob 30
82250 Laguépie 71 Oa 29
12210 Laguiole 71 Oa 30
40110 Laharie 70 Oa 26
21330 Laignes 57 Mb 32
55800 Laimont 58 Ma 33
12310 Laissac 71 Oa 30
24150 Lalinde 70 Oa 28
38930 Lalley 72 Oa 33
88320 Lamarche 58 Ma 33
21440 Lamargelle 58 Mb 32
07270 Lamastre 71 Oa 32
22400 Lamballe 58 Ma 25
41600 Lamotte-Beuvron 57 Mb 30
29242 Lampaul 43 Ma 22
38510 Lancin 71 Nb 33
29800 Landerneau 43 Ma 23
29400 Landivisiau 43 Ma 23
48300 Langogne 71 Oa 31
33210 Langon 70 Oa 27
52200 Langres 58 Mb 33
29620 Lanmeur 43 Ma 24

65300 Lannemezan 70 Ob 28
22300 Lannion 44 Ma 24
24270 Lanouaille 70 Nb 29
12350 Lanuéjouls 71 Oa 30
22290 Lanvollon 44 Ma 24
02000 Laon 45 Lb 31
03120 Lapalisse 57 Na 31
05300 Laragne-Montéglin 72 Oa 33
07110 Largentière 71 Oa 32
64560 Larrau 70 Ob 27
64440 Laruns 70 Pa 27
53110 Lassay-les-Châteaux
          56 Ma 27
34970 Lattes 71 Ob 31
82110 Lauzerte 70 Oa 29
53000 Laval 56 Ma 27
47230 Lavardac 70 Oa 28
81500 Lavaur 70 Ob 29
09300 Lavelanet 70 Pa 29
47390 Layrac 70 Oa 28
66420 le Barcarès 71 Pa 31
33114 le Barp 70 Oa 27
36300 le Blanc 56 Na 29
66160 le Boulou 71 Pa 30
38520 le Bourg-d'Oisans 72 Nb 34
24260 le Bugue 70 Oa 28
48100 le Buisson 71 Oa 31
06110 le Cannet 72 Ob 35
12520 le Caylar 71 Ob 31
42500 le Chambon-Feugerolles
          71 Nb 32
18170 le Châtelet 57 Na 30
08390 le Chesne 58 Lb 32
07160 le Cheylard 71 Oa 32
29217 le Conquet 43 Ma 23
71200 le Creusot 57 Na 32
03130 le Donjon 57 Na 31
87210 le Dorat 56 Na 29
29590 le Faou 55 Ma 23
56320 le Faouët 55 Ma 24
17590 le Gillieux 56 Na 26
72150 le Grand-Lucé 56 Mb 28
30240 le Grau-du-Roi 71 Ob 32
76600 le Havre 44 Lb 28
02120 le Hérie-la-Viéville 45 Lb 31
83980 le Lavandou 72 Ob 34
49220 le Lion-d'Angers 56 Mb 27
83340 le Luc 72 Ob 34
72000 le Mans 56 Ma 28
61170 le Mêle-sur-Sarthe 56 Ma 28
88270 le Ménil 58 Ma 34
51190 le Mesnil-sur-Oger 57 Ma 32
50170 le Mont-Saint Michel
          56 Ma 26
40410 le Muret 70 Oa 27
27110 le Neubourg 45 Lb 28
02170 le Nouvion-en-Thiérache
          45 La 31
56360 le Palais 55 Mb 24
62480 le Portel 45 La 29
43000 le Puy-en-Velay 71 Nb 31
59530 le Quesnoy 45 La 31
25210 le Russey 58 Mb 34
88160 le Thillot 58 Mb 34
62520 le Touquet-Paris-Plage
          45 La 29

38660 le Touvet 72 Nb 33
76470 Le Tréport 45 La 29
83143 le Val 72 Ob 34
15200 le Vigan 71 Ob 31
32700 Lectoure 70 Ob 28
33950 Lège-Cap-Ferret 70 Oa 26
86140 Lencloître 56 Na 28
62300 Lens 45 La 30
18220 les Aix-d'Angillon 57 Mb 30
27700 les Andelys 45 Lb 29
83460 les Arcs 72 Ob 34
58340 les Brunettes 57 Na 31
85148 les Essarts 56 Na 26
24620 les Eyzies-de-Tayac-Sireuil
          70 Oa 29
85500 les Herbiers 56 Na 26
73440 les Menuires 72 Nb 34
78130 les Mureaux 57 Ma 30
50340 les Pieux 44 Lb 26
49130 les Ponts-de-Cé 56 Mb 27
10340 les Riceys 57 Mb 32
39220 les Rousses 58 Na 34
85100 les Sables-d'Olonne
          56 Na 26
07140 les Vans 71 Oa 32
10500 Lesmont 58 Ma 32
29260 Lesneven 43 Ma 23
33340 Lesparre-Médoc 70 Nb 27
50430 Lessay 44 Lb 26
11370 Leucate 71 Pa 31
21290 Leuglay 58 Mb 32
25270 Levier 58 Na 34
36110 Levroux 57 Na 29
11200 Lézignan-Corbières
          71 Ob 30
63190 Lezoux 71 Nb 31
33500 Libourne 70 Oa 27
14170 Lieurey 45 Lb 28
62800 Liévin 45 La 30
88350 Liffol-le-Grand 58 Ma 33
35340 Liffré 56 Ma 26
18160 Lignières 57 Na 30
55500 Ligny-en-Barrois 58 Ma 33
59000 Lille 45 La 31
76170 Lillebonne 45 Lb 28
62190 Lillers 45 La 30
87000 Limoges 56 Nb 29
46240 Limogne-en-Quercy
          71 Oa 29
11300 Limoux 71 Ob 30
14100 Lisieux 44 Lb 28
46320 Livernon 71 Oa 29
26250 Livron-sur-Drôme 71 Oa 32
37600 Loches 57 Mb 29
56360 Locmaria 55 Mb 24
56500 Locmine 56 Mb 25
34700 Lodève 70 Ob 31
59160 Lomme 45 La 30
52250 Longeau 58 Mb 33
54260 Longuyon 58 Lb 33
21600 Longvic 58 Mb 33
54400 Longwy 58 Lb 33
39000 Lons-le-Saunier 58 Na 33
83510 Lorgues 72 Ob 34
56100 Lorient 55 Mb 24
26270 Loriol-sur-Drôme 71 Oa 32

58140 Lormes 57 Mb 31
22600 Loudéac 56 Ma 25
86200 Loudun 56 Mb 28
71500 Louhans 58 Na 33
65100 Lourdes 70 Ob 27
27400 Louviers 45 Lb 29
35420 Louvigné-du-Désert
          56 Ma 26
51150 Louvois 57 Lb 32
26310 Luc-in-Diois 72 Oa 33
28110 Luce 57 Ma 29
85400 Luçon 56 Na 26
28480 Luigny 57 Ma 29
62380 Lumbres 45 La 30
34400 Lunel 71 Ob 32
54300 Lunéville 58 Ma 34
70200 Lure 58 Mb 34
36220 Lureuil 57 Na 29
30580 Lussan 71 Oa 32
70300 Luxeuil-les-Bains 58 Mb 34
58170 Luzy 57 Na 31
69000 Lyon 71 Nb 32
44270 Machecoul 56 Na 26
21320 Mâcon 57 Na 32
40140 Magescq 70 Ob 26
03260 Magnat 54 Na 31
95420 Magny-en-Vexin 57 Lb 29
25120 Maîche 58 Mb 34
10230 Mailly-le-Camp 57 Ma 32
08220 Mainbressy 46 Lb 32
28300 Mainvilliers 57 Ma 29
91720 Maisse 57 Ma 30
45330 Malesherbes 57 Ma 30
71140 Maltat 57 Na 31
72600 Mamers 56 Ma 28
32370 Manciet 70 Ob 28
06210 Mandelieu-la-Napoule
          72 Ob 34
55160 Manheulles 58 Lb 33
04100 Manosque 72 Ob 33
16230 Mansle 56 Nb 28
78200 Mantes-la-Jolie 57 Lb 29
78200 Mantes-la-Ville 57 Ma 29
17230 Marans 56 Na 27
28200 Marboué 57 Ma 29
71110 Marcigny 57 Na 32
10290 Marcilly-le-Hayer 57 Ma 31
17320 Marennes 56 Nb 26
24340 Mareuil 70 Nb 28
60890 Mareuil-sur-Ourcq 57 Lb 31
08370 Margut 58 Lb 33
13700 Marignane 71 Ob 33
95640 Marines 57 Lb 29
02250 Marle 45 Lb 31
57155 Marly 58 Lb 34
71710 Marmagne 57 Na 32
47200 Marmande 70 Oa 28
13001 Marseille 71 Ob 33
60690 Marseille-en-Beauvaisis
          45 Lb 29
81150 Marssac-sur-Tarn 71 Ob 30
46600 Martel 71 Oa 29
35640 Martigné-Ferchaud 56 Mb 26
13500 Martigues 71 Ob 33
48100 Marvejols 71 Oa 31
87130 Masléon 71 Nb 29

139 INDEX WITH POST CODES · ORTSREGISTER MIT POSTLEITZAHLEN · INDICE CON CODICI
STEDREGISTER MED POSTNUMRE · PLAATSNAMENREGISTER MET POSTCODE · REJSTŘÍK

F

Massat F **Péronne**

09320 Massat 70 Pa 29	40000 Mont-de-Marsan 70 Ob 27	61400 Mortagne-au-Perche	89310 Nitry 57 Mb 31
32140 Masseube 70 Ob 28	66210 Mont-Louis 70 Pa 30	57 Ma 28	28210 Nogent-le-Roi 57 Ma 29
15500 Massiac 71 Nb 31	76130 Mont-Saint Aignan 45 Lb 29	85290 Mortagne-sur-Sèvre	28400 Nogent-le-Rotrou 57 Ma 28
22550 Matignon 56 Ma 25	39380 Mont-sous-Vaudrey 58 Na 33	56 Na 27	60180 Nogent-sur-Oise 57 Lb 30
59600 Maubeuge 46 La 31	34530 Montagnac 71 Ob 31	50140 Mortain 56 Ma 27	10400 Nogent-sur-Seine 57 Ma 31
65700 Maubourguet 70 Ob 28	85600 Montaigu 56 Na 26	25500 Morteau 58 Mb 34	42440 Noiretable 71 Nb 31
34130 Mauguio 71 Ob 32	31530 Montaigut-sur-Save	74110 Morzine 72 Na 34	85330 Noirmoutier-en-l'Ile 56 Na 25
79700 Mauléon 56 Na 27	70 Ob 29	39330 Mouchard 58 Na 33	21340 Nolay 57 Na 32
64130 Mauléon-Licharre 70 Ob 27	45200 Montargis 57 Mb 30	06250 Mougins 72 Ob 34	27320 Nonancourt 57 Ma 29
15200 Mauriac 71 Nb 30	60160 Montataire 57 Lb 30	03000 Moulins 57 Na 31	24300 Nontron 70 Nb 28
56430 Mauron 56 Ma 25	82000 Montauban 70 Oa 29	61380 Moulins-la-Marche 57 Ma 28	20217 Nonza 87 Pa 37
15600 Maurs 71 Oa 30	35360 Montauban-de-Bretagne	10800 Moussey 57 Ma 32	44390 Nort-sur-Erdre 56 Mb 26
32120 Mauvezin 70 Ob 28	56 Ma 25	40410 Moustey 70 Oa 27	37460 Nouans-les-Fontaines
79210 Mauzé-sur-le-Mignon	21500 Montbard 57 Mb 32	04360 Moustiers-Sainte Marie	57 Mb 29
56 Na 27	25200 Montbéliard 58 Mb 34	72 Ob 34	08270 Novion-Porcien 46 Lb 32
53100 Mayenne 56 Ma 27	42600 Montbrison 71 Nb 32	73600 Moûtiers 72 Nb 34	49700 Noyant-la-Plaine 56 Mb 27
81200 Mazamet 71 Ob 30	71300 Montceau-les-Mines	85440 Moutiers-les-Mauxfaits	60400 Noyon 45 Lb 30
09270 Mazères 70 Ob 29	57 Na 32	56 Na 26	44170 Nozay 56 Mb 26
77100 Meaux 57 Ma 30	77151 Montceaux-lès-Provins	08210 Mouzon 58 Lb 33	21700 Nuits-Saint Georges
74120 Mègève 72 Nb 34	57 Ma 31	57630 Moyenvic 58 Ma 34	58 Mb 32
18500 Mehun-sur-Yèvre 57 Mb 30	02340 Montcornet 46 Lb 32	68100 Mulhouse 58 Mb 35	26110 Nyons 71 Oa 33
79190 Melle 56 Na 27	46800 Montcuq 70 Oa 29	22530 Mûr-de-Bretagne 56 Ma 25	67210 Obernai 58 Ma 35
77350 Melun 57 Ma 30	80500 Montdidier 45 Lb 30	15300 Murat 71 Nb 30	70700 Oiselay-et-Grachaux
48000 Mende 71 Oa 31	50310 Montebourg 44 Lb 26	31600 Muret 70 Ob 29	58 Mb 33
06500 Menton 72 Ob 35	82700 Montech 70 Ob 29	52300 Mussey-sur-Marne 58 Ma 33	76350 Oissel 45 Lb 29
36500 Méobecq 57 Na 29	26200 Montélimar 71 Oa 32	24400 Mussidan 70 Nb 28	20232 Oletta 87 Pa 37
22230 Merdrignac 56 Ma 25	77130 Montereau-Fault-Yonne	10250 Mussy-sur-Seine 58 Mb 32	45160 Olivet 57 Mb 29
19340 Merlines 71 Nb 30	57 Ma 30	56190 Muzillac 56 Mb 25	64400 Oloron-Sainte Marie
60110 Méru 57 Lb 30	31310 Montesquieu-Volvestre	55500 Naives-Rosières 58 Ma 33	70 Ob 27
71310 Mervans 58 Na 33	70 Ob 29	18330 Nançay 57 Mb 30	40440 Ondres 70 Ob 26
53170 Meslay-du-Maine 56 Mb 27	84170 Monteux 71 Oa 32	54000 Nancy 58 Ma 34	04700 Oraison 72 Ob 33
57000 Metz 58 Lb 34	46240 Montfaucon 70 Oa 29	77370 Nangis 57 Ma 31	84100 Orange 71 Oa 32
45130 Meung-sur-Loire 57 Mb 29	88410 Monthureux-sur-Saône	92000 Nanterre 57 Ma 30	14290 Orbec 57 Lb 28
19250 Meymac 71 Nb 30	58 Ma 33	44000 Nantes 56 Mb 26	39270 Orgelet 58 Na 33
69330 Meyzieu 72 Nb 32	52220 Montier-en-Der 58 Ma 32	60440 Nanteuil-le-Haudouin	02390 Origny-Sainte Benoite
34140 Mèze 71 Ob 31	78180 Montigny-le-Bretonneux	57 Lb 30	45 Lb 31
87330 Mézières-sur-Issoire	57 Ma 30	01130 Nantua 72 Na 33	45000 Orléans 57 Mb 29
56 Na 28	52360 Montigny-le-Roi 58 Ma 33	11100 Narbonne 71 Ob 30	25290 Ornans 58 Mb 34
32170 Miélan 70 Ob 28	76290 Montivilliers 45 Lb 28	12800 Naucelle 71 Oa 30	64300 Orthez 70 Ob 27
41200 Millançay 57 Mb 29	12400 Montlaur 71 Ob 30	64800 Nay 70 Ob 27	44700 Orvault 56 Mb 26
66170 Millas 71 Pa 30	03100 Montluçon 57 Na 30	77140 Nemours 57 Ma 30	21260 Orville 58 Mb 33
12100 Millau 71 Oa 31	55600 Montmédy 58 Lb 33	47600 Nérac 70 Oa 28	64780 Ossès 70 Ob 26
40200 Mimizan 70 Oa 26	83670 Montmeyan 72 Ob 34	03310 Néris-les-Bains 57 Na 30	89560 Ouanne 57 Mb 31
69780 Mions 71 Nb 32	51210 Montmirail 57 Ma 31	18350 Nérondes 57 Na 30	41290 Oucques 57 Mb 29
13140 Miramas 71 Ob 33	86500 Montmorillon 56 Na 28	19600 Nespouls 70 Nb 29	14150 Ouistreham 44 Lb 27
17150 Mirambeau 70 Nb 27	41800 Montoire-sur-le-Loir	55800 Nettancourt 58 Ma 32	09140 Oust 70 Pa 29
32300 Mirande 70 Ob 28	57 Mb 28	68600 Neuf-Brisach 58 Ma 35	01100 Oyonnax 72 Na 33
86110 Mirebeau 56 Na 28	34000 Montpellier 71 Ob 31	88300 Neufchâteau 58 Ma 33	77330 Ozoir-la-Ferrière 57 Ma 30
21310 Mirebeau-sur-Bèze 58 Mb 33	24700 Montpon-Ménestérol	76270 Neufchâtel-en-Bray 45 Lb 29	27120 Pacy-sur-Eure 57 Lb 29
88500 Mirecourt 58 Ma 34	70 Nb 28	02190 Neufchâtel-sur-Aisne	09130 Pailhès 70 Ob 29
09500 Mirepoix 70 Ob 29	31210 Montréjeau 70 Ob 28	57 Lb 32	22500 Paimpol 44 Ma 24
77290 Mitry-Mory 57 Ma 30	62170 Montreuil 45 La 29	37360 Neuillé-Pont-Pierre 56 Mb 28	34250 Palavas-les-Flots 71 Ob 31
73500 Modane 72 Nb 34	49260 Montreuil-Bellay 56 Mb 27	15260 Neuvéglise 71 Oa 30	09100 Pamiers 70 Ob 29
39260 Moirans-en-Montagne	41400 Montrichard 57 Mb 29	24190 Neuvic/Périgueux 70 Nb 28	87350 Panazol 56 Nb 29
58 Na 33	86420 Monts-sur-Guesnes	19160 Neuvic/Tulle 71 Nb 30	71600 Paray-le-Monial 57 Na 32
82200 Moissac 70 Oa 29	56 Na 28	18330 Neuvy-sur-Barangeon	75001 Paris 57 Ma 30
41190 Molineuf 57 Mb 29	15120 Montsalvy 71 Oa 30	57 Mb 30	79200 Parthenay 56 Na 27
67120 Molsheim 58 Ma 35	58230 Montsauche-les-Settons	05100 Névache 72 Nb 34	64000 Pau 70 Ob 27
08260 Mon-Idée 46 Lb 32	57 Mb 32	58000 Nevers 57 Na 31	08310 Pauvres 58 Lb 32
14120 Mondeville 44 Lb 27	32160 Montsaunes 70 Ob 28	06000 Nice 72 Ob 34	46350 Payrac 70 Oa 29
64360 Monein 70 Ob 27	15150 Montvert 71 Oa 30	67110 Niederbronn-les-Bains	29760 Penmarch 55 Mb 23
05110 Monêtier-Allemont 72 Oa 33	39400 Morbier 58 Na 34	58 Ma 35	89360 Percy 44 Ma 24
43120 Monistrol-sur-Loire 71 Nb 32	35310 Mordelles 56 Ma 26	30000 Nîmes 71 Ob 32	50190 Périers 44 Lb 26
61470 Monnai 57 Ma 28	57340 Morhange 58 Ma 34	79000 Niort 56 Na 27	24000 Périgueux 70 Nb 28
37380 Monnaie 56 Mb 28	64160 Morlaàs 70 Ob 27	34440 Nissan-lez-Enserune	01960 Péronnas 72 Na 33
24540 Monpazier 70 Oa 28	29600 Morlaix 43 Ma 24	71 Ob 31	80200 Péronne 45 Lb 30

POSTALI · ÍNDICE CON CÓDIGOS POSTALES · INDICE DE LUGARES COM CÓDIGOS POSTAIS ·
MÍST S PSČ · ZOZNAM OBCÍ S PSČ · INDEKS MIEJSCOWOŚCI Z KOD POCZTOWY

140

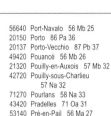

Perpignan — **F** — **Saint Jean-de-Daye**

F

66000 Perpignan 71 Pa 30	56640 Port-Navalo 56 Mb 25
22700 Perros-Guirec 44 Ma 24	20150 Porto 86 Pa 36
84120 Pertuis 72 Ob 33	20137 Porto-Vecchio 87 Pb 37
70140 Pesmes 58 Mb 33	49420 Pouancé 56 Mb 26
33600 Pessac 70 Oa 27	21320 Pouilly-en-Auxois 57 Mb 32
40300 Peyrehorade 70 Ob 26	42720 Pouilly-sous-Charlieu
34120 Pézenas 71 Ob 31	57 Na 32
20115 Piana 86 Pa 36	71270 Pourlans 58 Na 33
60350 Pierrefonds 57 Lb 30	43420 Pradelles 71 Oa 31
15230 Pierrefort 71 Oa 30	53140 Pré-en-Pail 56 Ma 27
26700 Pierrelatte 71 Oa 32	21390 Précy-sous-Thil 57 Mb 32
10220 Piney 57 Ma 32	58700 Prémery 57 Mb 31
43300 Pinols 71 Nb 31	86460 Pressac 56 Na 28
35550 Pipriac 56 Mb 26	37290 Preuilly-sur-Claise 56 Na 28
45300 Pithiviers 57 Ma 30	07000 Privas 71 Oa 32
58230 Planchez 57 Mb 32	20110 Propriano 86 Pb 36
22130 Plancoët 56 Ma 25	77160 Provins 57 Ma 31
27300 Plasnes 45 Lb 28	45390 Puiseaux 57 Ma 30
35380 Plélan-le-Grand 56 Ma 25	63290 Puy-Guillaume 71 Nb 31
22210 Plémet 56 Ma 25	46700 Puy-l'Évêque 70 Oa 29
22640 Plénée-Jugon 56 Ma 25	81700 Puylaurens 71 Ob 30
86450 Pleumartin 56 Na 28	66210 Puyvalador 70 Pa 30
29190 Pleyben 56 Ma 24	56230 Questembert 56 Mb 25
56270 Ploemeur 55 Mb 24	80710 Quevauvillers 45 Lb 30
56800 Ploërmel 56 Mb 25	56170 Quiberon 55 Mb 24
29180 Plogonnec 55 Ma 23	11500 Quillan 71 Pa 30
56270 Plouay 55 Mb 24	29000 Quimper 55 Mb 23
29830 Ploudalmézeau 43 Ma 23	29300 Quimperlé 55 Mb 24
29470 Plougastel-Daoulas	25440 Quingey 58 Mb 33
43 Ma 23	22800 Quintin 56 Ma 25
22580 Plouha 44 Ma 25	30260 Quissac 71 Ob 32
29780 Plouhinec 55 Ma 23	88700 Rambervillers 58 Ma 34
56770 Plouray 55 Ma 24	78120 Rambouillet 57 Ma 29
29280 Plouzané 43 Ma 23	15800 Raulhac 71 Oa 30
56930 Pluméliau 56 Mb 25	81120 Réalmont 71 Ob 30
56330 Pluvigner 56 Mb 24	35600 Redon 56 Mb 25
28300 Poisvilliers 57 Ma 29	67110 Reichshoffen 58 Ma 35
86000 Poitiers 56 Na 28	51100 Reims 58 Lb 32
08430 Poix-Terron 46 Lb 32	61110 Rémalard 57 Ma 28
39800 Poligny 58 Na 33	88200 Remiremont 58 Ma 34
17800 Pons 56 Na 27	30210 Remoulins 71 Ob 32
27500 Pont-Audemer 45 Lb 28	35000 Rennes 56 Ma 26
54700 Pont-à-Mousson 58 Ma 34	34160 Restinclières 71 Ob 32
12290 Pont-de-Salars 71 Oa 30	08300 Rethel 58 Lb 32
01190 Pont-de-Vaux 58 Na 32	39248 Retiers 56 Mb 26
29120 Pont-l'Abbé 55 Mb 23	36260 Reuilly 57 Mb 30
30130 Pont-Saint Esprit 71 Oa 32	31250 Revel 71 Ob 30
89140 Pont-sur-Yonne 57 Ma 31	08500 Revin 46 Lb 32
21270 Pontailler-sur-Saône	83560 Rians 72 Ob 33
58 Mb 33	24600 Ribérac 70 Nb 28
23250 Pontarion 57 Nb 29	37120 Richelieu 56 Mb 28
25300 Pontarlier 58 Na 34	31370 Rieumes 70 Ob 29
77340 Pontault-Combault 57 Ma 30	12240 Rieupeyroux 71 Oa 30
63380 Pontaumur 71 Nb 30	04500 Riez 72 Ob 34
38530 Pontcharra 72 Nb 34	37340 Rillé 56 Mb 28
44160 Pontchâteau 56 Mb 25	69140 Rillieux-la-Pape 71 Nb 32
20218 Ponte-Leccia 87 Pa 37	09420 Rimont 70 Pa 29
56300 Pontivy 56 Ma 25	63200 Riom 71 Nb 31
95300 Pontoise 57 Lb 30	42153 Riorges 71 Na 32
50170 Pontorson 56 Ma 26	42330 Riotord 71 Nb 32
44210 Pornic 56 Mb 25	70190 Rioz 58 Mb 34
13230 Port Saint Louis-du-Rhône	42800 Rive-de-Gier 71 Nb 32
71 Ob 32	42300 Roanne 71 Na 32
13110 Port-de-Bouc 71 Ob 32	42230 Roche-la-Molière 71 Nb 32
85350 Port-Joinville 56 Na 25	87600 Rochechouart 56 Nb 28
11210 Port-la-Nouvelle 71 Ob 31	17300 Rochefort 56 Nb 27

85620 Rocheservière 56 Na 26	86280 Saint Benoît 56 Na 28
08230 Rocroi 46 Lb 32	36170 Saint Benoît-du-Sault
12000 Rodez 71 Oa 30	57 Na 29
20247 Rogliano 87 Pa 37	55210 Saint Benoît-en-Woëvre
08190 Roizy 58 Lb 32	58 Ma 33
52260 Rolampont 58 Mb 33	22000 Saint Brieuc 56 Ma 25
26100 Romans-sur-Isère 71 Nb 33	72120 Saint Calais 57 Mb 28
10100 Romilly-sur-Seine 57 Ma 31	13760 Saint Cannat 71 Ob 33
41200 Romorantin-Lanthenay	42400 Saint Chamond 71 Nb 32
57 Mb 29	48200 Saint Chély-d'Apcher
70250 Ronchamp 58 Mb 34	71 Oa 31
06450 Roquebillière 72 Oa 35	34360 Saint Chinian 71 Ob 30
40120 Roquefort 70 Oa 27	95770 Saint Clair-sur-Epte
05150 Rosans 72 Oa 33	57 Lb 29
29680 Roscoff 43 Ma 24	16450 Saint Claud 56 Nb 28
29140 Rosporden 55 Mb 24	39200 Saint Claude 58 Na 33
22110 Rostrenen 55 Ma 24	05600 Saint Clément 72 Oa 34
59100 Roubaix 45 La 31	72110 Saint Cosme-en-Vairais
76000 Rouen 45 Lb 29	56 Ma 28
25680 Rougemont 58 Mb 34	66750 Saint Cyprien 71 Pa 31
16170 Rouillac 56 Nb 27	93200 Saint Denis 57 Ma 30
34320 Roujan 71 Ob 31	17650 Saint Denis-d'Oléron
25640 Roulans 58 Mb 34	56 Na 26
06420 Roussillon 72 Ob 35	88100 Saint Dié 58 Ma 34
08150 Rouvroy-sur-Audry 46 Lb 32	52100 Saint Dizier 58 Ma 32
58110 Rouy 57 Mb 31	38120 Saint Égrève 72 Nb 33
17200 Royan 56 Nb 26	03330 Saint Éloy-les-Mines
38940 Roybon 72 Nb 33	57 Na 30
80700 Roye 45 Lb 30	42000 Saint Étienne 71 Nb 32
23460 Royère-de-Vassivière	01370 Saint Étienne-du-Bois
57 Nb 29	58 Na 33
46120 Rudelle 71 Oa 29	76800 Saint Étienne-du-Rouvray
80120 Rue 45 La 29	45 Lb 29
16700 Ruffec 56 Na 28	89170 Saint Fargeau 57 Mb 31
74150 Rumilly 72 Nb 33	20217 Saint Florent 87 Pa 37
88360 Rupt-sur-Moselle 58 Mb 34	18400 Saint Florent-sur-Cher
72300 Sablé-sur-Sarthe 56 Mb 27	57 Na 30
40630 Sabres 70 Oa 27	89600 Saint Florentin 57 Mb 31
18600 Sagone 86 Pa 36	15100 Saint Flour 71 Nb 31
07320 Saint Agrève 71 Nb 32	37600 Saint Flovier 57 Na 29
41110 Saint Aignan 57 Mb 29	31800 Saint Gaudens 70 Ob 28
58310 Saint Amand-en-Puisaye	36800 Saint Gaultier 56 Na 29
57 Mb 31	69230 Saint Genis-Laval 71 Nb 32
18200 Saint Amand-Montrond	49170 Saint Georges-sur-Loire
57 Na 30	56 Mb 27
63890 Saint Amant-Roche-Savine	78100 Saint Germain-en-Laye
71 Nb 31	57 Ma 30
30500 Saint Ambroix 71 Oa 32	34610 Saint Gervais-sur-Mare
33240 Saint André-de-Cubzac	71 Ob 31
70 Oa 27	30800 Saint Gilles 71 Ob 32
34725 Saint André-de-Sangonis	09200 Saint Girons 70 Pa 29
71 Ob 31	87260 Saint Hilaire-Bonneval
04170 Saint André-les-Alpes	71 Nb 29
72 Ob 34	85270 Saint Hilaire-de-Riez
10120 Saint André-les-Vergers	56 Na 26
57 Ma 32	50600 Saint Hilaire-du-Harcouët
82140 Saint Antonin-Noble-Val	56 Ma 26
70 Oa 29	58300 Saint Hilaire-Fontaine
24110 Saint Astier 70 Nb 28	57 Na 31
04160 Saint Auban 72 Oa 33	50240 Saint James 56 Ma 26
33820 Saint Aubin-de-Blaye	17400 Saint Jean-d'Angély
70 Nb 27	56 Nb 27
35140 Saint Aubin-du-Cormier	45800 Saint Jean-de-Braye
56 Ma 26	57 Mb 29
37550 Saint Avertin 56 Mb 28	50620 Saint Jean-de-Daye
57500 Saint Avold 58 Lb 34	44 Lb 26

141

INDEX WITH POST CODES · ORTSREGISTER MIT POSTLEITZAHLEN · INDICE CON CODICI
STEDREGISTER MED POSTNUMRE · PLAATSNAMENREGISTER MET POSTCODE · REJSTŘÍK

45140	Saint Jean-de-la-Ruelle	86260	Saint Pierre-de-Maillé
	57 Mb 29		56 Na 28
64500	Saint Jean-de-Luz 69 Ob 26	58240	Saint Pierre-le-Moûtier
85160	Saint Jean-de-Monts		57 Na 31
	56 Na 25	14170	Saint Pierre-sur-Dives
12230	Saint Jean-du-Bruel		44 Lb 27
	71 Oa 31	29250	Saint Pol-de-Léon 43 Ma 24
64220	Saint Jean-Pied-de-Port	62130	Saint Pol-sur-Ternoise
	70 Ob 26		45 La 30
37600	Saint Jean-Saint Germain	34220	Saint Pons-de-Thomières
	57 Mb 29		71 Ob 30
48190	Saint Julien-du-Tournel	03500	Saint Pourçain-sur-Sioule
	71 Oa 31		57 Na 31
87200	Saint Junien 56 Nb 28	69800	Saint Priest 71 Nb 32
42170	Saint Just-Saint Rambert	19220	Saint Privat 71 Nb 30
	71 Nb 32	22410	Saint Quay-Portrieux
65170	Saint Lary-Soulan 70 Pa 28		44 Ma 25
33112	Saint Laurent Médoc	02100	Saint Quentin 45 Lb 31
	70 Nb 27	83700	Saint Raphaël 72 Ob 34
39150	Saint Laurent-en-Grandvaux	13210	Saint Rémy-de-Provence
	58 Na 33		71 Ob 32
14710	Saint Laurent-sur-Mer	58330	Saint Saulge 57 Mb 31
	44 Lb 27	30750	Saint Sauveur-Camprieu
87400	Saint Léonhard-de-Noblat		71 Oa 31
	57 Nb 29	50390	Saint Sauveur-le-Vicomte
50000	Saint Lô 44 Lb 26		44 Lb 26
31470	Saint Lys 70 Ob 29	06420	Saint Sauveur-sur-Tinée
79400	Saint Maixent-l'École		72 Oa 35
	56 Na 27	86310	Saint Savin 56 Na 28
35400	Saint Malo 56 Ma 26	21440	Saint Seine-l'Abbaye
03390	Saint Marcel-en-Murat		58 Mb 32
	57 Na 31	40500	Saint Sever 70 Ob 27
72470	Saint Mars-la-Brière	81370	Saint Sulpice 70 Ob 29
	56 Ma 28	31410	Saint Sulpice-sur-Lezé
24250	Saint Martial-de-Nabirat		70 Ob 29
	70 Oa 29	52150	Saint Thiébault 58 Ma 33
13310	Saint Martin-de-Crau	83990	Saint Tropez 72 Ob 34
	71 Ob 32	76460	Saint Valery-en-Caux
34380	Saint Martin-de-Londres		45 Lb 28
	71 Ob 31	26240	Saint Vallier/Annonay
17410	Saint Martin-de-Ré		71 Nb 32
	56 Na 26	23320	Saint Vaury 57 Na 29
29600	Saint Martin-des-Champs	40230	Saint Vincent-de-Tyrosse
	43 Ma 24		70 Ob 26
15140	Saint Martin-Valmeroux	25410	Saint Vit 58 Mb 33
	71 Nb 30	87500	Saint Yrieix-la-Perche
87440	Saint Mathieu 56 Nb 28		70 Nb 29
83470	Saint Maximin-la-Sainte	26150	Sainte Croix 72 Oa 33
	Baume 72 Ob 33	48210	Sainte Enimie 71 Oa 31
33160	Saint Médard-en-Jalles	33220	Sainte Foy-la-Grande
	70 Oa 27		70 Oa 28
35290	Saint Méen-le-Grand	91700	Sainte Genevieve-des-Bois
	56 Ma 25		57 Ma 30
51470	Saint Memmie 58 Ma 32	85210	Sainte Hermine 56 Na 26
55300	Saint Mihiel 58 Ma 33	20124	Sainte Lucie-de-Porte-Vecchio
44600	Saint Nazaire 56 Mb 25		87 Pb 37
62500	Saint Omer 45 La 30	68160	Sainte Marie-aux-Mines
31650	Saint Orens-de-Gameville		58 Ma 35
	70 Ob 29	37800	Sainte Maure-de-Touraine
64120	Saint Palais 70 Ob 26		56 Mb 28
66220	Saint Paul-de-Fenouillet	51800	Sainte Menehould 58 Lb 32
	71 Pa 30	10300	Sainte Savine 57 Ma 32
40990	Saint Paul-lès-Dax	36160	Sainte Sévère-sur-Indre
	70 Ob 26		57 Na 30
43350	Saint Paulien 71 Nb 31	17100	Saintes 56 Nb 27
07130	Saint Péray 71 Oa 32	41300	Salbris 57 Mb 30

15140	Salers 71 Nb 30	71330	Simard 58 Na 33
43150	Salettes 71 Oa 31	24170	Siorac-en-Périgord 70 Oa 28
84270	Salies-de-Béarn 70 Ob 27	04200	Sisteron 72 Oa 33
74700	Sallanches 72 Nb 34	83140	Six-Fours-les-Plages
13300	Salon-de-Provence 71 Ob 33		72 Ob 33
81630	Salvagnac 70 Ob 29	25600	Sochaux 58 Mb 34
31130	Samatan 70 Ob 28	02200	Soissons 57 Lb 31
62830	Samer 45 La 29	20145	Solenzara 87 Pb 37
55300	Sampigny 58 Ma 33	21540	Sombernon 58 Mb 32
18140	Sancergues 57 Mb 30	51600	Sommepy-Tahure 58 Lb 32
18300	Sancerre 57 Mb 30	30250	Sommières 71 Ob 32
25430	Sancey-le-Long 58 Mb 34	84700	Sorgues 71 Oa 32
18600	Sancoins 57 Na 30	37250	Sorigny 56 Mb 28
20228	Santa Severa 87 Pa 37	81580	Soual 71 Ob 30
06540	Saorge 72 Ob 35	79800	Soudan 56 Na 27
45770	Saran 57 Mb 29	41300	Souesmes 57 Mb 30
24200	Sarlat-la-Canéda 70 Oa 29	46200	Souillac 70 Oa 29
67260	Sarre-Union 58 Ma 35	55220	Souilly 58 Lb 33
57400	Sarrebourg 58 Ma 35	33780	Soulac-sur-Mer 56 Nb 26
57200	Sarreguemines 58 Lb 35	10200	Soulaines-Dhuys 58 Ma 32
40800	Sarron 70 Ob 27	53210	Soulgé-sur-Ouette 56 Ma 27
20100	Sartène 86 Pb 36	77460	Souppes-sur-Loing 57 Ma 30
56370	Sarzeau 56 Mb 25	46190	Sousceyrac 71 Oa 30
38360	Sassenage 72 Nb 33	16800	Soyaux 56 Nb 28
33920	Saugon 70 Nb 27	07130	Soyons 71 Oa 32
43170	Saugues 71 Oa 31	83120	Ste.-Maxime 72 Ob 34
17600	Saujon 56 Nb 27	55700	Stenay 58 Lb 33
21210	Saulieu 57 Mb 32	13460	Stes.-Maries-de-la-Mer
84390	Sault 72 Oa 33		71 Ob 32
64300	Sault-de-Navailles 70 Ob 27	67000	Strasbourg 58 Ma 35
49400	Saumur 56 Mb 27	20169	Suartone 87 Pb 37
13960	Sausset-les-Pins 71 Ob 33	51600	Suippes 58 Lb 32
33540	Sauveterre-de-Guyenne	45600	Sully-sur-Loire 57 Mb 30
	70 Oa 27	17700	Surgères 56 Na 27
79190	Sauzé-Vaussais 56 Na 28	21240	Talant 58 Mb 32
56360	Sauzon 55 Mb 24	85440	Talmont-Saint Hilaire
67700	Saverne 58 Ma 35		56 Na 26
77176	Savigny-le-Tempe 57 Ma 30	58110	Tamnay-en-Bazois 57 Mb 31
72160	Sceaux-sur-Huisne 56 Ma 28	54116	Tantonville 58 Ma 34
08200	Sedan 46 Lb 32	69170	Tarare 71 Nb 32
26560	Séderon 72 Oa 33	13150	Tarascon 71 Ob 32
61500	Sées 56 Ma 28	09400	Tarascon-sur-Ariege
49500	Segré 56 Mb 27		70 Pa 29
12290	Ségur 71 Oa 30	65000	Tarbes 70 Ob 28
15300	Ségur-les-Villas 71 Nb 30	40400	Tartas 70 Ob 27
19700	Seilhac 71 Nb 29	69160	Tassin-la-Demi-Lune
67600	Sélestat 58 Ma 35		71 Nb 32
41130	Selles-sur-Cher 57 Mb 29	66500	Taurinya 71 Pa 30
21260	Selongey 58 Mb 33	63690	Tauves 71 Nb 30
21140	Semur-en-Auxois 57 Mb 32	39500	Tavaux 58 Mb 33
60300	Senlis 57 Lb 30	20163	Tavera 86 Pa 37
71240	Sennecey-le-Grand 58 Na 32	83670	Tavernes 72 Ob 34
89100	Sens 57 Ma 31	95150	Taverny 57 Lb 30
09140	Sérac 70 Pa 29	06430	Tende 72 Oa 35
08220	Seraincourt 46 Lb 32	02700	Tergnier 45 Lb 31
34410	Sérignan 71 Ob 31	32400	Termes-d'Armagnac
45300	Sermaises 57 Ma 30		70 Ob 27
58000	Sermoise-sur-Loire 57 Na 31	68800	Thann 58 Mb 35
05700	Serres 72 Oa 33	24210	Thenon 70 Nb 29
34200	Sète 71 Ob 31	63300	Thiers 71 Nb 31
21250	Seurre 58 Na 33	57100	Thionville 58 Lb 34
12150	Sévérac-le-Château	01140	Thoissey 71 Na 32
	71 Oa 31	74200	Thonon-les-Bains 58 Na 34
51120	Sézanne 57 Ma 31	79100	Thouars 56 Na 27
11130	Sigean 71 Ob 30	14220	Thury-Harcourt 44 Ma 27
72140	Sille-le-Guillaume 56 Ma 27	45510	Tigy 57 Mb 30

POSTALI · ÍNDICE CON CÓDIGOS POSTALES · INDICE DE LUGARES COM CÓDIGOS POSTAIS ·
MÍST S PSČ · ZOZNAM OBCÍ S PSČ · INDEKS MIEJSCOWOŚCI Z KOD POCZTOWY

142

Tinchebray   (F) · (FIN)   Heinäaho

61800 Tinchebray 56 Ma 27	37600 Varennes 56 Mb 28	61120 Vimoutiers 56 Ma 28	42100 Arvaja 14 Eb 53
35190 Tinténiac 56 Ma 26	55270 Varennes-en-Argonne	41350 Vineuil 57 Mb 29	17320 Asikkala Vääsky 15 Eb 53
20111 Tiuccia 86 Pa 36	58 Lb 33	71260 Vire 56 Ma 27	99550 Aska 8 Bb 54
17380 Tonnay-Boutonne 56 Nb 27	03160 Varennes-sur-Allier 57 Na 31	35500 Vitré 56 Ma 26	97700 Asmunti 8 Cb 54
47400 Tonneins 70 Oa 28	58210 Varzy 57 Mb 31	13127 Vitrolles 71 Ob 33	21380 Aura 14 Fa 50
89700 Tonnerre 57 Mb 31	36150 Vatan 57 Mb 29	51300 Vitry-le-François 58 Ma 32	97655 Autti 9 Ca 55
50160 Torigni-sur-Vire 44 Lb 27	51210 Vauchamps 57 Ma 31	21350 Vitteaux 57 Mb 32	68555 Bosund 14 Db 50
76890 Tôtes 45 Lb 29	55140 Vaucouleurs 58 Ma 33	88800 Vittel 58 Ma 33	11020 Dálvadas 5 Ab 54
89130 Toucy 57 Mb 31	30600 Vauvert 71 Ob 32	20219 Vivario 87 Pa 37	22710 Degerby 30 Fa 48
54200 Toul 58 Ma 33	70210 Vauvillers 58 Mb 34	86370 Vivonne 56 Na 28	25900 Dalsbruk 30 Fa 50
83000 Toulon 72 Ob 33	21150 Venarey-les-Laumes	85770 Vix 56 Na 27	68870 Edsevö 14 Db 50
03400 Toulon-sur-Allier 57 Na 31	57 Mb 32	38500 Voiron 72 Nb 33	10600 Tammisaari 30 Fb 51
71320 Toulon-sur-Arroux 57 Na 32	06140 Vence 72 Ob 35	38340 Voreppe 72 Nb 33	47200 Elimäki 15 Fa 54
31000 Toulouse 70 Ob 29	10140 Vendeuvre-sur-Barse	10150 Voué 57 Ma 32	44910 Elämäjärvi 14 Db 53
59200 Tourcoing 45 La 31	58 Ma 32	86190 Vouillé 56 Na 28	81200 Eno 15 Ea 58
50110 Tourlaville 44 Lb 26	41100 Vendôme 57 Mb 29	89270 Voutenay-sur-Cure 57 Mb 31	58175 Enonkoski 15 Ea 56
65190 Tournay 70 Ob 28	55100 Verdun 58 Lb 33	08400 Vouziers 58 Lb 32	99400 Enontekiö 4 Ba 51
31170 Tournefeuille 70 Ob 29	89270 Vermenton 57 Mb 31	41600 Vouzon 57 Mb 30	56210 Erajärvi 15 Eb 56
47370 Tournon-d'Agenais 70 Oa 28	27130 Verneuil-sur-Avre 57 Ma 28	52130 Wassy 58 Ma 32	42100 Eräslahti 14 Eb 52
07300 Tournon-sur-Rhône 71 Nb 32	27200 Vernon 57 Lb 29	67160 Wissembourg 58 Lb 35	69150 Eskola 8 Db 52
71700 Tournus 58 Na 32	07240 Vernoux-en-Vivarais	68310 Wittelsheim 58 Mb 35	02100 Espoo 30 Fa 52
16560 Tourriers 56 Nb 28	71 Oa 32	57140 Woippy 58 Lb 34	68820 Esse 14 Db 51
37000 Tours 56 Mb 28	86410 Verrières 56 Na 28	88220 Xertigny 58 Ma 34	27510 Eura 14 Eb 50
28310 Toury 57 Ma 29	78000 Versailles 57 Ma 30	73170 Yenne 72 Nb 33	27100 Eurajoki 14 Eb 49
10140 Trannes 58 Ma 32	44120 Vertou 56 Mb 26	43200 Yssingeaux 71 Nb 32	62500 Evijärvi 14 Db 51
78190 Trappes 57 Ma 29	02140 Vervins 45 Lb 31	57970 Yutz 58 Lb 34	22220 Finström 29 Fa 47
20240 Travo 87 Pb 37	70000 Vesoul 58 Mb 34	76190 Yvetot 45 Lb 28	07700 Forsby 15 Fa 53
22220 Tréguier 44 Ma 24	89450 Vézelay 57 Mb 31	03400 Yzeure 57 Na 31	30100 Forssa 14 Fa 51
19260 Treignac 71 Nb 29	72320 Vibraye 57 Ma 28		65280 Gerby 14 Db 49
49340 Trémentines 56 Mb 27	65500 Vic-en-Biggore 70 Ob 28		22340 Geta 29 Fa 47
40630 Trensacq 70 Oa 27	32190 Vic-Fezensac 70 Ob 28	(FIN)	85800 Haapajärvi 14 Db 53
01600 Trévoux 71 Nb 32	15800 Vic-sur-Cère 71 Oa 30		68370 Haapala 14 Db 52
65220 Trie-sur-Baise 70 Ob 28	03200 Vichy 57 Na 31	98560 Aapajärvi 8 Bb 55	42800 Haapamäki 14 Ea 52
10000 Troyes 58 Ma 32	38200 Vienne 71 Nb 32	83950 Ahmovaara 15 Db 57	86600 Haapavesi 8 Da 53
61160 Trun 56 Ma 28	18100 Vierzon 57 Mb 30	92920 Ahokylä 9 Db 54	90480 Hailuoto 8 Cb 52
11350 Tuchan 71 Pa 30	49310 Vihiers 56 Mb 27	21037 Ahola 9 Cb 57	24800 Halikko 30 Fa 51
19000 Tulle 71 Nb 29	33730 Villandraut 70 Oa 27	72300 Ahveninen 15 Ea 54	35600 Halli 14 Eb 52
38210 Tullins 72 Nb 33	38250 Villard-de-Lans 72 Nb 33	58130 Ahvensalmi 15 Ea 56	21570 Halslahti 30 Fa 50
64490 Urdos 70 Pa 27	01330 Villars-les-Dombes 72 Nb 33	74740 Aittojärvi 15 Db 54	69510 Halsua 14 Db 52
86230 Usseau/Châtellerault	11420 Villautou 70 Ob 29	91088 Aittovaara 9 Cb 57	73350 Haluna 15 Db 56
56 Na 28	16320 Villebois-Lavalette 70 Nb 28	37801 Akaa 14 Eb 51	49400 Hamina 15 Fa 55
17220 Usseau/la Rochelle 56 Na 26	12580 Villecomtal 71 Oa 30	99800 Akujärvi 5 Ba 55	22320 Hamnsund 29 Fa 48
19200 Ussel/Neuvic 71 Nb 30	50800 Villedieu-les-Poêles	74500 Ala-Livo 9 Cb 54	44670 Hamula 15 Db 54
42550 Usson-en-Forez 71 Nb 31	44 Ma 26	97510 Ala-Nampa 8 Ca 54	86510 Hanhiperä 8 Da 52
22460 Uzel 56 Ma 25	36320 Villedieu-sur-Indre 57 Na 29	95300 Ala-Paakkola 8 Cb 52	62300 Hankamäki 15 Db 56
19140 Uzerche 71 Nb 29	16240 Villefagnan 56 Na 28	89830 Ala-Vuokki 9 Da 57	41520 Hankasalmi 15 Ea 54
30700 Uzès 71 Oa 32	38090 Villefontaine 72 Nb 33	62300 Alahärmä 14 Db 50	10900 Hanko 30 Fb 52
18260 Vailly-sur-Sauldre 57 Mb 30	48800 Villefort 71 Oa 31	86710 Alajoki 8 Db 53	81160 Harivaara 15 Ea 57
84110 Vaison-la-Romaine 71 Oa 33	31290 Villefranche-de-Lauragais	62900 Alajärvi 14 Ea 51	29200 Harjavalta 14 Eb 50
73150 Val d'Isère 72 Nb 34	70 Ob 29	89600 Alajärvi 9 Da 56	51440 Harjunmaa 15 Eb 55
25800 Valdahon 58 Mb 34	12430 Villefranche-de-Panat	97470 Alakylä 8 Bb 52	17840 Harjunsalmi 14 Eb 53
86300 Valdivienne 56 Na 28	71 Oa 30	95255 Alaniemi 8 Cb 53	17780 Harmoinen 14 Eb 53
36600 Valençay 57 Mb 29	12200 Villefranche-de-Rouergue	71910 Alapitkä 15 Db 55	19600 Hartola 15 Eb 54
26000 Valence 71 Oa 32	71 Oa 30	32440 Alastaro 14 Fa 50	22710 Hastersboda 30 Fa 48
32310 Valence-sur-Baïse 70 Ob 28	41200 Villefranche-sur-Cher	85200 Alavieska 8 Da 52	13880 Hattula 14 Eb 52
59300 Valenciennes 45 La 31	57 Mb 29	63300 Alavus 14 Ea 51	81650 Hattuvaara 15 Ea 59
25700 Valentigney 58 Mb 34	69400 Villefranche-sur-Saône	86460 Alpua 8 Da 53	14700 Hauho 14 Eb 52
07110 Valgorge 71 Oa 32	71 Nb 32	44860 Alvajärvi 14 Db 53	74100 Haukilahti 15 Db 55
44330 Vallet 56 Mb 26	82130 Villemade 70 Oa 29	46800 Anjalankoski 15 Fa 54	90830 Haukipudas 8 Cb 53
03190 Vallon-en-Sully 57 Na 30	40190 Villeneuve-de-Marsan	52100 Anttola 15 Eb 55	51600 Haukivuori 15 Ea 55
50700 Valognes 44 Lb 26	70 Ob 27	58200 Anttola 15 Eb 57	12210 Hausjärvi Oitti 14 Fa 53
84600 Valréas 71 Oa 33	47300 Villeneuve-sur-Lot 70 Oa 28	22010 Arkala 8 Cb 54	98950 Hautajärvi 9 Ca 57
54500 Vand-uvre-les-Nancy	89500 Villeneuve-sur-Yonne	95590 Arpela 8 Ca 52	18100 Heinola 15 Eb 54
58 Ma 34	57 Ma 31	17530 Arrakoski 14 Eb 53	18100 Heinola kk. 15 Eb 54
56000 Vannes 56 Mb 25	80200 Villers-Carbonnel 45 Lb 30	16200 Artjärvi 15 Fa 54	38100 Heinoo 14 Eb 50
44370 Varades 56 Mb 26	70110 Villersexel 58 Mb 34		82710 Heinäaho 15 Ea 58

143

INDEX WITH POST CODES · ORTSREGISTER MIT POSTLEITZAHLEN · INDICE CON CODICI
STEDREGISTER MED POSTNUMRE · PLAATSNAMENREGISTER MET POSTCODE · REJSTŘÍK

Heinävesi · FIN · **Käyrämö**

79700 Heinävesi 15 Ea 56	89320 Joukokylä 9 Cb 56	51900 Kaskii 15 Eb 56	98780 Koramoniemi 9 Ca 56
00100 Helsinki Helsingfors	19650 Joutsa 15 Eb 54	64260 Kaskinen 14 Ea 49	45610 Koria 15 Fa 54
30 Fa 52	54100 Joutseno 15 Eb 56	25930 Kasnäs 30 Fb 50	41800 Korpilahti 15 Ea 53
88900 Hietaperä 9 Da 57	98710 Joutsijärvi 9 Ca 55	61800 Kauhajoki 14 Ea 50	74100 Korpinen 15 Db 55
98800 Hihnavaara 5 Bb 56	73500 Juankoski 15 Db 56	61910 Kauhajärvi 14 Ea 50	83330 Korpivaara 15 Ea 57
68100 Himanka 8 Da 51	97870 Jumisko 9 Ca 56	62200 Kauhava 14 Db 51	21710 Korpo 30 Fa 49
27600 Hinnerjoki 14 Fa 49	21037 Juntusranta 9 Cb 57	99110 Kaukonen 8 Bb 52	74920 Korretoja 5 Ab 55
35320 Hirsilä 14 Eb 52	95640 Juoksenki 8 Ca 51	95635 Kaulinranta 8 Ca 51	65610 Korsholm 14 Db 49
74420 Hirvaskoski 9 Cb 55	88900 Juonto 9 Da 57	69600 Kaustinen 14 Db 51	66200 Korsnäs 14 Ea 49
52550 Hirvensalmi 15 Eb 54	66300 Jurva 14 Ea 49	72600 Keitele 15 Db 54	62420 Kortesjärvi 14 Db 51
75810 Hirvikoski 14 Fa 50	54530 Jurvala 15 Fa 55	90820 Kello 8 Cb 53	71320 Korvala 8 Ca 54
25940 Hitis 30 Fb 50	97645 Juujärvi 9 Ca 55	04500 Kellokoski 14 Fa 53	38840 Korvaluoma 14 Eb 50
62940 Hoisko 14 Db 51	83900 Juuka 15 Db 57	98920 Kelloselkä 9 Ca 56	86400 Korvenkylä 8 Da 53
15860 Hollola 15 Fa 53	35540 Juupajoki 14 Eb 52	99490 Kelottijärvi 4 Ba 50	90100 Korvensuora 8 Cb 53
38950 Honkajoki 14 Ea 50	51900 Juva 15 Eb 55	94100 Kemi 8 Cb 52	29340 Koski 14 Eb 50
29940 Honkajärvi 14 Eb 49	40100 Jyväskylä 15 Ea 53	98100 Kemijärvi 9 Ca 55	31500 Koski TI 14 Fa 51
93780 Hossa 9 Cb 57	38800 Jämijärvi 14 Eb 50	93720 Kemilä 9 Cb 57	61720 Koskue 14 Ea 50
32700 Huittinen 14 Eb 50	42100 Jämsä 14 Eb 53	94400 Keminmaa 8 Cb 52	99100 Kotakumpu 5 Bb 53
43640 Humppi 14 Ea 52	42300 Jämsänkoski 14 Eb 53	90440 Kempele 8 Da 53	42870 Kotala 14 Ea 52
31640 Humppila 14 Fa 51	77570 Jäppilä 15 Ea 55	04200 Kerava 14 Fa 53	98950 Kotala 9 Ca 56
52200 Huunkala 15 Eb 56	04400 Järvenpää 14 Fa 53	58200 Kerimäki 15 Eb 57	48100 Kotka 15 Fa 54
99910 Huutoniemi 5 Ab 54	97340 Jääskö 8 Bb 53	77700 Kerkonkoski 15 Ea 54	44790 Kotvala 14 Db 53
89400 Hyrynsalmi 9 Da 56	99910 Kaamanen 5 Ab 55	99660 Kersilö 5 Bb 54	61160 Koura 14 Ea 51
05800 Hyvinkää 14 Fa 52	99910 Kaamasmukka 5 Ab 54	62500 Kerttua 14 Db 51	45100 Kouvola 15 Fa 54
97900 Hyväniemi 9 Ca 56	34270 Kaanaa 14 Eb 51	92320 Keskikylä 8 Da 52	82710 Kovero 15 Ea 58
41900 Häkkiskylä 14 Ea 52	99470 Kaaresuvanto 4 Ba 50	90460 Keskipiiri 8 Da 53	64100 Kristinestad 14 Ea 49
16800 Hämeenkoski 14 Eb 53	20780 Kaarina 30 Fa 50	92700 Kestilä 9 Da 54	68500 Kronoby 14 Db 51
39100 Hämeenkyrö 14 Eb 51	73600 Kaavi 15 Ea 56	59800 Kesälahti 15 Eb 57	97700 Kuha 8 Cb 54
13100 Hämeenlinna 14 Fa 52	95610 Kainuunkylä 8 Ca 51	42700 Keuruu 14 Ea 52	36810 Kuhmalahti 14 Eb 52
88900 Härmänkylä 9 Da 57	46400 Kaipiainen 15 Fa 55	21037 Kiannanniemi 9 Cb 57	88900 Kuhmo 9 Da 57
49660 Ihamaa 15 Fa 55	88600 Kaitainsalmi 9 Da 56	95950 Kihlanki 4 Bb 51	17800 Kuhmoinen 14 Eb 53
27320 Ihode 14 Fa 49	87100 Kajaani 9 Da 55	39820 Kihniö 14 Ea 51	89430 Kuikkavaara 9 Da 56
91100 Ii 8 Cb 53	99830 Kakslauttanen 5 Ba 55	82140 Kiihtelysvaara 15 Ea 58	38950 Kuivakangas 14 Eb 50
74100 Iisalmi 15 Db 55	85900 Kalaja 14 Db 53	38360 Kiikoinen 14 Eb 50	95100 Kuivaniemi 8 Cb 53
14500 Iittala 14 Eb 52	85100 Kalajoki 8 Da 51	88930 Kiimavaara 9 Da 57	39750 Kuivasjärvi 14 Ea 50
47520 Iitti Kausala 15 Fa 54	61650 Kalakoski 14 Ea 51	90900 Kiiminki 8 Cb 53	37560 Kulju 14 Eb 51
39500 Ikaalinen 14 Eb 51	23600 Kalanti 14 Fa 49	34980 Killinkoski 14 Ea 51	97895 Kuloharju 9 Cb 56
60800 Ilmajoki 14 Ea 50	98440 Kallaanvaara 9 Ca 55	99490 Kilpisjärvi 4 Ab 48	91060 Kuolio 9 Cb 56
82900 Ilomantsi 15 Ea 58	34300 Kallio 14 Eb 51	51760 Kilpola 15 Eb 55	70100 Kuopio 15 Ea 55
55100 Imatra 15 Eb 56	98100 Kalliosalmi 8 Ca 54	25700 Kimito 30 Fa 50	63100 Kuortane 14 Ea 51
99870 Inari 5 Ba 55	58810 Kallislahti 15 Eb 56	47350 Kimonkylä 15 Fa 54	98850 Kuosku 9 Bb 56
10210 Ingå 30 Fa 52	98980 Kallunki 9 Ca 56	43900 Kinnula 14 Db 52	21900 Kurala 14 Fa 50
64900 Isojoki 14 Ea 49	43270 Kalmari 14 Ea 53	02400 Kirkkonummi 30 Fa 52	61300 Kurikka 14 Ea 50
61500 Isokyrö 14 Ea 50	43490 Kangasaho 14 Ea 52	82500 Kitee 15 Ea 58	98600 Kursu 9 Ca 56
73900 Issakka 15 Db 56	36200 Kangasala 14 Eb 52	81750 Kitsi 15 Db 58	95990 Kurtakko 8 Bb 52
44350 Istunmäki 15 Ea 54	85930 Kangaskylä 14 Db 52	99100 Kittilä 5 Bb 52	52400 Kurtti 9 Cb 56
99800 Ivalo 5 Ba 55	79480 Kangaslampi 15 Ea 56	27430 Kiukainen 14 Eb 50	34300 Kuru 14 Eb 51
47710 Jaala 15 Eb 54	51200 Kangasniemi 15 Eb 54	74700 Kiuruvesi 15 Db 54	23360 Kustavi 14 Fa 49
91740 Jaalanka 9 Da 55	99360 Kangosjärvi 4 Bb 51	43800 Kivijärvi 14 Db 53	99460 Kuttanen 4 Ba 50
97170 Jaatila 8 Ca 53	38700 Kankaanpää 14 Eb 50	99460 Kivilompolo 4 Ba 51	93600 Kuusamo 9 Cb 57
91210 Jakkukylä 8 Cb 53	43300 Kannonkoski 14 Ea 53	97670 Kivitaipale 8 Ca 53	45700 Kuusankoski 15 Fa 54
68600 Jakobstad 14 Db 50	69100 Kannus 14 Db 51	01800 Klaukkala 14 Fa 52	25330 Kuusjoki 14 Fa 51
61600 Jalasjärvi 14 Ea 50	31900 Kanteenmaa 14 Eb 50	51900 Kohiseva 15 Eb 55	37910 Kylmäkoski 14 Eb 51
81700 Jamali 15 Db 57	39940 Kantti 14 Ea 50	01360 Koivukylä 30 Fa 53	61450 Kylänpää 14 Ea 50
14240 Janakkala Turenki 14 Fa 52	48770 Karhula 15 Fa 54	32800 Kokemäki 14 Eb 50	39200 Kyröskoski 14 Eb 51
93350 Jaurakkajärvi 9 Cb 55	99950 Karigasniemi 5 Ab 53	67100 Kokkola 14 Db 51	43700 Kyyjärvi 14 Db 52
99770 Jeesiö 5 Bb 54	64350 Karijoki 14 Ea 49	95900 Kolari 8 Bb 51	68300 Kälviä 14 Db 51
10250 Joddböle 30 Fa 51	10300 Karis 30 Fa 51	35990 Kolho 14 Ea 52	34240 Kämmenniemi 14 Eb 51
80100 Joensuu 15 Ea 57	03600 Karkkila 14 Fa 52	83960 Koli 15 Db 57	66640 Kärklax 14 Ea 50
05400 Jokela 14 Fa 52	38100 Karkku 14 Eb 51	43100 Kolkanlahti 14 Ea 53	16610 Kärkölä Järvelä 15 Fa 53
75500 Jokikylä 15 Db 56	98230 Karsimus 9 Ca 55	44400 Konginkangas 15 Ea 53	25870 Kärra 30 Fa 50
31600 Jokioinen 14 Fa 51	43500 Karstula 14 Ea 52	44300 Konnevesi 15 Ea 54	92500 Kärsämä 8 Da 53
22150 Jomala 29 Fa 47	72100 Karttula 15 Ea 54	81100 Kontiolahti 15 Ea 57	86710 Kärsämäki 8 Da 53
62100 Jonkeri 9 Db 57	95530 Karunki 8 Ca 52	88470 Kontiomäki 9 Da 56	99320 Kätkäsuvanto 4 Ba 51
87950 Jormua 9 Da 56	39930 Karvia 14 Ea 50	95760 Konttajärvi 8 Ca 52	93850 Käylä 9 Ca 57
79600 Joroinen 15 Ea 55	79820 Karvio 15 Ea 56	92260 Kopsa 8 Da 52	71320 Käyrämö 8 Ca 54

POSTALI · ÍNDICE CON CÓDIGOS POSTALES · INDICE DE LUGARES COM CÓDIGOS POSTAIS ·
MÍST S PSČ · ZOZNAM OBCÍ S PSČ · INDEKS MIEJSCOWOŚCI Z KOD POCZTOWY

144

Kökar FIN Pori FIN

22730 Kökar 30 Fb 48	07900 Loviisa 15 Fa 54	35800 Mänttä 14 Ea 52	99960 Outakoski 5 Ab 53
99140 Köngäs 4 Bb 52	19950 Luhanka 15 Eb 53	52700 Mäntyharju 15 Eb 54	83500 Outokumpu 15 Ea 57
74390 Laakajärvi 9 Db 56	73670 Luikonlahti 15 Ea 56	97820 Mäntyjärvi 9 Cb 55	92430 Paavola 8 Da 53
99830 Laanila 5 Ba 55	91980 Lumijoki 8 Da 53	69980 Möttönen 14 Db 52	17500 Padasjoki 14 Eb 53
15100 Lahti 15 Fa 53	34540 Luode 14 Eb 51	21100 Naantali 14 Fa 50	10570 Padva 30 Fb 50
92350 Lahtiranta 8 Da 52	61230 Luopa 14 Ea 50	76850 Naarajärvi 15 Ea 55	21530 Paimio 14 Fa 50
66400 Laihia 14 Ea 50	99555 Luosto 8 Bb 54	21660 Nagu 30 Fa 49	72400 Pajuskylä 15 Db 54
89400 Laitila 14 Fa 49	54540 Luumäki Taavetti 15 Fa 55	29250 Nakkila 14 Eb 50	99450 Palojoensuu 4 Ba 51
47650 Lammi 14 Eb 53	98230 Luusua 9 Ca 55	51860 Narila 15 Ea 55	99460 Palojärvi 4 Ba 51
72400 Lampaanjärvi 15 Db 54	29100 Luvia 14 Eb 49	97675 Narkaus 8 Ca 54	79830 Palokki 15 Ea 56
29720 Lamppi 14 Eb 49	82915 Lylyvaara 15 Ea 58	15550 Nastola 15 Fa 53	16790 Palomaa 5 Ab 55
95770 Lankojärvi 8 Ca 52	35400 Länkipohja 14 Eb 52	68410 Nedervetil 14 Db 51	89600 Palovaara 9 Da 57
41270 Lannevesi 14 Ea 53	64300 Läppfjärd 14 Ea 49	89200 Neulikko 9 Da 55	88300 Paltamo 9 Da 55
27150 Lapijoki 14 Eb 49	12600 Läyliäinen 14 Fa 52	82675 Niirala 15 Ea 58	81750 Pankakoski 15 Db 58
07800 Lapinjärvi 15 Fa 54	22630 Långnäs 30 Fa 48	73300 Nilsiä 15 Db 56	21600 Pargas 30 Fa 50
73100 Lapinlahti 15 Db 55	71750 Maaninka 15 Db 55	39360 Niskala 9 Cb 55	59100 Parikkala 15 Eb 57
62600 Lappajärvi 14 Db 51	98780 Maaninkavaara 9 Ca 56	93600 Nissinvaara 9 Ca 57	39700 Parkano 14 Ea 51
53100 Lappeenranta 15 Eb 56	77460 Maavesi 15 Ea 55	85500 Nivala 8 Db 52	59100 Parkkila 15 Eb 55
68820 Lappfors 14 Db 51	43220 Mahlu 14 Ea 53	74260 Nivankylä 8 Ca 53	11002 Partakko 5 Ab 55
27230 Lappi 14 Eb 49	97340 Maijanen 8 Bb 53	73640 Njurkulahti 5 Ba 54	91700 Partalankylä 9 Da 54
10820 Lappohja 30 Fb 51	87100 Mainua 9 Da 55	37100 Nokia 14 Eb 51	90100 Pateniemi 8 Cb 53
62100 Lapua 14 Ea 51	51380 Makkola 15 Eb 56	80140 Noljakka 15 Ea 57	74120 Patoniva 5 Ab 55
68570 Larsmo 14 Db 50	66100 Malax 14 Ea 49	29600 Noormarkku 14 Eb 49	82140 Patrikka 15 Ea 59
92600 Latva 8 Da 53	22100 Mariehamn 29 Fa 47	64530 Norrnäs 14 Ea 49	92140 Pattijoki 8 Da 52
79940 Latvalampi 15 Ea 57	68210 Marinkainen 8 Db 51	98950 Nousu 9 Bb 56	71460 Paukarlahti 15 Ea 55
85900 Latvanen 14 Db 53	90480 Marjaniemi 8 Da 52	54230 Nuijamaa 15 Fa 56	81270 Paukkaja 15 Ea 58
41340 Laukaa 15 Ea 53	85320 Markkula 8 Db 52	03100 Nummela 30 Fa 52	68910 Pedersöre 14 Db 50
93600 Lautiosaari 8 Cb 52	97290 Marraskoski 8 Ca 53	09810 Nummi-Pusula 14 Fa 51	98500 Pelkosenniemi 9 Bb 55
88900 Lauvuskylä 9 Db 57	95590 Martimo 8 Ca 51	99430 Nunnanen 4 Ba 52	71480 Pellesmäki 15 Ea 55
93780 Lavala 9 Cb 57	98830 Martti 5 Bb 56	83940 Nunnanlahti 15 Db 57	95700 Pello 8 Ca 52
38600 Lavia 14 Eb 50	95340 Mattinen 8 Ea 53	25610 Nurkkila 30 Fa 51	74510 Peltosalmi 15 Db 55
63500 Lehtimäki 14 Ea 51	99490 Maunu 4 Ba 50	75500 Nurmes 15 Db 57	99420 Peltovuoma 4 Ba 52
97840 Lehtiniemi 9 Ca 55	92400 Meijerinkylä 8 Da 53	81950 Nurmijärvi 9 Db 57	89770 Peranka 9 Cb 57
74200 Lehtovaara 9 Cb 55	95690 Mellakoski 8 Ca 52	01900 Nurmijärvi 14 Fa 52	69950 Perho 14 Db 52
89200 Leipivaara 9 Da 55	97340 Meltaus 8 Ca 53	60550 Nurmo 14 Ea 50	25500 Perniö 30 Fa 51
41770 Leivonmäki 15 Eb 54	95675 Meltosjärvi 8 Ca 52	97700 Nuupas 8 Ca 54	07930 Pernå 15 Fa 54
54710 Lemi 15 Eb 55	73640 Menesjärvi 5 Ba 54	92830 Nuutila 9 Da 54	25360 Pertteli 14 Fa 51
22610 Lemland 29 Fa 48	28600 Meri-Pori 14 Eb 49	66900 Nykarleby 14 Db 50	19430 Pertunmaa 15 Eb 54
33880 Lempäälä 14 Eb 51	86220 Merijärvi 8 Da 52	22240 Näsby 29 Fa 47	97820 Perä-Posio 9 Ca 55
21230 Lemu 14 Fa 49	66510 Merikaarto 14 Db 49	72300 Närhilä 15 Ea 54	64720 Perälä 14 Ea 49
88930 Lentira 9 Da 57	29900 Merikarvia 14 Eb 49	64200 Närpes 14 Ea 49	29100 Peränkylä 14 Eb 49
99440 Leppäjärvi 4 Ba 51	27670 Mestilä 14 Eb 50	99940 Näätämö 5 Ab 57	61100 Peräseinäjoki 14 Ea 51
41310 Leppävesi 15 Ea 53	52190 Metsäkylä 9 Cb 56	95160 Oijärvi 8 Cb 53	75930 Petäiskylä 9 Db 57
79100 Leppävirta 15 Ea 55	49700 Miehikkälä 15 Fa 55	97610 Oikarainen 8 Ca 54	99700 Petäjäjärvi 9 Cb 54
69440 Lestijärvi 14 Db 52	99340 Mielsö 4 Ba 52	31400 Oinasjärvi 14 Fa 51	88350 Petäjälahti 9 Da 55
04940 Levanto 15 Fa 53	50100 Mikkeli 15 Eb 55	93600 Oivanki 9 Ca 57	56320 Petäjävesi 14 Ea 53
34930 Liedenpohja 14 Ea 51	66210 Molpe 14 Ea 49	85580 Ojakylä 14 Db 53	73800 Peurasuvanto 5 Bb 54
81700 Lieksa 15 Db 58	98740 Morottaja 9 Ca 56	92620 Ojakylä 8 Da 53	92220 Piehinki 8 Da 52
21420 Lieto 14 Fa 50	38460 Mouhijärvi 14 Eb 50	88270 Ojanperä 9 Da 54	76100 Pieksämäki 15 Ea 55
41400 Lievestuore 15 Ea 54	91500 Muhos 8 Da 53	85920 Oksava 14 Db 53	72400 Pielavesi 15 Db 54
42600 Lihjamo 14 Ea 52	75940 Mujejärvi 9 Db 57	91140 Olhava 8 Cb 53	81470 Pihlajavaara 15 Db 59
68940 Lillby 14 Db 51	42600 Multia 14 Ea 52	82360 Onkamo 15 Ea 58	44800 Pihtipudas 14 Db 53
91900 Liminka 8 Da 53	99300 Muonio 4 Bb 51	19230 Onkiniemi 15 Eb 54	21500 Piikkiö 30 Fa 50
92500 Liminkakylä 8 Da 52	93760 Murtovaara 9 Cb 57	88640 Ontojoki 9 Da 56	92620 Piippola 8 Da 53
39810 Linnankylä 14 Ea 51	73300 Mutalahti 16 Ea 59	95750 Orajärvi 8 Ca 52	93290 Pintamo 9 Cb 55
83100 Liperi 15 Ea 57	40950 Muurame 15 Ea 53	99600 Orakylä 8 Bb 54	38100 Pirkkala 14 Eb 51
58620 Lohilahti 15 Eb 56	44880 Muurasjärvi 14 Db 53	66800 Oravais 8 Db 50	29720 Pirttijärvi 14 Eb 49
97420 Lohiniva 8 Bb 52	97140 Muurola 8 Ca 53	58130 Oravi 15 Ea 56	97655 Pittisjärvi 8 Ca 54
08100 Lohja 30 Fa 52	88120 Muuttola 9 Db 56	16300 Orimattila 15 Fa 53	10420 Pohja 30 Fa 51
68230 Lohtaja 8 Db 51	61400 Myllykoski 14 Ea 50	35300 Orivesi 14 Eb 52	14810 Pohjoinen 14 Eb 52
32200 Loimaa 14 Fa 51	63900 Myllymäki 14 Ea 52	88220 Otanmäki 9 Da 55	34330 Poikelus 14 Eb 51
23450 Lokalahti 14 Fa 49	23100 Mynämäki 14 Fa 49	50670 Otava 15 Eb 55	99195 Pokka 5 Ba 53
99645 Lokka 5 Bb 55	07600 Myrskylä 15 Fa 53	91720 Oterma 9 Da 55	83700 Polvijärvi 15 Ea 57
99160 Lompolo 4 Ba 52	21450 Mäentaka 14 Fa 50	86300 Oulainen 8 Da 52	39570 Polviniemi 9 Cb 56
12700 Loppi 14 Fa 52	95645 Mämmilä 8 Ca 51	90100 Oulu 8 Cb 53	29630 Pomarkku 14 Eb 50
95340 Loue 8 Ca 52	04600 Mäntsälä 15 Fa 53	90460 Oulunsalo 8 Da 53	28100 Pori 14 Eb 49

145

INDEX WITH POST CODES · ORTSREGISTER MIT POSTLEITZAHLEN · INDICE CON CODICI
STEDREGISTER MED POSTNUMRE · PLAATSNAMENREGISTER MET POSTCODE · REJSTŘÍK

FIN

Pomainen | FIN | **Vehmaa**

07170 Pornainen 15 Fa 53	88400 Ristijärvi 9 Da 56	71800 Siilinjärvi 15 Db 55	41160 Tikkakoski 15 Ea 53
31320 Portimo 8 Ca 54	41520 Ristimäki 15 Ea 54	39300 Siivikko 9 Cb 55	95970 Tiurajärvi 4 Bb 52
06100 Porvoo 15 Fa 53	25500 Ristinkulma 30 Fa 51	73210 Sikovuono 5 Ba 54	82600 Tohmajärvi 15 Ea 58
97900 Posio 9 Ca 56	25950 Rosala 30 Fb 50	69750 Sillanpää 14 Db 51	69300 Toholampi 14 Db 52
93730 Poussu 9 Cb 57	96700 Rovaniemi 8 Ca 53	95200 Simo 8 Cb 53	41660 Toivakka 15 Ea 54
21660 Prostvik 30 Fa 50	34600 Ruhala 14 Eb 52	54330 Simola 15 Fa 56	97340 Tolonen 8 Ca 53
93100 Pudasjärvi 9 Cb 54	74940 Ruhkaperä 14 Db 53	97220 Sinettä 8 Ca 53	95400 Tornio 8 Cb 52
82430 Puhos 15 Ea 57	93600 Ruka 9 Ca 57	04130 Sipoo 15 Fa 53	99540 Torvinen 8 Bb 54
07560 Pukkila 15 Fa 53	56100 Ruokolahti 15 Eb 56	46710 Sippola 15 Fa 54	64320 Träskvik 14 Ea 49
99170 Pulju 4 Ba 52	98100 Ruopsa 9 Ca 55	99130 Sirkka 4 Bb 52	88120 Tuhkakylä 9 Da 56
92600 Pulkkila 8 Da 53	34600 Ruovesi 14 Eb 52	02580 Siuntio 30 Fa 52	71320 Tunturikylä 9 Ca 55
58450 Punkaharju 15 Eb 57	97330 Ruuhijärvi 8 Ca 52	99600 Sodankylä 8 Bb 54	46110 Tuohikotti 15 Eb 55
31900 Punkalaidun 14 Eb 51	36110 Ruutana 14 Eb 52	95255 Soikko 8 Cb 53	29790 Tuorila 14 Eb 49
89210 Puokio 9 Da 55	52270 Ryhälä 15 Eb 56	63800 Soini 14 Ea 52	91910 Tupos 8 Da 53
89200 Puolanka 9 Da 55	21140 Rymättylä 30 Fa 49	73640 Solojärvi 5 Ba 54	20100 Turku 14 Fa 50
43440 Puolimatka 14 Ea 52	93240 Rytinki 9 Cb 55	31400 Somero 14 Fa 51	95645 Turtola 8 Ca 51
69340 Purontaka 14 Db 52	98420 Rytylahti 9 Ca 55	74300 Sonkajärvi 15 Db 55	82730 Tuupovaara 15 Ea 58
52200 Puumala 15 Eb 56	71330 Räsälä 15 Ea 55	79130 Sorsakoski 15 Ea 55	63610 Tuuri 14 Ea 51
49270 Pyhtää 15 Fa 54	69820 Räyrinki 14 Db 51	88600 Sotkamo 9 Da 56	71200 Tuusniemi 15 Ea 56
86100 Pyhäjoki 8 Da 52	82300 Rääkkylä 15 Ea 57	22270 Storby 29 Fa 47	04300 Tuusula 14 Fa 52
86610 Pyhäjärvi 14 Db 53	95400 Röyttä 8 Cb 52	74340 Sukeva 9 Db 55	85140 Tynkä 8 Da 52
44660 Pyhältö 15 Fa 55	72840 Saarela 15 Db 54	58700 Sulkava 15 Eb 56	91800 Tyrnävä 8 Da 53
92930 Pyhäntä 9 Da 54	89547 Saarela 9 Db 57	44200 Suolahti 15 Ea 53	66295 Töjby 14 Ea 49
23950 Pyhäranta 14 Fa 49	43100 Saarijärvi 14 Ea 53	52830 Suomenniemi 15 Eb 55	38580 Törmänen 5 Ba 55
82200 Pyhäselkä 15 Ea 57	91440 Saarikoski 8 Cb 54	89600 Suomussalmi 9 Da 56	89110 Törmänmäki 9 Da 55
84100 Pyykangas 8 Da 52	99490 Saarikoski 4 Ba 49	77600 Suonenjoki 15 Ea 55	63600 Töysä 14 Ea 51
36600 Pälkäne 14 Eb 52	95920 Saaripudas 8 Bb 51	11020 Supru 5 Ab 56	81280 Uimaharju 15 Ea 58
61980 Pöntäne 14 Ea 50	99830 Saariselkä 5 Ba 55	51380 Synsiö 15 Ea 54	47710 Uimila 15 Eb 54
99490 Pättikä 4 Ba 49	82655 Saarivaara 15 Ea 58	69420 Syri 14 Db 52	81290 Ukkola 15 Ea 58
66270 Pörtom 14 Ea 49	70130 Saarivaara 9 Da 57	19700 Sysmä 15 Eb 53	83630 Ulla 15 Ea 56
77600 Pörölänmäki 15 Ea 55	36420 Sahalahti 14 Eb 52	99740 Syväjärvi 8 Bb 53	28400 Ulvila 14 Eb 49
21880 Pöytyä 14 Fa 50	98950 Saija 9 Bb 56	56310 Syyspohja 15 Eb 56	26910 Unaja 14 Eb 49
92100 Raahe 8 Da 52	54915 Saimaanharju 15 Eb 56	27800 Säkylä 14 Eb 50	73470 Unari 8 Bb 53
97250 Raanujärvi 8 Ca 52	74230 Salahmi 9 Db 54	73470 Särkijärvi 8 Ca 53	23840 Untamala 14 Fa 49
99340 Raatama 4 Ba 52	98900 Salla 9 Ca 56	91640 Särkijärvi 9 Da 55	31760 Urjala 14 Eb 51
21200 Raisio 14 Fa 50	98600 Sallatunturi 9 Ca 56	99130 Särkijärvi 4 Bb 51	91600 Utajärvi 9 Da 54
39610 Raivala 14 Eb 50	98660 Salmivaara 9 Ca 56	59310 Särkisalmi 15 Eb 57	99950 Utsjoki 5 Ab 55
99800 Raja-Jooseppi 5 Ba 56	24100 Salo 30 Fa 51	09100 Särkiä 30 Fa 51	41230 Uurainen 14 Ea 53
05200 Rajamäki 14 Fa 52	58260 Salonkylä 15 Ea 57	91760 Säräisniemi 9 Da 54	61980 Uuro 14 Ea 50
17380 Rantapalo 8 Ca 54	83700 Sammakkovaara 15 Ea 57	72550 Säviä 15 Db 54	23500 Uusikaupunki 14 Fa 49
58900 Rantasalmi 15 Ea 56	95750 Sammalvaara 8 Bb 52	71800 Säyneinen 15 Db 56	16100 Uusikylä 15 Fa 53
92500 Rantsila 8 Da 53	61720 Sammatti 30 Fa 51	74920 Säytsjärvi 5 Ab 55	73800 Uutela 15 Bb 54
97700 Ranua 8 Cb 54	53850 Sammonlahti 15 Eb 56	34240 Sääksjärvi 14 Eb 51	88400 Uva 9 Da 56
89200 Rasinkylä 9 Da 55	21660 Samslax 30 Fa 49	65930 Södra Vallgrund 14 Db 49	40800 Vaajakoski 15 Ea 53
21037 Rasivaara 15 Ea 57	91620 Sanginkylä 9 Da 54	44500 Taimoniemi 14 Db 53	91700 Vaala 9 Da 54
88900 Rastinkylä 9 Db 57	17800 Sappee 14 Eb 52	95270 Tainiemi 8 Cb 53	99710 Vaalajärvi 8 Bb 54
99300 Rauhala 4 Bb 52	39980 Sara 14 Ea 50	74200 Taipaleenharju 9 Cb 54	65100 Vaasa 14 Db 49
26100 Rauma 14 Eb 49	93250 Sarajärvi 9 Cb 55	54920 Taipalsaari 15 Eb 56	54270 Vainikkala 15 Fa 56
77700 Rautalampi 15 Ea 54	79100 Sarkamäki 15 Ea 56	93400 Taivalkoski 9 Cb 56	97130 Valajaskoski 8 Ca 53
73900 Rautavaara 15 Db 56	79985 Sarvikumpu 15 Ea 57	23310 Taivassalo 14 Fa 49	37600 Valkeakoski 14 Eb 52
85160 Rautio 8 Da 52	81360 Sarvinki 15 Ea 58	31300 Tammela 14 Fa 51	45360 Valkeala 15 Fa 54
56610 Rautjärvi 15 Eb 57	99650 Sattanen 5 Bb 54	33100 Tampere 14 Eb 51	74210 Valkeiskylä 15 Db 55
80330 Reijola 15 Ea 57	21570 Sauvo 30 Fa 50	99640 Tanhua 5 Bb 54	07910 Valko 15 Fa 54
85900 Reisjärvi 14 Db 52	75530 Savijärvi 9 Db 57	99695 Tankavaara 5 Ba 55	75700 Valtimo 9 Db 56
14300 Renko 14 Fa 52	31130 Saviniemi 14 Fa 51	91240 Tannila 8 Cb 53	38200 Vammala 14 Eb 50
65800 Replot 14 Db 49	86710 Saviselkä 8 Da 54	93780 Teeriranta 9 Cb 57	32610 Vampula 14 Eb 50
73130 Repojoki 5 Ba 53	54800 Savitaipale 15 Eb 55	25570 Teijo 30 Fa 50	01200 Vantaa Vanda 30 Fa 52
28900 Reposaari 14 Eb 49	57100 Savonlinna 15 Eb 56	62100 Teljo 9 Db 57	95300 Varajoki 9 Da 57
88460 Revonkanta 9 Da 56	58300 Savonranta 15 Eb 56	10520 Tenala 30 Fa 51	95300 Varajärvi 8 Ca 52
85410 Rieskaniemi 8 Db 52	98800 Savukoski 9 Bb 56	99150 Tepasto 4 Bb 52	78200 Varkaus 15 Ea 55
11100 Riihimäki 14 Fa 52	60100 Seinäjoki 14 Ea 50	99280 Tepsa 5 Bb 53	73200 Varpaisjärvi 15 Db 55
99720 Riipi 8 Bb 54	99930 Sevettijärvi 5 Ab 56	12400 Tervakoski 14 Fa 52	81820 Varpanen 15 Eb 54
95750 Riipisenvaara 8 Ca 52	95800 Sieppijärvi 8 Bb 51	72210 Tervo 15 Ea 54	88930 Vartius 9 Da 57
71160 Riistavesi 15 Ea 56	85410 Sievi 8 Db 52	95300 Tervola 8 Ca 52	25260 Vaskio 14 Fa 50
10570 Rilax 30 Fb 51	29810 Siikainen 14 Eb 49	64700 Teuva 14 Ea 49	34710 Vaskivesi 14 Ea 51
52100 Ristiina 15 Eb 55	92320 Siikajoki 8 Da 53	74980 Tihilänkangas 9 Db 54	23210 Vehmaa 14 Fa 49

POSTALI · ÍNDICE CON CÓDIGOS POSTALES · INDICE DE LUGARES COM CÓDIGOS POSTAIS ·
MÍST S PSČ · ZOZNAM OBCÍ S PSČ · INDEKS MIEJSCOWOŚCI Z KOD POCZTOWY

146

Vehmersalmi Brighton

71310 Vehmersalmi 15 Ea 56	63700 Ähtäri 14 Ea 52	Arisaig 20 Ha 22	Bedlington 25 Hb 26
02880 Veikkola 30 Fa 52	95970 Äkäslompolo 4 Bb 52	Armadale 20 Ga 23	Belcoo 23 Ja 20
89600 Veikkola 9 Cb 56	44100 Äänekoski 15 Ea 53	Armagh 23 Ja 21	Belfast 24 Ja 22
94830 Veitsiluoto 8 Cb 52	10660 Öby 30 Fb 51	Arnol 20 Ga 21	Belford 25 Hb 26
74440 Vesalanperä 8 Ca 53	64440 Ömossa 14 Ea 49	Ashbourne 24 Jab 26	Belleek 23 Ja 19
72300 Vesanto 15 Ea 54	66140 Övermalax 14 Ea 49	Ashford 45 Kb 28	Belmont 21 Fa 27
69700 Veteli 14 Db 51	64610 Övermark 14 Ea 49	Ashington 25 Hb 26	Belper 24 Jab 26
81850 Vieki 15 Db 57		Aspatria 24 Ja 24	Berriedale 21 Ga 24
74200 Vieremä 15 Db 55		Auchinleck 20 Hb 23	Berwick-upon-Tweed
19110 Vierumäki 15 Eb 53		Auchnagatt 21 Gb 25	21 Hb 25
86400 Vihanti 8 Da 53		Auchterader 20 Ha 24	Beverley 25 Jab 27
41330 Vihtavuori 15 Ea 53		Aultbea 20 Gb 22	Bicester 44 Kb 26
03400 Vihti 14 Fa 52	**FL**	Aviemore 20 Gb 24	Bideford 44 Kb 23
37830 Viiala 14 Eb 51		Axminster 44 La 25	Biggar 20 Hb 24
83400 Viinijärvi 15 Ea 57	9490 Vaduz 59 Mb37	Aylesbury 44 Kb 27	Biggleswade 45 Ka 27
69600 Viiperi 14 Db 51		Aylsham 25 Ka 29	Billingham 25 Ja 26
73710 Viitaniemi 15 Db 56		Ayr 20 Hb 23	Billinghay 25 Jab 27
44500 Viitasaari 15 Db 53	**GB**	Badcaul 20 Gb 22	Birmingham 24 Ka 26
97510 Vikajärvi 8 Ca 54		Bagh a Chaisteil 20 Ha 20	Bishop Auckland 25 Ja 26
58360 Villala 15 Ea 57	Aberaeron 24 Ka 23	Bagh a Tuath 20 Gb 20	Bishop`s Cleeve 44 Kb 25
35700 Vilppula 14 Ea 52	Aberdare 44 Kb 24	Baile Ailein 20 Ga 21	Bishop`s Stortford 45 Kb 28
62800 Vimpeli 14 Db 51	Aberdeen 21 Gb 25	Bala 24 Ka 24	Bixter 21 Fa 26
08700 Virkkala 30 Fa 52	Aberfeldy 20 Ha 24	Balbeggie 20 Ha 24	Blackburn 24 Jab 25
70600 Virkkunen 9 Cb 55	Aberffraw 24 Jab 23	Ballantrae 24 Hb 22	Blackpool 24 Jab 24
49900 Virolahti 15 Fa 55	Aberfoyle 20 Ha 23	Ballater 21 Gb 24	Blackwaterfoot 20 Hb 22
34800 Virrat 14 Ea 51	Abergavenny 44 Kb 24	Ballinamallard 23 Ja 20	Blairmore 20 Ha 23
77330 Virtasalmi 15 Ea 55	Abergele 24 Jab 24	Ballinluig 20 Ha 24	Blakeney 25 Ka 29
34870 Visuvesi 14 Ea 51	Abersoch 24 Ka 23	Ballycastle 20 Hb 21	Blandford Forum 44 La 25
62310 Voltti 14 Db 50	Aberystwyth 24 Ka 23	Ballygawley 23 Ja 20	Blyth 25 Hb 26
99530 Vuohijärvi 15 Eb 54	Abingdon 44 Kb 26	Ballymena 24 Ja 21	Blyth Bridge 20 Hb 24
73100 Vuohtomäki 15 Db 54	Abington 20 Hb 24	Ballymoney 20 Hb 21	Bodmin 43 La 23
88610 Vuokatti 9 Da 56	Aboyne 21 Gb 25	Ballynahinch 24 Ja 22	Bognor Regis 44 La 27
88270 Vuolijoki 9 Da 55	Acha Mor 20 Ga 21	Ballywalter 24 Ja 22	Boldon 25 Hb 26
99410 Vuontisjärvi 4 Ba 52	Achalader 20 Ha 23	Balmedie 21 Gb 25	Bolton 24 Jab 25
73200 Vuorela 15 Ea 55	Achavanich 21 Ga 24	Balmouth 24 Ka 23	Bolton Abbey 24 Jab 26
23360 Vuosnainen 14 Fa 49	Achnasheen 20 Gb 22	Baltasound 21 Fa27	Bonar Brigde 20 Gb 23
98360 Vuostimo 9 Ca 55	Airdrie 20 Hb 24	Banbridge 23 Ja 21	Bonnyrigg 20 Hb 24
99690 Vuotso 5 Ba 55	Aith 21 Fa 26	Banbury 44 Ka 26	Bootle 24 Ja 24
88210 Vuottolahti 9 Da 55	Aldeburgh 45 Ka 29	Banchory 21 Gb 25	Borehamwood 45 Kb 27
66500 Vähäkyrö 14 Db 50	Aldershot 44 Kb 27	Banff 21 Gb 25	Borgh 20 Ga 21
69100 Väli-Kannus 8 Db 51	Alness 20 Gb 23	Bangor 24 Ja 22	Borve 20 Gb 21
64140 Välikylä 14 Db 51	Alnwick 25 Hb 26	Bangor 24 Jab 23	Boston 25 Ka 27
98820 Värriö 5 Bb 55	Alston 24 Ja 25	Barabhas 20 Ga 21	Bothel 24 Ja 24
22610 Västeränga 30 Fa 48	Altnaharra 20 Ga 23	Barcaldine 20 Ha 22	Bourne 25 Ka 27
11012 Väylä 5 Ab 55	Alton 44 Kb 27	Barmouth 24 Ka 23	Bournemouth 44 La 26
43430 Väätäiskylä 14 Ea 52	Alyth 20 Ha 24	Barnard Castle 25 Ja 26	Brackley 44 Ka 26
66600 Vörå-Maxmo 14 Db 50	Amble 25 Hb 26	Barnsley 24 Jab 26	Bracknell 44 Kb 27
22550 Vårdö 30 Fa 48	Amersham 45 Kb 27	Barnstaple 44 Kb 23	Bradford 24 Jab 26
99340 Yli-Kyrö 4 Ba 52	Amesbury 44 Kb 26	Barrapoll 20 Ha 21	Brae 21 Fa 26
95270 Yli-Kärppä 8 Cb 53	Amlwch 24 Jab 23	Barrhill 24 Hb 23	Braemar 20 Gb 24
91200 Yli-Ii 8 Cb 53	Ammanford 44 Kb 24	Barrow-in-Furness 24 Ja 24	Braintree 45 Kb 28
89670 Yli-Näljänkä 9 Cb 56	Amulree 20 Ha 24	Barry 44 Kb 24	Brampton 24 Ja 25
95300 Yli-Paakkola 8 Ca 52	Andover 44 Kb 26	Barton-upon-Humber	Brandon 45 Ka 28
91300 Yli-Vuotto 9 Da 54	Annalong 24 Ja 22	25 Jab 27	Braunton 44 Kb 23
91300 Ylikiiminki 8 Cb 54	Annan 24 Ja 24	Basildon 45 Kb 28	Brechin 21 Ha 25
61400 Ylistaro 14 Ea 50	Anstruther 21 Ha 25	Basingstoke 44 Kb 26	Brecon 44 Kb 24
95600 Ylitornio 8 Ca 51	Antrim 24 Ja 21	Bath 44 Kb 25	Brenfield 20 Hb 22
84100 Ylivieska 8 Da 52	Anwoth 24 Ja 23	Bathage 20 Hb 24	Brentwood 45 Kb 28
95980 Ylläsjärvi 8 Bb 52	Appleby-in-Westmorland	Batley 24 Jab 26	Bride 24 Ja 23
54410 Ylämaa 15 Fa 56	24 Ja 25	Beadnell 25 Hb 26	Bridgend 20 Hb 21
80400 Ylämylly 15 Ea 57	Arbroath 21 Ha 25	Bearsden 20 Hb 23	Bridgend 44 Kb 24
21900 Yläne 14 Fa 50	Ardelve 20 Gb 22	Bearsted 45 Kb 28	Bridgwater 44 Kb 24
33470 Ylöjärvi 14 Eb 51	Ardglass 24 Ja 22	Beaumaris 24 Jab 23	Bridlington 25 Ja 27
86170 Yppäri 8 Da 52	Ardlui 20 Ha 23	Bebington 24 Jab 25	Bridport 44 La 25
32100 Ypäjä 14 Fa 51	Ardlussa 20 Ha 22	Beccles 45 Ka 29	Brigg 25 Jab 27
32740 Äetsä 14 Eb 50	Ardvasar 20 Gb 22	Bedale 25 Ja 26	Brigg 25 Jab 27
	Arileod 20 Ha 21	Bedford 45 Ka 27	Brighton 45 La 27

147

INDEX WITH POST CODES · ORTSREGISTER MIT POSTLEITZAHLEN · INDICE CON CODICI
STEDREGISTER MED POSTNUMRE · PLAATSNAMENREGISTER MET POSTCODE · REJSTŘÍK

GB

Bristol   GB   Glencoe

Bristol 44 Kb 25
Brixham 44 La 24
Broad Oak 45 La 28
Broadford 20 Gb 22
Broadmeadows 24 Hb 25
Broadstairs 45 Kb 29
Bromsgrove 24 Ka 25
Bromyard 24 Ka 25
Brora 20 Ga 24
Brough 24 Ja 25
Broughton in Furness
    24 Ja 24
Broxburn 20 Hb 24
Brynmawr 44 Kb 24
Buckhaven 20 Ha 24
Buckie 21 Gb 25
Buckingham 44 Kb 27
Buckley 24 Jab 24
Bude 43 La 23
Builth Wells 24 Ka 24
Bungay 45 Ka 29
Buntingford 45 Kb 27
Burgess Hill 45 La 27
Burnham Market 25 Ka 28
Burnley 24 Jab 25
Burton uponTrent 24 Ka 26
Burwick 21 Ga 25
Bury 24 Jab 25
Bury Saint Edmunds 45 Ka 28
Bushmills 20 Hb 21
Buxton 24 Jab 26
Byrness 24 Hb 25
Caernarfon 24 Jab 23
Caerphilly 44 Kb 24
Cairnbaan 20 Ha 22
Cairnryan 24 Ja 22
Caister-on-Sea 45 Ka 29
Calanais 20 Ga 21
Callander 20 Ha 23
Callington 43 La 23
Calvine 20 Ha 24
Camborne 43 La 22
Cambridge 45 Ka 28
Camelford 43 La 23
Campbeltown 20 Hb 22
Cannich 20 Gb 23
Cannock 24 Ka 25
Canterbury 45 Kb 29
Canvey Island 45 Kb 28
Caolas 20 Ha 21
Cardiff 44 Kb 24
Cardigan 24 Ka 23
Carlabhagh 20 Ga 21
Carlisle 24 Ja 25
Carluke 20 Hb 24
Carmarthen 24 Kb 23
Carnforth 24 Ja 25
Carnlough 24 Ja 22
Carnoustie 21 Ha 25
Carrbridge 20 Gb 24
Carrickfergus 24 Ja 22
Carterton 44 Kb 26
Castle Douglas 24 Ja 24
Castletown 21 Ga 24
Castletown 24 Ja 23
Castlewellan 24 Ja 22

Catterick 25 Ja 26
Cemaes 24 Jab 23
Chard 44 La 25
Chatham 45 Kb 28
Chatteris 45 Ka 28
Cheddar 44 Kb 25
Chelmsford 45 Kb 28
Cheltenham 44 Kb 25
Chepstow 44 Kb 25
Chesham 45 Kb 27
Chester 24 Jab 25
Chesterfield 24 Jab 26
Chichester 44 La 27
Chippenham 44 Kb 25
Chorley 24 Jab 25
Christchurch 44 La 26
Church Stretton 24 Ka 25
Churchdown 44 Kb 25
Cirencester 44 Kb 26
Clacton-on-Sea 45 Kb 29
Cleator Moor 24 Ja 24
Clevedon 44 Kb 25
Clitheroe 24 Jab 25
Cluanie Inn 20 Gb 22
Clydebank 20 Hb 23
Coalville 24 Ka 26
Cockermouth 24 Ja 24
Col 20 Ga 21
Colchester 45 Kb 28
Coldbackie 20 Ga 23
Coleraine 20 Hb 21
Collafirth 21 Fa 26
Collieston 21 Gb 26
Colne 24 Jab 25
Colpy 21 Gb 25
Colsterworth 25 Ka 27
Colwyn Bay 24 Jab 24
Comrie 20 Ha 24
Congleton 24 Jab 25
Coningsby 25 Jab 27
Connel 20 Ha 22
Consett 25 Ja 26
Conwy 24 Jab 24
Cookstown 23 Ja 21
Copplestone 44 La 24
Corby 45 Ka 27
Coupar Angus 20 Ha 24
Coventry 24 Ka 26
Cowdenbeath 20 Ha 24
Craig 20 Gb 22
Craigavon 23 Ja 21
Craigellachie 21 Gb 24
Craighouse 20 Hb 22
Cramlington 25 Hb 26
Cranleigh 44 Kb 27
Craven Arms 24 Ka 25
Crawley 45 Kb 27
Crediton 44 La 24
Crewe 24 Jab 25
Crewkerne 44 La 25
Crianlarich 20 Ha 23
Crieff 20 Ha 24
Cromer 25 Ka 29
Crook 25 Ja 26
Crosby 24 Jab 24
Crowborough 45 Kb 28

Cruden Bay 21 Gb 26
Cullivoe 21 Fa 26
Cullompton 44 La 24
Cumnock 20 Hb 23
Cupar 20 Ha 24
Cushendall 20 Hb 21
Cwmbran 44 Kb 24
Dalbeattie 24 Ja 24
Dalgety Bay 20 Ha 24
Dalhalvaig 21 Ga 24
Dalkeith 20 Hb 24
Dalmally 20 Ha 23
Dalmellington 24 Hb 23
Dalnaspidal 20 Ha 23
Darlington 25 Ja 26
Dartford 45 Kb 28
Dartmouth 44 La 24
Dava 20 Gb 24
Daventry 44 Ka 26
Daviot 20 Gb 23
Dawlish 44 La 24
Deal 45 Kb 29
Denbigh 24 Jab 24
Denholm 24 Hb 25
Derby 24 Ka 26
Dereham 45 Ka 28
Devizes 44 Kb 26
Dewsbury 24 Jab 26
Didcot 44 Kb 26
Dingwall 20 Gb 23
Dishforth 25 Ja 26
Diss 45 Ka 29
Dolgellau 24 Ka 24
Donaghadee 24 Ja 22
Doncaster 25 Jab 26
Donington 25 Ka 27
Dorchester 44 La 25
Dornoch 20 Gb 23
Douglas 24 Ja 23
Dover 45 Kb 29
Downham Market 45 Ka 28
Downpatrick 24 Ja 22
Driffield 25 Ja 27
Droitwich 24 Ka 25
Dronfield 24 Jab 26
Druid 24 Ka 24
Drummore 24 Ja 23
Drumnadrochit 20 Gb 23
Drynoch 20 Gb 21
Dudley 44 Ka 25
Dufftown 21 Gb 24
Dumbarton 20 Hb 23
Dumfries 24 Hb 24
Dunbar 21 Hb 25
Dunblane 20 Ha 24
Dundee 20 Ha 25
Dundonnell 20 Gb 22
Dundreggan 20 Gb 23
Dunfermline 20 Ha 24
Dungannon 23 Ja 21
Dungiven 19 Ja 21
Dunkeld 20 Ha 24
Dunoon 20 Hb 23
Dunstable 45 Kb 27
Dunvegan 20 Gb 21
Durness 20 Ga 23

Dursley 44 Kb 25
Earls Colne 45 Kb 28
Easingwold 25 Ja 26
East Grinstead 45 Kb 27
East Kilbride 20 Hb 23
Eastbourne 45 La 28
Eastleigh 44 La 26
Edinburgh 20 Hb 24
Eglwyswrw 24 Ka 23
Egremont 24 Ja 24
Elgin 21 Gb 24
Ellon 21 Gb 25
Elvanfoot 24 Hb 24
Ely 45 Ka 28
Enniskillen 23 Ja 20
Esher 45 Kb 27
Evesham 44 Ka 26
Exeter 44 La 24
Exmouth 44 La 24
Exton 44 Kb 24
Eyemouth 21 Hb 25
Fakenham 25 Ka 28
Falkirk 20 Ha 24
Falmouth 43 La 22
Farnborough 44 Kb 27
Farnham 44 Kb 27
Felixstowe 45 Kb 29
Feolin Ferry 20 Hb 21
Ferryhill 25 Ja 26
Filey 25 Ja 27
Findhorn 20 Gb 24
Fionnphort 20 Ha 21
Fishguard 24 Kb 23
Flamborough 25 Ja 27
Fleetwood 24 Jab 24
Fochabers 21 Gb 24
Folkestone 45 Kb 29
Fordingbridge 44 La 26
Forfar 21 Ha 25
Formby 24 Jab 24
Forres 20 Gb 24
Forsinard 21 Ga 24
Fort Augustus 20 Gb 23
Fort William 20 Ha 22
Fortrose 20 Gb 23
Fortuneswell 44 La 25
Fowey 43 La 23
Fraserburgh 21 Gb 25
Freshwater 44 La 26
Frinton-on-Sea 45 Kb 29
Frome 44 Kb 25
Gainsborough 25 Jab 27
Gairloch 20 Gb 22
Galashiels 20 Hb 25
Garelochhead 20 Ha 23
Garforth 25 Jab 26
Garve 20 Gb 23
Gateshead 25 Ja 26
Gillingham 45 Kb 28
Gills 21 Ga 24
Girvan 24 Hb 23
Glasbury 24 Ka 24
Glasgow 20 Hb 23
Glastonbury 44 Kb 25
Glenbarr 20 Hb 22
Glencoe 20 Ha 22

POSTALI · ÍNDICE CON CÓDIGOS POSTALES · INDICE DE LUGARES COM CÓDIGOS POSTAIS ·
MÍST S PSČ · ZOZNAM OBCÍ S PSČ · INDEKS MIEJSCOWOŚCI Z KOD POCZTOWY

148

Glendarud 20 Ha 22	High Wycombe 44 Kb 27	Kildonan 20 Hb 22	Livingston 20 Hb 24
Glenfinnan 20 Ha 22	Highbridge 44 Kb 24	Kilkeel 24 Ja 21	Lizard 43 Lb 22
Glenluce 24 Ja 23	Hinckley 24 Ka 26	Kilkenzie 20 Hb 22	Llanaelhaearn 24 Ka 23
Glenrothes 20 Ha 24	Hipswell 25 Ja 26	Killichonan 20 Ha 23	Llandeilo 44 Kb 23
Gloucester 44 Kb 25	Hollandstoun 21 Fb 25	Killin 20 Ha 23	Llandovery 24 Kb 24
Goole 25 Jab 27	Hollybush 20 Hb 23	Kilmaluag 20 Gb 21	Llandrindod Wells 24 Ka 24
Gosport 44 La 26	Holmrock 24 Ja 24	Kilmarnock 20 Hb 23	Llandudno 24 Jab 24
Grangemouth 20 Ha 24	Holsworthy 44 La 23	Kilmelfort 20 Ha 22	Llanelli 44 Kb 23
Grantham 25 Ka 27	Holt 25 Ka 29	Kilwinning 20 Hb 23	Llangollen 24 Ka 24
Grantown-on-Spey 20 Gb 24	Holyhead 24 Jab 23	Kinbrace 20 Ga 24	Llangurig 24 Ka 24
Grantshouse 21 Hb 25	Honiton 44 La 24	Kincraig 20 Gb 24	Llanrwst 24 Jab 24
Grasmere 24 Ja 24	Horncastle 25 Jab 27	King's Lynn 25 Ka 28	Loch Baghasdail 20 Gb 20
Gravesend 45 Kb 28	Hornsea 25 Jab 27	Kingarth 20 Hb 22	Loch nam Madadh 20 Gb 20
Grays 45 Kb 28	Horsham 45 Kb 27	Kingsbridge 44 La 24	Lochailort 20 Ha 22
Great Malvern 44 Ka 25	Houghton 45 Kb 27	Kingston upon Hull 25 Jab 27	Lochaline 20 Ha 22
Great Torrington 44 La 23	Houton 24 Ga 24	Kingussie 20 Gb 23	Locharbriggs 24 Hb 24
Great Yarmouth 45 Ka 29	Hucknall 25 Jab 26	Kinlochewe 20 Gb 22	Lochinver 20 Ga 22
Greenlaw 20 Hb 25	Huddersfield 24 Jab 26	Kintraw 20 Ha 22	Lockerbie 24 Hb 24
Greenock 20 Hb 23	Hungerford 44 Kb 26	Kirbister 21 Ga 24	Loddon 45 Ka 29
Greenodd 24 Ja 24	Hunmanby 25 Ja 27	Kirkby Lonsdale 24 Ja 25	Loftus 25 Ja 27
Gretna 24 Ja 24	Hunstanton 25 Ka 28	Kirkby Stephen 24 Ja 25	Logie Coldstone 21 Gb 25
Greysteel 19 Hb 20	Huntingdon 45 Ka 27	Kirkcaldy 20 Ha 24	London 45 Kb 27
Grimsby 25 Jab 27	Huntly 21 Gb 25	Kirkcolm 24 Ja 22	Londonderry 19 Ja 20
Guildford 44 Kb 27	Hynish 20 Ha 21	Kirkcudbright 24 Ja 23	Long Preston 24 Ja 25
Guisborough 25 Ja 26	Hythe 44 La 26	Kirkintilloch 20 Hb 23	Longtown 24 Hb 25
Gwaun-Cae-Gurwen 44 Kb 24	Hythe 45 Kb 29	Kirkwall 21 Ga 25	Looe 43 La 23
Hackland 21 Fb 24	Idrigill 20 Gb 21	Kirriemuir 20 Ha 24	Lossiemouth 21 Gb 24
Haddington 20 Hb 25	Ilchester 44 La 25	Knighton 24 Ka 24	Loughborough 24 Ka 26
Hailsham 45 La 28	Ilfracombe 44 Kb 23	Knutsford 24 Jab 25	Louth 25 Jab 27
Halesworth 45 Ka 29	Ilkeston 24 Ka 26	Kyle of Lochalsh 20 Gb 22	Lowestoft 45 Ka 29
Halifax 24 Jab 26	Ilkley 24 Jab 26	L'Erée 44 Lb 25	Ludlow 24 Ka 25
Halstead 45 Kb 28	Ilminster 44 La 25	Laggan 20 Gb 23	Lurgan 23 Ja 21
Haltwhistle 24 Ja 25	Immingham 25 Jab 27	Lairg 20 Ga 23	Luton 45 Kb 27
Hamilton 20 Hb 23	Inchnadamph 20 Ga 23	Lampeter 24 Ka 23	Lybster 21 Ga 24
Harlow 45 Kb 28	Ingleton 24 Ja 25	Lanark 20 Hb 24	Lydd 45 La 28
Harpenden 45 Kb 27	Ingoldmells 25 Jab 28	Lancaster 24 Ja 25	Lyme Regis 44 La 25
Harrogate 25 Jab 26	Inveran 20 Gb 23	Langholm 24 Hb 25	Lynton 44 Kb 24
Hartlepool 25 Ja 26	Inveraray 20 Ha 22	Largs 20 Hb 23	Lytham Saint Anne's
Harwich 45 Kb 29	Invergarry 20 Gb 23	Larne 24 Ja 22	24 Jab 24
Haslemere 44 Kb 27	Invergordon 20 Gb 23	Latheron 21 Ga 24	Mablethorpe 25 Jab 28
Haslingden 24 Jab 25	Invermoriston 20 Gb 23	Launceston 43 La 23	Macclesfield 24 Jab 25
Hastings 45 La 28	Inverness 20 Gb 23	Laxford Bridge 20 Ga 22	Macduff 21 Gb 25
Hatfield 25 Jab 26	Inverurie 21 Gb 25	Leadenham 25 Jab 27	Machynlleth 24 Ka 24
Hatfield 45 Kb 27	Ipswich 45 Ka 29	Leatherhead 45 Kb 27	Maesteg 44 Kb 24
Haverfordwest 23 Kb 23	Irvine 20 Hb 23	Ledbury 44 Ka 25	Maghera 23 Ja 21
Haverhill 45 Ka 28	Irvinestown 23 Ja 20	Ledmore 20 Ga 23	Magherafelt 23 Ja 21
Hawes 24 Ja 25	Isbister 21 Fa 24	Leeds 25 Jab 26	Maidenhead 44 Kb 27
Hawick 24 Hb 25	Islibhig 20 Ga 20	Leicester 24 Ka 26	Maidstone 45 Kb 28
Haxby 25 Ja 26	Jedburgh 24 Hb 25	Leigh 24 Jab 25	Maldon 45 Kb 28
Haywards Heath 45 La 27	John o'Groats 21 Ga 24	Leighton Buzzard 45 Kb 27	Mallaig 20 Gb 22
Helensburgh 20 Ha 23	Johnshaven 21 Ha 25	Leominster 24 Ka 25	Mallwyd 24 Ka 24
Helmsdale 21 Ga 24	Keighley 24 Jab 26	Lerwick 21 Fa 26	Maltby 25 Jab 26
Helmsley 25 Ja 26	Keith 21 Gb 25	Letchworth 45 Kb 27	Maltby le Marsh 25 Jab 28
Helston 43 La 22	Kelso 24 Hb 25	Leven 20 Ha 24	Malton 25 Ja 27
Hemel Hempstead 45 Kb 27	Kempston 45 Ka 27	Levenwick 21 Fb 26	Manchester 24 Jab 25
Hemsby 45 Ka 29	Kendal 24 Ja 25	Lewes 45 La 27	Mansfield 25 Jab 26
Henley-on-Thames 44 Kb 27	Kennacraig 20 Hb 22	Leyburn 24 Ja 26	March 45 Ka 28
Hereford 44 Ka 25	Kentallen 20 Ha 22	Leyland 24 Jab 25	Margate 45 Kb 29
Heriot 20 Hb 25	Kesh 23 Ja 20	Lichfield 24 Ka 26	Market Drayton 24 Ka 25
Herne Bay 45 Kb 29	Kessingland 45 Ka 29	Limavady 19 Hb 21	Market Harborough 45 Ka 27
Hessle 25 Jab 27	Keswick 24 Ja 24	Lincoln 25 Jab 27	Market Rasen 25 Jab 27
Hetton-le-Hole 25 Ja 26	Kettering 45 Ka 27	Lisburn 24 Ja 21	Market Weighton 25 Jab 27
Hexham 24 Ja 25	Keynsham 44 Kb 25	Liskeard 43 La 23	Marlborough 44 Kb 26
Heysham 24 Ja 25	Kidderminster 24 Ka 25	Lisnaskea 23 Ja 20	Maryport 24 Ja 24
Heywood 24 Jab 25	Kidlington 44 Kb 26	Littlehampton 44 La 27	Matlock 24 Jab 26
High Hawsker 25 Ja 27	Kidsgrove 24 Jab 25	Liverpool 24 Jab 25	Mauchline 20 Hb 23

149

INDEX WITH POST CODES · ORTSREGISTER MIT POSTLEITZAHLEN · INDICE CON CODICI
STEDREGISTER MED POSTNUMRE · PLAATSNAMENREGISTER MET POSTCODE · REJSTŘÍK

Maybole   20 Hb 23
Melksham   44 Kb 25
Melton Mowbray   25 Ka 27
Melvich   21 Ga 24
Mennock   24 Hb 24
Merthyr Tydfil   44 Kb 24
Miabhigh   20 Ga 21
Mid Yell   21 Fa 26
Middlesbrough   25 Ja 26
Middleton   24 Jab 25
Middlewich   24 Jab 25
Mildenhall   45 Ka 28
Milford Haven   23 Kb 22
Millom   24 Ja 24
Milton Keynes   45 Ka 27
Minehead   44 Kb 24
Mintlaw   21 Gb 25
Moffat   24 Hb 24
Monifieth   21 Ha 25
Monmouth   44 Kb 25
Montrose   21 Ha 25
Morecambe   24 Ja 25
Moreton in Marsh   44 Kb 26
Morpeth   25 Hb 26
Mossat   21 Gb 25
Moy   20 Ha 23
Muir of Ord   20 Gb 23
Muirkirk   20 Hb 23
Mybster   21 Ga 24
Na Buirgh   20 Gb 20
Nairn   20 Gb 24
Nantwich   24 Jab 25
Neath   44 Kb 24
Nelson   24 Jab 25
New Addington   45 Kb 27
New Galloway   24 Hb 23
New Grimsby   43 Lb 21
New Milton   44 La 26
New Quay   24 Ka 23
Newark-on-Trent   25 Jab 27
Newbury   44 Kb 26
Newcastle   24 Ja 22
Newcastle Emlyn   24 Ka 23
Newcastle upon Tyne   25 Ja 26
Newcastle-under-Lyme
      24 Jab 25
Newmarket   45 Ka 28
Newport   44 La 26
Newport   24 Ka 25
Newport   44 Kb 25
Newquay   43 La 22
Newry   23 Ja 21
Newton Abbot   44 La 24
Newton Aycliffe   25 Ja 26
Newton Mearns   20 Hb 23
Newton Stewart   24 Ja 23
Newton-le-Willows   24 Jab 25
Newtonabbey   24 Ja 22
Newtonhill   21 Gb 25
Newtonmore   20 Gb 23
Newtown   24 Ka 24
Newtownards   24 Ja 22
Newtownstewart   23 Ja 20
North Berwick   20 Ha 25
North Burlingham   45 Ka 29
North Shields   25 Hb 26

North Walsham   25 Ka 29
Northallerton   25 Ja 26
Northam   44 Kb 23
Northampton   44 Ka 27
Norwich   45 Ka 29
Norwick   21 fa27
Nottingham   25 Ka 26
Nuneaton   24 Ka 26
Oakham   25 Ka 27
Oban   20 Ha 22
Odie   21 Fb 25
Okehampton   44 La 23
Old Town   43 Lb 21
Oldham   24 Jab 25
Oldmeldrum   21 Gb 25
Omagh   23 Ja 20
Ormskirk   24 Jab 25
Oswestry   24 Ka 24
Otley   24 Jab 26
Otterburn   25 Hb 25
Oxford   44 Kb 26
Padstow   43 La 23
Paignton   44 La 24
Paisley   20 Hb 23
Patrington   25 Jab 27
Peel   24 Ja 23
Pembroke   43 Kb 23
Penarth   44 Kb 24
Penicuik   20 Hb 24
Penkridge   24 Ka 25
Penrith   24 Ja 25
Penryn   43 La 22
Pentrefoelas   24 Jab 24
Penzance   43 La 22
Perth   20 Ha 24
Peterborough   45 Ka 27
Peterculter   21 Gb 25
Peterhead   21 Gb 26
Peterlee   25 Ja 26
Petersfield   44 La 27
Pettigo   23 Ja 20
Pickering   25 Ja 27
Pitlochry   20 Ha 24
Plumpton   24 Ja 25
Plymouth   44 La 23
Pocklington   25 Jab 27
Polegate   45 La 28
Polmont   20 Hb 24
Pontefract   25 Jab 26
Ponteland   25 Hb 26
Poole   44 La 26
Poolewe   20 Gb 22
Port Charlotte   20 Hb 21
Port Einon   44 Kb 23
Port Ellen   20 Hb 21
Port Erin   24 Ja 23
Port Nis   20 Ga 21
Port nan Giuran   20 Ga 21
Port nan Long   20 Gb 20
Port Talbot   44 Kb 24
Port William   24 Ja 23
Portadown   23 Ja 21
Portaferry   24 Ja 22
Porthcawl   44 Kb 24
Porthmadog   24 Ka 23
Portlethen   21 Gb 25

Portnahaven   20 Hb 21
Portpatrick   24 Ja 22
Portree   20 Gb 21
Portrush   20 Hb 21
Portsmouth   44 La 26
Portsoy   21 Gb 25
Poulton-le-Fylde   24 Jab 25
Powburn   25 Hb 26
Preston   24 Jab 25
Preston   21 Hb 25
Prestwick   20 Hb 23
Pumsaint   24 Ka 24
Pwllheli   24 Ka 23
Quarff   21 Fa 26
Ramsey   24 Ja 23
Ramsgate   45 Kb 29
Rathen   21 Gb 25
Rathfriland   24 Ja 21
Rattray   20 Ha 24
Rawenworth   24 Ja 25
Rayleigh   45 Kb 28
Reading   44 Kb 27
Reay   21 Ga 24
Redditch   24 Ka 26
Redruth   43 La 22
Reigate-Redhill   45 Kb 27
Reiss   21 Ga 24
Retford   25 Jab 27
Rhayader   24 Ka 24
Rhiconich   20 Ga 23
Rhyl   24 Jab 24
Rhynie   21 Gb 25
Ringford   24 Ja 23
Ringwood   44 La 26
Ripon   25 Ja 26
Rochdale   24 Jab 25
Rochester   45 Kb 28
Roghadal   20 Gb 21
Romsey   44 La 26
Rosenhall   20 Gb 23
Ross-on-Wye   44 Kb 25
Rosyth   20 Ha 24
Rotherham   25 Jab 26
Rothesay   20 Hb 22
Royal Leamington Spa
      44 Ka 26
Royal Tunbridge Wells
      45 Kb 28
Roystone   45 Ka 27
Rubha Ban   20 Gb 20
Rugby   24 Ka 26
Runcorn   24 Jab 25
Rushden   45 Ka 27
Ryde   44 La 26
Rye   45 La 28
Saffron Walden   45 Ka 28
Saint Albans   45 Kb 27
Saint Andrews   20 Ha 25
Saint Austell   43 La 23
Saint Boswells   24 Hb 25
Saint Brelade   44 Lb 25
Saint Céré   71 Oa 29
Saint David`s   23 Kb 22
Saint Helens   24 Jab 25
Saint Helier   44 Lb 25
Saint Ives   43 La 22

Saint Ives   45 Ka 27
Saint John   44 Lb 25
Saint Just   43 La 22
Saint Margaret`s Hope
      21 Ga 25
Saint Martin   44 Lb 25
Saint Mary`s   21 Ga 25
Saint Neots   45 Ka 27
Saint Peter Port   44 Lb 25
Sainte Anne   44 Lb 25
Saintfield   24 Ja 22
Salcombe   44 La 24
Salen   20 Ha 22
Salen   20 Ha 22
Salisbury   44 Kb 26
Saltcoats   20 Hb 23
Sanaigmore   20 Hb 21
Sandness   21 Fa 26
Sandown   44 La 26
Sandy   45 Ka 27
Saxilby   25 Jab 27
Saxmundham   45 Ka 29
Scalby   25 Ja 27
Scalloway   21 Fa 26
Scarborough   25 Ja 27
Scourie   20 Ga 22
Scrabster   21 Ga 24
Scunthorpe   25 Jab 27
Seaford   45 La 28
Seaham   25 Ja 26
Sedbergh   24 Ja 25
Selby   25 Jab 26
Selkirk   24 Hb 25
Sennen   43 La 22
Settle   24 Ja 25
Sevenoaks   45 Kb 28
Sgiogarstaigh   20 Ga 21
Shaftesbury   44 Kb 25
Shanklin   44 La 26
Sheffield   24 Jab 26
Shepton Mallet   44 Kb 25
Sherborne   44 La 25
Sheringham   25 Ka 29
Shiel Bridge   20 Gb 22
Shieldaig   20 Gb 22
Shipdham   45 Ka 28
Shipston-on-Stour   44 Ka 26
Shipton   25 Ja 26
Shrewsbury   24 Ka 25
Siabost   20 Ga 21
Sidmouth   44 La 24
Sittingbourne   45 Kb 28
Skegness   25 Jab 28
Skipton   24 Jab 25
Sleaford   25 Ka 27
Sligachan   20 Gb 21
Slough   44 Kb 27
Solihull   24 Ka 26
Somercotes   24 Jab 26
South Molton   44 Kb 24
South Shields   25 Ja 26
Southampton   44 La 26
Southend-on-Sea   45 Kb 28
Southport   24 Jab 25
Southwold   45 Ka 29
Spalding   25 Ka 27

POSTALI · ÍNDICE CON CÓDIGOS POSTALES · INDICE DE LUGARES COM CÓDIGOS POSTAIS ·
MÍST S PSČ · ZOZNAM OBCÍ S PSČ · INDEKS MIEJSCOWOŚCI Z KOD POCZTOWY

150

Spean Bridge — GB · GR — Bralos

GB

GR

Spean Bridge 20 Ha 23
Spittal of Glenshee 20 Ha 24
St. Clears 24 Kb 23
Stafford 24 Ka 25
Staines 45 Kb 27
Stamford 25 Ka 27
Stanford-le-Hope 45 Kb 28
Stanhope 24 Ja 25
Staxton 25 Ja 27
Stenhousemuir 20 Ha 24
Steornabhagh 20 Ga 21
Stevenage 45 Kb 27
Stirling 20 Ha 24
Stockport 24 Jab 25
Stockton-on-Tees 25 Ja 26
Stoer 20 Ga 22
Stoke-on-Trent 24 Jab 25
Stokesley 25 Ja 26
Stone 24 Ka 25
Stonehaven 21 Ha 25
Stourbridge 24 Ka 25
Stow 20 Hb 25
Stowmarket 45 Ka 28
Strabane 19 Ja 20
Strachur 20 Ha 22
Stranraer 24 Ja 22
Stratford-upon-Avon 44 Ka 26
Strathcarron 20 Gb 22
Strathcoil 20 Ha 22
Strathyre 20 Ha 23
Stromness 21 Ga 24
Strontian 20 Ha 22
Stroud 44 Kb 25
Struy 20 Gb 23
Sudbury 45 Ka 28
Sulland 21 Fb 25
Sunderland 25 Ja 26
Sutton Coldfield 24 Ka 26
Sutton in Ashfield 25 Jab 26
Sutton on Sea 25 Jab 28
Swadlincote 24 Ka 26
Swaffham 45 Ka 28
Swanage 44 La 26
Swansea 44 Kb 24
Swindon 44 Kb 26
Syston 25 Ka 26
Tain 20 Gb 23
Tairbeart 20 Gb 21
Tamworth 24 Ka 26
Tarbert 20 Hb 22
Tarbet 20 Ha 23
Taunton 44 Kb 24
Tavistock 44 La 23
Tayinloan 20 Hb 22
Tebay 24 Ja 25
Teignmouth 44 La 24
Telford 24 Ka 25
Tenby 44 Kb 23
Tenderden 45 Kb 28
Ternhill 24 Ka 25
Tetbury 44 Kb 25
Tewkesbury 44 Kb 25
Thame 44 Kb 27
The Lhen 24 Ja 23
Thetford 45 Ka 28
Thirsk 25 Ja 26

Thornbury 44 Kb 25
Thorne 25 Jab 27
Thornhill 24 Hb 24
Thornton-Cleveleys 24 Jab 24
Thrumster 21 Ga 24
Thurso 21 Ga 24
Tigh a Ghearraidh 20 Gb 20
Tillicoultry 20 Ha 24
Timsgearraidh 20 Ga 20
Tiverton 44 La 24
Tobermore 23 Ja 21
Tobermory 20 Ha 21
Tobha Mor 20 Gb 20
Toft 21 Fa 26
Tolastadh 20 Ga 21
Tomintoul 20 Gb 24
Tonbridge 45 Kb 28
Tongue 20 Ga 23
Topsham 44 La 24
Tore 20 Gb 23
Torquay 44 La 24
Totnes 44 La 24
Totton 44 La 26
Toward 20 Hb 23
Towcester 44 Ka 27
Tregaron 24 Ka 24
Troon 20 Hb 23
Trowbridge 44 Kb 25
Truro 43 La 22
Turnberry 20 Hb 23
Turriff 21 Gb 25
Twatt 21 Fb 24
Tyndrum 20 Ha 23
Tywyn 24 Ka 23
Uckfield 45 La 28
Ullapool 20 Gb 22
Ulsta 21 Fa 26
Ulverston 24 Ja 24
Unapool 20 Ga 22
Uttoxeter 24 Ka 26
Veness 21 Fb 25
Vidlin 21 Fa 26
Voe 21 Fa 26
Wadebridge 43 La 23
Wainfleet 25 Jab 28
Wakefield 24 Jab 26
Wallasey 24 Jab 24
Walsall 24 Ka 25
Walton-on-Thames 45 Kb 27
Wantage-Grove 44 Kb 26
Wantage-Grove 44 Kb 26
Wareham 44 La 25
Warminster 44 Kb 25
Warrenpoint 23 Ja 21
Warrington 24 Jab 25
Warwick 24 Ka 26
Washington 25 Ja 26
Watford 45 Kb 27
Watten 21 Ga 24
Watton 45 Ka 28
Wellingborough 45 Ka 27
Wellington 44 La 24
Wellington 24 Ka 25
Wells 44 Kb 25
Welshpool 24 Ka 24
West Bromwich 24 Ka 25

Westhill 21 Gb 25
Weston-super-Mare 44 Kb 25
Wetheral 24 Ja 25
Wetherby 25 Jab 26
Weymouth 44 La 25
Whitburn 20 Hb 24
Whitby 25 Ja 26
Whitchurch 24 Ka 25
Whitehaven 24 Ja 24
Whitehead 24 Ja 22
Whithorn 24 Ja 23
Whitley Bay 25 Hb 26
Whittington 24 Ka 24
Whittlesey 45 Ka 27
Wick 21 Ga 24
Wigan 24 Jab 25
Wigton 24 Ja 24
Willersley 24 Ka 24
Wilmslow 24 Jab 25
Wilton 44 Kb 26
Wincanton 44 Kb 25
Winchester 44 Kb 26
Windermere 24 Ja 25
Windsor-Eton 44 Kb 27
Winsford 24 Jab 25
Wisbech 25 Ka 28
Wishaw 20 Hb 24
Witham 45 Kb 28
Withernsea 25 Jab 28
Witney 44 Kb 26
Woking 45 Kb 27
Wolverhampton 24 Ka 25
Woodbridge 45 Ka 29
Woodstock 44 Kb 26
Wooler 25 Hb 25
Wootton Bassett 44 Kb 26
Worcester 24 Ka 25
Workington 24 Ja 24
Worksop 25 Jab 26
Worthing 44 La 27
Wragby 25 Jab 27
Wrexham 24 Jab 25
Yarm 25 Ja 26
Yeovil 44 La 25
York 25 Jab 26

848 01 Adamas 105 Sa 52
530 75 Aetos 90 Qa 49
851 03 Afandou 10 Sa 56
740 56 Agia Galini 109 Sb 52
854 00 Agia Marina/Leros 106 Rb 54
197 07 Agia Marina/Nea Makri
                  105 Ra 52
802 00 Agia Pelagia 109 Sa 50
270 69 Agia Triada 104 Rb 49
700 03 Agia Varvara 110 Sb 52
700 12 Agii Deka 110 Sb 52
200 03 Agii Theodori 105 Rb 51
601 00 Agios Dimitrios 90 Qa 50
833 00 Agios Kirikos 106 Rb 54
350 06 Agios Konstandinos
                  105 Ra 50

630 78 Agios Nikolaos/Halkidiki
                  91 Qa 51
721 00 Agios Nikolaos/Ierapetra
                  110 Sb 53
330 58 Agios Nikolaos/Nafpaktos
                  105 Ra 50
420 37 Agios Nikolaos/Trikala
                  104 Qb 49
301 00 Agrinio 104 Ra 49
740 53 Akoumia 109 Sb 52
250 06 Akrata 105 Ra 50
593 00 Alexandria / Αλεξάνδρεια
                  91 Qa 50
681 00 Alexandroupoli /
                  Αλεξανδρούπολη
                  92 Qa 53
320 01 Aliartos 105 Ra 51
620 45 Alistrati 91 Pb 51
345 00 Aliveri 105 Ra 52
403 00 Almiros 105 Qb 50
370 05 Alonnisos 105 Qb 51
840 10 Alopronia 106 Sa 53
823 00 Amades 106 Ra 54
272 00 Amaliada 104 Rb 49
340 06 Amarinthos 105 Ra 51
350 02 Amfiklia 105 Ra 50
305 00 Amfilohia 104 Ra 49
620 52 Amfipoli 91 Qa 51
331 00 Amfissa 105 Ra 50
532 00 Amindeo 90 Qa 49
840 08 Amorgos 106 Sa 53
360 71 Anatoliki Frangista
                  104 Ra 49
853 02 Andimahia 106 Sa 55
270 51 Andravida 104 Rb 49
270 61 Andritsena 104 Rb 49
511 00 Anixi 90 Qb 49
843 02 Apiranthos 106 Rb 53
851 09 Apolakkia 106 Sa 55
843 01 Apollon 106 Rb 53
840 03 Apollonia 105 Sa 52
740 61 Apostoli 109 Sb 52
584 00 Apsalos 90 Qa 50
320 14 Arahova 105 Ra 50
212 00 Argos 105 Rb 50
522 00 Argos Orestiko 90 Qa 49
281 00 Argostoli 104 Ra 48
851 02 Arhangelos 106 Sa 56
584 00 Aridea 90 Qa 50
703 00 Arkalohori 110 Sb 53
352 00 Arkitsa 105 Ra 50
741 00 Armeni/Rethimno 109 Sb 52
630 74 Arnea 91 Qa 51
471 00 Arta / Άρτα 104 Qb 48
455 00 Asfaka 104 Qb 48
700 10 Asimi 110 Sb 53
730 13 Askifou 109 Sb 52
300 06 Astakos 104 Ra 49
859 00 Astipalea 106 Sa 54
220 01 Astros 105 Rb 50
352 00 Atalandi 105 Ra 50
104 41 Athina / Αθήνα 105 Rb 51
831 00 Avlakia 106 Ra 54
190 11 Avlonas 105 Ra 51
740 57 Bali 109 Sb 52
330 57 Bralos 105 Ra 50

151

INDEX WITH POST CODES · ORTSREGISTER MIT POSTLEITZAHLEN · INDICE CON CODICI
STEDREGISTER MED POSTNUMRE · PLAATSNAMENREGISTER MET POSTCODE · REJSTŘÍK

GR | **Delfi** | **GR** | **Ormos Panormou**

330 54 Delfi 105 Ra 50	341 00 Halkida / Χαλκίδα 105 Ra 51	470 40 Komboti 104 Qb 49	851 11 Megisti 107 Sa 57
700 10 Demati 110 Sb 53	731 00 Hania / Χανιά 109 Sb 52	310 82 Komilio 104 Ra 48	240 02 Meligalas 104 Rb 49
230 53 Demonia 105 Sa 50	821 00 Hios 106 Ra 54	691 00 Komotini / Κομοτηνή	300 16 Menidi 104 Qb 49
205 00 Dervenakia 105 Rb 50	642 00 Hrisoupoli 91 Qa 52	91 Pb 53	845 00 Mesaria 105 Rb 52
330 50 Desfina 105 Ra 50	692 00 Iasmos 91 Pb 53	441 00 Konitsa 90 Qa 48	302 00 Mesolongi 104 Ra 49
512 00 Deskati 90 Qb 49	180 40 Idra 105 Rb 51	422 00 Koridallos 104 Qb 49	490 80 Mesongi 104 Qb 47
857 00 Diafani 110 Sb 55	722 00 Ierapetra 110 Sb 53	600 62 Korinos 91 Qa 50	242 00 Messini 104 Rb 50
250 03 Diakofto 105 Ra 50	630 75 Ierissos 91 Qa 51	201 00 Korinthos 105 Rb 50	240 06 Methoni 104 Sa 49
570 08 Diavata / Διαβάτα 91 Qa 50	461 00 Igoumenitsa 104 Qb 48	520 50 Koromilea 90 Qa 49	442 00 Metsovo 104 Qb 49
213 00 Didima 105 Rb 51	455 00 Ioannina / Ιωάννινα	853 00 Kos 106 Sa 55	846 00 Mikonos 106 Rb 53
683 00 Didimotiho 92 Pb 54	104 Qb 48	220 20 Kosmas 105 Rb 50	370 13 Milina 105 Qb 51
220 07 Dimitsana 104 Rb 50	840 01 Ios 106 Sa 53	571 00 Koufalia 91 Qa 50	848 00 Milos 105 Sa 52
320 05 Distomo 105 Ra 50	624 00 Iraklia 91 Pb 51	212 00 Koutsopodi 105 Rb 50	704 00 Mires 109 Sb 52
280 81 Divarata 104 Ra 48	715 00 Iraklio / Ηράκλειο 110 Sb 53	720 55 Koutsouras 110 Sb 53	814 00 Mirina 91 Qb 53
610 03 Doirani 91 Pb 50	200 10 Isthmia 105 Rb 51	501 00 Kozani / Κοζάνη 90 Qa 49	720 56 Mirtos 110 Sb 53
350 10 Domokos 105 Qb 50	342 00 Istiea 105 Ra 51	510 31 Krania 104 Qb 49	811 08 Mithimna 106 Qb 54
663 00 Doxato 91 Pb 52	332 00 Itea 105 Ra 50	213 00 Kranidi 105 Rb 51	481 00 Mitikas 104 Ra 48
661 00 Drama / Δράμα 91 Pb 52	283 00 Ithaki 104 Ra 48	811 00 Kratigos 106 Qb 54	811 00 Mitilini 106 Qb 54
370 08 Drimonas 105 Qb 50	422 00 Kalambaka 104 Qb 49	270 55 Krestena 104 Rb 49	230 52 Molai 105 Sa 50
545 00 Drimos 91 Qa 50	730 02 Kakopetros 109 Sb 51	583 00 Kria Vrisi 90 Qa 50	350 09 Molos 105 Ra 50
844 00 Drios 106 Rb 53	551 10 Kalamaria / Καλαμαριά	305 00 Krikellos 104 Ra 49	851 00 Monolithos 106 Sa 55
740 54 Drosia 109 Sb 52	91 Qa 50	640 03 Krinides 91 Pb 52	480 60 Morfi 104 Qb 48
582 00 Edessa / Έδεσσα 90 Qa 50	241 00 Kalamata / Καλάματα	230 57 Krokees 105 Sa 50	430 67 Mouha 104 Qb 49
612 00 Efzoni 91 Pb 50	105 Rb 50	680 10 Ladi 92 Pb 54	733 00 Mournies 109 Sb 52
180 10 Egina 105 Rb 51	250 01 Kalavrita 105 Ra 50	290 92 Laganas 104 Rb 48	303 00 Nafpaktos 104 Ra 49
603 00 Eginio 91 Qa 50	852 00 Kalimnos 106 Sa 54	683 00 Lagos 91 Pb 53	211 00 Nafplio 105 Rb 50
251 00 Egio 104 Ra 50	190 10 Kalivia Thorikou 105 Rb 51	811 01 Lambou Mili 106 Qb 54	592 00 Naousa/Veria / Νάουσα/
402 00 Elassona 90 Qb 50	811 07 Kalloni 106 Qb 54	351 00 Lamia / Λαμία 105 Ra 50	Βέροια 90 Qa 50
192 00 Elefsina 105 Ra 51	440 04 Kalpaki 104 Qb 48	572 00 Langadas 91 Qa 51	844 01 Naousa/Paros 106 Rb 53
641 00 Eleftheroupoli 91 Qa 52	680 02 Kamariotissa 91 Qa 53	415 00 Larisa / Λάρισα 105 Qb 50	843 00 Naxos 106 Rb 53
455 00 Eleousa 104 Qb 48	350 08 Kamena Vourla 105 Ra 50	680 04 Lavara 92 Pb 54	374 00 Nea Anhialos 105 Qb 50
270 58 Epitalio 104 Rb 49	480 62 Kanallaki 104 Qb 48	195 00 Lavrio 105 Rb 52	210 54 Nea Epidavros 105 Rb 51
500 07 Eptahori 90 Qa 49	431 00 Karditsa / Καρδίτσα	311 00 Lefkada 104 Ra 48	570 07 Nea Halkidona /
811 05 Eresos 106 Qb 53	104 Qb 49	490 80 Lefkimmi 104 Qb 48	Νέα Χαλκηδόνα 91 Qa 50
340 08 Eretria 105 Ra 51	630 86 Karies 91 Qa 52	857 00 Lefkos 110 Sb 55	630 80 Nea Kallikratia 91 Qa 51
190 08 Erithres 105 Ra 51	340 01 Karistos 105 Ra 52	530 75 Lehovo 90 Qa 49	145 65 Nea Makri 105 Ra 51
841 00 Ermoupoli 105 Rb 52	857 00 Karpathos 110 Sb 55	223 00 Leonidi 105 Rb 50	632 00 Nea Moudania 91 Qa 51
304 00 Etoliko 104 Ra 49	361 00 Karpenisi 104 Ra 49	680 11 Leptokaria 92 Pb 53	545 00 Nea Sanda 91 Qa 50
833 02 Evdilos 106 Rb 54	630 77 Kassandria 91 Qa 51	220 02 Levidi 105 Rb 50	340 15 Nea Stira 105 Ra 52
851 00 Faliraki 107 Sa 56	591 00 Kastanea 90 Qa 50	210 52 Ligourio 105 Rb 51	620 42 Nea Zihni 91 Pb 51
833 00 Fanari 106 Rb 54	521 00 Kastoria / Καστορία 90 Qa 49	821 02 Limenas 106 Ra 53	724 00 Neapoli/Agios Nikolaos
420 31 Farkadonas 104 Qb 50	730 01 Kastri 109 Ta 52	700 14 Limin Hersonisou 110 Sb 53	110 Sb 53
403 00 Farsala / Φάρσαλα	601 00 Katerini / Κατερίνη 91 Qa 50	340 05 Limni 105 Ra 51	230 53 Neapoli/Demonia 105 Sa 51
105 Qb 50	252 00 Kato Ahaia 104 Ra 49	851 07 Lindos 106 Sa 56	500 01 Neapoli/Siatista 90 Qa 49
685 00 Feres 92 Qa 54	660 33 Kato Nevrokopi 91 Pb 51	720 59 Lithines 110 Sb 54	832 00 Neo Karlovasi 106 Rb 54
680 06 Filakio 92 Pb 54	350 15 Kato Tithorea 105 Ra 50	602 00 Litohoro 91 Qa 50	350 10 Neo Monastiri 105 Qb 50
482 00 Filippiada 104 Qb 48	851 09 Kattavia 110 Sb 55	321 00 Livadia 105 Ra 50	620 43 Neo Petrisi 91 Pb 51
847 00 Fira 106 Sa 53	650 00 Kavala / Καβάλα 91 Qa 52	480 61 Louros 104 Qb 48	370 10 Neohori 105 Qb 51
280 84 Fiskardo 104 Ra 48	840 02 Kea 105 Rb 52	343 00 Loutra Edipsou 105 Ra 51	300 01 Neohori 104 Ra 49
531 00 Florina / Φλώρινα 90 Qa 49	853 01 Kefalos 106 Sa 54	640 08 Loutra Eleftheron 91 Qa 52	630 81 Neos Marmaras 91 Qa 51
840 11 Folegandros 105 Sa 52	610 04 Kendriko 91 Pb 50	240 06 Loutraki 105 Rb 50	462 00 Neraida/Igoumenitsa
858 00 Fri 110 Sb 54	642 00 Keramoti 91 Qa 52	350 11 Makrakomi 104 Ra 50	104 Qb 48
630 73 Galatista 91 Qa 51	482 00 Kerasona 104 Qb 48	700 07 Malia 110 Sb 53	501 00 Neraida/Kozani 90 Qa 49
244 00 Gargaliani 104 Rb 49	491 00 Kerkira/Korfu / Κέρκυρα	340 04 Mandoudi 105 Ra 51	311 00 Nidri 104 Ra 48
845 01 Gavrio 105 Rb 52	104 Qb 47	196 00 Mandra 105 Ra 51	622 00 Nigrita 91 Qa 51
570 11 Gefira 91 Qa 50	202 00 Kiato 105 Ra 50	851 08 Mandriko 106 Sa 55	531 00 Niki 90 Qa 49
851 09 Gennadio 106 Sa 55	501 00 Kilas 90 Qa 49	220 12 Manthirea 105 Rb 50	630 88 Nikiti 91 Qa 51
631 00 Gerakini 91 Qa 51	611 00 Kilkis / Κιλκίς 91 Qa 50	190 03 Markopoulo 105 Rb 51	481 00 Nikopoli 104 Qb 48
741 00 Gerani 109 Sb 52	340 03 Kimi 105 Ra 52	694 00 Maronia 91 Qa 53	821 02 Olimbi 106 Ra 53
581 00 Giannitsa / Γιαννιτσά	245 00 Kiparissia 104 Rb 49	700 06 Mathia 110 Sb 53	270 65 Olimbia 104 Rb 49
91 Qa 50	734 00 Kissamos 109 Sb 51	350 05 Martino 105 Ra 51	857 00 Olimbos 110 Sb 55
232 00 Githio 105 Sa 50	801 00 Kithira 109 Sa 50	360 71 Mavrommata 104 Qb 49	682 00 Orestiada / Ορεστιάδα
613 00 Goumenissa 91 Qa 50	840 06 Kithnos 105 Rb 52	680 05 Mega Derio 92 Pb 54	92 Pb 54
491 00 Gouvia 104 Qb 47	811 04 Klio 106 Qb 54	455 00 Mega Peristeri 104 Qb 49	323 00 Orhomenos 105 Ra 50
511 00 Grevena / Γρεβενά	482 00 Klisoura 104 Qb 48	222 00 Megalopoli 105 Rb 50	680 07 Ormenio 92 Pb 54
90 Qa 49	250 07 Klitoria 105 Rb 50	191 00 Megara 105 Rb 51	842 01 Ormos Panormou 105 Rb 53

POSTALI · ÍNDICE CON CÓDIGOS POSTALES · INDICE DE LUGARES COM CÓDIGOS POSTAIS · MÍST S PSČ · ZOZNAM OBCÍ S PSČ · INDEKS MIEJSCOWOŚCI Z KOD POCZTOWY

152

Orologio ⓖⓇ · Ⓗ **Igal**

GR

H

340 09 Orologio 105 Ra 52	
630 75 Ouranopoli 91 Qa 51	
263 34 Ovria 104 Ra 49	
722 00 Pahia Ammos 110 Sb 53	
432 00 Palamas 104 Qb 50	
730 01 Paleohora 109 Sb 51	
421 00 Paleomonastiro 104 Qb 49	
300 12 Paleros 104 Ra 48	
630 85 Paliouri 91 Qb 51	
340 15 Panagia 105 Ra 52	
300 03 Panetolio 104 Ra 49	
552 36 Panorama / Πανόραμα 91 Qa 51	
740 57 Panormo 109 Sb 52	
462 00 Paramithia 104 Qb 48	
660 35 Paranesti 91 Pb 52	
480 60 Parga 104 Qb 48	
844 00 Paros 105 Rb 53	
265 00 Patra / Πάτρα 104 Ra 49	
490 82 Paxi 104 Qb 48	
455 00 Pedini 104 Qb 48	
500 07 Pendalofos 90 Qa 49	
455 00 Perdika 104 Qb 48	
570 19 Perea / Περαία 91 Qa 50	
240 01 Pilos 104 Sa 49	
185 31 Pireas / Πειραίας 105 Rb 51	
821 02 Pirgi 106 Ra 54	
244 00 Pirgos/Amaliada 104 Rb 49	
700 10 Pirgos/Iraklio 110 Sb 53	
831 04 Pirgos/Samos 106 Rb 54	
440 15 Pirsogianni 90 Qa 48	
530 76 Pisoderi 90 Qa 49	
831 03 Pithagorio 106 Rb 54	
683 00 Pithio 92 Pb 54	
590 32 Plati 91 Qa 50	
812 00 Plomari 106 Ra 54	
631 00 Poligiros 91 Qa 51	
813 00 Polihnitos 106 Qb 54	
612 00 Polikastro 91 Qa 50	
841 00 Posidonia 105 Rb 52	
840 08 Potamos 106 Sa 53	
640 02 Potos 91 Qa 52	
481 00 Preveza / Πρέβεζα 104 Ra 48	
623 00 Promahonas 91 Pb 51	
662 00 Prosotsani 91 Pb 51	
620 47 Proti 91 Qa 51	
344 00 Psahna 105 Ra 51	
502 00 Ptolemaida / Πτολεμαΐδα 90 Qa 49	
190 09 Rafina 105 Ra 52	
741 00 Rethimno 109 Sb 52	
265 04 Rio 104 Ra 49	
851 00 Rodos / Ρόδος 107 Sa 56	
189 00 Salamina 105 Rb 51	
280 80 Sami 104 Ra 48	
831 00 Samos 106 Rb 54	
693 00 Sapes 92 Pb 53	
840 05 Serifos 105 Rb 52	
621 00 Serres / Σέρρες 91 Pb 51	
505 00 Servia 90 Qa 49	
730 11 Sfakia 109 Sb 52	
320 09 Shimatari 105 Ra 51	
503 00 Siatista 90 Qa 49	
623 00 Sidirokastro 91 Pb 51	
660 38 Sidironero 91 Pb 52	

811 12 Sigri 106 Qb 53	
630 72 Sikia 91 Qa 51	
856 00 Simi 106 Sa 55	
530 74 Sitaria 90 Qa 49	
723 00 Sitia 110 Sb 54	
230 51 Skala 105 Sa 50	
811 05 Skala Eresou 106 Qb 53	
730 11 Skaloti 109 Sb 52	
370 02 Skiathos 105 Qb 51	
585 00 Skidra 90 Qa 50	
340 07 Skiros 105 Ra 52	
370 03 Skopelos 105 Qb 51	
433 00 Sofades 104 Qb 50	
570 02 Sohos 91 Qa 51	
732 00 Souda 109 Sb 52	
684 00 Soufli 92 Pb 54	
730 09 Sougia 109 Sb 51	
195 00 Sounio 105 Rb 52	
231 00 Sparti 105 Rb 50	
190 04 Spata 105 Rb 51	
180 50 Spetses 105 Rb 51	
740 53 Spili 109 Sb 52	
700 13 Stavrakia 110 Sb 53	
570 14 Stavros 91 Qa 51	
210 58 Sterna 105 Rb 50	
353 00 Stilida 105 Ra 50	
630 82 Stratoni 91 Qa 51	
692 00 Tangeo 91 Pb 53	
730 06 Tavronitis 109 Sb 51	
640 04 Thasos 91 Qa 52	
680 02 Therma 92 Qa 53	
570 01 Thermi / Θέρμη 91 Qa 51	
540 00 Thessaloniki / Θεσσαλονίκη 91 Qa 50	
322 00 Thiva 105 Ra 51	
240 09 Thouria 105 Rb 50	
680 03 Tihero 92 Pb 54	
702 00 Timbaki 109 Sb 52	
842 00 Tinos 105 Rb 53	
455 00 Tiria 104 Qb 48	
401 00 Tirnavos / Τύρναβος 105 Qb 50	
851 00 Trianda 106 Sa 56	
421 00 Trikala / Τρίκαλα 104 Qb 49	
370 09 Trikeri 105 Qb 51	
221 00 Tripoli 105 Rb 50	
270 63 Tripotama 104 Rb 49	
500 02 Tsotili 90 Qa 49	
270 52 Varda 104 Ra 49	
814 01 Varos 91 Qb 53	
310 82 Vasiliki 104 Ra 48	
340 02 Vasiliko 105 Ra 51	
813 00 Vatera 106 Qb 54	
530 76 Vatohori 90 Qa 49	
375 00 Velestino 105 Qb 50	
591 00 Veria Βέροια 90 Qa 50	
220 10 Vitina 105 Rb 50	
843 00 Vivlos 106 Rb 53	
821 03 Volissos 106 Ra 53	
385 00 Volos / Βόλος 105 Qb 50	
300 02 Vonitsa 104 Ra 48	
250 02 Vrahneika 104 Ra 49	
730 07 Vrises 109 Sb 52	
822 00 Vrondados 106 Ra 54	
440 17 Vrosina 104 Qb 48	
671 00 Xanthi / Ξάνθη 91 Pb 52	

204 00 Xilokastro 105 Ra 50	
370 01 Zagora 105 Qb 51	
270 54 Zaharo 104 Rb 49	
291 00 Zakinthos 104 Rb 48	
570 12 Zangliverio 91 Qa 51	

Ⓗ

3882 Abaújkér 62 Ma 49	
2740 Abony 62 Mb 48	
2941 Ács 61 Mb 46	
2683 Acsa 62 Mb 47	
2457 Adony 61 Mb 46	
3759 Aggtelek 62 Ma 48	
8400 Ajka 61 Mb 45	
2730 Albertirsa 62 Mb 47	
6750 Algyő 76 Na 48	
8675 Alsótold 62 Mb 47	
8675 Andocs 75 Na 45	
4253 Aradványpuszta 62 Mb 49	
6500 Baja 75 Na 46	
8945 Bak 75 Na 44	
4220 Bakóhát 62 Mb 49	
8056 Bakonycsernye 61 Mb 46	
2660 Balassagyarmat 61 Ma 47	
6764 Balástya 76 Na 48	
8220 Balatonalmádi 61 Mb 46	
8630 Balatonboglár 75 Na 45	
8312 Balatonederics 75 Na 45	
8230 Balatonfüred 61 Na 46	
8638 Balatonlelle 75 Na 45	
6800 Barattyos 76 Na 48	
7570 Barcs 75 Nb 45	
7140 Bátaszék 75 Na 46	
3070 Bátonyterenye 62 Ma 47	
5830 Battonya 76 Na 49	
6351 Bátya 75 Na 46	
5630 Békés 76 Na 49	
5600 Békéscsaba 76 Na 49	
2687 Bercel 62 Mb 47	
4103 Berettyószentmárton 62 Mb 49	
4100 Berettyóújfalu 62 Mb 49	
7516 Berzence 75 Na 45	
2060 Bicske 61 Mb 46	
8714 Bize 75 Na 45	
7754 Bóly 75 Nb 46	
7150 Bonyhád 75 Na 46	
3671 Borsodnádasd 62 Ma 48	
8719 Böhönye 75 Na 45	
9167 Bősárkány 61 Mb 45	
2040 Budaörs 61 Mb 47	
1000 Budapest 61 Mb 47	
2347 Bugyi 61 Mb 47	
9737 Bük 61 Mb 44	
7013 Cece 75 Na 46	
2700 Cegléd 62 Mb 47	
9500 Celldömölk 61 Mb 45	
3973 Cigánd 62 Ma 49	
6230 Csábor 76 Na 47	
8083 Csákvár 61 Mb 46	
5662 Csanádapáca 76 Na 48	
4844 Csaroda 62 Ma 50	
6239 Császártöltés 75 Na 47	

6448 Csávoly 75 Na 47	
5465 Cserkeszőlő 62 Na 48	
6640 Csongrád 76 Na 48	
6311 Csorna 61 Mb 45	
5920 Csorvás 76 Na 48	
4145 Csökmő 62 Mb 49	
8840 Csurgó 75 Na 45	
2370 Dabas 62 Mb 47	
4144 Darvas 62 Mb 49	
4000 Debrecen 62 Mb 49	
4130 Derecske 62 Mb 49	
7200 Dombóvár 75 Na 46	
2510 Dorog 61 Mb 46	
2344 Dömsöd 61 Mb 47	
7020 Dunaföldvár 75 Na 46	
7712 Dunaszekcső 75 Na 46	
6325 Dunatetétlen 75 Na 47	
2400 Dunaújváros 61 Na 46	
3780 Edelény 62 Ma 48	
3300 Eger 62 Mb 48	
8130 Enying 61 Na 46	
2451 Ercsi 61 Mb 46	
2030 Érd 61 Mb 46	
2500 Esztergom 61 Mb 46	
8582 Farkasgyepű 61 Mb 45	
6055 Felsőlajos 62 Mb 47	
9444 Fertőszentmiklós 61 Mb 44	
8732 Fonyód 75 Na 45	
4177 Földes 62 Mb 49	
3390 Füzesabony 62 Mb 48	
3815 Gadna 62 Ma 48	
3873 Garadna 62 Ma 49	
6111 Gátér 76 Na 47	
3444 Gelej 62 Mb 48	
9672 Gérce 61 Mb 45	
4803 Gergelyiugornya 62 Ma 50	
2131 Göd 61 Mb 47	
2100 Gödöllő 62 Mb 47	
7386 Gödre 75 Na 45	
4075 Görbeháza 62 Mb 49	
7553 Görgeteg 75 Na 45	
2360 Gyál 62 Mb 47	
9019 Gyirmót 61 Mb 45	
5500 Gyomaendrőd 62 Na 48	
2230 Gyömrő 62 Mb 47	
3200 Gyöngyös 62 Mb 47	
9000 Győr 61 Mb 45	
9121 Győrszemere 61 Mb 45	
5700 Gyula 76 Na 49	
8412 Gyulafirátót 61 Mb 45	
8771 Hahót 75 Na 44	
4220 Hajdúböszörmény 62 Mb 49	
4242 Hajdúhadház 62 Mb 49	
4251 Hajdúsámson 62 Mb 49	
4200 Hajdúszoboszló 62 Mb 49	
6136 Harkakötöny 76 Na 47	
8105 Harkány 75 Nb 46	
3000 Hatvan 62 Mb 47	
9631 Hegyfalu 61 Mb 44	
8442 Herend 61 Mb 45	
3360 Heves 62 Mb 48	
7696 Hidas 75 Na 46	
7693 Hird 75 Na 46	
6800 Hódmezővásárhely 76 Na 48	
7191 Hőgyész 75 Na 46	
7275 Igal 75 Na 45	

153

INDEX WITH POST CODES · ORTSREGISTER MIT POSTLEITZAHLEN · INDICE CON CODICI
STEDREGISTER MED POSTNUMRE · PLAATSNAMENREGISTER MET POSTCODE · REJSTŘÍK

H

HR

Iharosberény   (H) · (HR)   Čakovec

8725 Iharosberény 75 Na 45	3500 Miskolc 62 Ma 48	9600 Sárvár 61 Mb 44
7095 Iregszemcse 75 Na 46	7700 Mohács 75 Nb 46	7370 Sásd 75 Na 46
9545 Jánosháza 61 Mb 45	2200 Monor 62 Mb 47	3980 Sátoraljaújhely 62 Ma 49
5054 Jászalsószentgyörgy	8060 Mór 61 Mb 46	7562 Segesd 75 Na 45
62 Mb 48	6782 Mórahalom 76 Na 47	8111 Seregélyes 61 Mb 46
5130 Jászapáti 62 Mb 48	9200 Mosonmagyaróvár 61 Mb 45	7800 Siklós 75 Nb 46
5100 Jászberény 62 Mb 47	7500 Nagyatád 75 Na 45	7474 Simonfa 75 Na 45
4225 Józsa 62 Mb 49	7561 Nagybajom 75 Na 45	7081 Simontornya 75 Na 46
8988 Kálócfa 75 Na 44	9485 Nagycenk 61 Mb 44	8600 Siófok 61 Na 46
6300 Kalocsa 75 Na 46	7985 Nagydobsza 75 Na 45	3332 Sirok 62 Mb 48
9841 Kám 61 Mb 44	2942 Nagyigmánd 61 Mb 46	6320 Solt 75 Na 47
7409 Kaposfüred 75 Na 45	4320 Nagykálló 62 Mb 49	6230 Soltvadkert 76 Na 47
7400 Kaposvár 75 Na 45	8800 Nagykanizsa 75 Na 44	8698 Somogyvár 75 Na 45
9330 Kapuvár 61 Mb 45	2760 Nagykáta 62 Mb 47	9400 Sopron 61 Mb 44
5300 Karcag 62 Mb 48	2750 Nagykőrös 62 Mb 47	8072 Söréd 61 Mb 46
5948 Kaszaper 76 Na 48	2645 Nagyoroszi 61 Ma 47	8330 Sümeg 61 Na 45
3700 Kazincbarcika 62 Ma 48	6612 Nagytőke 76 Na 48	7192 Szakály 75 Na 46
6237 Kecel 75 Na 47	8948 Nova 75 Na 44	7213 Szakcs 76 Na 46
6000 Kecskemét 62 Na 47	6032 Nyárlőrinc 62 Na 47	7811 Szálanta 75 Nb 46
5331 Kenderes 62 Mb 48	3433 Nyékládháza 62 Mb 48	3754 Szalonna 62 Ma 48
3396 Kerecsend 62 Mb 48	4300 Nyírbátor 62 Mb 50	5008 Szandaszőlős 62 Mb 48
8360 Keszthely 75 Na 45	4361 Nyírbogát 62 Mb 50	5540 Szarvas 62 Na 48
8713 Kéthely 75 Na 45	4400 Nyíregyháza 62 Mb 49	2440 Százhalombatta 61 Mb 46
2870 Kisbér 61 Mb 46	4522 Nyírtass 62 Ma 50	7751 Szederkény 75 Nb 46
6200 Kiskőrös 76 Na 47	4461 Nyírtelek 62 Ma 49	7056 Szedres 75 Na 46
6100 Kiskunfélegyháza 76 Na 47	9082 Nyúl 61 Mb 45	6700 Szeged 76 Na 48
6400 Kiskunhalas 76 Na 47	5900 Orosháza 76 Na 48	5520 Szeghalom 62 Mb 49
6120 Kiskunmajsa 76 Na 47	2840 Oroszlány 61 Mb 46	3918 Szegilong 62 Ma 49
6421 Kisszállás 76 Na 47	3600 Ózd 62 Ma 48	8000 Székesfehérvár 61 Mb 46
5310 Kisújszállás 62 Mb 48	4755 Ököritófülpös 62 Mb 50	7100 Szekszárd 75 Na 46
4600 Kisvárda 62 Ma 50	2377 Örkény 62 Mb 47	6821 Székkuttas 76 Na 48
5359 Kócsújfalu 62 Mb 48	9153 Öttevény 61 Mb 45	2640 Szendehely 61 Mb 47
4138 Komádi 62 Na 49	8761 Pacsa 75 Na 45	2000 Szentendre 61 Mb 47
2900 Komárom 61 Mb 46	8451 Padragkút 61 Mb 45	6600 Szentes 76 Na 48
7300 Komló 75 Na 46	7030 Paks 75 Na 46	9970 Szentgotthárd 61 Na 44
5553 Kondoros 76 Na 48	3994 Pálháza 62 Ma 49	7936 Szentlászló 75 Na 45
9144 Kóny 61 Mb 45	9345 Páli 61 Mb 45	3900 Szerencs 62 Ma 49
9900 Körmend 61 Mb 44	9090 Pannonhalma 61 Mb 45	7900 Szigetvár 75 Na 45
2851 Környe 61 Mb 46	8500 Pápa 61 Mb 45	9312 Szilsárkány 61 Mb 45
5622 Köröstarcsa 62 Na 49	3240 Parád 62 Mb 48	2628 Szob 61 Mb 46
9730 Kőszeg 61 Mb 44	3060 Pásztó 62 Mb 47	5000 Szolnok 62 Mb 48
5340 Kunhegyes 62 Mb 48	2119 Pécel 62 Mb 47	9700 Szombathely 61 Mb 44
5321 Kunmadaras 62 Mb 48	7600 Pécs 75 Na 46	6771 Szőreg 76 Na 48
7551 Lábod 75 Na 45	9099 Pér 61 Mb 45	8541 Takácsi 61 Mb 45
6050 Lajosmizse 62 Mb 47	3250 Pétervására 62 Ma 48	7090 Tamási 75 Na 46
8960 Lenti 75 Na 44	2721 Pilis 62 Mb 47	2251 Tápiószecső 62 Mb 47
8132 Lepsény 61 Na 46	2085 Pilisvörösvár 61 Mb 46	8300 Tapolca 61 Na 45
8868 Letenye 75 Na 44	7084 Pincehely 75 Na 46	3073 Tar 62 Mb 47
3517 Lillafüred 62 Ma 48	4090 Polgár 62 Mb 49	2890 Tata 61 Mb 46
3186 Litke 62 Ma 47	8154 Polgárdi 61 Mb 46	2800 Tatabánya 61 Mb 46
3021 Lőrinci 62 Mb 47	2013 Pomáz 61 Mb 47	6451 Tataháza 76 Na 47
9461 Lövő 61 Mb 44	3388 Poroszló 62 Mb 48	3359 Tenk 62 Mb 48
3909 Mád 62 Ma 49	8291 Pula 61 Na 45	5430 Tiszaföldvár 62 Na 48
6900 Makó 76 Na 48	5125 Pusztamonostor 62 Mb 47	5350 Tiszafüred 62 Mb 48
4942 Mánd 62 Mb 50	3630 Putnok 62 Ma 48	5362 Tiszaörs 62 Mb 48
8700 Marcali 75 Na 45	4150 Püspökladány 62 Mb 49	3580 Tiszaújváros 62 Mb 49
2462 Martonvásár 61 Mb 46	4465 Rakamaz 62 Ma 49	4440 Tiszavasvári 62 Mb 49
4700 Mátészalka 62 Mb 50	6903 Rákos 76 Na 48	7130 Tolna 75 Na 46
4700 Mátészalka 62 Mb 50	9653 Répcelak 61 Mb 45	6422 Tompa 76 Na 47
4351 Merk 62 Mb 50	2651 Rétság 61 Mb 47	5200 Törökszentmiklós 62 Mb 48
5650 Mezőberény 62 Na 49	3770 Sajószentpéter 62 Ma 48	7811 Túrony 75 Nb 46
5800 Mezőkovácsháza 76 Na 48	3100 Salgótarján 62 Ma 47	4623 Tuzsér 62 Ma 50
3400 Mezőkövesd 62 Mb 48	7000 Sárbogárd 61 Na 46	7718 Udvar 75 Nb 46
9097 Mezőörs 61 Mb 45	5720 Sarkad 62 Na 49	4244 Újfehértó 62 Mb 49
7017 Mezőszilas 75 Na 46	8125 Sárkeresztúr 61 Mb 46	2367 Újhartyán 62 Mb 47
5400 Mezőtúr 62 Na 48	3950 Sárospatak 62 Ma 49	5052 Újszász 62 Mb 48

2225 Üllő 62 Mb 47	
2600 Vác 61 Mb 47	
7041 Vajta 75 Na 46	
7146 Várdomb 75 Na 46	
6033 Városföld 76 Na 47	
8100 Várpalota 61 Mb 46	
7691 Vasas 75 Na 46	
9800 Vasvár 61 Mb 44	
3431 Vatta 62 Mb 48	
2112 Veresegyház 61 Mb 47	
8721 Vése 75 Na 45	
8200 Veszprém 61 Mb 45	
7773 Villány 75 Nb 46	
3124 Zabar 62 Ma 48	
8971 Zalabaksa 75 Na 44	
8900 Zalaegerszeg 75 Na 44	
8751 Zalakomár 75 Na 45	
8999 Zalalövő 75 Na 44	
8790 Zalaszentgrót 61 Na 45	
8621 Zamárdi 61 Na 45	
8420 Zirc 61 Mb 45	
7173 Zomba 75 Na 46	
5537 Zsadány 62 Na 49	

(HR)

21246 Aržano 75 Ob 44
52445 Baderna 74 Nb 41
51523 Baška 74 Oa 42
21320 Baška Voda 89 Ob 44
31306 Batina 75 Nb 46
35410 Batrina 75 Nb 45
42253 Bednja 75 Na 43
34343 Bektež 75 Nb 45
31300 Beli Manastir 75 Nb 46
23420 Benkovac 74 Oa 43
22000 Bilice 75 Ob 43
23210 Biograd na Moru 74 Ob 43
53230 Bjelopolje 75 Oa 43
43000 Bjelovar 75 Nb 44
47243 Blagaj 74 Nb 43
20271 Blato 89 Pa 44
44231 Blinja 75 Nb 44
21420 Bol 89 Ob 44
32227 Borovo 75 Nb 46
47251 Bosanci 74 Nb 43
23285 Brbinje 74 Oa 43
34322 Brestovac 75 Nb 45
53260 Brinje 74 Oa 43
21230 Brnaze 75 Ob 44
51418 Brseč 74 Nb 42
23441 Bruvno 75 Oa 43
44202 Budaševo 75 Nb 44
52460 Buje 74 Nb 41
23420 Bulić 75 Oa 43
53235 Bunić 74 Oa 43
10417 Buševec 75 Nb 44
52420 Buzet 74 Nb 41
20210 Cavtat 89 Pa 46
21256 Cista Provo 75 Ob 44
51557 Cres 74 Oa 42
51260 Crikvenica 74 Nb 42
33514 Čačinci 75 Nb 45
40000 Čakovec 75 Na 44

POSTALI · ÍNDICE CON CÓDIGOS POSTALES · INDICE DE LUGARES COM CÓDIGOS POSTAIS ·
MÍST S PSČ · ZOZNAM OBCÍ S PSČ · INDEKS MIEJSCOWOŚCI Z KOD POCZTOWY

154

HR

I

Čazma (HR) . (I) **Ádria**

43240 Čazma 75 Nb 44	31309 Kneževi Vinogradi 75 Nb 46	53202 Perušić 74 Oa 43	10380 Sveti Ivan Zelina 75 Nb 44
31431 Čepin 75 Nb 46	22300 Knin 75 Oa 44	48321 Peteranec 75 Na 44	53284 Sveti Juraj 74 Oa 42
31553 Črnkovci 75 Nb 46	53226 Kompolje 74 Oa 43	44250 Petrinja 75 Nb 44	22000 Šibenik 75 Ob 43
51564 Čunski 74 Oa 42	49282 Konjščina 75 Na 44	52332 Pićan 74 Nb 42	23251 Šimuni 74 Oa 42
31326 Darda 75 Nb 46	48000 Koprivnica 75 Na 44	33405 Pitomača 75 Nb 45	34550 Španovica 75 Nb 45
43500 Daruvar 75 Nb 45	20264 Korčula 89 Pa 45	34310 Pleternica 75 Nb 45	33404 Špišić Bukovica 75 Nb 45
35425 Davor 75 Nb 45	53230 Korenica 75 Oa 43	20340 Ploče 89 Ob 45	43246 Štefanje 75 Nb 44
51300 Delnice 74 Nb 42	31224 Koška 75 Nb 46	52234 Plomin 74 Nb 42	32249 Tovarnik 75 Nb 47
53252 Doljani 75 Oa 44	51262 Kraljevica 74 Nb 42	21312 Podstrana 75 Ob 44	21240 Trilj 75 Ob 44
40328 Donja Dubrava 75 Na 44	49000 Krapina 75 Na 43	10090 Podsused 75 Nb 43	21220 Trogir 75 Ob 44
43531 Donja Vrijeska 75 Nb 45	10413 Kravarsko 75 Nb 44	10414 Pokupsko 75 Nb 44	20240 Trpanj 89 Ob 45
47271 Donje Stative 74 Nb 43	10314 Križ 75 Nb 44	23241 Poličnik 74 Oa 43	47241 Tušilović 74 Nb 43
31540 Donji Miholjac 75 Nb 46	48260 Križevci 75 Na 44	53231 Poljanak 74 Oa 43	52470 Umag 74 Nb 41
23445 Donji Srb 75 Oa 44	51500 Krk 74 Nb 42	52440 Poreč 74 Nb 41	51500 Valbiska 74 Nb 42
20246 Drače 89 Pa 45	44320 Kutina 75 Nb 44	51557 Porozina 74 Nb 42	31550 Valpovo 75 Nb 46
47313 Drežnica 74 Nb 43	52220 Labin 74 Nb 42	23242 Posedarje 74 Oa 43	42000 Varaždin 75 Na 44
22320 Drniš 75 Ob 44	20290 Lastovo 89 Pa 44	34000 Požega 75 Nb 45	20270 Vela Luka 89 Pa 44
21333 Drvenik 89 Ob 45	53226 Ličko Cerje 74 Oa 43	40323 Prelog 75 Na 44	34330 Velika 75 Nb 45
10342 Dubrava 75 Nb 44	53224 Ličko Lešće 74 Oa 43	52100 Premantura 74 Oa 41	10410 Velika Gorica 75 Nb 44
20000 Dubrovnik 89 Pa 46	34551 Lipik 75 Nb 45	21201 Prgomet 75 Ob 44	35221 Velika Kopanica 75 Nb 46
47250 Duga Resa 74 Nb 43	32246 Lipovac 75 Nb 47	53231 Prijeboj 74 Oa 43	43271 Velika Pisanica 75 Nb 45
21204 Dugopolje 75 Ob 44	52427 Livade 74 Nb 41	22202 Primošten 75 Ob 43	43293 Veliki Zdenci 75 Nb 45
53287 Dušikrava 74 Oa 42	43290 Lončarica 75 Nb 45	23420 Pristeg 75 Ob 43	47243 Veljun 74 Nb 43
31400 Đakovo 75 Nb 46	51415 Lovran 74 Nb 42	23233 Privlaka 74 Oa 43	32271 Vinkovci 75 Nb 46
48350 Đurđevac 75 Na 45	52470 Lovrečica 74 Nb 41	53287 Prizna 74 Oa 42	48326 Virje 75 Na 44
31512 Feričanci 75 Nb 45	42230 Ludbreg 75 Na 44	52100 Pula 74 Oa 41	33000 Virovitica 75 Nb 45
52450 Flengi 74 Nb 41	31328 Lug 75 Nb 46	51280 Rab 74 Oa 42	21480 Vis 89 Ob 44
43280 Garešnički Brestovac	53289 Lukovo Šugarje 74 Oa 43	47245 Rakovica 74 Oa 43	52447 Vižinada 74 Nb 41
75 Nb 44	52426 Lupoglav 74 Nb 42	23248 Ražanac 74 Oa 43	22211 Vodice 75 Ob 43
44400 Glina 75 Nb 44	44403 Maja 75 Nb 44	48305 Reka 75 Na 44	47220 Vojnić 75 Nb 43
51327 Gomirje 74 Nb 43	21300 Makarska 89 Ob 45	35403 Rešetari 75 Nb 45	51557 Vrana 74 Oa 42
23249 Gorica 74 Oa 43	51550 Mali Lošinj 74 Oa 42	51000 Rijeka 74 Nb 42	10340 Vrbovec 75 Nb 44
53244 Gornja Ploča 74 Oa 43	51304 Mali Lug 74 Nb 42	52210 Rovinj 74 Nb 41	21276 Vrgorac 89 Ob 45
44425 Gornje Taborište 75 Nb 44	52206 Marčana 74 Oa 41	43212 Rovišće 75 Nb 44	10450 Vrh Draganički 74 Nb 43
53000 Gospić 74 Oa 43	21430 Maslinica 89 Ob 44	51214 Rupa 74 Nb 42	21236 Vrhta 75 Ob 44
23440 Gračac 75 Oa 43	53205 Medak 74 Oa 43	34350 Ruševo 75 Nb 45	31403 Vuka 75 Nb 46
31500 Gradac Našički 75 Nb 46	20350 Metković 89 Ob 45	51213 Ružići 74 Nb 42	32000 Vukovar 75 Nb 46
43290 Grubišno Polje 75 Nb 45	47221 Miholjsko 74 Nb 43	10430 Samobor 75 Nb 43	49210 Zabok 75 Na 43
20215 Gruda 89 Pa 46	47303 Modruš 74 Nb 43	52475 Savudrija 74 Nb 41	23000 Zadar 75 Oa 43
44410 Gvozd 75 Nb 43	51325 Moravice 74 Nb 43	33405 Sedlarica 75 Nb 45	10000 Zagreb 75 Nb 43
44437 Gvozdansko 75 Nb 44	51315 Mrkopalj 74 Nb 42	53270 Senj 74 Oa 42	10290 Zaprešić 75 Nb 43
44430 Hrvatska Kostajnica	22243 Murter 74 Ob 43	10360 Sesvete 75 Nb 44	47264 Zdenac 74 Nb 43
75 Nb 44	53234 Mutilić 75 Oa 43	21230 Sinj 75 Ob 44	52341 Žminj 74 Nb 41
21450 Hvar 89 Ob 44	31500 Našice 75 Nb 46	44000 Sisak 75 Nb 44	32270 Županja 75 Nb 46
32236 Ilok 76 Nb 47	40305 Nedelišće 75 Na 44	22222 Skradin 75 Ob 43	
21260 Imotski 75 Ob 45	53291 Novalja 74 Oa 42	20232 Slano 89 Pa 45	
42240 Ivanec 75 Na 44	42220 Novi Marof 75 Na 44	33520 Slatina 75 Nb 45	
10310 Ivanić Grad 75 Nb 44	51250 Novi Vinodolski 74 Nb 42	33516 Slatinski Drenovac 75 Nb 45	(I)
31540 Ivankovo 75 Nb 46	10020 Novi Zagreb 75 Nb 44	35000 Slavonski Brod 75 Nb 46	
10297 Jakovlje 75 Nb 43	23312 Novigrad 74 Nb 41	47240 Slunj 74 Nb 43	35031 Abano Terme 73 Nb 39
34308 Jakšić 75 Nb 45	44330 Novska 75 Nb 44	23424 Smilčić 74 Oa 43	09071 Abbasanta 86 Qa 36
10450 Jastrebarsko 74 Nb 43	23450 Obrovac 74 Oa 43	20225 Sobra 89 Pa 45	20081 Abbiategrasso 73 Nb 36
53262 Jezerane 74 Nb 43	47300 Ogulin 74 Nb 43	21210 Solin 75 Ob 44	12021 Accéglio 72 Oa 34
47304 Jezero I Dio 74 Nb 43	35430 Okučani 75 Nb 45	32232 Sotin 75 Nb 47	04010 Acciarella 88 Pb 40
47303 Josipdol 74 Nb 43	21310 Omiš 75 Ob 44	21000 Split 75 Ob 44	85011 Acerenza 89 Qa 43
31221 Josipovac 75 Nb 46	51410 Opatija 74 Nb 42	21460 Stari Grad 89 Ob 44	00125 Acilia 87 Pb 40
53234 Jošan 75 Oa 43	20350 Opuzen 89 Ob 45	23244 Starigrad 74 Oa 43	95024 Acireale 102 Rb 43
52342 Juršići 74 Nb 41	20250 Orebič 89 Pa 45	21311 Stobreč 75 Ob 44	01021 Acquapendente 87 Pa 39
53288 Karlobag 74 Oa 43	31000 Osijek 75 Nb 46	20230 Ston 89 Pa 45	89832 Acquaro 103 Ra 44
47000 Karlovac 74 Nb 43	51554 Osor 74 Oa 42	22311 Strmica 74 Oa 44	05021 Acquasparta 88 Pa 40
23451 Kaštel Žegarski 75 Oa 43	53220 Otočac 74 Oa 43	23442 Sučevići 75 Oa 44	70021 Acquaviva delle Fonti
22310 Kijevo 75 Ob 44	32252 Otok 75 Nb 46	21469 Sućuraj 89 Ob 45	89 Qa 44
22305 Kistanje 75 Ob 43	22318 Pađene 75 Oa 44	23206 Sukošan 74 Oa 43	98070 Acquedolci 102 Ra 42
53286 Klada 74 Oa 42	23250 Pag 74 Oa 43	21426 Sumartin 89 Ob 44	15011 Acqui Terme 72 Oa 36
23441 Klapavica 75 Oa 43	34550 Pakrac 75 Nb 45	44210 Sunja 75 Nb 44	95031 Adrano 102 Rb 42
31000 Klisa 75 Nb 46	52000 Pazin 74 Nb 41	21400 Supetar 89 Ob 44	45011 Ádria 73 Nb 40

155

INDEX WITH POST CODES · ORTSREGISTER MIT POSTLEITZAHLEN · INDICE CON CODICI
STEDREGISTER MED POSTNUMRE · PLAATSNAMENREGISTER MET POSTCODE · REJSTŘÍK

Agria | I | **Catanzaro**

94011 Agira 102 Rb 42
86081 Agnone 88 Pb 42
32021 Àgordo 73 Na 40
92100 Agrigento 102 Rb 41
84043 Agrópoli 88 Qa 42
17021 Alássio 72 Oa 36
03011 Alatri 88 Pb 41
12051 Alba 72 Oa 36
64011 Alba Adriática 88 Pa 41
00041 Albano Laziale 88 Pb 40
17031 Albenga 72 Oa 36
58010 Albínia 87 Pa 39
24021 Albino 73 Nb 37
17012 Albisola Marina 72 Oa 36
91011 Àlcamo 102 Rb 40
15100 Alessándria 72 Oa 36
92010 Alessándria della Rocca
102 Rb 41
67030 Alfedena 88 Pb 42
48011 Alfonsine 73 Oa 40
07041 Alghero 86 Qa 36
98050 Alicudi Porto 102 Ra 42
81011 Alife 88 Pb 42
70022 Altamura 89 Qa 44
84011 Amalfi 88 Qa 42
63021 Amándola 88 Pa 41
87032 Amantea 103 Qb 44
02012 Amatrice 88 Pa 41
05022 Amélia 88 Ob 40
33021 Ampezzo 74 Na 40
03012 Anagni 88 Pb 41
60100 Ancona 74 Ob 41
83040 Andretta 88 Qa 43
70031 Àndria 89 Pb 44
52031 Anghiari 73 Ob 40
57100 Antignano 73 Ob 38
02013 Antrodoco 88 Pa 41
00042 Ànzio 88 Pb 40
11100 Aosta/Aoste 72 Nb 35
61042 Apécchio 74 Ob 40
71011 Apricena 88 Pb 43
04011 Aprília 88 Pb 40
64043 Aqualagna 74 Ob 40
33051 Aquiléia 74 Nb 41
13031 Arbório 72 Nb 36
60011 Arcéiva 74 Ob 40
58031 Arcidosso 87 Pa 39
38062 Arco 73 Nb 38
16011 Arenzano 72 Oa 36
52100 Arezzo 73 Ob 39
44011 Argenta 73 Oa 39
83031 Ariano Irpino 88 Pb 43
45012 Ariano nel Polésine
73 Oa 40
28041 Arona 73 Nb 36
00031 Artena 88 Pb 40
07021 Arzachena 87 Pb 37
36071 Arzignano 73 Nb 39
63100 Àscoli Piceno 88 Pa 41
71022 Àscoli Satriano 88 Pb 43
36012 Asiago 73 Nb 39
46041 Àsola 73 Nb 38
09032 Assémini 100 Qb 37
06081 Assisi 88 Ob 40
14100 Asti 72 Oa 36
64032 Atri 88 Pa 41

96011 Augusta 102 Rb 43
54011 Aulla 73 Oa 37
32041 Auronzo di Cadore 74 Na 40
83100 Avellino 88 Qa 42
81031 Aversa 88 Qa 42
67051 Avezzano 88 Pa 41
85021 Avigliano 88 Qa 43
96012 Àvola 102 Sa 43
33082 Azzano Décimo 74 Nb 40
45021 Badia Polésine 73 Nb 39
90011 Bagheria 102 Ra 41
48012 Bagnacavallo 73 Oa 39
89011 Bagnara Cálabra 102 Ra 43
12071 Bagnasco 72 Oa 36
47021 Bagno di Romagna 73 Ob 39
25021 Bagnolo Mella 73 Nb 38
10070 Balme 72 Nb 35
98051 Barcellona Pozzo di Gotto
102 Ra 43
33080 Bárcis 74 Na 40
43032 Bardi 73 Oa 37
70100 Bari 89 Pb 44
67021 Barisciano 88 Pa 41
70051 Barletta 89 Pb 44
94012 Barrafranca 102 Rb 42
36061 Bassano del Grappa
73 Nb 39
06083 Bastia Umbra 88 Ob 40
84091 Battipáglia 88 Qa 42
08040 Baunei 87 Qa 37
43041 Bedónia 73 Oa 37
06047 Belforte 88 Pa 40
22021 Bellágio 73 Nb 37
23822 Bellano 73 Na 37
47814 Bellária 74 Oa 40
32100 Belluno 74 Na 40
87021 Belvedere Maríttimo
103 Qb 43
82100 Benevento 88 Pb 42
43042 Berceto 73 Oa 37
24100 Bérgamo 73 Nb 37
75012 Bernalda 89 Qa 44
29021 Béttola 73 Oa 37
06031 Bevagna 88 Pa 40
95033 Biancavilla 102 Rb 42
89032 Bianco 103 Ra 44
13900 Biella 72 Nb 36
70010 Biscéglie 89 Pb 44
70032 Bitonto 89 Pb 44
08021 Bitti 87 Qa 37
29022 Bóbbio 73 Oa 37
86021 Bojano 88 Pb 42
20021 Bollate 73 Nb 37
40100 Bologna 73 Oa 39
90030 Bolognetta 102 Rb 41
01023 Bolsena 87 Pa 39
44012 Bondeno 73 Oa 39
07011 Bono 86 Qa 37
88021 Bórgia 103 Ra 44
02032 Borgo Quínzio 88 Pa 40
50032 Borgo San Lorenzo 73 Ob 39
43043 Borgo Val di Taro 73 Oa 37
18021 Borgomaro 72 Oa 35
13011 Borgosesia 72 Nb 36
23032 Bórmio 73 Na 38
08013 Bosa 86 Qa 36

89034 Bovalino Marina 103 Ra 44
71023 Bovino 88 Pb 43
37051 Bovolone 73 Nb 39
39100 Bozen/Bolzano 73 Na 39
46012 Bózzolo 73 Nb 38
12042 Bra 72 Oa 35
58030 Braccagni 87 Pa 39
00062 Bracciano 87 Pa 40
89036 Brancaleone Marina
103 Rb 44
39041 Brenner 59 Mb 39
25043 Breno 73 Nb 38
25100 Bréscia 73 Nb 38
11028 Breuil-Cervínia 72 Nb 35
89817 Briático 103 Ra 44
85050 Brienza 88 Qa 43
72100 Bríndisi 89 Qa 45
39042 Brixen/Bressanone 73 Na 39
95034 Bronte 102 Rb 42
39031 Bruneck/Brunico 59 Na 39
14051 Búbbio 72 Oa 36
07020 Buddusò 87 Qa 37
40054 Búdrio 73 Oa 39
33030 Búia 74 Na 41
53022 Buonconvento 87 Ob 39
12022 Busca 72 Oa 35
37012 Bussolengo 73 Nb 38
21052 Busto Arsízio 73 Nb 36
61043 Cagli 74 Ob 40
09100 Cágliari 100 Qb 37
71010 Cagnano Varano 89 Pb 43
81013 Caiazzo 88 Pb 42
91013 Calatafimi-Segesta
102 Rb 40
83045 Calitri 88 Qa 43
95041 Caltagirone 102 Rb 42
93100 Caltanissetta 102 Rb 42
90022 Caltavuturo 102 Rb 41
55041 Camaiore 73 Ob 38
62032 Camerino 88 Ob 41
22012 Campagna 103 Qb 44
87061 Campana 103 Qb 44
50013 Campi Bisénzio 73 Ob 39
73012 Campi Salentina 89 Qa 46
16013 Campo Lígure 72 Oa 36
86100 Campobasso 88 Pb 42
92023 Campobello di Licata
102 Rb 41
91021 Campobello di Mazara
102 Rb 40
90010 Campofelice di Roccella
102 Rb 41
90030 Campofiorito 102 Rb 41
36020 Campolongo 73 Na 39
86042 Campomarino 88 Pb 43
71024 Candela 88 Pb 43
92024 Canicattí 102 Rb 41
46013 Canneto sull' Òglio 73 Nb 38
28822 Cannóbio 73 Na 36
70053 Canosa di Púglia 89 Pb 44
22063 Cantù 73 Nb 37
30021 Cáorle 74 Nb 40
56033 Capánnoli 73 Ob 38
98071 Capo d'Orlando 102 Ra 42
25044 Capo di Ponte 73 Na 38
57032 Cápraia Ísola 87 Ob 37
80073 Capri 88 Qa 42

81043 Cápua 88 Pb 42
24043 Caravággio 73 Nb 37
09013 Carbónia 100 Qb 36
87062 Cariati 103 Qb 44
90044 Carini 102 Ra 41
09014 Carloforte 100 Qb 36
10022 Carmagnola 72 Oa 35
41012 Carpi 73 Oa 38
54033 Carrara 73 Oa 38
67061 Carsóli 88 Pa 41
81033 Casàl di Príncipe 88 Pb 42
15033 Casale Monferrato 72 Nb 36
40033 Casalécchio di Reno
73 Oa 39
26041 Casalmaggiore 73 Oa 38
26841 Casalpusterlengo 73 Nb 37
70010 Casamássima 89 Qa 44
73042 Casarano 89 Qa 46
56021 Cáscina 73 Ob 38
81100 Caserta 88 Pb 42
66043 Cásoli 88 Pa 42
87011 Cassano allo Jónio
103 Qb 44
03043 Cassino 88 Pb 41
67031 Castèl di Sangro 88 Pb 42
29015 Castèl San Giovanni
73 Nb 37
40024 Castèl San Pietro Terme
73 Oa 39
81030 Castèl Volturno 88 Pb 41
60022 Castelfidardo 74 Ob 41
50051 Castelfiorentino 73 Ob 38
41013 Castelfranco Emilia
73 Oa 39
31033 Castelfranco Véneto
73 Nb 39
84048 Castellabate 88 Qa 42
91014 Castellammare del Golfo
102 Ra 40
80053 Castellammare di Stábia
88 Qa 42
90020 Castellana Sicula
102 Rb 42
96017 Castellúccio 89 Qa 43
55032 Castelnovo di Garfagnana
73 Oa 38
42035 Castelnovo ne Monti
73 Oa 38
07031 Castelsardo 86 Qa 36
91022 Castelvetrano 102 Rb 40
52043 Castiglion Fiorentino
73 Ob 39
57016 Castiglioncello 73 Ob 38
40035 Castiglione dei Pépoli
73 Oa 39
06061 Castiglione del Lago
87 Ob 40
58043 Castiglione della Pescáia
87 Pa 39
46043 Castiglione delle Stiviere
73 Nb 38
66033 Castiglione Messer Marino
88 Pb 42
87012 Castrovillari 103 Qb 44
95100 Catánia 102 Rb 43
88100 Catanzaro 103 Ra 44

POSTALI · ÍNDICE CON CÓDIGOS POSTALES · INDICE DE LUGARES COM CÓDIGOS POSTAIS ·
MÍST S PSČ · ZOZNAM OBCÍ S PSČ · INDEKS MIEJSCOWOŚCI Z KOD POCZTOWY

156

Catanzaro Marina   **I**   Latisana

    I

88063 Catanzaro Marina 103 Ra 44	44022 Comácchio 73 Oa 40	44100 Ferrara 73 Oa 39	10094 Giaveno 72 Nb 35
47841 Cattólica 74 Ob 40	97013 Cómiso 102 Sa 42	29024 Ferriere 73 Oa 37	91024 Gibellina Nuova 102 Rb 40
84013 Cava de Tirreni 88 Qa 42	22100 Como 73 Nb 37	02023 Fiamignano 88 Pa 41	75016 Ginosa 89 Qa 44
33014 Cavárzere 73 Nb 40	25062 Concésio 73 Nb 38	05016 Ficulle 87 Pa 40	70023 Gióia del Colle 89 Qa 44
10061 Cavour 72 Oa 35	31015 Conegliano 74 Nb 40	43036 Fidenza 73 Oa 38	89013 Gióia Táuro 103 Ra 43
03023 Ceccano 88 Pb 41	84024 Contursi Terme 88 Qa 43	38054 Fiera di Primiero 73 Na 39	98063 Gioiosa Marea 102 Ra 42
57023 Cécina 73 Ob 38	70014 Conversano 89 Qa 45	50014 Fiésole 73 Ob 39	70054 Giovinazzo 89 Pb 44
90015 Cefalú 102 Ra 42	73043 Copertino 89 Qa 46	50063 Figline Valdarno 73 Ob 39	80014 Giugliano in Campánia
67043 Celano 88 Pa 41	44034 Coparo 73 Oa 39	98050 Filicudi Porto 102 Ra 42	88 Qa 42
44042 Cento 73 Oa 39	70033 Corato 89 Pb 44	41034 Finale Emília 73 Oa 39	64021 Giuliánova 88 Pa 41
03024 Ceprano 88 Pb 41	87064 Corigliano Cálabro	17024 Finale Lígure 72 Oa 36	07020 Golfo Aranci 87 Qa 37
90010 Cerda 102 Rb 41	103 Qb 44	50100 Firenze 73 Ob 39	09010 Gonnesa 100 Qb 36
37053 Cerea 73 Nb 39	90034 Corleone 102 Rb 41	50033 Firenzuola 73 Oa 39	34170 Gorizia 74 Nb 41
10080 Ceresole Reale 72 Nb 35	85012 Corleto Perticara 89 Qa 44	87010 Firmo 103 Qb 44	28024 Gozzano 72 Nb 36
71042 Cerignola 89 Pb 43	29016 Cortemaggiore 73 Oa 37	03014 Fiuggi 88 Pb 41	34073 Grado 74 Nb 41
00052 Cervéteri 87 Pb 40	12074 Cortemília 72 Oa 36	00054 Fiumicino 87 Pb 40	95042 Grammichele 102 Rb 42
48015 Cérvia 74 Oa 40	32043 Cortina d'Ampezzo	96014 Floridia 102 Rb 43	28883 Gravellona Toce 72 Nb 36
33052 Cervignano del Friuli	74 Na 40	07300 Florínas 86 Qa 36	70024 Gravina in Púglia 89 Qa 44
74 Nb 41	52044 Cortona 87 Ob 39	09010 Fluminimaggiore 100 Qb 36	11025 Gressoney-Saint-Jean
98033 Cesarò 102 Rb 42	39033 Corvara/Corvara in Badia	71100 Fóggia 88 Pb 43	72 Nb 35
47023 Cesena 74 Oa 40	73 Na 39	06034 Foligno 88 Pa 40	58100 Grosseto 87 Pa 39
47042 Cesenático 74 Oa 40	87100 Cosenza 103 Qb 44	58022 Follónica 87 Pa 38	74023 Grottáglie 89 Qa 45
87022 Cetraro 103 Qb 43	12024 Costigliole Saluzzo 72 Oa 35	04022 Fondi 88 Pb 41	83035 Grottaminarda 88 Pb 43
12073 Ceva 72 Oa 36	11013 Courmayeur 72 Nb 34	38013 Fondo 73 Na 39	63013 Grottammare 88 Pa 41
11020 Champoluc 72 Nb 35	26013 Crema 73 Nb 37	08023 Fonni 86 Qa 37	06023 Gualdo Tadino 88 Ob 40
11024 Châtillon 72 Nb 35	26100 Cremona 73 Nb 38	24010 Fóppolo 73 Na 37	82034 Guárdia Sanframondi
12062 Cherasco 72 Oa 35	13044 Crescentino 72 Nb 36	09083 Fordongiánus 86 Qb 36	88 Pb 42
36072 Chiampo 73 Nb 39	88900 Crotone 103 Qb 45	47100 Forlí 73 Oa 40	66016 Guardiagrele 88 Pa 42
60033 Chiaravalle 74 Ob 41	09073 Cúglieri 86 Qa 36	47034 Forlimpópoli 73 Oa 40	42016 Guastalla 73 Oa 38
88064 Chiaravalle Centrale	12100 Cúneo 72 Oa 35	04023 Fórmia 88 Pb 41	06024 Gúbbio 74 Ob 40
103 Ra 44	10082 Cuorgne 72 Nb 35	33020 Forni di Sotto 74 Na 40	86034 Guglionesi 88 Pb 42
25032 Chiari 73 Nb 37	66051 Cupello 88 Pa 42	43045 Fornovo di Taro 73 Oa 38	09036 Gúspini 100 Qb 36
52100 Chiassa 73 Nb 37	88842 Cutro 103 Qb 44	57020 Forte di Bibbona 73 Ob 38	25064 Gussago 73 Nb 38
23022 Chiavenna 73 Na 37	25047 Darfo 73 Nb 38	12045 Fossano 72 Oa 35	09016 Iglésias 100 Qb 36
10023 Chieri 72 Nb 35	23014 Delébio 73 Na 37	61034 Fossombrone 74 Ob 40	40026 Ímola 73 Oa 39
66100 Chieti 88 Pa 42	89012 Delianuova 103 Ra 43	66023 Francavilla al Mare 88 Pa 42	18100 Impéria 72 Ob 36
30015 Chióggia 74 Nb 40	25015 Desenzano del Garda	98034 Francavilla di Sicília	50023 Impruneta 73 Ob 39
12013 Chiusa di Pésio 72 Oa 35	73 Nb 38	102 Rb 43	08020 Írgoli 87 Qa 37
90033 Chiusa Scláfani 102 Rb 41	18013 Diano Marina 72 Ob 36	72021 Francavilla Fontana	75022 Irsina 89 Qa 44
10034 Chivasso 72 Nb 35	50062 Dicomano 73 Ob 39	89 Qa 45	80077 Íschia 88 Qa 41
13043 Cigliano 72 Nb 36	12063 Dogliani 72 Oa 35	96015 Francofonte 102 Rb 42	25049 Iseo 73 Nb 38
62011 Cíngoli 74 Ob 41	09041 Dolianova 100 Qb 37	00044 Frascati 88 Pb 40	86170 Isérnia 88 Pb 42
90045 Cínisi 102 Ra 40	30031 Dolo 73 Nb 40	00050 Fregene 87 Pb 40	37063 Ísola della Scala 73 Nb 38
88811 Cirò Marina 103 Qb 45	28845 Domodóssola 72 Na 36	53010 Frósini 87 Ob 39	88841 Ísola di Capo Rizzuto
35013 Citadella 73 Nb 39	08022 Dorgali 87 Qa 37	03100 Frosinone 88 Pb 41	103 Ra 45
06062 Città della Pieve 87 Pa 39	84013 Éboli 88 Qa 43	50054 Fucécchio 73 Ob 38	97014 Íspica 102 Sa 42
06012 Città di Castello 73 Ob 40	25048 Édolo 73 Na 38	91010 Fulgatore 102 Rb 40	07044 Íttiri 86 Qa 36
02015 Cittaducale 88 Pa 40	50053 Émpoli 73 Ob 38	04024 Gaeta 88 Pb 41	10015 Ivrea 72 Nb 35
33043 Cividale del Friuli 74 Na 41	94100 Enna 102 Rb 42	73034 Gagliano del Capo	60035 Jesi 74 Ob 41
01033 Civita Castellana 88 Pa 40	39057 Eppan/Appiano 73 Na 39	103 Qb 46	30016 Jésolo 74 Nb 40
62012 Civitanova Marche 88 Ob 41	30020 Eraclea 74 Nb 40	08040 Gáiro 87 Qb 37	67100 L'Àquila 88 Pa 41
00053 Civitavécchia 87 Pa 39	91016 Érice 101 Ra 40	73013 Galatina 89 Qa 46	07024 la Maddalena 87 Pb 37
64010 Civitella del Tronto 88 Pa 41	60044 Fabriano 88 Ob 40	47010 Galeata 73 Oa 39	19100 La Spézia 73 Oa 37
67054 Civitella Roveto 88 Pb 41	48018 Faenza 73 Oa 39	21012 Cassano Magnago 73 Nb 36	83046 Lacedónia 88 Pb 43
38023 Cles 73 Na 39	93012 Falconara 102 Rb 42	73014 Gallípoli 89 Qa 45	08034 Láconi 86 Qb 37
24023 Clusone 73 Nb 37	60015 Falconara Maríttima	37016 Garda 73 Nb 38	00055 Ladíspoli 87 Pb 40
35020 Codevigo 73 Nb 40	74 Ob 41	12075 Garéssio 72 Oa 36	85042 Lagonegro 88 Qa 43
44021 Codigoro 73 Oa 40	61032 Fano 74 Ob 41	16047 Gattorna 73 Oa 37	39011 Lana 73 Na 39
26845 Codogno 73 Nb 37	28073 Fara Novarese 72 Nb 36	93012 Gela 102 Rb 42	86040 Lanciano 88 Pa 42
33333 Codróipo 74 Nb 40	72015 Fasano 89 Qa 45	33013 Gemona del Friuli 74 Na 41	43013 Langhirano 73 Oa 38
11012 Cogne 72 Nb 35	92026 Favara 102 Rb 41	16100 Génova 73 Oa 36	08045 Lanusei 87 Qb 37
53034 Colle di Val d'Elsa 73 Ob 39	91023 Favignana 101 Rb 40	85013 Genzano di Lucánia	39030 Láppago 59 Na 39
00034 Colleferro 88 Pb 40	32032 Feltre 73 Na 39	89 Qa 44	86035 Larino 88 Pb 42
10093 Collegno 72 Nb 35	03013 Ferentino 88 Pb 41	09020 Gésturi 86 Qb 37	74014 Laterza 89 Qa 44
90016 Collesano 102 Rb 41	63023 Fermo 88 Ob 41	25016 Ghedi 73 Nb 38	04100 Latina 88 Pb 40
25060 Cóllio 73 Nb 38	75013 Ferrandina 89 Qa 44	09074 Ghilarza 86 Qa 36	33053 Latisana 74 Nb 41

157 INDEX WITH POST CODES · ORTSREGISTER MIT POSTLEITZAHLEN · INDICE CON CODICI
STEDREGISTER MED POSTNUMRE · PLAATSNAMENREGISTER MET POSTCODE · REJSTŘÍK

I

Latrónico | I | Pérgine Valsugana

85043 Latrónico 89 Qa 44
85014 Laurenzana 89 Qa 43
85040 Lauria 89 Qa 43
85024 Lavello 89 Pb 43
21014 Laveno 73 Nb 36
06080 le Pulci 88 Qb 40
52035 le Ville 73 Ob 40
73100 Lecce 89 Qa 46
23900 Lecco 73 Nb 37
37045 Legnago 73 Nb 39
20025 Legnano 73 Nb 36
35020 Legnaro 73 Nb 39
39055 Leifers/Láives 73 Na 39
10040 Leini 72 Nb 35
45026 Lendinara 73 Nb 39
24010 Lenna 73 Nb 37
96016 Lentini 102 Rb 43
94013 Leonforte 102 Rb 42
90025 Lercara Friddi 102 Rb 41
71010 Lésina 88 Pb 43
19015 Lévanto 73 Oa 37
91010 Lévanzo 101 Rb 40
38056 Levico Terme 73 Na 39
92027 Licata 102 Rb 41
00042 Lido dei Pini 88 Pb 40
30017 Lido di Jésolo 74 Nb 40
75010 Lido di Metaponto 89 Qa 44
00122 Lido di Óstia 87 Pb 40
33054 Lignano Sabbiadoro 74 Nb 41
20051 Limbiate 73 Nb 37
12015 Limone Piemonte 72 Oa 35
95055 Linguaglossa 102 Rb 43
98055 Lípari 102 Ra 42
57100 Livorno 73 Ob 38
24020 Lizzola 73 Na 38
70010 Locorotondo 89 Qa 45
89044 Locri 103 Ra 44
26900 Lodi 73 Nb 37
27034 Lomello 73 Nb 36
32013 Longarone 74 Na 40
36045 Lonigo 73 Nb 39
60025 Loreto 74 Ob 41
24065 Lóvere 73 Nb 38
55100 Lucca 73 Ob 38
71036 Lucera 88 Pb 43
86030 Lucito 88 Pb 42
48022 Lugo 73 Oa 39
21016 Luino 73 Nb 36
07020 Luogosanto 87 Pb 37
62100 Macerata 88 Ob 41
08015 Macomér 86 Qa 36
81024 Maddaloni 88 Pb 42
23020 Madesimo 73 Na 37
38084 Madonna di Campiglio 73 Na 38
25080 Magasa 73 Nb 38
20013 Magenta 73 Nb 36
02046 Magliano Sabina 88 Pa 40
73024 Máglie 89 Qa 46
39024 Málles Venosta 59 Na 38
39024 Mals im Vinschgau Málles Venosta 59 Na 38
08024 Mamoiada 86 Qa 37
58014 Manciano 87 Pa 39
09040 Mándas 100 Qb 37

87060 Mandatoriccio 103 Qb 44
74024 Mandúria 89 Qa 45
25025 Manérbio 73 Nb 38
71043 Manfredónia 89 Pb 43
33085 Maniago 74 Na 40
65024 Manoppello 88 Pa 42
31040 Mansuè 74 Nb 40
46100 Mántova 73 Nb 38
85046 Maratea 102 Qb 43
91010 Maréttimo 101 Rb 40
71044 Margherita di Savóia 89 Pb 44
58046 Marina di Grosseto 87 Pa 38
73030 Marina di Léuca 103 Qb 46
54100 Marina di Massa 73 Oa 38
97010 Marina di Ragusa 102 Sa 42
48100 Marina di Ravenna 74 Oa 40
91022 Marinella 102 Rb 40
00047 Marino 88 Pb 40
91025 Marsala 101 Rb 40
06055 Marsciano 87 Pa 40
85052 Mársico Nuovo 88 Qa 43
74015 Martina Franca 89 Qa 45
95030 Mascalucia 102 Rb 43
54100 Massa 73 Oa 38
48024 Massa Lombarda 73 Oa 39
58024 Massa Maríttima 87 Ob 38
74016 Massafra 89 Qa 45
55054 Massarosa 73 Ob 38
75100 Matera 89 Qa 44
71030 Mattinata 89 Pb 44
91026 Mazara del Vallo 101 Rb 40
93013 Mazzarino 102 Rb 42
27035 Mede 73 Nb 36
40059 Medicina 73 Oa 39
85025 Melfi 88 Pb 43
89063 Melito di Porto Salvo 102 Rb 43
92013 Menfi 102 Rb 40
39012 Meran/Merano 73 Na 39
84085 Mercato San Severino 88 Qa 42
72023 Mesagne 89 Qa 45
44026 Mésola 74 Oa 40
88838 Mesoraca 103 Qb 44
98100 Messina 102 Ra 43
38017 Mezzolombardo 73 Na 39
56019 Migliarino 73 Ob 38
20121 Milano 73 Nb 37
98057 Milazzo 102 Ra 43
89852 Mileto 103 Ra 44
70055 Minervino Murge 89 Pb 44
04026 Minturno 88 Pb 41
30034 Mira 73 Nb 40
41037 Mirándola 73 Oa 39
30035 Mirano 73 Nb 40
90036 Misilmeri 102 Ra 41
95045 Misterbianco 102 Rb 43
38073 Mistretta 102 Rb 42
41100 Módena 73 Oa 38
97015 Módica 102 Sa 42
47015 Modigliana 73 Oa 39
70032 Mogudno 89 Pb 44
33015 Móggio Udinese 74 Na 41
70042 Mola di Bari 89 Pb 45
70056 Molfetta 89 Pb 44

38030 Molina 73 Na 39
10024 Moncalieri 72 Nb 35
14036 Moncalvo 72 Nb 36
12084 Mondoví 72 Oa 35
81034 Mondragone 88 Pb 41
34074 Monfalcone 74 Nb 41
13888 Mongrando 72 Nb 35
70043 Monópoli 89 Qa 45
90046 Monreale 102 Ra 41
35043 Monsélice 73 Nb 39
51015 Monsummano Terme 73 Ob 38
35544 Montagnana 73 Nb 39
92010 Montallegro 102 Rb 41
01014 Montalto di Castro 87 Pa 39
04020 Monte San Biágio 88 Pb 41
52048 Monte San Savino 73 Ob 39
71037 Monte Sant'Ángelo 89 Pb 43
31044 Montebelluna 73 Nb 40
01027 Montefiascone 87 Pa 40
83048 Montella 88 Qa 43
86036 Montenero di Bisáccia 88 Pb 42
53045 Montepulciano 87 Ob 39
00015 Monterotondo 88 Pa 40
84033 Montesano sulla Marcellana 88 Qa 43
82016 Montesárchio 88 Pb 42
75024 Montescaglioso 89 Qa 44
65015 Montesilvano 88 Pa 42
52025 Montevarchi 73 Ob 39
07020 Monti 87 Qa 37
25018 Montichiari 73 Nb 38
53015 Monticiano 87 Ob 39
64046 Montório al Vomano 88 Pa 41
20052 Monza 73 Nb 37
82026 Morcone 88 Pb 42
07013 Móres 86 Qa 36
12033 Moretta 72 Oa 35
11017 Morgex 72 Nb 35
87026 Mormanno 103 Qb 43
27036 Mortara 73 Nb 36
74017 Móttola 89 Qa 45
09043 Muravera 101 Qb 37
85054 Muro Lucano 88 Qa 43
93014 Mussomeli 102 Rb 41
80121 Nápoli 88 Qa 42
73048 Nardò 89 Qa 46
05035 Narni 88 Pa 40
98074 Naso 102 Ra 42
16100 Nervi 73 Oa 37
00048 Nettuno 88 Pb 40
88046 Nicastro 103 Ra 44
10042 Nichelino 72 Oa 35
94014 Nicosia 102 Rb 42
89844 Nicótera 103 Ra 43
14049 Nizza Monferrato 72 Oa 36
88047 Nocera Terinese 103 Qb 44
06025 Nocera Umbra 88 Ob 40
70015 Noci 89 Qa 45
73020 Nocíglia 89 Qa 46
37054 Nogara 73 Nb 39
80035 Nola 88 Qa 42
41015 Nonántola 73 Oa 39
06046 Nórcia 88 Pa 41

96017 Noto 102 Sa 43
28100 Novara 73 Nb 36
15067 Novi Lígure 73 Oa 36
08100 Nuoro 87 Qa 37
31046 Oderzo 74 Nb 40
07026 Ólbia 87 Qa 37
28047 Oléggio 73 Nb 36
28887 Omegna 72 Nb 36
85015 Óppido Lucano 89 Qa 43
58015 Orbetello 87 Pa 39
87073 Oriolo 89 Qa 44
01010 Oriolo Romano 87 Pa 40
09170 Oristano 86 Qa 36
12078 Ormea 72 Oa 35
71045 Orta Nova 88 Pb 43
01028 Orte 87 Pa 40
66026 Ortona 88 Pa 42
05018 Orvieto 87 Pa 40
07027 Óschiri 86 Qa 36
60027 Ósimo 74 Ob 41
33010 Osoppo 74 Na 41
05010 Ospedaletto 87 Pa 40
44020 Ostellato 73 Oa 39
46035 Ostiglia 73 Nb 39
72017 Ostuni 89 Qa 45
73028 Otranto 89 Qa 46
08020 Ottana 86 Qa 37
29026 Ottone 73 Oa 37
10056 Oulx 72 Nb 34
15076 Ovada 72 Oa 36
07014 Ozieri 86 Qa 37
91027 Paceco 101 Rb 40
35100 Pádova 73 Nb 39
84034 Padula 88 Qa 43
12034 Paesana 72 Oa 35
31038 Paese 74 Nb 40
95046 Palagónia 102 Rb 42
07020 Pálau 87 Pb 37
25036 Palazzolo 73 Nb 37
96010 Palazzolo Acréide 102 Rb 42
90100 Palermo 102 Ra 41
00036 Palestrina 88 Pb 40
03018 Paliano 88 Pb 41
84064 Palinuro 88 Qa 43
89038 Palizzi Marina 103 Rb 43
92020 Palma di Montechiaro 102 Rb 41
33057 Palmanova 74 Nb 41
89015 Palmi 103 Ra 43
33026 Paluzza 74 Na 41
26025 Pandino 73 Nb 37
91017 Pantelleria 101 Sa 39
87027 Páola 103 Qb 44
73052 Parábita 89 Qa 46
43100 Parma 73 Oa 38
91028 Partanna 102 Rb 40
90151 Mondello-Partanna 102 Ra 41
90047 Partinico 102 Ra 41
95047 Paternò 102 Rb 42
98066 Patti 102 Ra 42
27100 Pavia 73 Nb 37
41026 Pavullo nel Frignano 73 Oa 38
65017 Penne 88 Pa 41
38057 Pérgine Valsugana 73 Na 39

POSTALI · ÍNDICE CON CÓDIGOS POSTALES · INDICE DE LUGARES COM CÓDIGOS POSTAIS ·
MÍST S PSČ · ZOZNAM OBCÍ S PSČ · INDEKS MIEJSCOWOŚCI Z KOD POCZTOWY

158

Pérgola Sássari

61045 Pérgola 74 Ob 40	63017 Porto San Giórgio 88 Ob 41	24058 Romano di Lombardia 73 Nb 37	71010 San Páolo di Civitate 88 Pb 43
06100 Perúgia 88 Ob 40	07026 Porto San Páolo 87 Qa 37	34077 Ronchi del Legionari 74 Nb 41	09043 San Priamo 101 Qb 37
61100 Pésaro 74 Ob 40	63018 Porto Sant'Elpídio 88 Ob 41	01037 Ronciglione 87 Pa 40	18038 San Remo 72 Ob 35
65100 Pescara 88 Pa 42	45018 Porto Tolle 74 Oa 40	89025 Rosarno 103 Ra 43	62027 San Severino Marche 88 Ob 41
67032 Pescasséroli 88 Pb 41	07046 Porto Tórres 86 Qa 36	64026 Roseto degli Abruzzi 88 Pa 42	71016 San Severo 88 Pb 43
71010 Pèschici 89 Pb 44	45014 Porto Viro 74 Nb 40	45010 Rosolina 74 Nb 40	87010 San Sosti 103 Qb 44
51017 Péscia 73 Ob 38	57037 Portoferráio 87 Pa 38	96019 Rosolini 102 Sa 42	57027 San Vincenzo/Piombino 87 Ob 38
01010 Péscia Romana 87 Pa 39	16034 Portofino 73 Oa 37	87067 Rossano 103 Qb 44	33078 San Vito al Tagliamento 74 Nb 40
86097 Pescolanciano 88 Pb 42	30026 Portogruaro 74 Nb 40	44020 Rovereto/Migliarino 73 Oa 39	72019 San Vito dei Normanni 89 Qa 45
85020 Pescopagano 88 Qa 43	44015 Portomaggiore 73 Oa 39	38068 Rovereto/Trento 73 Nb 39	39032 Sand in Taufers/Campo Túres 59 Na 39
90026 Petralia 102 Rb 42	84017 Positano 88 Qa 42	45100 Rovigo 73 Nb 39	39046 Sankt Ulrich/Ortisei 73 Na 39
29100 Piacenza 73 Nb 37	84026 Postiglione 88 Qa 43	20089 Rozzano 73 Nb 37	
65019 Pianella 88 Pa 42	85100 Potenza 89 Qa 43	48026 Russi 73 Oa 40	09025 Sanluri 100 Qb 36
94015 Piazza Armerina 102 Rb 42	97016 Pozzallo 102 Sa 42	98075 S. Fratello 102 Rb 42	52037 Sansepolcro 73 Ob 40
85055 Picerno 88 Qa 43	07018 Pozzomaggiore 86 Qa 36	04016 Sabáudia 88 Pb 41	98076 Sant'Agata Militello 102 Ra 42
81016 Piedimonte Matese 88 Pb 42	80078 Pozzuoli 88 Qa 42	84036 Sala Consilina 88 Qa 43	09017 Sant'Antíoco 100 Qb 36
32044 Pieve di Cadore 74 Na 40	87028 Prái a Mare 102 Qb 43	91018 Salemi 102 Rb 40	61048 Sant'Ángelo in Vado 74 Ob 40
18026 Pieve di Teco 72 Oa 35	59100 Prato 73 Ob 39	84100 Salerno 88 Qa 42	26866 Sant'Ángelo Lodigiano 73 Nb 37
52036 Pieve Santo Stéfano 73 Ob 40	39030 Prettau/Predoi 60 Mb 40	25087 Saló 73 Nb 38	85037 Sant'Arcángelo 89 Qa 44
41027 Pievepélago 73 Oa 38	96010 Priolo Gargallo 102 Rb 43	43039 Salsomaggiore Terme 73 Oa 37	09073 Santa Caterina di Pittinuri 86 Qa 36
10064 Pinerolo 72 Oa 35	90038 Prizzi 102 Rb 41	12037 Saluzzo 72 Oa 35	93018 Santa Caterina Villarmosa 102 Rb 42
64025 Pineto 88 Pa 42	70017 Putignano 89 Qa 45	12020 Sampéyre 72 Oa 35	08029 Santa Lucia 87 Qa 37
57025 Piombino 87 Pa 38	30020 Quarto d'Altino 74 Nb 40	82028 San Bartolomeo in Galdo 88 Pb 43	09010 Santa Margherita 100 Ra 36
35028 Piove di Sacco 73 Nb 40	09045 Quartu Sant'Élena 100 Qb 37	63039 San Benedetto del Tronto 88 Pa 41	16038 Santa Margherita Ligure 73 Oa 37
56100 Pisa 73 Ob 38	09043 Quirra 101 Qb 37	93017 San Cataldo/Caltanisetta 102 Rb 41	81055 Santa Maria Cápua Vétere 88 Pb 42
84066 Pisciotta 88 Qa 43	92020 Racalmuto 102 Rb 41	33038 San Daniele del Friuli 74 Na 41	07030 Santa Maria Coghínas 86 Qa 36
51100 Pistóia 73 Ob 38	12035 Racconigi 72 Oa 35	30027 San Donà di Piave 74 Nb 40	58010 Santa Maria di Rispéscia 87 Pa 39
58017 Pitigliano 87 Pa 39	53040 Radicófani 87 Pa 39	04017 San Felice Circeo 88 Pb 41	98050 Santa Marina Salina 102 Ra 42
Pizzo 103 Ra 44	92015 Raffadali 102 Rb 41	09037 San Gavino Monreale 100 Qb 36	00058 Santa Marinella 87 Pa 39
29027 Podenzano 73 Oa 37	97100 Ragusa 102 Sa 42	05029 San Gémini 88 Pa 40	98028 Santa Teresa di Riva 102 Ra 43
53036 Poggibonsi 73 Ob 39	95036 Randazzo 102 Rb 42	74027 San Giórgio Iónico 89 Qa 45	07028 Santa Teresa Gallura 87 Pb 37
46025 Póggio Rusco 73 Oa 39	16035 Rapallo 73 Oa 37	87055 San Giovanni in Fiore 103 Qb 44	47822 Santarcangelo di Romagna 74 Oa 40
02030 Póggio San Lorenzo 88 Pa 40	53040 Rapolano Terme 73 Ob 39	40017 San Giovanni in Persiceto 73 Oa 39	70029 Santéramo in Colle 89 Qa 44
Poirino 72 Oa 35	92029 Ravanusa 102 Rb 41	71013 San Giovanni Rotondo 88 Pb 43	13048 Santhià 72 Nb 36
75025 Policoro 89 Qa 44	48100 Ravenna 73 Oa 40	52027 San Giovanni Valdarno 73 Oa 39	98077 Santo Stéfano di Camastra 102 Ra 42
70044 Polignano a Mare 89 Pb 45	62019 Recanati 74 Ob 41	56017 San Giuliano Terme 73 Ob 38	92020 Santo Stéfano Quisquina 102 Rb 41
89024 Polístena 103 Ra 44	94017 Regalbuto 102 Rb 42	87038 San Lúcido 103 Qb 44	30029 Santo Stino di Livenza 74 Nb 40
84035 Polla 88 Qa 43	89100 Réggio di Calábria 102 Ra 43	87018 San Marco Argentano 103 Qb 44	84030 Sanza 88 Qa 43
32010 Polpét 74 Na 40	42100 Réggio nell'Emilia 73 Oa 38	82029 San Marco dei Cavoti 88 Pb 42	84073 Sapri 88 Qa 43
Pomarance 73 Ob 38	87036 Rende 103 Qb 44	39030 San Martino in Badia 73 Na 39	25068 Sarezzo 73 Nb 38
00040 Pomézia 88 Pb 40	20017 Rho 73 Nb 36	06024 San Martino in Colle 88 Ob 40	21047 Saronno 73 Nb 37
80045 Pompei 88 Qa 42	92016 Ribera 102 Rb 41	56027 San Miniato 73 Ob 38	47027 Sársina 73 Ob 40
44021 Pomposa 73 Oa 40	86016 Riccia 88 Pb 42	71015 San Nicandro Gargánico 88 Pb 43	19038 Sarzana 73 Oa 37
11026 Pont-Saint Martin 72 Nb 35	47838 Riccione 74 Ob 40	72026 San Pancrázio Salentino 89 Qa 45	07100 Sássari 86 Qa 36
50065 Pontassieve 73 Ob 39	93016 Riesi 102 Rb 42		
25056 Ponte di Legno 73 Na 38	02100 Rieti 88 Pa 40		
61010 Ponte Messa 73 Ob 40	00068 Rignano Flamínio 88 Pa 40		
24028 Ponte Nossa 73 Nb 37	47900 Rímini 74 Oa 40		
33016 Pontebba 74 Na 41	85028 Rionero in Vúlture 88 Qa 43		
03037 Pontecorvo 88 Pb 41	58022 Riotorto 87 Pa 38		
56025 Pontedera 73 Ob 38	38066 Riva del Garda 73 Nb 38		
29010 Pontenure 73 Oa 37	10098 Rívoli 72 Nb 35		
54027 Pontrémoli 73 Oa 37	87074 Rocca Imperiale 89 Qa 44		
04027 Ponza 88 Qa 40	47017 Rocca San Casciano 73 Oa 39		
65026 Pópoli 88 Pa 41	84069 Roccadáspide 88 Qa 43		
33080 Porcia 74 Nb 40	67037 Roccaraso 88 Pb 42		
33170 Pordenone 74 Nb 40	58036 Roccastrada 87 Ob 39		
07020 Porto Cervo 87 Pb 37	12018 Roccavione 72 Oa 35		
73010 Porto Cesáreo 89 Qa 45	89047 Roccella Jónica 103 Ra 44		
98050 Porto di Levante 102 Ra 42	71012 Rodi Gargánico 89 Pb 43		
92014 Porto Empédocle 102 Rb 41	87054 Rogliano 103 Qb 44		
58018 Porto Ércole 87 Pa 39	00118 Roma 88 Pb 40		
44022 Porto Garibaldi 74 Oa 40	38100 Romagnano 72 Nb 36		
62017 Porto Recanati 74 Ob 41			

159

INDEX WITH POST CODES · ORTSREGISTER MIT POSTLEITZAHLEN · INDICE CON CODICI
STEDREGISTER MED POSTNUMRE · PLAATSNAMENREGISTER MET POSTCODE · REJSTŘÍK

Sasso Marconi **Borrisokane**

40037 Sasso Marconi 73 Oa 39	39040 Sterzing/Vipiteno 59 Na 39	24047 Trevíglio 73 Nb 37
60041 Sassoferrato 74 Ob 40	52017 Stia 73 Ob 39	31100 Treviso 74 Nb 40
41019 Sassuolo 73 Oa 38	75018 Stigliano 89 Qa 44	20090 Trezzano sul Navíglio
74028 Sava 89 Qa 45	89049 Stilo 103 Ra 44	73 Nb 37
88825 Savelli 103 Qb 44	07040 Stintino 86 Qa 36	75019 Tricárico 89 Qa 44
12038 Savigliano 72 Oa 35	27049 Stradella 73 Nb 37	34100 Trieste 74 Nb 41
47039 Savignano sul Rubicone	91020 Strasatti 101 Rb 40	70019 Triggiano 89 Pb 44
74 Oa 40	38059 Strigno 73 Na 39	71029 Tróia 88 Pb 43
17100 Savona 72 Oa 36	Strómboli 102 Ra 43	94018 Troina 102 Rb 42
87029 Scalea 103 Qb 43	88816 Stróngoli 103 Qb 45	89861 Tropea 103 Ra 44
42019 Scandiano 73 Oa 38	00028 Subiaco 88 Pb 41	01017 Tuscánia 87 Pa 39
58054 Scansano 87 Pa 39	39029 Sulden/Solda 73 Na 38	33100 Údine 74 Na 41
06027 Schéggia 74 Ob 40	67039 Sulmona 88 Pa 41	73059 Ugento 103 Qb 46
24020 Schilpário 73 Na 38	10059 Susa 72 Nb 35	61049 Urbánia 74 Ob 40
36015 Schio 73 Nb 39	01015 Sutri 87 Pa 40	61029 Urbino 74 Ob 40
39029 Schlanders/Silandro	46029 Suzzara 73 Oa 38	08040 Ussássai 87 Qb 37
73 Na 38	18018 Tággia 72 Ob 35	10070 Usséglio 72 Nb 35
92019 Sciacca 102 Rb 41	08020 Tanaunella 87 Qa 37	90010 Ústica 102 Ra 41
97018 Scicli 102 Sa 42	98039 Taormina 102 Rb 43	36078 Valdagno 73 Nb 39
30037 Scorzè 73 Nb 40	74100 Táranto 89 Qa 45	01018 Valentano 87 Pa 39
07035 Sédini 86 Qa 36	33017 Tarcento 74 Na 41	15048 Valenza 72 Nb 36
88050 Sellía Marina 103 Ra 44	01016 Tarquínia 87 Pa 39	70010 Valenzano 89 Pb 44
60019 Senigállia 74 Ob 41	33018 Tarvísio 74 Na 41	84078 Vallo della Lucánia 88 Qa 43
85038 Senise 89 Qa 44	89029 Taurianova 103 Ra 44	06040 Vallo di Nera 88 Pa 40
24068 Seriate 73 Nb 37	33010 Tavagnaco 74 Na 41	23868 Valmadrera 73 Nb 37
89822 Serra San Bruno	88055 Taverna 103 Qb 44	00038 Valmontone 88 Pb 40
103 Ra 44	81057 Teano 88 Pb 42	75029 Valsinni 89 Qa 44
71010 Serracapriola 88 Pb 43	82037 Telese Terme 88 Pb 42	13019 Varallo 72 Nb 36
14100 Serravalle 73 Oa 36	07029 Témpio Pausánia 86 Qa 37	17012 Varazze 72 Oa 36
81037 Sessa Aurunca 88 Pb 42	64100 Téramo 88 Pa 41	21100 Varese 73 Nb 36
50019 Sesto Fiorentino 73 Ob 39	70038 Terlizzi 89 Pb 44	19028 Varese Lígure 73 Oa 37
16039 Sestri Levante 73 Oa 37	90018 Términi Imerese 102 Rb 41	27057 Varzi 73 Oa 37
10058 Sestriere 72 Oa 34	88140 Terminillo 88 Pa 40	66054 Vasto 88 Pa 42
09028 Sestu 100 Qb 37	86049 Térmoli 88 Pa 42	24010 Vedeseta 73 Nb 37
10036 Séttimo Torinese 72 Nb 35	05100 Terni 88 Pa 40	00049 Velletri 88 Pb 40
04018 Sezze 88 Pb 41	04019 Terracina 88 Pb 41	86079 Venafro 88 Pb 42
90148 Sferracavallo 102 Ra 41	09098 Terralba 86 Qb 36	30100 Venézia 74 Nb 40
89048 Siderno 103 Ra 44	08047 Tertenia 101 Qb 37	85029 Venosa 89 Qa 43
53100 Siena 73 Ob 39	09019 Teulada 100 Ra 36	18039 Ventimíglia 72 Ob 35
02010 Sigillo 88 Pa 41	36016 Thiene 73 Nb 39	33010 Venzone 74 Na 41
09010 Siliqua 100 Qb 36	38079 Tione di Trento 73 Na 38	28900 Verbánia 73 Nb 36
64028 Silvi 88 Pa 42	23037 Tirano 73 Na 38	13100 Vercelli 72 Nb 36
53048 Sinalunga 87 Ob 39	00019 Tívoli 88 Pb 40	40038 Vergato 73 Oa 39
08029 Siniscóla 87 Qa 37	39034 Toblach/Dobbiaco 74 Na 40	37100 Verona 73 Nb 38
09048 Sinnai 100 Qb 37	06059 Todi 88 Pa 40	11029 Verrès 72 Nb 35
96100 Siracusa 102 Rb 43	62039 Tolentino 88 Ob 41	25078 Vestone 73 Nb 38
25019 Sirmione 73 Nb 38	00059 Tolfa 87 Pa 40	01019 Vetralla 87 Pa 40
23027 Somággia 73 Na 37	33028 Tolmezzo 74 Na 41	38070 Vezzano/Trento 73 Na 39
26029 Soncino 73 Nb 37	08039 Tonara 86 Qa 37	46019 Viadana 73 Oa 38
23100 Sóndrio 73 Na 37	00040 Tor Vaiánica 88 Pb 40	55049 Viaréggio 73 Ob 38
03039 Sora 88 Pb 41	10100 Torino 72 Nb 35	89900 Vibo Valéntia 103 Ra 44
26015 Soresina 73 Nb 37	80059 Torre del Greco 88 Qa 42	90020 Vicari 102 Rb 41
08038 Sórgono 86 Qa 37	84047 Torre di Paestum 88 Qa 42	36100 Vicenza 73 Nb 39
80067 Sorrento 88 Qa 42	98164 Torre Faro 102 Ra 43	71019 Vieste 89 Pb 44
07037 Sorso 86 Qa 36	84077 Torre Orsáia 88 Qa 43	27029 Vigévano 73 Nb 36
30015 Sottomarina 74 Nb 40	10066 Torre Péllice 72 Oa 35	41058 Vignola 73 Oa 38
88068 Soverato 103 Ra 44	16029 Torríglia 73 Oa 37	38039 Vigo di Fassa 73 Na 39
88049 Soveria Mannelli	08048 Tortolì 87 Qb 37	89018 Villa San Giovanni
103 Qb 44	15057 Tortona 73 Oa 36	102 Ra 43
06038 Spello 88 Pa 40	90019 Trabía 102 Rb 41	33029 Villa Santina 74 Na 40
87019 Spezzano Albanese	07040 Tramaríglio 86 Qa 36	09039 Villacidro 100 Qb 36
103 Qb 44	70059 Trani 89 Pb 44	15057 Villalvérnia 73 Oa 36
15018 Spigno Monferrato 72 Oa 36	91100 Trápani 101 Ra 40	07019 Villanova Monteleone
33097 Spilimbergo 74 Na 40	87075 Trebisacce 103 Qb 44	86 Qa 36
70058 Spinazzola 89 Qa 44	38100 Trento 73 Na 39	09049 Villasimíus 101 Qb 37
06049 Spoleto 88 Pa 40	06039 Trevi 88 Pa 40	31050 Villorba 74 Nb 40

12010 Vinádio 72 Oa 35	
62039 Visso 88 Pa 41	
01100 Viterbo 87 Pa 40	
97019 Vittória 102 Sa 42	
31029 Vittório Véneto 74 Nb 40	
95049 Vizzini 102 Rb 42	
27058 Voghera 73 Oa 37	
10088 Volpiano 72 Nb 35	
56048 Volterra 73 Ob 38	
16158 Voltri 73 Oa 36	
71030 Voltura Appula	
88 Pb 43	

Abbeyfeale 23 Ka 18
Abbeyleix 23 Ka 20
Adare 23 Ka 19
An Clochán Liath 19 Ja 19
An Coireán 22 Kb 17
An Daingean 22 Ka 17
An Tearmann 19 Hb 20
Anascaul 22 Ka 17
Ardara 19 Ja 19
Ardee 23 Jab 21
Ardrahan 23 Jab 19
Arklow 23 Ka 21
Athboy 23 Jab 21
Athlone 23 Jab 20
Athy 23 Ka 21
Bagenalstown 23 Ka 21
Baile Bhuirne 23 Kb 18
Balbriggan 23 Jab 21
Ballina 23 Ja 18
Ballinasloe 23 Jab 19
Ballincollig 23 Kb 19
Ballinrobe 23 Jab 18
Ballon 23 Ka 21
Ballybofey 19 Ja 20
Ballycarney 23 Ka 21
Ballycroy 23 Ja 18
Ballydehob 22 Kb 18
Ballyhaunis 23 Jab 19
Ballymoe 23 Jab 19
Ballymore 19 Hb 20
Ballymote 23 Ja 19
Ballysadare 23 Ja 19
Ballyshannon 23 Ja 19
Ballyvaughan 23 Jab 18
Baltinglass 23 Ka 21
Banagher 23 Jab 20
Bandon 23 Kb 19
Bangor Erris 23 Ja 18
Banteer 23 Ka 18
Bantry 22 Kb 18
Béal an Mhuirthead
23 Ja 18
Belturbet 23 Ja 20
Birdhill 23 Ka 19
Birr 23 Jab 20
Blanchardstown 23 Jab 21
Blarney 23 Kb 19
Blessington 23 Jab 21
Borrisokane 23 Ka 19

POSTALI · ÍNDICE CON CÓDIGOS POSTALES · INDICE DE LUGARES COM CÓDIGOS POSTAIS ·
MÍST S PSČ · ZOZNAM OBCÍ S PSČ · INDEKS MIEJSCOWOŚCI Z KOD POCZTOWY

160

Boyle (IRL) . (IS) Siglufjörður

Boyle 23 Jab 19	Foxford 23 Jab 18	Newbridge 23 Jab 19	735	Eskifjörður 2 Cb 14
Bray 23 Jab 21	Freemount 23 Ka 19	Newcastle West 23 Ka 18	820	Eyrarbakki 1 Db 6
Broadford 23 Ka 19	Frenchpark 23 Jab 19	Oughterard 23 Jab 18	750	Fáskrúðsfjörður 2 Da 13
Bunbrosna 23 Jab 20	Galway 23 Jab 18	Portlaoise 23 Ka 20	701	Fellabær 2 Cb 13
Buncrana 19 Hb 20	Gaoth Dobhair 19 Hb 19	Portumna 23 Jab 19	425	Flateyri 1 Ca 4
Bundoran 23 Ja 19	Glenfarne 23 Ja 20	Quilty 23 Ka 18	845	Flúðir 1 Da 7
Cahersiveen 22 Kb 17	Glengarriff 22 Kb 18	Rathkeale 23 Ka 19	210	Garðabær 1 Da 6
Cahir 23 Ka 20	Glenties 19 Ja 19	Rathmullan 19 Hb 20	250	Garður 1 Da 5
Callan 23 Ka 20	Gorey 23 Ka 21	Roscommon 23 Jab 19	610	Grenivík 2 Cb 9
Camolin 23 Ka 21	Gort 23 Jab 19	Roscrea 23 Ka 20	611	Grímsey 2 Ca 9
Camp 22 Ka 18	Gort an Choirce 19 Hb 19	Rosslare 23 Ka 21	240	Grindavík 1 Db 5
Cappoquin 23 Ka 20	Gowran 23 Ka 20	Shannon 23 Ka 19	350	Grundarfjörður 1 Da 4
Carlow 23 Ka 21	Granard 23 Jab 20	Skerries 23 Jab 21	220	Hafnarfjörður 1 Da 6
Carndonagh 19 Hb 20	Grange 23 Ja 19	Skibbereen 22 Kb 18	235	Hafnir 1 Db 5
Carrick-on-Shannon	Greencastle 19 Hb 21	Sligo 23 Ja 19	700	Hallormsstaður 2 Cb 13
23 Jab 19	Greystones 23 Jab 21	Sneem 22 Kb 18	621	Hauganes 2 Cb 9
Carrick-on-Suir 23 Ka 20	Headford 23 Jab 18	Sraith Salach 23 Jab 18	850	Hella 1 Db 7
Carrickmacross 23 Jab 21	Inagh 23 Ka 18	Stranorlar 19 Ja 20	360	Hellisandur 1 Da 4
Carrigaline 23 Kb 19	Keel 23 Jab 17	Strokestown 23 Jab 19	601	Hjalteyri 2 Cb 9
Carrowkennedy 23 Jab 18	Kells 23 Jab 21	Swinford 23 Jab 19	401	Hnífsdalur 1 Ca 4
Cashel 23 Ka 20	Kells 22 Ka 17	Swords 23 Jab 21	565	Hofsós 2 Cb 8
Castlebar 23 Jab 18	Kenmare 22 Kb 18	Tagoat 23 Ka 21	851	Hólar 2 Cb 8
Castlebellingham 23 Jab 21	Kilbeggan 23 Jab 20	Tallaght 23 Jab 21	510	Holmavík 1 Cb 6
Castleblayney 23 Ja 21	Kilcolgan 23 Jab 19	Tallow 23 Ka 19	601	Hrafnagil 2 Cb 9
Castlecomer 23 Ka 20	Kilcormac 23 Jab 20	Tarbert 23 Ka 18	630	Hrísey 2 Cb 9
Castledermot 23 Ka 21	Kilkee 23 Ka 18	Templemore 23 Ka 20	640	Húsavík 2 Ca 10
Castleisland 22 Ka 18	Kilkenny 23 Ka 20	Thomastown 23 Ka 20	530	Hvammstangi 1 Cb 7
Castlerea 23 Jab 19	Killarney 22 Ka 18	Thurles 23 Ka 20	311	Hvanneyri 1 Da 6
Cathair Dónall 22 Kb 17	Killorglin 22 Ka 18	Tipperary 23 Ka 19	810	Hveragerði 1 Db 6
Cavan 23 Jab 20	Killybegs 19 Ja 19	Tobercurry 23 Ja 19	860	Hvolsvöllur 1 Db 7
Charlestown 23 Jab 19	Kilrush 23 Ka 18	Toomyvara 23 Ka 19	720	Höfn 2 Da 12
Charleville 23 Ka 19	Kinsale 23 Kb 19	Tralee 22 Ka 18	400	Ísafjörður 1 Ca 4
Clara 23 Jab 20	Kinvarra 23 Jab 19	Tramore 23 Ka 20	235	Keflavíkurflugvöllur
Claremorris 23 Jab 18	Knocktopher 23 Ka 20	Tuam 23 Jab 19		1 Db 5
Clifden 23 Jab 17	Leenane 23 Jab 18	Tullamore 23 Jab 20	233	Kevflavík 1 Da 5
Cloghan 23 Jab 20	Lemybrien 23 Ka 20	Tullow 23 Ka 21	880	Kirkjubæjarklaustur
Clonakilty 23 Kb 19	Letterfrack 23 Jab 18	Tulsk 23 Jab 19		1 Db 9
Clones 23 Ja 20	Letterkenny 19 Ja 20	Urlingford 23 Ka 20	670	Kópasker 2 Ca 11
Clonmel 23 Ka 20	Lifford 19 Ja 20	Virginia 23 Jab 20	200	Kópavogur 1 Da 6
Collon 23 Jab 21	Limerick 23 Ka 19	Waterford 23 Ka 20	380	Króksfjarðarnes 1 Cb 6
Cork/Corcaigh 23 Kb 19	Lisdoonvarna 23 Jab 18	Westport 23 Jab 18	641	Laugar 2 Cb 10
Crossmolina 23 Ja 18	Lismore 23 Ka 20	Wexford 23 Ka 21	801	Laugarás 1 Da 7
Crusheen 23 Ka 19	Lissycasey 23 Ka 18	Wicklow 23 Ka 21	531	Laugarbakki 1 Cb 7
Culleens 23 Ja 19	Listowel 23 Ka 18	Youghal 23 Kb 20	840	Laugarvatn 1 Da 7
Delvin 23 Jab 20	Littleton 23 Ka 20		620	Litli-Árskógssandur
Donegal 23 Ja 19	Longford 23 Jab 20			2 Cb 9
Doonbeg 23 Ka 18	Loughrea 23 Jab 19	(IS)	270	Mosfellsbær 1 Da 6
Drogheda 23 Jab 21	Lucan 23 Jab 21		780	Nesjahverfi 2 Da 12
Dromin 23 Jab 21	Macroom 23 Kb 19		740	Neskaupstaður
Drumshanbo 23 Ja 19	Maigh Cuilinn 23 Jab 18	300 Akranes 1 Da 5		2 Cb 14
Dublin/Baile Átha Cliath	Malahide 23 Jab 21	600 Akureyri 2 Cb 9	625	Ólafsfjörður 2 Ca 9
23 Jab 21	Mallow 23 Ka 19	225 Álftanes 1 Da 5	355	Ólafsvík 1 Da 4
Dún Loaghaire 23 Jab 21	Maynooth 23 Jab 21	685 Bakkafjörður 2 Ca 13	450	Patreksfjörður 1 Cb 4
Dundalk 23 Ja 21	Midleton 23 Kb 19	720 Bakkagerði 2 Cb 14	675	Raufarhöfn 2 Ca 12
Dunfanaghy 19 Hb 20	Milltown Malbay 23 Ka 18	465 Bildudalur 1 Cb 4	730	Reyðarfjörður 2 Cb 13
Dungarvan 23 Ka 20	Mitchelstown 23 Ka 19	540 Blönduós 1 Cb 7	380	Reykhólar 1 Cb 5
Dunshaughlin 23 Jab 21	Moll´s Gap 22 Kb 18	415 Bolungarvík 1 Ca 4	320	Reykholt 1 Da 6
Durrow 23 Ka 20	Monaghan 23 Ja 21	500 Borðeyri 1 Cb 6	801	Reykholt 1 Da 7
Edgeworthstown 23 Jab 20	Mountmellick 23 Jab 20	301 Borgarnes 1 Da 6	660	Reykjahlíð 2 Cb 11
Elton 23 Ka 19	Mullingar 23 Jab 20	760 Breiðdalsvík 2 Da 13	401	Reykjanes 1 Cb 5
Emyvale 23 Ja 21	Mulrany 23 Jab 18	370 Búðardalur 1 Cb 6	101	Reykjavík 1 Da 6
Ennis 23 Ka 19	Naas 23 Jab 21	620 Dalvík 2 Cb 9	245	Sandgerði 1 Da 5
Enniscorthy 23 Ka 21	Navan 23 Jab 21	765 Djúpivogur 2 Da 13	550	Sauðárkrókur 2 Cb 8
Ennistymon 23 Ka 18	Nenagh 23 Ka 19	520 Drangsnes 1 Cb 6	800	Selfoss 1 Db 7
Farranfore 22 Ka 18	New Ross 23 Ka 21	700 Egilsstaðir 2 Cb 13	710	Seyðisfjörður 2 Cb 13
Fermoy 23 Ka 19	Newbridge 23 Jab 21	701 Eiðar 2 Cb 13	580	Siglufjörður 2 Ca 9

161 INDEX WITH POST CODES · ORTSREGISTER MIT POSTLEITZAHLEN · INDICE CON CODICI
STEDREGISTER MED POSTNUMRE · PLAATSNAMENREGISTER MET POSTCODE · REJSTŘÍK

Skagaströnd   IS · KOS · L · LT   Svėdasai

545	Skagaströnd	1 Cb 7
861	Skogar	1 Db 8
825	Stokkseyri	1 Db 6
340	Stykkishólmur	1 Cb 5
755	Stöðvarfjörður	2 Da 14
420	Súðavík	1 Ca 4
430	Suðureyri	1 Ca 4
601	Svalbarðseyri	2 Cb 9
460	Tálknafjörður	1 Cb 4
560	Varmahlíð	2 Cb 8
311	Varmaland	1 Da 6
900	Vestmannaeyjar	1 Db 7
870	Vík	1 Db 8
190	Vogar	1 Db 5
690	Vopnafjörður	2 Cb 13
470	Þingeyri	1 Cb 4
815	Þorlákshöfn	1 Db 6
680	Þórshöfn	2 Ca 12
851	Þykkvibær	1 Db 7

KOS

11000	Besianë	90 Pa 49
	Brezovicë	90 Pa 48
51000	Deçan	90 Pa 48
70000	Ferizaj	90 Pa 49
12000	Fushë Kosovë	
		90 Pa 49
50000	Gjakovë	90 Pa 48
60000	Gjilan	90 Pa 49
31000	Istog	90 Pa 48
71000	Kaçanik	90 Pa 49
32000	Klinë	90 Pa 48
61050	Kllokot	90 Pa 49
	Kuistë	90 Pa 48
43500	Leposaviq	90 Ob 48
	Lutogllavë	90 Pa 48
14000	Lypjan	90 Pa 49
	Llapushnik	90 Pa 48
40000	Mitrovicë	90 Pa 48
15000	Obiliq	90 Pa 49
	Parllovë	90 Pa 49
30000	Pejë	90 Pa 49
10000	Prishtinë	90 Pa 49
20000	Prizreni	90 Pa 48
21000	Rahovec	90 Pa 48
	Strellc i Epërm	90 Pa 48
72000	Shtime	90 Pa 49
42000	Vushtrri	90 Pa 48
40650	Zubin Potok	90 Pa 48

L

9706	Clervaux	46 La 34
9202	Diekirch	46 Lb 34
6402	Echternach	46 Lb 34
4002	Esch-sur-Alzette	58 Lb 33
9001	Ettelbrück	46 Lb 34
5801	Hespérange	58 Lb 34
1009	Luxembourg	58 Lb 34
7410	Mersch	58 Lb 34
6905	Niederanven	58 Lb 34

LT

18039	Adutiškis	39 Hb 54
58053	Akademija	38 Hb 51
69047	Akmenynai	38 Ja 51
85022	Akmenė	38 Ha 50
33037	Alanta	39 Hb 53
62001	Alytus	39 Ja 52
29001	Andrioniškis	39 Hb 53
29001	Anykščiai	39 Hb 53
20030	Antakalnis	39 Ja 52
32019	Antazavė	39 Hb 53
60019	Ariogala	38 Hb 51
33013	Arnionys 1	39 Hb 53
65284	Ašašninkai	39 Jab 52
21034	Aukštadvaris	39 Ja 52
82025	Baisogala	38 Hb 51
17035	Baltoji Vokė	39 Ja 53
38241	Barklainiai	39 Hb 52
70021	Bartninkai	38 Ja 51
67267	Barzdžiūnai	39 Ja 51
33019	Bijutiškis	39 Hb 53
99072	Bikavėnai	38 Hb 49
59009	Birštonas	39 Ja 52
41001	Biržai	39 Ha 52
75493	Bytlaukis	38 Hb 50
80016	Bubiai	38 Hb 51
55075	Bukonys	39 Hb 52
54046	Čekiškė	38 Hb 51
97023	Darbėnai	38 Ha 49
64009	Daugai	39 Ja 52
28042	Daugaliai	39 Hb 53
73007	Dauglaukis	38 Hb 50
99008	Degučiai	39 Hb 53
30006	Didžiasalis	39 Hb 54
96011	Dovilai	38 Hb 49
66001	Druskininkai	39 Ja 51
30042	Dūkštas	39 Hb 54
14019	Dūkštos	39 Ja 52
32029	Dusetos	39 Hb 53
73004	Eičiai	38 Hb 50
17017	Eišiškės	39 Ja 52
26001	Elektrėnai	39 Ja 52
74021	Eržvilkas	38 Hb 50
96001	Gargždai	38 Hb 49
53030	Garliava	38 Ja 51
84007	Gataučiai	38 Ha 51
88237	Gaulėnai	38 Hb 50
83037	Gedučiai	38 Ha 52
55282	Geguėžinė	39 Hb 52
67307	Gerdašiai	39 Jab 51
33025	Giedraičiai	39 Hb 53
81033	Ginkūnai	38 Hb 51
60028	Girkalnis	38 Hb 51
27001	Grigiškės	39 Ja 53
82034	Grinkiškis	38 Hb 51
71041	Griškabūdis	38 Ja 51
81024	Gruzdžiai	38 Ha 51
69102	Igliškėliai	38 Ja 51
30001	Ignalina	39 Hb 54
53288	Ilgakiemis	38 Ja 51
33007	Inturke	39 Hb 53
55328	Išorai	39 Ja 52
17038	Jašiūnai	39 Ja 53
59058	Jieznas	39 Ja 52

97008	Jokūbavas	38 Hb 49
55001	Jonava	39 Hb 52
84001	Joniškis	38 Ha 51
39027	Joniškėlis	38 Ha 52
58017	Josvainiai	38 Hb 51
96032	Judrėnai	38 Hb 49
74042	Juodaičiai	38 Hb 51
98300	Juodeikiai	38 Ha 51
93017	Juodkrantė	38 Hb 49
42063	Juodupė	39 Ha 53
74001	Jurbarkas	38 Hb 50
56001	Kaišiadorys	39 Ja 52
75044	Kaltinėnai	38 Hb 50
69030	Kalvarija	38 Ja 51
28413	Kalviai	39 Hb 53
67039	Kapčiamiestis	38 Ja 51
97041	Kartena	38 Hb 49
44001	Kaunas	38 Ja 51
29021	Kavarskas	39 Hb 52
42039	Kazitiškis	39 Hb 54
86001	Kelmė	38 Hb 50
13146	Kena	39 Ja 53
70065	Kybartai	38 Ja 50
88237	Kirkliai	38 Hb 50
91001	Klaipėda	38 Hb 49
86026	Kražiai	38 Hb 50
38043	Krekenava	38 Hb 52
97001	Kretinga	38 Hb 49
96044	Kretingalė	38 Hb 49
84037	Kriukai	38 Ha 51
65272	Krokšlys	39 Ja 52
67071	Krosna	38 Ja 51
85007	Kruopiai	38 Ha 51
53093	Kulautuva	38 Ja 51
90024	Kuliai	38 Hb 49
40100	Kupiškis	39 Hb 52
39421	Kurpalaukis	39 Ha 52
81001	Kuršėnai	38 Ha 50
75039	Kvėdarna	38 Hb 49
57001	Kėdainiai	38 Hb 51
18035	Labanoras	39 Hb 53
86049	Laikšės	38 Hb 50
75038	Laukuva	38 Hb 50
67001	Lazdijai	38 Ja 51
67027	Leipalingis	38 Ja 51
71021	Lekėčiai	38 Ja 51
28027	Leliūnai	39 Hb 53
98038	Lenkimai	38 Ha 49
25001	Lentvaris	39 Ja 53
29290	Levaniškiai	39 Hb 52
80141	Lingailiai	38 Hb 51
83046	Linkuva	38 Ha 51
65319	Liškiava	39 Ja 52
64381	Luksnėnai	39 Ja 51
71005	Lukšiai	38 Ja 51
14025	Maišiagala	39 Ja 53
68001	Marijampolė	38 Ja 51
89001	Mažeikiai	38 Ha 50
92280	Melnragė	38 Hb 49
65035	Merkinė	39 Ja 52
81027	Meškuičiai	38 Ha 51
38004	Miežiškiai	39 Hb 52
37185	Molainiai	39 Hb 52
76476	Moline	38 Hb 50
33001	Molėtai	39 Hb 53
19017	Musninkai	39 Ja 52

84196	Mėdginai	38 Ha 51
85001	Naujoji Akmenė	
		38 Ha 50
15019	Nemenčinė	39 Ja 53
64021	Nemunaitis	39 Ja 52
83354	Nociūnai	38 Hb 52
53363	Noreikiškės	38 Ja 51
42006	Obeliai	39 Hb 53
21025	Onuškis	39 Ja 52
14031	Paberžė	39 Ja 53
17026	Pabradė	39 Ja 53
33243	Padustis	39 Hb 53
20278	Pageležiai	39 Hb 52
99032	Pagėgiai	38 Hb 49
83001	Pakruojis	38 Hb 51
00001	Palanga	38 Hb 49
42041	Pandėlys	39 Ha 53
35001	Panevėžys	39 Hb 52
54050	Panevėžiukas	38 Hb 51
40330	Papiliai	39 Hb 53
85010	Papilė	38 Ha 50
39187	Papyvesiai	39 Ha 52
41068	Parovėja	39 Ha 53
39001	Pasvalys	39 Ha 52
15140	Pikeliškės	39 Ja 53
70085	Pilviškiai	38 Ja 51
96014	Plikiai	38 Hb 49
90001	Plungė	38 Hb 49
96047	Priekulė	38 Hb 49
59001	Prienai	38 Ja 51
39012	Pumpėnai	39 Hb 52
64057	Punia	39 Ja 52
81009	Rabalvė	38 Ha 50
82001	Radviliškis	38 Hb 51
38031	Ramygala	39 Hb 52
86377	Ramučiai	38 Hb 50
60001	Raseiniai	38 Hb 51
90018	Rietavas	38 Hb 49
42001	Rokiškis	39 Hb 53
83013	Rozalimas	38 Hb 51
21016	Rūdiškės	39 Ja 52
99047	Rusnė	38 Hb 49
99357	Sakūčiai	38 Hb 49
97035	Salantai	38 Ha 49
18011	Sariai	39 Hb 54
73014	Sartininkai	38 Hb 49
99060	Saugos	38 Hb 49
89051	Seda	38 Ha 50
67010	Seirijai	38 Ja 51
21043	Semeliškės	39 Ja 52
74051	Seredžius	38 Hb 51
71057	Sintautai	38 Ja 50
38061	Skaistgiriai	39 Hb 52
73028	Skaudvilė	38 Hb 50
59030	Skriaudžiai	38 Ja 51
98001	Skuodas	38 Ha 49
82028	Skėmiai	38 Hb 51
74009	Smalininkai	38 Hb 50
38055	Smilgiai	38 Hb 52
33026	Stirniai	39 Hb 53
86030	Stulgiai	38 Hb 50
40033	Subačius	39 Hb 52
71077	Sudargas	38 Hb 50
58047	Surviliškis	38 Hb 52
89494	Svirkančiai	38 Ha 50
29048	Svėdasai	39 Hb 53

POSTALI · ÍNDICE CON CÓDIGOS POSTALES · INDICE DE LUGARES COM CÓDIGOS POSTAIS ·
MÍST S PSČ · ZOZNAM OBCÍ S PSČ · INDEKS MIEJSCOWOŚCI Z KOD POCZTOWY

162

Sėlynė   (LT) · (LV)   Riebiņi

Column 1 (LT)

42166 Sėlynė 39 Hb 53
71001 Šakiai 38 Ja 51
17001 Šalčininka 39 Ja 53
17041 Šalčininkėliai 39 Ja 53
82007 Šeduva 38 Hb 51
76001 Šiauliai 38 Hb 51
82043 Šiaulėnai 38 Hb 51
75001 Šilalė 38 Hb 50
99001 Šilutė 38 Hb 49
60052 Šiluva 38 Hb 51
19001 Širvintos 39 Hb 52
55041 Švejcarija 39 Hb 52
18001 Švenčionys 39 Hb 54
18002 Švenčionėliai 39 Hb 53
99056 Švėkšna 38 Hb 49
58005 Šėta 39 Hb 52
20054 Taujenai 39 Hb 52
72001 Tauragė 38 Hb 50
87001 Telšiai 38 Hb 50
39040 Tetirvinai 39 Ha 52
89031 Tirkšliai 38 Ha 50
86061 Tytuvėnai 38 Hb 51
21001 Trakai 39 Ja 52
29033 Troškūnai 39 Hb 52
40467 Tvirai 39 Hb 53
20001 Ukmergė 39 Hb 52
88028 Upyna 38 Hb 50
28001 Utena 39 Hb 53
86036 Užventis 38 Hb 50
98244 Vabaliai 38 Ha 49
41033 Vabalninkas 39 Hb 52
99069 Vainutas 38 Hb 49
17285 Valkininkai 39 Ja 52
88050 Varniai 38 Hb 50
65001 Varėna 39 Ja 52
67043 Veisiejai 38 Ja 51
74054 Veliuona 38 Hb 51
85019 Venta 38 Ha 50
99361 Ventė 38 Hb 49
65007 Vydeniai 39 Ja 52
20057 Vidiškiai 39 Hb 52
60037 Viduklė 38 Hb 50
89094 Viekšniai 38 Ha 50
29039 Viešintos 39 Hb 52
74012 Viešvilė 38 Hb 50
21058 Vievis 39 Ja 52
70001 Vilkaviškis 38 Ja 51
54015 Vilkija 38 Hb 51
99023 Vilkyškiai 38 Hb 50
01001 Vilnius 39 Ja 53
76103 Vinkšnėnai 38 Hb 51
31001 Visaginas 39 Hb 54
15001 Visalaukė 39 Ja 53
70037 Vištytis 38 Ja 50
28030 Vyžuonos 39 Hb 53
96008 Vėžaičiai 38 Hb 49
18189 Zalavas 39 Ja 53
32001 Zarasai 39 Hb 54
62187 Zervynos 39 Ja 52
84019 Žagarė 38 Ha 51
83034 Žeimelis 38 Ha 51
20015 Želva 39 Hb 53
99005 Žemaičių Naumiestis
       38 Hb 49
99317 Žemaitkiemis 38 Hb 49
89071 Židikai 38 Ha 50

56017 Žiežmariai 39 Ja 52
65374 Žiūrai 39 Ja 52

Column 2 (LV)

(LV)

2164 Ādaži 30 Gb 52
5304 Aglona 39 Ha 55
4035 Ainaži 30 Gb 52
5101 Aizkraule 39 Ha 53
3456 Aizpute 38 Ha 49
5208 Aknīste 39 Ha 53
4064 Aloja 38 Gb 52
3306 Alsunga 38 Ha 49
4301 Alūksne 31 Gb 55
3612 Ance 30 Gb 50
3706 Annenieki 38 Ha 51
3116 Apšuciems 30 Gb 51
4865 Ārini 39 Ha 54
4405 Atpūtas 31 Gb 54
3708 Auce 38 Ha 50
3709 Augstkalne 38 Ha 51
3882 Auniņi 38 Ha 50
4733 Baci 31 Gb 53
2160 Bādciems 30 Gb 52
2125 Baldone 39 Ha 52
4501 Balvi 31 Gb 55
3905 Bārbele 39 Ha 52
3482 Bārta 38 Ha 49
3901 Bauska 38 Ha 52
5439 Bebrene 39 Ha 54
3711 Bēne 38 Ha 51
4853 Bērzaune 31 Ha 54
4116 Bērzkrogs 31 Gb 53
4576 Bērzpils 31 Ha 55
3713 Biksti 38 Ha 50
4014 Bīriņi 31 Gb 52
3851 Broceni 38 Ha 50
5708 Brodaiža 39 Ha 55
2163 Carnikava 30 Gb 52
4567 Cērpene 31 Gb 55
4101 Cēsis 31 Gb 53
4871 Cesvaine 31 Ha 54
3910 Code 38 Ha 52
5476 Červonka 39 Hb 54
5674 Dagda 39 Ha 55
5107 Daudzese 39 Ha 53
1016 Daugavgrīva 30 Gb 52
5401 Daugavpils 39 Hb 54
3701 Dobele 38 Ha 51
3013 Dorupe 38 Ha 51
4615 Dricāni 39 Ha 55
4616 Dubuli 39 Ha 55
5213 Dubulti 39 Ha 53
3270 Dundaga 30 Gb 50
3309 Ēdas 38 Ha 50
3310 Ēdole 30 Gb 49
3023 Eleja 38 Ha 51
3436 Embūte 38 Ha 49
5226 Endželi 38 Ha 54
5133 Ērberģe 39 Ha 53
4840 Ērgli 31 Ha 54
5692 Ezernieki 39 Ha 55
4352 Fjuki 31 Gb 55
5311 Galēni 39 Ha 54

Column 3 (LV)

2137 Garkalne 31 Gb 52
3044 Garoza 38 Ha 51
4339 Gaujiena 31 Gb 54
3431 Gavieze 38 Ha 49
5704 Goliševa 31 Ha 55
5315 Gospori 39 Ha 54
5120 Gostini 39 Ha 53
3486 Gramzda 38 Ha 49
5655 Grāveri 39 Ha 55
3891 Grīvaiši 38 Ha 50
3430 Grobiņa 38 Ha 49
4401 Gulbene 31 Gb 54
5052 Ikšķile 39 Ha 52
5447 Ilūkste 39 Hb 54
2145 Inciems 31 Gb 52
4123 Ineši 31 Gb 53
5716 Istalsna 39 Ha 55
3717 Jaunbērze 38 Ha 51
4420 Jaungulbene 31 Gb 54
4860 Jaunkalsnava 39 Ha 53
4125 Jaunpiebalga 31 Gb 54
3145 Jaunpils 38 Ha 51
5316 Jaunsilavas 39 Ha 54
5201 Jēkabpils 39 Ha 53
3001 Jelgava 38 Ha 51
3626 Jūrkalne 38 Ha 49
2003 Jūrmala 30 Ha 51
3314 Kabile 38 Ha 50
5449 Kalkūni 39 Hb 54
3476 Kalnišļi 38 Ha 49
3443 Kalvene 38 Ha 49
3120 Kandava 30 Gb 50
5668 Kaplava 39 Hb 55
4577 Kapūne 31 Ha 55
4701 Karki 31 Gb 53
5717 Kārsava 31 Gb 55
4840 Katrina 31 Ha 53
5020 Kegums 39 Ha 52
4415 Keņģi 31 Gb 54
4116 Kleken 31 Gb 53
3434 Knīveri 38 Ha 49
5113 Koknese 39 Ha 53
3275 Kolka 30 Gb 50
5656 Kombuļi 39 Hb 55
5601 Krāslava 39 Hb 55
3720 Kroņauce 38 Ha 51
5222 Kūkas 39 Ha 54
3301 Kuldīga 38 Ha 49
3890 Kursīši 38 Ha 50
5062 Ķeipene 31 Ha 53
3114 Ķesterciems 30 Gb 51
3482 Ķīburi 38 Ha 49
3321 Ķimale 30 Gb 49
4022 Ķurmrags 30 Gb 52
3147 Lancenieki 38 Ha 51
5695 Landskorona 39 Ha 56
3285 Lauciene 30 Gb 50
4846 Lautere 31 Ha 54
3623 Leči 30 Gb 49
4412 Lejasciems 31 Gb 54
4224 Liči 31 Gb 53
3723 Lielauce 38 Ha 50
5070 Lielvārde 39 Ha 52
3401 Liepāja 38 Ha 49
5221 Liepas 39 Ha 54
4354 Liepna 31 Gb 54

Column 4 (LV)

4001 Limbaži 31 Gb 52
4624 Lipuški 39 Ha 55
5316 Līvāni 39 Ha 54
4347 Lizespasts 31 Gb 54
4425 Lizums 39 Gb 54
5012 Lobe 39 Ha 53
4830 Lubāna 31 Ha 54
5701 Ludza 39 Ha 55
4862 Ļaudona 39 Ha 54
5045 Madliena 39 Ha 53
4801 Madona 31 Ha 54
4580 Makšinava 31 Gb 55
2152 Mālpils 31 Gb 52
4630 Malta 39 Ha 55
3456 Marijas 38 Ha 49
4210 Matīši 31 Gb 53
3441 Mazilmāja 38 Ha 49
4215 Mazsalaca 31 Gb 53
4563 Medņi 31 Gb 55
3461 Medze 38 Ha 49
4885 Mēdzūla 31 Gb 53
4122 Meirāni 31 Ha 54
3276 Melnsils 30 Gb 50
3284 Mērsrags 30 Gb 51
5201 Mīļelāni 39 Ha 53
3621 Mīļeļtornis 30 Gb 49
3298 Mordanga 30 Gb 50
2106 Mucenieki 30 Ha 52
4835 Murmastiene 39 Ha 54
5462 Naujene 39 Hb 54
5666 Naukšēni 31 Gb 53
5118 Nereta 39 Ha 53
3271 Neveja 30 Gb 50
3473 Nica 38 Ha 49
5463 Nīcgale 39 Ha 54
3899 Nīgrande 38 Ha 50
4112 Nītaure 31 Gb 53
5001 Ogre 39 Ha 52
2114 Olaine 38 Ha 51
3877 Ošenieki 38 Ha 50
5737 Otrie Mežvidi 31 Ha 55
3621 Oviši 30 Gb 49
4001 Ozolaine 31 Gb 52
4063 Ozoli 31 Gb 52
4052 Pāle 31 Gb 52
3466 Pāvilosta 38 Ha 49
4729 Pidrikkalns 31 Gb 54
3620 Piltene 30 Gb 49
3270 Plintiņi 30 Gb 50
3253 Pobuži 30 Gb 50
3614 Pope 30 Gb 49
5301 Preiļi 39 Ha 54
3301 Priedaine 38 Ha 49
3434 Priekule 38 Ha 49
4126 Priekuļi 31 Gb 53
4618 Pudinova 39 Ha 55
3253 Pūņas 30 Gb 50
4635 Puša 39 Ha 55
5742 Pušmucova 39 Ha 55
5120 Pļaviņas 39 Ha 53
4131 Rauna 31 Gb 53
3871 Remte 38 Ha 50
4209 Rencēni 31 Gb 53
3319 Renda 30 Gb 50
4601 Rēzekne 39 Ha 55
5326 Riebiņi 39 Ha 54

163

INDEX WITH POST CODES · ORTSREGISTER MIT POSTLEITZAHLEN · INDICE CON CODICI
STEDREGISTER MED POSTNUMRE · PLAATSNAMENREGISTER MET POSTCODE · REJSTŘÍK

Rīga   LV . MA . MC . MD   **Camenca/Râbniţa**

1001 Rīga 30 Ha 52	3895 Vadakste 38 Ha 50	13100 Bouznika 95 Tb 20	35250 Sidi-Abdallah-des-Rhiata
4622 Rogs 39 Ha 55	3260 Valdemārpils 30 Gb 50	91026 Brikcha 95 Ta 22	96 Ta 23
3264 Roja 30 Gb 50	4701 Valka 31 Gb 53	20000 Casablanca 95 Tb 20	15250 Sidi-Allal-el-Bahraoui
2135 Ropaži 31 Ha 52	5106 Valle 39 Ha 52	91000 Chefchaouen 96 Sb 22	95 Ta 21
4041 Rožēni 31 Gb 52	4201 Valmiera 31 Gb 53	92000 Dar-Ben-Sadouk 95 Sb 22	14050 Sidi-Allal-Tazi 95 Ta 21
5327 Rožupe 39 Ha 54	3330 Valtaiji 38 Ha 49	20220 Dar-Bouâzza 95 Tb 20	13160 Sidi-Bettache 95 Tb 21
4227 Rubene 31 Gb 53	3281 Vandzene 30 Gb 50	44050 Dar-Caïd-Medboh 96 Ta 24	26600 Sidi-Hajjaj 95 Tb 20
5229 Rubene 39 Ha 53	2136 Vangaži 31 Gb 52	91000 Derdara 96 Sb 22	16000 Sidi-Kacem 95 Ta 22
3477 Rucava 38 Ha 49	4838 Varakļāni 39 Ha 54	26200 Deroua 95 Tb 20	14200 Sidi-Slimane 95 Ta 22
4240 Rūjiena 31 Gb 53	4211 Vecate 31 Gb 53	30006 Douyèt 96 Ta 22	14250 Sidi-Yahya-du-Rharb 95 Ta 21
3922 Rundāle 38 Ha 51	4122 Vecpiebalga 31 Gb 53	62250 Driouch 96 Ta 24	12050 Skhirat 95 Tb 20
4219 Rūpnieki 31 Gb 53	3933 Vecumnieki 39 Ha 52	60450 El-Aïoun 96 Ta 25	12050 Skhirat-Plage 95 Tb 20
3294 Sabile 30 Gb 50	4415 Velēna 31 Gb 54	62550 El-Batel 96 Ta 24	26300 Souk El-Had-des-~Moualine El
3464 Saka 38 Ha 49	4141 Velmeri 31 Gb 53	14200 El-Beggara 95 Ta 22	Oued 95 Tb 20
4033 Salacgrīva 30 Gb 52	3301 Venta 38 Ha 50	90000 El-Borj 96 Sb 22	14300 Souk-el-Arba du-Rharb
2121 Salaspils 38 Ha 52	3601 Ventspils 30 Gb 49	93000 El-Fendek 96 Sb 22	95 Ta 21
3801 Saldus 38 Ha 50	4647 Verēmi 39 Ha 55	62500 Es-Sebt 95 Tb 20	91000 Souk-el-Arba-des-Beni-
3627 Sārnate 30 Gb 49	5237 Viesīte 39 Ha 53	41150 Et-Tnine 95 Tb 21	Hassan 96 Sb 22
3138 Sāti 38 Ha 50	3026 Vilce 38 Ha 51	30000 Fès 96 Ta 23	92100 Souk-Khemis-du-Sahel
4701 Saule 31 Gb 53	4583 Viļaka 31 Gb 55	93100 Fnideq 96 Sb 22	95 Sb 21
2160 Saulkrasti 30 Gb 52	4650 Viļāni 39 Ha 54	62902 Hassi-Berkane 96 Ta 25	13000 Souk-Tleta-des-Ziaïda
3275 Saunags 30 Gb 50	4423 Virāne 31 Gb 54	35105 Hassi-Ouenzga 96 Ta 24	95 Tb 20
4841 Sausnēja 39 Ha 53	4355 Vireši 31 Gb 54	32250 Imzouren 95 Sb 24	42050 Taddert 96 Ta 24
5124 Sece 39 Ha 53	4032 Vitrupe 30 Gb 52	34050 Karia-Ba-Mohamed 96 Ta 22	34150 Tahar-Souk 96 Ta 23
4728 Seda 31 Gb 53	4352 Zaiceva 31 Gb 55	16202 Karrouba 96 Ta 22	90000 Tanger 95 Sb 22
2143 Sēja 31 Gb 52	4735 Zaki 31 Gb 54	62500 Kassita 96 Ta 24	34000 Taounate 96 Ta 23
5232 Sēlija 39 Ha 53	5112 Zalve 39 Ha 53	14000 Kénitra 95 Ta 21	34000 Taounate-el-Kchour 96 Ta 23
5123 Sērene 39 Ha 53	3011 Zaļenieki 38 Ha 51	32300 Ketama 96 Ta 23	60800 Taourirt 96 Ta 25
2150 Sigulda 31 Gb 52	3134 Zante 38 Ha 50	26000 Khemisset 95 Tb 21	32350 Targuist 96 Ta 23
3273 Sikrags 30 Gb 50	4113 Zaube 31 Ha 53	16100 Khénichèt 95 Ta 22	35000 Taza 96 Ta 23
5470 Silene 39 Hb 54	4345 Zeltiņi 31 Gb 54	92150 Ksar-el-Kebir 95 Sb 22	62500 Telat-Azlaf 96 Ta 24
2102 Skāduciems 38 Ha 51	3135 Zemīte 38 Ha 50	90000 Ksar-es-Seghir 96 Sb 22	12000 Témara 95 Tb 21
5671 Skaista 39 Hb 55		92000 Larache 95 Sb 21	93000 Tetouan 96 Sb 22
3924 Skaistkalne 39 Ha 52		15050 Mâaziz 95 Tb 21	24150 Thine-des Chtouka 95 Tb 19
3326 Skrunda 38 Ha 50		93150 Martil 96 Sb 22	15400 Tiflèt 95 Tb 21
4025 Skulte 30 Gb 52	MA	93200 Mdiq 96 Sb 22	34200 Tissa 96 Ta 23
4729 Smiltene 31 Gb 53		16150 Mechra-Bel-Ksiri 95 Ta 22	20640 Tit-Mellil 95 Tb 20
3298 Spāre 30 Gb 50	60050 Ahfir 97 Ta 25	60450 Mechra-Hammadi 96 Ta 25	35350 Tizi- Ouzli 96 Ta 24
4043 Staicele 31 Gb 52	34002 Aïn-Aïcha 96 Ta 23	20490 Médiouna 95 Tb 20	32008 Torres-de-Alcalá 96 Sb 23
4151 Stalbe 31 Gb 53	35006 Aïn-Bou-Kellal 96 Ta 24	50000 Meknès 95 Ta 22	62900 Zaïo 96 Ta 25
3604 Staldzene 30 Gb 49	16052 Aïn-Defali 95 Ta 22	35100 Merada 96 Ta 24	93000 Zinat 96 Sb 22
4821 Stalidyāni 31 Ha 54	Aïn-ej-Jmel 95 Tb 20	62500 Midar 96 Ta 24	
3031 Stalģene 38 Ha 51	12100 Aïn-el-Aouda 95 Tb 21	16303 Mjâra 96 Ta 22	
3257 Stende 31 Gb 50	50000 Aïn-el-Orma 95 Tb 22	20650 Mohammedia 95 Tb 20	MC
4358 Stradiņš 31 Gb 55	20630 Aïn-Harrouda 95 Tb 20	62550 Mont-Aroui 96 Sb 24	
4730 Strenči 31 Gb 53	30000 Aïn-Kansera 96 Ta 23	14000 Morhane 95 Ta 21	98000 Monte Carlo 72 Ob 35
4562 Sudarbe 31 Ha 55	32000 Ajdir 96 Sb 24	14302 Moulay-Bousselham 95 Ta 21	
4032 Svētciems 30 Gb 52	35050 Aknoul 96 Ta 24	50350 Moulay-Idriss 95 Ta 22	
4050 Šķirstiņi 31 Gb 52	32000 Al Hoceima 96 Sb 24	62000 Nador 96 Sb 25	MD
5481 Špoģi 39 Ha 54	14001 Arbaoua 95 Ta 22	60007 Naïma 97 Ta 25	
5711 Šuškova 39 Ha 56	90050 Asilah 95 Sb 21	84150 Nkheïla 95 Tb 21	6501 Anenii Noi 64 Na 57
3201 Talsi 30 Gb 50	24100 Azemmour 95 Tb 19	50352 Nzala-des-Béni-Ammar	7414 Balabanu 78 Nb 56
5132 Taurkalne 39 Ha 52	91050 Bab-Berret 96 Ta 23	95 Ta 22	4911 Balatina 64 Mb 55
4572 Tilža 31 Ha 55	35004 Bab-Marzouka 96 Ta 23	16200 Ouazzane 95 Ta 22	6701 Basarabeasca 64 Na 56
2138 Tiraine 38 Ha 52	91002 Bab-Taza 96 Sb 22	60000 Oujda 97 Ta 26	6812 Bācioi 64 Na 56
3015 Tirelī 38 Ha 51	14300 Barga 95 Ta 21	34009 Ourtzarh 96 Ta 23	3100 Bălţi 64 Mb 55
4424 Tirza 31 Gb 54	13000 Ben-Slimane 95 Tb 20	30016 Pont-du-Sebou 96 Ta 22	5512 Beloci 64 Mb 56
5238 Trepe 39 Ha 54	13050 Ben-Yakhlef 95 Tb 20	10000 Rabat 95 Ta 21	6202 Biruinţa 64 Mb 56
5211 Troškas 39 Ha 54	62050 Beni-Enzar 96 Sb 25	62200 Ras Kebdana 97 Sb 25	3415 Bozieni 64 Na 56
4022 Tūja 30 Gb 52	14000 Benmansour 95 Ta 21	Riffien 96 Sb 22	4414 Bravicea 64 Mb 56
3101 Tukums 30 Ha 51	60300 Berkane 97 Ta 25	15150 Rommani 95 Tb 21	4619 Brânzeni 64 Ma 55
3329 Turlava 38 Ha 49	26100 Berrechid 95 Tb 20	60450 Saf-Saf 96 Ta 25	4701 Briceni 64 Ma 55
3003 Tušļi 38 Ha 51	31150 Bir-Tam-Tam 96 Ta 23	60300 Saïdia 97 Sb 25	3901 Cahul 78 Nb 56
3615 Ugāle 30 Gb 50	32150 Bni-Hadifa 96 Sb 23	35105 Saka 96 Ta 24	
3266 Upesgrīva 30 Gb 50	35053 Boured 96 Ta 23	11000 Salé 95 Ta 21	
3627 Užava 30 Gb 49	20180 Bouskoura 95 Tb 20	62700 Selouane 96 Sb 25	6601 Camenca/Râbniţa 64 Ma 56

POSTALI · ÍNDICE CON CÓDIGOS POSTALES · INDICE DE LUGARES COM CÓDIGOS POSTAIS · MÍST S PSČ · ZOZNAM OBCÍ S PSČ · INDEKS MIEJSCOWOŚCI Z KOD POCZTOWY

164

Cazaclia (MD) . (MK) . (MNE) . (N) **Bjørkelangen**

MD

6113 Cazaclia 78 Na 56
4401 Călăraşi 64 Mb 56
4301 Căuşeni 64 Na 57
6101 Ceadâr-Lunga 78 Na 56
7419 Cealâc 78 Nb 56
3813 Chirsova 78 Na 56
6216 Chişcăreni 64 Mb 56
2000 Chişinău 64 Mb 56
4101 Cimişlia 64 Na 56
3818 Cioc-Maidan 64 Na 56
3801 Comrat 64 Na 56
3819 Congaz 78 Na 56
6416 Corneşti 64 Mb 56
5617 Costeşti 64 Mb 56
7216 Cotiujenii Mari 64 Mb 56
5706 Crasnoe 64 Na 57
2084 Cricova 64 Mb 56
6424 Cristeşti 64 Mb 56
4801 Criuleni 64 Mb 57
6644 Cunicea 64 Mb 56
3352 Dnestrovsc 64 Na 57
5101 Donduşeni 64 Ma 55
5201 Drochia 64 Ma 55
4501 Dubăsari 64 Mb 57
6224 Dumbrăvita 64 Mb 56
4601 Edineţ 64 Ma 55
5901 Fălești 64 Mb 55
5318 Giurgiuleşti 78 Nb 56
4901 Glodeni 64 Mb 55
7326 Goteşti 78 Na 56
4001 Grigoriopol 64 Mb 57
3401 Hânceşti 64 Na 56
4020 Hlinaia 64 Mb 57
6618 Hristovaia 64 Ma 56
6619 Hruşca 64 Ma 56
6801 Ialoveni 64 Na 56
3431 Lăpuşna 64 Na 56
6301 Leova 64 Na 56
4706 Lipcani 64 Ma 54
5933 Mărăndeni 64 Mb 55
5008 Mărculeşti 64 Mb 56
4125 Mihailovca 64 Na 56
5127 Moşana 64 Ma 55
5224 Nicoreni 64 Mb 55
6401 Nisporeni 64 Mb 56
3502 Orhei 64 Mb 56
7106 Otaci 64 Ma 55
3641 Pârliţa 64 Mb 55
3541 Peresecina 64 Mb 56
7725 Pervomaisc 64 Na 57
3640 Petreşti 64 Mb 56
5131 Pocrovca 64 Ma 55
4228 Popeasca 64 Na 57
5530 Popencu 64 Mb 57
6236 Prepeliţa 64 Mb 56
5033 Prodăneşti 64 Mb 56
5944 Pruteni 64 Mb 55
6237 Rădoaia 64 Mb 56
5945 Răuţel 64 Mb 55
7727 Răzeni 64 Na 56
5500 Râbniţa 64 Mb 56
5601 Râşcani 64 Mb 55
5636 Recea/Bălţi 64 Mb 55
3727 Recea/Călăraşi 64 Mb 56
5401 Rezina 64 Mb 56
4323 Sălcuţa 64 Na 57

3446 Sărata-Galbenă 64 Na 56
2091 Sângera 64 Na 56
6201 Sângerei 64 Mb 56
3644 Sculeni 64 Mb 55
4438 Sipoteni 64 Mb 56
5700 Slobozia 64 Na 57
5320 Slobozia Mare 78 Nb 56
3040 Soloneţ 64 Mb 56
3004 Soroca 64 Ma 56
3547 Step-Soci 64 Mb 56
3041 Stoicani 64 Ma 56
3701 Străşeni 64 Mb 56
5725 Sucleia 64 Na 57
3043 Şolcani 64 Na 56
7201 Şoldăneşti 64 Mb 56
7401 Taraclia/Ceadâr-Lunga
78 Nb 56
7730 Taraclia/Cimişlia 64 Na 57
4026 Taşlâc 64 Mb 57
5834 Tânţăreni 64 Mb 56
5140 Târnova 64 Ma 55
5801 Teleneşti 64 Mb 56
4739 Teţcani 64 Ma 54
6526 Tighina 64 Na 57
3300 Tiraspol 64 Na 57
7422 Tvardiţa 78 Na 56
3602 Ungheni 64 Mb 55
2046 Vadul lui Vodă 64 Mb 57
5301 Vulcăneşti 78 Nb 56
5644 Zăicani/Edineţ 64 Mb 55
3933 Zârneşti 78 Na 56
5234 Zgurița 64 Ma 56

MK

2330 Berovo 91 Pb 50
7000 Bitola 90 Pb 49
1220 Bogovinje 90 Pb 48
1250 Debar 90 Pb 48
7537 Debreşte 90 Pb 49
2320 Delčevo 91 Pb 50
7240 Demir Hisar 90 Pb 49
2737 Demir Kapija 90 Pb 50
Dolenci 90 Pb 49
6337 Dolno Lukovo 90 Pb 48
1480 Gevgelija 91 Pb 50
Gorno Konjari 90 Pa 49
1230 Gostivar 90 Pb 48
6256 Izvor/Kičevo 90 Pb 48
1414 Izvor/Veles 90 Pb 49
Janče 90 Pb 48
2464 Josifovo 91 Pb 50
1430 Kavadarci 90 Pb 50
7314 Kazani 90 Pb 49
6250 Kičevo 90 Pb 48
2300 Kočani 90 Pb 50
1330 Kriva Palanka 90 Pa 50
1300 Kumanovo 90 Pa 49
6336 Labuništa 90 Pb 48
2208 Lozovo 90 Pb 49
2304 Makedonska Kamenica
91 Pa 50
6530 Makedonski Brod 90 Pb 49
6342 Mešeišta 90 Pb 48

7216 Mogila 90 Pb 49
1235 Negotino 90 Pb 48
1440 Negotino/Kavadarci 90 Pb 50
1485 Novi Dojran 91 Pb 50
2434 Novo Selo 91 Pb 50
6000 Ohrid 90 Pb 48
1305 Orašac 90 Pa 49
2326 Pehčevo 91 Pb 50
1043 Petrovec 90 Pb 49
7500 Prilep 90 Pb 49
2434 Radičevo 91 Pb 50
2420 Radoviš 91 Pb 50
7310 Resen 90 Pb 49
1422 Rosoman 90 Pb 49
Saraj 90 Pb 49
1010 Skopje 90 Pa 49
2000 Štip 90 Pb 50
1361 Stracin 90 Pa 50
6330 Struga 90 Pb 48
2400 Strumica 91 Pb 50
2220 Sveti Nikole 90 Pb 49
1224 Tearce 90 Pa 49
1200 Tetovo 90 Pa 48
7512 Topolčani 90 Pb 49
Trojaci 90 Pb 49
2460 Valandovo 91 Pb 50
1400 Veles 90 Pb 49
2310 Vinica 91 Pb 50
Volkovija 90 Pb 48
1225 Vratnica 90 Pa 49
6253 Zajas 90 Pb 48
1226 Želino 90 Pb 49

MNE

84320 Andrijevica 90 Pa 47
85000 Bar 89 Pa 47
84300 Berane 90 Pa 47
84000 Bijelo Polje 90 Ob 47
85311 Budva 89 Pa 46
Bukovica 90 Ob 47
81250 Cetinje 89 Pa 46
81410 Danilovgrad 89 Pa 47
Goransko 89 Ob 46
Gradina 90 Ob 47
85340 Herceg Novi 89 Pa 46
81210 Kolašin 90 Pa 47
85330 Kotor 89 Pa 46
Kruta 90 Pa 47
Mijoska 90 Pa 47
84205 Mojkovac 90 Pa 47
81401 Nikšić 89 Pa 46
85300 Petrovac na moru 89 Pa 46
84210 Pljevlja 90 Ob 47
Poda 90 Pa 47
81101 Podgorica 90 Pa 47
Polje Bajovo 89 Ob 46
85337 Risan 89 Pa 46
84310 Rožaje 90 Pa 48
85355 Sutomore 89 Pa 47
Sviba 90 Pa 47
81450 Šavnik 89 Pa 47
85320 Tivat 89 Pa 46
81206 Tuzi 90 Pa 47

85360 Ulcinj 90 Pb 47
81423 Vilusi 89 Pa 46
81305 Virpazar 89 Pa 47
84220 Žabljak 89 Ob 47

N

7950 Abelvær 26 Da 39
9730 Áidejávri 4 Ba 51
9650 Akkarfjord 4 Aa 51
5570 Aksdal 27 Fb 33
7672 Aksnes 12 Db 39
8883 Alstahaug 26 Cb 40
9501 Alta 4 Ab 51
2560 Alvdal 12 Ea 38
3158 Andebu 27 Fb 38
8480 Andenes 3 Ab 44
9322 Andselv 3 Ab 46
4801 Arendal 27 Ga 36
Arsvågen 27 Fb 33
1370 Asker 28 Fb 38
1800 Askim 28 Fb 39
6980 Askvoll 11 Eb 33
7822 Asp 26 Da 39
2477 Atnbrua 12 Eb 38
2476 Atnosen 12 Eb 38
1927 Aulifeltet 28 Fa 39
7590 Aunet 12 Db 39
2910 Aurdal 11 Fa 37
6690 Aure 11 Db 36
1930 Aursmoen 28 Fb 39
7900 Austafjord 26 Da 38
3650 Austbygdi 27 Fb 36
8690 Austerkroken 26 Cb 42
9321 Austpollen 3 Ba 43
4262 Avaldsnes 27 Fb 33
9730 Badje Máze 4 Ab 51
2930 Bagn 11 Fa 37
6899 Balestrand 11 Eb 34
8373 Ballstad 3 Ba 41
Barkald 12 Eb 38
3157 Barkåker 28 Fb 38
Batnfjordsora 11 Ea 35
2953 Beitostølen 11 Eb 36
9982 Bekkarfjord 5 Aa 55
Berdalen 27 Fb 35
Berg 26 Cb 40
Berg 28 Fa 40
5001 Bergen 11 Fa 33
3075 Berger 28 Fb 38
Bergset 12 Eb 39
7391 Berkåk 12 Ea 38
9980 Berlevåg 5 Aa 57
Besstrond 11 Eb 36
Betna 11 Db 36
2836 Biri 12 Fa 38
4760 Birkeland 27 Ga 36
9147 Birtavarre 4 Ab 48
2690 Bismo 11 Eb 36
8643 Bjerka 26 Ca 41
8530 Bjerkvik 3 Ba 45
2676 Bjølstad 11 Eb 37
Bjørgo 11 Fa 37
1940 Bjørkelangen 28 Fb 39

165

INDEX WITH POST CODES · ORTSREGISTER MIT POSTLEITZAHLEN · INDICE CON CODICI
STEDREGISTER MED POSTNUMRE · PLAATSNAMENREGISTER MET POSTCODE · REJSTŘÍK

Bjørkåsen Hundorp

	Bjørkåsen 3 Ba 44	2662	Dovre 11 Eb 37		Flesberg 27 Fb 37	3525	Hallingby 28 Fa 38
	Bjørnevatn 5 AB 57		Drag 3 Ba 44	8448	Flesnes 3 Ba 43		Halmstad 28 Fb 38
9402	Bjørnå 3 Ba 44	3007	Drammen 27 Fb 38	2270	Flisa 12 Fa 40	8178	Halsa 26 Ca 41
	Blakstad 27 Ga 36	3750	Drangetal 27 Fb 37		Flora 12 Db 39		Haltdalen 12 Ea 39
8647	Bleikvasslia 26 Cb 41	2443	Drevsjø 12 Eb 40	6900	Florø 11 Eb 33	2301	Hamar 12 Fa 39
8001	Bodø 26 Bb 42	1440	Drøbak 28 Fb 38		Flå 11 Fa 37	9600	Hammerfest 4 Aa 51
	Bogen 3 Bb 43	7746	Dun 26 Da 39	7985	Foldereid 26 Da 40	8056	Hamsund 3 Ba 43
8533	Bogen 3 Ba 44	8392	Dyping 3 Bb 43	7120	Follafoss 26 Db 39	9130	Hansnes 4 Ab 47
9442	Bognes 3 Ba 44	4869	Dølemo 27 Ga 36	2580	Folldal 12 Ea 38	8056	Hanøy 3 Ba 43
	Bolfoss 28 Fb 39		Edøy 11 Db 36	2656	Follebu 12 Eb 38	6924	Hardbakke 11 Eb 32
8630	Bolna 7 Ca 43	4379	Egersund 27 Ga 34	5953	Fonnes 11 Fa 32	6060	Hareid 11 Ea 34
8360	Borge 3 Ba 41	3359	Eggedal 27 Fa 37	7761	Formofoss 26 Da 40	2743	Harestua 28 Fa 38
	Bostrak 27 Fb 36		Eida 27 Ga 34	9518	Forset/Alta 4 Ab 51	9402	Harstad 3 Ba 44
	Botnen 27 Fb 34	6490	Eide 11 Ea 35	2653	Forset/Lillehammer 12 Eb 38		Harsvika 26 Da 38
7127	Botngård 12 Db 37	5783	Eidfjord 11 Fa 35	6690	Forsnes 11 Db 36	9590	Hasvik 4 Aa 50
9373	Botnhamn 3 Ab 45	9020	Eidkjosen 4 Ab 46	8900	Forvika 26 Cb 40	3595	Haugastøl 11 Fa 35
2760	Brandbu 12 Fa 38	6215	Eidsdalen 11 Ea 35	6099	Fosnavåg 11 Ea 33	4380	Hauge 27 Ga 34
	Brandsøy 11 Eb 33		Eidskog 28 Fa 40	9350	Fossbakken 3 Ba 45	5501	Haugesund 27 Fb 33
9350	Brandvoll 3 Ba 46	5728	Eidslandet 11 Fa 33	1798	Fossby 28 Fb 39	3888	Haukeligrend 27 Fb 35
	Brannan 12 Db 39		Eidstod 27 Fb 36		Fosse 11 Fa 32		Haupe 28 Fb 38
2435	Braskereidfoss 12 Fa 39	2080	Eidsvoll 28 Fa 39	1601	Fredrikstad 28 Fb 38	9690	Havøysund 4 Aa 52
6270	Brattvåg 11 Ea 34	6460	Eidsvåg 11 Ea 36	5742	Freteim 11 Fa 35		Hedal 11 Fa 37
9709	Breiddalstua 4 Aa 52		Eikefjord 11 Eb 33	3870	Fyresdal 27 Fb 36		Heggeriset 12 Eb 40
9593	Breivikbotn 4 Aa 50	2843	Eina 12 Fa 38		Førde/Haugsund 27 Fb 33	7472	Heimdal 12 Db 38
9050	Breivikeidet 4 Ab 47	5967	Eivindvik 11 Fa 33	6800	Førde/Naustdal 11 Eb 33		Hella 11 Eb 34
	Brekken 12 Ea 39	2446	Elgå 12 Ea 39	2634	Fåvang 12 Eb 38		Helle 27 Ga 37
7896	Brekkvasselv 26 Da 41	6440	Elnesvågen 11 Ea 35		Gamvik 5 Aa 56		Helle/Oltedal 27 Ga 34
7130	Brekstad 12 Db 37	8432	Elvenes 3 Ba 43		Ganddal 27 Ga 33	7982	Hellesvikan 11 Db 36
6727	Bremanger 11 Eb 32	9334	Elverom 3 Ab 46		Gandvik 5 Aa 57	6218	Hellesylt 11 Ea 34
	Brenna 26 Cb 41	2406	Elverum 12 Fa 39		Garmo 11 Eb 36		Hellevike 11 Eb 33
	Brimnes 11 Fa 34		Elvestad 4 Ab 48	7870	Gartland 26 Da 40	1970	Hemnes 28 Fb 39
	Bru 11 Eb 33	9311	Elvevoll 3 Ab 45	6868	Gaupne 11 Eb 35	8640	Hemnesberget 26 Ca 41
2381	Brumunddal 12 Fa 38		Enden 12 Eb 38	3580	Geilo 11 Fa 36	3560	Hemsedal 11 Fa 36
4363	Brusand 27 Ga 33	2440	Engerdal 12 Eb 39	6216	Geiranger 11 Ea 35	8312	Henningsvær 3 Ba 42
6711	Bryggja 11 Eb 33		Engerneset 12 Eb 40	7970	Geisnes 26 Da 39	4766	Herefoss 27 Ga 36
4340	Bryne 27 Ga 33	5306	Erdal 11 Fa 33		Gjemnes 11 Ea 35		Hernes 12 Fa 39
8900	Brønnøysund 26 Cb 40	8100	Ertenvåg 26 Bb 42		Gjerde 27 Ea 34	3965	Herre 27 Fb 37
9311	Brøstadbotn 3 Ab 45	2338	Espa 12 Fa 39	5635	Gjermundshamn 27 Fa 33		Herøyholmen 26 Cb 40
	Brøttum 12 Eb 38		Estensvollar 12 Ea 38		Gjerstad 27 Ga 37		Hillesøy 3 Ab 46
6430	Bud 11 Ea 34	5590	Etne 27 Fb 33	9913	Gjøra 11 Ea 37		Hindaråvåg 27 Fb 33
9934	Bugøyfjord 5 Ab 57		Evje 27 Ga 35	2800	Gjøvik 12 Fa 38	3621	Hindrem 12 Db 38
9325	Buktmoen 4 Ab 46		Fagerheim 11 Fa 35	8900	Gladstad 26 Cb 39	8630	Hjartåsen 7 Ca 42
9161	Burfjord 4 Ab 50	2900	Fagernes 11 Fa 37	8285	Glein 26 Ca 40	4130	Hjelmeland 27 Fb 34
	Buvika 12 Ea 39	9050	Fagernes/Tromsø 4 Ab 47	8160	Glomfjord 26 Ca 41	2661	Hjerkinn 11 Ea 37
	Bygdin 11 Eb 36	2864	Fall 12 Fa 38	7372	Glåmos 12 Ea 39		Hodalen 12 Ea 39
4745	Bygland 27 Ga 35	8658	Fallmoen 26 Cb 41	3550	Gol 11 Fa 36	3300	Hokksund 27 Fb 37
4741	Byglandsfjord 27 Ga 35	5243	Fanahammaren 11 Fa 33	2750	Gran 28 Fa 38	3576	Hol 11 Fa 36
4754	Bykle 27 Fb 35	4550	Farsund 27 Ga 34	2636	Granrudmoen 12 Eb 38	8664	Holandsvika 26 Cb 41
9930	Byluft 5 Aa 57	8200	Fauske 7 Bb 43	5736	Granvin 11 Fa 34		Holla 12 Eb 39
6826	Byrkjelo 11 Eb 34		Femoen 28 Fa 40		Gratangen 3 Ba 45	6409	Hollingsholmen 11 Ea 34
3800	Bø 27 Fb 37	9402	Fenes 3 Ba 44		Gravvik 26 Da 39	6982	Holmedal 11 Eb 33
9716	Børselv 4 Aa 53		Fersund 28 Fb 39	4876	Grimstad 27 Ga 36	5642	Holmefjord 11 Fa 33
	Bøverdal 11 Eb 36	8220	Festvåg 7 Bb 42		Grindaheim 11 Eb 36	3080	Holmestrand 27 Fb 38
	Bøvertun 11 Eb 36		Festøya 11 Ea 34	2264	Grinder 28 Fa 40		Holøygal 12 Ea 39
	Bøyane 11 Eb 34	4870	Fevik 27 Ga 36	8001	Grindjorda 3 Ba 45	8960	Hommeistø 26 Cb 40
9990	Båtsfjord 5 Aa 57	9300	Finnsnes 3 Ab 45	7870	Grong 26 Da 40	7550	Hommelvik 12 Db 38
9716	Èaskilbekk 4 Aa 53	8322	Fiskebøl 3 Ba 42	2695	Grotli 11 Ea 35	9750	Honningsvåg 4 Aa 53
	Dagali 11 Fa 36	4122	Fiskå 11 Ea 33	9446	Grov 3 Ba 45	9174	Hopen 11 Db 36
	Dal 27 Fb 36	5419	Fitjar 27 Fb 33	2742	Grua 28 Fa 38	5108	Hordvik 11 Fa 33
	Dal/Jessheim 28 Fa 39	1472	Fjellhamar 28 Fb 38	9380	Gryllefjord 3 Ab 45	3191	Horten 28 Fb 38
	Dale 11 Eb 33		Fjellsrud 28 Fb 39		Gullstein 11 Db 36	2867	Hov 12 Fa 38
	Dale/Bergen 11 Fa 33		Flakstad 3 Ba 41	9670	Gunnarnes 4 Aa 52	4755	Hovden 27 Fb 35
3880	Dalen 27 Fb 35		Flatanger 26 Da 38	3810	Gvarv 27 Fb 37		Hove 12 Db 38
	Djupvik 4 Ab 48	1911	Flateby 28 Fb 39		Gåsvika 28 Fb 39	3577	Hovet 11 Fa 36
2870	Dokka 12 Fa 38		Flatøygarden 11 Fa 37	1752	Halden 28 Fb 39		Hufthammar 11 Fa 33
2660	Dombås 11 Ea 37	4400	Flekkefjord 27 Ga 34		Haljem 11 Fa 33	2647	Hundorp 12 Eb 37

POSTALI · ÍNDICE CON CÓDIGOS POSTALES · INDICE DE LUGARES COM CÓDIGOS POSTAIS ·
MÍST S PSČ · ZOZNAM OBCÍ S PSČ · INDEKS MIEJSCOWOŚCI Z KOD POCZTOWY

166

Hurdal · N · **Ofte** · N

2090 Hurdal 12 Fa 39	Kjøs 11 Eb 34	7800 Lauvsnes 26 Da 39	3658 Miland 27 Fb 36
5460 Husnes 27 Fb 33	Kleppe 27 Ga 33	9465 Lavangen 3 Ba 45	8220 Misten 7 Bb 42
3647 Hvittingfoss 27 Fb 38	5350 Kleppestø 11 Fa 33	6497 Lavik 11 Eb 33	8100 Misvær 7 Bb 42
Hyen 11 Eb 33	5373 Klokkarvik 11 Fa 33	9710 Leaibevuotna 4 Aa 53	3050 Mjøndalen 27 Fb 38
Hyllestad 11 Eb 33	2040 Kløfta 28 Fa 39	6750 Leikanger 11 Ea 33	Mjøsstrand 12 Fa 39
Hyttfossen 12 Db 38	Knappskog 11 Fa 33	8766 Leira 26 Ca 41	Mo 11 Fa 33
4720 Hægelandskrossen 27 Ga 35	5903 Knarrviki 11 Fa 33	2920 Leira 11 Fa 37	8601 Mo i Rana 26 Ca 42
Høle 27 Ga 34	Kobbevik 5 Aa 55	9532 Leirbotnvatn 4 Aa 51	Moane 11 Eb 37
3500 Hønefoss 28 Fa 38	9325 Kobbvågneset 4 Ab 46	5401 Leirvik 27 Fb 33	2390 Moelv 12 Fa 38
Høvag 27 Ga 36	9715 Kokelv 4 Aa 52	8672 Leirvika 26 Ca 41	4460 Moi 27 Ga 34
6993 Høyanger 11 Eb 34	1410 Kolbotn 28 Fb 38	8370 Leknes 3 Ba 41	6401 Molde 11 Ea 35
7977 Høylandet 26 Da 40	7970 Kolvereid 26 Da 39	7120 Leksvik 12 Db 38	Monstad 26 Db 38
Hålandsosen 27 Fb 34	3600 Kongsberg 27 Fb 37	Leland 26 Ca 40	Mortavika 27 Fb 33
Håra 27 Fb 34	9982 Kongsfjord 5 Aa 57	2850 Lena 12 Fa 38	4619 Mosby 27 Ga 35
9775 Ifjord Idjavuotna 5 Aa 55	4812 Kongshamn 27 Ga 36	7234 Ler 12 Db 38	8651 Mosjøen 26 Cb 41
8900 Igerøy 26 Cb 40	7976 Kongsmoen 26 Da 40	2665 Lesja 11 Ea 36	1503 Moss 28 Fb 38
Indre Ålvik 11 Fa 34	2200 Kongsvinger 28 Fa 40	8766 Levang 26 Ca 41	5447 Mosterhamn 27 Fb 33
2420 Innbygda 12 Eb 40	Kongsvoll 11 Ea 37	7600 Levanger 12 Db 39	7690 Mosvik 12 Db 39
Inndry 26 Bb 42	4525 Konsmo 27 Ga 35	4480 Liknes 27 Ga 34	Mundheim 11 Fa 33
8260 Innhavet 3 Bb 43	6149 Koparnes 11 Ea 33	2601 Lillehammer 12 Eb 38	9443 Myklebostad 3 Bb 43
9334 Innset 4 Ba 46	4250 Kopervik 27 Fb 33	Lillesand 27 Ga 36	Myra 27 Ga 36
Instefjord 11 Fa 33	2480 Koppang 12 Eb 39	2000 Lillestrøm 28 Fb 39	8488 Myre/Dverberg 3 Ab 43
6320 Isfjorden 11 Ea 35	8646 Korgen 26 Ca 41	5955 Lindås 11 Fa 33	8430 Myre/Lønskogen 3 Ba 43
9540 Isnestoften 4 Aa 50	Korsmo 28 Fa 39	2686 Lom 11 Eb 36	9419 Myre/Medby 3 Ba 45
Isterfossen 12 Eb 39	Kragerø 27 Ga 37	Lomsdalen 12 Fa 38	7746 Myrvika 26 Da 39
9305 Ivarrud 26 Cb 41	6926 Krakhella 11 Eb 33	8764 Lovund 26 Ca 40	1850 Mysen 28 Fb 39
4724 Iveland 27 Ga 35	4604 Kristiansand 27 Ga 35	7818 Lund 26 Da 39	7710 Mære 12 Db 39
9900 Jakobselv 5 Ab 58	6501 Kristiansund 11 Db 35	7232 Lundamo 12 Db 38	Møvik 11 Fa 33
2770 Jaren 12 Fa 38	Krossbu 11 Eb 36	3825 Lunde 4 Ba 46	9325 Målsnes 3 Ab 46
8750 Jektvika 26 Ca 41	Krossen 27 Fb 36	3825 Lunde 27 Fb 37	6700 Måløy 11 Eb 33
1134 Jelsa 27 Fb 34	4519 Krossen/Mandal 27 Ga 35	6872 Luster 11 Eb 35	7176 Råmyra 26 Da 38
9730 Jergol 4 Ab 52	Krossli 27 Fb 36	Lyfjord 4 Ab 46	8100 Mårnes 26 Bb 42
2052 Jessheim 28 Fa 39	7510 Krøkstadøra 12 Db 37	Lykling 27 Fb 33	7790 Namdalseid 26 Da 39
3520 Jevnaker 28 Fa 38	8413 Kråkberget 3 Ba 42	4580 Lyngdal 27 Ga 35	7800 Namsos 26 Da 39
5627 Jondal 11 Fa 34	9174 Kråkmo 3 Bb 43	9060 Lyngseidet 4 Ab 48	7890 Namsskogan 26 Da 41
2430 Jordet 12 Eb 40	9620 Kvalsund 4 Aa 51	6493 Lyngstad 11 Ea 35	Narbuvoll 12 Ea 39
Jostedal 11 Eb 35	2642 Kvam 11 Eb 37	4127 Lysebotn 27 Fb 34	8501 Narvik 3 Ba 45
4160 Judaberg 27 Fb 33	Kvam 26 Da 39	Lærdalsøyri 11 Eb 35	6817 Naustdal 11 Eb 33
2416 Jømna 12 Fa 39	Kvarme 12 Db 38	8020 Løding 7 Bb 42	9930 Neiden 5 Ab 57
4100 Jørpeland 27 Fb 34	7980 Kveina 26 Cb 40	9442 Lødingen 3 Ba 44	9305 Nerli 26 Cb 42
2617 Jørstadmoen 12 Eb 38	Kvenvær 11 Db 36	1960 Løken 28 Fb 39	3523 Nes 11 Fa 37
Jåvall 28 Fb 39	4473 Kvinlog 27 Ga 34	Lønset 11 Ea 37	3540 Nesbyen 11 Fa 37
9982 Kalak 5 Aa 55	3836 Kviteseid 27 Fb 36	2340 Løten 12 Fa 39	Nesgrenda 27 Ga 36
8447 Kaljord 3 Ba 43	6995 Kyrkjebø 11 Eb 33	2240 Magnor 28 Fb 40	Nesjestranda 11 Ea 35
6729 Kalvåg 11 Eb 32	7201 Kyrkseterøra 11 Db 37	7982 Majavatn 26 Cb 41	8700 Nesna 26 Ca 41
Kanestraum 11 Db 36	9768 Kåfjord/Honnigsvåg 4 Aa 53	7790 Malm 26 Da 39	1450 Nesoddtangen 28 Fb 38
9050 Kantornes 4 Ab 47	Kårhamm 4 Aa 51	4501 Mandal 27 Ga 35	9930 Nesseby 5 Aa 56
9730 Karasjok 4 Ab 53	Kårvåg 11 Db 35	5931 Manger 11 Fa 33	4645 Nodeland 27 Ga 35
Karlshus 28 Fb 38	9700 Lakselv 4 Aa 52	7622 Markabygd 12 Db 39	Nor 28 Fa 40
9322 Karlstad 3 Ab 46	2682 Lalm 11 Eb 37	9934 Måskejohka 5 Aa 56	3820 Nordagutu 27 Fb 37
6854 Kaupanger 11 Eb 35	Lampeland 27 Fb 37	5984 Matre 11 Fa 33	6770 Nordfjordeid 11 Eb 34
9730 Kautokeino 4 Ab 51	Lande 26 Cb 40	2032 Maura 28 Fa 39	8286 Nordfold 3 Bb 43
9730 Kentan 4 Ab 53	3947 Langangen 27 Fb 37	7580 Mebonden 12 Db 39	9442 Nordkil 3 Ba 43
Kinn 12 Fa 38	8056 Langbakken 3 Ba 43	9321 Meby 3 Ba 43	7260 Nordskaget 11 Db 36
5780 Kinsarvik 11 Fa 34	Langeid 27 Ga 35	4625 Mebø 27 Ga 36	6050 Nordstranda 11 Ea 34
Kippermoen 26 Cb 41	3970 Langesund 27 Ga 37	9770 Mehamn 5 Aa 55	Nordstumoen 12 Eb 39
Kirkehamn 27 Ga 34	Langevåg 27 Fb 33	8445 Melbu 3 Ba 42	9925 Nordvestbukta 5 Ab 57
9900 Kirkenes 5 Ab 58	6030 Langevåg 11 Ea 34	7336 Meldal 12 Db 37	3536 Noresund 27 Fa 37
2260 Kirkenær 12 Fa 40	9545 Langfjordbotn 5 Aa 55	Meldalen 28 Fa 40	5600 Norheimsund 11 Fa 34
7893 Kjelda 26 Cb 40	1405 Langhus 28 Fb 38	7224 Melhus 12 Db 38	3671 Notodden 27 Fb 37
8543 Kjeldebotn 3 Ba 44	9300 Langnes 3 Ab 46	7530 Meråker 12 Db 39	2422 Nybergsund 12 Eb 40
Kjellmyra 12 Fa 40	Langodden 12 Ea 38	2610 Mesnali 12 Eb 38	9620 Nyvoll 4 Aa 51
Kjerret 28 Fb 40	Langset 28 Fa 39	Messelt 12 Eb 39	4565 Nærbø 27 Ga 33
Kjerringøy 7 Bb 42	9180 Langslett 4 Ab 48	9054 Mestervik 4 Ab 46	5750 Odda 27 Fa 34
9790 Kjøllefjord 5 Aa 55	6084 Larsnes 11 Ea 33	6475 Midsund 11 Ea 34	9164 Odden 4 Ab 48
9442 Kjøpsvik 3 Ba 44	3251 Larvik 27 Fb 38	Mierojávri 4 Ab 51	Ofte 27 Fb 36

N   Okkelberg   N   **Teksnes**

	Okkelberg 12 Db 39	2960	Røn 11 Eb 37	2019	Skedsmokorset 28 Fa 39	8450	Stokmarknes 3 Ba 42
	Oldeide 11 Eb 33		Rønningen 27 Ga 37	6843	Skei 11 Eb 34		Stonglandseidet 3 Ab 45
6788	Olden 11 Eb 34	7672	Røra 12 Db 39		Skerpje 27 Ga 34		Stordalen 11 Ea 34
9050	Olderbakken 4 Ab 48	7374	Røros 12 Ea 39	1400	Ski 28 Fb 38	9441	Storfjord 4 Ab 47
9164	Olderdalen 4 Ab 48	7900	Rørvik 26 Da 39	3705	Skien 27 Fb 37	8630	Storforshei 26 Ca 42
	Olsøya 12 Db 38		Rørvik 27 Ga 34	9840	Skiippagurra 5 Aa 56	8275	Storjord 7 Ca 43
4333	Oltedal 27 Ga 34	8314	Rørvika 3 Ba 42	1816	Skipvet 28 Fb 39	9402	Stornes 3 Ba 44
	Opeland 11 Fa 34	8900	Rørøya 26 Cb 40	1746	Skjeberg 28 Fb 39	9151	Storslett 4 Ab 49
	Oppdal 12 Ea 37		Røssnesvågen 26 Bb 40	9180	Skjervøy 4 Aa 48	9518	Storvik 4 Ab 51
	Oppstryn 11 Eb 35		Røst 26 Bb 40	9054	Skjold 4 Ab 47	9595	Storvollen 26 Bb 42
7300	Orkanger 12 Db 37	8220	Røsvik 7 Bb 43	5574	Skjold/Haugesund 27 Fb 33	7334	Storås 12 Db 37
2550	Os 12 Ea 39	7893	Røyrvik 26 Da 41		Skjæret 4 Ab 47	9321	Strand 3 Ba 43
7190	Osen 26 Da 38		Råholt 28 Fa 39	1680	Skjærhalden 28 Fb 39	6200	Stranda 11 Ea 34
0101	Oslo 28 Fb 38	8533	Råna 3 Ba 45	1860	Skjønhaug 28 Fb 39	8664	Straum 26 Cb 41
2460	Osneset 12 Eb 39	5410	Sagvåg 27 Fb 33	9771	Skjånes 5 Aa 56		Straumbu 12 Eb 38
5200	Osøyro 11 Fa 33	7746	Salen 26 Da 39	6260	Skodje 11 Ea 34	8413	Straume 3 Ba 42
	Otnes 12 Eb 39	7960	Salsbruket 26 Da 39	9722	Skoganvarri 4 Ab 53	8226	Straumen/Bodø 7 Bb 43
2670	Otta 11 Eb 37	4230	Sand/Haugesund 27 Fb 34	7870	Skogmo 26 Da 40	7201	Straumen/Levanger 12 Db 39
	Otterøy 26 Da 39		Sand/Jessheim 28 Fa 39	7620	Skogn 12 Db 39	8413	Straumsnes 3 Ba 42
2477	Plassen 12 Eb 40	6823	Sandane 11 Eb 34		Skordal 11 Eb 37	9465	Straumsnes/Langnes 3 Ab 46
9062	Polleidet 4 Ab 48		Sande/Drøbak 27 Fb 38	7893	Skorovatn 26 Da 41	6783	Stryn 11 Eb 34
9934	Polmak 5 Aa 56		Sande/Hoyanger 11 Eb 33	2230	Skotterud 28 Fb 40		Stuggudalen 12 Ea 39
9709	Porsangermoen 4 Ab 52	3201	Sandefjord 27 Fb 38		Skottfoss 27 Fb 37		Stuguflotten 11 Ea 36
3901	Porsgrunn 27 Fb 37	9151	Sandelva 4 Ab 49	2848	Skreia 12 Fa 38	7290	Støren 12 Db 38
1796	Prestebakke 28 Ga 39		Sandes 5 Ab 47		Skråmestøi 11 Fa 33	4240	Suldal 27 Fb 34
3350	Prestfoss 27 Fa 37		Sandestølen 11 Fa 37	4280	Skudeneshavn 27 Fb 33	8210	Sulitjelma 7 Bb 44
1890	Rakkestad 28 Fb 39	4301	Sandnes 27 Ga 33		Skullerud 28 Fa 40		Sundan 11 Db 37
	Rakvågen 12 Db 38		Sandnes 26 Da 40	9982	Skuvgi 5 Aa 56	5450	Sunde 27 Fb 33
8380	Ramberg 3 Ba 41	5981	Sandnes/Amudsbotnen		Skåbu 11 Eb 37		Sundvollen 28 Fa 38
9442	Ramsund 3 Ba 44		11 Fa 33	5593	Skånevik 27 Fb 33	6600	Sunndalsøra 11 Ea 36
	Randsverk 11 Eb 37	8800	Sandnessjøen 26 Ca 40	2966	Slidre 11 Eb 36	9518	Suolovuobmi 4 Ab 51
7977	Ranemsletta 26 Da 39	7246	Sandstad 11 Db 37		Sløvåg 11 Fa 33	6650	Surnadalsøra 11 Ea 36
6710	Raudeberg 11 Eb 33	9430	Sandtorg 3 Ba 44		Slåtten 4 Aa 52	3275	Svarstad 27 Fb 37
	Raudsand 11 Ea 36	4272	Sandve 27 Fb 33	7980	Smalåsen 26 Cb 41		Svartevatn 27 Ga 34
2830	Raufoss 12 Fa 38		Sandvika 27 Fb 33		Smørfjord 4 Aa 56		Svartnes 5 Aa 59
8390	Reine 3 Bb 41		Sandvika 28 Fb 38		Snippen 12 Eb 39		Sveingardsbotn 11 Fa 35
2840	Reinsvoll 12 Fa 38	7660	Sandvika 12 Db 40	7761	Snåsa 26 Da 40	5550	Sveio 27 Fb 33
8146	Reipå 26 Ca 41	7761	Sandvika 26 Da 41	6856	Sogndalsfjøra 11 Eb 35	6723	Svelgen 11 Eb 33
2450	Rena 12 Eb 39	9151	Sappen 4 Ab 49	3534	Sokna 27 Fa 37	3060	Svelvik 28 Fb 38
	Rennebu 12 Ea 37	1702	Sarpsborg 28 Fb 39	7288	Soknedal 12 Ea 38	3622	Svene 27 Fb 37
6520	Rensvik 11 Db 35	4200	Sauda 27 Fb 34	4050	Sola 27 Ga 33	7982	Svenningrud 26 Cb 41
8750	Reppa 26 Ca 41	2672	Sel 11 Eb 37		Solholmen 11 Ea 34		Svensby 4 Ab 47
	Revsnes 3 Ba 44	7246	Selbekken 12 Db 37		Sollfjellsjøen 26 Ca 40	8300	Svolvær 3 Ba 42
2630	Ringebu 12 Eb 38	6740	Selje 11 Ea 33	1820	Sollia 12 Eb 38	5430	Svortland 27 Fb 33
	Ringvoll 28 Fb 38	3840	Seljord 27 Fb 36		Solstad 4 Ab 47	6230	Sykkylven 11 Ea 34
	Risan 11 Ea 37	9715	Selkopp 4 Aa 52		Solstad 26 Cb 40	6144	Sylte 11 Ea 35
	Risnes 27 Ga 34	3170	Sem 27 Fb 38	8210	Solvik 7 Bb 43		Sæbo 11 Ea 34
2216	Rissa 12 Db 37	9350	Setermoen 3 Ba 46		Solvorn 11 Eb 35	9442	Sætran 3 Ba 44
	Risør 27 Ga 37	8210	Setså 7 Bb 43	8266	Sommarset 7 Bb 43	4640	Søgne 27 Ga 35
8484	Risøyhamn 3 Ba 43	8266	Sildhopen 7 Bb 43	1555	Son 28 Fb 38		Søm 27 Ga 36
3660	Rjukan 27 Fb 36	7387	Singsås 12 Ea 38		Sortland 3 Ba 43		Søndre Rasan 12 Fa 39
2740	Roa 28 Fa 38	4438	Sira 27 Ga 34		Spangereid 27 Ga 35	9040	Sørkjos 4 Ab 47
9826	Roavvegieddi 5 Ab 55	4364	Sirevåg 27 Ga 33	1820	Spydeberg 28 Fb 39	8480	Sørli/Finnsnes 3 Ab 45
8250	Rognan 7 Bb 43		Sjoa 11 Eb 37	9775	Stabburstranda 5 Aa 55	7761	Sørli/Sandvika 26 Da 41
7295	Rognes 12 Db 38		Sjona 26 Ca 41	8340	Stamsund 3 Ba 41	9310	Sørreisa 3 Ab 46
5470	Rosendal 27 Fb 34		Sjøholt 11 Ea 34	2335	Stange 12 Fa 38	9445	Sørrollnes 3 Ba 44
5917	Rossland 11 Fa 33	9350	Sjøvegan 3 Ba 45	3960	Stathelle 27 Fb 37	9162	Sørstraumen 4 Ab 49
	Rotberget 12 Fa 40	7790	Sjøåsen 26 Da 39	4001	Stavanger 27 Ga 33	8392	Sørvågen 3 Bb 41
	Rotnes 28 Fa 38		Skáidi 4 Aa 52	3290	Stavern 27 Ga 38		Šuoššjávri 4 Ab 52
2216	Roverud 28 Fa 40		Skaiå 27 Ga 35		Steine 11 Fa 35	9845	Tana bru 5 Aa 56
5448	Rubbestadneset 27 Fb 33	9384	Skaland 3 Ab 45	7701	Steinkjer 26 Da 39	2337	Tangen 12 Fa 39
	Rutledalen 11 Eb 33	8264	Skard 26 Ca 40	8312	Steira 3 Ba 41		Tangen 12 Ea 38
	Rysjedalsvika 11 Eb 33	9442	Skardberget 3 Ba 44		Stengelsrud 27 Fb 37	4120	Tau 27 Fb 33
3630	Rødberg 27 Fa 36	5763	Skare 27 Fb 34	7500	Stjørdalshalsen 12 Db 38		Teigebyen 28 Fa 39
8256	Røkland 7 Ca 43	2100	Skarnes 28 Fa 39		Stodsbuøya 12 Ea 38	7114	Teksdalen 12 Db 37
5760	Røldal 27 Fb 34	4715	Skarpengland 27 Ga 35	8735	Stokkvågen 26 Ca 41		Teksnes 28 Fb 38

POSTALI · ÍNDICE CON CÓDIGOS POSTALES · INDICE DE LUGARES COM CÓDIGOS POSTAIS ·
MÍST S PSČ · ZOZNAM OBCÍ S PSČ · INDEKS MIEJSCOWOŚCI Z KOD POCZTOWY

168

7980 Terråk 26 Cb 40
6630 Tingvoll 11 Ea 36
5336 Tjeldstø 11 Fa 32
    Tjelle 11 Ea 35
8186 Tjong 26 Ca 41
8883 Tjotta 26 Cb 40
3145 Tjøme 27 Fb 38
    Todalen 11 Ea 36
3482 Tofte 28 Fb 38
2540 Tolga 12 Ea 39
6393 Tomra 11 Ea 34
4440 Tonstad 27 Ga 34
3579 Torpo 11 Fa 36
9381 Torsken 3 Ab 45
7982 Tosbotn 26 Cb 40
6391 Tresfjord 11 Ea 35
2635 Tretten 12 Eb 38
8680 Trofors 26 Cb 41
9001 Tromsø 4 Ab 46
7004 Trondheim 12 Db 38
8100 Tuv/Bodø 26 Bb 42
    Tuv/Hemsedal 11 Fa 36
    Tvedestrand 27 Ga 36
    Tveit 27 Fb 34
3855 Tveitsund 27 Fb 36
8100 Tverrvika 26 Bb 42
    Tyinholmen 11 Eb 36
2985 Tyinkrysset 11 Eb 36
2500 Tynset 12 Ea 38
5650 Tysse 11 Fa 33
5770 Tyssedal 27 Fa 34
5284 Tysso 11 Fa 33
    Tømmerneset 3 Bb 43
6590 Tømmervåg 11 Db 35
3101 Tønsberg 28 Fb 38
1950 Tørnby 28 Fb 39
3830 Ulefoss 27 Fb 37
6065 Ulsteinvik 11 Ea 33
    Ulsvåg 3 Ba 43
    Ulvastad 11 Eb 34
5730 Ulvik 11 Fa 34
8617 Umbukta 26 Ca 42
9162 Undereidet 4 Ab 49
5463 Uskedalen 27 Fb 33
5778 Utne 11 Fa 34
    Utvik 11 Eb 34
5453 Utåker 27 Fb 33
6996 Vadheim 11 Eb 33
9800 Vadsø 5 Aa 57
9925 Vaggatem 5 Ab 57
5725 Vaksdal 11 Fa 33
5451 Valen 26 Cb 39
4747 Valle 27 Fb 35
    Vålljohka 5 Ab 53
8215 Valnesfjord 7 Bb 43
    Valvika 7 Bb 42
6894 Vangsnes 11 Eb 34
9135 Vannråg 4 Aa 47
4560 Vanse 27 Ga 34
7125 Vanvikan 12 Db 38
9950 Vardø 5 Aa 59
4360 Varhaug 27 Ga 33
6265 Vatne 11 Ea 34
    Vatvet 28 Fb 39
3628 Veggli 27 Fa 37
    Vegusdal 27 Ga 36

9715 Veidneset 5 Aa 54
6690 Veiholmen 11 Db 35
7822 Vellamelen 26 Da 39
    Velta 12 Fa 40
    Vemundvik 26 Da 39
2632 Venabygd 12 Eb 38
    Venganeset 11 Fa 33
4700 Vennesla 27 Ga 36
7980 Vennesund 26 Cb 40
7650 Verdalsøra 12 Db 39
7120 Verrabotn 12 Db 38
4563 Vestbygd 27 Ga 34
8250 Vesterli 7 Bb 43
3320 Vestfossen 27 Fb 37
6399 Vestnes 11 Ea 35
8322 Vestre 3 Ba 42
    Vestre Åbu 12 Eb 39
    Vevelstad 26 Cb 40
4520 Vigeland 27 Ga 35
7354 Viggja 12 Db 37
7980 Vik 11 Eb 34
6392 Vikebukta 11 Ea 35
3370 Vikersund 27 Fb 37
4389 Vikeså 27 Ga 34
    Vikna 26 Da 38
9057 Vikran 4 Ab 46
6893 Vikøyri 11 Eb 34
    Vingnes 12 Eb 38
    Vingrom 12 Eb 38
7203 Vinjeøra 11 Db 37
    Vinjo 11 Fa 34
8643 Vinneidfjord 26 Ca 41
2639 Vinstra 11 Eb 37
    Vintervollen 5 Ab 58
7343 Vognill 11 Ea 37
6100 Volda 11 Ea 34
    Voll 11 Ea 35
    Vormstad 12 Db 37
5700 Voss 11 Fa 34
8185 Vågaholmen 26 Ca 41
5956 Vågseidet 11 Fa 33
2680 Vågåmo 11 Eb 37
2436 Våler 12 Fa 39
    Vålåsjø 11 Ea 37
    Yli 27 Fb 37
5265 Ytre Arna 11 Fa 33
    Ytre Oppedal 11 Eb 33
9550 Øksfjord 4 Aa 50
5580 Ølen 27 Fb 33
9545 Ørbakken 4 Aa 50
    Øresvika 26 Ca 41
1870 Ørje 28 Fb 39
8150 Ørnes 26 Ca 41
6150 Ørsta 11 Ea 34
    Ørvella 27 Fb 37
    Østerud 27 Fb 37
9054 Øvergård 4 Ab 47
6884 Øvre Årdal 11 Eb 35
    Øy 27 Ga 34
6196 Øye 11 Ea 34
    Øyslebø 27 Ga 35
5610 Øystese 11 Fa 34
6360 Åfarnes 11 Ea 35
8184 Ågskardet 26 Ca 41
4270 Åkrahamn 27 Fb 33
2482 Åkrestømmen 12 Eb 39

    Ålen 12 Ea 39
6010 Ålesund 11 Ea 34
    Ålfoten 11 Eb 33
4330 Ålgård 27 Ga 33
6622 Ålvund 11 Ea 36
4865 Åmli 27 Ga 36
3340 Åmot 27 Fb 37
3890 Åmot 27 Fb 35
6300 Åndalsnes 11 Ea 35
1484 Åneby 28 Fa 38
    Åraksbø 27 Ga 35
6885 Årdalstangen 11 Eb 35
    Årnes 26 Db 38
2150 Årnes 28 Fa 39
7893 Årsand 26 Cb 40
1430 Ås 28 Fb 38
7630 Åsen 12 Db 39
4540 Åseral 27 Ga 35

NL

1431 Aalsmeer 46 Ka 32
1811 Alkmaar 46 Ka 32
7607 Almelo 46 Ka 34
1312 Almere 46 Ka 33
2402 Alphen aan den Rijn 46 Ka 32
3811 Amersfoort 46 Ka 33
1181 Amstelveen 46 Ka 32
1012 Amsterdam 46 Ka 32
7311 Apeldoorn 46 Ka 33
9901 Appingedam 35 Jab 34
6811 Arnhem 46 Kb 33
9401 Assen 46 Ka 34
9781 Bedum 46 Jab 34
9411 Beilen 46 Ka 34
1861 Bergen/Alkmaar 46 Ka 32
5854 Bergen/Venray 46 Kb 34
4611 Bergen op Zoom 46 Kb 32
1944 Beverwijk 46 Ka 32
8701 Bolsward 46 Jb 33
9531 Borger 46 Ka 34
7622 Borne 46 Ka 34
5281 Boxtel 46 Kb 33
4811 Breda 46 Kb 32
4511 Breskens 46 Kb 31
9164 Buren 46 Jb 33
1401 Bussum 46 Ka 33
1902 Castricum 46 Ka 32
7741 Coevorden 46 Ka 34
5431 Cuijk 46 Kb 33
4101 Culemborg 46 Kb 33
1795 De Cocksdorp 46 Jb 32
1796 De Koog 46 Jb 32
9934 Delfzijl 35 Jab 34
1791 Den Burg 46 Jb 32
1782 Den Helder 46 Ka 32
1797 Den Hoorn 46 Jb 32
1779 Den Oever 46 Ka 33
5751 Deurne 46 Kb 33
7418 Deventer 46 Ka 34
7001 Doetinchem 46 Kb 34
9101 Dokkum 46 Jb 33
3311 Dordrecht 46 Kb 32
9203 Drachten 46 Jab 34

8251 Dronten 46 Ka 33
6711 Ede 46 Ka 33
5611 Eindhoven 46 Kb 33
8301 Emmeloord 46 Ka 33
7811 Emmen 46 Ka 34
1601 Enkhuizen 46 Ka 33
7511 Enschede 46 Ka 34
3851 Ermelo 46 Ka 33
4872 Etten-Leur 46 Kb 32
8802 Franeker 46 Jb 33
4191 Geldermalsen 46 Kb 33
4461 Goes 46 Kb 31
5051 Goirle 46 Kb 33
4201 Gorinchem 46 Kb 32
2801 Gouda 46 Ka 32
9712 Groningen 46 Jab 34
9861 Grootegast 46 Jab 34
7481 Haaksbergen 46 Ka 34
2012 Haarlem 46 Ka 32
7772 Hardenberg 46 Ka 34
3841 Harderwijk 46 Ka 33
8861 Harlingen 46 Jb 33
1964 Heemskerk 46 Ka 32
8181 Heerde 46 Ka 34
8442 Heerenveen 46 Ka 33
1702 Heerhugowaard 46 Ka 32
6411 Heerlen 46 La 33
3221 Hellevoetsluis 46 Kb 32
5701 Helmond 46 Kb 33
7255 Hengelo 46 Ka 34
1211 Hilversum 46 Ka 33
9161 Hollum 46 Jb 33
9151 Holwerd 46 Jb 33
2131 Hoofddorp 46 Ka 32
7801 Hoogeveen 46 Ka 34
9601 Hoogezand-Sappemeer
       46 Jab 34
8896 Hoorn 46 Ka 33
1271 Huizen 46 Ka 33
1972 IJmuiden 46 Ka 32
8261 Kampen 46 Ka 33
6461 Kerkrade 46 La 34
8723 Koudum 46 Ka 33
1721 Langedijk 46 Ka 32
8911 Leeuwarden 46 Jb 33
2312 Leiden 46 Ka 32
2261 Leidschendam 46 Ka 32
8232 Lelystad 46 Ka 33
8532 Lemmer 46 Ka 33
9919 Loppersum 35 Jab 34
7581 Losser 46 Ka 35
6211 Maastricht 46 La 33
8754 Makkum 46 Jb 33
7941 Meppel 46 Ka 34
4331 Middelburg 46 Kb 31
3434 Nieuwegein 46 Ka 33
3861 Nijkerk 46 Ka 33
6511 Nijmegen 46 Kb 33
7441 Nijverdal 46 Ka 34
2202 Noordwijk 46 Ka 32
8391 Noordwolde 46 Ka 34
8071 Nunspeet 46 Ka 33
7572 Oldenzaal 46 Ka 34
7731 Ommen 46 Ka 34
8899 Oost-Vlieland 46 Jb 33
4501 Oostburg 45 Kb 31

169

INDEX WITH POST CODES · ORTSREGISTER MIT POSTLEITZAHLEN · INDICE CON CODICI
STEDREGISTER MED POSTNUMRE · PLAATSNAMENREGISTER MET POSTCODE · REJSTŘÍK

NL

P

Oosterbierum

NL · P

Monforte

8854 Oosterbierum 46 Jb 33
8897 Oosterend 46 Jb 33
8897 Oosterend 46 Jb 32
4901 Oosterhout 46 Kb 32
8097 Oosterwolde 46 Ka 34
5341 Oss 46 Kb 33
3262 Oud-Beijerland 46 Kb 32
1441 Purmerend 46 Ka 32
8102 Raalte 46 Ka 34
2982 Ridderkerk 46 Kb 32
5121 Rijen 46 Kb 32
6041 Roermond 46 Kb 34
4701 Roosendaal 46 Kb 32
3011 Rotterdam 46 Kb 32
7261 Ruurlo 46 Ka 34
2511 `s-Gravenhage (den Haag)
46 Ka 32
5211 `s-Hertogenbosch 46 Kb 33
1741 Schagen 46 Ka 32
9679 Scheemda 46 Jab 34
3111 Schiedam 46 Kb 32
9076 Sint Annaparochie 46 Jb 33
8603 Sneek 46 Jb 33
3203 Spijkenisse 46 Kb 32
9501 Stadskanaal 46 Jab 34
7951 Staphorst 46 Ka 34
4651 Steenbergen 46 Kb 32
8331 Steenwijk 46 Ka 34
9561 Ter Apel 46 Ka 35
4531 Terneuzen 46 Kb 31
4001 Tiel 46 Kb 33
5011 Tilburg 46 Kb 33
7651 Tubbergen 46 Ka 34
5401 Uden 46 Kb 33
8321 Urk 46 Ka 33
3511 Utrecht 46 Ka 33
5554 Valkenswaard 46 Kb 33
9641 Veendam 46 Jab 34
3901 Veenendaal 46 Ka 33
5461 Veghel 46 Kb 33
5911 Venlo 46 Kb 34
5801 Venray 46 Kb 33
3131 Vlaardingen 46 Kb 32
9541 Vlagtwedde 46 Jab 35
4381 Vlissingen 46 Kb 31
7383 Voorst 46 Ka 34
5261 Vught 46 Kb 33
5141 Waalwijk 46 Kb 33
6701 Wageningen 46 Kb 33
2242 Wassenaar 46 Ka 32
6001 Weert 46 Kb 33
8881 West-Terschelling 46 Jb 33
7641 Wierden 46 Ka 34
6601 Wijchen 46 Kb 33
9671 Winschoten 46 Jab 35
8831 Winsum 46 Jab 34
7101 Winterswijk 46 Kb 34
8711 Workum 46 Ka 33
1501 Zaandam 46 Ka 32
3701 Zeist 46 Ka 33
7021 Zelhem 46 Ka 34
6901 Zevenaar 46 Kb 34
4301 Zierikzee 46 Kb 31
2711 Zoetermeer 46 Ka 32
9801 Zuidhorn 46 Jab 34
9785 Zuidwolde 46 Ka 34

7201 Zutphen 46 Ka 34
8011 Zwolle 46 Ka 34

P

2200 Abrantes 81 Qb 19
2000 Achete 81 Qb 19
2240 Águas Belas 81 Qb 19
3750 Águeda 67 Qa 19
3570 Aguiar da Beira 68 Qa 20
7250 Alandroal 81 Qa 20
8200 Albufeira 81 Rb 19
7580 Alcácer do Sal 81 Ra 19
7090 Alcáçovas 81 Ra 19
2460 Alcobaça 81 Qb 19
2890 Alcochete 81 Ra 19
2065 Alcoentre 81 Qb 19
8970 Alcoutim 81 Rb 20
7830 Aldeia Nova de São Bento
81 Rb 20
2580 Alenquer 81 Qb 19
6320 Alfaiates 82 Qa 21
8670 Alfambra 81 Rb 19
8365 Algoz 81 Rb 19
5070 Alijó 68 Pb 20
8670 Aljezur 81 Rb 19
7600 Aljustrel 81 Rb 19
2800 Almada 81 Ra 18
6350 Almeida 68 Qa 21
2080 Almeirim 81 Qb 19
7700 Almodôvar 81 Rb 19
6050 Alpalhão 81 Qb 20
2090 Alpiarça 81 Qb 19
7220 Alqueva 81 Ra 20
8100 Alte 81 Rb 19
7440 Alter do Chão 81 Qb 20
7565 Alvalade 81 Rb 19
6300 Alvendre 82 Qa 20
2615 Alverca do Ribatejo 81 Ra 18
7920 Alvito 81 Ra 20
4600 Amarante 67 Pb 19
7885 Amareleja 81 Ra 20
6120 Amêndoa 81 Qb 19
3780 Anadia 67 Qa 19
4740 Apúlia 67 Pb 19
3300 Arganil 81 Qa 19
7040 Arraiolos 81 Ra 20
7340 Arronches 81 Qb 20
2630 Arruda dos Vinhos 81 Ra 18
3800 Aveiro 67 Qa 19
7480 Avis 81 Qb 20
4750 Barcelos 67 Pb 19
7230 Barrancos 81 Ra 21
2830 Barreiro 81 Ra 18
2440 Batalha 81 Qb 19
7800 Beja 81 Ra 20
6250 Belmonte 82 Qa 20
2130 Benavente 81 Ra 19
7630 Bicos 81 Rb 19
2540 Bombarral 81 Qb 18
7150 Borba 81 Ra 20
4700 Braga 67 Pb 19
5300 Bragança 68 Pb 21
2670 Bucelas 81 Ra 18

4540 Burgo 67 Qa 19
4860 Cabeceiras de Basto
67 Pb 20
7050 Cabrela 81 Ra 19
8800 Cachopo 81 Rb 20
2500 Caldas da Rainha
81 Qb 18
4910 Caminha 67 Pb 19
7370 Campo Maior 81 Qb 20
4920 Campos 67 Pb 19
2985 Canha 81 Ra 19
4400 Canidelo 67 Pb 19
3060 Cantanhede 67 Qa 19
4905 Capareiros 67 Pb 19
6230 Capinha 81 Qa 20
8670 Carrapateira 81 Rb 19
3430 Carregal do Sal 81 Qa 20
3100 Carriço 81 Qb 19
2070 Cartaxo 81 Qb 19
7470 Casa Branca 81 Ra 20
8550 Casais 81 Rb 19
2750 Cascais 81 Ra 18
5200 Castelo Branco/Mogadouro
68 Pb 21
6000 Castelo Branco/Sarrnades de
Ródão 81 Qb 20
7320 Castelo de Vide 81 Qb 20
4900 Castelo do Neiva 67 Pb 19
3600 Castro Daire 67 Qa 20
7780 Castro Verde 81 Rb 19
6360 Celorico da Beira 68 Qa 20
7555 Cercal 81 Rb 19
6320 Cerdeira 82 Qa 20
2140 Chamusca 81 Qb 19
5400 Chaves 68 Pb 20
4690 Cinfães 67 Pb 19
3000 Coimbra 81 Qa 19
7630 Colos 81 Rb 19
7580 Comporta 81 Ra 19
3150 Condeixa-a-Nova 81 Qa 19
2100 Coruche 81 Ra 19
2825 Costa da Caparica 81 Ra 18
2100 Couço 81 Ra 19
6200 Covilhã 81 Qa 20
7430 Crato 81 Qb 20
7940 Cuba 81 Ra 20
5320 Edral 68 Pb 20
7350 Elvas 81 Ra 20
2330 Entroncamento 81 Qb 19
2655 Ericeira 81 Ra 18
7540 Ermidas Sado 81 Ra 19
4500 Espinho 67 Pb 19
4740 Esposende 67 Pb 19
3860 Estarreja 67 Qa 19
2765 Estoril 81 Ra 18
7100 Estremoz 81 Ra 20
7000 Évora 81 Ra 20
4970 Extremo 67 Pb 19
4820 Fafe 67 Pb 19
8000 Faro 81 Rb 20
2495 Fátima 81 Qb 19
7900 Ferreira do Alentejo 81 Ra 19
3080 Figueira da Foz 81 Qa 19
6440 Figueira de Castelo Rodrigo
68 Qa 21
3260 Figueiró dos Vinhos 81 Qb 19

5180 Fornos 68 Pb 21
2435 Freixianda 81 Qb 19
7460 Fronteira 81 Qb 20
6230 Fundão 81 Qa 20
3830 Gafanha da Nazaré
67 Qa 19
4890 Gandarela 67 Pb 19
6030 Gardete 81 Qb 20
4420 Gondomar 67 Pb 19
2080 Gorjão 81 Qb 20
5470 Gralhós 68 Pb 20
7570 Grândola 81 Ra 19
7240 Granja 81 Ra 20
5300 Guadramil 68 Pb 21
6300 Guarda 82 Qa 20
4810 Guimarães 67 Pb 19
6060 Idanha-a-Nova 82 Qb 20
3830 Ílhavo 67 Qa 19
8400 Lagoa 81 Rb 19
8600 Lagos 81 Rb 19
2550 Lamas 81 Qb 18
5100 Lamego 67 Pb 20
7050 Lavre 81 Ra 19
2400 Leiria 81 Qb 19
1000 Lisboa 81 Ra 18
8100 Loulé 81 Rb 19
2670 Loures 81 Ra 18
3100 Louriçal 81 Qa 19
2530 Lourinhã 81 Qb 18
3200 Lousã 81 Qa 19
3050 Luso 67 Qa 19
8600 Luz 81 Rb 19
7665 Luzianes 81 Rb 19
6120 Mação 81 Qb 20
3885 Maceda 67 Qa 19
5340 Macedo de Cavaleiros
68 Pb 21
3660 Macieira 67 Qa 19
2640 Mafra 81 Ra 18
2380 Malhou 81 Qb 19
6000 Malpica do Tejo 81 Qb 20
3530 Mangualde 67 Qa 20
6260 Manteigas 81 Qa 20
2965 Marateca 81 Ra 19
4630 Marco de Canaveses
67 Pb 19
2430 Marinha Grande 81 Qb 19
2125 Marinhais 81 Qb 19
6430 Meda 68 Qa 20
6060 Medelim 82 Qa 20
4620 Meinedo 67 Pb 19
4960 Melgaço 67 Pa 19
7570 Melides 81 Ra 19
7750 Mértola 81 Rb 20
7750 Mina de São Domingos
81 Rb 20
3070 Mira 67 Qa 19
3220 Miranda do Corvo 81 Qa 19
5210 Miranda do Douro 68 Pb 21
5370 Mirandela 68 Pb 20
5320 Mofreita 68 Pb 21
5200 Mogadouro 68 Pb 21
3620 Moimenta da Beira 68 Qa 20
6150 Moitas 81 Qb 20
8550 Monchique 81 Rb 19
7450 Monforte 81 Qb 20

POSTALI · ÍNDICE CON CÓDIGOS POSTALES · INDICE DE LUGARES COM CÓDIGOS POSTAIS ·
MÍST S PSČ · ZOZNAM OBCÍ S PSČ · INDEKS MIEJSCOWOŚCI Z KOD POCZTOWY

170

Monfortinho

P · PL

Bogdaniec

6060 Monfortinho 82 Qa 21	7630 Porto das Barcas 81 Rb 19	7470 Sousel 81 Ra 20
6050 Montalvão 81 Qb 20	2625 Póvoa de Santa Iria 81 Ra 18	3420 Tábua 81 Qa 19
7425 Montargil 81 Qb 19	4490 Póvoa de Varzim 67 Pb 19	3610 Tarouca 67 Pb 20
2425 Monte Redondo 81 Qb 19	4730 Prado 67 Pb 19	8800 Tavira 81 Rb 20
7050 Montemor-o-Novo 81 Ra 19	3060 Praia da Tocha 67 Qa 19	3060 Tocha 67 Qa 19
2870 Montijo 81 Ra 19	8125 Quarteira 81 Rb 19	2300 Tomar 81 Qb 19
7200 Montoito 81 Ra 20	3080 Quiaios 81 Qa 19	3460 Tondela 67 Qa 19
7490 Mora 81 Ra 19	7300 Rabaça 81 Qb 20	7595 Torrão 81 Ra 19
7860 Moura 81 Ra 20	5300 Rabal 68 Pb 21	5385 Torre de Dona Chama
7240 Mourão 81 Ra 20	2565 Ramalhal 81 Qb 18	68 Pb 20
7540 Muda 81 Rb 19	5335 Rebordelo 68 Pb 20	5160 Torre de Moncorvo 68 Pb 20
5090 Murça 68 Pb 20	7170 Redondo 81 Ra 20	3870 Torreira 67 Qa 19
3870 Murtosa 67 Qa 19	7200 Reguengos de Monsaraz	2350 Torres Novas 81 Qb 19
6355 Nave de Haver 82 Qa 21	81 Ra 20	2560 Torres Vedras 81 Qb 18
7665 Nave Redonda 81 Rb 19	2635 Rio de Mouro 81 Ra 18	5155 Touça 68 Pb 20
2450 Nazaré 81 Qb 18	2040 Rio Maior 81 Qb 19	6420 Trancoso 68 Qa 20
6050 Nisa 81 Qb 20	8670 Rogil 81 Rb 19	7800 Trindade/Beja 81 Rb 20
7630 Odemira 81 Rb 19	6060 Rosmaninhal 82 Qb 20	5360 Trindade 68 Pb 20
8600 Odiáxere 81 Rb 19	5060 Sabrosa 68 Pb 20	3840 Vagos 67 Qa 19
7900 Odivelas 81 Ra 19	6320 Sabugal 82 Qa 20	4930 Valença 67 Pa 19
6160 Oleiros 81 Qb 20	8650 Sagres 81 Rb 19	7830 Vales Mortos 81 Rb 20
2580 Olhalvo 81 Qb 18	6060 Salvaterra do Extremo	5430 Valpaços 68 Pb 20
8700 Olhão 81 Rb 20	82 Qb 21	5470 Venda Nova 67 Pb 20
3680 Oliveira de Frades 67 Qa 19	4415 Sandim 67 Pb 19	7080 Vendas Novas 81 Ra 19
3400 Oliveira do Hospital	8800 Santa Catarina da Fonte do	7090 Viana do Alentejo 81 Ra 20
81 Qa 20	Bispo 81 Rb 20	4900 Viana do Castelo 67 Pb 19
6230 Orca 81 Qa 20	3440 Santa Comba Dão 81 Qa 19	5425 Vidago 68 Pb 20
7370 Ouguela 81 Qb 20	5300 Santa Comba de Rossas	6285 Vide 81 Qa 20
2490 Ourém 81 Qb 19	68 Pb 21	7960 Vidigueira 81 Ra 20
7670 Ourique 81 Rb 19	7580 Santa Susana 81 Ra 19	2430 Vieira de Leiria 81 Qb 19
3880 Ovar 67 Qa 19	7670 Santana da Serra 81 Rb 19	5470 Vila da Ponte 68 Pb 20
2780 Paço de Arcos 81 Ra 18	2000 Santarém 81 Qb 19	3720 Vila de Cucujães 67 Qa 19
7580 Palma 81 Ra 19	3100 Santiago de Litém 81 Qb 19	8650 Vila do Bispo 81 Rb 19
2950 Palmela 81 Ra 19	7540 Santiago do Cacém 81 Ra 19	4480 Vila do Conde 67 Pb 19
3320 Pampilhosa da Serra	7875 Santo Aleixo da Restauração	7350 Vila Fernando 81 Ra 20
81 Qa 20	81 Ra 20	5360 Vila Flor 68 Pb 20
4940 Paredes de Coura 67 Pb 19	7500 Santo André 81 Ra 19	2600 Vila Franca de Xira
2445 Pataias 81 Qb 19	2130 Santo Estêvão 81 Ra 19	81 Ra 19
2200 Paúl 81 Qa 20	6040 São Bartolomeu 81 Qb 20	4760 Vila Nova de Famalicão
7490 Pavia 81 Ra 19	8375 São Bartolomeu de Messines	67 Pb 19
7960 Pedrógão 81 Ra 20	81 Rb 19	5150 Vila Nova de Foz Côa
3360 Penacova 81 Qa 19	8150 São Brás de Alportel 81 Rb 20	68 Pb 20
6090 Penamacor 82 Qa 20	7540 São Domingos 81 Rb 19	7645 Vila Nova de Milfontes
3650 Pendilhe 67 Qa 20	3700 São João da Madeira	81 Rb 19
3640 Penedono 68 Qa 20	67 Qa 19	3650 Vila Nova de Paiva 67 Qa 20
6060 Penha Garcia 82 Qa 20	2695 São João da Talha 81 Ra 18	5450 Vila Pouca de Aguiar
2520 Peniche 81 Qb 18	7630 São Luís 81 Rb 19	68 Pb 20
4455 Perafita 67 Pb 19	3660 São Pedro do Sul 67 Qa 19	4910 Vila Praia de Âncora 67 Pb 19
3140 Pereira 81 Qa 19	7630 São Teotónio 81 Rb 19	5000 Vila Real 68 Pb 20
5200 Peso 68 Pb 21	5460 Sapiãos 68 Pb 20	8900 Vila Real de Santo António
5050 Peso da Régua 67 Pb 20	2230 Sardoal 81 Qb 19	81 Rb 20
2955 Pinhal Novo 81 Ra 19	6030 Sarnadas de Ródão 81 Qb 20	6030 Vila Velha de Ródão
5085 Pinhão 68 Pb 20	6000 Sarzedas 81 Qb 20	81 Qb 20
4830 Pinheiro 67 Pb 19	3560 Sátão 67 Qa 20	5400 Vila Verde da Raia 68 Pb 20
6400 Pinhel 68 Qa 20	6060 Segura 82 Qb 21	7830 Vila Verde de Ficalho
7750 Pomarão 81 Rb 20	6270 Seia 81 Qa 20	81 Rb 20
3100 Pombal 81 Qb 19	7830 Serpa 81 Rb 20	8125 Vilamoura 81 Rb 19
4980 Ponte da Barca 67 Pb 19	2970 Serra do Cabo 81 Ra 18	6355 Vilar Formoso 82 Qa 21
4990 Ponte de Lima 67 Pb 19	6100 Sertã 81 Qb 19	5140 Vilarinho da Castanheira
7400 Ponte de Sor 81 Qb 20	2970 Sesimbra 81 Ra 18	68 Pb 20
7300 Portalegre 81 Qb 20	2900 Setúbal 81 Ra 19	5000 Vilarinho de Samardã
7220 Portel 81 Ra 20	2560 Silveira 81 Qb 18	68 Pb 20
8500 Portimão 81 Rb 19	8300 Silves 81 Rb 19	7040 Vimieiro 81 Ra 20
4000 Porto 67 Pb 19	7520 Sines 81 Rb 19	5230 Vimioso 68 Pb 21
7330 Porto da Espada 81 Qb 20	2710 Sintra 81 Ra 18	5320 Vinhais 68 Pb 21
	7875 Sobral de Adiça 81 Ra 20	3500 Viseu 67 Qa 20

PL

87 700 Aleksandrów Kujawski 49 Ka 46
95 070 Aleksandrów Łódzki 49 Kb 47
34 120 Andrychów 61 Lb 47
16 300 Augustów 38 Jab 50
62 620 Babiak/Konin 49 Ka 46
11 122 Babiak/Lidzbark Warmiński 38 Ja 48
11 711 Babięta 38 Jab 49
66 110 Babimost 49 Ka 43
37 758 Bachórz 62 Lb 50
16 423 Bakałarzewo 38 Ja 50
74 110 Banie 48 Jab 42
19 520 Banie Mazurskie 38 Ja 50
11 410 Barciany 38 Ja 49
88 190 Barcin 49 Ka 45
11 010 Barczewo 38 Jab 48
77 314 Barkowo 49 Jab 45
74 320 Barlinek 48 Ka 43
11 200 Bartoszyce 38 Ja 48
78 460 Barwice 37 Jab 44
87 704 Bądkowo 49 Ka 46
99 311 Bedlno 50 Ka 47
05 662 Belsk Duży 50 Kb 48
97 400 Bełchatów 49 Kb 47
22 670 Bełżec 51 La 51
11 222 Bezledy 38 Ja 48
48 210 Biała 49 La 45
12 230 Biała Piska 38 Jab 50
21 500 Biała Podlaska 50 Ka 51
96 230 Biała Rawska 50 Kb 48
86 005 Białe Błota 49 Jab 45
16 311 Białobrzegi/Augustów 38 Jab 50
26 800 Białobrzegi/Warka 50 Kb 48
78 200 Białogard 37 Ja 43
17 230 Białowieża 51 Ka 51
78 425 Biały Bór 37 Jab 44
15 000 Białystok 50 Jab 51
38 340 Biecz 62 Lb 49
58 260 Bielawa 49 La 44
99 423 Bielawy 50 Ka 47
39 220 Bielowy 62 Lb 49
09 230 Bielsk 50 Ka 47
17 100 Bielsk Podlaski 50 Ka 51
43 300 Bielsko-Biała 61 Lb 47
56 420 Bierutów 49 Kb 45
09 320 Bieżuń 50 Ka 47
23 400 Biłgoraj 50 La 50
13 340 Biskupiec 49 Jab 47
11 300 Biskupiec 38 Jab 48
11 230 Bisztynek 38 Ja 48
98 235 Błaszki 49 Kb 46
21 306 Błonie/Biała Podlaska 50 Ka 51
05870 Błonie/Warszawa 50 Ka 48
76 020 Bobolice 37 Jab 44
38 350 Bobowa 62 Lb 48
16 042 Bobrowniki 51 Jab 51
32 700 Bochnia 62 Lb 48
59 920 Bogatynia 48 La 42
66 450 Bogdaniec 48 Ka 43

171

INDEX WITH POST CODES · ORTSREGISTER MIT POSTLEITZAHLEN · INDICE CON CODICI
STEDREGISTER MED POSTNUMRE · PLAATSNAMENREGISTER MET POSTCODE · REJSTŘÍK

PL

Bojanowo   (PL)   **Jarocin**

63 940 Bojanowo 49 Kb 44
59 700 Bolesławiec 49 Kb 43
59 420 Bolków 49 La 44
16 053 Bondary 51 Ka 51
76 009 Bonin 37 Ja 44
63 810 Borek Wielkopolski
      49 Kb 45
21 145 Borki 50 Kb 50
22 423 Borów 50 La 50
62 307 Borzykowo 49 Ka 45
14 500 Braniewo 38 Ja 47
17 120 Brańsk 50 Ka 50
87 300 Brodnica 49 Jab 47
68 343 Brody 48 Kb 42
07 306 Brok 50 Ka 49
05 610 Broniszew 50 Kb 48
89 632 Brusy 37 Jab 45
49 300 Brzeg 49 La 45
56 120 Brzeg Dolny 49 Kb 44
28 304 Brzegi 50 La 48
32 800 Brzesko 62 Lb 48
96 140 Brzeziny 50 Kb 47
86 061 Brzoza 49 Jab 46
36 200 Brzozów 62 Lb 50
98 113 Buczek 49 Kb 47
64 840 Budzyń 49 Ka 44
64 320 Buk 49 Ka 44
38 505 Bukowsko 62 Lb 50
28 100 Busko-Zdrój 50 La 48
66 510 Buszów 48 Ka 43
46 220 Byczyna 49 Kb 46
85 001 Bydgoszcz 49 Jab 45
57 500 Bystrzyca Kłodzka 49 La 44
41 900 Bytom 49 La 46
77 100 Bytów 37 Ja 45
74 520 Cedynia 48 Ka 42
84 100 Celbowo 37 Ja 46
08 322 Ceranów 50 Ka 50
72 342 Cerkwica 36 Ja 43
97 421 Chabielice 49 Kb 47
22 100 Chełm/Krasnystaw 51 Kb 51
86 200 Chełmno 49 Jab 46
87 140 Chełmża 49 Jab 46
66 624 Chlebowo 48 Ka 42
26 020 Chmielnik 50 La 48
34 513 Chochołów 62 Lb 47
59 140 Chocianów 49 Kb 43
96 213 Chociw 50 Kb 48
73 120 Chociwel 48 Jab 43
87 860 Chodecz 49 Ka 47
24 210 Chodel 50 Kb 50
08 100 Chodów 50 Ka 50
64 800 Chodzież 49 Ka 44
74 500 Chojna 48 Ka 42
89 600 Chojnice 37 Jab 45
59 225 Chojnów 49 Kb 43
41 500 Chorzów 49 La 47
73 200 Choszczno 48 Jab 43
16 003 Chraboly 50 Jab 50
32 500 Chrzanów 61 La 47
83 306 Chwaszczyno 37 Ja 46
62 404 Ciążeń 49 Ka 45
18 230 Ciechanowiec 50 Ka 50
06 400 Ciechanów 50 Ka 48
87 720 Ciechocinek 49 Ka 46
19 212 Ciemnoszyje 50 Jab 50

37 611 Cieszanów 50 La 51
56 330 Cieszków 49 Kb 45
43 400 Cieszyn 61 Lb 46
34 350 Cięcina 61 Lb 47
19 405 Cimochy 38 Jab 50
36 105 Cmolas 50 La 49
66 630 Cybinka 48 Ka 42
22 140 Cyców 50 Kb 51
83 100 Czarlin 37 Ja 46
16 020 Czarna Białostocka
      50 Jab 51
77 116 Czarna Dąbrówka 37 Ja 45
83 262 Czarna Woda 37 Jab 46
77 330 Czarne 37 Jab 44
64 700 Czarnków 49 Ka 44
98 310 Czarnożyły 49 Kb 46
34 470 Czarny Dunajec 62 Lb 47
17 304 Czartajew 50 Ka 50
43 500 Czechowice-Dziedzice
      61 Lb 46
64 020 Czempiń 49 Ka 44
59 731 Czerna 48 Kb 43
87 640 Czernikowo 49 Ka 46
89 650 Czersk 37 Jab 45
09445 Czerwińsk nad Wisłą
      50 Ka 48
44 230 Czerwionka-Leszczyny
      61 La 46
42 200 Częstochowa 49 La 47
78 630 Człopa 49 Jab 44
77 300 Człuchów 49 Jab 45
18 220 Czyżew-Osada 50 Ka 50
38 525 Daliowa 62 Lb 49
76 150 Darłowo 37 Ja 44
76 150 Darłówko 37 Ja 44
99 107 Daszyna 49 Ka 47
11 430 Dąb 50 Jab 48
62 660 Dąbie/Koło 49 Ka 46
70 001 Dąbie/Szczecin 48 Jab 42
88 306 Dąbrowa/Mogilno 49 Ka 45
16 200 Dąbrowa Białostocka
      38 Jab 51
41 300 Dąbrowa Górnicza 49 La 47
33 200 Dąbrowa Tarnowska
      62 La 48
14 120 Dąbrówno 50 Jab 48
77 310 Debrzno 49 Jab 45
39 200 Dębica 62 La 49
08 520 Dęblin 50 Kb 49
74 400 Dębno/Gorzów Wielkopolski
      48 Ka 42
98 281 Dębołęka 49 Kb 46
12 100 Dębówko 50 Jab 48
55 090 Długołęka 49 Kb 45
32 410 Dobczyce 62 Lb 48
66 520 Dobiegniew 49 Ka 43
72 010 Dobieszczyn 48 Jab 42
62 730 Dobra 49 Kb 46
72 210 Dobra/Nowogard 48 Jab 43
05 307 Dobre 50 Ka 49
11 040 Dobre Miasto 38 Jab 48
42 780 Dobrodzień 49 La 46
29 121 Dobromierz 50 La 47
98 150 Dobroń 49 Kb 47
28 152 Dobrowoda 50 La 48
09 522 Dobrzyków 50 Ka 47

63 140 Dolsk 49 Kb 45
21 516 Dołhobrody 50 Kb 51
38 607 Dołżyca 62 Lb 50
36 230 Domaradz 62 Lb 49
73 220 Drawno 49 Jab 43
64 733 Drawsko 49 Ka 44
78 500 Drawsko Pomorskie
      49 Jab 43
21 355 Drelów 50 Kb 50
77 203 Dretyń 37 Ja 44
66 530 Drezdenko 49 Ka 43
09 210 Drobin 50 Ka 47
05 651 Drwalew 50 Kb 49
12 240 Drygały 38 Jab 50
62 661 Drzewce 49 Ka 46
38 428 Drzewiany 37 Jab 44
37 750 Dubiecko 62 Lb 50
19 411 Dunajek 38 Ja 50
37 551 Duńkowice 62 Lb 50
64 550 Duszniki 49 Ka 44
78 113 Dygowo 37 Ja 43
46 043 Dylaki 49 La 46
07 422 Dylewo 50 Jab 49
17 306 Dziadkowice 50 Ka 50
13 200 Działdowo 50 Jab 48
98 620 Działoszyn 49 Kb 46
82 440 Dzierzgoń 37 Jab 47
58 200 Dzierżoniów 49 La 44
32 008 Dziewin 62 La 48
72 420 Dziwnów 36 Ja 42
12 120 Dźwierzuty 38 Jab 48
83 312 Egiertowo 37 Ja 46
82 300 Elbląg 37 Ja 47
19 300 Ełk 38 Jab 50
97 568 Fałków 50 Kb 48
21 136 Firlej 50 Kb 50
85 900 Fordon 49 Jab 46
23 440 Frampol 50 La 50
16 507 Frącki 38 Jab 51
14 530 Frombork 38 Ja 47
24 180 Garbów 50 Kb 50
82 520 Gardeja 49 Jab 46
08 400 Garwolin 50 Kb 49
78 226 Gawroniec 37 Jab 44
09 530 Gąbin 50 Ka 47
80 001 Gdańsk 37 Ja 46
32 420 Gdów 62 Lb 48
81 001 Gdynia 37 Ja 46
42 272 Gidle 49 La 47
22 454 Giełczew 50 La 50
63 308 Gizałki 49 Ka 45
11 500 Giżycko 38 Ja 49
06 450 Glinojeck 50 Ka 48
44 100 Gliwice 49 La 46
14 521 Głębock 38 Ja 48
67 200 Głogów 49 Kb 44
26 903 Głowaczów 50 Kb 49
95 015 Głowno 50 Kb 47
48 100 Głubczyce 61 La 45
83 220 Głuche 37 Jab 46
48 340 Głuchołazy 49 La 45
46 134 Głuszyca 49 La 44
83 140 Gniew 37 Jab 46
88 140 Gniewkowo 49 Ka 46
62 200 Gniezno 49 Ka 45
14 407 Godkowo 38 Ja 47

83 209 Godziszewo 37 Ja 46
47 320 Gogolin 49 La 46
72 410 Golczewo 36 Jab 42
72 100 Goleniów 48 Jab 42
63 211 Golina/Jarocin 49 Kb 45
62 590 Golina/Konin 49 Ka 46
59 707 Golnice 49 Kb 43
87 400 Golub-Dobrzyń 49 Jab 47
62 130 Gołańcz 49 Ka 45
24 101 Gołąb 50 Kb 49
19 500 Gołdap 38 Ja 50
63 322 Gołuchów 49 Kb 45
06 420 Gołymin-Ośrodek 50 Ka 48
08 405 Gończyce 50 Kb 49
38 300 Gorlice 62 Lb 49
66 400 Gorzów Wielkopolski
      48 Ka 43
64 425 Gorzyń 49 Ka 43
78 627 Gostomia 49 Jab 44
09 500 Gostynin 49 Ka 47
63 800 Gostyń 49 Kb 45
84 241 Gościcino 37 Ja 46
84 241 Gościno 37 Ja 43
56 200 Góra/Głogów 49 Kb 44
09 431 Góra/Płock 50 Ka 48
05 530 Góra Kalwaria 50 Kb 49
69 113 Górzyca 48 Ka 42
63 520 Grabów nad Prosną
      49 Kb 46
21 222 Grabówka 50 Kb 51
19 200 Grajewo 38 Jab 50
49 200 Grodków 49 La 45
05 825 Grodzisk Mazowiecki
      50 Ka 48
62 065 Grodzisk Wielkopolski
      49 Ka 44
13 204 Gródki 50 Jab 48
05 600 Grójec 50 Kb 48
06 460 Grudusk 50 Jab 48
86 300 Grudziądz 49 Jab 46
33 330 Grybów 62 Lb 48
72 300 Gryfice 38 Jab 43
74 100 Gryfino 48 Jab 42
59 620 Gryfów Śląski 48 Kb 43
78 450 Grzmiąca 37 Jab 44
66 620 Gubin 48 Kb 42
78 422 Gwda Mała 37 Jab 44
17 200 Hajnówka 50 Ka 51
37 413 Harasiuki 50 La 50
84 150 Hel 37 Ja 46
22 500 Hrubieszów 51 La 51
36 024 Hyżne 62 Lb 50
14 200 Iława 49 Jab 47
68 120 Iłowa 48 Kb 43
88 100 Inowrocław 49 Ka 46
76 003 Iwięcino 37 Ja 44
87 865 Izbica Kujawska 49 Ka 46
83 211 Jabłowo 37 Jab 46
46 034 Jagienna 49 Ka 45
22 151 Janów/Chełm 50 Kb 51
42 253 Janów/Częstochowa
      49 La 47
16 130 Janów/Mońki 50 Jab 51
98 311 Janów/Wieluń 49 Kb 46
23 300 Janów Lubelski 50 La 50
63 200 Jarocin 49 Kb 45

POSTALI · ÍNDICE CON CÓDIGOS POSTALES · INDICE DE LUGARES COM CÓDIGOS POSTAIS ·
MÍST S PSČ · ZOZNAM OBCÍ S PSČ · INDEKS MIEJSCOWOŚCI Z KOD POCZTOWY

172

Jarosław   PL   **Mielno**   PL

37 500 Jarosław 62 La 50	63 507 Kobyla Góra 49 Kb 45	66 435 Krzeszyce 48 Ka 43	59 600 Lwówek Śląski 49 Kb 43
68 320 Jasień 48 Kb 43	63 740 Kobylin 49 Kb 45	16 400 Krzywe 38 Ja 51	89 210 Łabiszyn 49 Ka 45
38 200 Jasło 62 Lb 49	09 455 Kobylniki 50 Ka 48	64 010 Krzywiń 49 Kb 44	22 437 Łabunie 50 La 51
21 002 Jastków 50 Kb 50	05 230 Kobyłka 50 Ka 49	28 503 Krzyż 50 La 48	55 061 Łagiewniki 49 La 44
64 915 Jastrowie 49 Jab 44	21 150 Kock 50 Kb 50	64 761 Krzyż Wielkopolski 49 Ka 44	99 306 Łanięta 49 Ka 47
44 330 Jastrzębie-Zdrój 61 Lb 46	42 233 Kokawa 49 La 47	32 210 Książ Wielki 50 La 48	37 100 Łańcut 62 La 50
21 120 Jawidz 50 Kb 50	36 100 Kolbuszowa 50 La 49	63 130 Książ Wielkopolski 49 Ka 45	18 100 Łapy 50 Ka 50
59 400 Jawor 49 Kb 44	12 500 Kolno 50 Jab 49	21 550 Kukuryki 50 Ka 51	86 320 Łasin 49 Jab 47
32 510 Jaworzno 61 La 47	97 140 Koluszki 50 Kb 47	46 082 Kup 49 La 45	98 100 Łask 49 Kb 47
26 660 Jedlińsk 50 Kb 49	38 213 Kołaczyce 62 Lb 49	18 317 Kurpiki 50 Jab 50	22 650 Łaszczów 51 La 51
18 420 Jedwabne 50 Jab 50	77 140 Kołczygłowy 37 Ja 45	37 303 Kurylówka 50 La 50	09 520 Łąck 50 Ka 47
12 122 Jedwabno 50 Jab 48	62 600 Koło 49 Ka 46	99 300 Kutno 49 Ka 47	84 360 Łeba 37 Ja 45
58 500 Jelenia Góra 49 La 43	78 100 Kołobrzeg 37 Ja 43	76 252 Kwakowo 37 Ja 45	21 010 Łęczna 50 Kb 50
37 310 Jelna 50 La 50	42 230 Koniecpol 50 La 47	82 500 Kwidzyn 37 Jab 46	99 100 Łęczyca/Ozorków 49 Ka 47
64 006 Jerka 49 Kb 44	62 500 Konin 49 Ka 46	11 008 Kwiecewo 38 Jab 48	73 112 Łęczyca/Stargard Szczeciński
11 320 Jeziorany 38 Jab 48	78 500 Konotop/Drawsko Pomorskie	26 025 Lagów 50 La 49	48 Jab 43
12 213 Jeże 50 Jab 49	49 Jab 43	86 130 Laskowice 49 Jab 46	97 412 Łękawa 49 Kb 47
16 073 Jeżewo 50 Jab 50	68 134 Konotop/Zielona Góra	62 406 Lądek 49 Ka 45	62 105 Łękno 49 Ka 45
37430 Jeżowe 50 La 50	49 Kb 43	05 118 Legionowo 50 Ka 48	73 150 Łobez 49 Jab 43
96 134 Jeżów 50 Kb 47	05 510 Konstancin-Jeziorna	59 200 Legnica 49 Kb 44	89 310 Łobżenica 49 Jab 45
28 300 Jędrzejów 50 La 48	50 Ka 49	09 212 Lelice 50 Ka 47	07 130 Łochów 50 Ka 49
05 410 Józefów 50 Ka 49	21 543 Konstantynów 50 Ka 51	42 235 Lelów 50 La 47	34 325 Łodygowice 61 Lb 47
16 053 Juszkowy Gród 51 Ka 51	95 050 Konstantynów Łódzki	64 100 Leszno 49 Kb 44	21 532 Łomazy 50 Kb 51
07 420 Kadzidło 50 Jab 49	49 Kb 47	59 820 Leśna 48 Kb 43	05 092 Łomianki 50 Ka 48
19 314 Kalinowo 38 Jab 50	26 200 Końskie 50 Kb 48	49 340 Lewin Brzeski 49 La 45	18 400 Łomża 50 Jab 50
62 800 Kalisz 49 Kb 46	27 660 Koprzywnica 50 La 49	37 300 Leżajsk 50 La 50	08 200 Łosice 50 Ka 50
78 540 Kalisz Pomorski 49 Jab 43	49 137 Korfantów 49 La 45	84 300 Lębork 37 Ja 45	99 400 Łowicz 50 Ka 47
05 310 Kałuszyn 50 Ka 49	83 409 Korne 37 Ja 45	64 916 Lędyczek 49 Jab 44	90 001 Łódź 49 Kb 47
58 400 Kamienna Góra 49 La 44	86 010 Koronowo 49 Jab 45	72 350 Lędzin 36 Ja 43	62 260 Łubowo/Gniezno 49 Ka 45
97 360 Kamiensk 50 Kb 47	11 430 Korsze 38 Ja 49	13 320 Lidzbark 50 Jab 47	78 445 Łubowo/Złocieniec
36 053 Kamień/Nowa Dęba	16 140 Korycin 50 Jab 51	11 100 Lidzbark Warmiński	49 Jab 44
50 La 50	32 088 Korzkiew 62 La 47	38 Ja 48	27 641 Łukawa 50 La 49
87 605 Kamień Kotowy 49 Ka 47	08 330 Kosów-Lacki 50 Ka 50	34 600 Limanowa 62 Lb 48	21 400 Łuków 50 Kb 50
72 400 Kamień Pomorski 36 Jab 42	66 470 Kostrzyn 48 Ka 42	74 240 Lipiany 48 Jab 42	14 105 Łukta 38 Jab 48
96 331 Kamion 50 Kb 48	75 001 Koszalin 37 Ja 44	77 420 Lipka 49 Jab 45	07 437 Łyse 50 Jab 49
05 480 Karczew 50 Ka 49	64 000 Kościan 49 Ka 44	87 212 Lipnica/Golub-Dobrzyń	99 420 Łyszkowice 50 Kb 47
66 120 Kargowa 49 Ka 43	62 604 Kościelec 49 Ka 46	49 Jab 47	08 480 Maciejowice 50 Kb 49
78 230 Karlino 37 Ja 43	83 400 Kościerzyna 37 Ja 45	77 130 Lipnica/Miastko 37 Jab 45	26 910 Magnuszew 50 Kb 49
83 300 Kartuzy 37 Ja 46	87 820 Kowal 49 Ka 47	64 111 Lipno 49 Ka 47	98 600 Makowiska 49 Kb 47
84 120 Karwia 37 Ja 46	19 420 Kowale Oleckie 38 Ja 50	87 600 Lipno 49 Ka 47	06 200 Maków Mazowiecki
67 416 Kaszczor 49 Kb 44	87 410 Kowalewo Pomorskie	16 315 Lipsk 38 Jab 51	50 Ka 49
40 001 Katowice 49 La 47	49 Jab 46	27 300 Lipsko 50 Kb 49	34 220 Maków Podhalański
55 080 Kąty Wrocławskie	58 530 Kowary 49 La 43	86 230 Lisewo 49 Jab 46	62 Lb 47
49 Kb 44	19 500 Kozaki 38 Ja 50	21 515 Liszna 51 Kb 51	82 200 Malbork 37 Ja 47
89 240 Kcynia 49 Ka 45	26 900 Kozienice 50 Kb 49	07 121 Liw 50 Ka 49	39 331 Malinie 50 La 49
47 200 Kędzierzyn-Koźle 49 La 46	63 720 Koźmin Wielkopolski	86 141 Lniano 49 Jab 46	17 136 Malinniki 50 Ka 51
77 230 Kępice 37 Ja 44	49 Kb 45	37 600 Lubaczów 50 La 51	07 320 Małkinia Górna 50 Ka 50
63 600 Kępno 49 Kb 45	67 120 Kożuchów 49 Kb 43	59 800 Lubań 48 Kb 43	64 830 Margonin 49 Ka 45
11 400 Kętrzyn 38 Ja 49	62 035 Kórnik 49 Ka 45	21 100 Lubartów 50 Kb 50	05 270 Marki 50 Ka 49
32 650 Kęty 61 Lb 47	77 430 Krajenka 49 Jab 44	64 720 Lubasz 49 Ka 44	14 121 Marwałd 50 Jab 47
25 001 Kielce 50 La 48	30 000 Kraków 62 La 47	14 260 Lubawa 50 Jab 47	22 160 Marynin 50 Kb 51
87 620 Kikół 49 Ka 47	06 212 Krasnosielc 50 Jab 49	58 420 Lubawka 49 La 43	72 130 Maszewo 48 Jab 43
14 220 Kisielice 49 Jab 47	22 300 Krasnystaw 50 La 51	36 042 Lubenia 62 Lb 49	86 013 Mąkowarsko 49 Jab 45
18 405 Kisielnica 50 Jab 50	23 200 Kraśnik 50 La 50	66 628 Lubiatów 48 Kb 43	38 606 Mchawa 62 Lb 50
62 540 Kleczew 49 Ka 46	78 446 Krągi 49 Jab 44	59 300 Lubin 49 Kb 44	06 315 Mchowo 50 Jab 48
17 250 Kleszczele 50 Ka 51	63 840 Krobia 49 Kb 44	20 001 Lublin 50 Kb 50	06 445 Mdzewo 50 Ka 48
27 640 Klimontów 50 La 49	38 400 Krosno 62 Lb 49	42 700 Lubliniec 49 La 46	89 631 Męcikał 37 Jab 45
46 200 Kluczbork 49 La 46	66 600 Krosno Odrzańskie	69 210 Lubniewice 48 Ka 43	76 231 Mianowice 37 Ja 45
97 522 Kluczewsko 50 La 47	48 Ka 43	78 607 Lubno 49 Jab 44	77 200 Miastko 37 Jab 44
83 321 Klukowa Huta 37 Ja 45	99 340 Krośniewice 49 Ka 47	62 030 Luboń 49 Ka 44	16 050 Michałowo 50 Jab 51
66 415 Kłodawa/Gorzów	63 700 Krotoszyn 49 Kb 45	56 208 Luboszyce 49 Kb 44	28 411 Michałów 50 La 48
Wielkopolski 48 Ka 43	11 612 Kruklanki 38 Ja 49	87 890 Lubraniec 49 Ka 46	32 200 Miechów 50 La 48
62 650 Kłodawa/Koło 49 Ka 46	88 150 Kruszwica 49 Ka 46	68 300 Lubsko 48 Kb 42	26 211 Miedzierza 50 Kb 48
57 300 Kłodzko 49 La 44	82 120 Krynica Morska 37 Ja 47	38 112 Lutcza 62 Lb 49	63 910 Miejska Górka 49 Kb 44
44 190 Knurów 61 La 46	16 120 Krynki 51 Jab 51	99 135 Lutomiersk 49 Kb 47	39 300 Mielec 50 La 49
16 015 Knyszyn 50 Jab 50	42 160 Krzepice 49 La 46	64 310 Lwówek 49 Ka 44	76 032 Mielno 37 Ja 44

74 133 Mieszkowice 48 Ka 42	76 241 Nowa Dąbrowa 37 Ja 45	27 400 Ostrowiec Świętokrzyski	24 320 Poniatowa 50 Kb 50
56 513 Międzybórz 49 Kb 45	39 460 Nowa Dęba 50 La 49	50 La 49	07 442 Ponikiew Duża 50 Ka 49
64 400 Międzychód 49 Ka 43	83 404 Nowa Karczma 37 Ja 46	14 100 Ostróda 38 Jab 47	07 205 Porządzie 50 Ka 49
21 350 Międzyrzec Podlaski	57 400 Nowa Ruda 49 La 44	21 110 Ostrów Lubelski 50 Kb 50	18 112 Poświętne 50 Ka 50
50 Kb 50	67 100 Nowa Sól 49 Kb 43	07 300 Ostrów Mazowiecka	22 653 Poturzyn 51 La 51
66 300 Międzyrzecz 49 Ka 43	19 321 Nowa Wieś Ełcka 38 Jab 50	50 Ka 49	26 414 Potworów 50 Kb 48
72 500 Międzyzdroje 36 Jab 42	86 170 Nowe 49 Jab 46	63 400 Ostrów Wielkopolski	11 610 Pozezdrze 38 Ja 49
11 730 Mikołajki 38 Jab 49	32 120 Nowe Brzesko 62 La 48	49 Kb 45	60 001 Poznań 49 Ka 44
05 822 Milanówek 50 Ka 48	67 124 Nowe Miasteczko 49 Kb 43	63 500 Ostrzeszów 49 Kb 45	82 550 Prabuty 37 Jab 47
17 332 Milejczyce 50 Ka 51	09 120 Nowe Miasto 50 Ka 48	69 220 Ośno Lubuskie 48 Ka 42	46 320 Praszka 49 Kb 46
56 300 Milicz 49 Kb 45	13 300 Nowe Miasto Lubawskie	32 600 Ościęcim 61 La 47	59 230 Prochowice 49 Kb 44
34 360 Milówka 61 Lb 47	49 Jab 47	05 400 Otwock 50 Ka 49	48 200 Prudnik 49 La 45
14 310 Miłakowo 38 Ja 48	63 460 Nowe Skalmierzyce	19 227 Owieczki 50 Jab 50	55 110 Prusice 49 Kb 44
62 733 Miłkowice 49 Kb 46	49 Kb 45	46 040 Ozimek 49 La 46	83 000 Pruszcz Gdański 37 Ja 46
14 140 Miłomłyn 38 Jab 47	72 022 Nowe Warpno 36 Jab 42	95 035 Ozorków 49 Kb 47	05 800 Pruszków 50 Ka 48
62 320 Miłosław 49 Ka 45	72 200 Nowogard 36 Jab 43	95 200 Pabianice 49 Kb 47	06 300 Przasnysz 50 Jab 48
05 300 Mińsk Mazowiecki 50 Ka 49	18 514 Nowogród 50 Jab 49	98 600 Pajęczno 49 Kb 46	16 422 Przedbórz 50 Kb 47
37 200 Mirocin 62 La 50	66 010 Nowogród Bobrzański	88 170 Pakość 49 Ka 46	59 170 Przemków 49 Kb 43
78 650 Mirosławiec 49 Jab 44	48 Kb 43	42 140 Panki 49 La 46	37 700 Przemyśl 62 Lb 50
59 870 Mirsk 48 La 43	17 211 Nowosady 50 Ka 51	37 224 Pantalowice 62 Lb 50	21 202 Przewłoka 50 Kb 50
06 500 Mława 50 Jab 48	82 100 Nowy Dwór Gdański	07 102 Paplin 50 Ka 49	37 200 Przeworsk 62 La 50
14 420 Młynary 38 Ja 47	37 Ja 47	21 200 Parczew 50 Kb 50	72 110 Przybiernów 36 Jab 42
09 214 Mochowo 49 Ka 47	05 100 Nowy Dwór Mazowiecki	42 164 Parzymiechy 49 Kb 46	49 351 Przylesie 49 La 45
18 230 Moczydły 50 Ka 50	50 Ka 48	14 400 Pasłęk 38 Ja 47	26 400 Przysucha 50 Kb 48
05 640 Mogielnica 50 Kb 48	38 545 Nowy Łupków 62 Lb 50	12 130 Pasym 38 Jab 48	21 146 Przytoczno 50 Kb 50
88 300 Mogilno 49 Ka 45	33 300 Nowy Sącz 62 Lb 48	89 100 Paterek 49 Jab 45	18 423 Przytuły 50 Jab 50
08 124 Mokobody 50 Ka 50	34 400 Nowy Targ 62 Lb 48	17 124 Patoki 50 Ka 50	26 650 Przytyk 50 Kb 48
13 324 Montowo 50 Jab 47	64 300 Nowy Tomyśl 49 Ka 44	11 015 Pawłowo 50 Jab 48	84 100 Puck 37 Ja 46
19 100 Mońki 50 Jab 50	38 230 Nowy Żmigród 62 Lb 49	83 130 Pelplin 37 Jab 46	24 100 Puławy 50 Kb 49
26 026 Morawica 50 La 48	18 322 Nur 50 Ka 50	73 205 Piasecznik 48 Jab 43	06 100 Pułtusk 50 Ka 49
14 300 Morąg 38 Jab 47	48 300 Nysa 49 La 45	05 500 Piaseczno 50 Ka 49	39 205 Pustków 62 La 49
08 140 Mordy 50 Ka 50	64 600 Oborniki 49 Ka 44	21 050 Piaski 50 Kb 50	55 040 Pustków Wilczkowski
14 100 Morliny 38 Jab 47	55 120 Oborniki Śląskie 49 Kb 44	99 120 Piątek 49 Ka 47	49 La 44
62 050 Mosina 49 Ka 44	64 520 Obrzycko 49 Ka 44	58 573 Piechowice 49 La 43	74 200 Pyrzyce 48 Jab 42
76 011 Mostowo 37 Ja 44	23 413 Obsza 50 La 50	11 710 Piecki 38 Jab 49	34 700 Rabka Zdrój 62 Lb 47
11 700 Mrągowo 38 Jab 49	63 430 Odolanów 49 Kb 45	26 065 Piekoszów 50 La 48	09 140 Raciąż 50 Ka 48
89 115 Mrocza 49 Jab 45	26 425 Odrzywół 50 Kb 48	14 520 Pieniężno 38 Ja 48	87 721 Raciążek 49 Ka 46
34 730 Mszana Dolna 62 Lb 48	06 456 Ojrzeń 50 Ka 48	11 223 Pieszkowo 38 Ja 48	22 136 Raciborowice 51 La 51
08 200 Mszanna 50 Ka 50	64 965 Okonek 49 Jab 44	58 250 Pieszyce 49 La 44	47 400 Racibórz 61 La 46
96 320 Mszczonów 50 Kb 48	23 231 Olbięcin 50 La 50	39 220 Pilzno 62 Lb 49	16 420 Raczki 38 Jab 50
76 031 Mścice 37 Ja 44	19 400 Olecko 38 Ja 50	64 920 Piła 49 Jab 44	33 130 Radłów 62 La 48
62 095 Murowana-Goślina 49 Ka 45	46 300 Olesno 49 La 46	28 400 Pińczów 50 La 48	26 600 Radom 50 Kb 48
33 370 Muszyna 62 Lb 48	37 630 Oleszyce 50 La 51	26 670 Pionki 50 Kb 49	97 500 Radomsko 49 Kb 47
41 400 Mysłowice 49 La 47	56 400 Oleśnica 49 Kb 45	28 111 Piotrkowice 50 La 48	59 160 Radwanice 49 Kb 43
42 300 Myszków 49 La 47	38 622 Olszanica 62 Lb 50	97 300 Piotrków Trybunalski	88 200 Radziejów 49 Ka 46
07 430 Myszyniec 50 Jab 49	42 256 Olsztyn/Częstochowa	50 Kb 47	19 213 Radziłów 50 Jab 50
32 400 Myślenice 62 Lb 47	49 La 47	12 200 Pisz 38 Jab 49	05 250 Radzymin 50 Ka 49
74 300 Myślibórz 48 Ka 42	10 001 Olsztyn/Ostróda 38 Jab 48	12 160 Piwnice Wielkie 50 Jab 48	86 333 Radzyń Chełmiński
89 100 Nakło nad Notecią	11 015 Olsztynek 50 Jab 48	63 300 Pleszew 49 Kb 45	49 Jab 46
49 Jab 45	55 200 Oława 49 La 45	09400 Płock 50 Ka 47	21 300 Radzyń Podlaski 50 Kb 50
46 100 Namysłów 49 Kb 45	64 330 Opalenica 49 Ka 44	22 426 Płonka 50 La 50	19 206 Rajgród 38 Jab 50
13 242 Napierki 50 Jab 48	28 520 Opatowiec 50 La 48	09 100 Płońsk 50 Ka 48	62 067 Rakoniewice 49 Ka 44
56 202 Naratów 49 Kb 44	27 500 Opatów 50 La 49	72 310 Płoty 36 Jab 43	27 435 Raków 50 La 49
17 210 Narew 50 Ka 51	62 860 Opatówek 49 Kb 46	62 045 Pniewy/Międzychód	37 111 Rakszawa 50 La 50
17 220 Narewka 51 Ka 51	26 300 Opoczno 50 Kb 48	49 Ka 44	36 130 Raniżów 50 La 49
37 610 Narol 50 La 51	45 001 Opole 49 La 45	99 200 Poddębice 49 Kb 46	96 200 Rawa Mazowiecka 50 Kb 48
09 152 Naruszewo 50 Ka 48	24 300 Opole Lubelskie 50 Kb 49	64 965 Podgaje 49 Jab 44	63 900 Rawicz 49 Kb 44
06 130 Nasielsk 50 Ka 48	11 130 Orneta 38 Ja 48	70 405 Podjuchy 48 Jab 42	34 700 Rdzawka 62 Lb 47
33 335 Nawojowa 62 Lb 48	12 250 Orzysz 38 Jab 49	76 010 Polanów 37 Ja 44	73 210 Recz 49 Jab 43
13 100 Nidzica 50 Jab 48	86 150 Osie 49 Jab 46	33 385 Polany 62 Lb 48	84 240 Reda 37 Ja 46
97 341 Niechcice 50 Kb 47	64 113 Osieczna 49 Kb 44	72 010 Police 48 Jab 42	62 093 Rejowiec 49 Ka 45
24 222 Niedrzwica Kościelna	59 724 Osiecznica 48 Kb 43	23 316 Polichna 50 La 50	06 330 Rembielin 50 Jab 48
50 Kb 50	28 221 Osiek 50 La 49	59 100 Polkowice 49 Kb 44	73 310 Resko 36 Jab 43
49 100 Niemodlin 49 La 45	88 220 Osięciny 49 Ka 46	64 710 Pojałwie 49 Ka 44	11 440 Reszel 38 Ja 49
26 205 Nieświń 50 Kb 48	07 400 Ostrołęka 50 Jab 49	28 230 Połaniec 50 La 49	42 242 Rędziny 49 La 47
37 400 Nisko 50 La 50	64 560 Ostroróg 49 Ka 44	78 320 Połczyn Zdrój 37 Jab 44	32 311 Rodaki 50 La 47

POSTALI · ÍNDICE CON CÓDIGOS POSTALES · INDICE DE LUGARES COM CÓDIGOS POSTAIS ·
MÍST S PSČ · ZOZNAM OBCÍ S PSČ · INDEKS MIEJSCOWOŚCI Z KOD POCZTOWY

174

Rogowo PL   **Tuliszków** PL

88 420 Rogowo 49 Ka 45	76 004 Sianów 37 Ja 44	82 220 Stare Pole 37 Ja 47	87 800 Szpetal Górny 49 Ka 47
64 610 Rogożno 49 Ka 45	55 011 Siechnice 49 Kb 45	67 412 Stare Strącze 49 Kb 44	67 300 Szprotawa 49 Kb 43
96 135 Rogów 50 Kb 47	08 100 Siedlce 50 Ka 50	73 100 Stargard Szczeciński	16 310 Sztabin 38 Jab 51
39 100 Ropczyce 62 La 49	66 613 Siedlisko/Krosno Odrzańskie	48 Jab 43	82 400 Sztum 37 Jab 47
76 042 Rosnowo 37 Ja 44	48 Ka 42	73 312 Stargard 37 Jab 43	89 200 Szubin 49 Jab 45
07 433 Rozogi 50 Jab 49	64 910 Siedlisko/Trzcianka	83 200 Starogard Gdański	26 500 Szydłowiec 50 Kb 48
57 530 Roztoki 61 La 44	49 Ka 44	37 Jab 46	14 241 Szymbark 49 Jab 47
74 312 Rów 48 Ka 42	28 200 Sielec 50 La 49	21 134 Staroścín 50 Kb 50	59 330 Ścinawa 49 Kb 44
06 230 Różan 50 Ka 49	17 300 Siemiatycze 50 Ka 50	09 440 Starożreby 50 Ka 47	62 561 Ślesin 49 Ka 46
66 146 Różanki 48 Ka 43	05 332 Siennica 50 Ka 49	82 450 Stary Dzierzgoń 37 Jab 47	89 530 Śliwice 37 Jab 46
12 220 Ruciane-Nida 38 Jab 49	98 200 Sieradz 49 Kb 46	99 220 Stary Gostków 49 Kb 47	64 030 Śmigiel 49 Ka 44
11 513 Ruda 38 Jab 49	64 410 Sieraków 49 Ka 44	26 805 Stary Gózd 50 Kb 49	64 811 Śmiłowo 49 Jab 44
59 305 Rudna 49 Kb 44	42 437 Sierbowice 50 La 47	33 340 Stary Sącz 62 Lb 48	18 411 Śniadowo 50 Jab 49
27 230 Rudnik/Starachowice	09 200 Sierpc 50 Ka 47	06 220 Stary Szelków 50 Ka 49	63 100 Śrem 49 Ka 45
50 La 49	42 267 Silniczka 50 La 47	28 200 Staszów 50 La 49	55 300 Środa Śląska 49 Kb 44
37 420 Rudnik/Nisko 50 La 50	26 640 Skaryszew 50 Kb 49	11 034 Stawiguda 38 Jab 48	63 000 Środa Wielkopolska
21 201 Rudno/Parczew 50 Kb 50	26 100 Skarżysko Kamienna	83 430 Stawiska 37 Ja 46	49 Ka 45
11 604 Rudziszki 38 Ja 49	50 Kb 48	18 520 Stawiski 50 Jab 50	58 100 Świdnica/Wałbrzych
84 230 Rumia 37 Ja 46	32 050 Skawina 62 Lb 47	26 220 Stąporków 50 Kb 48	49 La 44
98 365 Rusiec 49 Kb 46	66 213 Skąpe 48 Ka 43	82 103 Stegna 37 Ja 47	66 008 Świdnica/Zielona Góra
78 640 Rusinowo 49 Jab 44	87 630 Skępe 49 Ka 47	72 112 Stepnica 48 Jab 42	48 Kb 43
59 950 Ruszów 48 Kb 43	96 100 Skierniewice 50 Kb 48	62 060 Stęszew 49 Ka 44	21 040 Świdnik 50 Kb 50
16 406 Rutka-Tartak 38 Ja 50	62 085 Skoki 49 Ka 45	21 450 Stoczek Łukowski 50 Kb 49	78 300 Świdwin 37 Jab 43
18 321 Rutki Kossaki 50 Jab 50	83 220 Skórcz 37 Jab 46	86 212 Stolno 49 Jab 46	58 160 Świebodzice 49 La 44
44 200 Rybnik 61 La 46	08 114 Skórzec 50 Ka 50	19 325 Straduny 38 Jab 50	66 200 Świebodzin 49 Ka 43
16 064 Ryboły 50 Ka 51	08 306 Skrzeszew 50 Ka 50	95 010 Stryków 50 Kb 47	86 100 Świecie 49 Jab 46
14 411 Rychliki 37 Jab 47	62 560 Skulsk 49 Ka 46	06 123 Strzegocin 50 Ka 48	59 850 Świeradów Zdrój 48 La 43
98 313 Rychłocice 49 Kb 46	66 440 Skwierzyna 49 Ka 43	58 150 Strzegom 49 La 44	58 540 Świerzawa 49 Kb 43
14 106 Rychnowo 50 Jab 48	67 410 Sława 49 Kb 44	66 500 Strzelce Krajeńskie	64 224 Świętno 49 Ka 44
63 630 Rychtal 49 Kb 45	76 100 Sławno 37 Ja 44	49 Ka 43	06 317 Świniary 50 Jab 48
62 570 Rychwał 49 Ka 46	78 314 Sławoborze 37 Jab 43	47 100 Strzelce Opolskie 49 La 46	72 600 Świnoujście 36 Jab 42
34 115 Ryczów 62 Lb 47	62 400 Słupca 49 Ka 45	47 364 Strzeleczki 49 La 45	72 004 Tanowo 48 Jab 42
26 912 Ryczywół 50 Kb 49	09 472 Słupno 50 Ka 47	57 100 Strzelin 49 La 45	21 104 Tarło 50 Kb 50
44 280 Rydułtowy 61 La 46	76 200 Słupsk 37 Ja 45	88 320 Strzelno 49 Ka 46	27 515 Tarłów 50 La 49
18 413 Rydzewo 50 Jab 49	64 825 Smogulec 49 Jab 45	38 100 Strzyżów 62 Lb 49	39 400 Tarnobrzeg 50 La 49
82 514 Ryjewo 37 Jab 46	16 508 Smolany 38 Ja 51	22 230 Stulno 51 Kb 51	23 420 Tarnogród 50 La 50
08 500 Ryki 50 Kb 49	76 214 Smołdzino 37 Ja 45	34 200 Sucha Beskidzka 62 Lb 47	62 080 Tarnowo Podgórne 49 Ka 44
78 125 Rymań 37 Jab 43	22 231 Sobibór 51 Kb 51	73 132 Suchań 48 Jab 43	42 600 Tarnowskie Góry 49 La 46
11 520 Ryn 38 Jab 49	63 450 Sobótka 49 Kb 45	26 030 Suchedniów 50 Kb 48	33 100 Tarnów 62 La 48
87 500 Rypin 49 Jab 47	96 500 Sochaczew 50 Ka 48	77 233 Suchorze 37 Ja 45	83 100 Tczew 37 Ja 46
89 642 Rytel 37 Jab 45	09 110 Sochocin 50 Ka 48	16 150 Suchowola 38 Jab 51	05 240 Tłuszcz 50 Ka 49
33 343 Rytro 62 Lb 48	16 131 Sokolany 50 Jab 51	58 540 Suchów 49 Ka 43	82 340 Tolkmicko 37 Ja 47
77 304 Rzeczenica 37 Jab 45	98 420 Sokolniki 49 Kb 46	97 330 Sulejów 50 Kb 47	18 121 Tołcze 50 Jab 51
34 451 Rzeka 62 Lb 48	36 140 Sokołów Małopolski	05 070 Sulejówek 50 Ka 49	22 600 Tomaszów Lubelski
69 110 Rzepin 48 Ka 42	50 La 50	69 200 Sulęcin 48 Ka 43	51 La 51
35 000 Rzeszów 62 La 49	08 300 Sokołów Podlaski 50 Ka 50	14 240 Susz 37 Jab 47	97 200 Tomaszów Mazowiecki
16 072 Rzędziany 50 Jab 50	18 218 Sokoły 50 Ka 50	16 400 Suwałki 38 Ja 50	50 Kb 48
27 580 Rzuchów 50 La 49	16 100 Sokółka 50 Jab 51	62 020 Swarzędz 49 Ka 45	17 133 Topczewo 50 Ka 50
26 423 Rzuców 50 Kb 48	86 050 Solec Kujawski 49 Jab 46	56 500 Syców 49 Kb 45	11 221 Toprzyny 38 Ja 48
89 110 Sadki 49 Jab 45	62 610 Sompolno 49 Ka 46	98 540 Szadek 49 Kb 46	87 100 Toruń 49 Jab 46
27 600 Sandomierz 50 La 49	81 001 Sopot 37 Ja 46	64 500 Szamotuły 49 Ka 44	66 235 Torzym 48 Ka 43
09 540 Sanniki 50 Ka 47	11 731 Sorkwity 38 Jab 49	38 541 Szczawne 62 Lb 50	37 204 Tryńcza 50 La 50
38 500 Sanok 62 Lb 50	41 200 Sosnowiec 49 La 47	34 460 Szczawnica 62 Lb 48	86 011 Tryszczyn 49 Jab 45
26 070 Sarbice 50 La 48	78 531 Sośnica 49 Jab 44	22 460 Szczebrzeszyn 50 La 50	64 980 Trzcianka 49 Jab 44
64 705 Sarbka 49 Ka 44	49 140 Sowin 49 La 45	70 001 Szczecin 48 Jab 42	66 320 Trzciel 49 Ka 43
08 220 Sarnaki 50 Ka 50	12 150 Spychowo 50 Jab 49	78 400 Szczecinek 37 Jab 44	72 320 Trzebiatów 36 Ja 43
42 245 Secemin 50 La 47	11 420 Srokowo 38 Ja 49	42 255 Szczekociny 50 La 47	21 404 Trzebieszów 50 Kb 50
16 500 Sejny 38 Ja 51	37 450 Stalowa Wola 50 La 50	33 230 Szczucin 50 La 49	55 100 Trzebnica 49 Kb 45
05 140 Serock 50 Ka 49	21 422 Stanin 50 Kb 50	19 230 Szczuczyn 50 Jab 50	62 240 Trzemeszno 49 Ka 45
08 116 Seroczyn 50 Ka 49	16 111 Stara Kamionka 50 Jab 51	06 211 Szczuki 50 Ka 48	17 213 Trześcianka 50 Ka 51
21 413 Serokomla 50 Kb 50	83 430 Stara Kiszewa 37 Jab 46	32 820 Szczurowa 62 La 48	89 500 Tuchola 38 Jab 45
39 120 Sędziszów Małopolski	23 104 Stara Wieś 50 La 50	09 227 Szczutowo 49 Ka 47	77 133 Tuchomie 37 Ja 45
62 La 49	27 200 Starachowice 50 Kb 48	12 100 Szczytno 50 Jab 48	33 170 Tuchów 62 Lb 49
38 307 Sękowa 62 Lb 49	17 205 Stare Berezowo 50 Ka 51	11 703 Szestno 38 Jab 49	13 215 Tuczki 50 Jab 47
89 400 Sępólno Krajeńskie	74 106 Stare Czarnowo 48 Jab 42	58 580 Szklarska Poręb 48 La 43	78 640 Tuczno 49 Jab 44
49 Jab 45	66 520 Stare Osieczno 49 Jab 43	67 407 Szlichtyngowa 49 Kb 44	62 740 Tuliszków 49 Ka 46

175

INDEX WITH POST CODES · ORTSREGISTER MIT POSTLEITZAHLEN · INDICE CON CODICI
STEDREGISTER MED POSTNUMRE · PLAATSNAMENREGISTER MET POSTCODE · REJSTŘÍK

PL

RO

Tuplice (PL) · (RO) Brad

68 219 Tuplice 48 Kb 42	22 200 Włodawa 51 Kb 51	57 220 Ziębice 49 La 45
62 700 Turek 49 Ka 46	29 100 Włoszczowa 50 La 47	78 520 Złocieniec 49 Jab 44
22 465 Turobin 50 La 50	28 330 Wodzisław 50 La 48	98 270 Złoczew 49 Kb 46
21 320 Turów 50 Kb 50	44 300 Wodzisław Śląski 61 Lb 46	62 002 Złotniki 49 Ka 44
97 315 Tuszyn 50 Kb 47	32 830 Wojnicz 62 Lb 48	59 500 Złotoryja 49 Kb 43
56 416 Twardogóra 49 Kb 45	06 404 Wola Wierzbowska 50 Ka 48	77 400 Złotów 49 Jab 45
42 690 Tworóg 49 La 46	97 320 Wolbórz 50 Kb 47	22 470 Zwierzyniec 50 La 50
43 100 Tychy 61 La 47	42 340 Wolbrom 50 La 47	26 700 Zwoleń 50 Kb 49
16 080 Tykocin 50 Jab 50	72 510 Wolin 36 Jab 42	28 134 Żabiec 50 La 49
38 535 Tyrawa Wołoska 62 Lb 50	64 200 Wolsztyn 49 Ka 44	74 200 Żabów 48 Jab 42
07 406 Tyszki Nadbory 50 Ka 49	46 250 Wołczyn 49 Kb 46	68 100 Żagań 48 Kb 43
22 510 Uchanie 51 La 51	05 200 Wołomin 50 Ka 49	42 310 Żarki 49 La 47
97 170 Ujazd 50 Kb 47	56 100 Wołów 49 Kb 44	68 200 Żary 48 Kb 43
64 850 Ujście 49 Jab 44	50 900 Wrocław 49 Kb 45	22 305 Żdżanne 50 Kb 51
21 307 Ulan-Majorat 50 Kb 50	64 510 Wronki 49 Ka 44	32 731 Żegocina 62 Lb 48
99 210 Uniejów 49 Kb 46	62 300 Września 49 Ka 45	57 361 Żelazno 49 La 44
22 234 Urszulin 50 Kb 51	67 400 Wschowa 49 Kb 44	08 430 Żelechów 50 Kb 49
76 270 Ustka 37 Ja 44	11 510 Wydminy 38 Jab 50	33 260 Żelichów 50 La 48
78 111 Ustronie Morskie 37 Ja 43	07 430 Wydmusy 50 Jab 49	46 061 Żlinice 49 La 45
43 450 Ustroń 61 Lb 46	88 432 Wylatowo 49 Ka 45	55 140 Żmigród 49 Kb 44
38 700 Ustrzyki Dolne 62 Lb 50	89 300 Wyrzysk 49 Jab 45	88 400 Żnin 49 Ka 45
13 214 Uzdowo 50 Jab 48	23 145 Wysokie/Krásnik 50 La 50	44 240 Żory 61 La 46
97 402 Wadlew 49 Kb 47	19 311 Wysokie/Ełk 38 Jab 50	16 411 Żubryn 38 Ja 50
34 100 Wadowice 62 Lb 47	18 200 Wysokie Mazowieckie	83 330 Żukowo 37 Ja 46
58 300 Wałbrzych 49 La 44	50 Ka 50	22 207 Żuków 50 Kb 51
78 600 Wałcz 49 Jab 44	07 200 Wyszków 50 Ka 49	09 300 Żuromin 50 Jab 47
05 660 Warka 50 Kb 49	09 450 Wyszogród 50 Ka 48	99 320 Żychlin 50 Ka 47
00 001 Warszawa 50 Ka 49	26 811 Wyśmierzyce 50 Kb 48	62 241 Żydowo 49 Ka 45
98 290 Warta 49 Kb 46	16 060 Zabłudów 50 Jab 51	96 300 Żyrardów 50 Ka 48
16 010 Wasilków 50 Jab 51	16 411 Zaboryszki 38 Ja 51	19 505 Żytkiejmy 38 Ja 50
42 119 Ważne Młyny 49 Kb 47	32 840 Zakliczyn 62 Lb 48	34 300 Żywiec 61 Lb 47
87 200 Wąbrzeźno 49 Jab 46	37 470 Zaklików 50 La 50	
62 100 Wągrowiec 49 Ka 45	34 500 Zakopane 62 Lb 47	
56 210 Wąsosz 49 Kb 44	26 652 Zakrzew 50 Kb 48	
24 160 Wąwolnica 50 Kb 50	14 320 Zalewo 37 Jab 47	(RO)
84 200 Wejherowo 37 Ja 46	26 704 Załazy 50 Kb 49	
32 090 Wesoła 50 La 48	89 665 Zamarte 49 Jab 45	515100 Abrud 77 Na 51
11 600 Węgorzewo 38 Ja 49	18 300 Zambrów 50 Ka 50	447005 Acáş 62 Mb 50
73 155 Węgorzyno 49 Jab 43	22 400 Zamość 50 La 51	727005 Adâncata 63 Mb 54
07 100 Węgrów 50 Ka 50	07 211 Zamość 50 Jab 49	625100 Adjud 78 Na 55
84 352 Wicko 37 Ja 45	63 020 Zaniemyśl 49 Ka 45	077010 Afumaţi 78 Oa 54
74 120 Widuchowa 48 Jab 42	33 530 Zarszyn 62 Lb 50	607005 Agăş 63 Na 54
12 160 Wielbark 50 Jab 48	32 640 Zator 62 Lb 47	907015 Agigea 78 Oa 56
64 730 Wieleń 49 Ka 44	42 276 Zawada/Lubliniec 49 La 47	555100 Agnita 77 Nb 52
32 020 Wieliczka 62 Lb 48	96 108 Zawady 50 Ka 48	515200 Aiud 77 Na 51
19 404 Wieliczki 38 Jab 50	46 059 Zawadzkie 49 La 46	510000 Alba Iulia 77 Na 51
86 133 Wielki Lubień 49 Jab 46	27 630 Zawichost 50 La 49	517005 Albac 77 Na 50
98 300 Wieluń 49 Kb 46	59 970 Zawidów 48 Kb 43	107010 Albeşti-Paleologu 77 Oa 54
26 432 Wieniawa 50 Kb 48	42 400 Zawiercie 49 La 47	415100 Aleşd 62 Mb 50
98 400 Wieruszów 49 Kb 46	14 331 Zawroty 38 Jab 47	140000 Alexandria 77 Ob 53
26 680 Wierzbica/Radom 50 Kb 49	41 300 Ząbkowice 49 La 47	317005 Almaş 76 Na 50
22 150 Wierzbica/Chełm 50 Kb 51	57 200 Ząbkowice Śląskie 49 La 44	547035 Aluniş 63 Na 52
23 250 Wierzbica/Kraśnik 50 Kb 50	64 360 Zbąszyń 49 Ka 43	927020 Amara 78 Oa 55
78 411 Wierzchowo 37 Jab 44	62 830 Zbiersk-Cukrownia 49 Kb 46	927025 Andrăşeşti 78 Oa 55
99 233 Wierzchy 49 Kb 46	83 210 Zblewo 37 Ja 46	325100 Anina 76 Nb 49
14 531 Wilczęta 38 Ja 47	08 106 Zbuczyn Poduchowny	137005 Aninoasa 77 Oa 53
08 470 Wilga 50 Kb 49	50 Ka 50	407035 Apahida 63 Na 51
42 295 Winowno 49 La 47	70 001 Zdroje 48 Jab 42	310000 Arad 76 Na 49
56 160 Wińsko 49 Kb 44	63 760 Zduny 49 Kb 45	310144 Aradu Nou 76 Na 49
21 225 Wisznice 50 Kb 51	98 500 Zduńska Wola 49 Kb 46	447020 Ardud 62 Mb 50
28 160 Wiślica 50 La 48	47 330 Zdzieszowice 49 La 46	517040 Arieşeni 76 Na 50
32 412 Wiśniowa 62 Lb 48	11 536 Zelki 38 Jab 50	327005 Armeniş 76 Nb 50
62 425 Witkowo 49 Ka 45	95 100 Zgierz 49 Kb 47	417035 Avram Iancu 76 Na 49
99 335 Witonia 49 Ka 47	59 900 Zgorzelec 48 Kb 43	555200 Avrig 77 Nb 52
84 120 Władysławowo 37 Ja 46	65 001 Zielona Góra 49 Kb 43	557025 Axente Sever 77 Na 52
87 800 Włocławek 49 Ka 47	05 220 Zielonka 50 Ka 49	825100 Babadag 78 Oa 56

		600000 Bacău 64 Na 54
		407055 Baciu 63 Na 51
		827005 Baia 78 Oa 56
		225100 Baia de Aramă 77 Nb 50
		515300 Baia de Arieş 77 Na 51
		337005 Baia de Criş 76 Na 50
		430000 Baia Mare 63 Mb 51
		435100 Baia Sprie 63 Mb 51
		147005 Balaci 77 Oa 52
		927040 Balaciu 78 Oa 54
		235100 Balş 77 Oa 52
		807005 Barcea 78 Nb 55
		905100 Basarabi 78 Oa 56
		117045 Bascov 77 Oa 52
		245100 Băbeni 77 Oa 52
		737050 Băceşti 64 Na 55
		105200 Băicoi 77 Nb 53
		337346 Băieşti 77 Nb 51
		245300 Băile Olăneşti 77 Nb 52
		205100 Băileşti 77 Oa 51
		407065 Băişoara 77 Na 51
		547100 Bălăuşeri 77 Na 52
		217045 Băleşti 77 Nb 51
		617025 Bălţăteşti 63 Mb 54
		907035 Băneasa 78 Oa 55
		817005 Bărăganul 78 Oa 55
		107055 Bărcăneşti 77 Oa 54
		731000 Bârlad 78 Na 55
		317025 Bârsa 76 Na 50
		317030 Bârzava 76 Na 49
		425100 Beclean 63 Mb 52
		415200 Beiuş 76 Na 50
		317040 Beliu 76 Na 49
		457035 Benesat 63 Mb 51
		217067 Bengeşti 77 Nb 51
		127035 Berca 78 Nb 54
		327025 Berzasca 76 Oa 49
		327030 Berzovia 76 Nb 49
		615100 Bicaz 63 Na 54
		617062 Bicaz-Chei 63 Na 53
		307060 Biled 76 Nb 48
		207065 Bistreţ 77 Ob 51
		420000 Bistriţa 63 Mb 52
		707055 Bivolari 64 Mb 55
		515400 Blaj 77 Na 51
		407085 Bobâlna 63 Mb 51
		457040 Bobota 62 Mb 51
		317055 Bocsig 76 Na 49
		325300 Bocşa 76 Nb 49
		105300 Boldeşti-Scăeni 77 Nb 54
		127070 Boldu 78 Nb 55
		407471 Bologa 62 Na 50
		617075 Borca 63 Na 53
		917015 Borcea 78 Oa 55
		927050 Borduşani 78 Oa 55
		727040 Boroaia 63 Mb 54
		417065 Borod 62 Na 50
		535300 Borsec 63 Na 53
		435200 Borşa 63 Mb 53
		617090 Boteşti 64 Mb 54
		147025 Botoroaga 77 Oa 53
		710000 Botoşani 63 Mb 54
		327040 Bozovici 76 Oa 49
		335200 Brad 76 Na 50

POSTALI · ÍNDICE CON CÓDIGOS POSTALES · INDICE DE LUGARES COM CÓDIGOS POSTAIS ·
MÍST S PSČ · ZOZNAM OBCÍ S PSČ · INDEKS MIEJSCOWOŚCI Z KOD POCZTOWY

176

Bradu   (RO)   **Leş**   (RO)

117140 Bradu 77 Oa 52	077045 Chitila 77 Oa 53	147115 Dobroteşti 77 Oa 52	407310 Gilău 63 Na 51
507025 Bran 77 Nb 53	437095 Cicârlău 63 Mb 51	320003 Doman 76 Nb 49	617210 Girov 63 Na 54
500000 Braşov 77 Nb 53	917035 Ciocăneşti 78 Oa 55	117370 Domneşti 77 Nb 52	080000 Giurgiu 77 Ob 53
207095 Bratovoeşti 77 Oa 51	077050 Ciolpani 77 Oa 54	917055 Dor Mărunt 78 Oa 54	327220 Glimboca 76 Nb 50
207105 Brădeşti 77 Oa 51	107155 Ciorani 78 Oa 54	727190 Dorna Candrenilor	117385 Godeni 77 Nb 52
810000 Brăila 78 Nb 55	555300 Cisnădie 77 Nb 52	63 Mb 53	207310 Goieşti 77 Oa 51
105400 Breaza 77 Nb 53	407225 Ciucea 62 Na 50	715200 Dorohoi 63 Mb 54	707210 Gorban 64 Na 56
527060 Breţcu 77 Na 54	827055 Ciucurova 78 Oa 56	447130 Dorolţ 62 Mb 50	547280 Gorneşti 63 Na 52
245500 Brezoi 77 Nb 52	707080 Ciurea 64 Mb 55	917080 Dragalina 78 Oa 55	327230 Grădinari 76 Nb 49
727075 Broşteni/Vatra Dornei	087045 Clejani 77 Oa 53	137210 Dragomireşti/Târguvişte	307216 Grănicerii 76 Nb 48
63 Mb 53	400000 Cluj-Napoca 63 Na 51	77 Oa 53	727290 Grăniceşti 63 Mb 54
227050 Broşteni/Motru 77 Oa 50	907065 Cobadin 78 Oa 56	737200 Dragomireşti/Bacău	927145 Griviţa 78 Oa 55
407441 Bucea 62 Na 50	505100 Codlea 77 Nb 53	64 Na 55	237210 Grojdibodu 77 Ob 52
337135 Buceş 77 Na 50	907070 Cogealac 78 Oa 56	235400 Drăgăneşti-Olt 77 Oa 52	317392 Groşi 76 Na 50
327055 Buchin 76 Nb 50	105700 Comarnic 77 Nb 53	147135 Drăgăneşti-Vlaşca	627155 Gugeşti 78 Nb 55
107110 Bucov 77 Oa 54	605200 Comăneşti 77 Na 54	77 Oa 53	725300 Gura Humorului 63 Mb 53
327017 Bucova 76 Nb 50	900000 Constanţa 78 Oa 56	245700 Drăgăşani 77 Oa 52	337245 Gurasada 76 Nb 50
927060 Bucu 78 Oa 55	717060 Copălău 64 Mb 54	417260 Drăgeşti 62 Na 50	447145 Halmeu 62 Mb 51
010000 Bucureşti 77 Oa 54	235300 Corabia 77 Ob 52	217225 Drăguţeşti 77 Oa 51	335500 Haţeg 77 Nb 50
915100 Budeşti 78 Oa 54	117275 Corbeni 77 Nb 52	220000 Drobeta-Turnu Severin	705100 Hârlău 64 Mb 54
070000 Buftea 77 Oa 53	137135 Corbii Mari 77 Oa 53	76 Oa 50	905400 Hârşova 78 Oa 55
605100 Buhuşi 64 Na 54	137150 Corneşti 77 Oa 53	227170 Dubova 76 Oa 50	607230 Helegiu 78 Na 54
215100 Bumbeşti-Jiu 77 Nb 51	327160 Coronini 76 Oa 49	307155 Dumbrava 76 Nb 50	227245 Hinova 77 Oa 50
105500 Buşteni 77 Nb 53	537060 Corund 77 Na 53	555500 Dumbrăveni/Sighişoara	507095 Hoghiz 77 Nb 53
317065 Buteni 76 Na 50	127200 Costeşti/Buzău 78 Nb 54	77 Na 52	245800 Horezu 77 Nb 51
137075 Butimanu 77 Oa 53	115200 Costeşti/Piteşti 77 Oa 52	727225 Dumbrăveni/Suceava	317407 Horia 76 Na 49
120000 Buzău 78 Nb 54	707115 Costuleni 64 Mb 55	63 Mb 54	405400 Huedin 63 Na 51
205200 Calafat 77 Ob 50	927095 Coşereni 78 Oa 54	427075 Dumitra 63 Mb 52	331000 Hunedoara 77 Nb 50
235200 Caracal 77 Oa 52	707120 Cotnari 64 Mb 54	417161 Duşeşti 62 Na 50	417290 Husasău de Tinca 62 Na 49
325400 Caransebeş 76 Nb 50	200000 Craiova 77 Oa 51	905350 Eforie Nord 78 Oa 56	735100 Huşi 64 Na 56
327065 Caraşova 76 Nb 49	317095 Craiva 76 Na 49	905360 Eforie Sud 78 Oa 56	727315 Iacobeni 63 Mb 53
445100 Carei 62 Mb 50	737007 Crasna/Vaslui 64 Na 55	927110 Făcăeni 78 Oa 55	817066 Ianca 78 Nb 55
907040 Castelu 78 Oa 56	527156 Crasna/Săcele 77 Nb 54	505200 Făgăraş 77 Nb 52	700000 Iaşi 64 Mb 55
827076 Cataloi 78 Nb 56	547180 Crăieşti 63 Na 52	607207 Făget/Comăneşti 63 Na 54	407335 Iclod 63 Na 51
527153 Catroşa 77 Na 52	137180 Crevedia 77 Oa 53	305300 Făget/Hunedoara 76 Nb 50	545100 Iernut 77 Na 52
807065 Cavadineşti 78 Na 56	707145 Cristeşti 63 Mb 54	737245 Fălciu 78 Na 56	917130 Ileana 78 Oa 54
607095 Căiuţi 78 Na 54	330003 Cristur 77 Nb 50	725200 Fălticeni 63 Mb 54	457190 Ileanda 63 Mb 51
335300 Călan 77 Nb 50	535400 Cristuru Secuiesc 77 Na 53	815100 Făurei 78 Nb 55	337270 Ilia 76 Nb 50
910000 Călăraşi 78 Oa 55	337200 Crişcior 77 Na 50	327200 Fârliug 76 Nb 49	807165 Independenţa/Galaţi
117190 Căldăraru 77 Oa 52	417215 Criştioru de Jos 76 Na 50	247165 Fârtăţeşti 77 Oa 51	78 Nb 55
245600 Călimăneşti 77 Nb 52	907095 Crucea 78 Oa 56	507065 Feldioara 77 Nb 53	917140 Independenţa/Călăraşi
725100 Câmpulung Moldovenesc	457218 Cuciulat 63 Mb 51	427080 Feldru 63 Mb 52	78 Oa 55
63 Mb 53	515600 Cugir 77 Nb 51	407270 Feleacu 63 Na 51	315300 Ineu 76 Na 49
217125 Căpreni 77 Oa 51	227150 Cujmir 77 Oa 50	925100 Feteşti 78 Oa 55	307446 Iohanisfeld 76 Nb 48
317032 Căpruţa 76 Na 50	917040 Curcani 78 Oa 54	135100 Fieni 77 Nb 52	907150 Ion Corvin 78 Oa 55
407145 Căpuşu Mare 63 Na 51	115300 Curtea de Argeş 77 Nb 52	205300 Filiaşi 77 Oa 51	247270 Ioneşti 77 Oa 52
307090 Cărpiniş 76 Nb 48	715100 Darabani 63 Ma 54	607175 Filipeşti 64 Na 54	825200 Isaccea 78 Nb 56
217145 Câlnic 77 Oa 51	207220 Dăbuleni 77 Ob 52	620000 Focşani 78 Nb 55	207340 Işalniţa 77 Oa 51
087040 Călugăreni 77 Oa 53	605300 Dărmăneşti/Comăneşti	807130 Folteşti 78 Nb 56	807157 Iveşti 78 Nb 55
515500 Câmpeni 77 Na 51	78 Na 54	727245 Frasin 63 Mb 53	107320 Izvoarele 77 Nb 54
457047 Câmpia 62 Mb 50	137185 Dărmăneşti/Ploieşti	087080 Frăteşti 77 Ob 53	516108 Izvoru Ampoiului 77 Na 51
405100 Câmpia Turzii 77 Na 51	77 Oa 53	717160 Frumuşica 64 Mb 54	817066 Însurăţei 78 Oa 55
105600 Câmpina 77 Nb 53	727155 Dărmăneşti/Suceava	915200 Fundulea 78 Oa 54	525300 Întorsura Buzăului 77 Nb 54
115100 Câmpulung 77 Nb 53	547205 Deda 63 Na 52	147145 Furculeşti 77 Ob 53	307230 Jamu Mare 76 Nb 49
827045 Cerna 78 Nb 56	405200 Dej 63 Mb 51	800000 Galaţi 78 Nb 56	307235 Jebel 76 Nb 49
905200 Cernavodă 78 Oa 56	907110 Deleni 78 Oa 56	207270 Galicea Mare 77 Oa 51	917145 Jegălia 78 Oa 55
077035 Cernica 78 Oa 54	437135 Deseşti 63 Mb 51	135200 Găeşti 77 Oa 53	455200 Jibou 63 Mb 51
447100 Certeze 63 Mb 51	305200 Deta 76 Nb 49	127240 Gâlbinaşi 78 Nb 54	077120 Jilava 77 Oa 54
147070 Cervenia 77 Ob 53	330000 Deva 77 Nb 50	237185 Găneasa 77 Oa 52	927155 Jilavele 78 Oa 54
207190 Cetate 77 Oa 51	417235 Diosig 62 Mb 50	457140 Gâlgău 63 Mb 51	305400 Jimbolia 76 Nb 48
517235 Cetatea de Baltă 77 Na 52	207230 Dioşti 77 Oa 52	517310 Gârda de Sus 76 Na 50	537130 Joseni 63 Na 53
107356 Cheia 77 Nb 53	537090 Ditrău 63 Na 53	535500 Gheorgheni 63 Na 53	337280 Lăpugiu de Jos 76 Nb 50
457027 Chendrea 63 Mb 51	327302 Divici 76 Oa 49	405300 Gherla 63 Mb 51	307234 Lăţunaş 76 Nb 49
827050 Chilia Veche 78 Nb 57	617155 Dobreni 63 Na 54	087095 Ghimpaţi 77 Oa 53	915300 Lehliu-Gară 78 Oa 54
315100 Chişineu Criş 76 Na 49	207235 Dobreşti 77 Ob 51	547265 Ghindari 77 Na 52	717220 Leorda 63 Mb 54
307221 Chişoda 76 Nb 49		307215 Giera 76 Nb 48	417348 Leş 62 Na 49

RO

Leţcani   **RO**   Şibot

707280 Leţcani 64 Mb 55	125100 Nehoiu 77 Nb 54	727440 Pojorâta 63 Mb 53	537260 Sărmaş 63 Na 53
207350 Leu 77 Oa 52	307406 Nerău 76 Nb 48	717300 Pomârla 63 Ma 54	547515 Sărmaşu 63 Na 52
807180 Lieşti 78 Nb 55	607355 Nicolae Bălcescu/Bacău	247599 Popeşti 77 Nb 52	517660 Săsciori 77 Nb 51
315400 Lipova 76 Na 49	64 Na 54	077160 Popeşti-Leordeni 78 Oa 54	317270 Săvârşin 76 Na 50
717362 Lişna 63 Ma 54	907210 Nicolae Bălcescu/Tulcea	707380 Popricani 64 Mb 55	715300 Săveni 64 Mb 54
727335 Liteni 63 Mb 54	78 Oa 56	557190 Porumbacu de Jos	537275 Sândominic 63 Na 53
447180 Livada 63 Mb 51	215300 Novaci 77 Nb 51	77 Nb 52	547530 Sângeorgiu de Mureş
307250 Lovrin 76 Nb 48	457260 Nuşfalău 62 Mb 50	127485 Poşta Câlnău 78 Nb 54	77 Na 52
545200 Luduş 77 Na 52	515700 Ocna Mureş 77 Na 51	537240 Praid 77 Na 53	547535 Sângeorgiu de Pădure
305500 Lugoj 76 Nb 49	535600 Odorheiu Secuiesc	507165 Prejmer 77 Nb 53	77 Na 52
517578 Lunca 77 Na 51	77 Na 53	327305 Prigor 76 Oa 50	425300 Sângeorz-Băi 63 Mb 52
117435 Lunca Corbului 77 Oa 52	317089 Odvoş 76 Na 49	247525 Prudeni 77 Oa 52	417495 Sânmartin/Oradea
827120 Luncaviţa 78 Nb 56	607365 Oituz 78 Na 54	087180 Prundu 78 Oa 54	62 Mb 49
337310 Luncoiu de Jos 76 Na 50	527125 Ojdula 77 Nb 54	427230 Prundu Bârgăului 63 Mb 52	537280 Sânmartin/Miercurea-Ciuc
407322 Lungeşti 77 Na 51	247440 Olanu 77 Oa 52	107485 Puchenii Mari 77 Oa 54	77 Na 53
137280 Lunguleţu 77 Oa 53	737380 Olteneşti 64 Na 55	135400 Pucioasa 77 Nb 53	457305 Sânmihaiu Almaşului
335600 Lupeni 77 Nb 51	915400 Olteniţa 78 Oa 54	237365 Radomireşti 77 Oa 52	63 Mb 51
900001 Mamaia 78 Oa 56	507252 Olteţ 77 Nb 52	207485 Radovan 77 Oa 51	305600 Sânnicolau Mare 76 Na 48
905500 Mangalia 78 Ob 56	601000 Oneşti 78 Na 54	207490 Rast 77 Ob 51	927210 Scânteia 78 Oa 55
905500 Mangalia 78 Ob 56	410000 Oradea 62 Mb 49	417400 Răbăgani 62 Na 50	087200 Schitu 77 Oa 53
717230 Manoleasa 64 Mb 55	325600 Oraviţa 76 Nb 49	607480 Răcăciuni 78 Na 55	707435 Schitu Duca 64 Mb 55
415300 Marghita 62 Mb 50	335700 Orăştie 77 Nb 51	725400 Rădăuţi 63 Mb 53	235600 Scornicesti 77 Oa 52
307270 Maşloc 76 Nb 49	227170 Orşova 76 Oa 50	717315 Rădăuţi-Prut 63 Ma 54	515800 Sebeş 77 Nb 51
825300 Măcin 78 Nb 56	307305 Ortişoara 76 Nb 49	147290 Rădoieşti 77 Oa 52	147335 Segarcea 77 Oa 51
107365 Măneciu-Ungureni	237310 Osica de Sus 77 Oa 52	707400 Răducăneni 64 Na 55	435400 Seini 63 Mb 51
77 Nb 53	207440 Ostroveni 77 Ob 51	407107 Răscruci 63 Na 51	520000 Sfântu Gheorghe/Braşov
327265 Măureni 76 Nb 49	247455 Oteşani 77 Nb 52	547485 Răciu 63 Na 52	77 Nb 53
917170 Mânăstirea 78 Oa 54	075100 Otopeni 77 Oa 54	125300 Râmnicu Sărat 78 Nb 55	827195 Sfântu Gheorghe/Tulcea
905600 Medgidia 78 Oa 56	905900 Ovidiu 78 Oa 56	240000 Râmnicu Vâlcea 77 Nb 52	78 Oa 57
551000 Mediaş 77 Na 52	527130 Ozun 77 Nb 53	505400 Râşnov 77 Nb 53	550000 Sibiu 77 Nb 52
327270 Mehadia 76 Oa 50	127410 Padina 78 Oa 55	737455 Rebricea 64 Na 55	537295 Siculeni 77 Na 53
207385 Melineşti 77 Oa 51	077145 Pantelimon 78 Oa 54	307340 Recaş 76 Nb 49	435500 Sighetu-Marmaţiei
147116 Merişani 77 Oa 52	705200 Paşcani 64 Mb 54	227414 Recea 77 Oa 52	63 Mb 51
517445 Meteş 77 Na 51	447128 Paulian 62 Mb 50	545300 Reghin 63 Na 52	545400 Sighişoara 77 Na 52
547400 Mica 77 Na 52	327295 Pâltiniş 76 Nb 50	320000 Reşita 76 Nb 49	335900 Simeria 77 Nb 51
527115 Micfalău 77 Na 53	127430 Pătârlagele 78 Nb 54	717325 Ripiceni 64 Mb 55	106100 Sinaia 77 Nb 53
557150 Miercurea Sibiului	315600 Pâncota 76 Na 49	427245 Rodna 63 Mb 52	725500 Siret 63 Mb 54
77 Nb 51	617305 Pângăraţi 63 Na 54	217238 Rogojel 77 Oa 51	230000 Slatina 77 Oa 52
530000 Miercurea-Ciuc 77 Na 53	127450 Pârscov 78 Nb 54	610000 Roman 64 Na 54	327360 Slatina-Timiş 76 Nb 50
247375 Mihăeşti/Râmnicu Vâlcea	317235 Pecica 76 Na 49	457280 Românaşi 63 Mb 51	557240 Slimnic 77 Nb 52
77 Nb 52	325201 Pecinişca 76 Oa 50	427250 Romuli 63 Mb 52	920000 Slobozia 78 Oa 55
117470 Mihăeşti/Mioveni 77 Nb 53	147240 Peretu 77 Oa 53	437250 Rona de Sus 63 Mb 52	627305 Slobozia Bradului 78 Nb 55
085200 Mihăileşti/Bucureşti	917195 Perişoru 78 Oa 55	145100 Roşiori de Vede 77 Oa 52	127595 Smeeni 78 Nb 54
77 Oa 53	217335 Peştişani 77 Nb 51	215400 Rovinari 77 Oa 51	317305 Socodor 76 Na 49
127375 Mihăileşti/Urziceni	137350 Petreşti 77 Oa 53	617390 Roznov 63 Na 54	545500 Sovata 63 Na 53
78 Oa 54	335800 Petrila 77 Nb 51	117630 Rucăr 77 Nb 53	737485 Stănileşti 64 Na 56
337532 Mintia 77 Nb 50	332000 Petroşani 77 Nb 51	707420 Ruginoasa 64 Mb 54	117675 Stoeneşti 77 Nb 53
115400 Mioveni 77 Oa 52	610000 Piatra-Neamţ 63 Na 54	505500 Rupea 77 Nb 53	217480 Stoina 77 Oa 51
707325 Mirosloveşti 64 Mb 54	235500 Piatra-Olt 77 Oa 52	437260 Ruscova 63 Mb 52	225300 Strehaia 77 Oa 51
105800 Mizil 78 Nb 54	147250 Pietroşani 77 Ob 53	327325 Sacu 76 Nb 50	237445 Studina 77 Ob 52
077130 Moara Vlăsiei 78 Oa 54	317255 Pilu 76 Na 49	207046 Sadova 77 Ob 51	720000 Suceava 63 Mb 54
407420 Mociu 63 Na 52	617325 Pipirig 63 Mb 54	415500 Salonta 62 Na 49	727510 Suceviţa 63 Mb 53
605400 Moineşti 64 Na 54	307325 Pişchia 76 Nb 49	427255 Salva 63 Mb 52	147350 Suhaia 77 Ob 53
137310 Moroeni 77 Nb 53	447250 Pişcolt 62 Mb 50	717345 Santa Mare 64 Mb 55	825400 Sulina 78 Nb 57
207077 Mosna 77 Na 52	110000 Piteşti 77 Oa 52	337345 Sarmizegetusa 77 Nb 50	415535 Suplacu de Barcău
215200 Motru 77 Oa 50	100000 Ploieşti 77 Oa 54	607520 Sascut 78 Na 55	62 Mb 50
207417 Moţăţei-Gara 77 Oa 51	607440 Plopana 64 Na 55	440000 Satu Mare 63 Mb 51	447300 Supuru de Jos 62 Mb 50
817100 Movila Miresii 78 Nb 55	217345 Plopşoru 77 Oa 51	437270 Satulung 63 Mb 51	457347 Sutoru 63 Na 51
807200 Munteni 78 Nb 55	147265 Plosca 77 Oa 53	617400 Săbăoani 64 Mb 54	307395 Şag 76 Nb 49
737370 Murgeni 78 Na 56	327272 Plugova 76 Oa 50	437290 Săcel 63 Mb 52	317310 Şagu 76 Na 49
315500 Nădlac 76 Na 48	207465 Podari 77 Oa 51	505600 Săcele 77 Nb 53	307065 Şandra 76 Nb 48
425200 Năsăud 63 Mb 52	707365 Podu Iloaiei 64 Mb 55	417435 Săcueni 62 Mb 50	427285 Şant 63 Mb 52
905700 Năvodari 78 Oa 56	607450 Podu Turcului 78 Na 55	557225 Sălişte 77 Nb 51	727525 Scheia 63 Mb 54
735200 Negreşti 64 Na 55	125200 Pogoanele 78 Oa 54	437300 Sălsig 63 Mb 51	807290 Şendreni 78 Nb 55
445200 Negreşti-Oaş 63 Mb 51	207470 Poiana Mare 77 Ob 51	607530 Sânduleni 64 Na 54	507195 Şercaia 77 Nb 53
905800 Negru Vodă 78 Ob 56	327300 Pojejena 76 Oa 49	427301 Sărăţel 63 Mb 52	517750 Şibot 77 Nb 51

POSTALI · ÍNDICE CON CÓDIGOS POSTALES · INDICE DE LUGARES COM CÓDIGOS POSTAIS ·
MÍST S PSČ · ZOZNAM OBCÍ S PSČ · INDEKS MIEJSCOWOŚCI Z KOD POCZTOWY

178

Şieu-Măgheruş   (RO) · (RSM) · (RUS)   Berežok

427295 Şieu-Măgheruş 63 Mb 52	925200 Ţăndărei 78 Oa 55	182815 Aševo 32 Gb 57
317335 Şimand 76 Na 49	217535 Ţânţăreni 77 Oa 51	140512 Astapovo 42 Ja 67
227445 Şimian 77 Oa 50	215600 Ţicleni 77 Oa 51	391525 Avdot`inka 42 Ja 68
207550 Şimnicu de Sus 77 Oa 51	147420 Ţigăneşti 78 Ob 53	186606 Avneporog 10 Cb 61
507206 Şinca Veche 77 Nb 53	417358 Ucuriş 76 Na 49	142645 Avsjunino 34 Hb 67
417550 Şinteu 62 Mb 50	307445 Uivar 76 Nb 48	152080 Babaevo/Danilov 34 Ga 68
317340 Şiria 76 Na 49	127645 Ulmeni/Buzău 78 Nb 54	162480 Babaevo/Kaduj /
737495 Ştefan cel Mare 64 Na 55	917260 Ulmeni/Olteniţa 78 Oa 54	Бабаево/Кадуй 17 Fb 63
717385 Ştefăneşti/Botoşani	117780 Ungheni/Slatina 77 Oa 52	152854 Babino/Čerepovec
64 Mb 52	547605 Ungheni/Târgu Mureş	33 Ga 66
117715 Ştefăneşti/Piteşti 77 Oa 52	77 Na 52	171394 Babino/Kuršinovo 33 Ha 62
415600 Ştei 76 Na 50	717415 Ungureni 64 Mb 54	162240 Babino/Sokol 18 Fb 68
517775 Şugag 77 Nb 51	517785 Unirea 77 Na 51	249210 Babynino 41 Ja 63
417570 Tarcea 62 Mb 50	336100 Uricani 77 Nb 51	161457 Badanki 18 Fb 72
555706 Tălmăcel 77 Nb 52	925300 Urziceni 78 Oa 54	238420 Bagrationovsk 38 Ja 48
417058 Tămăşeu 62 Mb 49	727560 Vadu Moldovei 63 Mb 54	249640 Bahmutovo/Kirov 41 Ja 62
445300 Tăşnad 62 Mb 50	415700 Valea lui Mihai 62 Mb 50	172361 Bahmutovo/Ržev 33 Ha 62
130000 Târgovişte 77 Oa 53	907163 Vama Veche 78 Ob 56	161471 Bajdarovo 18 Fb 73
215500 Târgu Cărbuneşti 77 Oa 51	917280 Vasilaţi 78 Oa 54	162013 Baklanka 18 Ga 68
705300 Târgu Frumos 64 Mb 55	730000 Vaslui 64 Na 55	302504 Baklanovo 41 Jab 63
210000 Târgu Jiu 77 Nb 51	415800 Vaşcău 76 Na 50	140703 Bakšeevo / Бакшеево
435600 Târgu Lăpuş 63 Mb 51	725700 Vatra Dornei 63 Mb 53	34 Hb 67
217293 Târgu Logereşti 77 Oa 51	727595 Vatra Moldoviţei 63 Mb 53	249800 Balabanovo / Балабаново
540000 Târgu Mureş 77 Na 52	737565 Văleni/Vaslui 64 Na 55	41 Hb 64
615200 Târgu Neamţ 63 Mb 54	106400 Vălenii de Munte 77 Nb 54	143900 Balašiha / Балашиха
605600 Târgu Ocna 78 Na 54	547635 Vânători 77 Na 52	34 Hb 66
525400 Târgu Secuiesc 77 Na 54	225400 Vânju Mare 77 Oa 50	238520 Baltijsk / Балтийск
545600 Târnăveni 77 Na 52	717450 Vârfu Câmpului 63 Mb 54	38 Ja 47
427345 Teaca 63 Na 52	317390 Vârfurile 76 Na 50	309732 Bankino 54 La 66
805300 Tecuci 78 Nb 55	457355 Vârşolţ 62 Mb 50	399020 Baranovo 42 Ka 66
515900 Teiuş 77 Na 51	117815 Vedea/Piteşti 77 Oa 52	174523 Barsaniha 33 Ga 63
427355 Telciu 63 Mb 52	087260 Vedea/Giurgiu 77 Ob 53	216522 Barsuki/Desnogorsk
337468 Teliucu Superior 77 Nb 50	127675 Verneşti 78 Nb 54	41 Ja 61
327390 Teregova 76 Nb 50	737570 Vetrişoaia 64 Na 56	216145 Barsuki/Počinok 40 Ja 60
457321 Tihău 63 Mb 51	727610 Vicovu de Sus 63 Mb 53	306511 Basovo 54 Kb 64
417585 Tileagd 62 Mb 50	307460 Victor Vlad Delamarina	306240 Bavykino 54 Kb 64
300000 Timişoara 76 Nb 49	76 Nb 49	249806 Bebelevo 41 Ja 64
417595 Tinca 62 Na 49	145300 Videle 77 Ob 52	161216 Bečevinka 17 Fb 65
135500 Titu 77 Oa 53	627415 Vidra 78 Nb 54	188423 Begunicy 31 Fb 57
707515 Tomeşti 64 Mb 55	317400 Vinga 76 Na 49	182500 Begunovo / Бегуново
417618 Topa de Criş 62 Mb 50	517160 Vinţu de Jos 77 Nb 51	40 Ha 57
407500 Topa Mică 63 Na 51	127705 Vipereşti 78 Nb 54	175340 Bel`-2 32 Gb 60
327400 Topleţ 76 Oa 50	435700 Vişeu de Sus 63 Mb 52	161344 Belehovo 18 Fb 71
535700 Topliţa 63 Na 53	817215 Viziru 78 Oa 55	301530 Belev / Белев 41 Jab 64
617352 Topoliceni 63 Mb 53	317405 Vladimirescu 76 Na 49	308000 Belgorod / Белгород
827200 Topolog 78 Oa 56	927250 Vlădeni 78 Oa 55	54 La 64
115500 Topoloveni 77 Oa 53	807335 Vlădeşti 78 Nb 56	307906 Belica 54 Kb 63
907285 Topraisar 78 Oa 56	535800 Vlăhiţa 77 Na 53	181500 Beljaevo/Ostrov 31 Gb 56
147405 Traian/Turnu Măgurele	247750 Voineasa 77 Nb 51	216299 Beljaevo/Vitebsk 40 Hb 59
77 Ob 52	137525 Voineşti 77 Nb 52	309273 Beljanka 54 La 65
607635 Traian/Bacău 64 Na 55	307470 Voiteg 76 Nb 49	184664 Belokamenka 6 Ab 61
707520 Trifeşti 64 Mb 55	337540 Vulcan 77 Nb 51	186500 Belomorsk 10 Da 62
717400 Truşeşti 64 Mb 55	450000 Zalău 63 Mb 51	249160 Belousovo/Obninsk /
817180 Tudor Vladimirescu	337550 Zam 76 Na 50	Белоусово/Обнинск
78 Nb 55	547615 Zau de Câmpie 77 Na 52	41 Hb 64
417600 Tulca 62 Na 49	505800 Zărneşti 77 Nb 53	162930 Belousovo/Vytegra
820000 Tulcea 78 Nb 56	327435 Zăvoi 77 Nb 50	17 Fa 64
537330 Tulgheş 63 Na 53	317427 Zimandcuz 76 Na 49	161200 Belozersk / Белозерск
627365 Tulnici 78 Nb 54	145400 Zimnicea 77 Ob 53	17 Fa 65
807300 Tuluceşti 78 Nb 56	737635 Zorleni 78 Na 55	241902 Belye Berega / Белые
217520 Turceni 77 Oa 51		Берега 41 Jab 62
217530 Turcineşti 77 Nb 51		172530 Belyj 40 Hb 60
401000 Turda 77 Na 51		187414 Berežki 16 Fb 60
145200 Turnu Măgurele 77 Ob 52	(RSM)	165234 Bereznik 18 Eb 71
537335 Tuşnad 77 Na 53		215866 Berežnjany 40 Ja 60
737356 Tutova 78 Na 55	47890 San Marino 74 Ob 40	160542 Berežok 17 Fb 67

Middle column RUS section:

(RUS)	
164120 Abakumovo 17 Eb 66	
309834 Afanas`evka 54 La 66	
171130 Afim`ino 33 Gb 62	
188653 Agalatovo 16 Fa 58	
214541 Agaponovo 40 Ja 59	
399331 Aksaj 42 Ka 67	
157200 Aksenovo/Galič 18 Ga 70	
601571 Aksenovo/Kurlovo 34 Hb 68	
165171 Aksenovskaja 18 Eb 70	
142854 Aksin`ino/Kolomna	
42 Hb 66	
301307 Aksin`ino/Venev 42 Ja 66	
162900 Akulovo 17 Eb 64	
391070 Akulovo 42 Ja 68	
184060 Alakurtti 9 Ca 58	
187719 Alehovščina 16 Fa 61	
391240 Aleksandro-Nevskij	
42 Jab 68	
601650 Aleksandrov / Александров	
34 Ha 66	
391924 Aleksandrovka/Sapožok	
42 Jab 68	
396150 Aleksandrovka/Voronež	
54 Kb 67	
309850 Alekseevka 54 La 66	
171408 Alekseevskoe 33 Gb 64	
301360 Aleksin / Алексин 42 Ja 65	
187439 Aleksino 16 Fa 60	
303240 Alešinka 41 Ka 63	
242414 Alešok 53 Ka 62	
165221 Alferovskaja 18 Eb 72	
242505 Alymova 41 Jab 63	
155070 An`kovo 34 Ha 68	
162961 Anciferovskaja 17 Fa 65	
172800 Andreapol` 32 Ha 60	
301900 Andreevka 42 Jab 65	
601370 Andreevo / Андреево	
34 Hb 69	
152031 Andrianovo 34 Ha 66	
150513 Androniki 34 Gb 68	
399253 Anikeevka 42 Ka 66	
161348 Anikovo 18 Fb 71	
301335 Anišino 42 Ja 65	
309233 Annovka 54 La 65	
164134 Antonovskaja 17 Eb 66	
157260 Antropovo 18 Ga 71	
161210 Antušovo 17 Fb 65	
164034 Anufrievo 17 Fa 67	
184215 Apatity 6 Bb 61	
143360 Aprelevka / Апрелевка	
41 Hb 65	
306530 Apuhtina 54 Kb 64	
303213 Arbuzovo 41 Ka 63	
301096 Arhangel`skoe/Efremov	
42 Jab 65	
309153 Arhangel`skoe/Gubkin	
54 Kb 65	
214523 Arhipovka 40 Ja 59	
170526 Arininskoe 33 Gb 64	
601530 Arsamaki 34 Hb 68	
301510 Arsen`evo/Belev 42 Jab 64	
301692 Arsen`evo/Novomoskovsk	
42 Ja 66	

179

INDEX WITH POST CODES · ORTSREGISTER MIT POSTLEITZAHLEN · INDICE CON CODICI
STEDREGISTER MED POSTNUMRE · PLAATSNAMENREGISTER MET POSTCODE · REJSTŘÍK

161396 Berezovaja Slobodka
18 Fa 72
157222 Berezovec 18 Ga 70
393086 Berezovka/Grjazi 42 Ka 68
165322 Berezovka/Kotlas 18 Eb 73
Berezovka/Poljarnye Zori
6 Bb 62
161364 Berezovka/Tot`ma
18 Fb 71
171356 Bernovo 33 Ha 62
309283 Beršakovo 54 La 65
305501 Besedino 54 Kb 64
165250 Bestuževo 18 Eb 71
391342 Betino 42 Ja 69
182840 Bežanicy 32 Ha 57
171980 Bežeck / Бежецк 33 Gb 64
162116 Birjakovo 18 Fb 69
242121 Bjakovo 41 Ka 62
301537 Bobriki 41 Jab 64
172410 Bobrovka 33 Ha 61
309170 Bobrovy Dvory 54 Kb 65
301546 Bogdanovo/Belev
41 Jab 64
216524 Bogdanovo/Desnogorsk
41 Ja 61
215642 Bogoljubovo/Kanjutino
41 Hb 60
601270 Bogoljubovo/Vladimir
34 Ha 68
301801 Bogorodick / Богородицк
42 Jab 66
391812 Bogoslovo 42 Jab 67
155625 Bokari 34 Ha 70
187650 Boksitogorsk / Бокситогорск
32 Fb 61
171961 Bol`šaja Bereža 33 Gb 64
162000 Bol`šaja Dvorišča 18 Ga 68
198504 Bol`šaja Ižora 31 Fb 57
172211 Bol`šaja Koša 33 Ha 61
162646 Bol`šaja Novinka 33 Ga 66
162354 Bol`šaja Sloboda 18 Fa 73
165210 Bol`šaja Virova 18 Fa 71
161214 Bol`šaje Noviški 17 Fb 65
238620 Bol`šakovo 38 Ja 49
307333 Bol`šenizovcevo 53 Kb 62
399634 Bol`šie Izbišči 42 Ka 67
301864 Bol`šie Medvedki 42 Jab 66
301878 Bol`šie Ploty 42 Jab 66
216223 Bol`šoe Beresnevo
40 Hb 60
171733 Bol`šoe Ovsjanikovo
33 Ga 64
188907 Bol`šoe Pole 15 Fa 56
307862 Bol`šoe Soldatskoe
53 Kb 63
307115 Bol`šoe Žirovo 54 Kb 63
391126 Bol`šoe Žokovo 42 Ja 67
161321 Bol`šoj Goroch 18 Fb 70
187717 Bol`šoj Kokoviči 16 Fa 61
188444 Bol`šoj Sabsk 33 Gb 64
182363 Bolgatovo 32 Ha 56
303162 Bolhov / Болхов 41 Jab 64
171070 Bologoe 33 Gb 62
301280 Bolohovo / Болохово
42 Ja 65
301545 Boloto 41 Jab 64

216320 Boltutino 41 Ja 60
Bond 34 Gb 71
182250 Bondari 39 Ha 56
188279 Bor/Luga 32 Ga 57
187540 Bor/Tihvin 16 Fb 61
186304 Bor-Pudancev 16 Ea 63
140740 Borduki 34 Hb 67
391875 Borec 42 Jab 69
398510 Borinskoe 42 Ka 67
152170 Borisoglebskij 34 Gb 67
188672 Borisova Griva 16 Fa 58
309340 Borisovka / Борисовка
54 La 64
173516 Borki 32 Ga 59
161446 Borok/Nikolsk 18 Fb 72
152742 Borok/Rybinsk 33 Ga 66
171977 Borok Suležskij 33 Gb 64
174400 Boroviči/Okulovka /
Боровичи/Окуловка
32 Ga 61
182641 Boroviči/pORHOV 32 Gb 57
157955 Borovikovo 34 Gb 69
Borovoj 10 Da 60
249010 Borovsk / Боровск
41 Hb 64
396816 Borščevo 54 Kb 67
157293 Borskij 18 Ga 71
162693 Botovo 17 Fb 65
390000 Božatkovo 42 Ja 67
140500 Bračevo 42 Ja 67
216632 Bratkovaja 40 Ja 60
171391 Bratkovo 33 Ha 62
152771 Brejtovo 33 Ga 65
241000 Brjansk / Брянск 41 Jab 62
155571 Brodki 34 Gb 69
164122 Bronevo 17 Eb 67
140170 Bronnicy / Бронницы
34 Hb 66
306005 Brusovoe 42 Ka 64
249310 Bryn` 41 Jab 63
172540 Budino 40 Hb 60
216294 Budnica 40 Hb 59
249623 Budnjanskij 41 Ja 61
187120 Budogošč 32 Fb 60
172063 Budovo 33 Gb 62
157000 Buj Буй 18 Ga 69
602204 Bulatnikovo 34 Hb 69
153502 Bun`kovo 34 Gb 68
303271 Bunino 41 Ka 63
175253 Burakovo 32 Gb 59
157452 Burdovo 18 Ga 72
174750 Burilovo 32 Ga 61
307917 Bušmeno 54 Kb 63
157244 Bušnevo 18 Ga 70
215133 Bušukovo 41 Hb 61
140324 Butovo 34 Hb 67
171604 Buzykovo 33 Gb 65
303240 Byčki 41 Ka 63
306732 Byčok 54 Kb 66
171542 Bykovo 33 Gb 64
306814 Bykovo 54 Kb 65
242670 Bytoš` 41 Jab 62
Čalna 16 Eb 62
181125 Capel`ka 31 Ga 56
399900 Čaplygin / Чаплыгин
42 Jab 67

215004 Carevo-Zajmišče 41 Hb 62
186321 Čebino 16 Ea 62
243556 Čechovka 41 Ka 61
173525 Čečulino 32 Ga 59
142300 Čehov / Чехов 42 Hb 65
238423 Čehovo 38 Ja 48
301414 Čekalin 41 Ja 64
162111 Čekšino 18 Fb 68
215800 Čelnovaja 41 Ja 60
187501 Čemihino 16 Fb 61
157084 Čencovo 34 Ga 69
157434 Central`nyj 18 Fb 73
180560 Čereha 31 Gb 56
164131 Čerelaševskaja 17 Eb 66
306440 Čereminsinovo 54 Kb 65
307704 Čeremoški 53 Kb 63
306440 Čeremošnoj 54 Kb 63
188515 Čeremykino 31 Fb 57
162430 Čerenskoe 33 Ga 63
162600 Čerepovec / Череповец
17 Fb 65
216624 Čerepovo 40 Ja 60
242750 Čerkasskaja Alešnja
41 Jab 61
143720 Čerlenkovo 33 Hb 63
157454 Čermenino 18 Fb 71
301090 Čern` 42 Jab 64
399024 Černava/Livny 42 Ka 66
391772 Černava/Skopin 42 Jab 67
181637 Černečki 31 Ga 56
152632 Černicyno 33 Gb 66
601291 Černiž 34 Ha 68
238100 Černjahovsk / Черняховск
38 Ja 49
309560 Černjanka / Чернянка
54 La 65
142432 Černogolovka /
Черноголовка 34 Hb 66
303155 Černogrjazka 41 Jab 64
243072 Černookovo 53 Ka 60
188578 Černovskoe 31 Fb 56
174418 Černozem` 32 Ga 61
181307 Čerskaja 31 Gb 56
602335 Čertkovo 34 Hb 70
396023 Čertovicy 42 Kb 67
157163 Čertovo 18 Fb 71
391344 Činur 42 Ja 69
161261 Čisti 17 Fa 66
157000 Čistye Bory 34 Ga 69
Čkalovsk 34 Ha 71
391420 Čučkovo/Sasovo /
Чучково/Сасово 42 Ja 69
162115 Čučkovo/Sokol 18 Fb 69
174210 Čudovo / Чудово 32 Fb 59
157130 Čuhloma 18 Ga 70
186670 Čupa 9 Ca 61
182573 Čurilovo 40 Hb 58
353545 Čuška 66 Nb 64
249656 Cvetovka 41 Ja 62
Cypnavolok 6 Ab 61
301304 D`jakonovo/Venev 42 Ja 66
161057 D`jakonovo/Vologda
18 Fb 68
157092 D`jakovka 34 Ga 69
309200 Dal`njaja Igumenka
54 La 64

152070 Danilov / Данилов
34 Ga 68
399850 Dankov / Данков 42 Jab 67
171392 Dar`ino 33 Ha 62
241517 Darkoviči 41 Jab 62
Darovica 18 Ga 71
161321 Davydicha 18 Fb 70
397940 Davydovka 54 Kb 67
301543 Davydovo/Belev 41 Jab 64
175220 Davydovo/Staraja Russa
32 Gb 59
391007 Davydovo/Velikodvorskij
34 Hb 68
182710 Dedoviči 32 Gb 57
391975 Degtjanoe 42 Jab 68
162940 Delo 17 Fa 64
243036 Demenka 53 Ka 59
216240 Demidov 40 Hb 59
165133 Demidovskoe 18 Eb 70
161401 Demino 18 Fb 73
162560 Deminovo 17 Fb 66
172541 Demjahi 40 Hb 60
175310 Demjansk 32 Gb 60
155839 Denisovo/Kinešma
34 Gb 70
Denisovo/Suvorov 41 Ja 64
185510 Derevjannoe 16 Eb 62
182330 Derganovo 31 Ha 56
152004 Dertniki 34 Ha 67
140765 Derzekovskaja 34 Hb 67
216400 Desnogorsk / Десногорск
41 Ja 61
249080 Dečino 41 Ja 64
Detkovo 31 Ga 56
396942 Devica 54 Kb 67
242600 Djat`kovo 41 Jab 62
171141 Djatlovo 33 Gb 62
306534 Dlinnaja 54 Ka 64
307500 Dmitriev-L`govskij 53 Ka 63
393000 Dmitrievka/Mičurinsk
Дмитриевка/Мичуринск
42 Ka 68
309322 Dmitrievka/Rakitnoe
54 La 64
309262 Dmitrievka/Volokonovka
54 La 65
391357 Dmitrievo 34 Hb 69
301022 Dmitrievskoe 42 Ja 65
141800 Dmitrov / Дмитров
33 Ha 65
303240 Dmitrovsk 41 Ka 63
140750 Dmitrovskij Pogost
34 Hb 67
182670 Dno 32 Gb 57
242836 Dobraja Korna 41 Jab 60
339430 Dobrinka / Добринка
42 Ka 68
238221 Dobrino 38 Ja 48
601580 Dobrjatino 34 Hb 69
215463 Dobroe 41 Ja 62
175458 Dobrosti 32 Ga 60
238743 Dobrovol`sk 38 Ja 50
181613 Dobruči 31 Ga 55
302520 Dobryj 41 Ka 63
142044 Dobryniha 42 Hb 65
307923 Dolgie Budy 54 Kb 63

Dolgorukovo (RUS) **Ignatovo/Anciferovskaja** (RUS)

399510 Dolgorukovo 42 Ka 66
301083 Dolmatovo/Mcensk
  42 Jab 64
165133 Dolmatovo/Njandoma
  18 Eb 70
162833 Dolockoe 33 Ga 63
182263 Doloscy 40 Ha 56
303251 Domacha 41 Ka 62
249210 Domašovka 41 Ja 63
142000 Domodedovo / Домодедово
  42 Hb 65
187715 Domožirovo 16 Fa 61
306440 Domra 54 Kb 63
301760 Donskoj/Novomoskovsk
  Донской/Новомосковск
  42 Jab 66
157046 Dor/Buj 34 Ga 69
143722 Dor/Šahovskaja 41 Hb 63
162840 Dora 33 Ga 64
301914 Dorobino 42 Jab 65
215710 Dorogobuž / Дрогобуж
  41 Ja 61
143160 Dorohovo 41 Hb 64
238437 Dorožnoe 38 Ja 48
607034 Doščatoe / Досчатое
  34 Hb 70
216152 Dosugovo 40 Ja 59
174752 Dregli 32 Fb 61
303180 Droskovo 42 Ka 65
306230 Drozdy 54 Kb 64
188377 Družnaja Gorka 32 Fb 58
152771 Dubec 33 Ga 66
601768 Dubki 34 Ha 67
141980 Dubna/Kimry
  Дубна/Кимры 33 Ha 65
301160 Dubna/Suvorov 42 Ja 65
302539 Dubovaja Rošča 41 Jab 64
  Dubovec 54 Kb 64
399945 Dubovoe / Дубовое
  42 Jab 68
242306 Dubrovka/Navlja 41 Ka 62
182272 Dubrovka/Opočka 39 Ha 56
182714 Dubrovka/Porhov 32 Gb 57
174525 Dubrovo/Pestovo 33 Ga 63
175031 Dubrovo/Porhov 32 Ga 58
182457 Dubrovy/Opočka 32 Ha 57
175143 Dubrovy/Staraja Russa
  32 Ga 59
216200 Duhovščina 40 Hb 60
215850 Duhovskaja 40 Ja 60
181307 Dulovka 31 Gb 56
172025 Dumanovo 33 Ha 63
175274 Dunaevo 32 Gb 58
  Dupljan` 34 Gb 71
187350 Dus`evo 16 Fb 59
243507 Dušatin 41 Jab 60
183000 Dva Ruč`ja 6 Ba 60
175135 Dvorec 32 Gb 59
601622 Dvoriki 34 Ha 66
161457 Dvorišćenskij 18 Fb 73
  Dvory 54 Kb 64
187613 Dymi 16 Fb 61
152951 Dymovskoe 33 Ga 66
353539 Džiginka 66 Nb 65
175429 Edrovo 32 Gb 61
187731 Efremkovo 16 Fa 62

301840 Efremov / Ефремов
  42 Jab 66
306626 Efrosimovka 54 Kb 65
140300 Egor`evsk / Егорьевск
  34 Hb 67
157983 Ekaterinkino 34 Gb 71
399752 Ekaterinovka 42 Ka 66
216533 Ekimoviči 41 Ja 61
172212 El`cy 33 Ha 61
  El`mus 16 Ea 61
216330 El`nja / Ельня 41 Ja 61
399770 Elec Елец 42 Ka 66
399263 Eleckaja Lozovka 42 Ka 67
  Elehovo 33 Fb 65
144000 Ėlektrostal` / Электросталь
  34 Hb 66
181310 Eliny 31 Gb 56
157323 Elizarovo 18 Ga 72
188653 Elizavetinka 16 Fa 58
174514 Elkino 33 Ga 64
155441 Elnat` 34 Gb 70
161401 Emel`janov Dor 18 Fb 73
186966 Emel`janovka 9 Db 58
186655 Ėngozero 10 Cb 61
184120 Enskij 5 Bb 59
301740 Epifan` 42 Jab 66
391344 Erahtur 34 Ja 69
152490 Ermakovo 34 Ga 69
155030 Ermoliha 34 Ha 68
249026 Ermolino / Ермолино
  41 Hb 64
216580 Eršiči 41 Jab 60
180520 Eršovo 31 Gb 56
186137 Ėssojla 16 Eb 61
  Evgora 16 Db 61
162325 Evseevskaja 18 Fa 71
  Fadeiha 18 Ga 72
399073 Faščevka 42 Ka 67
307100 Fatež 54 Ka 63
141333 Fedorcovo 34 Ha 66
171533 Fedorovka 33 Ha 65
157474 Fedorovskoe 18 Ga 72
161331 Fedotovo 18 Fa 70
164273 Fedovo/Oksovskij 17 Ea 67
174521 Fedovo/Pestovo 33 Ga 63
161120 Ferapontovo 17 Fb 66
249800 Ferzikovo 41 Ja 64
186150 Filimonovskaja 17 Eb 64
162240 Filinskaja/Babino 18 Fb 68
  Filinskaja/Jukovskaja
  18 Fa 69
606162 Filinskoe 34 Hb 70
  Filippovo 17 Fb 65
601471 Fominki 34 Hb 70
161327 Fominskoe 18 Fb 70
353550 Fontalovskaja 66 Nb 64
187022 Fornosovo 32 Fb 58
141146 Frjanovo / Фряново
  34 Ha 66
155520 Furmanov / Фурманов
  34 Gb 69
184670 Gadžievo 6 Ab 61
215010 Gagarin / Гагарин
  41 Hb 63
171545 Gajnovo 33 Gb 64
152854 Gajutino 33 Ga 66

186162 Gakugsa 17 Eb 64
157200 Galič / Галич 18 Ga 70
162656 Galinskoe 17 Fb 66
187520 Gan`kovo 16 Fb 61
155450 Gar` 34 Gb 70
188658 Garbolovo 16 Fa 58
309810 Garbuzovo 54 La 66
171918 Garusovo 33 Gb 63
238602 Gastellovo 38 Hb 49
188300 Gatčina / Гатчина 32 Fb 58
152240 Gavrilov-Jam / Гаврилов-Ям
  34 Gb 67
182386 Gavry 31 Ha 55
181600 Gdov 31 Ga 55
165104 Georgievskoe 18 Eb 69
309916 Geraščenkovo 54 La 67
306811 Gerasimovo 54 Kb 65
309840 Gezov 54 La 66
186955 Gimoly 16 Ea 60
186214 Girvas 16 Ea 61
187126 Glaževo 32 Fb 60
150511 Glebovskoe/Jaroslavl`
  34 Gb 67
  Glebovskoe/Pereslavl`-
  Zalesskij 34 Ha 66
307450 Gluškovo 53 Kb 62
302100 Gnezdilovo 41 Jab 63
181623 Gnilišče 31 Ga 56
155520 Golčanovo 34 Gb 69
391733 Goldino 42 Ja 67
393015 Golicyno 42 Ka 68
157490 Golodaicha 34 Gb 71
309376 Golovčino 54 La 64
  Goloven`ki 41 Hb 64
238634 Golovkino 38 Ja 49
303030 Golovlevo 42 Jab 64
353521 Golubickaja 66 Nb 65
216740 Golynki 40 Ja 59
187754 Gomoroviči 16 Fa 62
181318 Gorai 18 Ga 56
171540 Goricy 33 Gb 64
162341 Gorka/Kotlas 18 Fa 74
187435 Gorka/Volhov 16 Fb 60
175111 Gorki Ratickie 32 Gb 58
391810 Gorlovo 42 Jab 67
188286 Gorodec 32 Ga 57
243160 Gorodečnja 40 Ka 59
187501 Gorodišče 16 Fb 61
161383 Gorodišćna 18 Fa 72
143716 Gorodkovo 33 Ha 63
306800 Goršečnoe 54 Kb 66
188520 Gostilicy 31 Fb 57
309370 Grajvoron 54 La 63
249121 Gremjačevo 41 Ja 64
  Gremjačij 18 Fb 70
305000 Gremjačka/Kursk 54 Kb 64
391832 Gremjačka/Skopin
  42 Jab 67
301327 Gribovka 42 Ja 66
175229 Grigorovo 32 Gb 59
243540 Grinevo 53 Ka 61

242727 Grišina 41 Jab 61
249716 Grišinsk 41 Ja 63
399050 Grjazi / Грязи 42 Ka 68
162000 Grjazovec / Грязовец
  18 Ga 68
164273 Grjazovo 17 Ea 67
157878 Grudki 34 Gb 69
161340 Grušino 18 Fb 72
172067 Gruziny 33 Ha 63
309180 Gubkin / Губкин 54 Kb 65
399681 Gudanovka 42 Ka 66
157920 Guljaevka 34 Gb 70
162920 Guljaevo 41 Jab 64
  Gumarino 16 Ea 61
238300 Gur`evsk / Гурьевск
  38 Ja 48
188460 Gurlevo 31 Fb 56
601500 Gus`-Hrustal`nyj /
  Гусь-Хрустальний
  34 Hb 68
391320 Gus`-Železnyj /
  Гус Железный 34 Hb 69
172752 Guša 32 Gb 60
155360 Gusarinki 34 Ha 71
238050 Gusev / Гусев 38 Ja 50
216117 Gusino 40 Ja 59
307721 Gustomoj 53 Kb 63
303420 Gustye 42 Ka 65
238210 Gvardejsk / Гвардейск
  38 Ja 49
171651 Habockoe 33 Ga 65
301054 Harino 42 Ja 65
186877 Hautavaara 16 Ea 60
216450 Hicovka 40 Ja 60
186700 Hijtola 15 Eb 57
141400 Himki / Химки 33 Hb 65
216620 Hislaviči 40 Ja 60
399260 Hlevnoe 42 Ka 67
216117 Hlystovka 40 Ja 59
216334 Hlysty 41 Ja 61
243351 Hmelevo 41 Jab 61
215153 Hmelita 41 Hb 61
214503 Hohlovo 40 Ja 59
396830 Hohol 54 Kb 66
175270 Holm 32 Gb 59
215650 Holm-Žirkovskij 41 Hb 61
309026 Holodnoe 54 Kb 65
301324 Holtobino 42 Ja 66
307540 Homutovka 53 Kb 62
303620 Homutovo 42 Ka 65
141370 Hot`kovo / Хотьково
  34 Ha 66
171097 Hotilino 33 Gb 62
303930 Hotynec 41 Jab 62
143260 Hrabrovo 41 Hb 63
181121 Hredino 32 Ga 57
397752 Hrenišče 54 Kb 67
309805 Hreščatyj 54 La 66
601211 Hrjaotovo 34 Ha 68
301320 Hruslovka 42 Ja 66
187435 Hvalovo 16 Fb 60
339410 Hvorostjanka 42 Ka 68
161342 Ida 18 Fb 71
161388 Igmas 18 Fa 71
162961 Ignatovo/Anciferovskaja
  17 Fa 65

181

INDEX WITH POST CODES · ORTSREGISTER MIT POSTLEITZAHLEN · INDICE CON CODICI
STEDREGISTER MED POSTNUMRE · PLAATSNAMENREGISTER MET POSTCODE · REJSTŘÍK

 Ignatovo/Ržev

 Kolpino / Колпино

172315 Ignatovo/Ržev 33 Hb 62
186877 Ignojla 16 Eb 60
161572 Igumnovskaja 18 Fa 71
141860 Ikša 33 Ha 65
601535 Ikševo 34 Hb 69
353548 Il`ič 66 Nb 64
396355 Il`iča 54 Kb 67
309802 Il`inka 54 La 66
398507 Il`ino/Lipeck 42 Ka 67
601363 Il`ino/Sudogda 34 Hb 68
186004 Il`inskij 16 Fa 60
171520 Il`inskoe/Kimry 33 Ha 65
602340 Il`inskoe/Krasnaja Gorbatka
34 Hb 69
249062 Il`inskoe/Malojaroslavec
41 Ja 64
152630 Il`inskoe/Uglič 34 Gb 66
155060 Il`inskoe-Hovanskoe
34 Ha 67
602131 Il`kino 34 Hb 69
157170 Ilejkino 18 Ga 70
309830 Ilovka 54 La 66
186801 Impilahti 16 Eb 59
Indel` 6 Ca 63
Inšinskij 42 Ja 65
391514 Iricy 42 Ja 69
157091 Isaevo 34 Ga 69
182300 Isakovo 40 Ha 57
390517 Iskra 42 Ja 67
181377 Issa 31 Ha 56
187430 Issad 16 Fa 60
309160 Istobnoe/Gubkin 54 Kb 65
396384 Istobnoe/Novovoronež
54 Kb 66
175325 Istošno 32 Gb 60
143500 Istra Истра 33 Hb 64
301040 Ivan`kovo 42 Ja 65
188490 Ivangorod / Ивангород
31 Fb 56
307220 Ivanino 53 Kb 63
153000 Ivanovo/Šuja / Иваново/Шуя
34 Ha 69
171710 Ivanovo/Ves`egonsk
33 Ga 65
161271 Ivanovskaja 17 Fa 65
Ivanovskoe 18 Ga 72
162753 Ivanovskoe/Čerepovec
17 Fb 65
307340 Ivanovskoe/L`gov
53 Kb 62
157325 Ivanovskoe/Manturovo
18 Ga 72
187025 Ivanovskoe/Toho 32 Fb 59
160545 Ivlevskoe 17 Fb 67
309110 Ivnja 54 Kb 64
242650 Ivot 41 Jab 62
181518 Izborsk 31 Gb 55
399000 Izmalkovo 42 Ka 66
161350 imeni Babuškina 18 Fb 71
396818 Jabločnoe 54 Kb 67
393097 Jablonovec 42 Ka 68
175435 Jablonovka 32 Gb 60
307610 Jaceno 53 Kb 63
141840 Jahroma / Яхрома
33 Ha 65
249436 Jakimovo/Kirov 41 Ja 62

157480 Jakimovo/Makar`ev
34 Gb 71
215710 Jakovlevo/Dorogobuž
41 Ja 61
157442 Jakovlevo/Kologriv
18 Ga 72
301002 Jakovlevo/Serpuhov
42 Ja 65
309076 Jakovlevo/Stroitel`
54 La 64
172062 Jakovlevskoe 33 Gb 63
162952 Jakšino 17 Fa 65
215530 Jakuškino 41 Hb 61
243155 Jalovka 52 Ka 59
243650 Jamnoe 40 Ka 59
175460 Jamskaja 32 Ga 60
182900 Jamy 32 Ha 58
187727 Janega 14 Fa 61
186206 Janšipole 16 Ea 62
215800 Jarcevo / Ярцево 40 Hb 60
171562 Jarinskoe 33 Ha 66
393748 Jarok 42 Ka 68
143632 Jaropolec 33 Ha 63
150000 Jaroslavl` / Ярославль
34 Gb 67
399824 Jaroslavy 42 Jab 66
249316 Jasenok 41 Jab 62
238613 Jasnoe 38 Hb 49
301030 Jasnogorsk / Ясногорск
42 Ja 65
187719 Javšinicy 16 Fa 62
175411 Jaželbicy 32 Ga 60
182623 Jazno 40 Ha 57
601956 Judiha 34 Ha 69
141900 Judino 33 Ha 65
161404 Jugskij 18 Fb 73
165133 Juhnevo 18 Eb 70
249910 Juhnov 41 Ja 63
182930 Juhovo 32 Ha 58
162240 Jukovskaja 18 Fa 69
Juma 10 Cb 61
601800 Jur`ev-Pol`skij /
Юрьев-Польский
34 Ha 67
155450 Jur`evec 34 Gb 71
171372 Jur`evskoe 33 Ha 63
140318 Jurcovo 34 Hb 67
186143 Jurgilica 16 Eb 60
161207 Jurino 17 Fa 65
Jurkino 18 Fb 71
161342 Jurkino/Anikovo 18 Fb 71
171974 Jurkino/Bežeck 33 Gb 64
186214 Jurkostrov 16 Ea 61
162030 Jurovo 18 Ga 68
181316 Juršino 31 Gb 56
165231 Jurtinskaja 18 Eb 71
181606 Juškino 31 Gb 56
186902 Juškozero 9 Da 60
Justozero 16 Ea 61
155630 Juža 34 Ha 70
162430 Kaboža 33 Fb 63
162107 Kadnikov 18 Fb 68
162510 Kaduj / Кадуй 17 Fb 65
157980 Kadyj 34 Gb 71
184060 Kajraly 9 Ca 57
186910 Kalevala 9 Cb 59

236000 Kaliningrad / Калининград
38 Ja 48
161463 Kalinino 18 Fb 73
157874 Kalinki 34 Gb 69
152070 Kalitino 34 Ga 68
171571 Kaljazin / Калязин
33 Gb 65
248000 Kaluga / Калуга 41 Ja 64
155315 Kamenka/Kinešma
34 Gb 69
396510 Kamenka/Ostrogožsk
54 La 67
399559 Kamenka/Voronež 42 Ka 66
188827 Kamenka/Zelenogorsk
15 Fa 57
188950 Kamennogorsk 15 Fa 57
601300 Kameškovo / Камешково
34 Ha 69
184056 Kandalakša 6 Bb 60
606552 Kandaurovo 34 Ha 71
215640 Kanjutino 41 Hb 61
Kaplino 18 Ga 71
215250 Kapyrevščina 41 Hb 60
601642 Karabanovo / Карабаново
34 Ha 66
391492 Karabuchino 42 Ja 69
242500 Karačev / Карачев
41 Jab 63
180528 Karamyševo 31 Gb 56
249855 Karavaj 41 Ja 64
215850 Kardymovo 40 Ja 69
164100 Kargopol` 17 Eb 66
161200 Kargulino 17 Fa 66
174201 Karlovka 32 Fb 59
396521 Karpenkovo 54 La 67
399521 Kartašovka 42 Ka 66
391300 Kasimov / Касимов
34 Ja 69
171640 Kašin / Кашин 33 Gb 65
161311 Kašinskoe 18 Fb 70
142900 Kašira / Кашира 42 Ja 66
396350 Kaširskoe 54 Kb 67
184711 Kaškarancy 10 Ca 63
185516 Kaskesručej 16 Eb 63
243014 Katiči 52 Ka 59
Katunki 34 Ha 71
214522 Katyn` 40 Ja 59
309527 Kazačok 54 Kb 65
399759 Kazaki 42 Ka 66
309966 Kazinka 54 La 65
165266 Kazovo 18 Eb 72
391021 Kel`cy 42 Ja 68
165129 Kelareva Gorka 18 Eb 69
186610 Kem` 10 Da 62
186916 Kepa 9 Cb 60
188469 Kerstovo 31 Fb 56
171701 Kes`ma 33 Gb 65
171470 Kesova Gora 33 Gb 65
186664 Kesten`ga 9 Cb 59
161400 Kičmengskij Gorodok
18 Fb 73
188400 Kikerino 31 Fb 57
186966 Kimovaara 9 Db 59
301720 Kimovsk / Кимовск
42 Jab 66
171500 Kimry / Кимры 33 Ha 65

155800 Kinešma / Кинешма
34 Gb 70
188455 Kingisepp / Кингисепп
31 Fb 56
301260 Kireevsk / Киреевск
42 Jab 65
391093 Kiricy 42 Ja 68
161100 Kirillov 17 Fb 66
187710 Kiriši / Кириши 32 Fb 60
249440 Kirov / Киров 41 Ja 62
184250 Kirovsk 6 Bb 61
188855 Kirovskoe 15 Fa 57
601010 Kiržač / Киржач 34 Ha 66
187413 Kisel`nja 16 Fa 60
157130 Kislovo 18 Ga 70
155927 Kitovo 34 Ha 69
182570 Kivaly 40 Hb 58
165262 Kizema 18 Eb 72
162952 Kjabelovo 17 Fa 65
164886 Kjanda 10 Da 66
186148 Kjasnjasel`ga 16 Eb 60
143211 Klement`evo 41 Hb 64
161411 Klepikovo 18 Fa 73
242820 Kletnja / Клетня 41 Jab 61
157928 Klevancevo 34 Gb 70
171920 Kleviči 33 Gb 64
249902 Klimov Zavod 41 Ja 62
243040 Klimovo/Novozybkov
Климово/Новозыбков
53 Ka 60
181323 Klimovo/Ostrov 31 Gb 56
188836 Klimovo/Zelenogorsk
15 Fa 57
142180 Klimovsk / Климовск
42 Hb 65
164034 Klimovskaja 17 Fa 67
141600 Klin Клин 33 Ha 64
243110 Klincy / Клинцы 53 Ka 60
174752 Klišino 32 Fb 61
172124 Ključi 33 Gb 61
242435 Knjaginino 53 Ka 62
182280 Knjazevo/Isakovo 40 Ha 56
396033 Knjazevo/Usman` 42 Ka 67
171945 Knjažiha 33 Gb 64
601952 Knjažskaja 34 Ha 69
187353 Kobona 16 Fa 59
165221 Kočkurga 18 Eb 72
153510 Kohma 34 Ha 69
186801 Kojrinoja 16 Eb 59
186666 Kokkosalma 9 Cb 59
186260 Kokorevo 32 Gb 57
161355 Kokšarka 18 Fb 72
601780 Kol`čugino / Кольчугино
34 Ha 67
184380 Kola 6 Ba 61
186522 Koležma 10 Da 63
171543 Koljubeevo 33 Gb 65
155933 Kolobovo 34 Ha 69
157440 Kologriv 18 Ga 72
188550 Kologriv 31 Fb 56
140400 Kolomna / Коломна
42 Hb 66
171113 Kolomno 33 Gb 62
397921 Kolomycevo 54 La 67
188730 Koloskovo 15 Fa 58
196641 Kolpino / Колпино 32 Fb 58

POSTALI · ÍNDICE CON CÓDIGOS POSTALES · INDICE DE LUGARES COM CÓDIGOS POSTAIS ·
MÍST S PSČ · ZOZNAM OBCÍ S PSČ · INDEKS MIEJSCOWOŚCI Z KOD POCZTOWY

182

Kolpny (RUS) | **Liski / Лиски** (RUS)

303410 Kolpny 42 Ka 65
170552 Koltalovo 33 Ha 63
184015 Kolvica 6 Bb 60
601385 Kolyčevo 34 Hb 69
242400 Komariči 41 Ka 62
242231 Komjagino 41 Ka 61
188320 Kommunar / Коммунар
        32 Fb 58
396031 Komsomol`skij 42 Kb 67
399281 Kon`-Kolodez` 42 Ka 67
171250 Konakovo / Конаково
        33 Ha 64
164223 Konda 17 Eb 67
188908 Kondrat`evo 15 Fa 56
249830 Kondrovo / Кондрово
        41 Ja 63
162900 Kondušskij Pogost
        17 Fa 64
164284 Konevo 17 Ea 67
164010 Konoša 17 Fa 68
141340 Konstantinovo 33 Ha 66
152321 Konstantinovskij 34 Gb 67
215241 Kopariha 41 Hb 62
188525 Kopor`e 31 Fb 57
391226 Korablino / Кораблино
        42 Jab 68
249144 Korekozevo 41 Ja 64
307410 Korenevo 53 Kb 62
171365 Koreničino 33 Ha 62
152961 Kornilovskoe 34 Gb 67
309210 Koroča 54 La 65
141060 Korolev / Королев
        34 Hb 65
152252 Koromyslovo 34 Gb 67
174157 Korostyn` 32 Ga 59
175221 Korovitčino 32 Gb 59
157192 Korovnovo 18 Ga 70
184405 Korzunovo 5 Ab 54
242746 Kosik 41 Jab 61
161363 Kosikovo 18 Fb 71
242724 Kosilovo 41 Jab 61
171660 Kosjakovo 33 Ga 65
216530 Koski 41 Ja 61
171536 Koškino 33 Gb 64
188472 Koskolovo 31 Fb 56
157214 Kostoma 34 Ga 69
186930 Kostomukša 9 Da 58
186855 Kostomuksi 16 Ea 60
156000 Kostroma / Кострома
        34 Gb 68
        Kostrovo 34 Gb 71
216524 Kostyri 41 Ja 61
186012 Kotkozero 16 Eb 61
165300 Kotlas 18 Eb 74
157982 Kotlovo 34 Gb 70
391242 Kotlovy-Borki 42 Jab 68
309807 Kovalevo 54 La 65
184141 Kovdor 5 Bb 58
601900 Kovrov / Ковров 34 Ha 69
        Koz`ja Rečka 43 Ga 71
187633 Kožakovo 33 Fb 62
249720 Kozel`sk / Козельск
        41 Ja 63
307364 Kozino 53 Kb 62
301233 Krapivna 42 Jab 65
216543 Krapivna 41 Ja 61

187121 Krapivno 32 Fb 60
155056 Krapivnovo 34 Ha 68
175332 Kraseja 32 Gb 60
393733 Krasivoe 42 Jab 68
243160 Krasnaja Gora 40 Ka 59
602332 Krasnaja Gorbatka /
        Красная Горбатка
        34 Hb 69
157343 Krasnaja Osyp` 18 Ga 72
303623 Krasnaja Zarja 42 Ka 65
143090 Krasnoarmejsk /
        Красноармейск
        34 Ha 66
152882 Krasnoe/Čerepovec
        33 Ga 67
161572 Krasnoe/Igumnovskaja
        18 Fa 71
399670 Krasnoe/Lebedjan`
        42 Ka 66
309912 Krasnoe/Novyj Oskol
        54 La 66
391140 Krasnoe/Pronsk 42 Ja 67
157940 Krasnoe-na-Volge 34 Gb 69
174214 Krasnofarfornyj 32 Fb 59
157467 Krasnogor`e 34 Gb 71
182370 Krasnogorodskoe 31 Ha 56
143400 Krasnogorsk / Красногорск
        33 Hb 65
601263 Krasnogvardejskij 34 Ha 68
309920 Krasnogvardejskoe/
        Alekseevka 54 La 66
243321 Krasnoviči 41 Ka 60
143090 Krasnozavodsk /
        Краснозаводск 34 Ha 66
238730 Krasnoznamensk 38 Ja 50
216100 Krasnyj 40 Ja 59
171660 Krasnyj Holm 33 Ga 65
188440 Krasnyj Luč 31 Fb 57
601975 Krasnyj Majak 34 Ha 69
601973 Krasnyj Oktjabr`/Andreevo
        34 Ha 69
243340 Krasnyj Rog 41 Ka 61
150522 Krasnyj Tkači 34 Gb 67
171934 Krasuha 33 Ga 63
164154 Krečetovo 17 Fa 66
249185 Kremenki / Кременки
        41 Ja 65
249962 Kremenskoe 41 Hb 63
152861 Krestcy 33 Ga 67
306622 Krestice 54 Kb 65
301951 Kresty/Bogorodick
        42 Jab 66
301089 Kresty/Efremov 42 Jab 65
391021 Kriuša 42 Ja 67
172503 Krivcovo 40 Ha 59
186170 Krivcy 17 Eb 64
162532 Krivec/Čerepovec 17 Fb 65
307023 Krivec/Gubkin 54 Kb 65
399174 Krivec/Mičurinsk 42 Ka 68
186622 Krivoj Porog 10 Cb 61
216415 Krivoles 41 Jab 60
303200 Kromy 41 Ka 63
197760 Kronštadt / Кронштадт
        15 Fa 57
186141 Krošnozero 16 Eb 61
393732 Krugloe/Mičurinsk 42 Ka 68

216790 Kruglovka 40 Ja 59
238542 Kruglovo 38 Ja 48
307360 Krupec 53 Kb 62
157290 Krusanovo 18 Ga 71
174474 Krutec 33 Ga 62
303802 Krutoe/Livny 42 Ka 65
142930 Krutoe/Zarajsk
        42 Ja 66
238414 Krylovo 38 Ja 49
306600 Kšenskij 54 Kb 65
160533 Kubenskoe 17 Fb 67
143070 Kubinka 41 Hb 64
161457 Kudanga 18 Fb 73
152030 Kudrino 34 Ha 66
301332 Kuhtinka 42 Ja 66
152450 Kukoboj 18 Ga 67
243517 Kulagi 41 Ka 60
187507 Kulatino 32 Fb 61
303620 Kuleši 42 Ka 65
306817 Kulevka 54 Kb 66
        Kulivertovo 18 Fb 70
186322 Kumsa 16 Ea 61
        Kun`ja 40 Ha 58
161349 Kunož 18 Fb 71
184215 Kuolajarvi 9 Ca 57
140324 Kuplijam 34 Ha 66
601542 Kupreevo 34 Hb 69
182142 Kupuj 40 Ha 58
182500 Kurakino 40 Ha 58
307250 Kurčatov / Курчатов
        53 Kb 63
157240 Kurilovo 18 Ga 71
186734 Kurkieki 15 Eb 59
301940 Kurkino 42 Jab 66
601570 Kurlovo / Курлово
        34 Hb 68
188470 Kurovicy 31 Fb 56
142620 Kurovskoe / Куровское
        34 Ha 66
249850 Kurovskoj 41 Ja 64
305000 Kursk / Курск 54 Kb 64
307004 Kus`kino 54 Kb 65
171422 Kušalino 33 Gb 64
        Kuševanda 9 Cb 58
187100 Kusino 32 Fb 59
186915 Kuusiniěmi 9 Cb 59
172110 Kuvšinovo / Кувшиново
        33 Gb 62
303111 Kuz`minka 41 Jab 63
157341 Kužbal 18 Ga 72
186620 Kuzema 10 Cb 62
157184 Kuzemino 18 Fb 70
249640 Kuzemki 41 Ja 64
171055 Kuženkino 33 Gb 61
188751 Kuznečnoe 15 Eb 57
175411 Kuznecovka 32 Ga 60
156420 Kuznecovo/Kostroma
        34 Gb 69
188245 Kuznecovo/Siverskij
        32 Fb 57
184713 Kuzomen` 10 Ca 64
301812 Kuzovka 42 Jab 66
187761 Kuzura 16 Fa 62
242220 Kvetun` 53 Ka 61
301880 Kytino 42 Jab 66
307750 L`gov / Льгов 53 Kb 63

142155 L`vovskij / Львовский
        42 Hb 65
186730 Lachdenpoh`ja 15 Eb 58
306720 Lačinovo 54 Kb 65
182459 Ladino 32 Ha 57
238460 Laduškin 38 Ja 48
249144 Ladygino 41 Ja 64
242413 Lagerevka 53 Ka 62
186521 Lapino 10 Da 63
184530 Laplandija 6 Ba 61
182360 Laptevo 31 Ha 56
171960 Laptiha 33 Gb 64
390523 Laskovo 42 Ja 66
391334 Lašma / Лашма 34 Ja 69
152952 Lavrent`evo 33 Ga 66
302521 Lavrovo 41 Ka 64
152115 Lazarcevo 34 Gb 67
399610 Lebedjan` / Лебедянь
        42 Ka 67
303900 Ledno 41 Ka 63
182533 Lehovo 40 Hb 58
172555 Lejkino 40 Hb 60
186985 Lendery 15 Db 59
162820 Lent`evo 33 Ga 64
216330 Leonidovo 41 Ja 63
157311 Leont`evo 18 Ga 72
171554 Leont`evskoe 33 Gb 66
186870 Leppjaniemi 16 Ea 60
236000 Lermontovo 38 Ja 48
303560 Leski 42 Ka 64
173509 Lesnaja 32 Ga 58
601563 Lesnikovo 34 Hb 69
309881 Lesnoe Ukolovo 54 La 66
140451 Lesnoj/Kolomna 42 Hb 66
238534 Lesnoj/Zelenogradsk
        38 Hb 48
188960 Lesogorskij 15 Eb 56
391016 Lesunovo 34 Hb 68
188416 Letošicy 31 Fb 57
242732 Letošniki 41 Jab 61
161306 Levaš 18 Fa 71
155120 Ležnevo 34 Ha 68
171667 Lihačevo 33 Ga 65
171210 Lihoslavl` / Лихославль
        33 Gb 63
        Lihun 41 Ja 64
142670 Likino-Dulevo /
        Ликино-Дулево 34 Hb 66
188553 Likovskoe 31 Fb 56
182300 Linec/Begunovo 40 Ha 57
307145 Linec/Železnogorsk
        53 Ka 63
165221 Linjaki 18 Eb 72
398000 Lipeck / Липецк 42 Ka 67
301098 Lipicy-Zybino 42 Jab 65
161250 Lipin Bor 17 Fa 65
391773 Lipjagi 42 Jab 67
301264 Lipki   Липки 42 Jab 65
216330 Lipnja 41 Ja 63
238606 Lipovka/Černjahovsk
        38 Ja 49
216561 Lipovka/Roslavl` 41 Jab 61
601623 Lisavy 34 Ha 66
215856 Lisičino 40 Hb 60
187023 Lisino-Korpus 32 Fb 58
397900 Liski / Лиски 54 La 67

183

INDEX WITH POST CODES · ORTSREGISTER MIT POSTLEITZAHLEN · INDICE CON CODICI
STEDREGISTER MED POSTNUMRE · PLAATSNAMENREGISTER MET POSTCODE · REJSTŘÍK

Litovka   (RUS)   **Nikitovka**

601470 Litovka 34 Ha 70
182440 Litovo 32 Gb 57
303850 Livny / Ливны 42 Ka 65
186220 Ližma 16 Ea 62
602144 Ljahi 34 Hb 69
186804 Ljaskelja 16 Eb 59
187050 Ljuban` 32 Fb 59
140000 Ljubercy / Люберцы
    34 Hb 65
175443 Ljubnica 32 Gb 60
142380 Ljubučany 42 Hb 65
174760 Ljubytino 32 Ga 61
249400 Ljudinovo / Людиново
    41 Jab 62
249942 Ljudkovo 41 Ja 62
187700 Ljugoviči 16 Fa 61
170544 Ljušino 33 Ha 63
141055 Lobnja / Лобня 33 Ha 65
182528 Lobok 40 Hb 57
186341 Lobskoe 16 Ea 63
215103 Loc`mino 41 Hb 62
162353 Lodejka 18 Fa 73
187700 Lodejnoe Pole 16 Fa 61
161358 Logduz 18 Fb 72
186850 Lojmola 16 Eb 59
182900 Loknja 32 Ha 58
242300 Lokot` / Локоть 41 Ka 62
243271 Lomakovka 53 Ka 60
157918 Lomki 34 Gb 70
162365 Lomovatka 18 Eb 73
184340 Loparskaja 6 Ba 61
243130 Lopatni 41 Ka 60
180541 Lopatovo 31 Gb 56
243513 Lopazna 41 Jab 60
171932 Loščemlja 33 Gb 63
143800 Lotošino 33 Ha 63
182517 Lovec 40 Ha 57
184591 Lovozero 6 Ba 63
175225 Loznicy 32 Gb 59
303247 Lubjanki 41 Ka 63
181120 Ludoni 31 Ga 57
188229 Luga / Луга 32 Ga 57
171863 Luginino 33 Gb 63
140500 Luhovicy / Луховицы
    42 Ja 67
216103 Lukiniči 40 Ja 59
301225 Lukino 42 Jab 65
186733 Lumivaara 15 Eb 58
238715 Lunino 38 Ja 50
184413 Luostari 5 Ab 59
186523 Lušnaja 10 Da 62
309677 Lutovinovo 54 La 66
186918 Luusalmi 9 Cb 59
184015 Luven`ga 6 Bb 60
187413 Luža 16 Fb 59
188472 Lužicy 31 Fb 56
188840 Lužki 15 Fa 57
171066 Lykošino 32 Ga 61
243311 Lyščiči 41 Ka 60
140080 Lytkarino / Лыткарино
    34 Hb 65
182220 Maevo 40 Ha 57
307147 Magnitnyj 41 Ka 63
181125 Majakovo 31 Ga 57
238033 Majakovskoe 38 Ja 50
309503 Majskij/Belgorod 54 La 64

238044 Majskoe 38 Ja 50
157460 Makar`ev 34 Gb 71
164200 Makarov Dvor 17 Eb 68
171055 Makarovo 32 Gb 61
171900 Maksatiha 33 Gb 63
602353 Mal`yševo 34 Hb 69
307835 Malaja Loknja 53 Kb 63
152850 Malaja Lucha 33 Ga 67
396100 Malaja Privalovka
    42 Kb 67
174260 Malaja Višera / Малая
    Вишера 32 Ga 60
140746 Malan`inskaja 34 Hb 67
141620 Maleevka 33 Ha 64
142850 Malino 42 Hb 66
391583 Malinovka/Sarai 42 Jab 69
171524 Maloe Vasilevo 33 Ha 65
249090 Malojaroslavec /
    Малоярославец
    41 Hb 64
171930 Malyševo 33 Gb 63
391155 Mamonovo/Pronsk
    42 Jab 67
238450 Mamonovo/Svetlyj
    38 Ja 47
242235 Mancurovo 41 Ka 62
187426 Manihino 16 Fa 60
249415 Manino 41 Jab 62
186821 Mansila 16 Eb 60
307000 Manturovo 54 Kb 65
396662 Mar`evka 54 La 67
301932 Mar`inka 42 Jab 66
162584 Mar`ino/Čerepovec
    17 Fb 66
301900 Mar`ino/Plavsk 42 Jab 65
399546 Mar`ino-Nikolaevka
    42 Ka 66
165210 Mareninskaja 18 Fa 71
175350 Marevo 32 Gb 60
307705 Marica 53 Kb 63
162923 Marino 17 Eb 64
    Markovka 42 Jab 65
181335 Marševicy 31 Gb 56
182150 Mart`janovo 40 Ha 58
186350 Masel`gskaja 10 Db 62
309276 Maslova Pristan` 54 La 64
186338 Maslozero 10 Db 60
397821 Mastjugino 54 Kb 67
186131 Matrosy 16 Eb 61
181620 Mazicha 31 Ga 56
303030 Mcensk / Мценск
    42 Jab 64
152781 Meduhovo 33 Ga 66
174160 Medved` 32 Ga 58
161304 Medvedevo 18 Fa 71
165390 Medvedka 18 Eb 74
307030 Medvenka 54 Kb 64
186350 Medvež`egorsk 16 Ea 62
249950 Medyn` 41 Ja 63
174470 Meglecy 33 Ga 62
    Megorskij Pogost
    17 Fa 63
186020 Megrega 16 Fa 61
188765 Mel`nikovo 15 Fa 57
391425 Melehovo/Čučkovo
    42 Ja 69

601966 Melehovo/Kovrov /
    Мелехово/Ковров
    34 Ha 69
602100 Melenki / Меленки
    34 Hb 69
188271 Merevo 32 Ga 58
249240 Meščovsk 41 Ja 63
188423 Mestanovo 31 Fb 57
187713 Mexbaza 16 Fa 61
184363 Meždureč`e 6 Ab 60
162833 Mezga 33 Ga 64
243220 Mglin 41 Jab 60
602353 Mičkovo 34 Hb 69
393730 Mičurinsk / Мичуринск
    42 Ka 68
391710 Mihajlov 42 Jab 67
161306 Mihajlovka 18 Fa 71
303640 Mihajlovka/Efremov
    42 Ka 65
216480 Mihajlovka/Počinok
    41 Ja 60
152118 Mihajlovskoe/Rostov
    34 Gb 67
    Mihajlovskoe/Ruza
    33 Hb 64
155932 Mihalevo 34 Ha 69
165274 Mihalevo 18 Eb 72
140343 Mihali 34 Hb 67
157980 Miheevo 34 Gb 71
391955 Mihei 42 Ja 68
162363 Mihninskaja 18 Fa 74
143822 Mikulino 33 Ha 63
602131 Mil`na 34 Hb 69
391770 Miloslavskoe 42 Jab 67
162035 Min`kino 18 Ga 67
161340 Min`kovo 18 Fb 71
175400 Mironegi 32 Gb 61
215825 Miropol`e 41 Hb 60
174510 Mirovo 33 Ga 63
157235 Mitino/Galič 34 Ga 70
214580 Mitino/Smolensk 40 Ja 60
    Mjačkovo 34 Ha 70
162646 Mjaksa 33 Ga 66
249875 Mjatlevo 41 Ja 63
162832 Močala 33 Ga 64
142954 Močily 42 Ja 66
172124 Mogilevka 33 Gb 61
303410 Mohovoe/Ščigny 42 Ka 64
303217 Mohovoe/Železnogorsk
    41 Ka 63
162311 Moiseevskaja 18 Fa 69
182620 Moločišče 32 Gb 57
160507 Moločnoe 17 Fb 67
243216 Molod`kovo 41 Jab 60
197720 Molodežnoe 15 Fa 57
175340 Molvoticy 32 Gb 60
606162 Monakovo 34 Hb 70
216130 Monastyrščina 40 Ja 59
184505 Mončegorsk 6 Bb 60
    Monza 18 Fa 72
171962 Morkiny Gory 33 Gb 64
309162 Morozovo 54 Kb 65
    Mortki 34 Ha 71
601566 Morugino 34 Hb 68
249930 Mosal`sk 41 Ja 63
396357 Mosal`skoe 54 Kb 67

172041 Moški 33 Ha 63
101000 Moskva / Москва 34 Hb 65
186984 Motko 16 Db 59
171894 Motyli 33 Ga 63
143200 Možajsk / Можайск
    41 Hb 64
188268 Mšinskaja 32 Fb 57
601408 Mstera 34 Ha 69
186960 Muezerskij 10 Db 59
183000 Murmansk 6 Ba 61
184355 Murmaši 6 Ba 60
602205 Murom / Муром 34 Hb 70
216466 Murygino 40 Ja 60
215834 Muškoviči 40 Hb 60
152830 Myškin 33 Gb 66
238616 Mysovska 38 Hb 49
155200 Myt 34 Ha 70
141000 Mytišči / Мытищи 34 Hb 65
399570 Naberežnoe 42 Kb 66
162656 Nadporož`e/Čerepovec
    17 Fb 66
187733 Nadporož`e/Lodejnoe Pole
    16 Fa 62
186430 Nadvoicy 10 Db 62
309745 Nagol`noe 54 Lb 67
152030 Nagor`e/Kimry 34 Ha 66
309750 Nagor`e/Rossoš` 54 La 67
171562 Nagorskoe 33 Ha 66
175211 Nagovo 32 Ga 59
238215 Nahimovo 38 Ja 49
601408 Naleskino 34 Ha 69
143300 Naro-Fominsk /
    Наро-Фоминск 41 Hb 64
    Našči 32 Ga 58
182225 Nasva 32 Ha 58
607100 Navašino / Навашино
    34 Hb 70
242130 Navlja / Навля 41 Ka 62
175292 Navolok 32 Gb 59
152150 Naževorka 34 Gb 67
174755 Nebolči 32 Fb 61
309238 Nečaevo 54 La 66
180502 Neelovo 31 Gb 56
172066 Negonovo 33 Ha 62
157330 Neja 18 Ga 71
170551 Nekrasovo 33 Ha 63
162672 Nelazskoe 17 Fb 65
172520 Nelidovo / Нелидово
    32 Ha 60
249383 Neloboč` 41 Jab 62
238710 Neman 38 Hb 50
186348 Nemino 3-e 16 Ea 63
301016 Nenaševo 42 Ja 65
140473 Nepecino 42 Hb 66
302532 Nepolod` 41 Jab 64
160510 Nepotjagovo 18 Fb 67
    Nereg 34 Gb 72
157800 Nerehta / Нерехта
    34 Gb 68
238010 Nesterov 38 Ja 50
182500 Nevel` / Невель 40 Ha 57
175455 Nevskaja 32 Ga 60
186212 Nigižma 17 Eb 64
184420 Nikel` 5 Ab 58
165102 Nikiforovo 18 Eb 69
309905 Nikitovka 54 La 66

POSTALI · ÍNDICE CON CÓDIGOS POSTALES · INDICE DE LUGARES COM CÓDIGOS POSTAIS ·
MÍST S PSČ · ZOZNAM OBCÍ S PSČ · INDEKS MIEJSCOWOŚCI Z KOD POCZTOWY

184

Nikitskoe/Bogorodick (RUS)   Petrovskaja (RUS)

301574 Nikitskoe/Bogorodick
       42 Jab 66
140168 Nikitskoe/Bronnicy
       42 Hb 66
161440 Nikol`sk 18 Fb 73
161111 Nikol`skij Toržok 17 Fb 66
162520 Nikol`skoe/Kaduj 17 Fb 65
188357 Nikol`skoe/Siverskij
       32 Fb 57
       Nikol`skoe/Usman`
       42 Ka 67
161326 Nikol`skoe/Uspen`e
       18 Fb 70
243234 Nikolaevka 41 Jab 60
181120 Nikolaevo 32 Ga 57
152435 Nikolo-Gora 34 Ga 68
157290 Nikolo-Poloma 18 Ga 71
153000 Nikul`skoe 34 Ha 69
302502 Nikuliči 41 Ka 64
170518 Nikulino 33 Ha 63
309606 Ninovka 54 La 65
396870 Nišnedevick 54 Kb 66
216117 Nitjaži 40 Ja 59
184374 Nivankjul` 5 Ba 58
238434 Nivenskoe 38 Ja 48
339412 Nižnjaja Matrenka 42 Ka 68
161232 Nižnjaja Mondoma
       17 Fa 65
       Njamozero 9 Ca 59
164200 Njandoma 17 Eb 68
182303 Nočlegovo 40 Ha 57
142400 Noginsk / Ногинск
       34 Hb 66
164010 Norinskaja 17 Fa 68
187643 Nosovo 32 Fb 61
140532 Nosovo 2-e 42 Ja 67
186523 Nottovarakka 10 Da 62
601385 Novaja 34 Hb 69
174215 Novaja 32 Fb 59
391491 Novaja Derevnja/Čučkovo
       42 Ja 69
238645 Novaja Derevnja/Kaliningrad
       38 Ja 49
309761 Novaja Ivanovka 54 La 66
307535 Novaja Peršina 53 Ka 63
396310 Novaja Usman` 42 Kb 67
181375 Novgorodka 31 Gb 56
175291 Novički 32 Gb 59
301680 Noviki 42 Ja 66
187713 Novinka/Alehovščina
       16 Fa 61
187522 Novinka/Bol`šoj Kokoviči
       16 Fa 61
       Novinka/Lodejnoe Polje
       16 Eb 60
188375 Novinka/Siverskij 32 Fb 58
       Noviny 17 Ea 67
160542 Novlenskoe 17 Fb 67
602337 Novljanka 34 Hb 69
249620 Novoaleksandrovskij
       41 Ja 62
393756 Novoe Hmelevoe 42 Ka 68
186902 Novoe Juškozero 9 Da 60
175009 Novoe Ovsino 32 Ga 58
175450 Novoe Rahino 32 Ga 60
157191 Novoe Samylovo 18 Ga 70

242430 Novojamskoe 53 Ka 62
391160 Novomičurinsk 42 Ja 67
301650 Novomoskovsk /
       Новомосковск 42 Ja 66
143570 Novopetrovskoe 33 Hb 64
182440 Novoržev 32 Gb 57
       Novoselki 34 Hb 70
393717 Novoseslavino 42 Jab 68
303500 Novosil` 42 Ka 65
396930 Novosil`skoe 42 Kb 66
165322 Novošino 18 Eb 73
182200 Novosokol`niki 40 Ha 58
       Novospasskoe 41 Ja 61
161122 Novostrojka 17 Fa 66
391240 Novotiševoe 42 Jab 68
396070 Novovoronež / Нововоронеж
       54 Kb 67
171270 Novozavidovskij 33 Ha 64
243200 Novozybkov / Новозыбков
       53 Ka 59
301536 Novye Dol`cy 41 Jab 64
309640 Novyj Oskol / Новый Оскол
       54 La 65
303153 Novyj Sinec 41 Jab 64
157130 Nožkino 18 Ga 70
141623 Nudol` 33 Ha 64
249030 Obninsk / Обнинск
       41 Hb 64
306230 Obojan` / Обоянь 54 Kb 64
142279 Obolensk 42 Ja 65
175332 Obryni 32 Gb 60
238050 Očakovo 38 Ja 50
143000 Odincovo / Одинцово
       33 Hb 65
301440 Odoev 42 Jab 66
188838 Ogonki 15 Fa 57
249357 Ogor` 41 Jab 62
152835 Ohotino 33 Gb 66
164205 Ohtoma 17 Eb 69
174423 Okladnevo 32 Ga 61
602133 Okšovo 34 Hb 69
152700 Oktjabr` 33 Gb 65
186181 Oktjabr`skaja 16 Ea 63
249802 Oktjabr`skij/Kaluga
       41 Ja 64
157320 Oktjabr`skij/Manturovo
       18 Ga 72
391720 Oktjabr`skij/Pronsk
       42 Ja 66
       Oktjabr`skij/Tula 42 Ja 65
165210 Oktjabr`skij/Vel`sk 18 Eb 71
399331 Oktjabr`skoe 42 Ka 67
174350 Okulovka / Окуловка
       32 Ga 61
161567 Okulovskaja 18 Fa 71
602217 Ol`gino 34 Hb 70
396670 Ol`hovatka/Rossoš`
       54 La 67
306018 Ol`hovatka/Železnogorsk
       42 Ka 64
399828 Ol`hovec 42 Jab 67
307555 Ol`hovka 53 Kb 62
309590 Ol`šanka 54 La 68
162101 Olarevo 18 Fb 68
301300 Olen`kovo 42 Ja 66
184530 Olenegorsk 6 Ba 61

184710 Olenica 10 Ca 63
152710 Olisavino 33 Gb 65
186000 Olonec 16 Fa 61
164840 Onega 10 Db 66
155270 Onoškovo 34 Gb 70
162820 Opel 33 Ga 64
182330 Opočka / Опочка 31 Ha 56
188220 Oredež 32 Ga 58
172353 Orehovo/Ržev 33 Ha 62
601220 Orehovo/Sobinka 34 Ha 67
142600 Orehovo-Zuevo /
       Орехово-Зуево 34 Hb 67
302000 Orel   Orel 41 Ka 64
171395 Oreški 33 Ha 62
396306 Orlovo 42 Kb 67
       Osinovskie 41 Jab 62
174218 Oskuj 32 Fb 60
152130 Osokino 34 Ha 67
164141 Ostaševskaja 17 Eb 66
172730 Ostaškov / Осташков
       32 Gb 61
216537 Oster 41 Ja 60
       Oštinskij Pogost 16 Fa 63
142931 Ostroga 42 Ja 66
397806 Ostrogožsk / Острогожск 54
       La 67
161270 Ostrov/Lipin Bor 17 Fa 65
181350 Ostrov/Pečory /
       Остров/Печоры 31 Gb 56
182262 Osyno 39 Ha 56
215150 Otnosovo 41 Hb 62
188750 Otradnoe/Priozersk
       15 Fa 58
187330 Otradnoe/Sankt Peterburg
       Отрадное/Санкт
       Петербург 32 Fb 58
182153 Ovečkovo 40 Ha 59
142920 Ožerel`e / Ожерелье
       42 Ja 66
215747 Ozerišče 41 Ja 61
161383 Ozerki 18 Fa 72
216239 Ozernyj 40 Hb 60
238120 Ozersk 38 Ja 50
140560 Ozery / Озеры 42 Ja 66
186333 Padany 10 Db 60
165151 Pajtovskaja 18 Eb 70
391124 Pal`nye 42 Ja 67
161448 Palagino 18 Fb 72
186147 Palalahta 16 Eb 60
309902 Palatovo 54 La 66
155620 Paleh 34 Ha 69
157240 Palkino 18 Ga 70
181270 Palkino/Ostrov 31 Gb 56
216100 Palkino/Smolenslk 40 Ja 59
157990 Pan`kovo 34 Gb 71
181511 Panikoviči 31 Gb 55
399148 Panino/Lipeck 42 Ka 67
396140 Panino/Voronež 42 Kb 68
172316 Panjukovo 33 Ha 62
173526 Pankovka / Панковка
       32 Ga 59
157164 Pankratovo 18 Fb 71
186609 Panozero 10 Da 60
188667 Pappolovo 16 Fa 58
602215 Papulino 34 Hb 69
       Papušino 17 Fb 67

157270 Parfen`evo 18 Ga 71
175130 Parfino 32 Gb 59
170515 Pasinkovo 33 Ha 64
161111 Paunino 17 Fb 66
391837 Pavelec 42 Jab 67
391531 Pavlovka 42 Ja 69
196620 Pavlovskij/Puškin /
       Павловск/Пушкин
       32 Fb 58
601977 Pavlovskoe/Melehovo
       34 Ha 69
601273 Pavlovskoe/Suzdal`
       34 Ha 68
182645 Pavy 32 Ga 57
301456 Pčel`na 42 Jab 64
184410 Pčenega 5 Ab 59
187507 Pečenga 32 Fb 61
181500 Pečory / Печоры 31 Gb 55
185511 Pedasel`ga 16 Eb 62
162362 Peganovo 18 Fa 74
391230 Pehlec 42 Jab 68
601106 Pekša 34 Hb 67
186950 Peninga 10 Db 60
172770 Peno 42 Ja 66
243560 Peregon 53 Ka 61
396180 Perelešino 42 Kb 68
249130 Peremyšl` 41 Ja 64
152020 Pereslavl`-Zalesskij /
       Переславль-Залесский
       34 Ha 66
353522 Peresyp` 66 Nb 65
243369 Peretorgi 41 Ka 62
164022 Peršinskaja 17 Fa 68
164292 Peršlahta 17 Ea 66
161262 Pervomajskij/Lipin bor
       17 Fa 65
393700 Pervomajskij/Mičurinsk
       Первомайский/Мичуринск
       42 Jab 68
       Pervomajskij/Navašino
       34 Hb 70
188855 Pervomajskoe 15 Fa 57
186183 Peščanoe 16 Ea 63
216520 Peščiki 41 Ja 60
182643 Peski 32 Ga 57
301416 Pesočenskij 41 Ja 64
391511 Pesočnja/Sapožok 42 Ja 68
242726 Pesočnja/Žukovka
       41 Jab 61
       Pesočnoe 34 Gb 68
155650 Pestjaki 34 Ha 70
174510 Pestovo/Boroviči /
       Пестово/Боровичи
       33 Ga 63
601966 Pestovo/Melehovo
       34 Ha 69
182655 Peti 31 Gb 57
602212 Petrakovo 34 Hb 70
215010 Petrecovo 41 Hb 63
249104 Petriševo/Aleksin 41 Ja 64
216216 Petriščevo/Jarcevo
       40 Hb 67
198504 Petrodvorec / Петродворец
       31 Fb 57
397814 Petropavlovka 54 La 67
165197 Petrovskaja 18 Ea 70

185

INDEX WITH POST CODES · ORTSREGISTER MIT POSTLEITZAHLEN · INDICE CON CODICI
STEDREGISTER MED POSTNUMRE · PLAATSNAMENREGISTER MET POSTCODE · REJSTŘÍK

RUS Petrovskoe   **RUS**   Sapernoe

393070 Petrovskoe 42 Ka 68	309118 Pokrovka 54 La 64	171420 Prudovo 33 Gb 64	155250 Rodniki / Родники
185000 Petrozavodsk 16 Eb 62	164884 Pokrovskoe 10 Da 66	188425 Pružicy 31 Fb 57	34 Gb 69
301382 Petrušino 42 Ja 65	303170 Pokrovskoe/Livny 42 Ka 64	216270 Prževal`skoe 40 Hb 59	141880 Rogačevo 33 Ha 65
601140 Petuški / Петушки	175140 Pola 32 Gb 59	180000 Pskov / Псков 31 Gb 56	309551 Rogovatoe 54 Kb 66
34 Hb 67	238630 Polessk 38 Ja 49	306125 Psolec 54 Kb 64	172747 Rogoža 32 Gb 61
215662 Pigulino 41 Hb 61	306530 Polevoe 54 Kb 65	155360 Pučež 34 Ha 71	152952 Rokanovo 33 Ga 66
162365 Pihtovo 18 Fa 73	186437 Polga 10 Db 62	186150 Pudož 17 Eb 64	301807 Romancevskij 42 Jab 66
186860 Pijtsieki 16 Ea 60	186312 Polja 16 Ea 63	186184 Pudožgorskij 16 Ea 63	307545 Romanovo 53 Kb 62
187600 Pikalevo / Пикалево	391511 Poljaki 42 Ja 68	187300 Puholovo 32 Fb 59	140730 Rošal` / Рошаль 34 Hb 67
16 Fb 62	215131 Poljanovo 41 Hb 62	186758 Pujkkola 15 Ea 58	188820 Roščino 15 Fa 57
Pinduši 16 Ea 62	188824 Poljany 15 Fa 57	606552 Pureh 34 Ha 71	216500 Roslavl` / Рославль
187716 Pirozero 16 Fa 61	184230 Poljarnye Zori 6 Bb 60	142290 Puščino / Пущино	41 Jab 60
243323 Pisarevka/Uneča 41 Ka 60	184650 Poljarnyj 6 Ab 61	42 Ja 65	161360 Rosljatino 18 Fb 72
155130 Piscovo 34 Gb 68	249340 Polom 41 Jab 62	307413 Puškarnoe 53 Kb 62	157213 Rossolovo 18 Ga 70
391630 Pitelino 42 Ja 69	Polomka 18 Ga 72	196600 Puškin / Пушкин 32 Fb 58	162011 Rostilovo 18 Ga 68
186810 Pitkjaranta 16 Eb 59	249844 Polotnjanyj Zavod 41 Ja 64	141200 Puškino/Moskva /	152150 Rostov / Ростов 34 Gb 67
188327 Pižma 32 Fb 58	309225 Polovka 54 La 65	Пушкино/Москва	309740 Roven`ki 54 Lb 66
181115 Pjatčino 31 Ga 57	161383 Polovniki 18 Fa 72	34 Hb 65	188861 Rovnoe 15 Fa 57
309665 Pjatnickoe 54 La 65	307505 Polozovka 53 Ka 63	242466 Puškino/Novojamskoe	152845 Roždestveno 33 Gb 65
301160 Plastovo 42 Ja 65	243366 Poluž`e 41 Jab 62	53 Ka 62	187070 Ruč`i/Čudovo 32 Fb 59
301470 Plavsk / Плавск 42 Jab 65	306000 Ponyri 42 Ka 64	170556 Puškino/Redkino 33 Ha 63	184030 Ruč`i/Kandalakša 9 Bb 60
155555 Ples 34 Gb 69	391845 Poplevinskij 42 Jab 67	181370 Puškinskie Gory 31 Gb 56	601971 Ručej 34 Ha 69
172352 Pleški 33 Ha 62	301119 Popovka/Aleksin 42 Ja 65	182300 Pustoška 40 Ha 57	396820 Rudkino 54 Kb 67
142322 Pleškino 42 Hb 65	171622 Popovka/Kašin 33 Gb 65	174750 Pustoški 32 Ga 61	182250 Rudnja/Glubočica
181000 Pljussa 31 Ga 57	152850 Popovka/Rybinsk 33 Ga 66	161446 Putilovo 18 Fb 72	39 Ha 56
249920 Ploskoe 41 Ja 63	171551 Poreč`e 33 Gb 65	181410 Pytalovo 31 Gb 55	216790 Rudnja/Smolensk
238735 Pobedino 38 Ja 50	182620 Porhov / Порхов 32 Gb 57	393091 Rachmanino 42 Ka 68	Рудня/Смоленск
157485 Poboišnja 34 Gb 71	186855 Porosozero 16 Ea 60	171267 Radčenko 33 Ha 64	40 Ja 59
243400 Počep / Почеп 41 Ka 61	306206 Porozők 32 Fb 58	172370 Radjukino 33 Ha 62	186968 Rugozero 10 Da 60
174443 Počinnaja Sopka 33 Ga 62	155284 Porzdni 32 Gb 70	186882 Rajsten`jarvi 16 Ea 60	186759 Ruskeala 15 Eb 58
216450 Počinok/El`nja /	152850 Pošehon`e 33 Ga 67	309310 Rakitnoe / Ракитное	309545 Russkaja Halan` 54 La 65
Починок/Ельня 40 Ja 60	303802 Postojal`skaja 42 Ka 65	54 La 63	238542 Russkoe/Svetlogorsk
171143 Počinok/Udomlja 33 Gb 63	396677 Postojalyj 54 La 67	143716 Ramen`e 33 Ha 63	38 Ja 48
182924 Podberez`e/Juhovo	187423 Potanino 16 Fa 60	140315 Ramenki 42 Hb 67	143100 Ruza / Руза 41 Hb 64
32 Ha 58	186326 Povenec 16 Ea 62	Rameški/Galič 18 Ga 70	238535 Rybačij 38 Hb 48
172508 Podberez`e/Nelidovo	391730 Pozdnoe 42 Ja 67	171400 Rameški/Lihoslavl`	152900 Rybinsk / Рыбинск
32 Ha 60	182730 Poževicy 32 Gb 57	33 Gb 64	33 Ga 66
303013 Podberezovo 42 Jab 64	238400 Pravdinsk 38 Ja 49	306641 Rashovec 54 Kb 65	391110 Rybnoe / Рыбное 42 Ja 67
249718 Podborki 41 Ja 63	152430 Prečistoe/Danilov 34 Ga 68	157876 Raslovo 34 Gb 69	185516 Rybreka 16 Eb 63
175144 Podborov`e 32 Ga 59	216230 Prečistoe/Ozernyj 40 Hb 60	141912 Rastovc` 33 Ha 65	307370 Ryl`sk / Рыльск 53 Kb 62
175260 Poddor`e 32 Gb 59	238616 Pričaly 38 Hb 49	391247 Ratmanovo 42 Jab 68	249913 Ryljaki 41 Ja 63
170520 Poddubki 33 Ha 63	214518 Prigorskoe 40 Ja 60	306728 Razdol`e 54 Kb 66	171580 Rylovo 33 Gb 66
161400 Podgorka 18 Fa 73	307605 Prilepy/L`gov 53 Kb 63	309510 Razumnoe / Разумное	303544 Ržanoe 42 Ka 64
238717 Podgornoe/Černjahovsk	307577 Prilepy/Puškino 53 Ka 62	54 La 64	172380 Ržev / Ржев 33 Ha 62
38 Ja 49	165100 Priluk 18 Eb 70	186966 Reboly 9 Db 58	215500 Safonovo/Jarcevo /
238415 Podlipovo 38 Ja 49	238510 Primorsk/Baltijsk 38 Ja 48	171260 Redkino / Редкино	Сафоново/Ярцево
142100 Podol`sk / Подольск	188910 Primorsk/Zelenogorsk	33 Ha 64	41 Hb 61
42 Hb 65	15 Fa 58	161572 Regiševskaje 18 Fa 71	242244 Sagut`evo 53 Ka 61
155136 Podozerskij 34 Gb 68	309980 Princevka 54 La 65	396370 Rep`evka 54 Kb 66	303208 Šahovo 41 Ka 63
187780 Podporož`e 16 Fa 62	188760 Priozersk 15 Eb 58	Retkino 42 Ja 67	143700 Šahovskaja / Шаховская
390000 Podvislovo 42 Jab 68	184420 Prirečnyj 5 Ab 58	186790 Reuskula 15 Eb 58	33 Ha 63
396326 Pogačevka 54 Kb 67	182225 Priskucha 32 Ha 58	143960 Reutov / Реутов 34 Hb 65	186214 Sajatnavolok 16 Ea 61
243550 Pogar / Погар 53 Ka 61	165391 Privodino 18 Eb 74	184580 Revda 6 Bb 62	249455 Šajkovka 41 Ja 62
171423 Pogorel`cy 33 Gb 64	155550 Privolžsk / Приволжск	186184 Rimskoe 16 Ea 63	Sal`mijarvi 5 Ab 58
172310 Pogoreloe-Gorodišče	34 Gb 69	391021 Rjabinovka 42 Hb 68	186167 Šal`skij 16 Eb 63
33 Ha 62	309020 Priznačnoe 54 Kb 64	187040 Rjabovo 32 Fb 59	391532 Salaury 42 Ja 69
309220 Pogorelovka 54 La 65	305000 Prjamicyno 54 Kb 63	186822 Rjajmjalja 16 Eb 59	186337 Šalgovaara 10 Db 61
164132 Pogost 17 Eb 66	186120 Prjaža 16 Eb 61	390000 Rjazan` / Рязань	186821 Salmi 16 Eb 59
238441 Pograničnoe 38 Ja 48	309000 Prohorovka / Прохоровка	42 Ja 67	249240 Šalovo 41 Ja 63
186821 Pogrankonduši 16 Eb 60	54 Kb 64	140753 Rjazanovskij 42 Hb 67	162927 Saminskij Pogost 17 Eb 64
242305 Pogreby 41 Ka 62	173530 Proletarij 32 Ga 59	390000 Rjažsk / Ряжск 42 Jab 68	164292 Samkovo 17 Ea 66
391715 Pojarkovo 42 Ja 67	309300 Proletarskij 54 La 63	243313 Rjuchov 41 Ka 60	187681 Samojlovo 16 Fb 62
601120 Pokrov/Orehovo-Zuevo	391140 Pronsk / Пронск 42 Ja 67	186760 Rjuttju 15 Eb 58	190000 Sankt Peterburg /
Покров/Орехово-Зуево	309263 Protopopovka 54 La 65	157430 Rodino 18 Ga 72	Санкт-Петербург
34 Hb 67	142280 Protvino / Протвино	187754 Rodinovo 16 Fa 63	16 Fb 58
152985 Pokrov/Rybinsk 33 Gb 66	42 Ja 65	142323 Rodionovka 42 Hb 65	188742 Sapernoe 15 Fa 57

POSTALI · ÍNDICE CON CÓDIGOS POSTALES · INDICE DE LUGARES COM CÓDIGOS POSTAIS ·
MÍST S PSČ · ZOZNAM OBCÍ S PSČ · INDEKS MIEJSCOWOŚCI Z KOD POCZTOWY

186

Sapožok / Сапожок   (RUS)   Sudislavl   (RUS)

391940 Sapožok / Сапожок
     42 Jab 68
161414 Saraevo 18 Fa 73
391870 Sarai / Сараи 42 Jab 69
165210 Sarbala 18 Fa 71
161415 Sarmas 18 Fa 73
152470 Šarna 34 Ga 68
187516 Saroža 16 Fb 61
157161 Šartanovo 18 Fb 71
249809 Saškino 41 Ja 64
309550 Šatalovka 54 Kb 66
238315 Šatrovo 38 Ja 48
140700 Šatura / Шатура 34 Hb 67
140700 Šaturtorf 34 Hb 67
157260 Savino/Galič 18 Ga 71
155710 Savino/Kovrov 34 Ha 69
162430 Sazonovo 33 Fb 63
301212 Ščekino / Щекино
     42 Jab 65
187758 Ščelejki 16 Eb 63
249921 Ščelkanovo 41 Ja 63
141100 Ščelkovo / Щелково
     34 Hb 66
396515 Ščerbakovo 54 La 67
142170 Ščerbinka / Щербинка
     42 Hb 65
303140 Ščerbovskij 41 Jab 64
305511 Ščetinka 54 Kb 64
162648 Ščetinskoe 33 Ga 66
306530 Ščigry / Щигры 54 Kb 64
181111 Ščir 31 Ga 57
309290 Šebekino 54 La 64
182250 Sebež 39 Ha 56
186420 Segeža 10 Db 62
155382 Segot` 34 Gb 71
     Šeino 34 Ga 69
162560 Šeksna / Шексна 17 Fb 66
241550 Sel`co/Brjansk
     Сельцо/Брянск 41 Jab 62
242671 Sel`co/Djal`kovo 41 Jab 62
140495 Sel`nikovo 42 Hb 67
309974 Šelaevo 54 La 66
165198 Šelaša 18 Eb 70
216134 Šelegovka 40 Ja 59
150522 Selifontovo 34 Gb 67
307524 Selino 53 Ka 62
172200 Seližarovo 32 Ha 61
173505 Selo-Gora 32 Ga 59
187125 Šelogino 32 Fb 60
185514 Šeltozero 16 Eb 63
243411 Semcy 41 Ka 61
187757 Šemeniči 16 Fa 62
306500 Semenovka 1-ja 54 Kb 64
186166 Semenovo 16 Eb 64
152445 Semenovskoe 34 Ga 67
152101 Semibratovo 34 Gb 67
396854 Semidesjatnoe 54 Kb 66
396900 Semiluki / Семилуки
     54 Kb 67
     Serbino 31 Ga 56
142970 Serebrjanye Prudy
     42 Ja 66
157142 Serebrjanyj Brod 18 Ga 71
143721 Sereda 33 Hb 63
180530 Seredka 31 Ga 56
140760 Serednikovo 34 Hb 67

141300 Sergiev Posad / Сергиев
     Посад 34 Ha 66
186344 Sergievo 16 Ea 64
161563 Sergievskaja 18 Fa 71
182362 Serovo 31 Ha 56
142200 Serpuhov / Серпухов
     42 Ja 65
188650 Sertolovo / Сертолово
     16 Fa 58
242760 Sešča 41 Jab 61
152751 Šestihino 33 Gb 66
197700 Sestroreck / Сестрорецк
     15 Fa 57
309888 Setišče 54 La 66
161567 Ševelevskaja 18 Fa 72
157092 Severnoe 34 Ga 69
157830 Severnyj 54 La 64
184610 Severomorsk 6 Ab 61
184603 Severomorsk III 6 Ba 61
141642 Ševljakovo 33 Ha 64
242440 Sevsk 53 Ka 62
238402 Sevskoe 38 Ja 49
606554 Sickoe 34 Ha 71
162063 Sidorovo/Grjazovec
     18 Ga 58
215283 Sidorovo/Ržev 41 Hb 62
155828 Šilekša 34 Gb 70
161100 Šiljakovo 17 Fb 66
391500 Šilovo/Čučkovo /
     Шилово/Чучково
     42 Ja 68
301885 Šilovo/Lebedjan`
     42 Jab 66
394000 Šilovo/Voronež 54 Kb 67
165150 Šilovskaja 18 Eb 70
     Simankovo 34 Ga 70
143393 Simbuhovo 41 Hb 64
601410 Simoncevo 34 Ha 69
174150 Šimsk 32 Ga 58
301088 Sinegubovo 1-e 42 Jab 64
175343 Šinkovo 32 Gb 60
187507 Sitomlja 32 Fb 61
188330 Siverskij / Сиверский
     32 Fb 58
162220 Sjamža 18 Fa 69
187420 Sjas`stroj 16 Fa 60
161250 Skokovo 17 Fa 65
172037 Skomorochovo 33 Ha 63
391800 Skopin / Скопин 42 Jab 67
164150 Skorjukovo 17 Eb 66
309163 Skorodnoe 54 Kb 65
602115 Skripino 34 Hb 69
188560 Slancy / Сланцы 31 Fb 56
339441 Slava 42 Ka 64
162580 Slavjanka 17 Fb 66
187320 Šlissel`burg / Шлиссельбург
     16 Fb 59
306125 Šljah 54 Kb 64
152076 Sloboda 34 Ga 68
242621 Slobodišče/Djat`kovo
     41 Jab 62
142651 Slobodišče/Egor`evsk
     34 Hb 66
601464 Slobodišči 34 Ha 70
152004 Slobodka 34 Ha 67
157244 Slovinka 34 Ga 71

181320 Smechino 31 Gb 56
606536 Smirkino 34 Ha 71
182655 Šmojlovo 31 Gb 56
214000 Smolensk / Смоленск
     40 Ja 60
606081 Smolino 34 Ha 71
187120 Smolino 32 Fb 60
181370 Smoliny 31 Ha 56
243118 Smotrova Buda 53 Ka 60
184682 Snežnogorsk 6 Ab 61
601200 Sobinka / Собинка
     34 Hb 68
391170 Sobolevo 42 Ja 68
141270 Sofrino 34 Ha 65
601361 Sojma 34 Hb 68
162130 Sokol / Сокол 18 Fb 68
606670 Sokol`skoe 34 Gb 71
175237 Sokolovo 32 Gb 59
185512 Šokša 16 Eb 63
175040 Sol`cy 32 Ga 58
397822 Soldatskoe/Ostrogožsk
     54 Kb 67
399550 Soldatskoe/Voronež
     42 Ka 66
165129 Solginskij 18 Eb 69
157170 Soligalič 18 Fb 70
306120 Solncevo 54 Kb 64
141501 Solnečnogorsk /
     Солнечногорск 33 Ha 65
172370 Šolochovo 33 Ha 61
186220 Soloha 16 Ea 62
390523 Solotča 42 Ja 67
152951 Solov`evskoe 33 Ga 66
243270 Solova 53 Ka 60
399924 Solovoe 42 Jab 66
157335 Soltanovo 18 Ga 71
164154 Solza 17 Fa 66
186609 Šomba 10 Cb 61
187632 Somino 33 Fb 62
301444 Somovo 41 Jab 64
171450 Sonkovo 33 Gb 65
174435 Sopiny 32 Ga 62
175273 Sopki/Holm 32 Gb 58
171066 Sopki/Valdaj 32 Ga 61
171150 Soroki 33 Gb 62
391335 Sorokino/Lašma 42 Ja 69
182731 Sorokino/Porhov 32 Gb 57
164123 Sorokinskaja 17 Eb 67
186790 Sortavala 15 Eb 58
249710 Sosenskij / Сосенский
     41 Ja 62
186530 Sosnovec 10 Da 62
238641 Sosnovka/Černjahovsk
     38 Ja 49
160523 Sosnovka/Vologda
     17 Fb 67
186662 Sosnovyj 9 Cb 60
174164 Sosnovyj Bor/Hredine
     32 Ga 57
188510 Sosnovyj Bor/Petrodvorec
     Сосновый Бор/
     Петродворец 31 Fb 57
     Sovdozero 16 Ea 61
238750 Sovetsk / Советск
     38 Hb 49
157440 Sovetskij/Kologriv 18 Ga 72

161320 Sovetskij/Tot`ma 18 Fb 70
188370 Špan`kovo 32 Fb 57
249611 Spas-Demensk 41 Ja 62
391030 Spas-Klepiki 34 Hb 68
141667 Spas-Zaulok 33 Ha 64
391050 Spassk-Rjazanskij /
     Спасск-Рязанский
     42 Ja 68
165129 Spasskaja 18 Fa 69
186203 Spasskaja Guba 16 Ea 61
174207 Spasskaja Polist` 32 Ga 59
397961 Srednij Ikorec 54 Kb 67
309586 Stanovoe/Černjanka
     54 La 66
399710 Stanovoe/Elec 42 Ka 66
307081 Stanovoe/Ščigry 54 Kb 65
302510 Stanovoj Kolodez`
     42 Ka 64
175200 Staraja Russa / Старая
     Русса 32 Ga 59
172630 Staraja Toropa 40 Ha 59
171360 Starica 33 Ha 62
155650 Starilovo 34 Ha 70
243240 Starodub / Стародуб
     53 Ka 60
152430 Starodvorskoe 34 Ga 68
171733 Staroe/Pestovo 33 Ga 64
172312 Staroe/Ržev 33 Ha 62
188477 Staroe Garkolovo 31 Fb 56
215541 Staroe Istomino 41 Hb 61
303635 Starogol`skoe 42 Jab 65
393801 Starojur`evo 42 Jab 68
353530 Starotitarovskaja /
     Старотитаровская
     66 Nb 65
601220 Starovo 34 Ha 68
216244 Starye Peresudy 40 Hb 59
309500 Staryj Oskol / Старый Оскол
     54 Kb 65
162363 Staryj Počinok 18 Fa 74
398520 Stebaevo 42 Ka 67
164100 Stegnevskaja 17 Eb 67
162801 Stepačevo 33 Ga 64
157227 Stepanovo 18 Ga 70
140222 Stepanščino 42 Hb 66
216470 Stodolišče 41 Ja 60
171936 Stolbiha 33 Gb 63
308511 Streleckoe 54 La 64
157335 Strelica 18 Ga 71
161393 Strelka 18 Fa 73
180568 Stremutka 31 Gb 56
309351 Striguny 1-e 54 La 64
165240 Stroevskoe 18 Eb 71
309070 Stroitel` / Строитель
     54 La 64
181110 Strugi Krasnye 31 Ga 57
215750 Strukovo 41 Hb 61
601670 Strunino / Струнино
     34 Ha 66
175460 Stukov`ja 32 Ga 60
142800 Stupino 42 Ja 66
306132 Subbotino 54 Kb 64
397805 Šubnoe 54 La 66
157150 Sudaj 18 Ga 71
303643 Sudbišči 42 Ka 67
157860 Sudislavl` 34 Gb 69

187

INDEX WITH POST CODES · ORTSREGISTER MIT POSTLEITZAHLEN · INDICE CON CODICI
STEDREGISTER MED POSTNUMRE · PLAATSNAMENREGISTER MET POSTCODE · REJSTŘÍK

Sudogda / Судогда   (RUS)   **Verhnjaja Hava**

601315 Sudogda / Судогда 34 Hb 68
307800 Sudža 53 Kb 63
215840 Suetovo 41 Hb 60
398504 Suhaja Lubna 42 Ka 67
175434 Suhaja Niva 32 Gb 60
301756 Suhanovo 42 Jab 66
249270 Suhiniči / Сухиничи 41 Ja 63
186532 Suhoe 10 Da 62
157455 Suhoverhovo 18 Ga 72
155900 Šuja / Шуя 34 Ha 69
Šujskaja 16 Eb 62
186956 Sukkozero 16 Db 60
171970 Sukromny 33 Gb 64
156539 Suljatino 34 Gb 68
390545 Šumaš` 42 Ja 67
172511 Šumily 40 Ha 60
186521 Sumskij Posad 10 Da 63
186870 Suojarvi 16 Ea 60
241520 Suponevo 41 Jab 62
243500 Suraž / Сураж 41 Jab 60
162660 Surkovo 17 Ga 66
391911 Šurovo 42 Jab 68
171425 Sutoki 33 Gb 64
301430 Suvorov / Суворов 41 Ja 64
601291 Suzdal / Суздаль 34 Ha 68
242190 Suzemka 53 Ka 62
172746 Svapušče 32 Gb 60
241518 Sven` 41 Jab 62
238553 Svetlogorsk / Светлогорск 38 Ja 48
238340 Svetlyj/Baltijsk / Светлый/Балтийск 38 Ja 48
399720 Svetlyj/Elec 42 Ka 66
188990 Svetogorsk 15 Eb 56
307019 Svinec 54 Kb 65
187726 Svir`stroj 16 Fa 61
391621 Sviš* čovo 42 Ja 69
216235 Svity 40 Hb 60
186122 Svjatozero 16 Eb 61
238162 Svoboda/Gusev 38 Ja 49
306050 Svoboda/Kursk 54 Kb 64
215280 Syčevka 41 Hb 62
398000 Syrskij 42 Ka 67
172370 Syt`kovo 33 Ha 62
184321 Tajbola 6 Ba 61
172210 Tal`cy 33 Ha 61
182513 Talankino 40 Ha 57
601542 Talanovo 34 Hb 69
141900 Taldom / Талдом 33 Ha 65
164885 Tamica 10 Da 66
175314 Tarasovo 32 Gb 60
249100 Tarusa / Таруса 42 Ja 65
601542 Taščilovo 34 Hb 69
306055 Tazovo 54 Kb 64
155040 Tejkovo / Тейково 34 Ha 68
150000 Teliščevo 34 Gb 68
141950 Tempy 33 Ha 65
353501 Temrjuk / Темрюк 66 Nb 65
399831 Teploe/Dankov 42 Jab 66
399640 Teploe/Lebedjan` 42 Ka 67
301900 Teploe/Plavsk 42 Jab 65

399540 Terbuny 42 Ka 66
165105 Terebino 18 Fa 70
175007 Tereboni 32 Ga 58
301530 Terebuš 42 Ja 66
391622 Terenteevo 42 Ja 69
186734 Tervu 15 Eb 58
173519 Tesovo-Netyl`skij 32 Ga 59
307490 Tetkino 53 Kb 62
306005 Tifinskoe 42 Ka 64
187549 Tihvin / Тихвин 16 Fb 61
Tihvin Bor 16 Ea 63
188458 Tikopis` 31 Fb 56
186963 Tikša 10 Da 60
307060 Tim 54 Kb 65
155612 Timenka 34 Ha 69
303189 Timirjazevo/Orel 42 Ka 64
238611 Timirjazevo/Sovetsk 38 Hb 49
171061 Timkovo 33 Gb 62
182531 Timofeevka 40 Hb 58
162011 Timonino/Grjazovec 18 Ga 68
165144 Timonino/Njandoma 18 Eb 69
Tipinicy 16 Ea 63
238422 Tišino 38 Ja 48
184245 Titan 6 Bb 61
171614 Tivolino 33 Gb 65
390507 Tjuševo 42 Ja 67
180523 Toblica 31 Ga 56
164150 Tobolkino 17 Eb 66
187000 Toho / Тохо 32 Fb 58
186881 Tojvola 16 Ea 60
157470 Tokari 18 Ga 71
238741 Tolstovo 38 Ja 50
186862 Tolvojarvi 16 Ea 59
186306 Tolvuja 16 Ea 63
309085 Tomarovka 54 La 64
162677 Tonšalovo 17 Fb 65
182731 Toporevo 32 Gb 57
215221 Torbeevo 41 Hb 62
182460 Torčani 31 Gb 57
601264 Torčino 34 Ha 68
172840 Toropec / Торопец 32 Ha 59
186012 Torosozero 16 Eb 61
172000 Toržok / Торжок 33 Gb 63
161300 Tot`ma 18 Fb 70
249855 Tovarkovo / Товарково 41 Ja 63
301824 Tovarkovskij 42 Jab 66
174203 Tregubovo 32 Ga 59
216222 Tret`jakovo 40 Hb 60
161355 Tretnica 18 Fa 72
242455 Troebortnoe 53 Kb 62
399626 Troekurovo 42 Ka 67
174111 Trofimovskaja 17 Eb 67
391067 Troica 42 Ja 68
142190 Troick / Троицк 41 Hb 65
399882 Troickoe 42 Jab 67
303450 Trosna 41 Ka 63
243020 Trostan` 53 Ka 60
142813 Trostniki 42 Ja 66
242220 Trubčevsk / Трубчевск 41 Ka 61
399151 Trubetčino 42 Ka 67

399768 Trubicyno 42 Ka 66
187070 Trubnikov Bor 32 Fb 59
143130 Tučkovo / Тучково 41 Hb 64
162900 Tudozerskij Pogost 17 Eb 64
152084 Tufanovo 34 Gb 68
186668 Tuhkala 9 Cb 58
300000 Tula Тула 42 Ja 65
186007 Tuloksa 16 Eb 60
140454 Tumenskoe 42 Ja 65
186668 Tungozero 9 Cb 59
150501 Tunošna 34 Gb 68
161342 Tupanovo 18 Fb 71
157240 Turilovo 18 Ga 70
393010 Turovka/Mičurinsk 42 Ka 68
307505 Turovka/Orel 42 Ka 65
152445 Turybarovo 34 Ga 67
152300 Tutaev / Тутаев 34 Gb 67
170000 Tver` / Тверь 33 Ha 63
393081 Tynkovo 42 Ka 68
391151 Tyrnovo 42 Ja 67
152830 Učma 33 Ga 63
243357 Udel`nye Uty 41 Ka 61
171840 Udomlja / Удомля 33 Gb 63
182570 Udvjaty 40 Hb 58
152610 Uglič / Углич 33 Gb 66
181126 Ugly 31 Gb 56
215430 Ugra 41 Ja 62
391920 Uholovo / Ухолово 42 Jab 68
161261 Uhtoma 17 Fa 66
249292 Ukolovo 41 Ja 63
307822 Ulanok 53 Kb 63
184701 Umba 10 Ca 62
243300 Uneča / Унеча 41 Ka 60
157471 Unža 18 Ga 72
Upolokša 6 Bb 59
184371 Ura-Guba 6 Ab 60
309887 Urakovo 54 La 66
309970 Urazovo 54 La 66
186410 Urosozero 10 Db 62
187025 Ušaki 32 Fb 59
182100 Ušicy 40 Ha 58
399370 Usman` / Усмань 42 Ka 67
242420 Usoža 53 Ka 62
309662 Uspenka 54 La 66
215162 Uspenskoe 41 Hb 62
182513 Ust`-Dolyssy 40 Ha 57
165172 Ust`-Paden`ga 18 Eb 70
186174 Ust`-Reka 17 Eb 65
162840 Ustjužna / Устюжна 33 Ga 62
215722 Usvjat`e 41 Ja 61
182570 Usvjaty 40 Hb 58
182900 Utehino 32 Ha 58
249223 Uteševo 41 Ja 63
174159 Utorgoš 32 Ga 58
186817 Uuksu 16 Eb 59
155120 Uval`evo 34 Ha 68
143260 Uvarovka 41 Hb 63
301600 Uzlovaja / Узловая 42 Jab 66
157452 Užuga 18 Ga 72
174755 Vagan 32 Fb 61

157227 Vaganovo 18 Ga 70
161464 Vahnevo 18 Fb 73
152495 Vahramejka 34 Ga 68
Vahrušino 18 Ga 72
186756 Valaam 16 Eb 58
186434 Valdaj/Segeža 10 Db 63
175400 Valdaj/Višnij Voloček Валдай/Вышний Волочек 32 Gb 61
243414 Valuec 41 Ka 61
182900 Valuevskoe 32 Ha 58
309990 Valujki / Валуйки 54 La 66
164050 Vandyš 17 Eb 68
Vanevskaja 18 Fa 71
396542 Varvarovka/Alekseevka 54 La 67
249961 Varvarovka/Malojaroslavec 41 Hb 63
184712 Varzuga 10 Ca 64
165266 Vas`kovskaja 18 Eb 72
172610 Vasil`evo 32 Ha 60
175146 Vasil`evščina 32 Gb 59
162240 Vasil`evskaja 41 Ja 61
172214 Vasil`evskoe 33 Ha 61
152610 Vasil`ki 33 Gb 66
161207 Vasjutino 17 Fa 64
164134 Vatamanovskaja 17 Eb 66
173519 Vdicko 32 Fb 59
161446 Vedeniha 18 Fb 72
186862 Vegarus 16 Ea 60
309720 Vejdelevka 54 La 66
175254 Vekšino 32 Gb 59
155150 Vel`sk 18 Eb 70
175000 Veleši 32 Ga 58
215001 Velikovo 41 Hb 63
Velikaja 17 Fb 65
186312 Velikaja Niva 16 Ea 63
182100 Velikie Luki / Великие луки 40 Ha 58
161344 Velikij Dvor 18 Fb 71
173000 Velikij Novgorod / Великий Новгород 32 Ga 59
162390 Velikij Ustjug 18 Fa 74
601590 Velikodvorskij / Великодворский 34 Hb 68
162527 Velikoe/Babaevo 17 Fb 65
152250 Velikoe/Gavrilov-Jam 34 Gb 67
Velikovo 18 Fb 70
216290 Veliž 40 Hb 59
301320 Venev / Венев 42 Ja 66
249400 Verbežiči 41 Jab 62
141930 Verbilki 33 Ha 65
143330 Vereja 41 Hb 64
140333 Verejka 34 Hb 67
182345 Veresenec 31 Ha 56
397842 Veret`e 54 La 66
Verhnaja Pel`šma 18 Fa 71
215750 Verhnedneprovskij / Верхнеднепровский 41 Ja 61
396892 Verhnee Turovo 54 Kb 66
184374 Verhnetulomskij 5 Ba 59
307120 Verhnij Ljubaž 53 Ka 63
396110 Verhnjaja Hava 42 Kb 67

POSTALI · ÍNDICE CON CÓDIGOS POSTALES · INDICE DE LUGARES COM CÓDIGOS POSTAIS ·
MÍST S PSČ · ZOZNAM OBCÍ S PSČ · INDEKS MIEJSCOWOŚCI Z KOD POCZTOWY

188

Verhopujskij ⓇⓊⓈ · Ⓢ **Alster**

165104 Verhopujskij 17 Eb 69
214540 Verhov`e 40 Ja 59
303270 Verhov`e 42 Ka 65
157222 Verkovo 18 Ga 70
606553 Veršilovo 34 Ha 71
171720 Ves`egonsk 33 Ga 65
188902 Veščevo 15 Fa 57
186877 Veškelica 16 Eb 60
215461 Veški 41 Ja 62
238742 Vesnovo 38 Ja 50
155330 Vičuga / Вичуга 34 Gb 69
186007 Vidlica 16 Eb 60
142700 Vidnoe / Видное 34 Hb 65
185507 Vilga 16 Eb 62
607040 Vilja Виля 34 Hb 70
187760 Vinnicy 16 Fa 62
187522 Vinogora 16 Fb 61
175317 Visjučij Bor 32 Gb 60
157454 Vjal`cevo 18 Fb 71
186757 Vjartsilja 15 Ea 58
215110 Vjaz`ma / Вязьма 41 Hb 62
601440 Vjazniki / Вязники
        34 Ha 70
399630 Vjazovo 42 Jab 67
600000 Vladimir / Владимир
        34 Ha 68
301824 Vladimirovka 42 Jab 66
160542 Vladyčnevo 17 Fb 67
152890 Vladyčnoe 18 Ga 67
161107 Vlasovo/Belozersk
        17 Fb 66
140720 Vlasovo/Rošal` 34 Hb 67
601470 Vnukovo 34 Ha 70
399550 Voejkovo 42 Ka 66
162042 Vohtoga 18 Ga 69
186203 Vohtozero 16 Ea 61
249413 Vojlovo 41 Jab 62
        Vojnica 9 Cb 58
602130 Vojutino 34 Hb 69
186942 Voknovolok 9 Da 58
175010 Vol`naja Gorka 32 Ga 58
186420 Voldozero 10 Db 61
152750 Volga 33 Gb 66
174420 Volgino 32 Ga 61
156901 Volgorečensk /
        Волгореченск 34 Gb 69
187400 Volhov / Волхов 16 Fb 60
173000 Volhovskij 32 Ga 59
188225 Volkino 32 Ga 58
160000 Vologda / Вологда
        18 Fb 67
        Volojarvi 16 Fa 58
143600 Volokolamsk / Волоколамск
        33 Ha 63
309596 Volokonovka/Černjanka
        54 Kb 65
309650 Volokonovka/Valujki
        Волоконовка/Валуйки
        54 La 65
186951 Voloma 10 Db 59
188410 Volosovo 31 Fb 57
175100 Volot 32 Gb 58
301570 Volovo/Bogorodick
        42 Jab 66
399580 Volovo/Naberežnoe
        42 Ka 65

164205 Volovskaja 17 Eb 68
155382 Vonjavino 34 Gb 70
        Vorenža 10 Db 63
162113 Vorob`ovo 18 Fb 68
        Vorobino 18 Eb 74
157866 Voron`e 34 Gb 70
394000 Voronež / Воронеж
        54 Kb 67
155720 Voroniha 34 Ha 69
175011 Voronino 32 Ga 58
249875 Voronki 41 Ja 63
182440 Voronkova Niva 32 Gb 57
140200 Voskresensk / скресенск
        42 Hb 66
152710 Voskresenskoe/Bežeck
        33 Gb 65
301150 Voskresenskoe/Ščekino
        42 Ja 65
        Vostočnoe Munozero
        6 Bb 62
162160 Vožega 17 Fa 68
157344 Vožerovo 18 Ga 72
155714 Voznesen`e/Kovrov
        34 Ha 69
187750 Voznesen`e/Podporož`e
        16 Eb 63
309130 Voznesenovka/Obojan`
        54 Kb 64
309259 Voznesenovka/Volokonovka
        54 La 65
215155 Vsevolodkino 41 Hb 62
188640 Vsevoložsk / Всеволожск
        16 Fa 58
601310 Vtorovo 34 Ha 68
393870 Vtorye Levye Lamki
        42 Jab 69
307072 Vvedenka 54 Kb 65
143069 Vvedenskoe 33 Hb 64
175045 Vybiti 32 Ga 58
188800 Vyborg 15 Fa 56
171174 Vydropužsk 33 Gb 62
243361 Vygoniči 41 Jab 62
157471 Vygorki 18 Ga 72
607060 Vyksa / Выкса 34 Hb 70
391082 Vypolzovo/Rjazan`
        42 Ja 68
171053 Vypolzovo/Valdaj 32 Gb 61
188356 Vyra 32 Fb 57
188830 Vyrica / Вырица 32 Fb 58
215524 Vyšegor 41 Hb 61
181420 Vyšhorodok 31 Gb 56
188578 Vyskatka 31 Fb 56
309316 Vyšnie Peny 54 La 64
171150 Vyšnij Voloček / Вышний
        Волочек 33 Gb 62
174760 Vysočka 32 Ga 61
216575 Vysokij Borok 41 Jab 60
249180 Vysokiniči 41 Ja 64
172030 Vysokoe/Bernovo 33 Ha 62
249316 Vysokoe/Ljudinovo
        41 Jab 62
307030 Vysokonskie Dvory
        54 Kb 64
141650 Vysokovsk / Высоковск
        33 Ha 64
162900 Vytegra 17 Eb 64

216261 Zabor`e 40 Hb 59
172630 Zadem`jan`e 32 Ha 59
399200 Zadonsk 42 Ka 66
243332 Zaduben`e 41 Ka 61
161383 Zaglubockaja 18 Fa 72
187631 Zagolodno 32 Fb 62
188553 Zagor`e 31 Fb 56
391740 Zaharovo/Pronsk 42 Ja 67
601362 Zaharovo/Vladimir
        34 Hb 68
187765 Zajackaja 16 Fa 62
188980 Zajcevo/Priozersk 15 Eb 57
175453 Zajcevo/Velikij Novgorod
        32 Ga 60
171409 Zaklin`e/Alekseevskoe
        33 Gb 64
181624 Zaklin`e/Serbino 31 Ga 56
303226 Zakromskij Hutor 41 Ka 63
216256 Zakrut`e 40 Hb 59
303560 Zalegošč` 42 Ka 64
162840 Zales`e 33 Ga 64
175224 Zaluč`e 32 Gb 59
173532 Zamlen`e 32 Ga 59
181608 Zamogil`e 31 Ga 55
301000 Zaokskij 42 Ja 65
187724 Zaostrov`e/Lodejnoe Pole
        16 Fa 61
188750 Zaostrov`e/Priozersk
        16 Fa 58
152638 Zaozer`e/Kaljazin 33 Gb 66
187719 Zaozer`e/Lodejnoe Pole
        16 Fa 61
216760 Zaozer`e/Rudnja 40 Hb 59
186174 Zaozer`e/Ust` Reka
        17 Eb 65
184310 Zaozersk 5 Ab 60
172610 Zapadnaja Dvina 32 Ha 60
165151 Zapan` 18 Eb 70
181012 Zapljus`e 32 Ga 57
181012 Zapol`e/Zapljus`e 32 Ga 57
184430 Zapoljarnyj 5 Ab 58
188734 Zaporožskoe 16 Fa 58
238612 Zapovednoe 38 Hb 49
141960 Zaprudnja / Запрудня
        33 Ha 63
140600 Zarajsk / Зарайск 42 Ja 66
162035 Zareč`e/Grjazovec
        18 Ga 67
182321 Zareč`e/Pustoška
        40 Ha 57
184004 Zarečensk 9 Ca 59
186930 Zarečnyj 9 Da 58
172460 Žarkovskij 40 Hb 60
156552 Zarubino 34 Gb 68
171976 Zaruč`e 33 Gb 64
171917 Zaseka 33 Gb 63
171421 Zastolb`e 33 Gb 64
445554 Zavolž`e 34 Ha 71
186306 Zažoginskaja 16 Ea 63
181119 Ždani 31 Ga 56
172769 Ždanovo 32 Gb 61
188255 Žel`cy 32 Ga 57
188846 Zelenaja Rošča 15 Fa 57
161468 Zelencovo 18 Fb 72
184020 Zelenoborskij 9 Ca 60

197720 Zelenogorsk / Зеленогорск
        15 Fa 57
101000 Zelenograd / Зеленоград
        33 Hb 65
238530 Zelenogradsk /
        Зеленоградск 38 Ja 48
301382 Železnja 42 Ja 65
216134 Železnjak 40 Ja 59
307170 Železnogorsk /
        Железногорск 53 Ka 63
175260 Žemčugovo 32 Gb 59
396920 Zemljansk 42 Kb 66
303450 Žernovec 41 Ka 63
216252 Žičicy 40 Hb 59
307612 Žigarevo 53 Ka 63
157180 Žilino 18 Ga 69
172769 Žilino/Ostaškov 33 Gb 61
238725 Žilino/Sovetsk 38 Ja 49
391244 Zimarovo 42 Jab 68
187600 Zinov`ja Gora 16 Fb 62
188903 Žitkovo 15 Fa 57
249340 Žizdra 41 Jab 62
243600 Zlynka 52 Ka 59
303320 Zmievka 42 Ka 64
302520 Znamenka/Orel /
        Знаменка/Орел 41 Ka 64
215463 Znamenka/Vjaz`ma
        41 Ja 62
238200 Znamensk 38 Ja 49
303100 Znamenskoe/Bolhov
        41 Jab 63
303100 Znamenskoe/Orel 42 Ka 64
171621 Zobnino 33 Gb 65
399887 Zolotuha 42 Jab 67
306053 Zolotuhino 54 Ka 64
181119 Zovka 31 Ga 56
172333 Zubcov 33 Ha 62
142920 Zubovo/Ožerel`e 42 Ja 66
162430 Zubovo/Ustjužna 33 Ga 63
174200 Zuevo 32 Fb 59
249190 Žukov / Жуков 41 Hb 64
242700 Žukovka / Жуковка
        41 Jab 61
301530 Žukovo 41 Jab 64
140180 Žukovskij 34 Hb 66
172345 Zvjagino 33 Ha 61
186605 20-j kilometr 10 Da 62

Ⓢ

984 91 Aareavaara 8 Bb 51
930 82 Abborrträsk 7 Cb 47
981 07 Abisko 4 Ba 46
920 64 Ajaureforsen 7 Cb 43
933 91 Akkavare 7 Cb 47
833 96 Alanäs 7 Da 43
640 40 Alberga 29 Fb 44
841 94 Alby 13 Ea 43
826 94 Alebo 13 Eb 44
822 01 Alfta 13 Eb 44
441 01 Alingsås 28 Gb 40
910 60 Almsele 7 Da 45
593 95 Almvik 29 Gb 44
655 90 Alster 28 Fb 41

ⓇⓊⓈ

Ⓢ

S Alsterbro ◯**S** Grimsmark

380 44 Alsterbro 37 Ha 43	920 41 Björksele 7 Da 46	943 31 Böle 8 Cb 49	946 99 Finnliden 7 Cb 48
981 92 Alttajärvi 4 Bb 48	890 50 Björna 13 Db 46	792 94 Börka 12 Eb 42	612 01 Finspång 29 Ga 43
747 01 Alunda 29 Fa 46	640 50 Björnlunda 29 Fb 45	673 01 Charlottenberg 28 Fb 40	933 99 Fiskträsk 7 Cb 46
342 01 Alvesta 36 Ha 42	920 72 Blattniksele 7 Cb 45	872 97 Dala 13 Ea 46	450 71 Fjällbacka 28 Ga 39
975 92 Alvik 8 Cb 49	471 96 Bleket 28 Gb 39	780 44 Dala-Floda 12 Fa 42	933 91 Fjällnäs 12 Ea 40
680 52 Ambjörby 12 Fa 41	660 60 Blombacka 28 Fb 41	780 51 Dala-Järna 12 Fa 42	740 83 Fjärdhundra 29 Fb 44
514 93 Ambjörnarp 28 Gb 41	830 76 Boberg 13 Db 43	130 54 Dalarö 29 Fb 46	790 90 Fjätervällen 12 Eb 41
451 91 Ammarnäs 7 Cb 44	860 41 Boda 13 Eb 43	680 60 Dalby 12 Fa 41	642 01 Flen 29 Fb 44
937 95 Andersfors 7 Da 48	961 01 Boden 8 Cb 49	790 70 Dalfors 13 Eb 43	572 95 Flivik 29 Gb 44
231 73 Anderslöv 36 Hb 41	880 51 Bodum 13 Db 44	464 91 Dals Rostock 28 Ga 40	520 40 Floby 28 Ga 41
578 01 Aneby 28 Gb 42	936 01 Boliden 7 Da 48	297 94 Degeberga 36 Hb 42	448 01 Floda 28 Gb 40
830 05 Anjan 12 Db 40	517 01 Bollebygd 28 Gb 40	693 01 Degerfors 28 Fb 42	743 93 Fors 29 Fa 44
524 42 Annelund 28 Gb 41	821 01 Bollnäs 13 Eb 44	380 65 Degerhamn 37 Ha 44	929 64 Forsbäck 7 Cb 43
905 82 Ansmark 13 Db 48	873 01 Bollstabruk 13 Ea 45	961 95 Degernäs 28 Fb 41	667 01 Forshaga 28 Fb 41
975 92 Antnäs 8 Cb 49	830 05 Bonäset 12 Db 41	955 95 Degerselet 8 Ca 49	330 12 Forsheda 28 Gb 41
984 91 Anttis 8 Bb 50	711 92 Boo 29 Fb 46	820 60 Delsbo 13 Eb 44	923 97 Forsmark 7 Cb 43
732 01 Arboga 29 Fb 43	330 15 Bor 28 Gb 42	933 91 Deppis 7 Cb 47	742 94 Forsmark 29 Fa 46
820 10 Arbrå 13 Eb 44	590 30 Borensberg 29 Ga 43	780 41 Djurås 12 Fa 43	546 73 Forsvik 28 Ga 42
532 95 Ardala 28 Ga 41	590 30 Borghamn 28 Ga 42	918 93 Djäkneboda 14 Da 48	790 90 Foskvallen 12 Eb 40
930 90 Arjeplog 7 Ca 45	387 01 Borgholm 37 Ha 44	870 33 Docksta 13 Db 46	910 50 Fredrika 7 Da 46
290 37 Arkelstorp 36 Ha 42	841 97 Borgsjö 13 Ea 43	982 92 Dokkas 8 Bb 49	360 10 Fridafors 36 Ha 42
943 31 Arnemark 8 Cb 49	781 01 Borlänge 29 Fa 43	917 01 Dorotea 7 Da 44	620 16 Fridhem 29 Gb 46
891 96 Arnäsvall 13 Db 46	501 01 Borås 28 Gb 40	790 91 Drosbacken 12 Eb 40	820 62 Friggesund 13 Eb 44
912 92 Aronsjö 7 Da 44	147 85 Botkyrka 29 Fb 45	830 15 Duved 12 Db 40	513 01 Fristad 28 Gb 41
933 01 Arvidsjaur 7 Cb 47	922 77 Botsmark 7 Da 48	830 41 Dvärsätt 12 Db 42	511 06 Fritsla 28 Gb 40
671 60 Arvika 28 Fb 40	560 25 Bottnaryd 28 Gb 41	668 01 Ed 28 Ga 39	840 12 Fränsta 13 Ea 44
374 02 Asarum 36 Ha 42	450 47 Bovallstrand 28 Ga 39	673 92 Eda glasbruk 28 Fb 40	598 95 Fröding 29 Gb 44
696 01 Askersund 28 Ga 42	590 10 Boxholm 28 Ga 43	860 13 Ede 13 Ea 44	718 01 Frövi 29 Fb 43
436 39 Askim 28 Gb 39	830 02 Brasta 12 Db 42	763 91 Edebo 29 Fa 46	780 67 Fulunäs 12 Eb 41
611 91 Aspa 29 Ga 45	680 60 Brattmon 12 Fa 40	683 92 Edebäck 28 Fa 41	840 95 Funäsdalen 12 Ea 40
933 91 Auktsjaur 7 Cb 47	360 42 Braås 36 Gb 43	760 31 Edsbro 29 Fb 46	671 92 Furtan 28 Fb 40
955 99 Avafors 8 Ca 50	895 01 Bredbyn 13 Db 46	590 98 Edsbruk 29 Ga 44	360 51 Furuby 36 Ha 43
774 01 Avesta 29 Fa 44	865 92 Bredsand 13 Ea 45	828 01 Edsbyn 13 Eb 43	790 70 Furudal 13 Eb 43
532 02 Axvall 28 Ga 41	942 95 Bredsel 7 Cb 48	880 41 Edsele 13 Db 44	804 29 Furuvik 13 Fa 45
370 11 Backaryd 36 Ha 43	621 72 Brissund 29 Gb 46	660 52 Edsvalla 28 Fb 41	610 42 Fyrudden 29 Ga 44
880 50 Backe 13 Db 44	864 91 Bro 29 Fb 45	260 51 Ekeby 36 Hb 41	370 45 Fågelmara 37 Ha 43
585 93 Bankeryd 28 Gb 42	280 72 Broby 36 Ha 42	574 02 Ekenässjön 28 Gb 43	830 22 Fåker 12 Db 42
923 96 Barsele 7 Cb 45	942 91 Brokind 29 Ga 43	980 61 Ekorrbäcken 8 Bb 50	572 96 Fårbo 29 Gb 44
231 76 Beddingestrand 36 Hb 41	542 91 Brommösund 28 Ga 41	680 50 Ekshärad 28 Fa 41	620 35 Fårösund 29 Gb 47
666 00 Bengtsfors 28 Fb 40	295 01 Bromölla 36 Ha 42	575 01 Eksjö 28 Gb 42	930 90 Fälloheden 7 Cb 46
542 92 Berga 28 Ga 41	834 01 Brunflo 12 Db 42	780 50 Eldforsen 28 Fa 42	820 41 Färila 13 Eb 43
311 95 Bergagård 36 Ha 40	380 62 Brunneby 37 Ha 44	310 31 Eldsberga 36 Ha 41	386 01 Färjestaden 37 Ha 44
817 02 Bergby 13 Fa 45	671 94 Brunnsberg 12 Eb 41	474 92 Ellös 28 Ga 39	830 60 Föllinge 12 Db 42
860 33 Bergeforsen 13 Ea 45	460 65 Brålanda 28 Ga 40	361 01 Emmaboda 37 Ha 43	780 41 Gagnef 12 Fa 43
972 53 Bergnäset 13 Cb 49	277 03 Brösarp 36 Hb 42	830 15 Enafors 12 Db 40	971 01 Gammelstaden 8 Cb 50
760 10 Bergshammra 29 Fb 46	796 99 Bunkris 12 Eb 41	745 01 Enköping 29 Fb 45	923 99 Gammhem 7 Cb 45
820 70 Bergsjö 13 Eb 45	930 15 Bureå 8 Da 49	680 51 Ennarbolsmon 28 Fa 41	923 99 Gardsjöbäcken 7 Cb 44
941 48 Bergsviken 8 Cb 49	620 10 Burgsvik 37 Gb 46	122 01 Enskede 29 Fb 46	683 91 Geijersholm 28 Fa 41
640 33 Bettna 29 Ga 44	330 26 Burseryd 28 Gb 41	790 26 Enviken 13 Fa 43	240 13 Genarp 36 Hb 41
641 96 Bie 29 Fb 44	937 01 Burträsk 8 Da 48	825 02 Enånger 13 Eb 45	830 15 Gevsjön 12 Db 40
427 41 Billdal 28 Gb 39	918 02 Bygdeå 8 Da 48	361 94 Eriksmåla 37 Ha 43	747 02 Gimo 29 Fa 46
660 11 Billingsfors 28 Ga 40	930 47 Byske 8 Da 49	630 03 Eskilstuna 29 Fb 44	332 80 Gislaved 28 Gb 41
871 93 Billsta 13 Db 46	842 94 Byvallen 12 Ea 42	241 01 Eslöv 36 Hb 41	930 81 Glommersträsk 7 Cb 47
840 73 Bispgården 13 Ea 44	746 93 Bålsta 29 Fb 45	297 02 Everöd 36 Hb 42	820 77 Gnarp 13 Ea 45
916 01 Bjurholm 13 Db 47	269 01 Båstad 36 Ha 40	570 84 Fagerås 29 Gb 43	646 01 Gnesta 29 Fb 45
790 21 Bjursås 13 Fa 43	680 65 Båtstad 12 Fa 40	566 92 Fagerhult 28 Ga 42	335 01 Gnosjö 28 Gb 41
975 91 Bjurträsk 7 Da 47	380 44 Bäckebo 37 Ha 44	737 01 Fagersta 29 Fa 44	620 30 Gothem 29 Gb 46
280 20 Bjärnum 36 Ha 41	668 94 Bäckefors 28 Ga 40	311 01 Falkenberg 36 Ha 40	680 51 Granberg 12 Fa 41
893 01 Bjästa 13 Db 46	681 83 Bäckhammar 28 Fb 42	521 01 Falköping 28 Ga 41	917 99 Granberget 7 Da 44
780 40 Björbo 28 Fa 43	620 30 Bäl 29 Gb 46	791 01 Falun 13 Fa 43	380 75 Grankullavik 29 Gb 45
921 93 Björkberg 7 Da 45	740 22 Bälinge 29 Fb 45	840 50 Fanbyn 13 Ea 44	920 70 Grannäs 7 Cb 45
980 41 Björkberget 8 Ca 49	912 90 Bäskele 7 Da 44	291 11 Farlöv 36 Ha 42	922 95 Granö 7 Da 47
519 02 Björketorp 28 Gb 40	912 93 Bäsksjö 7 Da 45	685 93 Fensbol 28 Fa 41	585 95 Grebo 29 Ga 43
830 76 Björkhöjden 13 Db 44	781 95 Bäsna 13 Fa 43	620 10 Fidenäs 29 Gb 46	881 95 Grilom 13 Db 45
981 93 Björkliden 4 Ba 46	380 74 Böda 29 Gb 45	682 01 Filipstad 28 Fb 42	340 32 Grimslöv 36 Ha 42
740 30 Björklinge 29 Fa 45		695 02 Finnerödja 28 Ga 42	915 94 Grimsmark 8 Da 49

Grinneröd · S · **Köarskär**

459 91 Grinneröd 28 Ga 39	620 20 Hejde 29 Gb 46	579 01 Högsby 29 Gb 44	823 91 Kilafors 13 Eb 44
760 45 Grisslehamn 29 Fa 46	250 02 Helsingborg 36 Ha 40	944 91 Högsböle 8 Cb 49	280 72 Killeberg 36 Ha 42
664 91 Grums 28 Fb 41	920 66 Hemevan/Bierke 7 Cb 43	450 63 Högsäter 28 Ga 40	511 01 Kinna 28 Gb 40
942 91 Grundsel 7 Cb 48	890 51 Hemling 13 Db 44	840 94 Högvälen 12 Ea 40	981 01 Kiruna 4 Bb 48
792 92 Gruvoma 12 Fa 42	620 12 Hemse 29 Gb 46	722 31 Hökåsen 29 Fb 44	590 40 Kisa 29 Gb 43
790 20 Grycksbo 13 Fa 43	820 46 Hennan 13 Ea 43	680 65 Höljes 12 Fa 40	984 99 Kitkiöjärvi 4 Bb 51
712 02 Grythyttan 28 Fb 42	473 01 Henån 28 Ga 39	236 41 Höllviken 36 Hb 40	680 65 Klaråsen 12 Fa 40
772 02 Grängesberg 28 Fa 43	524 01 Herrljunga 28 Ga 41	153 07 Hölö 29 Fb 45	840 32 Klavsjö 12 Ea 42
920 42 Grästorp 7 Cb 46	620 16 Herrvik 29 Gb 46	430 91 Hönö 28 Gb 39	Klintehamn 29 Gb 46
467 01 Grästorp 28 Ga 40	573 94 Hestra 28 Gb 43	242 01 Hörby 36 Hb 41	264 01 Klippan 36 Ha 41
579 93 Grönskåra 37 Gb 43	430 63 Hindås 28 Gb 40	772 94 Hörken 28 Fa 42	920 66 Klippen 7 Cb 43
833 96 Gubbhögen 7 Da 43	287 93 Hinneryd 36 Ha 41	910 20 Hörnefors 13 Db 47	714 91 Kloten 29 Fb 43
880 37 Gulkäl 13 Db 45	956 92 Hirvijärvi 8 Ca 51	243 01 Höör 36 Hb 41	671 95 Klässbol 28 Fb 40
79596 Gulleråsen 13 Eb 43	903 45 Hissjön 13 Db 48	790 91 Idre 12 Eb 40	975 91 Klöverträsk 8 Cb 49
590 81 Gullringen 29 Gb 43	544 01 Hjo 28 Ga 42	825 01 Iggesund 13 Eb 45	680 50 Knappåsen 28 Fa 41
547 01 Gullspång 28 Ga 42	590 91 Hjorted 29 Gb 44	860 40 Indal 13 Ea 45	289 01 Knislinge 36 Ha 42
920 51 Gunnarn 7 Cb 45	697 93 Hjortkvarn 29 Ga 43	360 44 Ingelstad 36 Ha 42	741 01 Knivsta 29 Fb 45
590 93 Gunnebo 29 Gb 44	342 93 Hjortsberga 36 Ha 42	793 04 Insjön 12 Fa 43	740 12 Knutby 29 Fb 46
739 92 Gunnilbo 29 Fb 43	712 91 Hjulsjö 28 Fb 42	984 92 Jarhois 8 Ca 51	442 97 Kode 28 Gb 39
713 02 Gyttorp 28 Fb 42	813 01 Hofors 13 Fa 44	920 70 Jillesnåle 7 Cb 44	730 40 Kolbäck 29 Fb 44
386 92 Gårdby 37 Ha 44	450 84 Holkekärr 28 Ga 39	792 92 Johannisholm 12 Fa 42	730 30 Kolsva 29 Fb 43
880 30 Gårelehöjden 13 Db 44	860 41 Holm 13 Ea 44	962 99 Jokkmokk 7 Ca 47	714 01 Kopparberg 28 Fb 43
755 96 Gåvsta 29 Fb 45	880 30 Holme 13 Db 44	984 91 Juhonpieti 8 Bb 51	670 41 Koppom 28 Fb 40
830 70 Gåxsjö 13 Db 43	672 94 Holmedal 28 Fb 39	981 91 Jukkasjärvi 4 Bb 48	980 60 Korpilombolo 8 Ca 51
830 90 Gäddede 26 Da 42	920 73 Holmfors 7 Cb 46	980 62 Junosuando 8 Bb 50	372 94 Korsanäs 36 Ha 43
982 01 Gällivare 7 Bb 48	370 34 Holmsjö 37 Ha 43	880 37 Junsele 13 Db 44	570 10 Korsberga 28 Gb 43
840 50 Gällo 13 Ea 43	913 01 Holmsund 13 Db 48	957 23 Juoksengi 8 Ca 51	957 95 Koutojärvi 8 Ca 51
520 10 Gällstad 28 Gb 41	512 64 Holsljunga 28 Gb 41	930 90 Jutis 7 Ca 45	860 25 Kovland 13 Ea 45
800 02 Gävle 13 Fa 45	828 92 Homna 13 Eb 43	982 99 Jutsarova 7 Bb 48	872 01 Kramfors 13 Ea 45
533 94 Gössäter 28 Ga 41	597 92 Horn 29 Gb 43	930 90 Jäkkvik 7 Ca 44	570 91 Kristdala 29 Gb 44
400 10 Göteborg 28 Gb 39	774 04 Horndal 29 Fa 44	373 00 Jämjö 37 Ha 43	291 01 Kristianstad 36 Ha 42
533 01 Götene 28 Ga 41	519 01 Horred 28 Gb 40	811 02 Järbo 13 Fa 44	681 01 Kristinehamn 28 Fb 42
732 97 Götlunda 29 Fb 43	791 47 Hosjö 13 Fa 43	740 21 Järlåsa 29 Fb 45	841 94 Krok 12 Db 41
566 01 Habo 28 Gb 42	830 80 Hoting 7 Da 44	153 95 Järna 29 Fb 45	618 92 Krokek 29 Ga 44
830 23 Hackås 12 Ea 42	548 01 Hova 28 Ga 42	830 05 Järpen 12 Db 41	835 01 Krokom 12 Db 42
683 01 Hagfors 28 Fa 41	360 51 Hovmantorp 36 Ha 43	Järps 28 Ga 41	981 29 Krokvik 4 Bb 48
980 41 Hakkas 8 Ca 49	705 91 Hovsta 29 Fb 44	681 91 Järsberg 28 Fb 42	666 92 Kråkviken 28 Fb 40
314 91 Hallaböke 36 Ha 41	141 01 Huddinge 29 Fb 45	830 01 Järsta 12 Db 42	620 23 Kräklingbo 29 Gb 46
Hallen 12 Db 42	824 01 Hudiksvall 13 Eb 45	820 40 Järvsjö 13 Eb 44	895 93 Kubbe 13 Db 46
734 01 Hallstahammar 29 Fb 44	575 92 Hult 28 Gb 43	820 76 Jättendal 13 Eb 45	953 91 Kukkola 8 Cb 52
833 92 Hallviken 13 Db 43	577 01 Hultsfred 29 Gb 43	944 94 Jävre 8 Cb 49	692 02 Kumla 28 Fb 43
301 01 Halmstad 36 Ha 40	450 46 Hunnebostrand 28 Ga 39	550 02 Jönköping 28 Gb 42	434 01 Kungsbacka 28 Gb 40
696 94 Hammar 28 Ga 42	241 94 Hurva 36 Hb 41	930 55 Jörn 7 Cb 48	812 03 Kungsgården 13 Fa 44
840 70 Hammarstrand 13 Db 44	921 91 Husbondliden 7 Da 46	952 01 Kalix 8 Cb 51	826 94 Kungsgården 13 Eb 44
276 02 Hammenhög 36 Hb 42	561 01 Huskvarna 28 Gb 42	830 05 Kall 12 Db 41	456 01 Kungshamn 28 Ga 39
830 70 Hammerdal 13 Db 43	890 35 Husum 13 Db 47	830 05 Kallsedet 12 Db 40	736 01 Kungsör 29 Fb 44
820 51 Hamra 13 Ea 43	314 01 Hyltebruk 36 Gb 41	390 02 Kalmar 37 Ha 44	442 01 Kungälv 28 Gb 40
840 98 Hamra 12 Ea 40	830 90 Håkafot 26 Da 42	930 82 Kalvträsk 7 Cb 47	980 16 Kuusilaki 4 Ba 50
817 93 Hamrångefjärden 13 Fa 45	770 13 Håksberg 29 Fa 43	936 91 Kankberg 7 Da 48	984 92 Kuusilaki 8 Ca 51
136 01 Handen 29 Fb 46	880 30 Hålaforsen 13 Db 44	760 15 Kapellskär 29 Fb 47	794 98 Kvarnberg 12 Eb 42
953 01 Haparanda 8 Cb 52	830 30 Häggenäs 12 Db 42	620 34 Kappelshamn 29 Gb 46	922 93 Kvarntorp 29 Fb 43
960 24 Harads 8 Ca 48	830 60 Häggsjövik 12 Db 42	980 16 Karesuando 4 Ba 50	310 34 Kvibille 36 Ha 40
740 47 Harbo 29 Fa 45	910 60 Hälla 13 Db 45	810 64 Karlholmsbruk 13 Fa 45	570 16 Kvillsfors 29 Gb 43
742 95 Harg 29 Fa 46	712 01 Hällefors 28 Fb 42	820 50 Karlsberg 13 Eb 43	862 01 Kvissleby 13 Ea 45
742 95 Hargshamn 29 Fa 46	474 94 Hälleviksstrand 28 Ga 39	952 71 Karlsborg 28 Ga 42	471 90 Kyrkesund 28 Ga 39
820 75 Harmånger 13 Eb 45	430 64 Hällingsjö 28 Gb 40	374 01 Karlshamn 36 Ha 42	960 24 Kåbdalis 7 Ca 47
982 60 Harspränget 7 Ca 47	922 73 Hällnäs 7 Da 47	691 01 Karlskoga 28 Fb 42	934 01 Kåge 8 Da 48
820 78 Hassela 13 Ea 44	820 46 Hälsingenybo 13 Ea 43	371 01 Karlskrona 37 Ha 43	820 43 Kårböle 13 Eb 43
370 23 Hasslö 37 Ha 43	793 92 Häradsbygden 12 Fa 43	651 01 Karlstad 28 Fb 41	380 30 Kåremo 37 Ha 44
620 11 Havdhem 29 Gb 46	871 01 Härnösand 13 Ea 45	840 90 Karlstrand 13 Ea 43	820 40 Kårsjö 13 Eb 44
744 01 Heby 29 Fb 44	281 01 Hässleholm 36 Ha 41	820 50 Karsvall 13 Eb 43	840 64 Kälarne 13 Ea 44
840 93 Hede 12 Ea 41	263 01 Höganäs 36 Ha 40	953 93 Karungi 8 Ca 51	691 91 Källmo 28 Fb 42
776 01 Hedemora 29 Fa 43	930 55 Högberg 7 Cb 47	380 62 Kastlösa 37 Ha 44	590 93 Kallviken 29 Gb 44
957 95 Hedenäset 8 Ca 51	665 93 Högboda 28 Fb 41	641 01 Katrineholm 29 Ga 44	873 92 Kärr 13 Db 45
810 40 Hedesunda 29 Fa 45	833 93 Högbränna 13 Db 44	665 01 Kil 28 Fb 41	244 01 Kävlinge 36 Hb 41
827 95 Hedsta 13 Eb 43	671 95 Högerud 28 Fb 40	733 94 Kila 29 Fb 44	780 67 Köarskär 12 Eb 41

191

INDEX WITH POST CODES · ORTSREGISTER MIT POSTLEITZAHLEN · INDICE CON CODICI
STEDREGISTER MED POSTNUMRE · PLAATSNAMENREGISTER MET POSTCODE · REJSTŘÍK

S

Kölsillre   (S)   **Rosvik**

841 93 Kölsillre 13 Ea 43	820 50 Los 13 Eb 43	311 93 Morup 36 Ha 40	295 04 Näsum 36 Ha 42
731 01 Köping 29 Fb 43	771 01 Ludvika 29 Fa 43	930 86 Moskosel 7 Cb 47	833 92 Näsviken 13 Db 43
760 18 Köpmansholm 29 Fb 46	872 95 Lugnvik 13 Ea 45	591 01 Motala 28 Ga 43	880 30 Näsåker 13 Db 44
893 92 Köpmanholmen 13 Db 46	542 94 Lugnäs 28 Ga 41	565 01 Mullsjö 28 Gb 41	668 91 Nössemark 28 Fb 39
464 71 Köpmannebro 28 Ga 40	971 01 Luleå 8 Cb 50	455 01 Munkedal 28 Ga 39	913 02 Obbola 13 Db 48
830 24 Kövra 12 Ea 42	620 33 Lummelunda 29 Gb 46	684 01 Munkfors 28 Fb 41	816 01 Ockelbo 13 Fa 44
820 42 Laforsen 13 Eb 43	220 02 Lund 36 Hb 41	984 95 Muodoslompolo 4 Bb 51	521 92 Odensberg 28 Ga 41
340 14 Lagan 36 Ha 42	840 64 Lund 13 Ea 44	982 99 Muorjevaara 8 Bb 48	830 30 Ollsta 13 Db 43
312 01 Laholm 36 Ha 41	872 93 Lunde 13 Ea 45	471 60 Myggenäs 28 Ga 39	293 01 Olofström 36 Ha 42
360 30 Lammhult 28 Gb 42	835 92 Lungsjön 13 Db 44	830 24 Myrviken 12 Db 42	696 93 Olshammar 28 Ga 42
314 04 Landeryd 28 Gb 41	830 80 Lunne 7 Da 44	570 82 Målilla 29 Gb 43	380 40 Orrefors 37 Ha 43
261 01 Landskrona 36 Hb 40	921 01 Lycksele 7 Da 46	815 03 Månkarbo 29 Fa 45	956 92 Orrfors 8 Ca 50
830 51 Landön 12 Db 42	453 01 Lysekil 28 Ga 39	830 01 Månsåsen 12 Db 42	794 01 Orsa 12 Eb 42
956 98 Lansjärv 8 Ca 50	452 05 Långegärde 28 Ga 39	922 75 Mårdsele 7 Da 47	842 91 Ortholmen 12 Ea 41
982 05 Lappeasuanto 8 Bb 49	840 73 Långliden 13 Ea 44	195 01 Märsta 29 Fb 45	283 01 Osby 36 Ha 42
952 96 Lappträsk 8 Ca 51	882 01 Långsele 13 Db 45	260 42 Mölle 36 Ha 40	572 01 Oskarshamn 29 Gb 44
912 94 Latikberg 7 Da 45	770 70 Långshyttan 29 Fa 44	546 02 Mölltorp 28 Ga 42	313 01 Oskarström 36 Ha 40
830 60 Laxsjö 12 Db 42	880 37 Långvattnet 13 Db 44	435 01 Mölnlycke 28 Gb 40	934 91 Ostvik 8 Da 49
780 50 Laxtjärn 28 Fa 42	755 92 Läby 29 Fa 45	383 01 Mönsterås 37 Gb 44	380 65 Ottenby 37 Ha 44
305 95 Laxvik 36 Ha 40	942 05 Längträsk 7 Cb 48	380 62 Mörbylånga 37 Ha 44	547 02 Otterbäcken 28 Ga 42
830 60 Laxviken 12 Db 42	761 93 Länna 29 Fb 45	570 84 Mörlunda 29 Gb 43	830 60 Ottsjön 12 Db 42
695 01 Laxå 28 Ga 42	643 95 Läppe 29 Fb 43	375 05 Mörrum 36 Ha 42	828 94 Ovanåker 13 Eb 43
914 91 Ledusjö 13 Db 47	463 71 Lödöse 28 Ga 40	830 04 Mörsil 12 Db 41	613 01 Oxelösund 29 Ga 45
560 28 Lekeryd 28 Gb 42	910 50 Lögdasund 7 Da 46	370 43 Nabben 37 Ha 43	960 30 Padjerim 7 Ca 48
793 01 Leksand 12 Fa 43	914 92 Lögdeå 13 Db 47	956 98 Naisheden 8 Ca 50	980 16 Paittasjärvi 4 Ba 50
360 73 Lenhovda 36 Gb 43	280 70 Lönsboda 36 Ha 42	880 40 Nassjö 13 Db 44	984 01 Pajala 8 Bb 51
434 93 Lerkill 28 Gb 39	380 74 Löttorp 29 Gb 44	795 92 Nedre Gärdsjö 13 Fa 43	984 99 Parkajoki 4 Bb 51
443 01 Lerum 28 Gb 40	930 71 Lövberg 7 Cb 46	980 10 NedreSoppero 4 Ba 49	895 93 Pengsjö 13 Db 45
680 96 Lesjöfors 28 Fb 42	833 95 Lövberga 13 Db 43	955 95 Niemisel 8 Ca 49	682 40 Persberg 28 Fb 42
360 50 Lessebo 36 Ha 43	930 10 Lövånger 8 Da 49	982 99 Nietsak 7 Bb 48	284 01 Perstorp 36 Ha 41
343 74 Liatorp 36 Ha 42	777 93 Malingsbo 29 Fb 43	523 99 Nitta 28 Gb 41	975 97 Persön 8 Cb 50
860 41 Liden 13 Ea 44	983 01 Malmberget 7 Bb 48	514 54 Nittorp 28 Gb 41	840 58 Pilgrimstad 13 Ea 43
340 10 Lidhult 36 Ha 41	570 12 Malmbäck 28 Gb 42	862 02 Njurundabommen 13 Ea 45	941 01 Piteå 8 Cb 49
531 01 Lidköping 28 Ga 41	640 32 Malmköping 29 Fb 44	825 92 Njutånger 13 Eb 45	982 60 Porjus 7 Ca 48
830 86 Lidsjöberg 7 Da 43	200 10 Malmö 36 Hb 41	294 95 Nogersund 36 Ha 42	840 90 Prinsbacken 12 Ea 42
937 96 Lidsjön 7 Da 48	782 01 Malung 12 Fa 41	794 98 Noppikoski 12 Eb 42	916 93 Provåker 13 Da 47
982 92 Liikavaara 8 Bb 49	782 02 Malungsfors 12 Fa 41	738 02 Norberg 29 Fa 43	946 99 Pålsboda 29 Fb 43
463 32 Lilla Edet 28 Ga 40	930 70 Malå 7 Cb 46	880 40 Nordankäl 13 Db 44	952 04 Påläng 8 Cb 50
830 60 Lillholmsjö 12 Db 42	570 30 Mariannelund 29 Gb 43	912 99 Nordanå 13 Ea 45	388 99 Påryd 37 Ha 43
910 60 Lillögda 7 Da 45	647 01 Mariefred 29 Fb 44	914 01 Nordmaling 13 Db 47	570 90 Påskallavik 29 Gb 44
780 64 Limedsforsen 12 Fa 41	542 01 Mariestad 28 Ga 41	682 93 Nordmark 28 Fb 42	450 73 Rabbalshede 28 Ga 39
956 92 Liminkajärvi 8 Ca 50	285 01 Markaryd 36 Ha 41	294 76 Norje 36 Ha 42	730 60 Ramnäs 29 Fb 44
290 11 Linderöd 36 Hb 41	440 30 Marstrand 28 Gb 39	571 63 Norra Sandsjö 28 Gb 42	880 40 Ramsele 13 Db 44
711 01 Lindesberg 29 Fb 43	360 70 Massamåla 29 Gb 43	920 70 Norra Örnäs 7 Cb 45	820 46 Ramsjö 13 Ea 43
437 40 Lindome 28 Gb 40	980 10 Masugnsbyn 8 Bb 50	945 31 Norrfjärden 8 Cb 49	870 16 Ramvik 13 Ea 45
380 30 Lindsdal 37 Ha 44	864 01 Matfors 13 Ea 45	360 71 Norrhult-Klavreström	680 60 Ransby 12 Fa 40
816 92 Lingbo 13 Eb 44	830 02 Mattmar 12 Db 41	28 Gb 43	842 91 Ransjö 12 Ea 41
580 01 Linköping 29 Ga 43	921 91 Medelås 7 Da 46	600 02 Norrköping 29 Ga 44	684 93 Ransäter 28 Fb 41
842 91 Linsell 12 Ea 41	815 93 Mehedeby 29 Fa 45	761 01 Norrtälje 29 Fb 46	330 21 Reftele 28 Gb 41
830 30 Lit 12 Db 42	890 42 Mellansel 13 Db 46	610 21 Norsholm 29 Ga 43	981 29 Rensjön 4 Ba 49
740 81 Litslena 29 Fb 45	820 46 Mellansjö 13 Ea 43	465 01 Nossebro 28 Ga 40	936 93 Renström 7 Da 48
605 91 Ljunga 29 Ga 44	464 01 Mellerud 28 Ga 40	792 04 Nusnäs 12 Fa 42	730 91 Riddarhyttan 29 Fb 43
840 10 Ljungaverk 13 Ea 44	980 10 Merasjärvi 8 Bb 49	952 50 Nyborg 8 Cb 51	981 94 Riksgränsen 3 Ba 46
341 01 Ljungby 36 Ha 41	912 90 Meselefors 7 Da 44	382 01 Nybro 37 Ha 43	762 01 Rimbo 29 Fb 46
260 70 Ljungbyhed 36 Ha 41	880 41 Meåstrand 13 Db 44	570 03 Nydala 28 Gb 42	590 41 Rimforsa 29 Ga 43
590 70 Ljungsbro 29 Ga 43	572 95 Misterhult 29 Gb 44	620 13 Nygårds 29 Gb 46	960 30 Rimjokk 7 Ca 48
840 67 Ljungå 13 Ea 44	595 01 Mjölby 28 Ga 43	770 14 Nyhammar 28 Fa 42	610 41 Ringarum 29 Ga 44
827 01 Ljusdal 13 Eb 44	684 92 Mjönas 28 Fb 41	680 90 Nykroppa 28 Fb 42	930 90 Ringselet 7 Ca 44
610 10 Ljusfallshammar 29 Ga 43	780 40 Mockfjärd 28 Fa 42	591 97 Nykyrka 28 Ga 42	291 14 Rinkaby 36 Hb 42
820 20 Ljusne 13 Eb 45	826 92 Mohed 13 Eb 44	611 00 Nyköping 29 Ga 45	915 01 Robertsfors 8 Da 48
828 93 Lobonäs 13 Eb 43	894 03 Moliden 13 Db 46	916 95 Nyliden 13 Db 46	946 91 Roknäs 8 Cb 49
590 95 Loftahammar 29 Gb 44	660 60 Molkom 28 Fb 41	149 01 Nynäshamn 29 Ga 45	430 16 Rolfstorp 28 Gb 40
620 12 Lojsta 29 Gb 46	474 70 Mollösund 28 Ga 39	Nyåker 13 Db 48	620 23 Roma 29 Gb 46
234 01 Lomma 36 Hb 41	792 01 Mora 29 Fa 43	914 94 Nyåker 13 Db 47	372 01 Ronneby 36 Ha 43
920 72 Lomselenäs 7 Cb 45	792 01 Mora 12 Eb 42	780 53 Näs 28 Fa 42	880 51 Rossön 13 Db 44
830 70 Lorås 13 Db 43	950 42 Morjärv 8 Ca 50	571 01 Nässjö 28 Gb 42	945 02 Rosvik 8 Cb 49

POSTALI · ÍNDICE CON CÓDIGOS POSTALES · INDICE DE LUGARES COM CÓDIGOS POSTAIS ·
MÍST S PSČ · ZOZNAM OBCÍ S PSČ · INDEKS MIEJSCOWOŚCI Z KOD POCZTOWY

192

Rot Ⓢ **Tösse** Ⓢ

796 90 Rot 12 Eb 42	917 99 Skavåsen 7 Da 44	711 04 Storå 28 Fb 43	562 02 Taberg 28 Gb 42
360 40 Rottne 28 Gb 42	452 94 Skee 28 Ga 39	922 95 Strandåker 7 Da 47	910 50 Tallsjö 7 Da 46
686 94 Rottneros 28 Fb 41	932 01 Skelleftehamn 8 Da 49	920 66 Strimasund 7 Ca 42	956 32 Tallvik 8 Ca 50
920 66 Rukkon 7 Ca 43	931 01 Skellefteå 8 Da 48	645 01 Strängnäs 29 Fb 45	827 02 Tallåsen 13 Eb 44
744 93 Runhällen 29 Fa 44	446 40 Skepplanda 28 Gb 40	287 01 Strömsnäsbruk 36 Ha 41	830 21 Tandsbyn 12 Db 42
921 94 Ruksele 7 Da 46	568 01 Skillingaryd 28 Gb 42	452 01 Strömstad 28 Ga 39	780 67 Tandådalen 12 Eb 40
975 96 Rutvik 8 Cb 50	276 03 Skillinge 36 Hb 42	833 01 Strömsund 13 Db 43	457 91 Tanumshede 28 Ga 39
360 10 Ryd 36 Ha 42	739 01 Skinnskatteberg 29 Fb 43	923 99 Strömsund 7 Cb 44	560 27 Tenhult 28 Gb 42
330 17 Rydaholm 36 Ha 42	747 91 Skoby 29 Fa 45	830 76 Stugun 13 Db 43	980 60 Teurajärvi 8 Ca 50
439 95 Rydet 28 Gb 40	820 29 Skog 13 Eb 44	828 95 Styggbo 13 Eb 43	543 01 Tibro 28 Ga 42
570 60 Rydsnäs 28 Gb 43	663 01 Skoghall 28 Fb 41	870 52 Styrnäs 13 Db 45	522 01 Tidaholm 28 Ga 41
611 94 Råby-Rönö 29 Ga 44	312 96 Skogstorp 29 Fb 44	620 13 Stånga 29 Gb 46	549 91 Tidan 28 Ga 42
683 03 Råda 28 Fb 41	980 41 Skröven 8 Ca 49	860 13 Stöde 13 Ea 44	815 01 Tierp 29 Fa 44
882 93 Rådom 13 Db 44	893 91 Skule 13 Db 46	680 51 Stöllet 28 Fa 41	861 01 Timrå 13 Ea 45
955 92 Råneå 8 Cb 50	814 01 Skutskär 13 Fa 45	541 91 Stöpen 28 Ga 41	362 01 Tingsryd 36 Ha 43
516 93 Rångedala 28 Gb 41	830 76 Skyttmon 13 Db 43	671 93 Sulvik 28 Fb 40	590 34 Tjällmo 29 Ga 43
950 42 Räktfors 8 Ca 50	922 95 Skålboda 7 Da 47	830 05 Sulviken 12 Db 41	621 98 Tofta 29 Gb 46
387 92 Rälla 37 Ha 44	635 50 Skåre 28 Fb 41	130 55 Sundby 29 Fb 46	290 10 Tollarp 36 Hb 41
840 30 Rätan 12 Ea 42	596 01 Skänninge 28 Ga 43	172 02 Sundbyberg 29 Fb 45	273 03 Tomelilla 36 Hb 41
795 01 Rättvik 13 Fa 43	617 01 Skärblacka 29 Ga 43	573 73 Sundhultsbrunn 28 Gb 42	260 93 Torekov 36 Ha 40
904 03 Röbäck 13 Db 48	471 31 Skärhamn 28 Gb 39	863 02 Sundsbruk 13 Ea 45	373 00 Torhamn 37 Ha 43
370 30 Rödeby 37 Ha 43	810 65 Skärplinge 29 Fa 45	851 00 Sundsvall 13 Ea 45	981 29 Torneträsk 4 Ba 47
933 91 Rönnberg 7 Cb 47	541 01 Skövde 28 Ga 41	683 95 Sunnemo 28 Fb 41	380 65 Torngård 37 Ha 44
931 92 Rönnbäcken 8 Da 48	930 91 Slagnäs 7 Cb 46	860 41 Sunnås 13 Ea 44	148 95 Torpa skog 29 Fb 46
570 01 Rörvik 28 Gb 42	620 30 Slite 29 Gb 46	735 01 Surahammar 29 Fb 44	840 13 Torpshammar 13 Ea 44
260 24 Röstånga 36 Ha 41	923 97 Slussfors 7 Cb 44	790 26 Svabensverk 13 Eb 43	685 01 Torsby 28 Fa 40
830 60 Rötviken 12 Db 42	545 91 Slätte 28 Ga 42	957 94 Svanstein 8 Ca 51	644 01 Torshälla 29 Fb 44
984 91 Sahavaara 8 Bb 51	777 90 Smedjebacken 29 Fa 43	980 20 Svappavaara 8 Bb 49	813 02 Torsåker 29 Fa 44
980 16 Saivomuotka 4 Ba 51	333 01 Smålandsstenar 28 Gb 41	956 93 Svartbyn 8 Ca 50	385 01 Torsås 37 Ha 43
733 01 Sala 29 Fb 44	930 81 Snödbränna 7 Cb 47	920 70 Svarttjärn 7 Cb 44	314 03 Torup 36 Ha 41
890 35 Saluböle 13 Db 47	680 50 Solberg 13 Db 45	693 93 Svartå 28 Fb 42	514 01 Tranemo 28 Gb 41
518 90 Sandared 28 Gb 40	466 01 Sollebrunn 28 Ga 40	233 01 Svedala 36 Hb 41	780 68 Transtrand 12 Eb 41
620 20 Sandhamn 29 Gb 46	881 01 Sollefteå 13 Db 45	842 01 Sveg 12 Ea 42	573 01 Tranås 28 Ga 42
860 41 Sandnäset 13 Ea 44	191 01 Sollentuna 29 Fb 45	512 01 Svenljunga 28 Gb 41	287 92 Traryd 36 Ha 41
870 52 Sandslån 13 Db 45	171 01 Solna 29 Fb 45	946 40 Svensbyn 8 Cb 49	231 01 Trelleborg 36 Hb 41
380 74 Sandvik 37 Gb 44	920 70 Sorsele 7 Cb 45	840 40 Svenstavik 12 Ea 42	461 01 Trollhättan 28 Ga 40
930 90 Sandviken 7 Ca 44	640 34 Sparreholm 29 Fb 44	745 93 Svinnegarn 29 Fb 45	619 92 Trosa 29 Ga 45
811 01 Sandviken 13 Fa 44	620 20 Sproge 29 Gb 46	376 06 Svängsta 36 Ha 42	830 47 Trångsviken 12 Db 42
952 72 Sangis 8 Cb 51	245 01 Staffanstorp 36 Hb 41	605 98 Svärtinge 29 Ga 43	520 26 Trädet 28 Gb 41
277 02 Sankt Olof 36 Hb 42	671 95 Stavnäs 28 Fb 40	923 99 Svärtträsk 7 Cb 45	830 51 Tulleråsen 12 Db 42
984 92 Sattajärvi 8 Bb 51	840 50 Stavre 13 Ea 43	680 60 Sysslebäck 12 Fa 40	147 01 Tumba 29 Fb 45
830 15 Saxvallen 12 Db 40	824 94 Steg 13 Eb 45	661 90 Säffle 28 Fb 40	856 34 Tunadall 13 Ea 45
660 40 Segmon 28 Fb 41	981 07 Stenbacken 4 Ba 47	780 67 Sälen 12 Eb 41	661 94 Tveta 28 Fb 40
880 30 Selsjön 13 Db 45	310 40 Steninge 36 Ha 40	840 90 Sänna 12 Ea 42	370 33 Tving 37 Ha 43
830 76 Selsålandet 13 Db 43	916 92 Stennäs 13 Db 46	429 02 Särö 28 Gb 39	922 94 Tväralund 7 Da 47
857 51 Selånger 13 Ea 45	923 41 Stensele 7 Cb 45	872 96 Säter 29 Fa 43	770 10 Tyfors 28 Fa 42
823 91 Sibo 13 Eb 44	571 91 Stensjön 28 Gb 42	918 01 Sävar 14 Db 48	457 91 Tyft 28 Ga 39
893 95 Sidensjö 13 Db 46	520 50 Stenstorp 28 Ga 41	961 47 Sävast 8 Cb 49	302 73 Tylösand 36 Ha 40
780 41 Sifferbo 13 Fa 43	930 55 Stensträsk 7 Cb 47	576 01 Sävsjö 28 Gb 42	282 01 Tyringe 36 Ha 41
672 95 Sillerud 28 Fb 40	920 70 Stensund 7 Cb 46	826 92 Söderala 13 Eb 44	614 98 Tyrislöt 29 Ga 44
310 38 Simlångsdalen 36 Ha 41	840 90 Stensån 13 Ea 43	761 75 Söderby-Karl 29 Fb 46	260 22 Tågarp 36 Hb 40
616 91 Simonstorp 29 Ga 44	962 99 Stenträsk 7 Ca 47	777 03 Söderbärke 29 Fa 43	930 47 Tåme 8 Da 49
272 01 Simrishamn 36 Hb 42	444 01 Stenungssund 28 Ga 39	815 04 Söderfors 29 Fa 45	962 99 Tärrajaur 7 Ca 47
460 20 Sjuntorp 28 Ga 40	610 55 Stigtomta 29 Ga 44	826 01 Söderhamn 13 Eb 45	183 01 Täby 29 Fb 46
275 01 Sjöbo 36 Hb 41	105 00 Stockholm 29 Fb 46	614 01 Söderköping 29 Ga 44	840 98 Tänndalen 12 Ea 40
514 94 Sjötofta 28 Gb 41	715 02 Stora Mellösa 29 Fb 43	151 01 Södertälje 29 Fb 45	890 94 Tänsta 12 Ea 40
540 66 Sjötorp 28 Ga 41	981 07 Stordalen 4 Ba 47	385 03 Söderåkra 37 Ha 44	980 61 Tärendö 8 Bb 50
443 74 Sjövik 28 Gb 40	590 83 Storebro 29 Gb 43	544 94 Södra Fågelås 28 Ga 42	920 64 Tärnaby 7 Cb 43
840 60 Sjöändan 12 Eb 42	688 01 Storfors 28 Fb 42	972 41 Södra Sunderbyn 8 Cb 49	740 45 Tärnsjö 29 Fa 44
239 01 Skanör med Falsterbo 36 Hb 40	830 15 Storlien 12 Db 40	294 01 Sölvesborg 36 Ha 42	891 96 Tävra 13 Db 47
	933 91 Stormyrheden 7 Cb 47	840 67 Sörbygden 13 Ea 44	833 93 Täxan 13 Db 43
532 01 Skara 28 Ga 41	912 99 Storseleby 7 Da 44	790 90 Sörfors 12 Eb 41	670 10 Töcksfors 28 Fb 39
916 95 Skarda 7 Da 46	920 70 Storsjö 7 Cb 46	864 92 Sörfors 13 Db 48	820 29 Tönnebro 13 Eb 44
923 98 Skarvsjöby 7 Da 45	923 01 Storuman 7 Cb 45	820 65 Sörforsa 13 Eb 44	950 40 Töre 8 Cb 50
794 91 Skattungbyn 12 Eb 42	830 15 Storvallen 12 Db 40	780 69 Sörsjön 12 Eb 41	545 01 Töreboda 28 Ga 42
982 04 Skaulo 8 Bb 49	743 01 Storvreta 29 Fb 45	860 35 Söråker 13 Ea 45	662 98 Tösse 28 Ga 40

Uddeholm   Ⓢ · ⓈⓇⒷ   **Draginac**

683 02 Uddeholm 28 Fa 41	280 22 Vittsjö 36 Ha 41	910 60 Åsele 7 Da 45
451 01 Uddevalla 28 Ga 39	921 91 Vormträsk 7 Da 46	796 90 Åsen 12 Eb 41
310 60 Ullared 28 Gb 40	828 93 Voxnabruk 13 Eb 43	920 51 Åskilje 7 Da 45
982 42 Ullatti 8 Bb 49	610 56 Vrena 29 Ga 44	961 91 Åskogen 8 Cb 49
870 32 Ullånger 13 Db 46	570 03 Vrigstad 28 Gb 42	265 01 Åstorp 36 Ha 40
523 01 Ulricehamn 28 Gb 41	960 30 Vuollerim 7 Ca 48	860 33 Åsäng 13 Ea 45
840 60 Ulvsjö 13 Ea 43	933 91 Vuotner 7 Cb 47	693 70 Åtorp 28 Fb 42
901 00 Umeå 13 Db 48	585 92 Vårdsberg 29 Ga 43	921 99 Åttonträsk 7 Da 46
921 91 Umgransele 7 Da 46	447 01 Vårgårda 28 Ga 40	597 01 Åtvidaberg 29 Ga 44
830 10 Undersåker 12 Db 41	820 62 Våtmor 13 Eb 44	870 10 Ålandsbro 13 Ea 45
194 01 Upplands-Väsby 29 Fb 45	312 98 Våxtorp 36 Ha 41	840 31 Åldsandet 12 Ea 42
750 02 Uppsala 29 Fb 45	590 21 Väderstad 28 Ga 42	545 02 Älgarås 28 Ga 42
360 13 Urshult 36 Ha 42	921 93 Vägsele 7 Da 46	910 60 Älgsjö 7 Da 45
932 03 Ursviken 8 Da 49	685 94 Vägsjöfors 28 Fa 41	343 01 Älmhult 36 Ha 42
870 15 Utansjö 13 Ea 45	620 10 Vändburg 37 Ha 46	760 40 Älmsta 29 Fb 46
130 56 Utö 29 Ga 46	462 01 Vänersborg 28 Ga 40	796 01 Älvdalen 12 Ea 42
592 01 Vadstena 28 Ga 42	740 20 Vänge 29 Fb 45	814 02 Älvkarleby 13 Fa 45
610 70 Vagnhärad 29 Ga 45	916 95 Vänjaurbäck 7 Da 46	842 92 Älvros 12 Ea 42
962 99 Vajmat 7 Ca 47	672 93 Vännacka 28 Fb 40	660 60 Älvsbacka 28 Fb 41
818 01 Valbo 13 Fa 44	916 91 Vännäs 13 Db 47	942 01 Älvsbyn 8 Cb 49
615 01 Valdemarsvik 29 Ga 44	911 02 Vännäsby 13 Db 47	310 63 Älvsered 28 Gb 40
621 93 Vall 29 Gb 46	842 93 Vänsjö 12 Eb 43	794 98 Åmådalen 12 Eb 42
840 64 Valla 13 Db 44	956 92 Vänäsberget 8 Ca 50	680 51 Ångan 12 Fa 41
655 93 Vallargärdet 28 Fb 41	661 93 Värmlandsbro 28 Fb 41	830 51 Ånge 12 Db 42
186 01 Vallentuna 29 Fb 46	331 01 Värnamo 28 Gb 42	262 01 Ängelholm 36 Ha 40
830 67 Valsjöbyn 26 Da 42	680 51 Värnäs 28 Fa 41	780 54 Äppelbo 28 Fa 42
620 10 Vamlingbo 37 Ha 46	796 91 Väse 28 Fb 41	610 25 Årkosund 29 Ga 44
780 50 Vansbro 12 Fa 42	920 64 Västansjö 7 Cb 43	882 93 Årtrik 13 Db 44
833 40 Vaplan 12 Db 42	864 92 Västansjön 13 Ea 44	640 25 Åsköping 29 Fb 44
534 01 Vara 28 Ga 40	820 50 Västbacka 12 Eb 42	310 61 Åtran 28 Gb 40
432 01 Varberg 28 Gb 40	830 51 Västbyn 7 Da 48	599 01 Ödeshög 28 Ga 42
468 01 Vargön 28 Ga 40	812 90 Västerberg 13 Fa 44	560 27 Ödestugu 28 Gb 42
931 98 Varuträsk 8 Da 48	730 70 Västerfärnebo 29 Fb 44	668 95 Ödskölt 28 Ga 40
792 97 Vattnäs 12 Eb 42	620 20 Västergarn 29 Gb 46	943 01 Öjebyn 8 Cb 49
430 20 Veddige 28 Gb 40	137 01 Västerhaninge 29 Fb 46	661 91 Ölserud 28 Fb 41
711 02 Vedevåg 29 Fb 43	593 01 Västervik 29 Gb 44	748 02 Örbyhus 29 Fa 45
312 92 Veinge 36 Ha 41	720 02 Västerås 29 Fb 44	700 02 Örebro 29 Fb 43
260 83 Vejbystrand 36 Ha 40	686 95 Västra Ämtervik 28 Fb 41	790 90 Örebäcken 12 Eb 40
235 01 Vellinge 36 Hb 41	880 45 Västvattnet 13 Db 44	286 01 Örkelljunga 36 Ha 41
840 92 Vemdalen 12 Ea 41	350 03 Växjö 36 Ha 42	891 01 Örnsköldsvik 13 Db 46
840 92 Vemdalsskalet 12 Ea 41	271 01 Ystad 36 Hb 41	563 91 Örserum 28 Ga 42
597 91 Vena 29 Gb 43	840 90 Ytterhogdal 12 Ea 42	382 97 Örsjö 37 Ha 43
574 01 Vetlanda 28 Gb 43	782 91 Yttermalung 12 Fa 41	740 82 Örsundsbro 29 Fb 45
942 92 Vidsel 7 Cb 48	920 64 Yttervik 7 Cb 43	195 93 Ösby 29 Fb 45
840 40 Vigge 12 Ea 42	830 44 Ytterån 12 Db 42	148 01 Ösmo 29 Ga 45
452 97 Vik 28 Ga 39	830 05 Åbo 12 Db 40	864 92 Östansjö 7 Ca 45
795 95 Vikarby 12 Fa 43	296 01 Åhus 36 Hb 42	360 13 Östavall 13 Ea 43
260 40 Viken 36 Ha 40	640 60 Åkers styckebruk 29 Fb 45	748 01 Österbybruk 29 Fa 45
713 92 Viker 28 Fb 42	184 01 Åkersberga 29 Fb 46	570 60 Österbymo 29 Gb 43
912 01 Vilhelmina 7 Da 44	933 90 Åkroken 7 Cb 48	882 91 Österforse 13 Db 45
598 01 Vimmerby 29 Gb 43	384 02 Ålem 37 Ha 44	895 93 Östersel 13 Db 45
922 01 Vindeln 7 Da 47	670 40 Åmotfors 28 Fb 40	831 01 Östersund 12 Db 42
643 91 Vingåker 29 Fb 43	922 75 Åmsele 7 Da 47	681 95 Östervik 28 Fa 42
531 03 Vinninga 28 Ga 41	662 00 Åmål 28 Fb 40	740 46 Östervåla 29 Fa 45
719 91 Vintrosa 28 Fb 42	611 93 Ånge 13 Ea 43	742 01 Östhammar 29 Fa 46
572 92 Virkvam 29 Gb 44	830 15 Ånn 12 Db 40	792 95 Östnor 12 Eb 42
570 80 Virserum 29 Gb 43	915 02 Ånäset 8 Da 49	610 31 Östra Husby 29 Ga 44
984 92 Virtala 8 Bb 51	830 13 Åre 12 Db 41	830 60 Östra Lövsjön 12 Db 42
621 01 Visby 29 Gb 46	672 90 Årjäng 28 Fb 40	242 97 Östraby 36 Hb 41
830 13 Viskan 13 Ea 44	820 77 Årskogen 13 Ea 45	842 94 Överberg 12 Ea 42
340 30 Vislanda 36 Ha 42	311 97 Årstad 36 Ha 40	921 88 Överbo 7 Da 46
942 91 Vistheden 7 Cb 48	810 22 Årsunda 29 Fa 44	960 24 Överedet 8 Ca 48
942 95 Vitberget 7 Cb 48	830 43 Ås 12 Db 42	746 93 Övergran 29 Fb 45
957 95 Vitsaniemi 8 Ca 51	430 31 Åsa 28 Gb 40	894 02 Överhörnäs 13 Db 46
980 10 Vittangi 4 Bb 49	840 31 Åsarne 12 Ea 42	956 01 Överkalix 8 Ca 50
961 96 Vittjärv 8 Cb 49	690 45 Åsbro 28 Ga 43	957 01 Övertorneå 8 Ca 51

590 96 Överum 29 Gb 44
961 98 Överäng 8 Cb 49
930 15 Övre Bäck 8 Da 49
980 14 Övre Soppero 4 Ba 49
942 92 Övre Tväråsel 8 Cb 48

ⓈⓇⒷ

36203 Adrani 76 Ob 48
18220 Aleksinac 76 Ob 49
26310 Alibunar 76 Nb 48
25260 Apatin 75 Nb 46
34300 Arandelovac 76 Oa 48
31230 Arilje 76 Ob 48
18330 Babušnica 90 Ob 50
21400 Bačka Palanka 76 Nb 47
24300 Bačka Topola 76 Nb 47
25276 Bački Breg 75 Nb 46
31250 Bajina Bašta 76 Ob 47
24210 Bajmok 76 Nb 47
26314 Banatsko Novo Selo 76 Oa 48
31337 Banja 76 Ob 47
15316 Banja Koviljača 75 Oa 47
23316 Bašaid 76 Nb 48
12311 Batuša 76 Oa 49
21220 Bečej 76 Nb 48
26340 Bela Crkva 76 Oa 49
18310 Bela Palanka 90 Ob 50
18424 Beloljin 90 Ob 49
11000 Beograd / Београд 76 Oa 48
25270 Bezdan 75 Nb 46
17522 Biljača 90 Pa 49
18420 Blace 90 Ob 49
23252 Boka 76 Nb 48
19370 Boljevac 76 Ob 49
19210 Bor 76 Oa 50
11211 Borča 76 Oa 48
37262 Bošnjane 76 Ob 49
16253 Brestovac/Leskovac 90 Ob 49
19229 Brestovac/Bor 76 Oa 50
19323 Brza Palanka 76 Oa 50
17520 Bujanovac 90 Pa 49
13260 Bukovi 76 Oa 47
34322 Cerovac 76 Oa 48
26213 Crepaja 76 Nb 48
15318 Crnča 76 Oa 47
25220 Crvenka 76 Nb 47
32101 Čačak 76 Ob 48
31310 Čajetina 76 Ob 47
23266 Čenta 76 Nb 48
31213 Čestobrodica 76 Ob 48
34322 Čumić 76 Oa 48
37210 Čićevac 76 Ob 49
35230 Ćuprija 76 Ob 49
19250 Debeli Lug 76 Oa 49
15214 Debrc 76 Oa 47
25254 Deronje 75 Nb 47
18320 Dimitrovgrad 91 Ob 50
11272 Dobanovci 76 Oa 48
17538 Donja Lisina 90 Pa 50
25243 Doroslovo 75 Nb 47
15311 Draginac 76 Oa 47

POSTALI · ÍNDICE CON CÓDIGOS POSTALES · INDICE DE LUGARES COM CÓDIGOS POSTAIS ·
MÍST S PSČ · ZOZNAM OBCÍ S PSČ · INDEKS MIEJSCOWOŚCI Z KOD POCZTOWY

194

Draginje   SRB · SK   Kolárovo

SRB · SK

15226 Draginje 76 Oa 47	18440 Malo Selo 90 Pa 49
35257 Drenovac 76 Ob 49	18415 Malošište 90 Ob 49
15220 Družetić 76 Oa 47	26364 Margita 76 Nb 49
11561 Dudovica 76 Oa 48	16240 Medveda 90 Pa 49
36312 Duga Poljana 90 Ob 48	19322 Mihajlovac/Negotin 76 Oa 50
19335 Dušanovac 76 Oa 50	11312 Mihajlovac 76 Oa 48
11450 Đurinci 76 Oa 48	19222 Miloševa Kula 76 Oa 50
23203 Ečka 76 Nb 48	19328 Milutinovac 76 Oa 50
21410 Futog 76 Nb 47	19340 Minićevo 76 Ob 50
12223 Golubac 76 Oa 49	15000 Mišar 76 Oa 47
19352 Gornja Kamenica	11400 Mladenovac 76 Oa 48
76 Ob 50	24435 Mol 76 Nb 48
32300 Gornji Milanovac 76 Oa 48	19222 Mosna 76 Oa 50
31305 Gostun 90 Ob 47	32210 Mrčajevci 76 Ob 48
34230 Gruža 76 Ob 48	36300 Mur 90 Ob 48
24410 Horgoš 76 Na 47	32312 Mutanj 76 Oa 48
22427 Hrtkovci 76 Oa 47	34313 Natalinci 76 Oa 48
23323 Iđoš 76 Nb 48	19300 Negotin 76 Oa 50
22319 Inđija 76 Nb 48	18000 Niš / Ниш 76 Oa 49
22406 Irig 76 Nb 47	18205 Niška Banja 90 Ob 50
32250 Ivanjica 76 Ob 48	22330 Nova Pazova 76 Oa 48
35000 Jagodina 76 Ob 49	31320 Nova Varoš 76 Ob 47
19332 Jasenica 76 Oa 50	22304 Novi Banovci 76 Oa 48
31215 Jelen Do 76 Ob 48	23272 Novi Bečej 76 Nb 48
21241 Kać 76 Nb 47	23330 Novi Kneževac
19352 Kalna 76 Ob 50	76 Na 48
24420 Kanjiža 76 Na 48	36300 Novi Pazar 90 Ob 48
23300 Kikinda 76 Nb 48	21000 Novi Sad / Нови Сад
23211 Klek 76 Nb 48	76 Nb 47
19222 Klokočevac 76 Oa 50	23273 Novo Miloševo 76 Nb 48
19350 Knjaževac 76 Ob 50	11500 Obrenovac 76 Oa 48
19316 Kobišnica 76 Oa 50	25250 Odžaci 76 Nb 47
11431 Kolari 76 Oa 48	16221 Oraovica 90 Pa 50
23253 Konak 76 Nb 48	23263 Orlovat 76 Nb 48
36340 Konarevo 76 Ob 48	14253 Osečina 76 Oa 47
31260 Kosjerić 76 Oa 47	23326 Ostojićevo 76 Nb 48
26210 Kovačica 76 Nb 48	11251 Ostružnica 76 Oa 48
26220 Kovin 76 Oa 48	26101 Pančevo 76 Oa 48
34000 Kragujevac / Крагујевац	35250 Paraćin 76 Ob 49
76 Oa 48	12300 Petrovac 76 Oa 49
36000 Kraljevo 76 Ob 48	21131 Petrovaradin 76 Nb 47
31242 Kremna 76 Ob 47	18300 Pirot 91 Ob 50
12316 Krepoljin 76 Oa 49	26360 Plandište 76 Nb 49
37000 Kruševac 76 Ob 49	12000 Požarevac 76 Oa 49
12240 Kučevo 76 Oa 49	31210 Požega 76 Ob 48
22224 Kukujevci 76 Nb 47	17523 Preševo 90 Pa 49
25230 Kula 76 Nb 47	31330 Priboj 76 Ob 47
32255 Kumanica 76 Ob 48	14251 Pričević 76 Oa 47
18430 Kuršumlija 90 Ob 49	31300 Prijepolje 90 Ob 47
22223 Kuzmin 76 Nb 47	15306 Prnjavor 76 Oa 47
22221 Laćarak 76 Nb 47	18400 Prokuplje 90 Ob 49
34220 Lapovo 76 Oa 49	17523 Rajince 90 Pa 49
11550 Lazarevac 76 Oa 48	36350 Raška 90 Ob 48
23241 Lazarevo 76 Nb 48	36212 Ratina 76 Ob 48
16230 Lebane 90 Pa 49	35260 Ratković 76 Ob 49
16000 Leskovac / Лесковац	19214 Rgotina 76 Oa 50
90 Pa 49	17538 Ribarci 91 Pa 50
35255 Lešje 76 Ob 49	36309 Ribarice 90 Pa 48
15307 Lešnica 76 Oa 47	15224 Riđake 76 Oa 47
15200 Loznica 76 Oa 47	11232 Ripanj 76 Oa 48
19371 Lukovo 76 Ob 49	31255 Rogačica 76 Oa 47
15320 Ljubovija 76 Oa 47	22400 Ruma 76 Nb 47
19250 Majdanpek 76 Oa 49	12311 Salakovac 76 Oa 49
12221 Majilovac 76 Oa 49	23240 Sečanj 76 Nb 48
15353 Majur 76 Oa 47	24000 Sel 76 Na 47
24309 Mali Beograd 76 Nb 47	24400 Senta 76 Nb 48

25223 Sivac 76 Nb 47	
36310 Sjenica 90 Ob 47	
14223 Slovac 76 Oa 48	
11300 Smederevo 76 Oa 48	
25000 Sombor 75 Nb 47	
21481 Srbobran 76 Nb 47	
11253 Sremčica 76 Oa 48	
21202 Sremska Kamenica	
76 Nb 47	
22000 Sremska Mitrovica 76 Oa 47	
23220 Srpska Crnja 76 Nb 48	
25240 Stapar 75 Nb 47	
22300 Stara Pazova 76 Oa 48	
11564 Stepojevac 76 Oa 48	
26345 Straža 76 Oa 49	
17535 Strezimirovci 90 Pa 50	
35215 Strmosten 76 Oa 49	
31255 Strmovo 76 Oa 47	
11507 Stubline 76 Oa 48	
24000 Subotica 76 Na 47	
11271 Surčin 76 Oa 48	
17530 Surdulica 90 Pa 50	
25211 Svetozar Miletić 75 Nb 47	
35210 Svilajnac 76 Oa 49	
18360 Svrljig 76 Ob 50	
15000 Šabac 76 Oa 47	
22240 Šid 76 Nb 47	
19234 Tanda 76 Oa 50	
21235 Temerin 76 Nb 47	
18355 Temska 91 Ob 50	
34310 Topola 76 Oa 48	
37240 Trstenik 76 Ob 48	
14206 Tubravić 76 Oa 47	
16247 Tulare 90 Pa 49	
12257 Turija 76 Oa 49	
14210 Ub 76 Oa 48	
32314 Ugrinovci 76 Oa 48	
26330 Uljma 76 Nb 49	
36342 Ušće 76 Ob 48	
26216 Uzdin 76 Nb 48	
31000 Užice 76 Ob 47	
14000 Valjevo 76 Oa 47	
11320 Velika Plana 76 Oa 49	
23316 Velike Livade 76 Nb 48	
37222 Veliki Kupci 76 Ob 49	
17510 Vladičin Han 90 Pa 50	
17532 Vlasina Okruglica 90 Pa 50	
16210 Vlasotince 90 Pa 50	
11329 Vranovo 76 Oa 48	
17501 Vranje 90 Pa 49	
17542 Vranjska Banja 90 Pa 50	
19344 Vratarnica 76 Ob 50	
21460 Vrbas 76 Nb 47	
36217 Vrnjačka Banja 76 Ob 48	
26300 Vršac 76 Nb 49	
26344 Zagajica 76 Oa 49	
19000 Zaječar 76 Ob 50	
11080 Zemun 76 Oa 48	
23101 Zrenjanin 76 Nb 48	
19227 Zvezdan 76 Ob 50	
21230 Žabalj 76 Nb 48	
12320 Žagubica 76 Oa 49	
12309 Ždrelo 76 Oa 49	
24224 Žednik 76 Nb 47	
23210 Žitište 76 Nb 48	
18412 Žitorađa 90 Ob 49	

SK

991 11 Balog nad Ipľom 61 Ma 47	
957 04 Bánovce nad Bebravou	
61 Ma 46	
974 01 Banská Bystrica 61 Ma 47	
969 01 Banská Štiavnica 61 Ma 46	
085 01 Bardejov 62 Lb 49	
018 61 Beluša 61 Lb 46	
935 74 Bielovce 61 Mb 46	
919 08 Boleráz 61 Ma 45	
908 77 Borský Mikuláš 61 Ma 45	
810 00 Bratislava 61 Ma 45	
977 01 Brezno 62 Ma 47	
90613 Brezová pod Bradlom	
61 Ma 45	
014 01 Bytča 61 Lb 46	
022 01 Čadca 61 La 46	
900 89 Častá 61 Ma 45	
979 01 Čerenčany 62 Ma 47	
976 52 Čierny Balog 62 Ma 47	
935 85 Demandice 61 Ma 46	
962 11 Detva 62 Ma 47	
84107 Devínska Nova Ves	
61 Ma 44	
026 01 Dolný Kubín 61 Lb 47	
922 41 Drahovce 61 Ma 45	
082 04 Drienov 62 Ma 49	
018 14 Dubnica nad Váhom	
61 Ma 46	
929 01 Dunajská Streda 61 Mb 45	
920 56 Dvorníky 61 Ma 45	
986 01 Fiľakovo 62 Ma 47	
930 05 Gabčíkovo 61 Mb 45	
924 01 Galanta 61 Ma 45	
943 42 Gbelce 61 Mb 46	
086 04 Gerlachov 62 Lb 49	
087 01 Giraltovce 62 Lb 49	
972 51 Handlová 61 Ma 46	
976 03 Harmanec 61 Ma 47	
044 46 Herľany 62 Ma 49	
966 01 Hliník nad Hronom 61 Ma 46	
020 62 Hlohovec 61 Ma 45	
981 01 Hnúšťa 62 Ma 47	
908 51 Holíč 61 Ma 45	
962 65 Hontianske Nemce	
61 Ma 46	
067 35 Hostovice 62 Lb 50	
029 52 Hruštín 61 Lb 47	
034 91 Hubová 61 Lb 47	
066 01 Humenné 62 Ma 49	
977 01 Hurbanovo 61 Mb 46	
951 12 Ivanka pri Nitre 61 Ma 46	
906 32 Jablonica 61 Ma 45	
055 61 Jaklovce 62 Ma 48	
985 01 Kalinovo 62 Ma 47	
935 32 Kalná nad Hronom	
61 Ma 46	
082 12 Kapušany 62 Lb 49	
060 01 Kežmarok 62 Lb 48	
072 36 Klokočov 61 Lb 46	
985 05 Kokava nad Rimavicou	
62 Ma 47	
013 54 Kolárovice 61 Lb 46	
946 03 Kolárovo 61 Mb 45	

195

INDEX WITH POST CODES · ORTSREGISTER MIT POSTLEITZAHLEN · INDICE CON CODICI
STEDREGISTER MED POSTNUMRE · PLAATSNAMENREGISTER MET POSTCODE · REJSTŘÍK

SK
SLO
TN

Kolonica   SK · SLO · TN   **Kelibia**

067 61 Kolonica 62 Ma 50
945 01 Komárno 61 Mb 46
941 06 Komjatice 61 Ma 46
040 01 Košice 62 Ma 49
966 15 Kozelník 61 Ma 46
980 45 Kráľ 62 Ma 48
077 01 Kráľovský Chlmec 62 Ma 49
962 04 Kriváň 62 Ma 47
053 42 Krompachy 62 Ma 48
963 01 Krupina 61 Ma 47
024 01 Kysucké Nové Mesto
61 Lb 46
934 01 Levice 61 Ma 46
054 01 Levoča 62 Lb 48
049 14 Licince 62 Ma 48
082 71 Lipany 62 Lb 48
034 73 Liptovská Osada 61 Ma 47
031 01 Liptovský Mikuláš 62 Lb 47
976 53 Lom nad Rimavicou
62 Ma 47
985 54 Lovinobaňa 62 Ma 47
984 01 Lučenec 62 Ma 47
023 56 Makov 61 Lb 46
901 01 Malacky 61 Ma 45
036 01 Martin 61 Lb 46
980 41 Martinová 62 Ma 48
930 07 Medvedov 61 Mb 45
044 25 Medzev 62 Ma 48
068 01 Medzilaborce 62 Lb 49
071 01 Michalovce 62 Ma 49
053 76 Mlynky 62 Ma 48
055 64 Mníšek nad Hnilcom
62 Ma 48
946 37 Moča 61 Mb 46
900 01 Modra 61 Ma 45
045 01 Moldava nad Bodvou
62 Ma 48
976 02 Motyčky 61 Ma 47
049 01 Muráň 62 Ma 48
907 01 Myjava 61 Ma 45
029 01 Námestovo 62 Lb 47
949 01 Nitra 61 Ma 46
972 13 Nitrianske Pravno 61 Ma 46
094 07 Nižná Sitnica 62 Lb 49
018 51 Nová Dubnica 61 Ma 46
972 71 Nováky 61 Ma 46
915 01 Nové Mesto nad Váhom
61 Ma 45
940 01 Nové Zámky 61 Mb 46
029 47 Oravská Polhora 62 Lb 47
958 06 Partizánske 61 Ma 46
072 14 Pavlovce nad Uhom
62 Ma 50
900 53 Pernek 61 Ma 45
908 44 Petrova Ves 61 Ma 45
902 01 Pezinok 61 Ma 45
921 01 Piešťany 61 Ma 45
065 03 Podolínec 62 Lb 48
976 66 Polomka 62 Ma 47
058 01 Poprad 62 Lb 48
017 01 Považská Bystrica 61 Lb 46
080 01 Prešov 62 Lb 49
038 42 Príbovce 61 Lb 46
971 01 Prievidza 61 Ma 46
018 52 Pruské 61 Lb 46
020 01 Púchov 61 Lb 46

985 58 Radzovce 62 Ma 47
086 41 Raslavice 62 Lb 49
050 01 Revúca 62 Ma 48
979 01 Rimavská Sobota
62 Ma 48
90638 Rohožník 61 Ma 45
048 01 Rožňava 62 Ma 48
034 01 Ružomberok 61 Lb 47
083 01 Sabinov 62 Lb 49
943 61 Salka 61 Mb 46
078 01 Sečovce 62 Ma 49
044 58 Seňa 62 Ma 49
903 01 Senec 61 Ma 45
905 01 Senica 61 Ma 45
962 43 Senohrad 61 Ma 47
926 01 Sereď 61 Ma 45
909 01 Skalica 61 Ma 45
976 13 Slovenská Ľupča 61 Ma 47
069 01 Snina 62 Ma 50
073 01 Sobrance 62 Ma 50
059 04 Spišské Hanušovce
62 Lb 48
064 01 Stará Ľubovňa 62 Lb 48
916 01 Stará Turá 61 Ma 45
013 24 Strečno 61 Lb 46
091 01 Stropkov 62 Lb 49
067 15 Svetlice 62 Lb 50
089 01 Svidník 62 Lb 49
936 01 Šahy 61 Ma 46
927 01 Šaľa 61 Ma 45
931 01 Šamorín 61 Ma 45
082 37 Široké 62 Lb 48
943 01 Štúrovo 61 Mb 46
991 01 Šuľa 62 Ma 47
942 01 Šurany 61 Ma 46
972 48 Tále 62 Ma 47
93541 Tekovské Lužany 61 Ma 46
935 21 Tlmače 61 Ma 46
955 01 Topoľčany 61 Ma 46
982 01 Tornaľa 62 Ma 48
075 01 Trebišov 62 Ma 49
913 11 Trenčianske Stankovce
61 Ma 45
911 01 Trenčín 61 Ma 45
917 01 Trnava 61 Ma 45
919 05 Trstín 61 Ma 45
039 01 Turčianske Teplice 61 Ma 46
023 54 Turzovka 61 Lb 46
027 44 Tvrdošín 62 Lb 47
941 10 Tvrdošovce 61 Ma 46
032 61 Važec 62 Lb 47
079 01 Veľké Kapušany 62 Ma 50
935 65 Veľké Ludince 61 Mb 46
990 01 Veľký Krtíš 62 Ma 47
932 01 Veľký Meder 61 Mb 45
059 17 Vernár 62 Ma 48
962 02 Vígľaš 61 Ma 47
049 24 Vlachovo 62 Ma 48
925 84 Vlčany 61 Ma 45
952 01 Vráble 61 Ma 46
093 01 Vranov nad Topľou
62 Ma 49
991 21 Závada 62 Ma 47
027 05 Zázrivá 61 Lb 47
086 33 Zborov 62 Lb 49
930 39 Zlaté Klasy 61 Ma 45

953 01 Zlaté Moravce 61 Ma 46
027 32 Zuberec 62 Lb 47
960 01 Zvolen 61 Ma 47
966 81 Žarnovica 61 Ma 46
991 06 Želovce 62 Ma 47
935 02 Žemberovce 61 Ma 46
965 01 Žiar nad Hronom 61 Ma 46
010 01 Žilina 61 Lb 46

SLO

5270 Ajdovščina 74 Nb 41
4260 Bled 74 Na 42
4264 Bohinjska Bistrica 74 Na 41
5230 Bovec 74 Na 41
8250 Brežice 74 Nb 43
3000 Celje 74 Na 42
1380 Cerknica 74 Nb 42
5282 Cerkno 74 Na 41
9232 Črenšovci 75 Na 44
2393 Črna na Koroškem 74 Na 42
6275 Črni Kal 74 Nb 41
8340 Črnomelj 74 Nb 43
3320 Črnova 74 Na 43
1230 Domžale 74 Na 42
2370 Dravograd 74 Na 43
8361 Dvor 74 Nb 42
1336 Fara 74 Nb 42
9250 Gornja Radgona 75 Na 43
2382 Gornji Dolič 74 Na 43
1430 Hrastnik 74 Na 42
5280 Idrija 74 Na 42
5222 Idrsko 74 Na 41
6250 Ilirska Bistrica 74 Nb 42
3254 Imeno 74 Na 43
6310 Izola 74 Nb 41
4270 Jesenice 74 Na 42
1240 Kamnik 74 Na 42
5213 Kanal 74 Na 41
1330 Kočevje 74 Nb 42
6101 Koper 74 Nb 41
6240 Kozina 74 Nb 41
2286 Kozminci 75 Na 43
4000 Kranj 74 Na 42
4280 Kranjska Gora 74 Na 41
8270 Krško 74 Nb 43
1270 Litija 74 Na 42
1000 Ljubljana 74 Na 42
9240 Ljutomer 75 Na 44
1370 Logatec 74 Nb 42
3334 Luče ob Savinji 74 Na 42
9202 Mačkovci 75 Na 44
8312 Malo Mraševo 74 Nb 43
2000 Maribor 75 Na 43
8330 Metlika 74 Nb 43
2204 Miklavž na Dravskem polju
75 Na 43
1338 Moravče 74 Nb 42
9000 Murska Sobota 75 Na 44
5101 Nova Gorica 74 Nb 41
8000 Novo mesto 74 Nb 43
2270 Ormož 75 Na 44
6257 Pivka 74 Nb 42
6232 Planina 74 Nb 42

3257 Podsreda 74 Na 43
6230 Postojna 74 Nb 42
2250 Ptuj 75 Na 43
1386 Pudob 74 Nb 42
4240 Radovljica 74 Na 42
1315 Rašica 74 Nb 42
2390 Ravne na Koroškem 74 Na 42
3250 Rogaška Slatina 74 Na 43
2342 Ruše 74 Na 43
8290 Sevnica 74 Na 43
6210 Sežana 74 Nb 41
2380 Slovenj Gradec 74 Na 43
2310 Slovenska Bistrica 74 Na 43
8351 Soteska 74 Nb 43
6244 Starod 74 Nb 42
8344 Suhor 74 Nb 43
2212 Šentilj v Slovenskih goricah
75 Na 43
4220 Škofja Loka 74 Na 42
5220 Tolmin 74 Na 41
1420 Trbovlje 74 Na 43
8210 Trebnje 74 Nb 43
1222 Trojane 74 Na 42
4290 Tržič 74 Na 42
4205 Tupaliče 74 Na 42
3320 Velenje 74 Na 43
8333 Vrcice 74 Nb 43
1360 Vrhnika 74 Nb 42
1432 Zidani Most 74 Na 43
3310 Žalec 74 Na 43
4228 Železniki 74 Na 42
4226 Žiri 74 Na 42
1310 Žlebič 74 Nb 42

TN

4092 Aïn Errahma 101 Sa 38
1100 Aïn Sallaj 100 Sa 37
1141 Aouja 101 Sa 37
2080 Ariana 101 Sa 38
8035 Azmour 101 Sa 39
6170 Bargou 100 Sa 37
9000 Béja 100 Sa 37
2013 Ben Arous 101 Sa 38
8021 Beni Khalled 101 Sa 38
8042 Bir Bouregba 101 Sa 38
1163 Bir Chaouch 101 Sa 38
7000 Bizerte 101 Rb 37
6180 Bou Arada 100 Sa 37
8170 Bou Salem 100 Sa 36
2016 Carthage 101 Sa 38
7016 El Alia 101 Rb 38
6116 El Aroussa 100 Sa 37
1140 El Fahs 101 Sa 38
8045 El Haouaria 101 Rb 39
7100 Le Kef 100 Sa 36
9010 Fatnassa 100 Sa 37
8160 Ghardimaou 100 Sa 36
8030 Grombalia 101 Sa 38
2050 Hammam Lif 101 Sa 38
8050 Hammamet 101 Sa 38
8100 Jendouba 100 Sa 36
2022 Kaalat El Andalous 101 Rb 38
8090 Kelibia 101 Sa 39

POSTALI · ÍNDICE CON CÓDIGOS POSTALES · INDICE DE LUGARES COM CÓDIGOS POSTAIS ·
MÍST S PSČ · ZOZNAM OBCÍ S PSČ · INDEKS MIEJSCOWOŚCI Z KOD POCZTOWY

196

Korba (TN) · (TR) **Çıtak**

TN
TR

8070 Korba 101 Sa 38	54400 Akyazı 93 Qa 58	10200 Bandırma 92 Qa 55	35390 Buca 106 Ra 55
2078 La Marsa 101 Sa 38	06750 Akyurt 94 Qa 61	71800 Barakobası 94 Qb 61	15300 Bucak 107 Rb 58
2015 El Kram 101 Sa 38	19600 Alaca/Sungurlu 94 Qa 62	59000 Barbaros 92 Qa 55	70000 Bucakkışla 108 Sa 61
6120 Le Krib 100 Sa 37	55800 Alaçam/Bafra 94 Pb 63	32530 Barla 107 Ra 58	40500 Budak 94 Qb 62
7180 Le Sers 100 Sa 37	35937 Alaçatı 106 Ra 54	74000 Bartın 93 Pb 60	10900 Buğdaylı 92 Qa 55
7030 Mateur 101 Rb 37	07400 Alanya 108 Sa 60	66000 Başıbüyüklü 94 Qb 62	09670 Buharkent 107 Rb 56
9070 Mejez El-Bab 100 Sa 37	67850 Alaplı 93 Pb 59	71520 Battalobası 94 Qa 61	37400 Bukköy 94 Pb 61
7050 Menzel Bourguiba 101 Rb 37	45600 Alaşehir 107 Ra 56	18280 Bayanpınar 94 Qa 62	20400 Buldan 107 Ra 56
8080 Menzel Temine 101 Sa 38	55760 Alayurt 94 Qa 63	03780 Bayat/Emirdağ 107 Ra 58	15000 Burdur 107 Rb 58
8080 Meroua 101 Sa 38	22370 Alıç 92 Pb 54	19800 Bayat/İskilip 94 Qa 62	10700 Burhaniye 106 Qb 54
1145 Mohammédia 101 Sa 38	35800 Aliağa 106 Ra 54	35840 Bayındır 106 Ra 55	16010 Bursa 93 Qa 57
2090 Mornag 101 Sa 38	26850 Alpu 93 Qb 58	16700 Bayramdere 92 Qa 56	37300 Bürnük 94 Pb 62
8000 Nabeul 101 Sa 38	42450 Altınekin 108 Ra 60	17700 Bayramiç 92 Qb 54	34500 Büyükçekmece 92 Pb 56
2056 Raouad 101 Sa 38	10280 Altınova 106 Qb 54	18320 Bayramören 94 Qa 61	39780 Büyükkarıştıran 92 Pb 55
7070 Rass Jebel 101 Rb 38	43800 Altıntaş 107 Qb 58	66500 Bazlambaç 94 Qa 63	16990 Büyükorhan 93 Qb 56
1115 Saouef 101 Sa 38	15420 Altınyayla 107 Rb 57	39650 Beğendik 92 Pb 56	66400 Büyüköz 94 Qb 63
7010 Sejnane 100 Rb 37	10870 Altınoluk 92 Qb 54	17860 Behram 106 Qb 54	39300 Cevizköy 92 Pb 55
9034 Sidi Mediene 101 Sa 37	51600 Altınhisar 108 Ra 62	51800 Bekarlar 108 Ra 62	07650 Cevizli 108 Rb 59
2020 Sidi Zine 100 Sa 36	74300 Amasra 93 Pb 60	20930 Bekilli 107 Ra 57	37600 Cide 94 Pb 61
6100 Siliana 100 Sa 37	05000 Amasya 94 Qa 63	07985 Beldibi 107 Sa 58	42850 Cihanbeyli 108 Ra 60
8020 Soliman 101 Sa 38	33630 Anamur 108 Sa 60	42355 Belkaya 108 Rb 61	78000 Cumayanı 94 Pb 60
8110 Tabarka 100 Sa 36	03050 Anıtkaya 107 Ra 58	42630 Belören/Çankırı 94 Qa 61	19300 Çardıhüyük 94 Qa 62
1130 Tébourba 101 Sa 37	06105 Ankara 94 Qb 60	40300 Benzer 94 Qb 61	10440 Çağış 92 Qb 56
9040 Téboursouk 100 Sa 37	07000 Antalya 107 Sa 58	35700 Bergama 106 Qb 55	07131 Çakırlar 107 Sa 58
9060 Testour 100 Sa 37	37800 Araç 94 Pb 61	57710 Beyardıç 94 Pb 63	20700 Çal 107 Ra 57
7112 Touiref 100 Sa 36	38800 Araplı 108 Ra 63	59600 Beyazköy 92 Pb 55	66000 Çalatlı 94 Qb 62
1001 Tunis 101 Sa 38	42610 Argıthanı 108 Ra 59	67980 Beycuma 93 Pb 59	07230 Çalkaya 107 Sa 58
1100 Zaghouan 101 Sa 38	74020 Arıt 94 Pb 60	35790 Beydağ 106 Ra 56	55900 Çaltı/Durağan 94 Pb 63
	77500 Armutlu 92 Qa 56	19910 Beygircioğlu 94 Pb 62	16510 Çaltılıbük 92 Qb 56
	33315 Arslanköy 108 Rb 62	34820 Beykoz 93 Pb 57	51660 Çamardı 108 Rb 63
	55400 Asar 94 Pb 63	26750 Beylikova 93 Qb 59	20980 Çameli 107 Rb 57
(TR)	19400 Asarcık/İskilip 94 Qa 62	06730 Beypazarı 93 Qa 59	06740 Çamlıdere 94 Qa 60
	37300 Aşağı Dikmen 94 Qa 62	42700 Beyşehir 108 Rb 59	33560 Çamlıyayla 108 Rb 62
68600 Abalı/Ortaköy 94 Ra 61	06920 Aşağı Kavacık 93 Qa 59	37700 Bıngıldayık 94 Pb 61	17400 Çan/Biga 92 Qa 55
57000 Abalı/Sinop 80 Pa 63	18000 Aşağı Pelitözu 94 Qa 61	17200 Biga 92 Qa 55	17000 Çanakkale 92 Qa 54
66400 Abdilli 94 Qb 63	03610 Aşağı Piribeyli 107 Ra 59	10440 Bigadiç 106 Qb 56	35985 Çandarlı 106 Ra 54
43610 Abide 107 Ra 57	32670 Atabey 107 Rb 58	11000 Bilecik 93 Qa 57	06870 Çandır/Çubuk 94 Qa 61
06950 Acıkuyu/Şereflikoçhisar	18310 Atkaracalar 94 Qa 61	48400 Bodrum 106 Rb 55	06551 Çankaya 94 Qb 60
94 Qb 61	50500 Avanos 94 Ra 62	74000 Boğaz 93 Pb 60	18000 Çankırı 94 Qa 61
20800 Acıpayam 107 Rb 57	06916 Avdanlı 94 Qb 60	19310 Boğazkale 94 Qa 62	20350 Çardak 107 Rb 57
45320 Adala 106 Ra 56	07410 Avsallar 108 Sa 59	05000 Boğazköy/Amasya 94 Qa 63	34550 Çatalca 92 Pb 56
54000 Adapazarı 93 Qa 58	57400 Ayancık 94 Pb 62	66400 Boğazlıyan 94 Qb 63	68600 Çatalçeşme 94 Ra 61
03030 Afyonkarahisar 107 Ra 58	06710 Ayaş 94 Qa 60	17350 Bolayır 92 Qa 54	37940 Çatalzeytin 94 Pb 62
68600 Ağaçören 94 Ra 61	09000 Aydın 106 Rb 55	14030 Bolu 93 Qa 59	43710 Çavdarhisar 107 Qb 57
70000 Ağılönü 108 Rb 61	33840 Aydıncık/Bozyazı 108 Sa 61	03300 Bolvadin 107 Ra 59	15900 Çavdır 107 Rb 57
15800 Ağlasun 107 Rb 58	26620 Aydınlı 93 Qb 59	51700 Bor 108 Rb 62	42360 Çavuş 108 Rb 59
37920 Ağlı 94 Pb 61	70500 Ayrancı 108 Rb 61	45940 Borlu 106 Ra 56	03700 Çay 107 Ra 59
34990 Ağva 93 Pb 57	17860 Ayvacık 92 Qb 54	35040 Bornova 106 Ra 55	67900 Çaycuma 93 Pb 60
64500 Ahat 107 Ra 57	10400 Ayvalık 106 Qb 54	37230 Bostan 94 Pb 61	06920 Çayırhan 93 Qa 59
39770 Ahmetbey 92 Pb 55	37750 Azdavay 94 Pb 61	57200 Boyabat 94 Pb 62	37300 Çaykapı 94 Pb 62
45450 Ahmetli 106 Ra 55	39200 Babaeski 92 Pb 55	78500 Boyalı 94 Pb 61	66500 Çekerek 94 Qa 63
81650 Akçakoca 93 Pb 59	55400 Bafra 94 Pb 63	57200 Bozburun 106 Sa 56	22750 Çelebi/Enez 92 Qa 54
41600 Akçaova/Kandıra 93 Pb 57	48200 Bağdamları 106 Rb 55	50500 Bozca 94 Ra 63	71810 Çelebi/Keskin 94 Qb 61
51650 Akçaören/Niğde 108 Ra 62	51030 Bağlama 108 Ra 62	19600 Bozdoğan/Alaca 94 Qa 63	55700 Çelikalan 94 Pb 63
07770 Akçay 107 Sa 57	59600 Bahçeköy 92 Pb 56	09760 Bozdoğan/Çine 106 Rb 56	42920 Çeltik 93 Qb 59
33940 Akdere/Silifke 108 Sa 61	17290 Bakacak 92 Qa 55	07550 Bozkaya 107 Rb 59	15070 Çeltikçi/Bucak 107 Rb 58
45200 Akhisar 106 Ra 55	34141 Bakırköy 92 Qa 56	68470 Bozkır/Ortaköy 94 Ra 62	06894 Çeltikçi/Kazan 94 Qa 61
03710 Akkonak 107 Ra 58	06720 Bala 94 Qb 61	42630 Bozkır/Seydişehir 108 Rb 60	71600 Çerikli 94 Qb 62
42460 Akören 108 Rb 60	26800 Balçıkhisar 94 Qb 60	20370 Bozkurt/Çardak 107 Rb 57	18600 Çerkeş 94 Qa 60
10245 Aksakal 92 Qa 56	10000 Balıkesir 92 Qb 55	37680 Bozkurt/İnebolu 94 Pb 62	59500 Çerkezköy 92 Pb 56
68000 Aksaray 108 Ra 62	17270 Balıklıçeşme 92 Qa 55	07810 Bozova 107 Rb 58	35930 Çeşme 106 Ra 54
43587 Aksaz 107 Qb 56	71520 Balışeyh 94 Qb 61	02000 Bozüyük 93 Qb 58	33870 Çeşmeli 108 Sa 62
07630 Akseki 108 Rb 59	42613 Balkı 108 Ra 59	33830 Bozyazı 108 Sa 60	32420 Çetince 107 Ra 59
07110 Aksu/Antalya 107 Sa 58	10840 Balya 92 Qb 55	70500 Böğecik 108 Rb 61	30700 Çığlı 106 Ra 55
32510 Aksu/Isparta 107 Rb 59	59010 Banarlı 92 Pb 55	42850 Böğrüdelik 108 Ra 60	77300 Çınarcık 93 Qa 57
42550 Akşehir 107 Ra 59	64500 Banaz 107 Ra 57	35727 Bölcek 106 Qb 55	20690 Çıtak 107 Ra 57

197

INDEX WITH POST CODES · ORTSREGISTER MIT POSTLEITZAHLEN · INDICE CON CODICI
STEDREGISTER MED POSTNUMRE · PLAATSNAMENREGISTER MET POSTCODE · REJSTŘÍK

TR

Çiftehan   TR   Kaklık

51900 Çiftehan 108 Rb 62	32500 Eğirdir 107 Rb 58	51070 Gölcük/Derinkuyu 108 Ra 62	10560 Havran 92 Qb 55
26700 Çifteler 93 Qb 59	18700 Eldivan 94 Qa 61	10330 Gölcük/Sındırgı 106 Qb 56	22500 Havsa 92 Pb 54
51800 Çiftlik/Aksaray 108 Ra 62	19700 Elköy 94 Qa 63	15400 Gölhisar 107 Rb 57	55700 Havza 94 Qa 63
77600 Çiftlikköy 93 Qa 57	06780 Elmadağ 94 Qb 61	40000 Göllü/Çiçekdağı 94 Qb 62	06860 Haymana 94 Qb 60
68000 Çimeli 108 Ra 61	07700 Elmalı 107 Sa 57	45580 Gölmarmara 106 Ra 55	59400 Hayrabolu 92 Pb 55
09500 Çine 106 Rb 56	33740 Elvanlı 108 Sa 62	07720 Gölova 107 Sa 58	54300 Hendek 93 Qa 58
20600 Çivril 107 Ra 57	48900 Emecik 106 Sa 55	11700 Gölpazarı 93 Qa 58	41800 Hereke 93 Qa 57
03060 Çobanlar 107 Ra 58	43700 Emet 93 Qb 57	81800 Gölyaka 93 Qa 59	38100 Himmetdede 94 Ra 63
59860 Çorlu 92 Pb 55	35670 Emiralem 106 Ra 55	42870 Gölyazı 108 Ra 61	40300 Hirfanlar 94 Qb 61
33600 Çortak 108 Sa 61	03600 Emirdağ 107 Qb 59	07780 Gömbe 107 Sa 57	43780 Hisarcık 107 Qb 57
19000 Çorum 94 Qa 62	22750 Enez 92 Qa 54	10715 Gömeç 106 Qb 54	67660 Hisarönü 93 Pb 60
33600 Çömelek 108 Sa 61	42564 Engilli 107 Ra 59	03680 Gömü 93 Qb 59	64000 Hocalar 107 Ra 57
22280 Çöpköy 92 Pb 54	10500 Erdek 92 Qa 55	10990 Gönen/Biga 92 Qa 55	20330 Honaz 107 Rb 57
06760 Çubuk 94 Qa 61	33740 Erdemli 108 Sa 62	32090 Gönen/Isparta 107 Rb 58	09950 Horsunlu 107 Rb 56
57200 Çulhalı 94 Pb 62	42310 Ereğli/Karaman 108 Rb 62	45750 Gördes 106 Ra 56	42400 Hotamış 108 Rb 61
42500 Çumra 108 Rb 60	67300 Ereğli/Zonguldak 93 Pb 59	05900 Göynücek 94 Qa 63	51000 Hüyük/Niğde 108 Ra 62
37870 Daday 94 Pb 61	57800 Erfelek 94 Pb 62	14780 Göynük 93 Qa 58	42690 Hüyük/Şarki Karaağaç
43580 Dağardı 93 Qb 57	70400 Ermenek 108 Sa 60	33325 Gözne 108 Rb 62	108 Rb 59
48770 Dalaman 107 Sa 56	43750 Esatlar 93 Qa 57	06840 Güdül 94 Qa 61	18400 Ilgaz 94 Qa 61
10840 Danışment 92 Qb 55	34226 Esenler 92 Pb 56	26620 Gülçayır 93 Qb 59	42600 Ilgın 108 Ra 59
41700 Darıca/Gebze 93 Qa 57	68800 Eskil 108 Ra 61	33530 Gülek 108 Rb 62	10000 Ilıca 92 Qb 55
10470 Darıca/Gönen 92 Qa 55	78400 Eskipazar 94 Qa 60	33700 Gülnar 108 Sa 61	55702 Ilıca/Vezirköprü 94 Pb 63
48900 Datça 106 Sa 55	26000 Eskişehir 93 Qb 58	17880 Gülpınar 106 Qb 54	07600 Ilıcaköy 108 Sa 59
03630 Davulga 107 Ra 59	43264 Eskiyüreğil 93 Qb 57	50900 Gülşehir 94 Ra 62	32000 Isparta 107 Rb 58
03950 Dazkırı 107 Rb 58	35580 Gümüldür 106 Ra 54	20650 Işıklı/Çivril 107 Ra 57	
43680 Dedeköy/Gediz 107 Ra 57	06250 Eşen 107 Sa 57	05700 Gümüşhacıköy 94 Qa 63	33115 Işıktepe 108 Sa 62
18000 Dedeköy/Kızılırmak	64600 Eşme 74 Ra 56	50900 Gümüşkent 94 Ra 62	19700 İbek 94 Qa 63
94 Qa 61	68810 Eşmekaya 108 Ra 61	81850 Gümüşova 93 Qa 58	07680 İbradı 108 Rb 59
71700 Delice/Kırıkkale 94 Qb 62	17400 Etili 92 Qb 54	20620 Gümüşsu 107 Ra 58	22910 İbrikbaba 92 Qa 54
43587 Demirci 107 Qb 56	06790 Etimesgut 94 Qb 60	07860 Gündoğmuş 108 Sa 60	33000 İçel (Mersin) 108 Sa 62
39500 Demirköy 92 Pb 55	17720 Eviciler 94 Qb 54	20460 Güney/Sarıgöl 107 Ra 57	42970 İçeriçumra 108 Rb 60
07570 Demre 107 Sa 58	06770 Evren 94 Qb 61	15220 Güney/Serinhisar 107 Rb 57	37850 İğdir 94 Pb 61
20000 Denizli 107 Rb 57	66760 Eymir/Çekerek 94 Qa 63	42190 Güneysınır 108 Rb 60	60475 İğdir/Zile 94 Qa 63
42480 Derebucak 108 Rb 59	34051 Eyüp 92 Pb 56	26650 Günyüzü 93 Qb 59	39650 İğneada 92 Pb 55
39040 Dereköy 92 Pb 55	17600 Ezine 92 Qb 54	64370 Gürün 107 Ra 57	37250 İhsangazi 94 Pb 61
50700 Derinkuyu 108 Ra 62	34080 Fatih 93 Pb 56	16580 Gürsu 93 Qa 57	06860 İkizce 94 Qb 60
16520 Devecikonağı 92 Qb 56	54110 Ferizli 93 Qa 58	06892 Güvem 94 Qa 60	18900 İkizören 94 Qa 61
67800 Devrek 93 Pb 59	48300 Fethiye 107 Sa 57	48450 Güvercinlik 106 Rb 55	11220 İlyasbey 93 Qa 57
37700 Devrekani 94 Pb 61	33115 Fındıkpınarı 108 Sa 62	07860 Güzelbağ 108 Sa 59	33940 İmamlı 108 Sa 61
09270 Didim 106 Rb 55	07740 Finike 107 Sa 58	35310 Güzelbahçe 106 Ra 54	19500 İnal 94 Pb 62
35700 Dikili 106 Qb 54	35680 Foça 106 Ra 54	33740 Güzeloluk 108 Sa 62	38560 İncesu/Hacılar 94 Ra 63
03400 Dinar 107 Ra 58	35410 Gaziemir 106 Ra 55	38800 Güzelöz 108 Ra 62	09600 İncirliova 106 Rb 55
42502 Dinek 108 Rb 60	07900 Gazipaşa 108 Sa 60	68500 Güzelyurt 108 Ra 62	57800 İncirpınarı 80 Pb 62
19060 Dodurga/Osmancık 94 Qa 62	07540 Gebiz 107 Rb 58	50800 Hacıbektaş 94 Ra 62	37500 İnebolu 94 Pb 61
43276 Doğalar 93 Qb 58	41400 Gebze 93 Qa 57	19400 Hacıhalil/Osmancık	39050 İnece 92 Pb 55
54700 Doğançay 93 Qa 58	43600 Gediz 107 Qb 57	94 Qa 62	59000 İnecik 92 Qa 55
06920 Doğandere 93 Qa 59	45370 Gelenbe 106 Qb 55	45600 Hacıhaliller 107 Ra 56	16400 İnegöl 93 Qa 57
42930 Doğanhisar 108 Ra 59	32900 Gelendost 107 Ra 59	19910 Hacıhamza 94 Pb 62	11640 İnhisar 93 Qa 58
37550 Doğanyurt/İnebolu 94 Pa 61	17500 Gelibolu 92 Qa 54	15000 Hacılar 107 Rb 58	42000 İnlice 108 Rb 60
43850 Domaniç 93 Qb 57	16600 Gemlik 93 Qa 57	42830 Hadım 108 Sa 60	26670 İnönü 93 Qb 58
68000 Dorukini 108 Ra 62	14900 Gerede 93 Qa 59	34555 Hadımköy 92 Pb 56	22400 İpsala 92 Qa 54
14910 Dörtdivan 93 Qa 60	09700 Germencik 106 Rb 55	42280 Halkapınar/Ereğli 108 Rb 62	03750 İscehisar 107 Ra 58
38800 Dörtyol/Yeşilhisar 94 Ra 63	57600 Gerze 94 Pb 63	66800 Hallaçlı/Yozgat 94 Qb 62	19400 İskilip 94 Qa 62
40000 Dulkadirli İnlimurat 94 Qb 62	17610 Geyikli 92 Qb 54	33600 Hamamköy 108 Sa 61	42400 İslik 108 Rb 61
43820 Dumlupınar 107 Ra 57	54700 Geyve 93 Qa 58	05720 Hamamözü 94 Qa 63	66700 İsmailhacılı 94 Qb 63
57700 Durağan 94 Pb 63	10610 Göbel 92 Qa 56	68000 Hamidiye/Aksaray 108 Ra 61	35700 İsmailli 106 Ra 55
10800 Dursunbey 92 Qb 56	70000 Gökçe 108 Rb 61	26800 Hamidiye/Eskişehir 93 Qb 58	42300 İsmil 108 Rb 61
19000 Dutköy 94 Qa 62	17760 Gökçeada 92 Qa 53	39400 Hamidiye/Saray 92 Pb 55	34000 İstanbul 93 Pb 57
10330 Düvertepe 106 Qb 56	57200 Gökçeağaçsakızı 94 Pb 62	40440 Hamitköy/Kaman 94 Qb 61	10770 İvrindi 92 Qb 55
81100 Düzce 93 Qa 59	67670 Gökçebey 93 Pb 60	55400 Harız 94 Pb 63	35000 İzmir 106 Ra 55
17900 Eceabat 92 Qa 54	45180 Gökçeören 106 Ra 56	16770 Harmancık 93 Qb 57	41000 İzmit 93 Qa 57
10640 Edincik 92 Qa 55	70400 Gökçeseki 108 Sa 61	71470 Hasandede 94 Qb 61	16860 İznik 93 Qa 57
22130 Edirne 92 Pb 54	10095 Gökçeyazı 92 Qb 55	37400 Hasanlı 94 Pb 62	57030 Kabalı/Gerze 94 Pb 63
10300 Edremit 92 Qb 55	66500 Gökdere/Sorgun 94 Qa 63	06870 Hasayaz 94 Qa 61	34711 Kadıköy 93 Qa 57
78300 Eflani 94 Pb 60	42360 Gökhüyük 108 Rb 60	22540 Hasköy 92 Pb 54	42800 Kadınhanı 108 Ra 60
67840 Eğerci 93 Pb 59	06830 Gölbaşı 94 Qb 60	37220 Hatipoğlu 94 Pb 61	20240 Kaklık 107 Rb 57
	41650 Gölcük 93 Qa 57		

POSTALI · ÍNDICE CON CÓDIGOS POSTALES · INDICE DE LUGARES COM CÓDIGOS POSTAIS ·
MÍST S PSČ · ZOZNAM OBCÍ S PSČ · INDEKS MIEJSCOWOŚCI Z KOD POCZTOWY

198

Kale · TR · **Reşadiye/Zile** · TR

20570 Kale 107 Rb 56
06870 Kalecik/Kırıkkale 94 Qa 61
33115 Kaleköy/İcel 108 Sa 62
07960 Kalkan 107 Sa 57
17560 Kalkım 92 Qb 55
40300 Kaman/Kırşehir 94 Qb 61
19400 Kamışağa M. 94 Qa 62
01480 Kamışlı/Pozantı 108 Rb 62
19500 Kamil 94 Pb 62
41600 Kandıra 93 Pb 58
55800 Kapaklı 94 Pb 63
03830 Karaadili 107 Ra 58
71810 Karaağıl/Keskin 94 Qb 61
40500 Karaarkaç 94 Qb 62
20980 Karabayr/Çameli 107 Sa 57
17950 Karabiga 92 Qa 55
35960 Karaburun 106 Ra 54
78000 Karabük 94 Pb 60
16700 Karacabey 92 Qa 56
39200 Karacaoğlan/Lüleburgaz
        92 Pb 55
19910 Karacaoğlan/OsmancıK
        94 Pb 62
09370 Karacasu 107 Rb 56
03550 Karadirek 107 Ra 58
19000 Karadona/Sungurlu 94 Qa 62
67400 Karahallı 107 Ra 57
06720 Karahamzalı 94 Qb 61
50610 Karahasanlı 94 Qa 62
71500 Karakeçili 94 Qb 61
70000 Karaman/Kazımkarabekir
        108 Rb 61
15700 Karamanlı 107 Rb 57
41500 Karamürsel 93 Qa 57
45080 Karaoğlanlı 106 Ra 55
42240 Karapınar/Ereğli 108 Rb 61
54430 Karapürçek 93 Qa 58
54500 Karasu 93 Pb 58
06730 Karaşar 93 Qa 60
42000 Karatay 108 Rb 60
66700 Karaveli 94 Qb 63
19900 Kargı/Osmancık 94 Pb 62
33940 Kargıcak/Silifke 108 Sa 61
09540 Karpuzlu 107 Rb 56
35510 Karşıyaka 106 Ra 55
34860 Kartal 93 Qa 57
07580 Kasaba 107 Sa 57
37000 Kastamonu 94 Pb 61
07580 Kaş 107 Sa 57
10800 Kavacık 92 Qb 56
17350 Kavak 92 Qa 54
48570 Kavaklıdere 107 Rb 56
51660 Kavlaktepe 108 Rb 63
05000 Kayabaşı/Amasya 94 Qa 63
42400 Kayalı/Karapınar 108 Rb 61
66650 Kayapınar/Sarıkaya
        94 Qb 63
35765 Kaymakçı 106 Ra 56
50760 Kaymaklı 108 Ra 62
26640 Kaymaz 93 Qb 59
56650 Kaynarca 93 Pb 58
51700 Kaynarca/Bor 108 Rb 62
81900 Kaynaşlı 93 Qa 59
06980 Kazan 94 Qa 60
70460 Kazancı 108 Sa 60
42400 Kazanhüyüğü 108 Rb 61

33281 Kazanlı 108 Sa 62
32700 Keçiborlu 107 Rb 58
06301 Keçiören 94 Qa 60
16740 Keles 93 Qb 57
35730 Kemalpaşa 106 Ra 55
07980 Kemer/Antalya 107 Sa 58
09760 Kemer/Çine 107 Rb 56
48850 Kemer/Fethiye 107 Sa 57
15090 Kemer/Korkuteli 107 Rb 58
51730 Kemerhisar 108 Rb 62
07190 Kepez 107 Sa 58
10660 Kepsut 92 Qb 56
57660 Kerim 94 Pb 63
06860 Kerpiçköy 94 Qb 60
19700 Kertme 94 Qa 63
71800 Keskin 94 Qb 61
16450 Kestel 93 Qa 57
22880 Keşan 92 Qa 54
14610 Kıbrıscık 93 Qa 59
70120 Kılbasan 108 Rb 61
03110 Kılıçaslan 107 Ra 58
35990 Kınık 106 Qb 55
37400 Kıran/Taşköprü 94 Pb 62
22260 Kırcasalih 92 Pb 54
71000 Kırıkkale 94 Qb 61
26970 Kırka 93 Qb 58
45700 Kırkağaç 106 Qb 55
42850 Kırkışla 108 Ra 60
39160 Kırklareli 92 Pb 55
33940 Kırobası 108 Sa 61
40000 Kırşehir 94 Qb 62
39480 Kıyıköy 92 Pb 56
20950 Kızılcabölük 107 Rb 57
07820 Kızılcadağ 107 Rb 57
06890 Kızılcahamam 94 Qa 60
40000 Kızılcaköy 94 Qb 62
18280 Kızılırmak 94 Qa 62
15310 Kızılkaya 107 Rb 58
42225 Kızılören/Meram 108 Rb 60
70000 Kızılyaka/Karaman
        108 Rb 60
48640 Kızılyaka/Marmaris
        107 Rb 56
55800 Kızlan 94 Pb 63
42000 Kızören 108 Ra 61
67500 Kilimli 93 Pb 59
19000 Kiranlık 94 Qa 62
35890 Kiraz 106 Ra 56
17090 Kirazlı 92 Qa 54
10800 Kireç 92 Qb 56
54800 Kocaali 93 Pb 58
37400 Koçanlı 94 Pb 62
06970 Koçarlı 106 Rb 55
39700 Kofcaz 92 Pb 55
51900 Kolsuz 108 Rb 62
81620 Konuralp 93 Qa 59
42000 Konya 108 Rb 60
07130 Konyaaltı 107 Sa 58
18260 Korgun 94 Qa 61
07800 Korkuteli 107 Rb 58
10770 Korucu 106 Qb 55
66500 Koyunculu 94 Qa 63
50600 Kozaklı 94 Qa 62
74400 Kozcağız 93 Pb 60
67600 Kozlu 93 Pb 59
39400 Kömürköy 92 Pb 55

45930 Köprübaşı/Kula 106 Ra 56
55900 Köprübaşı/Vezirköprü
        94 Pb 63
07860 Köprülü 108 Sa 60
43320 Köprüören 93 Qb 57
41780 Körfez 93 Qa 57
40000 Körpınar 94 Qb 62
33705 Köseçobanlı 108 Sa 61
17880 Kösedere 92 Qb 54
33600 Köselerli 108 Sa 61
09570 Köşk 106 Rb 56
48800 Köyceğiz 107 Sa 56
45170 Kula 107 Ra 56
42770 Kulu 94 Qb 61
20800 Kumavşarı 107 Rb 57
32440 Kumdanlı 107 Ra 59
33780 Kumkuyu/Erdemli 108 Sa 62
74600 Kumluca/Karabük 94 Pb 60
07350 Kumluca/Kemer 107 Sa 58
18300 Kurşunlu 94 Qa 61
42800 Kurthasanlı 108 Ra 60
57200 Kurtlu 94 Pb 62
74500 Kurucaşile 94 Pb 60
09400 Kuşadası 106 Rb 55
19000 Kuşsaray 94 Qa 63
09930 Kuyucak 107 Rb 56
66510 Kuyuköy 94 Qa 63
66800 Kuzayca 94 Qb 62
37230 Kuzyaka/Kastamonu
        94 Pb 61
35960 Küçükbahçe 106 Ra 54
17980 Küçükkuyu 106 Qb 54
66700 Külhüyük/Sorgun 94 Qb 63
11210 Küplü 93 Qa 58
37900 Küre/İnebolu 94 Pb 61
43000 Kütahya 93 Qb 58
19020 Laçin/Çorum 94 Qa 62
55760 Ladik 94 Qa 63
54800 Lahna 93 Pb 58
22950 Lalapaşa 92 Pb 54
17800 Lapseki 92 Qa 54
39750 Lüleburgaz 92 Pb 55
50500 Mahmat 94 Ra 62
66700 Mahmatlı 94 Qb 63
26800 Mahmudiye 93 Qb 59
07450 Mahmutlar 108 Sa 60
33630 Malaklar 108 Sa 60
59300 Malkara 92 Qa 54
34845 Maltepe 93 Qa 57
06261 Mamak 94 Qb 60
07600 Manavgat 108 Sa 59
45000 Manisa 106 Ra 55
10470 Manyas 92 Qa 55
10360 Marmara 92 Qa 55
59740 Marmara Ereğlisi 92 Qa 55
48700 Marmaris 107 Sa 56
19700 Mecitözü 94 Qa 63
35470 Menderes 106 Ra 55
35660 Mengen 94 Pb 60
14840 Mengen 93 Qa 60
42000 Meram 108 Rb 60
05300 Merzifon 94 Qa 63
55400 Meşelitürkmenler 94 Pb 63
26880 Mihalgazi 93 Qa 58
26900 Mihalıççik 93 Qb 59
48200 Milas 106 Rb 55

35965 Mordoğan 106 Ra 54
40500 Mucur 94 Qb 62
16940 Mudanya 93 Qa 56
14800 Mudurnu 93 Qa 59
48000 Muğla 107 Rb 56
45140 Muradiye 106 Ra 55
59700 Muratlı 92 Pb 55
07230 Muratpaşa 107 Sa 58
66000 Musabeyli/Yozgat 94 Qb 62
16500 Mustafa Kemalpaşa
        92 Qa 56
33600 Mut 108 Sa 61
59560 Mürefte 92 Qa 55
06920 Nallıhan 93 Qa 59
35320 Narlıdere 106 Ra 55
09800 Nazilli 106 Rb 56
50000 Nevşehir 94 Ra 62
51000 Niğde 108 Rb 62
16370 Nilüfer 93 Qa 56
06714 Oltan 94 Qb 60
55420 Ondokuzmayıs 94 Pb 64
16980 Orhaneli 93 Qb 57
16800 Orhangazi 93 Qa 57
67380 Ormanlı 93 Pb 59
18800 Orta 94 Qa 61
48800 Ortaca 107 Sa 56
68400 Ortaköy/Aksaray 94 Ra 62
33630 Ortaköy/Anamur 108 Sa 60
37680 Ortasökü 94 Pb 62
19500 Osmancık 94 Qa 62
11500 Osmaneli 93 Qa 58
16370 Osmangazi 93 Qa 57
19000 Osmaniye/Çorum 94 Qa 62
57000 Osmaniye/Sinop 80 Pb 63
57200 Osmanköy/Boyabat 94 Pb 62
66140 Osmanpaşa 94 Qb 62
57500 Otmanlı 94 Pb 62
78500 Ovacık 94 Pb 60
51310 Ovacık/Niğde 108 Ra 62
78640 Ovacuma 94 Pb 60
35769 Ovakent 106 Ra 56
43843 Oysu 107 Ra 57
35750 Ödemiş 106 Ra 55
57500 Ömerdüz 94 Pb 62
40300 Ömerkahya 94 Qb 61
48220 Ören 106 Rb 55
55400 Örencik/Bafra 94 Pb 63
43750 Örencik/Emet 93 Qb 57
10000 Pamukçu 92 Qb 55
20280 Pamukkale 107 Rb 57
54900 Pamukova 93 Qa 58
14860 Pazarköy 93 Qa 60
11800 Pazaryeri 93 Qa 57
39600 Pehlivanköy 92 Pb 54
06740 Pelitçik 94 Qa 60
67960 Perşembe 93 Pb 60
37770 Pınarbaşı 94 Pb 61
19700 Pınarbaşı/Çorum 94 Qa 63
70000 Pınarbaşı/Karaman
        108 Rb 61
39300 Pınarhisar 92 Pb 55
06900 Polatlı 94 Qb 60
51900 Porsuk/Pozantı 108 Rb 62
39300 Poyralı 92 Pb 55
01470 Pozantı 108 Rb 62
60700 Reşadiye/Zile 94 Qa 63

199

INDEX WITH POST CODES · ORTSREGISTER MIT POSTLEITZAHLEN · INDICE CON CODICI
STEDREGISTER MED POSTNUMRE · PLAATSNAMENREGISTER MET POSTCODE · REJSTŘÍK

TR

UA

Saçıkara

 TR . UA

Balaklija/Izjum / Балаклія/Ізюм

42800 Saçıkara 108 Ra 60
78600 Safranbolu 94 Pb 60
45300 Salihli 106 Ra 56
03500 Sandıklı 107 Ra 58
54600 Sapanca 93 Qa 58
59600 Saray/Çerkezköy 92 Pb 55
42530 Saray/Yunak 108 Ra 59
05700 Saraycık/Gümüşhacıköy
94 Qa 63
55900 Saraycık/Vezirköprü
94 Pb 63
57300 Saraydüzü 94 Pb 62
66320 Saraykent 94 Qb 63
20300 Sarayköy/Denizli 107 Rb 56
66920 Sarayköy/Yozgat 94 Qb 62
42430 Sarayönü 108 Ra 60
05300 Sarıbuğday 94 Qa 63
26870 Sarıcakaya 93 Qa 58
45470 Sarıgöl/Alaşehir 107 Ra 56
66650 Sarıkaya/Saraykent
94 Qb 63
10900 Sarıköy 92 Qa 55
45200 Sarılar 106 Qb 56
19000 Sarımbey 94 Qa 62
70800 Sarıveliler 108 Sa 60
06920 Sarıyar 93 Qa 59
34450 Sarıyer 93 Pb 57
45800 Saruhanlı 106 Ra 55
10580 Savaştepe 106 Qb 55
40410 Savcılı 94 Qb 61
14750 Seben 93 Qa 59
17900 Seddülbahir 92 Qa 54
35460 Seferihisar 106 Ra 54
66900 Sekili 94 Qb 62
35920 Selçuk 106 Rb 55
42000 Selçuklu 108 Rb 60
45970 Selendi 107 Ra 56
48230 Selimiye 106 Rb 55
32600 Senirkent 107 Ra 58
07500 Serik 107 Sa 59
20430 Serinhisar 107 Rb 57
37270 Seydiler 94 Pb 61
42360 Seydişehir 108 Rb 59
26950 Seyitgazi 93 Qb 58
40000 Sıdıklı Küçükoba 94 Qb 61
10330 Sındırgı 106 Qb 56
66400 Sırçalı/Boğazlıyan 94 Qb 63
33940 Silifke 108 Sa 61
34570 Silivri 92 Pb 56
43500 Simav 107 Qb 56
06930 Sincan 94 Qb 60
17260 Sinekçi 92 Qa 55
57000 Sinop 80 Pa 63
37450 Sirkeköy 94 Pb 62
06762 Sirkeli 94 Qa 60
64600 Sivaslı 107 Ra 57
26600 Sivrihisar 93 Qb 59
45500 Soma 106 Qb 55
66700 Sorgun/Yozgat 94 Qb 63
11600 Söğüt/Eskişehir 93 Qa 58
15930 Söğüt/Korkuteli 107 Rb 57
16516 Söğütalan 92 Qa 56
54160 Söğütlü 93 Qa 58
09200 Söke 106 Rb 55
03900 Sultandağı 107 Ra 59
09470 Sultanhisar 106 Rb 56

05500 Suluova 94 Qa 63
19300 Sungurlu 94 Qa 62
10600 Susurluk 92 Qb 56
50700 Suvermez/Derinkuyu
108 Ra 62
38560 Süksün 94 Ra 63
22370 Süleymaniye 92 Pb 54
22560 Süloğlu 92 Pb 54
42573 Sülüklü 94 Ra 60
32950 Sütçüler 107 Rb 59
18650 Şabanözü 94 Qa 61
59300 Şahin 92 Pb 54
10000 Şamlı 92 Qb 55
32800 Şarki Karaağaç 107 Ra 59
59800 Şarköy 92 Qa 55
66800 Şefaatli 94 Qb 62
37650 Şenpazar 94 Pb 61
06950 Şereflikoçhisar 94 Ra 61
34980 Şile 93 Pb 57
03800 Şuhut 107 Ra 58
16417 Tahtaköprü 93 Qb 57
54750 Taraklı 93 Qa 58
07550 Taşağıl 107 Sa 59
42960 Taşkent 108 Sa 60
37400 Taşköprü/Boyabat 94 Pb 62
68220 Taşpınar/Aksaray 108 Ra 62
33900 Taşucu 108 Sa 61
71700 Tavaözü 94 Qb 61
20500 Tavas 107 Rb 57
42780 Tavşançalı 94 Ra 61
43300 Tavşanlı 93 Qb 57
15600 Tefenni 107 Rb 57
34980 Teke 93 Pb 57
59000 Tekirdağ 92 Qa 55
07995 Tekirova 107 Sa 58
06909 Temelli 94 Qb 60
34537 Tepecik 92 Pb 56
81650 Tepeköy 93 Pb 57
51900 Tepeköy/Ereğli 108 Rb 62
51000 Tepeköy/Niğde 108 Ra 62
35900 Tire 106 Ra 55
40110 Tokluman 94 Qb 61
50880 Topaklı/Kırşehir 94 Qb 62
33400 Topaklı/Tarsus 108 Rb 62
35860 Torbalı 106 Ra 55
40000 Tosunburnu 94 Qb 62
37300 Tosya 94 Pb 62
43900 Tunçbilek 93 Qb 57
42585 Turgut 108 Ra 59
39750 Turgutbey 92 Pb 55
45400 Turgutlu 106 Ra 55
48960 Turgutreis 106 Rb 55
34941 Tuzla 93 Qa 57
19000 Tuzluburun 94 Qa 62
42290 Tuzlukçu 107 Ra 59
05900 Tuzsuz 94 Qa 63
57900 Türkeli/Ayancık 94 Pb 62
10900 Tütüncü 92 Qa 55
19410 Uğurludağ 94 Qa 62
48640 Ula 107 Rb 56
64900 Ulubey 107 Ra 57
32650 Uluborlu 107 Ra 58
51900 Ulukışla/Ereğli 108 Rb 62
74600 Ulus 94 Pb 60
17820 Umurbey 92 Qa 54
35430 Urla 106 Ra 54

64000 Uşak 107 Ra 57
22360 Uzunköprü 92 Pb 54
35430 Uzunkuyu 106 Ra 54
55850 Üçhanlar 94 Pb 63
42670 Üçpınar 108 Rb 60
03650 Ümraniye/Emirdağ 93 Qb 59
34761 Ümraniye/İstanbul 93 Pb 57
50400 Ürgüp 94 Ra 62
07210 Varsak 107 Rb 58
11130 Vezirhan 93 Qa 58
55900 Vezirköprü 94 Pb 63
39400 Vize 92 Pb 55
01000 Yağcılar 92 Qb 56
71450 Yahşihan 94 Qb 61
55810 Yakakent 94 Pb 63
41500 Yalakdere 93 Qa 57
68900 Yalman 94 Ra 62
77000 Yalova 93 Qa 57
32400 Yalvaç 107 Ra 59
57600 Yamacık 94 Pb 63
18900 Yapraklı 94 Qa 61
51000 Yarhisar/Niğde 108 Ra 62
26000 Yarımca 93 Qa 58
42265 Yarma 108 Rb 60
48500 Yatağan 106 Rb 56
57600 Yaykıl 94 Pb 63
66400 Yazıçepni 94 Qb 63
17550 Yenice 92 Qb 55
78700 Yenice/Karabük 94 Pb 60
09370 Yenice/Nazilli 107 Rb 56
42890 Yeniceoba 94 Ra 60
14650 Yeniçağa 93 Qa 59
59760 Yeniçiftlik 92 Pb 55
42270 Yenidoğan 108 Rb 59
66470 Yenifakılı 94 Qb 63
35687 Yenifoça 106 Ra 54
10000 Yeniköy/Balıkesir 92 Qb 56
16900 Yeniköy/Bor 108 Rb 62
19070 Yeniköy/Osmancık 94 Qa 62
43930 Yeniköy/Tavşanlı 93 Qb 57
06171 Yenimahalle 94 Qb 60
57200 Yenimehmetli/Boyabat
94 Pb 62
66475 Yenipazar/Boğazlıyan
94 Qb 63
09350 Yenipazar/Nazilli 106 Rb 56
11780 Yenipazar/Sarıcakaya
93 Qa 58
32850 Yenişarbademli 107 Rb 59
16900 Yenişehir 93 Qa 57
33840 Yeniyürük 108 Sa 61
66900 Yerköy 94 Qb 62
19400 Yerli 94 Qa 62
22850 Yerlisu 92 Qa 54
70160 Yeşildere/Karaman
108 Rb 61
38800 Yeşilhisar 108 Ra 63
68250 Yeşilova/Aksaray 108 Ra 61
15500 Yeşilova/Denizli 107 Rb 57
71900 Yeşilyazı/Sulakyurt 94 Qa 61
81950 Yığılca 93 Qa 59
16350 Yıldırım 93 Qa 57
66000 Yozgat 94 Qb 62
55900 Yukarı Narlı 94 Pb 63
35700 Yukaribey 106 Qb 55
42530 Yunak 107 Ra 59

26900 Yunusemre 93 Qb 59
18900 Yüklü 94 Qa 61
42345 Zengen 108 Rb 62
16970 Zeytinbağı 92 Qa 56
67000 Zonguldak 93 Pb 59

 UA

27620 Adžamka / Аджамка
65 Ma 60
98676 Alupka / Алупка 80 Oa 62
98500 Alušta / Алушта 80 Oa 62
66400 Anan`jiv 64 Mb 57
42087 Andrijašivka 53 La 61
67021 Andrijevo-Ivanivka 65 Mb 58
62642 Andrijivka/Dvorična 54 Lb 65
64031 Andrijivka/Krasnohrad
54 Lb 63
85540 Andrijivka/Kurachove
66 Ma 65
71140 Andrijivka/Smyrnove
66 Mb 64
87120 Andrijivka/Volnovacha
66 Mb 65
64220 Andrijivka/Zmijiv 54 Lb 64
13400 Andrušivka / Андрушівка
52 La 57
13543 Andrušky 52 Lb 57
92133 Anoškyne 54 Lb 66
31022 Antoniny 63 Lb 54
56630 Antonivka 65 Mb 60
53800 Apostolove / Апостолве
65 Mb 59
55300 Arbuzynka 65 Mb 59
74022 Archanhel`ske 65 Mb 61
68400 Arcyz / Арциз 78 Nb 57
96012 Armjans`k / Армянськ
66 Na 61
62821 Artemivka/Pečenihy
54 Lb 65
38813 Artemivka/Valky 54 Lb 63
84500 Artemivs`k / Артемівськ
54 Ma 66
75230 Askanija-Nova 66 Na 61
52310 Auly 65 Ma 62
67806 Avanhard 65 Na 58
16110 Avdijivka 53 Kb 60
52072 Aviators`ke 66 Ma 63
20351 Babanka 64 Ma 58
24132 Babčynci 64 Ma 56
22224 Babync 64 Lb 57
98400 Bachčysaraj / Бахчисарай
80 Oa 61
16500 Bachmač / Бахмач 53 Kb 60
97650 Bahate/Bilohirs`k 80 Nb 62
51224 Bahate/Pereščepyne
54 Ma 63
85530 Bahatyr 66 Mb 64
22350 Bahrynivci 64 Lb 55
66230 Bakša 64 Ma 58
28314 Balachivka 65 Ma 61
99000 Baklakava 80 Oa 61
64200 Balaklija/Izjum / Балаклія/Ізюм
54 Lb 64

POSTALI · ÍNDICE CON CÓDIGOS POSTALES · INDICE DE LUGARES COM CÓDIGOS POSTAIS ·
MÍST S PSČ · ZOZNAM OBCÍ S PSČ · INDEKS MIEJSCOWOŚCI Z KOD POCZTOWY

200

UA

Balaklija/Smila (UA) Demeči UA

20721 Balaklija/Smila 65 Lb 59
66100 Balta / Балта 64 Mb 57
32440 Balyn 63 Ma 54
41462 Banyči 53 Kb 61
23000 Bar / Бар 64 Lb 55
12700 Baranivka / Баранівка
　　　　52 La 55
11255 Baraši 52 La 56
57370 Barativka 65 Na 60
70151 Barvinivka 66 Mb 63
64700 Barvinkove / Барвінкове
　　　　54 Ma 65
7500 Baryšivka 53 La 59
70643 Basan` 66 Mb 64
42312 Basivka 53 Kb 63
56100 Baštanka / Баштанка
　　　　65 Mb 60
98216 Batal`ne 80 Nb 63
16512 Baturyn 53 Kb 60
30650 Bazalija 63 Lb 54
11452 Bazar 52 Kb 57
80062 Belz 51 La 52
71100 Berdjans`k / Бердянськ
　　　　66 Na 64
87430 Berdjans`ke 66 Mb 65
13300 Berdyčiv / Бердичів
　　　　52 Lb 56
59233 Berehomet 63 Ma 53
98179 Berehove/Feodosija
　　　　80 Nb 63
90200 Berehove/Vynohradiv /
　　　　Берегове/Виноградів
　　　　62 Ma 50
45765 Berestečko 51 La 53
7811 Berestjanka 52 La 57
71130 Berestove 66 Mb 64
41437 Bereza 53 Kb 61
7540 Berezan` / Березань
　　　　53 La 59
47500 Berežany / Бережани
　　　　63 Lb 52
30053 Berezdiv 51 La 55
24111 Berezivka/Mohyliv-Podil`s`kyj
　　　　64 Ma 56
67300 Berezivka/Nova Odesa /
　　　　Березівка/Нова Одеса
　　　　65 Mb 58
15622 Berezna 53 Kb 59
34600 Berezne / Березне 51 La 54
56200 Bereznehuvate 65 Mb 60
34164 Berežnycja 51 Kb 54
68542 Berezyne 64 Na 57
24400 Beršad` / Бершадь 64 Ma 57
74300 Beryslav / Берислав
　　　　65 Na 61
52440 Bezborod`kove 66 Ma 62
87660 Bezimenne 66 Mb 65
62489 Bezljudivka 54 Lb 64
81220 Bibrka 63 Lb 52
9100 Bila Cerkva / Біла Церквал
　　　　52 Lb 58
70441 Bilen`ke 66 Mb 63
67700 Bilhorod-Dnistrovs`kyj /
　　　　Білгород-Дністровський
　　　　65 Na 58
67600 Biljajivka 65 Na 58

97600 Bilohirs`k / Білогірськ
　　　　80 Nb 62
30343 Bilohorodka 51 La 54
92200 Bilokurakyne / Білокуракине
　　　　54 Lb 66
68130 Bilolissja 78 Nb 57
92332 Biloluc`k 54 Lb 67
41800 Bilopillja / Білопілля
　　　　53 Kb 62
56576 Bilousivka/Nova Odesa
　　　　65 Mb 59
60233 Bilousivka/Sokyrjany
　　　　64 Ma 55
75000 Bilozerka 65 Na 60
85012 Bilozers`ke / Білозерське
　　　　66 Ma 65
19635 Bilozir`ja 65 Lb 59
85043 Bilyc`ke / Білицьке
　　　　66 Ma 65
62540 Bilyj Kolodjaz` 54 La 65
44240 Birky 51 Kb 53
55325 Blahodatne 65 Mb 59
71050 Blahoviščenka 66 Mb 64
16071 Blystova 53 Kb 60
64800 Blyznjuky / Близнюки
　　　　54 Ma 64
17400 Bobrovycja / Бобровиця
　　　　53 La 59
66531 Bobryk Peršyj 64 Mb 58
27200 Bobrynec` / Бобринець
　　　　65 Ma 60
90645 Bohdan 83 Ma 52
41121 Bohdanivka/Šostka 53 Kb 61
52612 Bohdanivka/Synel`kove
　　　　66 Ma 63
62100 Bohoduchiv / Богодухів
　　　　54 La 63
77700 Bohorodčany 63 Ma 52
9700 Bohuslav / Богуслав
　　　　52 Lb 58
63810 Bohuslavka 54 Lb 65
8150 Bojarka / Боярка 52 La 58
77200 Bolechiv / Болехів 63 Lb 51
68700 Bolhrad / Болград 78 Nb 56
24123 Borivka 64 Ma 56
7800 Borodjanka 52 La 57
42621 Boromlja 53 La 63
48700 Borščiv / Борщів 63 Ma 54
82547 Borynja 62 Lb 50
82300 Boryslav / Борислав
　　　　63 Lb 51
8300 Boryspil` / Бориспіль
　　　　52 La 58
16400 Borzna / Борзна 53 Kb 60
22870 Braclav 64 Ma 56
42455 Brancivka 53 La 63
28512 Bratoljubivka 65 Ma 60
55400 Brats`ke 65 Mb 59
94100 Brjanka / Брянка 54 Ma 66
81244 Brjuchovyči 63 Lb 52
80600 Brody / Броди 51 La 53
77611 Brošniv-Osada 63 Ma 52
7400 Brovary / Бровари 52 La 58
12600 Brusyliv 52 La 57
75143 Brylivka 65 Na 61
48400 Bučač / Бучач 63 Lb 53

81363 Buchovyči 62 Lb 51
11056 Bučmany 52 Kb 56
42238 Budylka 53 La 62
85764 Buhas 66 Mb 65
89114 Bukovec` 62 Ma 50
20114 Buky 64 Lb 58
15143 Burivka 52 Kb 59
77111 Burštyn / Бурштин 63 Lb 52
41700 Buryn` / Буринь 53 Kb 61
80500 Bus`k 63 Lb 52
90556 Buštyno 63 Ma 51
39213 Butenky 53 Lb 62
15135 Butivka 53 Kb 59
19333 Bužanka 64 Lb 58
8072 Byšiv 52 La 57
78436 Bystrycja 63 Ma 52
34644 Bystryei 51 La 54
41330 Bystryk 53 Kb 61
34579 Čabel` 51 Kb 54
75200 Čaplynka 65 Na 61
51820 Čaplynka 66 Ma 62
51000 Caryčanka 65 Ma 62
84551 Časiv Jar / Часів Яр
　　　　54 Ma 65
24800 Čečel`nyk 64 Ma 57
31600 Čemerivci 63 Lb 54
90361 Čepa 62 Ma 51
18000 Čerkasy / Черкаси 53 Lb 60
41740 Černeča Sloboda 53 Kb 61
31052 Černelivka 63 Lb 54
14000 Černihiv / Чернігів 52 Kb 59
75572 Černihivka/Heničes`k 66 Na 62
71200 Černihivka/Tokmak 66 Mb 64
24100 Černivci/Mohyliv-Podil`s`kyj
　　　　64 Ma 56
58000 Černivci/Storožynec` /
　　　　Чернівці 63 Ma 53
12300 Černjachiv 52 La 56
51310 Černjavščyna 54 Ma 63
19604 Červona Sloboda 53 Lb 60
13434 Červone/Andrušivka
　　　　52 La 56
64731 Červone/Barvinkove
　　　　54 Lb 65
41432 Červone/Hluchiv 53 Kb 62
17130 Červoni Partyzany 53 La 59
12000 Červonoarmijs`k 52 La 56
68720 Červonoarmijs`ke 78 Nb 56
80100 Červonohrad / Червоноград
　　　　51 La 52
92924 Červonopopivka 54 Lb 65
37240 Červonozavods`ke /
　　　　Червонозаводське
　　　　53 La 61
67211 Červonoznam`janka
　　　　65 Mb 58
74370 Červonyj Majak 65 Na 61
86700 Charcyz`k / Харцизьк
　　　　66 Ma 66
61000 Charkiv / Харків 54 Lb 64
73000 Cherson / Херсон 65 Na 60
78234 Chlibyčyn 63 Ma 52
16112 Chodor`janyky 53 Kb 60
71223 Chmel`nyc`ke 66 Mb 63
29000 Chmel`nyc`kyj /
　　　　Хмельницький 63 Lb 54

96435 Chmel`ove/Jevpatorija
　　　　79 Nb 61
26225 Chmel`ove/Mala Vyska
　　　　64 Lb 59
42034 Chmeliv 53 La 61
22000 Chmil`nyk / Хмільник
　　　　64 Lb 55
8473 Choc`ky 53 Lb 59
11011 Chočyne 52 Kb 55
81750 Chodoriv / Ходорів 63 Lb 52
13520 Chodorkiv 52 La 57
15331 Cholmy 53 Kb 60
47235 Chomivka 63 Lb 54
87620 Chomutove 66 Mb 66
75813 Chorly 65 Na 61
37800 Chorol / Хорол 53 Lb 61
42320 Chotin` 53 Kb 62
60000 Chotyn / Хотин 63 Ma 54
63311 Chrestyšče 54 Lb 63
20000 Chrystynivka / Христинівка
　　　　64 Ma 57
42750 Chuchra 53 La 62
20923 Chudolijivka 65 Lb 60
90400 Chust / Хуст 63 Ma 51
82060 Chyriv 62 Lb 50
75100 Cjurupyns`k / Цюрупинськ
　　　　65 Na 60
75320 Čkalove/Heničes`k 66 Na 62
72212 Čkalove/Vesele 66 Mb 62
75570 Čonhar 66 Na 62
89500 Čop 62 Ma 50
11621 Čopovyči 52 La 56
67911 Čorna 64 Mb 57
　　　　(Čornobyl`) / (Чорнобиль)
　　　　52 Kb 58
67570 Čornomors`ke 65 Na 58
96400 Čornomors`ke 79 Nb 60
16121 Čornotyči 53 Kb 60
72511 Čornozemne 66 Na 62
37100 Čornuchy 53 La 60
31310 Čornyj Ostriv 63 Lb 54
15472 Čornyj Rih 53 Kb 60
48500 Čortkiv / Чортків 63 Lb 53
55393 Čortomlyk 65 Mb 62
13200 Čudniv 63 La 56
63500 Čuhujiv / Чугуїв 54 Lb 64
54510 Čumaky 66 Mb 62
42722 Čupachivka 53 La 62
9185 Čupyra 52 Lb 58
38800 Čutove 54 Lb 63
27430 Cybuleve 65 Ma 60
19114 Cybuliv 64 Lb 57
20900 Čyhyryn / Чигирин
　　　　65 Lb 60
97570 Čysten`ke 80 Oa 62
98023 Dačne 80 Oa 63
96412 Daleke 79 Nb 61
48146 Darachiv 63 Lb 53
22740 Dašiv 64 Ma 57
74120 Davydiv Brid 65 Mb 63
31341 Davydkivci 64 Lb 55
84700 Debal`ceve / Дебальцеве
　　　　54 Ma 66
62110 Dehtjari 54 La 63
78442 Deljatyn 63 Ma 52
89464 Demeči 62 Ma 50

UA

Demydiv   UA   **Južne/Feodosija**

7335 Demydiv 52 La 58
35200 Demydivka 51 La 53
67312 Demydove 65 Mb 58
92110 Demyno-Oleksandrivka
   54 La 66
32200 Deražnja / Деражня
   64 Lb 55
62300 Derhači / Дерачі 54 La 64
68341 Desantne 78 Nb 57
17024 Desna 52 La 58
53132 Devladove 65 Ma 61
17332 Dihtjari 53 La 60
22341 Djakivci 64 Lb 55
71153 Dmytrivka/Berdjans`k
   66 Na 64
16572 Dmytrivka/Ičnja 53 La 60
53261 Dmytrivka/Marhanec`
   66 Mb 62
57545 Dmytrivka/Parutyne / Дмит-
   рівка/Парутине 65 Na 59
52740 Dmytrivka/Peršotravens`k
   66 Ma 64
27422 Dmytrivka/Znam`janka
   65 Ma 60
74987 Dniprjany 65 Na 61
51900 Dniprodzeržyns`kŽ` /
   Дніпродзержинс`к
   66 Ma 62
49000 Dnipropetrovs`k /
   Днипропетровськ
   66 Ma 63
71630 Dniprorudne / Дніпрорудне
   66 Mb 62
56156 Dobre 65 Mb 60
15011 Dobrjanka 52 Ka 59
70221 Dobropillja/Huljapole
   66 Mb 64
85000 Dobropillja/Rodyns`ke /
   Добропілля/Родинське
   66 Ma 65
80410 Dobrotvir 51 La 52
27000 Dobrovelyčkivka 65 Ma 59
85740 Dokučajevs`k / Докучаєвск
   66 Mb 65
44232 Dol`s`k 51 Kb 53
59240 Dolišnij Šepit 63 Ma 53
77500 Dolyna / Долина 63 Ma 52
28500 Dolyns`ka / Долинська
   65 Ma 60
66442 Dolyns`ke 64 Mb 57
56400 Domanivka 65 Ma 59
83000 Donec`k / Донецьк
   66 Mb 65
45133 Dorocyni 51 La 53
70234 Dorožnjanka 66 Mb 64
12724 Dovbyš 52 La 56
90154 Dovhe 66 Ma 51
19800 Drabiv 53 Lb 60
90432 Drahovo 63 Ma 51
16352 Drimajlivka 53 Kb 59
82100 Drohobyc / Дрогобич
   63 Lb 51
41220 Družba/Šostka 53 Ka 61
48130 Družba/Terebovlja 63 Lb 53
84200 Družkivka / Дружківка
   54 Ma 65

35600 Dubno / Дубно 51 La 53
41655 Dubov`jazivka 53 Kb 61
90531 Dubove 63 Ma 51
12736 Dubrivka 52 La 55
34100 Dubrovycja / Дубровиця
   51 Kb 54
74233 Dudčany 65 Mb 61
32400 Dunajivci / Дунаївці
   63 Ma 54
62700 Dvorična 54 Lb 65
38500 Dykan`ka 53 Lb 62
7330 Dymer 52 La 58
85320 Dymytrov / Димитров
   66 Ma 65
96100 Džankoj / Джанкой 66 Nb 62
24450 Džuryn 64 Ma 57
23545 Džuryn 64 Ma 56
24531 Dzyhivka 64 Ma 56
71500 Enerhodar / Енергодар
   66 Mb 62
8500 Fastiv / Фастів 52 La 57
67920 Fedosijivka 64 Mb 57
98100 Feodosija / Феодосія
   80 Nb 63
98690 Foros 80 Oa 61
66700 Frunzivka 64 Mb 59
9150 Fursy 52 Lb 58
37300 Hadjač / Гадяч 53 La 62
23700 Hajsyn / Гайсин 64 Ma 57
26300 Hajvoron / Гайворон
   64 Ma 57
77100 Halyč 63 Lb 52
16671 Halycja 53 La 60
64740 Havrylivka 54 Ma 64
19715 Hel`mjaziv 53 Lb 59
75500 Heničes`k / Генічеськ
   66 Na 62
60500 Herca 63 Ma 54
64634 Hersevanivka 54 Lb 64
15211 Hirs`k 53 Ka 59
76533 Hladkivka 65 Na 60
11115 Hladkovyči 52 Kb 56
68434 Hlavani 78 Nb 57
39000 Hlobyne / Глобине 53 Lb 61
41400 Hluchiv / Глухів 53 Kb 61
80720 Hlynjany 63 Lb 52
87261 Hlynka 66 Mb 66
27532 Hlyns`k 65 Ma 60
59355 Hlynycja 63 Ma 53
23310 Hnivan` / Гнівань 64 Lb 56
7452 Hoholiv 52 La 59
75600 Hola Prystan` / Гола
   Пристань 65 Na 60
45070 Holoby 51 Kb 53
31535 Holoskiv 63 Lb 55
26500 Holovanivs`k 64 Ma 58
44323 Holovne 51 Kb 52
12325 Holovyne 52 La 56
51230 Holubivka 54 Ma 63
99811 Hončarne 80 Oa 61
90430 Horinčovo 63 Ma 51
84600 Horlivka / Горлівка 66 Ma 66
98241 Hornostajivka 66 Nb 64
45700 Horochiv 51 La 52
63822 Horochuvatka 54 Lb 65
34381 Horodec` 51 Kb 54

78100 Horodenka / Городенка
   63 Ma 53
15100 Horodnja / Городня
   52 Kb 59
32000 Horodok/Chmel`nyc`kyj /
   Городок/Хмельницький
   63 Lb 54
81500 Horodok/Pustomyty /
   Городок/Пустомити
   63 Lb 51
30423 Horodyšče/Šepetivka
   51 La 55
19500 Horodyšče/Smila /
   Городище/Сміла
   65 Lb 59
11560 Horščyk 52 La 56
35400 Hoška 51 La 54
8290 Hostomel` 52 La 58
67640 Hradenyci 64 Na 58
39070 Hradyz`k 53 Lb 61
63542 Hrakove 54 Lb 64
87123 Hranitne 66 Mb 65
42620 Hrebenykivka 53 La 63
67144 Hrebenyky 64 Na 57
37400 Hrebinka / Гребінка
   53 La 60
8662 Hrebinky 53 Lb 58
16020 Hrem`jač 53 Ka 61
95493 Hresivs`kyj 80 Nb 62
31544 Hruškivci 64 Lb 55
64720 Hrušuvacha 54 Lb 64
41324 Hruz`ke 53 Kb 61
30455 Hryciv 52 Lb 55
52660 Hryhorivka 66 Ma 64
48210 Hrymajliv 63 Lb 54
13337 Hryškivci 53 Lb 56
15081 Hubyči 52 Kb 58
51250 Hubynycha 66 Ma 63
23042 Huli 64 Ma 55
45051 Hulivka 51 Kb 53
70200 Huljajpole / Гуляйполе
   66 Mb 64
51110 Hupalivka 54 Lb 62
28540 Hurivka 66 Ma 61
98640 Hurzuf 80 Oa 62
64264 Husarivka 54 Lb 64
48200 Husjatyn 63 Lb 54
77745 Huta 63 Ma 52
51270 Hvardijs`ke/Novomoskovs`k
   66 Ma 63
97513 Hvardijs`ke/Simferopol`
   80 Nb 62
78260 Hvizdec` 63 Ma 53
80191 Hyrnik 51 La 52
16700 Ičnja / Ічня 53 La 60
11163 Ihnatpil` 52 Kb 56
97230 Illičeve 80 Nb 63
68000 Illičivs`k / Іллічівськ
   65 Na 58
22700 Illinci / Іллінці 64 Lb 57
86793 Ilovajs`k / Іловайськ
   66 Mb 66
99703 Inkerman / Інкерман
   80 Oa 61
72142 Inzivka 66 Na 64
19630 Irdyn` 53 Lb 59

19950 Irklijiv 53 Lb 60
8200 Irpin` / Ірпінь 52 La 58
12110 Iršans`k 52 La 56
90100 Iršava / Іршава 62 Ma 51
96025 Išun` 66 Nb 61
20132 Ivan`ky 64 Ma 58
16710 Ivanhorod/Borzna 53 Kb 60
60144 Ivanivci 64 Ma 55
15432 Ivanivka//Semenivka
   53 Ka 60
63551 Ivanivka/Bakaklija 54 Lb 64
67200 Ivanivka/Baranove 65 Na 58
15562 Ivanivka/Černihiv 52 Kb 59
75623 Ivanivka/Hola Prystan`
   65 Na 60
9145 Ivanivka/Uzyn 52 Lb 58
8335 Ivankiv/Boryspil` 52 La 59
7200 Ivankiv/Malyn / Іванків/Малин
   52 La 57
76000 Ivano-Frankivs`k /
   Івано-Франківськ
   63 Ma 52
45300 Ivanyči 51 La 52
13420 Ivnycja 52 La 57
30300 Izjaslav / Ізяслав 51 La 54
64300 Izjum / Ізюм 54 Lb 63
68600 Izmajil / Ізмаїл 78 Nb 56
11250 Jablunec` 52 La 56
78621 Jabluniv 63 Ma 52
9154 Jablunivka 52 Lb 57
7700 Jahotyn / Яготин 53 La 59
64225 Jakovenkove 54 Lb 64
98600 Jalta/Alupka / Ялта/Алупка
   80 Oa 62
87450 Jalta/Mariupol` 66 Na 65
23021 Jaltuškiv 64 Ma 55
30231 Jampil`/Kremenec` 51 Lb 54
24500 Jampil`/Mohyliv-Podil`s`kyj /
   Ямпіль/Могилів-
   Подільський 64 Ma 56
41200 Jampil`/Šostka 53 Kb 61
90233 Janoši 62 Ma 50
78500 Jaremča 63 Ma 52
32100 Jarmolynci 63 Lb 54
80661 Jaseniv 63 Lb 53
9430 Jasenivka 64 Lb 58
86000 Jasynuvata / Ясинувата
   66 Ma 65
56165 Javkyne 65 Mb 60
81000 Javoriv / Яворів 63 Lb 51
55500 Jelanec` 65 Ma 59
52433 Jelizarove 66 Ma 62
11200 Jemil`čyne 52 La 55
86400 Jenakijeve / Єнакієве
   66 Ma 66
20505 Jerky 65 Ma 59
96123 Jermakove 66 Nb 62
17071 Jevmynka 52 La 58
97400 Jevpatorija / ЄвпаторіяЄ
   79 Nb 61
77411 Jezupil` 63 Ma 52
56325 Josypivka 65 Mb 58
42317 Junakivka 53 Kb 63
22112 Jurivka 52 La 57
11014 Jurove 52 Kb 55
98183 Južne/Feodosija 80 Oa 63

POSTALI · ÍNDICE CON CÓDIGOS POSTALES · INDICE DE LUGARES COM CÓDIGOS POSTAIS ·
MÍST S PSČ · ZOZNAM OBCÍ S PSČ · INDEKS MIEJSCOWOŚCI Z KOD POCZTOWY

202

Južne/Odesa / Южне/Одеса (UA) **Lunačars`ke** (UA)

65481 Južne/Odesa / Южне/Одеса 65 Na 59
55000 Južnoukrajins`k / Южноукраїнськ 65 Mb 59
99804 Kača 80 Oa 61
74800 Kachovka / Каховка 65 Na 61
9200 Kaharlyk / Кагарлик 52 Lb 58
74612 Kajiry 65 Na 61
92711 Kalmykivka 54 Lb 66
77300 Kaluš / Калуш 63 Lb 52
22400 Kalynivka / Калинівка 64 Lb 56
32300 Kam`janec`- Podil`s`kyj / Камʼянець-Подільський 63 Ma 54
53830 Kam`janka/Apostolove 65 Mb 61
63352 Kam`janka/Krasnohrad 54 Lb 63
57520 Kam`janka/Rivne / Камʼянка/Рівне 65 Na 59
41053 Kam`janka/Seredyna-Buda 53 Ka 61
20800 Kam`janka/Smila / Камʼянка/Сміла 65 Lb 60
80400 Kam`janka-Buz`ka / Камʼянка Бузька 51 La 52
71300 Kam`janka Dniprovs`ka / Камʼянка Дніпровська 66 Mb 62
71612 Kam`jans`ke 66 Mb 63
44500 Kamin`- Kašyrs`kyj / Камінь-Каширський 51 Kb 52
19000 Kaniv / Канів 53 Lb 59
7754 Kapustynci 53 La 59
8841 Karapyši 52 Lb 58
39500 Karlivka / Карлівка 54 Lb 63
17023 Karpylivka 52 La 58
9812 Kašperivka 64 Lb 57
20500 Katerynopil` 65 Ma 59
7313 Katjužanka 52 La 58
56000 Kazanka 65 Mb 60
64000 Kehyčivka / Кегичівка 54 Lb 63
60100 Kel`menci 63 Ma 54
98300 Kerč / Керч 66 Nb 64
59300 Kicman` 63 Ma 53
68300 Kilija / Кілія 78 Nb 57
17050 Kipti 52 Kb 59
16060 Kirove 53 Kb 61
25000 Kirovohrad / Кіровоград 65 Ma 60
93800 Kirovs`k/Teplohirs`k / Кіровськ/Теплогірськ 54 Ma 66
86300 Kirovs`ke/Šachtars`k / Кіровське/Шахтарськ 66 Ma 66
45200 Kiverci / Ківерці 51 La 53
7850 Klavdijevo-Tarasove 52 La 58
34550 Klesiv 51 Kb 54

35311 Klevan` 51 La 53
60014 Kliškivci 63 Ma 54
15210 Kljusy 53 Ka 59
39200 Kobeljaky / Кобеляки 53 Lb 62
57453 Kobleve 65 Na 59
90620 Kobylec`ka Poljana 63 Ma 52
17411 Kobyžča 53 La 59
12264 Kočeriv 52 La 57
66000 Kodyma 64 Ma 57
44661 Kolky 51 Kb 53
90043 Koločava 63 Ma 51
63100 Kolomak / Коломак 54 Lb 63
78200 Kolomyja / Коломия 63 Ma 53
62030 Kolontajiv 53 Lb 63
63235 Komintern 54 Lb 63
67500 Kominternivs`ke 65 Na 58
28400 Kompanijivka 65 Ma 60
39800 Komsomol`s`k / Комсомольськ 65 Lb 61
73490 Komyšany 65 Na 60
37613 Komyšnja 53 La 61
70530 Komyšuvacha 66 Mb 63
87420 Komyšuvate 66 Mb 65
41600 Konotop / Конотоп 53 Kb 61
23053 Kopajhorod 64 Ma 55
11010 Kopišče 52 Kb 55
48260 Kopyčynci 63 Lb 53
8033 Kopyliv 52 La 57
34700 Korec` 51 La 55
15300 Korjukivka / Корюківка 53 Kb 60
13514 Kornyn 52 La 57
63540 Korobočkine 54 Lb 64
16200 Korop / Короп 53 Kb 60
11500 Korosten` / Коростень 52 La 56
82630 Korostiv 63 Lb 51
12500 Korostyšiv / Коростишів 52 La 57
42140 Korovynci 53 La 61
19400 Korsun`-Ševčenkivs`kyj / Корсунь-Шевченківський 53 Lb 59
78600 Kosiv 63 Ma 53
32155 Kosohirka 63 Lb 54
85100 Kostjantynivka/Kramators`k / Костянтинівка/ Краматорськ 54 Ma 65
72364 Kostjantynivka/Melitopol` 66 Na 63
15443 Kostobobriv 53 Ka 60
35000 Kostopil` / Костопіль 51 La 54
66344 Kosy 64 Mb 57
38600 Kotel`va 53 La 62
51112 Kotovo 64 Mb 57
66300 Kotovs`k / Котовськ 64 Mb 57
63021 Kov`jahy 54 Lb 63
45000 Kovel` / Ковель 51 Kb 52
82631 Koz`ova 63 Ma 51
41644 Kozac`ke 53 Kb 61
17000 Kozelec` 52 La 59

22100 Kozjatyn / Козятин 52 Lb 56
47600 Kozova 63 Lb 53
35523 Kozyn/Kremenec 51 La 53
8711 Kozyn/Ukrajinka 52 La 58
57525 Kozyrka / Козирка 65 Na 59
84300 Kramators`k / Краматорськ 54 Ma 65
7053 Krasjatyči 52 Kb 57
85571 Krasna Poljana 66 Mb 65
68552 Krasne/Arcyz 78 Na 57
80560 Krasne/Zoločiv 63 Lb 52
67900 Krasni Okny 64 Mb 57
85300 Krasnoarmijs`k / Красноармійськ 66 Ma 65
87612 Krasnoarmijs`ke 66 Mb 65
97221 Krasnoflots`ke 80 Nb 62
63300 Krasnohrad / Красноград 54 Lb 63
97000 Krasnohvardijs`ke 80 Nb 62
59022 Krasnojil`s`k 63 Ma 53
62000 Krasnokuts`k / Краснокутськ 54 La 63
96000 Krasnoperekops`k / Красноперекопськ 66 Nb 61
42400 Krasnopillja / Краснопілля 53 La 63
13234 Krasnosilka 52 Lb 56
27326 Krasnosillja 65 Ma 60
75640 Krasnoznam`janka 65 Na 60
84400 Krasnyj Lyman / Красний Лиман 54 Ma 65
31000 Krasyliv / Красилів 63 Lb 54
17031 Krasylivka 52 Kb 59
39600 Kremenčuk / Кременчук 65 Lb 61
47000 Kremenec` / Кременець 51 La 53
87031 Kremenivka 66 Mb 65
92900 Kreminna / Кремінна 54 Lb 66
41300 Krolevec` / Кролевець 19763 Kropyvna 53 Lb 60
52300 Krynyčky 66 Ma 62
68742 Krynyčne 78 Nb 56
55100 Kryve Ozero 64 Mb 58
50000 Kryvyj Rih / Кривий Ріг 65 Mb 61
24600 Kryžopil` 64 Ma 56
57030 Kudrjavcivka 65 Mb 59
31523 Kudynka 64 Lb 55
98470 Kujbyševe/Bachčysaraj 80 Oa 61
71000 Kujbyševe/Polohy 66 Mb 64
16631 Kukšyn 53 Kb 59
80362 Kulykiv 63 Lb 52
16300 Kulykivka 53 Kb 59
87260 Kumačove 66 Mb 66
64323 Kun`je 54 Lb 65
63700 Kup`jans`k / Купʼянськ 54 Lb 65
62112 Kup`jevacha 54 La 63
31226 Kupil` 63 Lb 54
44852 Kupyčiv 51 La 52

80725 Kurovyči 63 Lb 52
51840 Kurylivka 66 Ma 62
90151 Kušnycja 63 Ma 51
30542 Kustivci 52 Lb 55
87321 Kutejnykove 66 Mb 66
78663 Kuty 63 Ma 53
92620 Kuzemivka 54 Lb 66
34400 Kuznecovs`k / Кузнецовськ 51 Kb 53
62801 Kycivka 54 Lb 64
15505 Kyjinka 52 Kb 59
1000 Kyjiv / Київ 52 La 58
2257 Kyrnasivka 64 Ma 55
68650 Kyrnyčky 78 Nb 57
42830 Kyrylivka 66 Na 63
63742 Kyslivka 54 Lb 65
53530 Kyslyčuvata 66 Mb 62
11040 Kyšyn 52 Kb 55
79000 L`viv / Львів 63 Lb 52
17583 Ladan 53 La 60
31183 Ladyhy 64 Lb 55
24320 Ladyžyn / Ладижин 64 Ma 57
20382 Ladyžynka 64 Ma 58
71052 Lanceve 66 Ma 64
78455 Lančyn 63 Ma 52
47400 Lanivci 63 Lb 54
90633 Lazeševyna 63 Ma 52
42200 Lebedyn / Лебедин 53 La 62
20435 Lehedzyne 64 Ma 58
98200 Lenine 65 Na 63
98232 Lenins`ke 66 Nb 63
11580 Lisivščyna 52 La 56
68530 Lisne 64 Na 57
34121 Lisove/Dubrovycja 51 Kb 54
16600 Lisove/Nižyn 53 Kb 60
7411 Litky 52 La 58
22300 Lityn 64 Lb 56
44235 Ljub`jaz` 51 Kb 53
13100 Ljubar 52 Lb 55
66500 Ljubašivka 64 Ma 57
15041 Ljubeč 52 Kb 58
44200 Ljubešiv 51 Kb 53
44300 Ljuboml` / Любомль 51 Kb 52
62433 Ljubotyn / Любітин 54 Lb 63
71760 Ljubymivka 66 Mb 63
34140 Ljutyns`k 51 Kb 54
96150 Lobanove 66 Nb 62
37200 Lochvycja / Лохвиця 53 La 62
45500 Lokači 51 La 52
80261 Lopatyn 51 La 52
92211 Lozno-Oleksandrivka 54 Lb 66
64600 Lozova / Лозова 54 Ma 64
53020 Lozuvatka 65 Ma 61
37500 Lubny 53 La 61
43000 Luc`k / Луцьк 51 La 53
98206 Luhove 80 Nb 63
9544 Luka 52 Lb 58
23015 Luka-Bars`ka 64 Lb 55
80654 Lukaši 51 Lb 53
37751 Lukim`ja 53 Lb 60
44810 Lukiv 51 Kb 52
71154 Lunačars`ke 66 Na 64

203

INDEX WITH POST CODES · ORTSREGISTER MIT POSTLEITZAHLEN · INDICE CON CODICI
STEDREGISTER MED POSTNUMRE · PLAATSNAMENREGISTER MET POSTCODE · REJSTŘÍK

UA

Lyčkove

UA

Novotrojic`ke/Heničes`k

51140 Lyčkove 54 Lb 63
67452 Lymans`ke 64 Na 58
57284 Lymany 65 Na 59
17584 Lynovycja 53 La 60
27015 Lyrpnjažka 65 Ma 59
42500 Lypova Dolyna / Липова
 Долина 53 La 61
39021 Lypove 53 Lb 60
22500 Lypovec` 64 Lb 57
55250 Lysa Hora 65 Ma 59
77452 Lysec` 63 Ma 52
19300 Lysjanka 64 Lb 58
26012 Lystopadove 65 Ma 59
93100 Lysyčans`k / Лисичанськ
 54 Ma 66
51100 Mahdalynivka 54 Ma 62
75362 Majačka 66 Na 62
67654 Majaky 65 Na 58
82195 Majdan/Boryslav 63 Lb 51
90024 Majdan/Svaljava 63 Ma 51
8000 Makariv 52 La 57
66840 Makarove 64 Mb 58
86100 Makijivka / Макіївка
 66 Ma 65
17020 Maksym 52 Kb 58
62145 Maksymivka/Bohoduchiv
 54 La 63
39510 Maksymivka/Poltava
 54 Lb 63
62341 Mala Danylivka 54 La 64
17523 Mala Divycja 53 La 60
70550 Mala Tokmačka 66 Mb 63
26200 Mala Vyska / Мала Виска
 65 Ma 59
87010 Malojanysol` 66 Mb 65
98520 Maloričens`ke 80 Oa 62
52371 Malosofijivka 65 Ma 62
89040 Malyj Bereznyj 62 Ma 50
11600 Malyn / Малин 52 La 57
60364 Mamaliha 63 Ma 54
20100 Man`kivka 64 Ma 58
44600 Manevcyi 51 Kb 53
87400 Manhuš / Мангуш 66 Mb 65
32244 Manykivci 64 Lb 55
66710 Mar`janivka/Frunzivka
 64 Mb 57
45744 Mar`janivka/Novovolyns`k
 51 La 52
66814 Mar`janivka/Šyrjajeve
 64 Mb 58
53842 Mar`jans`ke 65 Mb 61
53400 Marhanec` / Марганець
 66 Mb 62
87500 Mariupol` / Маріуполь
 66 Mb 65
17421 Markivci 52 La 59
15460 Maševe 53 Ka 60
39400 Mašivka 54 Lb 62
8850 Maslivka 53 Lb 59
82563 Matkiv 62 Ma 51
72222 Matvijivka 66 Mb 63
82129 Medenyči 63 Lb 51
20930 Medvedivka/Čyhyryn
 65 Lb 60
64012 Medvedivka/Krasnohrad
 54 Lb 63

9751 Medvyn 64 Lb 58
31530 Medžybiž 64 Lb 55
48751 Mel`nycja-Podil`s`ka
 63 Ma 54
87441 Melekyne 66 Na 65
11576 Meleni 52 La 56
51217 Melioratyvne 66 Ma 63
72300 Melitopol` / Мелітополь
 66 Na 63
15600 Mena / Мена 53 Kb 60
62472 Merefa / Мерефа 54 Lb 64
93491 Met`olkine 54 Ma 66
42253 Mezenivka 54 La 64
52900 Mežova 66 Ma 64
32430 Micivci 63 Lb 54
87130 Mičurine 66 Mb 66
63111 Mirošnykivka 54 Lb 63
92654 Mistky 54 Lb 66
90000 Mižhir`ja 63 Ma 51
35740 Mizoč 51 La 54
96420 Mižvodne 79 Nb 60
19511 Mlijiv 65 Lb 59
35100 Mlyniv 51 La 53
51040 Mohyliv 65 Ma 62
24000 Mohyliv-Podil`s`kyj /
 Могилів-Подільський
 64 Ma 55
20540 Mokra Kalyhirka 65 Ma 59
34634 Mokvyn 51 La 54
71716 Moločans`k / Молочанськ
 66 Mb 63
67744 Monaši 65 Na 58
48300 Monastyrys`ka 63 Lb 53
19100 Monastyryšče/Chrystynivka
 65 Lb 59
16726 Monastyryšče/Ičnja 53 La 60
34022 Moročne 51 Kb 53
98033 Mors`ke 66 Oa 62
82482 Moršyn 63 Lb 51
83492 Mospyne / Моспине
 66 Mb 66
56470 Mostove 65 Mb 59
81300 Mostys`ka 62 Lb 51
19615 Mostyv 53 Lb 59
17113 Mryn 53 Kb 59
89600 Mukačeve / Мукачеве
 62 Ma 51
23400 Murovani Kurylivci 64 Ma 55
34023 Mutvycja 51 Kb 54
41351 Mutyn 53 Kb 61
87170 Mychajlivka/Novoazovs`k
 66 Mb 66
75710 Mychajlivka/Skadovs`k
 65 Na 60
72000 Mychajlivka/Tokmak
 66 Mb 63
70030 Mychajlivka/Vil`njans`k
 66 Mb 63
67210 Mychajlopil` 65 Mb 58
38013 Mychajlyky 53 Lb 62
70521 Mykil`s`ke 66 Mb 63
54000 Mykolajiv/Cherson /
 Миколаїв/Херсон
 65 Na 60
81600 Mykolajiv/L`viv /
 Миколаїв/Львів 63 Lb 51

67794 Mykolajivka/Bilhorod-
 Dnistrovs`kyj 79 Nb 58
52060 Mykolajivka/Dniprodzeržyns`k
 66 Ma 62
75572 Mykolajivka/Heničes`k
 66 Na 62
64423 Mykolajivka/Krasnohrad
 54 Lb 63
64511 Mykolajivka/Lozova 54 Lb 64
56009 Mykolajivka/Novyj Buh
 65 Mb 60
67813 Mykolajivka/Ovidiopol`
 65 Na 58
67000 Mykolajivka/Petrivka
 65 Mb 58
97546 Mykolajivka/Simferopol`
 80 Oa 61
48120 Mykulynci 63 Lb 53
37600 Myrhorod / Миргород
 53 Lb 61
62203 Myronivka 54 La 64
8800 Myronivka / Миронівка
 53 Lb 59
13035 Myropil` 52 La 55
89112 Myslivka 63 Ma 51
73483 Naddniprjans`ke 65 Na 60
38531 Nadežda 53 Lb 62
64680 Nadeždivka 54 Lb 64
78400 Nadvirna / Надвірна
 63 Ma 52
68821 Nahirne 78 Nb 56
11400 Narodyči 52 Kb 57
9633 Nastaška 52 Lb 58
98180 Nasypne 80 Nb 63
63351 Natalyne 54 Lb 63
57140 Nečajane 65 Na 59
11610 Nedašky 52 La 57
60035 Nedobojivci 63 Ma 54
42100 Nedryhajliv / Недригайлів
 53 La 61
34540 Nemovyči 51 Kb 54
22800 Nemyriv/Illinci / Немирів/
 Іллінці 64 Ma 56
81013 Nemyriv/Javoriv 51 La 51
68122 Nerušaj 78 Nb 57
92252 Neščeretove 54 Lb 66
30100 Netišyn / Нетішин 51 La 54
78118 Nezvys`ko 63 Ma 53
32320 Nihyn 63 Ma 54
53200 Nikopol` / Нікополь
 66 Mb 62
74700 Nižny Sirohozy 66 Na 62
16600 Nižyn / Ніжин 53 Kb 60
17100 Nosivka / Носівка 53 La 59
23151 Noskivci 64 Ma 56
92940 Nova Astrachan` 54 Lb 66
17461 Nova Basan` 53 La 59
12114 Nova Borova 52 La 56
39140 Nova Haleščyna 53 Lb 61
64670 Nova Ivanivka 54 Ma 64
75900 Nova Kachovka / Нова
 Каховка 65 Na 61
56600 Nova Odesa / Нова Одеса
 65 Mb 59
28042 Nova Praha 65 Ma 60
32600 Nova Ušycja 64 Ma 55

63200 Nova Vodolaha / Нова
 Водолага 54 Lb 63
25491 Nove / Нове 65 Ma 60
30374 Nove Selo 51 Lb 54
16000 Novhorod-Sivers`kyj /
 Новгород-Сіверський
 53 Kb 61
28200 Novhorodka 65 Ma 60
67550 Novi Biljari 65 Na 59
11050 Novi Bilokorovyči 52 Kb 56
15214 Novi Borovyči 53 Kb 59
15013 Novi Jarylovyči 52 Ka 59
81714 Novi Strilyšča 63 Lb 52
39200 Novi Sanžary 53 Lb 62
97511 Novoandrijivka 80 Nb 62
26100 Novoarchangel`s`k 64 Ma 58
87600 Novoazovs`k / Новоазовськ
 66 Mb 66
92310 Novobila 54 Lb 67
70505 Novodanylivka 66 Mb 63
60236 Novodnistrovs`k /
 Новодністровськ
 64 Ma 55
93193 Novodružes`k 54 Ma 66
11700 Novohrad-Volyns`kyj /
 Новоград-Волинський
 52 La 55
56522 Novohryhorivka 65 Mb 59
72400 Novoivanivka 66 Na 63
51313 Novoivanivs`ke 54 Ma 64
81053 Novojavorivs`ke /
 Новояворівське 63 Lb 51
87240 Novokaterynivka 66 Mb 66
87022 Novokrasnivka 66 Mb 65
70320 Novomlynivka 66 Mb 65
51200 Novomoskovs`k /
 Новомосковськ 66 Ma 63
75410 Novomykolajivka/
 Persotravneve 66 Na 62
75712 Novomykolajivka/Skadovs`k
 65 Na 60
70100 Novomykolajivka/Viln`jans`k
 66 Mb 63
26000 Novomyrhorod /
 Новомиргород 65 Ma 59
93530 Novoochtyrka 54 Ma 66
55480 Novooleksandrivka 65 Mb 59
75560 Novooleksijivka 66 Na 62
85372 Novoolenivka 66 Ma 65
67103 Novopetrivka/Rozdil`na
 64 Mb 57
57330 Novopetrivka/Snihurivka
 65 Mb 60
56650 Novopetrivs`ke 65 Mb 59
52441 Novopokrovka 66 Ma 62
55642 Novopoltavka 65 Mb 60
71721 Novoprokopivka 66 Mb 63
92300 Novopskov / Новопсков
 54 Lb 67
96274 Novoselivs`ke 80 Nb 61
68830 Novosil`s`ke 78 Nb 56
47133 Novostav 51 La 54
85732 Novotrojic`ke/Dokučajevs`k
 66 Mb 65
75300 Novotrojic`ke/Heničes`k
 66 Na 62

POSTALI · ÍNDICE CON CÓDIGOS POSTALES · INDICE DE LUGARES COM CÓDIGOS POSTAIS ·
MÍST S PSČ · ZOZNAM OBCÍ S PSČ · INDEKS MIEJSCOWOŚCI Z KOD POCZTOWY

204

Novotrojic`ke/Krasnoarmijs`k Rivne/Novoukrajinka

85370 Novotrojic`ke/Krasnoarmijs`k 66 Ma 65	11000 Olevs`k / Олевськ 52 Kb 55	22134 Peremoha/Kalynivka 64 Lb 56
27100 Novoukrajinka/Pomična / Новоукраїнка/Помічна 65 Ma 59	70522 Omel`nyk 66 Mb 63	81200 Peremyšljany 63 Lb 52
	38154 Opišnja 53 Lb 62	63043 Perepelycivka 54 Lb 63
	82655 Oporec` 63 Ma 51	57220 Peresadivka 65 Mb 60
	7250 Orane 52 Kb 58	51220 Pereščepyne 54 Lb 63
67441 Novoukrajinka/Rozdil`na 65 Na 58	22600 Orativ 64 Lb 57	48420 Perevoloka 63 Lb 53
71128 Novovasylivka/Berdjans`k 66 Na 64	53300 Ordžonikidze / Орджонікідзе 65 Mb 62	74712 Peršopokrovka 66 Mb 62
	67800 Orichiv / Оріхів 66 Mb 63	52800 Peršotravens`k / Першотравенськ 66 Ma 64
75432 Novovasylivka/Peršotravneve 66 Na 62	68831 Orlivka 78 Nb 56	
	19515 Orlovec` 65 Lb 59	
45400 Novovolyns`k / Нововолинськ 51 La 52	53620 Orly 66 Ma 64	64441 Peršotravneve 54 Lb 63
	32331 Orynyn 63 Ma 54	55200 Pervomajs`k/Južnoukrajins`k / Первомайськ/ Южноукраїнськ 65 Ma 58
74200 Novovoroncovka 65 Mb 61	37700 Oržyčia 53 Lb 60	
22620 Novožyvotiv 64 Lb 57	77672 Osmoloda 63 Ma 52	
55600 Novyj Buh / Новий Буг 65 Mb 60	17044 Oster 52 La 58	93200 Pervomajs`k/Zolote / Первомайськ/Золоте 54 Ma 66
	35800 Ostroh / Острог 51 La 54	
17452 Novyj Bykiv 53 La 59	78223 Otynija 63 Ma 52	
80465 Novyj Jaryčiv 63 Lb 52	67800 Ovidiopol` 65 Na 58	97323 Pervomajs`ke/Feodosija 80 Nb 63
81652 Novyj Rozdil / Новий Роздiл 63 Lb 52	11100 Ovruč / Овруч 52 Kb 56	
	27633 Ovsjanykivka / Овсянківка 65 Ma 60	87051 Pervomajs`ke/Mariupol` 66 Mb 65
28310 Novyj Starodub 65 Ma 61		
53810 Nyva Trudova 65 Mb 61	9129 Ozerna/Bila Cerkva 52 Lb 58	57232 Pervomajs`ke/Mykolajiv 65 Mb 60
97100 Nyžn`ohirs`kyj 66 Nb 62		
92714 Nyžn`opokrovka 54 Lb 66	47264 Ozerna/Ternopil` 63 Lb 53	64100 Pervomajs`kyj / Первомайський 54 Lb 64
74741 Nyžni Torhaji 66 Na 62	80530 Ožydiv 63 Lb 52	
89130 Nyžni Vorota 62 Ma 51	52100 P`jatychatky / Пʼятихатки 65 Ma 61	67240 Petrivka/Ivanivka 65 Na 58
92612 Nyžnja Duvanka 54 Lb 66		75511 Petrivka/Partyzany 66 Na 62
78060 Obertyn 63 Ma 53	64252 P`jatyhirs`ke 54 Lb 64	67512 Petrivka/Volkove 65 Na 58
24353 Obodivka 64 Ma 57	9841 P`jatyhory 64 Lb 57	28300 Petrove 65 Ma 61
16223 Obolonnja 53 Kb 60	15543 Pakul` 52 Kb 58	51800 Petrykivka 66 Ma 62
8700 Obuchiv / Обухiв 52 La 58	42516 Panasivka 53 La 61	88512 Piddubne 66 Mb 64
57500 Očakiv / Очакiв 65 Na 59	71244 Panfilivka 66 Mb 64	48000 Pidhajci 63 Lb 53
71750 Očeretuvate 66 Mb 63	64660 Panjutyne 64 Ma 62	52001 Pidhorodne / Підгородне 66 Ma 63
72562 Ochrimivka 66 Na 63	28023 Pantajivka 65 Ma 60	
42700 Ochtyrka / Охтирка 53 La 62	16730 Parafijivka 53 La 60	11225 Pidluby 52 La 55
	98542 Partenit 80 Oa 62	63820 Pidvysoke 65 Ma 58
65000 Odesa / Одеса 65 Na 58	75550 Partyzany 66 Na 62	8811 Piji 53 Lb 59
90365 Okli 62 Ma 51	57540 Parutyne / Парутине 65 Na 59	44010 Pišča 51 Kb 51
97060 Oktjabrs`ke/Simferopol` 80 Nb 62		66110 Pišana 64 Ma 57
	63452 Pasiky 54 Lb 64	39701 Pišane/Kremenčuk 53 Lb 61
24830 Ol`hopil` 64 Ma 57	92222 Pavlivka/Bilourakyne 54 Lb 66	
9635 Ol`šanycja 52 Lb 58		19723 Piščane/Zolotonoša 53 Lb 59
28000 Oleksandrija/Adžamka / Олександрія 65 Ma 61	15053 Pavlivka/Černihiv 52 Kb 58	24700 Piščanka/Jampil` 64 Ma 56
	45342 Pavlivka/Novovolyns`k 51 La 52	63332 Piščanka/Krasnohrad 54 Lb 63
35320 Oleksandrija/Rivne 51 La 54		
84000 Oleksandrivka/Barvinkove / Олександрівка/Барвінкове 54 Ma 64	74441 Pavlivka/Verchnij Rohačyk 66 Mb 62	27037 Piščanyj Brid 65 Ma 59
		7820 Piskivka 52 La 57
	85672 Pavlivka/Volnovacha 66 Mb 65	16542 Pisky/Bachmač 53 Kb 60
57375 Oleksandrivka/Cherson 65 Na 60		62714 Pisky/Dvorična 54 Lb 65
62214 Oleksandrivka/Derhači 54 La 63	51400 Pavlohrad / Павлоград 66 Ma 63	78633 Pistyn` 63 Ma 53
		26245 Pletenyj Tašlyk 65 Ma 59
53630 Oleksandrivka/Huljajpole 66 Mb 64	28110 Pavlyš 65 Ma 61	89311 Ploske 62 Ma 50
	23610 Pečera 64 Ma 56	30320 Plužne 51 La 54
27300 Oleksandrivka/Kam`janka 65 Ma 60	23521 Pen`kivka 64 Ma 56	22252 Plyskiv 64 Lb 57
	96100 Peredmistne 66 Nb 62	16453 Plysky 53 Kb 60
66040 Oleksandrivka/Kodyma 64 Mb 57	77662 Perehins`ke 63 Ma 52	96167 Pobjedne 66 Nb 62
	26522 Perehonivka 64 Ma 58	47025 Počajiv / Почаїв 51 Lb 53
62156 Oleksandrivka/Valky 54 La 63	8400 Perejaslav-Chmel`nyc`kyj / Переяслав-Хмельницький 53 La 59	38343 Podil 53 Lb 61
		27522 Podorožne 65 Lb 61
56530 Oleksandrivka/Voznesens`k 65 Mb 59		63421 Pohorile 54 Lb 64
	66124 Perejma 64 Ma 57	39053 Pohreby 53 La 61
	7510 Peremoha/Berezan` 53 La 59	22200 Pohrebyšče / Погребище 64 Lb 57
64122 Oleksijivka 54 Lb 64		
97651 Olenivka 80 Oa 62	41460 Peremoha/Hluchiv 53 Kb 61	92135 Pokrovs`ke 54 Lb 66
44356 Oles`k 51 Kb 52		70600 Polohy / Пологи 66 Mb 64

30500 Polonne / Полонне 52 La 55	
44000 Položeve 51 Kb 51	
36000 Poltava / Полтава 53 Lb 62	
55264 Poltavka/Pervomajs`k 65 Mb 58	
97036 Poltavka/Petrivka 80 Nb 62	
51150 Polyvanivka 66 Ma 63	
27030 Pomična / Помічна 65 Ma 59	
16220 Ponornycja 53 Kb 60	
93300 Popasna / Попасна 54 Ma 66	
13500 Popil`nja 52 Lb 57	
37633 Popivka 53 La 61	
75010 Posad-Pokrovs`ke 65 Na 60	
12225 Potijivka 52 La 56	
51613 Pravobereżne 65 Ma 62	
51022 Prjadivka 54 Ma 62	
16262 Proletars`ke 53 Kb 61	
53610 Prosjana 66 Ma 64	
63230 Prosjane 54 Lb 63	
90421 Protyven` 63 Ma 51	
72400 Pryazovs`ke 66 Na 63	
28026 Pryjutivka 65 Ma 61	
62630 Prykolotne 54 La 65	
44614 Prylisne 51 Kb 53	
11100 Pryluky/Ovruč 52 Kb 56	
17500 Pryluky/Pryjatyn / Прилуки 53 La 60	
72100 Prymors`k / Приморськ 66 Na 64	
87643 Prymors`ke 66 Mb 65	
81100 Pustomyty / Пустомити 63 Lb 51	
59100 Putyla 63 Mb 53	
41500 Putyvl` / Путивль 53 Kb 61	
66112 Pužajkove 64 Ma 57	
37000 Pyrjatyn / Пирятин 53 La 60	
39045 Pyrohy 53 Lb 61	
90600 Rachiv / Paxiв 63 Ma 52	
23536 Rachny-Lisovi 64 Ma 57	
11411 Radča 52 Kb 57	
80200 Radechiv 51 La 52	
76113 Radens`k 65 Na 60	
67212 Radisne 65 Na 58	
12200 Radomyšl`/Korostyšiv / Радомишль/Коростишів 52 La 57	
45664 Radomyšl`/Luc`k 51 La 53	
35500 Radyvyliv / Радивилiв 51 La 53	
34371 Rafalivka 51 Kb 54	
84150 Rajhorodok 54 Ma 65	
37343 Rašivka 53 La 61	
44100 Ratne 51 Kb 52	
67308 Rauchivka 65 Mb 58	
80316 Rava-Rus`ka 51 La 51	
68800 Reni / Рені 78 Nb 56	
38400 Rešetylivka 53 Lb 62	
41343 Reutynci 53 Kb 61	
62550 Revoljucijne 54 La 64	
15000 Ripky 52 Kb 59	
57530 Rivne/Mykolajiv / Рiвне/ Миколаїв 65 Na 59	
27160 Rivne/Novoukrajinka 65 Ma 59	

33000 Rivne/Zdolbuniv / Рівне/Здолбунів 51 La 54
81521 Rodatyči 63 Lb 51
12722 Rohačiv 52 La 55
62481 Rohan` 54 Lb 64
77000 Rohatyn 63 Lb 52
8351 Rohoziv 52 La 59
45626 Rokyni 51 La 53
38353 Rokyta 53 Lb 61
9600 Rokytne/Bila Cerkva 52 Lb 58
34200 Rokytne/Sarny 51 Kb 55
13000 Romaniv 52 La 55
60226 Romankivci 64 Ma 55
42000 Romny / Ромни 53 La 61
37650 Romodan 53 Lb 61
20726 Rotmistrivka 65 Lb 59
81650 Rozdil 63 Lb 52
67400 Rozdil`na / Роздільна 64 Na 58
96200 Rozdol`ne/Krasnoperekops`k 65 Nb 61
74840 Rozdol`ne/Tavrijs`k 65 Na 61
64151 Rozdollja 54 Lb 64
82512 Rozluč 62 Lb 50
70424 Rozumivka 66 Mb 63
45100 Rožyšče / Рожище 51 La 53
74531 Rubanivka 66 Na 62
93000 Rubižne / Рубіжне 54 Ma 66
15514 Rudka 52 Kb 59
44561 Rudka-Červyns`ka 51 Kb 53
81440 Rudky 63 Lb 51
24723 Rudnycja 64 Ma 56
13600 Ružyn 52 Lb 57
92350 Ryb`janceve 54 Lb 67
9230 Ržyščiv 53 Lb 59
67770 Šabo 65 Na 58
44001 Šac`k 51 Kb 51
64500 Sachnovščyna 54 Lb 63
86200 Šachtars`k / Шахтарськ 66 Ma 66
85560 Šachtars`ke 66 Mb 65
81420 Sadkovyči 62 Lb 51
52173 Saksahan` 65 Ma 61
96500 Saky / Саки 80 Nb 61
81400 Sambir / Самбір 62 Lb 51
22163 Samhorodok/Kozjatyn 64 Lb 56
9040 Samhorodok/Skvyra 52 Lb 57
68200 Sarata 78 Na 57
23500 Šarhorod 64 Ma 56
34500 Sarny / Сарни 51 Kb 54
32034 Sataniv 63 Lb 54
32445 Šatava 63 Ma 54
66200 Savran` 64 Ma 58
37722 Savynci 53 Lb 60
56415 Ščaslyvka 65 Mb 58
98187 Ščebetovka 80 Oa 63
98213 Ščolkine / Щолкіне 66 Nb 63
15200 Ščors / Щорс 53 Kb 59
52323 Ščors`k 65 Ma 62
81160 Ščyrec` 63 Lb 51
59131 Seljatyn 63 Mb 53
62103 Semeniv Jar 54 La 63
38200 Semenivka/Chorol 53 Lb 61
15400 Semenivka/Korjukivka / Семенівка/Корюківка 53 Ka 60
72355 Semenivka/Melitopol` 66 Na 63
7423 Semypolky 52 La 58
15120 Sen`kivka 53 Ka 59
63752 Sen`kove 54 Lb 65
30400 Šepetivka / Шепетівка 51 La 55
59133 Šepit 63 Mb 53
31144 Serbynivka 52 Lb 55
41000 Seredyna-Buda / Середина-Буда 53 Ka 62
67780 Serhijivka/Bilhorod-Dnistrovs`kyj 79 Na 58
84191 Serhijivka/Kramators`k 54 Ma 65
53505 Serhijivka/Marhanec` 66 Mb 62
34052 Sernyky 51 Kb 54
68522 Serpneve 64 Na 57
99000 Sevastopol` / Севастополь 80 Oa 61
51160 Ševčenkivka 66 Ma 62
68332 Ševčenkove/Kilija 78 Nb 57
41667 Ševčenkove/Konotop 53 Kb 61
63600 Ševčenkove/Kup`jans`k 54 Lb 65
57200 Ševčenkove/Mykolajiv 65 Na 60
64263 Ševelivka 54 Lb 64
51131 Ševs`ke 54 Ma 62
95000 Simferopol` / Симферополь 80 Oa 62
84522 Sivers`k / Сіверськ 54 Ma 66
89432 Sjurte 62 Ma 50
75700 Skadovs`k / Скадовськ 65 Na 60
48720 Skala-Podil`s`ka 63 Ma 54
47845 Skalat 63 Lb 53
82600 Skole 63 Lb 51
9000 Skvyra / Сквира 52 Lb 57
15013 Skytok 52 Ka 58
15555 Slabyn 52 Kb 59
42456 Slavhorod 54 La 63
30000 Slavuta / Славута 51 La 54
7100 Slavutyč 52 Kb 58
24432 Šljachova 64 Ma 57
66050 Slobidka 64 Mb 57
41714 Sloboda/Buryn` 53 Kb 61
15564 Sloboda/Černihiv 52 Kb 59
41436 Slout 53 Kb 61
52911 Slov`janka 66 Ma 64
84100 Slov`jans`k / Слов'янськ 54 Ma 65
20700 Smila / Сміла 65 Lb 59
42033 Smile 53 La 61
16030 Smjač 53 Ka 61
16333 Smoljanka 53 Kb 59
32423 Smotrye 63 Ma 54
15161 Smyčyn 53 Kb 59
35680 Smyha 51 La 53
71040 Smyrnove 66 Mb 64
57300 Snihurivka / Снігурівка 65 Mb 60
78300 Snjatyn / Снятин 63 Ma 53
23820 Sobolivka 64 Ma 57
53100 Sofijivka 65 Ma 61
84397 Sofijivka/Kramators`k 54 Ma 65
70113 Sofijivka/Novomykolajivka 66 Ma 63
80000 Sokal` / Сокаль 51 La 52
19253 Sokolivka 64 Lb 58
75521 Sokolohirne 66 Na 62
60200 Sokyrjany / Сокиряни 64 Ma 55
17312 Sokyrynci 53 La 60
84545 Soledar / Соледар 54 Ma 66
32162 Solobkivci 63 Lb 54
52400 Solone 66 Ma 62
62368 Solonycivka 54 Lb 64
77753 Solotvyn 63 Ma 52
90220 Šom 62 Ma 50
98025 Sonjačna Dolyna 80 Oa 63
70417 Sonjačne 66 Mb 63
80193 Sosnivka / Соснівка 51 La 52
34652 Sosnove 51 La 55
16100 Sosnycja / Сосниця 53 Kb 60
41100 Šostka / Шостка 53 Kb 61
44543 Sošyčne 51 Kb 52
97200 Sovjets`kyj 80 Nb 62
20600 Špola / шпола 65 Lb 59
23614 Špykiv 64 Ma 56
19812 Šramkivka 53 La 60
17300 Sribne 53 La 60
94000 Stachanov / Стаханов 54 Ma 66
9210 Stajky 52 La 58
75051 Stanislav 65 Na 60
23160 Stanislavčyk 64 Ma 56
63232 Stanyčne 54 Lb 63
31400 Stara Synjava 64 Lb 55
44400 Stara Vyživka 51 Kb 52
87200 Starobeševe 66 Mb 66
92700 Starobil`s`k / Старобільськ 54 Lb 66
31100 Starokostjantyniv / Старокостянтинів 64 Lb 55
85552 Staromlynivka 66 Mb 64
63250 Starovirivka 54 Lb 63
97345 Staryi Krym 80 Nb 63
30063 Staryj Kryvyn 51 La 54
62560 Staryj Saltiv 54 La 64
67940 Stavrove 64 Mb 57
9400 Stavyšče 64 Lb 58
19451 Stebliv 65 Lb 59
82172 Stebnyk / Стебник 63 Lb 51
70535 Stenohirs`k 66 Mb 63
34560 Stepan` 51 Kb 54
84043 Stepanivka/Bilozers`ke 54 Ma 65
28611 Stepanivka/Bobrynec` 65 Ma 60
42304 Stepanivka/Sumy 53 La 62
42220 Štepivka 53 La 62
57107 Stepove 65 Mb 59
93510 Štormove 54 Lb 66
59000 Storožynec` / Сторожинець 63 Ma 53
89655 Strabyčovo 62 Ma 50
34512 Stril`s`k 51 Kb 54
82092 Strilky 62 Lb 51
67050 Strjukove 65 Mb 58
68120 Strumok 78 Nb 57
82400 Stryj / Стрий 63 Lb 51
23210 Stryžavka 64 Lb 56
27444 Subotci 65 Ma 60
98000 Sudak / Судак 80 Oa 63
35766 Sujmy 51 La 54
92764 Šul`hynka 54 Lb 66
47100 Šums`k 51 La 54
40000 Sumy / СУМИ 53 La 62
52410 Surs`ko-Mychajlivka 66 Ma 62
96526 Suvorovs`ke 79 Nb 61
89300 Svaljava / Свалява 62 Ma 50
34120 Svarycevyči 51 Kb 54
92600 Svatove / Сватове 54 Lb 66
72340 Svitlodolyns`ke 66 Mb 63
27500 Svitlovods`k / Світловодськ 65 Lb 61
84130 Svjatohirs`k 54 Lb 65
92642 Svystunivka 54 Lb 66
20615 Syhnajivka 65 Lb 59
38124 Šylivka 53 La 62
66432 Šymkove 64 Mb 58
92314 Synel`nykove/Bilokurakyne 54 Lb 66
52500 Synel`nykove/Dnipropetrovs`k / Синельникове/Дніпропетровськ 66 Ma 63
90041 Synevyr 63 Ma 51
42533 Synivka 53 La 62
89642 Synjak 62 Ma 50
15630 Synjavka 53 Kb 60
66800 Šyrjajeve 64 Mb 58
53700 Šyroke 65 Mb 61
38000 Šyšaky 53 Lb 62
27167 Šyškyne 65 Ma 59
96177 Tabačne 66 Nb 62
20400 Tal`ne / Тальне 64 Ma 58
16651 Talalajivka/Nižyn 53 La 59
17200 Talalajivka/Romny 53 La 61
60430 Tarašany 63 Ma 54
9500 Tarašča / Тараща 52 Lb 58
75140 Tarasivka 65 Na 61
68500 Tarutyne 78 Na 57
68100 Tatarbunary / Татарбунари 78 Nb 57
74988 Tavrijs`k / Таврійськ 65 Na 61
87100 Tel`manove / Тельманове 66 Mb 66
30600 Teofipol` 63 Lb 54
65490 Teplodar / Теплодар 65 Na 58

POSTALI · ÍNDICE CON CÓDIGOS POSTALES · INDICE DE LUGARES COM CÓDIGOS POSTAIS · MÍST S PSČ · ZOZNAM OBCÍ S PSČ · INDEKS MIEJSCOWOŚCI Z KOD POCZTOWY

206

Teplyk — UA — **Žaškiv / Жяшків** — UA

24357 Teplyk 64 Ma 57	57116 Uljanivka/Mykolajiv 65 Mb 59	9030 Velykopolovec`ke 52 Lb 57	37140 Voron`ky 53 La 61
90550 Tereblja 63 Ma 51	20300 Uman` / Умань 64 Ma 58	62600 Velykyj Burluk / Великий Бурлук 54 La 65	41140 Voroniž 53 Kb 61
48100 Terebovlja / Теребовля 63 Lb 53	67663 Usatove 65 Na 58	90615 Velykyj Byčkiv 63 Mb 52	23252 Voronovycja 64 Lb 56
45724 Tereškivci 51 La 52	41230 Usok 53 Kb 61	19854 Velykyj Chutir 53 Lb 60	41811 Vorožba/Bilopillja 53 Kb 62
16674 Tereškivka 53 La 59	41732 Uspenka 53 Kb 61	59052 Velykyj Kučuriv 63 Ma 53	42240 Vorožba/Lebedyn 53 La 62
7240 Termachivka 52 Kb 57	90520 Ust`-Čorna 63 Ma 51	15160 Velykyj Lystven 52 Kb 59	57210 Voskresens`ke 65 Mb 60
24443 Ternivka 64 Ma 57	44731 Ustylun 51 La 52	15207 Velykyj ŠČymel` 53 Kb 59	62500 Vovčans`k / Вовчанськ 54 La 64
46000 Ternopil` / Тернопіль 63 Lb 53	28600 Ustynivka 65 Mb 60	7136 Vendyčany 64 Ma 55	72551 Vovčans`ke 66 Na 63
42110 Terny 53 La 62	62471 Utkivka 54 Lb 64	13610 Veorajše 52 Lb 57	32223 Vovkovynci 64 Lb 55
9800 Tetijiv / Тетіїв 64 Lb 57	68645 Utkonosivka 78 Nb 56	35670 Verba/Dubno 51 La 53	56500 Voznesens`k / Бознесенськ 65 Mb 59
90500 Tjačiv / Тячів 63 Ma 51	88000 Užhorod / Ужгород 62 Ma 50	44721 Verba/Volodymyr-Volyns`kyj 51 La 52	56543 Voznesens`ke 65 Mb 59
74300 Tjahynka 65 Na 61	9161 Uzyn / Узин 52 Lb 58	28223 Verbljužka 65 Ma 60	55542 Vozsijats`ke 65 Mb 60
78000 Tlumač 63 Ma 53	63000 Valky / Валки 54 Lb 63	51326 Verbuvatyka 66 Ma 63	56300 Vradijivka 65 Mb 58
71700 Tokmak / Токмак 66 Mb 63	24222 Vanjarky 64 Ma 56	51660 Verchivceve / Верхіцеве 66 Ma 62	44520 Vyderta 51 Kb 53
53500 Tomakivka 66 Mb 62	2257 Vapnjarka 64 Ma 56		77552 Vyhoda/Dolyna 63 Ma 51
24200 Tomašpil` 64 Ma 56	35612 Varkovyči 51 La 53	99802 Verchn`osadove 80 Oa 61	67620 Vyhoda/Teplodar 65 Na 58
12134 Toporyšče 52 La 56	17600 Varva / Варва 53 La 60	74400 Verchnij Rohačyk 66 Mb 62	70000 Vyl`njans`k / Вільнянськ 66 Mb 63
45612 Torčyn 51 La 53	70221 Varvarivka 66 Mb 64		
48630 Tovste 63 Ma 53	11522 Vas`kovyči 52 Kb 56	42351 Verchnja Syrovatka 53 La 62	68355 Vylkove / Вилкове 78 Nb 57
97051 Traktove 80 Nb 61	59210 Vaškivci 63 Ma 53	78700 Verchovyna 63 Ma 52	90351 Vylok 62 Ma 50
72336 Travneve 66 Na 63	8600 Vasyl`kiv / Васильків 52 La 58	16624 Vertijivka 53 Kb 59	79495 Vynnyky / Винники 63 Lb 52
7454 Trebuchiv 52 La 58		72200 Vesele 66 Mb 62	
92100 Trojic`ke/Anoškyne 54 Lb 66	52600 Vasyl`kivka 66 Ma 64	57000 Veselynove 65 Mb 59	90300 Vynohradiv / Виноградів 62 Ma 51
67641 Trojic`ke/Teplodae 64 Na 58	68752 Vasylivka/Bolhrad 78 Nb 56	31256 Vijtivci 63 Lb 54	68722 Vynohradne 78 Nb 57
66560 Trojic`ke/Viktorivka 64 Mb 58	71600 Vasylivka/Dniprorudne / Василівка/Дніпрорудне 66 Mb 63	62620 Vil`chuvatka 54 La 65	37263 Vyrišal`ne 53 La 61
56050 Trojic`ko-Safonove 65 Mb 60		44115 Vil`na Sloboda 53 Kb 62	7300 Vyšhorod / Вишгород 52 La 58
12345 Trokovyči 52 La 56		16234 Vil`ne/Krolevec` 53 Kb 61	
45214 Trostjanec`/Kiverci 51 La 53	87252 Vasylivka/Komsomol`s`ke 66 Mb 63	42820 Vil`ne/Ochtyrka 54 La 63	47432 Vyšhorodok 63 Lb 53
24300 Trostjanec`/Ladyžyn 64 Ma 57		51700 Vil`nohirs`k / Вільногірськ 65 Ma 62	64231 Vyšneva 54 Lb 65
	20250 Vatutine / Ватутіне 65 Lb 59		15070 Vyšneve/Černihiv 52 Kb 59
42600 Trostjanec`/Ochtyrka / Тростянець/Охтирка 53 La 63	27520 Velyka Andrusivka 65 Lb 60	19523 Vil`šana/Horodyšče 65 Lb 59	8132 Vyšneve/Kyjiv / Вишневе/Київ 52 La 58
	38300 Velyka Bahačka 53 Lb 61	42127 Vil`šana/Romny 53 La 62	
81620 Trudove 63 Lb 51	47725 Velyka Berezovycja 63 Lb 53	24624 Vil`šanka/Jampil` 64 Ma 56	47313 Vyšnivec` 63 Lb 53
82200 Truskavec` / Трускавець 63 Lb 51	71340 Velyka Bilozerka 66 Mb 62	26600 Vil`šanka/Puškove 65 Ma 58	37860 Vyšnjaky 53 Lb 61
	19940 Velyka Burimka 53 La 60	92123 Vil`šany 54 Lb 66	70331 Vyšnjuvate 66 Mb 65
56535 Trykraty 65 Mb 59	44221 Velyka Hluša 51 Kb 53	32500 Vin`kivci 64 Lb 55	12424 Vysoka Pie 52 La 56
8552 Trylisy 52 Lb 57	64722 Velyka Komyšuvacha 54 Lb 65	21000 Vinnycja / Вінниця 64 Lb 56	72020 Vysoke 66 Mb 63
82644 Tuchol`ka 63 Ma 51		97320 Vladyslavivka 80 Nb 63	74000 Vysokopillja 65 Mb 61
35415 Tučyn 51 La 54	90330 Velyka Kopanja 63 Ma 51	96033 Vojinka 66 Nb 62	62459 Vysokyj 54 Lb 64
34110 Tumen` 51 Kb 54	74500 Velyka Lepetycha 65 Mb 61	77316 Vojnylv 63 Lb 52	11110 Vystupovyči 52 Kb 57
22513 Turbiv 64 Lb 56		85700 Volnovacha / Волноваха 66 Mb 65	24640 Žabokryč 64 Ma 57
13510 Turbivka 52 La 57	67100 Velyka Mychajlivka 64 Mb 57		78315 Zabolotiv 63 Ma 53
44800 Turijs`k 51 Kb 52	85500 Velyka Novosilka / Велика Новосілка 66 Mb 64	63552 Volochiv Jar 54 Lb 65	64400 Začepylivka 54 Lb 63
35031 Tyche 51 La 54		31200 Voločys`k / Волочиськ 63 Lb 54	15461 Žadove 53 Ka 60
23600 Tyl`čyn / Тильчин 64 Ma 56	74100 Velyka Oleksandrivka 65 Mb 61		7823 Zahal`ci 52 La 57
66052 Tymkove 64 Mb 57	38112 Velyka Pavlivka 53 La 62	9300 Volodarka 64 Lb 57	90040 Zahorb 63 Ma 51
72030 Tymošivka 66 Mb 63	42800 Velyka Pysarivka / Велика Писарівка 54 La 63	12100 Volodars`k-Volyns`kyj 52 La 56	31614 Zakupne 63 Lb 54
19220 Tynivka 64 Lb 58		87000 Volodars`ke / Володарське 66 Mb 65	48600 Zališčyky / Заліщики 63 Ma 53
34544 Tynne 51 Kb 54	38623 Velyka Rublivka 53 Lb 62		
89111 Tyšiv 62 Ma 51	8671 Velyka Vil`šanka 52 La 58	44700 Volodymyr-Volyns`kyj / Володимир-Волинський 51 La 52	47234 Zalizci 63 Lb 53
77220 Tysiv 63 Lb 51	26241 Velyka Vyska 65 Ma 59		13000 Zalužne 52 La 55
27013 Tyškivka 65 Ma 58	44740 Velyki Birky 63 Lb 53	34300 Volodymyrec` 51 Kb 54	74860 Zaozerne 66 Na 61
77400 Tysmenycja 63 Ma 52	75131 Velyki Kopani 65 Na 60	27611 Volodymyrivka/Kirovohrad / Володимирівка/ Кіровоград 65 Ma 60	70031 Zaporiz`ke 66 Na 63
23300 Tyvriv 64 Lb 56	39032 Velyki Krynky 53 Lb 61		72240 Zaporižžja/Melitopol` 66 Na 63
98435 Uhlove 80 Oa 61	34725 Velyki Mežyryčy 51 La 54		
80064 Uhniv 51 La 51	80074 Velyki Mosty 51 La 52		69000 Zaporižžja/Vil`njans`k / Запоріжжя/Вільнянськ 66 Mb 63
8720 Ukrajinka / Украïнка 52 La 58	67832 Velykodolyns`ke 65 Na 58	72530 Volodymyrivka/Melitopol 66 Na 63	
26400 Ul`janovka 64 Ma 58	56040 Velykooleksandrivka/Novyj Buh 65 Mb 60	15632 Voloskivci 53 Kb 60	71333 Zapovitne 66 Mb 62
22032 Ulaniv 64 Lb 56		13424 Volycja 52 La 57	90124 Zariččja 62 Ma 51
41856 Uljanivka/Bilopillja 53 La 62	52610 Velykooleksandrivka/ Pavlohrad 66 Ma 63	16131 Volynka 53 Kb 60	97575 Zarične 80 Oa 62
71664 Uljanivka/Dniprorudne 66 Mb 63	67140 Velykoploske 64 Na 57	78595 Vorochta 63 Ma 52	19200 Žaškiv / Жяшків 64 Lb 58

207

INDEX WITH POST CODES · ORTSREGISTER MIT POSTLEITZAHLEN · INDICE CON CODICI POSTALI · ÍNDICE CON CÓDIGOS POSTALES · INDICE DE LUGARES COM CÓDIGOS POSTAIS · STEDREGISTER MED POSTNUMRE · PLAATSNAMENREGISTER MET POSTCODE · REJSTŘÍK MÍST S PSČ · ZOZNAM OBCÍ S PSČ · INDEKS MIEJSCOWOŚCI Z KOD POCZTOWY

Zastavna / Заставна

Roma

59400 Zastavna / Заставна
    63 Ma 53
67772 Zatoka 65 Na 58
45523 Zaturci 51 La 52
66325 Zatyššja 64 Mb 57
48523 Zavods`ke 63 Ma 53
47300 Zbaraž / Збараж 63 Lb 53
47200 Zboriv 63 Lb 53
89120 Ždenijevo 62 Ma 50
35700 Zdolbuniv / Здолбунів
    51 La 54
8832 Zelen`ky 52 Lb 58
60133 Zelena 63 Ma 54
72113 Zelenivka 66 Na 64
53860 Zelenodol`s`k / Зеленодольск
    65 Mb 61
66513 Zelenohirs`ke 64 Mb 58
51327 Žemčužne 54 Ma 64

97154 Žemčužyna 80 Nb 62
7600 Zhurivka 53 La 59
38100 Zin`kiv / Зіньків 53 La 62
23100 Žmerynka / Жмеринка
    64 Lb 56
63400 Zmijiv / Зміїв 54 Lb 64
27400 Znam`janka / Знамьянка
    65 Ma 60
41022 Znob-Novhorods`ke
    53 Ka 61
62200 Zoločiv/Derhači 54 La 64
80700 Zoločiv/Ternopil / Золочів/Тер-
    нопіль
    63 Lb 52
85560 Zolota Nyva 66 Mb 65
19700 Zolotonoša / Золотоноша
    53 Lb 60
7733 Žoravka 53 La 60

68251 Zorja 78 Nb 57
97114 Zorkine 66 Nb 62
80300 Žovkva / Жовка 51 La 51
80431 Žovtanci 63 Lb 52
52130 Žovte 65 Ma 61
66860 Žovten` 65 Mb 58
52200 Žovti Vody / Жовті Води
    65 Ma 61
8421 Žovtneve/Jahotyn 53 La 59
53172 Žovtneve/Kryvyj Rih
    65 Mb 61
62724 Žovtneve/Kup`jans`k
    54 Lb 65
38413 Žovtneve/Poltava 53 Lb 62
41854 Žovtneve/Sumy 53 La 62
56443 Žovtneve/Voznesens`k
    65 Mb 59
68152 Žovtyj Jar 78 Nb 57

97630 Zuja 80 Nb 62
15334 Žuklja 53 Kb 60
7341 Žukyn 52 La 58
17620 Žuravka 53 La 60
97321 Žuravky 80 Nb 63
81780 Žuravno 63 Lb 52
20200 Zvenyhorodka / Звенигородка
    65 Lb 58
81700 Žydačiv / Жидачів 63 Lb 52
10000 Žytomyr / Житомир 52 La 56

00120 Roma 88 Pb 40